JNLE—See JG.

JNO *target*—Jump short to *target* if Overflow flag is clear. 142

JNP *target*—Jump short to *target* if Parity flag is clear. 143 ·

JNS *target*—Jump short to *target* if Sign flag is clear. 143

JNZ—See JNE.

JO *target*—Jump short to *target* if Overflow flag is set. 142

JP *target*—Jump short to *target* if Parity flag is set. 143

JPE—See JP.

JPO—See JNP.

JS *target*—Jump short to *target* if Sign flag is set. 142

JZ—See JE.

LODS—Copy byte or word value from DS:[SI] to AL or AX; adjust SI. 382

LOOP *target*—Decrement CX; jump short to target if CX not zero. 151

LOOPE *target*—Decrement CX; jump short to target if CX not zero and Zero flag was set before decrementing CX. 152

LOOPNE *target*—Decrement CX; jump short to target if CX not zero and Zero flag was clear before decrementing CX. 153

LOOPNZ—See LOOPNE.

LOOPZ—See LOOPE.

MOV *dest, source*—Copy *source* value into *dest*. 121

MOVS—Copy byte or word value from DS:[SI] to ES:[DI]; adjust SI and DI. 381

MUL *source*—Multiply unsigned AL (or AX if *source* is word) by unsigned *source*; product to AX (or DX:AX if *source* is word). 376

NEG *dest*—Negate (twos complement) *dest*. 125

NOP—Do nothing; synonym for XCHG AX, AX. 153

NOT *dest*—Do logical NOT (ones complement) on *dest*. 129

OR
dest. 128

OUT *byte_immed*, AL—Output byte from AL to I/O port *byte_immed*. 288

OUT *byte_immed*, AX—Output word from AX to I/O port *byte_immed*. 288

OUT DX, AL—Output byte from AL to I/O port specified by DX. 288

OUT DX, AX—Output word from AX to I/O port specified by DX. 288

POP *dest*—Move word value from SS:[SP] to *dest*; add 2 to SP. 121

POPF—Move word value from SS:[SP] to Flags register; add 2 to SP. 122

PUSH *source*—Subtract 2 from SP; move word value from *source* to SS:[SP]. 121

PUSHF—Subtract 2 from SP; move word value from Flags register to SS:[SP]. 122

RCL *dest*, 1—Rotate *dest* left once through Carry flag. 133

RCL *dest*, CL—Rotate *dest* left CL times through Carry flag. 133

RCR *dest*, 1—Rotate *dest* right once through Carry flag. 133

RCR *dest*, CL—Rotate *dest* right CL times through Carry flag. 133

REP—Repeat String instruction CX times, unless string instruction clears Carry flag. 387

REPE—See REP.

REPNE—Repeat String instruction CX times, unless string instruction sets Carry flag. 387

REPNZ—See REPNE.

REPZ—See REP.

RET [*n*]—POP IP (and CS if Far); add *n* to IP if specified. 145, 243

ROL *dest*, 1—Rotate *dest* left once. 132

ROL *dest*, CL—Rotate *dest* left CL times. 132

ROR *dest*, 1—Rotate *dest* right once. 132

ROR *dest*, CL—Rotate *dest* right CL times. 132

SAL—See SHL.

SAR *dest*, 1—Shift *dest* right once, copying high bit

continues on back endpaper

INTRODUCTION TO PROGRAMMING IN ASSEMBLY LANGUAGE (IBM PC)

INTRODUCTION TO PROGRAMMING IN ASSEMBLY LANGUAGE (IBM PC)

GEORGE DRIVER

Bakersfield College

West Publishing Company

Minneapolis/St. Paul • New York • Los Angeles • San Francisco

West's Commitment to the Environment

In 1906, West Publishing Company began recycling materials left over from the production of books. This began a tradition of efficient and responsible use of resources. Today, up to 95 percent of our legal books and 70 percent of our college and school texts are printed on recycled, acid-free stock. West also recycles nearly 22 million pounds of scrap paper annually—the equivalent of 181,717 trees. Since the 1960s, West has devised ways to capture and recycle waste inks, solvents, oils, and vapors created in the printing process. We also recycle plastics of all kinds, wood, glass, corrugated cardboard, and batteries, and have eliminated the use of styrofoam book packaging. We at West are proud of the longevity and the scope of our commitment to our environment.

Copyediting: Bonnie Gruen
Design: The Book Company
Composition: American Composition & Graphics, Inc.
Illustrations: Precision Graphics
Cover Design: Randy Miyake, Miyake Illustration and Design
Production, Prepress, Printing and Binding by West Publishing Company.

Photo Credits
10, 16, 42 Courtesy of International Business Machines Corporation.
84 Courtesy of Intel Corporation.

Library of Congress Cataloging in Publication Data

Driver, George.
    Introduction to programming in assembly language (IBM PC)/ George Driver.
        p. cm.
    Includes index.
    ISBN 0-314-01040-8
    1. IBM Personal Computer—Programming.   2. Assembler language
(Computer program language)   I. Title.
QA76.8.I2594D75   1992
005.265—dc20
                                                            92-1638
                                                            CIP

Contents

Chapter 3   PC Operation and System Software   39

Chapter 9 **Keyboard Input**   **332**

Preface

INTRODUCTION

Introduction to Programming in Assembly Language (IBM PC) is a textbook that the student can and will read. It is intended for use in a semester or two-quarter course in introductory assembly-language programming for sophomore or community-college students. The basic assumption throughout is that the student has had no prior experience with assembly language and may have had no experience with the IBM PC or compatibles. However, it is recommended that the student be proficient in at least one high-level programming language, preferably two.

Throughout the text, emphasis is placed on general assembly-language programming techniques and skills. The IBM family of personal computers (IBM PC, XT, AT, PS/2 and compatible machines) is used as the target hardware; however, most of the major concepts are common in one form or another to all processors and can easily be adapted to other hardware.

KEY FEATURES OF THE TEXT

In a nutshell, this text differs from most other available books in its emphasis, organization, and thoroughness. While other books teach assembly language, this text emphasizes programming in assembly language. Rather than the too-common hodgepodge of random topics, the text follows a logical progression from basic concepts through more-complex ideas. While many texts provide only an introduction to important topics (with suggestions that the student refer to the appropriate manuals for the important details), this text assumes that the student may not have ready access to manuals and so provides thorough, in-depth coverage of each major topic. Some of the unusual features include:

1. The text emphasizes a methodical approach to programming in assembly language with the effective use of macros and procedures, use of macro and object libraries, and effective parameter-passing techniques. Emphasis is placed on a modular building-block approach, structured logic design with pseudocode, good internal documentation, and many other habits and techniques essential to successful assembly-language programming.

2. Difficult concepts are presented as a progression of simpler concepts. Just as the student is taught to solve complex problems as a sequence of simpler problems, so the text develops difficult concepts as a logical sequence of simpler ideas. This systematic thorough coverage of concepts enables a greatly-reduced reliance on example programs (many programming examples have been included, however, where appropriate).

   While many programming examples are presented, they have been carefully chosen to illustrate key concepts but to avoid the "cookbook" or "copy-the-example-and-use-it" approach taken by many texts. The student is made to understand each concept and to apply that understanding to particular problem solutions.

3. For those instructors who might wish to provide more example programs than are included in the text, a supplement of additional programming examples is available from the publisher. Its use is left entirely up to the instructor:
   a) Adopt it as a required text, making the additional examples available to all students.
   b) Adopt it as an optional text, making it available to only those students who desire additional examples.
   c) Do not make it available to students but obtain a desk copy and integrate the examples into lectures.
   d) Ignore it completely.

4. Each chapter begins with an introduction listing the major topics to be discussed and ends with a summary to reinforce the major concepts and ideas. Key terms and phrases are highlighted upon introduction. Summary, Review, and Relevance-of-Topic boxes are included at appropriate points throughout each chapter. In addition to programming assignments, each chapter contains a vocabulary review as well as a wide variety of probing review questions.

5. No prior experience with the IBM PC is required. Included are discussions and exercises to familiarize the student with hardware operation, the most commonly used DOS commands, debugging utilities, the assembler, the

linker, the object-library manager, and EXE2BIN. Extensive discussions are included of much information extracted from the DOS manual, the assembler manual, the Technical Reference manual, and the author's own extensive experience.

6. Complete coverage is given to the hardware, BIOS operations, and DOS functions for video and printer output and keyboard input. String/numeric conversion algorithms (for the input and output of numeric data) are discussed in depth. Disk storage is covered thoroughly, beginning with the fundamentals. Major disk topics include: principles of magnetism, disk organization, BIOS operations for non-file-structured disk access, DOS disk-allocation structures, data file organizations, and the DOS functions for file-structured disk access.

7. The text seeks to overcome the "throw-away" nature of most classroom programming. Each chapter (from chapter seven on) presents suggested building blocks to provide easy future access to the hardware, BIOS operations, and DOS functions discussed in the chapter. Assignments result in the creation of libraries of commonly needed building blocks to be retained for later use. Upon completion, the student will have created macro and object libraries for console I/O, printer output, and disk storage.

8. Emphasis is on the principles of assembly-language programming common to all systems rather than on the latest in system-specific technological developments. With the exception of Chapter 12, which requires DOS version two or later, the text can be completed on any member of the IBM PC family running any version of DOS and with any version of the Microsoft or IBM macro assembler or Borland Turbo assembler.

   However, in order to satisfy curiosity and stimulate further interest, succinct discussions of more recent technology have been included at appropriate points throughout the text. Some such topics are: descendants of the 8086/8088 (through the 80586), enhancements of later versions of DOS (through version four), OS/2, more recent versions of the Microsoft macro assembler (through version five) and Borland International's Turbo assembler.

9. The text includes thorough coverage of many essential topics that are often neglected. Some of the most-often-neglected topics that are covered in the text are:
   Electronic data storage and arithmetic
   PC operation and system software
   Clear explanations of assembler directives
   The development of libraries (toolboxes) of easy-to-use building-blocks
   Use of macros and procedures, including effective parameter-passing techniques
   Good internal documentation
   Use of pseudocode and structured-programming constructs for program design

Debugging hints
Thorough coverage of disk storage
Differences between COM and EXE files
Creating COM files with EXE2BIN
Interfacing with high-level languages
Interrupt-service routines
TSR (Terminate-and-Stay-Resident) programs

10. An Instructor's Manual and Diskette are available free of charge upon adoption of the text. Changing textbooks (usually a difficult, time-consuming process) is made much easier by the chapter synopses, suggested lesson plans, and source and executable solutions to all building blocks and programming assignments, which are included in the manual and on diskette.

TEXT ORGANIZATION

Much time and effort have been devoted to a systematic presentation of the material. Concepts are presented in a methodical step-by-step manner. Such an approach necessarily places some restrictions on any alterations to the sequence of the material. However, a great deal of flexibility is still possible!

Since all building blocks and programming assignments are included on the Instructor's Diskette, the instructor may choose to skip, abbreviate, advance or delay the presentation of many topics, making available to the student (from the Instructor's diskette) any necessary building blocks or problem solutions.

Additionally, an instructor may choose to skip over much of Chapters 4 (Processor Fundamentals) and 5 (Instruction Set), presenting the material a little at a time as needed throughout the rest of the text. See the Instructor's Manual for details of the implementation of any deviation from the sequence of the text.

INSTRUCTOR SUPPLEMENTS

An Instructor's Manual with Transparency Masters and an Instructor's Diskette are available from the publisher at no cost to adopters of the text. The Instructor's Manual includes:

Camera-ready transparency masters of key figures from the text.

Suggested schedule and lesson plans for a 15-week semester.

Brief chapter-by-chapter suggestions for the teaching of the material.

Solutions to all vocabulary and review questions and problems.

Source code listings of all building blocks (macros and subprocedures) and programming assignments.

The Instructor's Diskette contains:

Suggested schedule and lesson plans as text files.

Vocabulary, review-question, and problem solutions as text files.

Macro libraries: CONSOLE.MLB, PRINTER.MLB and DISK.MLB

Object libraries: CONSOLE.LIB, PRINTER.LIB and DISK.LIB

Source files of all building-block subprocedures.

Source and executable files of all programming assignments.

ACKNOWLEDGMENTS

A special thank you to Richard Mixter and Keith Dodson, Editors, for their guidance and encouragement throughout the preparation of the manuscript.

I also wish to thank the following reviewers for their many helpful comments and suggestions: Richard A. Beebe, Simpson College; Richard Easton, Indiana State University; John V. Erhart, Northeast Missouri State University; Donald Gustafson, Texas Tech University; James Kittelsrud, Glendale Community College; Douglas Knight, University of Southern Colorado; Cary Laxer, Rose-Hulman Institute of Technology; James F. Leach, Metropolitan State College; Ronald Lipsky, Foothill and West Valley Colleges; Bernard McIntyre, University of Houston; James Peters, University of Arkansas—Fayette-ville; Maria Petrie, Florida Atlantic University; Mark Steele, Mesa State University; Robert Sterling, Tidewater Community College; John B. Tappen, University of Southern Colorado; James van Speybroeck, St. Ambrose University; Richard Walker, Moorhead State University; Layne Wallace, University of North Florida; Michael J. Walton, Miami-Dade Community College; Ronald Williams, Central Piedmont Community College.

Above all others I wish to thank my wife for her infinite patience and support. Thank you, Helen, for not complaining too much about the missed vacations or all the many other things left undone. I promise not to take on another project at least until I have completed the new shed and pasture fence.

1

Introduction

WHAT IS ASSEMBLY LANGUAGE?

Your previous experience with computers has probably involved programming in **high-level** languages, such as BASIC, COBOL, FORTRAN, or PASCAL, or possibly in **nonprocedural** or **fourth-generation** languages, such as SQL, provided by relational-model database management systems. Now that you have embarked on a study of assembly language, your first questions should be, What is assembly language, and how does it differ from the high-level languages with which I am familiar?

In very simple terms, programming in a high-level language might be likened to giving directions to a taxicab driver, while programming in assembly language is akin to driving the vehicle yourself. A cab driver understands directions such as "Go north ten blocks on B Street. Turn left on 14th Avenue, and go eight and one-half blocks. Stop at 524 14th Avenue." Such directions are analogous to high-level language statements. If the cabby knows the city well enough, you might be able to simply say, "Go to 524 14th Avenue," which would be analogous to programming in a fourth-generation language.

In either case, the driver translates each one of your broad, general directions into a long, complex, and detailed sequence of manipulations of the taxi's pedals, steering wheel, and gearshift lever. In the analogy, the driver performs much the same function as a high-level language's compiler or interpreter, translating each high-level statement into the many machine-level actions necessary to carry it out. Programming in assembly language then is like driving the vehicle yourself, instead of taking a taxi. When doing your own driving, you "communicate" directly with the machine, providing the many detailed, low-level "instructions" necessary to bring your vehicle safely to its destination; when programming in assembly language, you also must provide the many machine-level instructions necessary to achieve the desired results.

Doing your own driving, as opposed to taking a taxi, requires a great deal more skill, more attention to detail, more work, and possibly involves more risk (unless you are a good driver). On the other hand, doing your own driving provides you with a great deal more control over your vehicle and, if you are a skillful driver and know the city well, may get you to your destination more quickly. Similarly, assembly-language programming requires more of the programmer than does a high-level language, but also provides much more control. In simple terms, assembly-language programming puts you directly into the driver's seat, giving you much greater control over the machine as well as much greater responsibility.

This simple analogy should provide you with a general understanding of the differences between assembly language and high-level languages. But to understand assembly language in more detail requires that you know what a computer is and how it is programmed to do a specific job. Every computer contains a piece of hardware called a **Central Processing Unit (CPU)** or simply **the processor**; the major function of the CPU is to examine instructions stored electronically in the computer's memory and to do what the instructions tell it to do. The instructions that the CPU understands are called **machine language** and consist of binary codes or patterns of ones and zeros. Each instruction represents one fundamental operation that the processor is capable of carrying out. For example, consider the following:

    10001001 11011000

That pattern of ones and zeros tells the 8086/8088 microprocessor to copy the value stored in a register called BX into another register called AX. We will discuss registers later in the text; for now, a register is simply a place within the CPU to store a binary value.

The 8086/8088 machine-language instruction to store the number 5 into the AX register is as follows:

    10111000 00000101 00000000

The following pattern tells the CPU to add 5 to the value currently in the BX register and store the result back into BX:

    10000011 11000011 00000101

The following instruction tells the CPU to increment (add 1 to) the value in the register called DX:

01000010

You can imagine how difficult it would be to program a computer in machine language. The programmer would have to remember all the different machine-language instructions and meticulously enter the patterns of ones and zeros to tell the processor what to do. Programmers are usually relieved of that kind of detail by **language translators.** A language translator is a system program that examines a program written in an English-like programming language, such as BASIC or PASCAL, and converts it to the machine-language instructions necessary to perform the desired functions.

In your high-level language programming classes, you have used a **compiler** or **interpreter** to translate your English-like statements into the required machine-language instructions. An **assembler** is also a language translator in that it is a system program that translates English-like instructions into machine language. The fundamental difference between a compiler and an assembler lies in the manner in which they perform the translation.

There is a one-to-many correspondence between high-level language statements and the resulting machine-language instructions; a compiler or interpreter translates each high-level language statement into one or more (often dozens or even hundreds) of machine-language instructions. A single fourth-generation-language statement may result in many thousands of machine-language instructions. An assembler on the other hand translates each assembly-language instruction into exactly one machine-language instruction; there is a one-to-one correspondence between assembly-language instructions and machine-language instructions.

When working in a high-level language such as BASIC, a programmer might write the following statement:

```
PRINT "This is a test"
```

Many many machine-language instructions are required to cause the above message to appear on the screen. The interpreter or compiler generates all the needed machine-language instructions from the single statement written by the programmer.

An assembly-language programmer might write the following instruction:

```
MOV      AX, BX
```

The assembler translates that instruction into the single machine-language instruction:

```
10001001 11011000
```

The resulting instruction merely copies the value currently stored in the BX register into the AX register; that is all it does. Similarly, consider the following 8086/8088 assembly-language instruction:

```
ADD       BX, 5
```

It is assembled to the single machine-language instruction:

10000011 11000011 00000101

That instruction then tells the CPU to add five to the value in the BX register, storing the result back into BX.

There is no machine-language instruction to display a message to the screen; displaying a message requires many machine-language instructions. Even getting a single character from the keyboard requires many machine-language instructions. Consequently, an assembly-language programmer must write many assembly-language instructions to accomplish what is done by each of the single BASIC statements:

```
PRINT "This is a test"
```

or

```
INPUT X$
```

Additionally, assembly language is machine specific. Every CPU has its own instruction set; different processors recognize different machine-language instructions. In high-level languages, the differences between processors are taken care of by the compiler or interpreter. A program written in COBOL for one machine can be transported, with few changes, to a different machine; the compiler on the new machine translates it to that processor's machine-language instructions. Assembly-language programs do not allow such transportability. Since there is one assembly-language instruction for each machine-language instruction, two different processors may have very different assembly-language instruction sets. An assembly-language program must be completely rewritten for another processor; assembly language is not transportable between different machines.

In this textbook we will learn the assembly language for the Intel 8086/8088 microprocessor. Actually, the same basic instruction set is utilized by an entire family of processors manufactured by Intel corporation: 8086, 8088, 80186, 80286, 80386, 80386SX, 80486, and 80586. Thus the assembly language learned in this class can be used on any of the machines (IBM PC, XT, AT, PS/2, and compatibles) that use that family of processors. In addition, although other processors have different instruction sets, the fundamental principles of assembly-language programming are the same on any machine. Most of the programming techniques presented in this text can be carried over to the programming of virtually any processor in assembly language.

WHY USE ASSEMBLY LANGUAGE?

From the above discussion, it should be clear that an assembly-language programmer must work much harder than a BASIC or COBOL programmer to achieve the same results. Why then would anyone other than a masochist want to work in assembly language? Why not write everything using high-level languages? The answer lies in the fact that assembly language provides the programmer with much more control over the CPU.

When working in a high-level language, the programmer uses the language syntax to describe, in rather broad terms, what needs to be done. The compiler or interpreter then chooses the many machine-language instructions necessary to perform all the minute steps required by each statement written by the programmer. Thus, while the programmer controls the process in broad, general terms, he or she has little control over the minute details of processing.

In assembly language, on the other hand, the programmer is given complete control over the processor; he or she is able to choose the exact sequence of machine-language instructions with which to solve the problem. Given this control, the programmer can often develop executable programs that are a good deal smaller and execute much more quickly than those generated through a compiler.

The programmer understands the specific problem to be solved and so can choose the optimum sequence of machine-language instructions for solving that particular problem. A high-level language, on the other hand, is designed to solve many different types of problems; consequently, its compiler or interpreter often generates machine-language instructions that, while they do solve the problem, may do so in an inefficient manner. A program written in assembly language will almost always be smaller and execute more quickly than the same program written in a high-level language.

Besides machine inefficiency, high-level languages also limit the programmer to those operations that are supported by the syntax of the language. If the designers of the language chose not to include (or overlooked the need for) some capability, then the programmer may be unable to perform a desired operation or may be required to use the available capabilities to perform it in a very roundabout and awkward manner. Since there is a one-to-one correspondence between assembly-language instructions and machine-language instructions, the programmer in assembly-language is limited only by the capabilities of the CPU; the programmer can do anything the CPU is capable of doing.

Of course, along with the greater control over the processor that assembly language provides comes much greater responsibility; the assembly-language programmer must address a multitude of picky details that are attended to by the compiler or interpreter in a high-level language. Consequently, while a program written in assembly language is usually smaller and executes more quickly than the same program written in a high-level language, it usually takes the programmer much longer to write it, and any program maintenance that must be done later also requires a great deal more programmer time.

In a nutshell, then, an assembler does very little for the programmer but allows the programmer to do anything that is within the processor's capabilities. Stated another way, assembly-language programs are much less efficient for programmers but much more efficient for the hardware than are programs written in a high-level language.

Consequently, assembly language is called for whenever a problem cannot be easily solved within the confines of a high-level language. If the problem requires the manipulation of specific hardware or the use of operating system services on a level not provided by high-level languages, assembly-language programming becomes necessary. Additionally, assembly language should be used whenever machine efficiency (size and speed of execution of the program) are more important than programmer efficiency (the time it takes a programmer to write and/or maintain the program). If a program must run within a limited memory space or is used very very often in situations where speed is important, then it probably should be written in assembly language.

Two types of programs that most often fit those criteria are **system programs** and **communications-control programs**. Communications-control programs such as Local Area Network programs control the flow of data among the various pieces of hardware in teleprocessing or distributed-processing systems. They often must deal directly with communications hardware at a low level that is difficult to achieve in most high-level programming languages. Additionally, they need to be very fast; any delay in the flow of data between machines would result in a degradation of the overall system performance. Consequently, assembly language is often used in the development of communications-control programs.

System programs control the hardware and provide an environment for applications processing; they include **operating systems, utility programs,** and **language processors**. An operating system must be capable of controlling hardware such as video screens, keyboards, disk-drive controllers, and serial and parallel communications devices; additionally, an operating system must be able to quickly provide system services for the use of applications programs. Thus an operating system must be made up of fast code that is able to communicate directly with different hardware devices and so is often written in assembly language.

Utility programs perform commonly needed general tasks such as preparing magnetic media for use (FORMAT.COM), verifying media (CHKDSK.COM), backing up of data (BACKUP.COM/RESTORE.COM), copying data (DISKCOPY.COM), comparing files or disks of data (COMP.COM, DISKCOMP.COM), and so forth. These programs often must perform low-level hardware functions, and they also must be fast, since they are used frequently in a variety of situations; consequently, utility programs are commonly written in assembly language.

Language processors, especially interpreters, are also often written in assembly language. A slow or very large compiler will merely decrease the productivity of application programmers. A slow or unnecessarily large interpreter, however, would produce extremely unpleasant results. Since it resides in memory and translates the application program line-by-line as it executes it, an interpreter must be made up of very fast, compact code. Interpreters are very often written in assembly language in order to keep them as small and fast as possible.

In addition to the writing of system programs and communications-control programs, one more perfectly valid reason for using assembly language is, quite simply, that it can be very personally satisfying. One of the reasons for the dramatic proliferation of microcomputers over the last few years is the growth of computing as a hobby as well as a profession. Many people, whose professions may or may not involve computers, derive great pleasure from learning to manipulate and control a tool as powerful as a computer. For any person who enjoys programming for its own sake, nothing is quite as gratifying as taking direct control of the CPU through assembly language. Like mountain climbers, programmers sometimes use assembly language purely for the challenge of it—"just because it's there."

There is nothing wrong with this attitude, but we must include one word of caution. If you are employed as a programmer, then you are paid by your employer, not for your personal fulfillment, but for getting a job done as cheaply and quickly as possible. It is all right to use assembly language "just because it's there" on your own time, but when working for someone else you should use assembly language only when it is required by the problem.

WHO SHOULD STUDY ASSEMBLY LANGUAGE?

Obviously, anyone who plans to work as a software engineer writing system programs or communications-control programs needs to know assembly language very well. Any hobbyist who wishes to truly understand and control his or her computer should also learn assembly language. It is also this author's firm belief that anyone who intends to make a career in the computer professions should have a good background knowledge of assembly language. Even application programmers who work only in high-level languages such as COBOL, FORTRAN, or even RPG need to study assembly language in order to better understand the machines with which they work.

All high-level languages, especially nonprocedural or fourth-generation languages, tend to give the programmer a false view of how a computer works; the compiler or interpreter provides the programmer with a greatly distorted perspective of the hardware. By communicating more directly with the processor through assembly language the programmer is able to perceive the true functioning of the machine. Through assembly language, a programmer can achieve a genuine understanding of the computer.

This understanding of the internal workings of the computer usually results in better high-level language programs. By understanding the machine, a programmer can often make a more intelligent choice among several algorithms for solving the same problem. Similarly, a programmer who knows the machine well can frequently choose the specific high-level language that is best suited for a particular application. Consequently, we believe that all future computer professionals should study assembly language.

CLASSROOM VERSUS "REAL WORLD" PROGRAMMING

Throughout this class, as well as in all your other programming classes, you should keep in mind the fact that the classroom is an artificial programming environment that is very different from the "real world." Due to the instructor's desire for the student to write many different programs, involving all the different concepts introduced in the class, and within the limited time allowed by the quarter or semester system, each classroom programming assignment is typically kept relatively short and simple. Outside the classroom, problems tend to be more complex and less quickly solved. The problems encountered by a professional programmer are usually much more involved, require much more time to solve, and result in programs that are much larger and more complicated than the typical classroom assignment. As a result, the professional programmer needs to develop techniques and programming habits that lend themselves to the development of extremely large, complex programs.

Classroom programming also tends to be somewhat throwaway in nature. The student writes the program, turns it in, gets it back with a grade, and then throws it away and moves on to the next programming assignment. The completed and graded program is usually never seen again; consequently, clarity or readability by others is unimportant in the classroom (unless, of course, the instructor emphasizes those qualities). In the real world, programs, once written and tested, are put into production and typically remain in constant use for many years. Throughout its life a program usually needs to be modified many times, often by someone other than the original programmer. Consequently, readability of programs is extremely important; a program must be written to be as easily and quickly understood as possible. No matter how well a program accomplishes its function, it is useless if future programmers cannot understand and maintain it.

Another characteristic of the classroom, which often leads to bad programming habits, is that a primary goal of the student is to impress the instructor with his or her knowledge of the language and general abilities as a programmer. This desire to impress the instructor, in hopes of a better grade, often leads to unnecessary complexity in programs. In real life programming it is very important not to make a program any more complex than necessary just to impress others; the more complex a program is the more difficult it is to maintain, and real world problems tend to be complex enough already.

As a student programmer, you should try to overcome the artificiality of the classroom environment by following some simple rules:

Rules for "Real World" Programming

1) Get in the habit of breaking apart a problem and modularizing the program. This habit will prove invaluable when you later tackle large, complex problems.

2) Write programs as if you are going to have to live with them for a long time. Include ample, well-thought-out internal documentation (remarks and comments) to make the program as easy to read and understand as possible. Remember that someone less talented than yourself may have to maintain your programs someday.

3) Follow the "KISS" principle (Keep It Short and Simple). Do not make the problem more difficult than it needs to be; take the simplest, most-direct, easiest-to-understand route to the solution.

WHAT YOU WILL NEED FOR THIS CLASS

All assignments in this text must be completed on an IBM PC, XT, AT, PS/2, or compatible machine. Your school probably has such machines available for your use; ask your instructor about the location and schedule of operation of the PC lab. Check with your instructor if you intend to use your own PC instead of the school's PC lab; some schools require lab attendance.

Additionally, you will need four personal flexible diskettes (floppies): one for your working diskette, one for a backup diskette, and two for use with your later programs that involve disk access. You will use your working diskette to store your programs; it is the one you will normally work with throughout this course.

As you work, you must periodically copy all your files from your working diskette to your backup diskette; the more often you back up the better. If at any time your working diskette becomes unusable (wears out or is damaged), you should purchase a new diskette and copy all your files onto it from the backup diskette. You should use your backup diskette *only* for that purpose, to maintain a backup copy of the data on your working diskette. You will not use the other two diskettes until chapter 11 when we study disk access.

Check with your instructor to determine the type of diskettes that are required by your school's PCs. Chances are that you will need double-sided, soft-sectored diskettes, either 5¼-inch or 3½-inch, and either double-density or high-density. Your school's bookstore probably sells the correct diskettes. Diskettes are also readily available from any computer store and most business-supply stores as well as many department stores.

Make sure you purchase double-sided diskettes. Many hobbyists and some professionals make a habit of using single-sided diskettes in machines with double-sided disk drives. This is a bad practice and may even be prohibited in your school's PC lab!

Figure 1-1   Flexible Diskettes

Most diskette manufacturers set out to produce only double-sided diskettes; most single-sided diskettes started out to be double-sided. Sometimes manufacturers, for marketing reasons, package and sell perfectly good double-sided diskettes as single-sided; often, however, diskettes are sold as single-sided because one side is defective, perhaps because the magnetic coating is improperly bonded to the diskette surface. Use of such a diskette in a double-sided disk drive is dangerous. When used in a double-sided drive, the coating may rub off onto the second read-write head, causing diskette errors for the user and for every subsequent user of the machine until the heads are cleaned.

If you plan to do all work in your school's PC lab, then the Macro Assembler will probably be available for your use in the lab, either on diskette or from a network file server. If, however, you plan to use your own PC, then you will also need to purchase a copy of the Microsoft or IBM Macro Assembler or the Turbo Assembler from Borland International. Any current version of the Macro Assembler or Turbo Assembler will work for all programming examples in this text. You will also need DEBUG.COM or SYMDEB.COM, which were supplied with earlier versions of the Macro Assembler; you should already have DEBUG.COM since it is included on the DOS diskette.

SOME ETHICAL AND LEGAL CONCERNS

Throughout your study of assembly language, you will make use of copyrighted software, and it is important that you not violate copyright laws. You must be especially careful if you plan to use the hardware and software provided by your school's PC lab. *Under no circumstances* should you make any copy of the programs provided for your use in the lab, however tempted you may be to do so. This admonishment applies to the operating system (MS-DOS, PC-DOS, or OS/2) as well as to the assembler and all programs supplied with it.

Your school has paid for a license (or licenses) to use the software in the PC laboratory under controlled conditions; you have not paid for any such license and so must not make any personal copies. If you plan to do your work on your own PC, you must purchase your own legal copy of the assembler and your own legal copy of DOS or OS/2, if you do not already own one. You must not copy your school's or anyone else's assembler or DOS diskette, nor should you go together with others to purchase one copy for use by several people. To do so constitutes theft and is both *illegal* and *unethical*!

Unfortunately, there is a widespread attitude among many computer hobbyists that such copying and/or sharing of copyrighted software is a harmless practice, that it hurts no one and so is permissible. This is not true! Such **software piracy** does indeed hurt others; it hurts all the many honest computer users who pay for what they use!

Software companies invest huge sums of money in the development of their products. In order to survive, they must take in enough money from the sale of licenses to repay that investment; they must also make a profit for investment in the development of new software and/or improvements to existing software. Software piracy constitutes huge losses of income for such companies, losses that must then be passed on to their honest customers in the form of increased prices. Any illegal copy of a copyrighted program is really stolen from the many honest computer users.

As a last word of warning, most educational institutions have very rigorous policies regarding any form of computer crime. In many cases, the copying of copyrighted software constitutes grounds for expulsion from the institution! In any case, always treat computer software just as you would other kinds of products: pay for what you use, and use only what you have paid for.

VOCABULARY

V1-1   In your own words, define each of the following terms:

a) High-level language

c) CPU

b) Fourth-generation language

d) Machine language

e) Language translator

k) Operating

f) Compiler

l) Utility program

g) Interpreter

m) Language processor

h) Assembler

n) KISS principle

j) System program

o) Software piracy

j) Communications-control program

REVIEW QUESTIONS

Q1-1   Describe the fundamental difference between a compiler and an assembler.

Q1-2   Why is assembly language not transportable?

Q1-3   Which gives the programmer the most freedom, a compiler or an assembler? Why?

Q1-4   Which requires the greatest degree of responsibility of the programmer, a compiler or an assembler? Why?

Q1-5   Which generates the most efficient machine-language code, assembly language or a high-level language? Why?

Q1-6   Which is most efficient for the programmer, assembly language or a high-level language? Why?

Q1-7   How does learning assembly language help one become a better programmer in high-level languages?

Q1-8   What are some of the differences between classroom programming and "real world" programming?

Q1-9   True or false: the operating system (MS-DOS, PC-DOS, or OS/2) is copyrighted software.

Q1-10   Is it permissible to copy the operating system when you have not purchased it?

Q1-11   Is it permissible for two or more people to share the cost of copyrighted software and then make extra copies for each?

Q1-12   Ultimately, who is hurt by software piracy?

2

Electronic Data Storage and Arithmetic

INTRODUCTION

In this chapter we will discuss some important basic ideas that are essential to an understanding of how computers function. Among other topics, we will discuss the manner in which data is stored, the organization of the data, and the way that the processor performs arithmetic. We will learn that all data is stored within the computer using the binary numeral system; consequently, we will discuss the binary numeral system, including binary arithmetic, in some detail. Since much computer documentation makes use of hexadecimal number representations, we will also discuss the hexadecimal numeral system.

ELECTRONIC DATA STORAGE

All data storage within a computer is provided by a collection of electronic "switches," each of which may be either on or off at any given moment. The processor has the ability to check the status of the switches whenever necessary. Also, with the exception of read-only memory, which will be discussed later, the processor is capable of turning switches on or off at will. The computer stores data by setting the appropriate group of switches to the correct positions. Numbers are stored by treating each switch as a single digit in a numeral. Since each switch has only two possible states, on or off, each digit in the numeral can be only one of two possibilities, one or zero.

Compare this with the **decimal numeral system**, in which each digit may be any one of ten possibilities, 0 through 9. The name decimal derives from the fact that ten different characters may be used to construct numerals; *decimus* is Latin for tenth. In the decimal numeral system, the numbers from zero through nine can all be represented by a single digit. The number ten requires two digits and is represented as 10.

The computer's system for representing numbers is called the **binary numeral system**; *binarius* is Latin for two or double. In binary, only the numbers zero and one can be represented by a single digit; the number two behaves like ten in the decimal system and must be represented by two digits: 10. Later in this chapter we will discuss the binary numeral system in detail.

DATA HIERARCHY

Each electronic switch within a computer's storage represents one **binary digit** and is commonly called a **bit** for short. In order to allow for the representation of numerals of more than one binary digit (required for any number greater than one), the computer's storage is organized into groups of bits. Although the grouping of bits varies with different processors, we will concern ourselves only with the grouping utilized by the 8086/8088.

In the IBM PC (or any other 8086/8088-based machine), a group of eight bits is called a **byte** and can store an eight-digit binary numeral. Sixteen bits (two bytes) taken as a group are referred to as a **word**. Sometimes sixteen binary digits are not sufficient, so we may group thirty-two bits together and call them a **double-word** (two words, four bytes). A **quad-word** is a group of sixty-four bits (four words, eight bytes). Occasionally we may wish to refer to half of a byte. The low four bits or high four bits of a byte are often called a **nibble**.

Later, we will discuss the ranges of values that can be stored in each of these groups of bits. For now, you should review and remember these terms:

KEY TERMS TO REMEMBER

Bit	=	BInary digiT, always zero or one.
Byte	=	A group of eight bits.
Word	=	A group of sixteen bits, two bytes.
Double-word	=	Two words, four bytes, thirty-two bits.

| Quad-word | = | Four words, eight bytes, sixty-four bits. |
| Nibble | = | Low four bits or high four bits of a byte. |

TYPES OF STORAGE

The processor has direct access to three types of data storage: **registers, read-only memory (ROM)** and **random-access memory (RAM)**. All are special integrated circuits (ICs), designed for the storage of data. Registers are groups of bits located within the processor itself. They are limited in number and are referred to by name, such as AX, BX, and SI. Since they are located within the processor, they are much more quickly accessible for the reading or writing of data than is memory, either RAM or ROM. The fourteen registers within the 8086/8088 are all **word registers**, made up of sixteen bits; however, four of them allow access to one-half the register at a time, as **byte registers**. We will discuss the 8086/8088 register set in much more detail in chapter 4.

Memory, both RAM and ROM, is external to the processor and is made up of a collection of integrated circuits (ICs) that plug into sockets on the system circuit board along with the processor. The processor "reads" the data in the memory or "writes" new data to memory through a collection of conductors called the System Bus. Since the memory is external to the processor, more time is required to access the data than is required to access registers.

Most of the IBM PC's memory is made up of random-access memory (RAM), which is really **read/write memory**; perhaps it should be called RWM instead of RAM. "Random access" refers to the fact that the processor can access any particular memory location just as quickly as any other; the term RAM is used to distinguish modern memory from the magnetic-drum main memory used by early computers, which did not provide such immediate access to any memory location. Although it allows both read and write access, random-access memory has one disadvantage; it is **volatile**. In chemistry, volatile refers to a liquid that evaporates when exposed to air; when referring to computer memory, it means that the contents of the memory are lost whenever the power is shut off to the computer.

Read-only memory also provides random access but is called ROM to distinguish it from RAM. ROM differs from RAM in two ways. First, ROM can only be read by the processor; it cannot be altered by it. Data or instructions are burned in at the factory and cannot thereafter be changed. The second difference, and the reason that ROM is used, is that it is **nonvolatile**; it does not lose its data when power is turned off. Normally, ROM is used to store basic operating system services that must be available immediately upon power up of the machine.

Figure 2-1   **System Board**

Bus
expansion
slots (5)

8088
microprocessor

128 K memory
(2 banks)

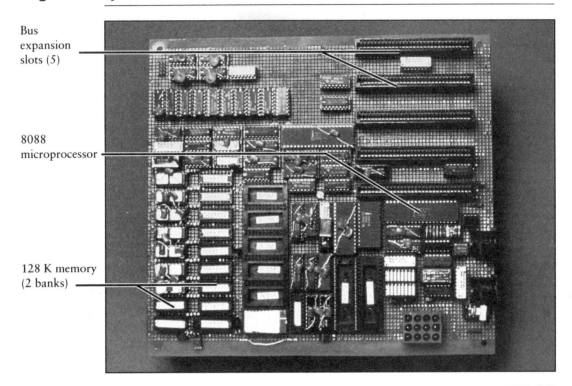

THE BINARY NUMERAL SYSTEM

Before beginning our discussion of the binary numeral system, we should clarify the difference between the terms, **number** and **numeral**. A number is a quantity, independent of the way in which it is represented. A numeral is the manner in which a number is written or represented. The same number may be represented in many ways. For example, twelve, 12, XII and 10+2 are four different *numerals*; however, they all represent the same *number*, the same quantity.

The binary numeral system is simply one more method for representing numbers. You should understand, then, that there is no such thing as a binary number! A number is a quantity, independent of its representation in binary or decimal or Roman numerals, or whatever.

To understand the binary system of numerals, we should first think about how we count in decimal numerals. In decimal, all the numbers from zero through nine are represented by a single digit. Once we go above nine, we are required to use two digits; the number ten is written as 10. Binary works the same way except that a single digit can only represent the numbers from zero through one. We must use more than one digit to represent any number above one; in binary, two must be written as 10.

A PAUSE IN THE ACTION

Why Binary Is Important

All computer storage is made up of electronic switches that are either on or off (two possible states). As a result, all data must be stored inside a computer in the binary numeral system, as a combination of ones and zeros. Additionally, all calculations are performed by the computer in binary. Consequently, an assembly-language programmer must be comfortable with the binary numeral system. You must understand how numbers are represented in binary and how the processor performs fundamental mathematical operations (addition, subtraction, multiplication, and division) in binary.

That could lead to a great deal of confusion, however. When presented with the numeral 10, how do we know if it is a decimal numeral representing the number ten, or a binary numeral representing the number two? Throughout this textbook, we will use the same convention as that used by the assembler. Binary numerals will be indicated by the letter B following the numeral. Thus 10 is a decimal numeral meaning ten, and 10B is a binary numeral representing the number two.

With that in mind, let us try counting in both decimal and binary numerals in order to see the pattern:

Figure 2-2 Counting Pattern in Decimal and Binary

Decimal	Binary	Decimal	Binary
0	0B	*	*
1	1B	*	*
2	10B	*	*
3	11B	97	1100001B
4	100B	98	1100010B
5	101B	99	1100011B
6	110B	100	1100100B
7	111B	101	1100101B
8	1000B	102	1100110B
9	1001B	103	1100111B
10	1010B	*	*
11	1011B	*	*
12	1100B	*	*

Notice that in decimal nine is the highest number that can be represented with a single digit (9); ten requires two digits (10). Also, in decimal ninety nine is the highest number that can be represented with two digits (99); one hundred requires three digits (100). Similarly the highest three-digit decimal numeral is nine hundred and ninety-nine (999); the number one thousand requires four digits (1000). Consequently, the **place values** of the decimal digits, from right to left, are ones, tens, hundreds, thousands, and so on. Stated as powers of ten, they are 10^0 (anything to the zero power is one), 10^1, 10^2, 10^3, 10^4, and so on.

The binary numeral system behaves much the same way except that one is the highest number that can be represented by a single digit (1B); two requires two digits (10B). The highest two-digit binary numeral (11B) represents the number three; four requires three digits (100B). Continuing the pattern, the highest three-digit binary numeral is seven (111B); eight requires four digits (1000B). The binary place values are 1, 2, 4, 8, 16, 32, 64, 128, 256, 512, 1024, and so on. Stated as exponents, the binary place values are 2^0, 2^1, 2^2, 2^3, 2^4, and so on.

Notice that 2^{10} is 1024, which is close to 1000; the prefix **kilo** is often used to mean 1024 when referring to computer memory. Kilo, often abbreviated as K, traditionally means one thousand; when referring to computer memory, however, kilo or K means 2^{10} or 1024. 64 kilobytes or 64 K, for example, means 64 times 1024 or 65536 bytes. Similarly the terms **mega** and **giga** traditionally mean one million (1000^2) and one billion (1000^3), respectively; in computer terminology, however, mega is used to mean 1024^2 or 2^{20}, and giga is used to denote 1024^3 or 2^{30}. One megabyte of memory, or one meg, means 1,048,576 bytes; one gigabyte is 1,073,741,824 bytes.

We have all grown up with the decimal numeral system and so have developed an intuitive feel for the quantity (number) represented by a decimal numeral; we have an immediate idea of the size of a decimal numeral such as 3467. Most of us however, have not the slightest intuitive feel for the magnitude of binary numerals since binary is not our native numeral system; most people have no immediate notion of the size of a binary numeral such as 1001101011B. To understand the size of a number, we must see it represented as a decimal numeral. Consequently, we often need to convert a binary numeral to its equivalent decimal numeral, so that we may understand the number it represents.

KEY TERMS TO REMEMBER

Decimal numeral system	RAM
Binary numeral system	Volatile, Nonvolatile
Register	Number vs. numeral
ROM	Kilo, mega, giga

CONVERTING FROM BINARY TO DECIMAL

You may recall, from elementary school math classes, having been required to express decimal numerals in terms of the sum of the digits times their place values. For example, 34,816 is equal to 3 * 10000 plus 4 * 1000 plus 8 * 100 plus 1 * 10 plus 6 * 1 ("*" means "times"). A similar process may be used to convert a binary numeral to decimal, with two major differences. First, the place values are all powers of two rather than powers of ten. Second, all digits are either one or zero; consequently, the value to be added for each digit is either the place value itself or zero.

To convert a binary numeral to a decimal numeral, first list the binary place values for all the digits. Then add up all the place values where the digit is 1. We will use the binary numeral, 1001101011B, as an example.

```
1 0 0 1 1 0 1 0 1 1 B   Binary numeral

5 2 1 6 3 1 8 4 2 1     Place values written
1 5 2 4 2 6             as decimal numerals
2 6 8                   (Read down)
```

The value, in decimal, of the binary numeral is simply the sum of all the place values in which the digit is 1.

```
   512
    64
    32
     8
     2
+    1
   619
```

Since decimal is our native numeral system, we understand the size of 619 and so can now comprehend the magnitude of 1001101011B; they are both the same number: six hundred and nineteen. Another algorithm, sometimes called the **double-dabble algorithm,** can be used to convert from binary to decimal numerals. In pseudocode, the double-dabble method is as follows:

```
Start with zero for the decimal numeral
Get the first binary digit (left-most)
Repeat while you have a digit
     Double the decimal numeral
     Add the binary digit (0 or 1) to the decimal numeral
     Get the next binary digit, if any (from left to right)
End repeat
```

Following is an example using the same binary numeral —1001101011B:

0	Start with zero
× 2	Double the decimal numeral
0	
+ 1	Add first (left-most) digit
1	
× 2	Double the decimal numeral
2	
+ 0	Add second digit (from left)
2	
× 2	Double again
4	
+ 0	Third digit (from left)
4	
× 2	
8	
+ 1	Fourth digit (from left)
9	
× 2	
18	
+ 1	Fifth digit (from left)
19	
× 2	
38	
+ 0	Sixth digit (from left)
38	
× 2	
76	
+ 1	Seventh digit (from left)
77	
× 2	
154	
+ 0	Eighth digit (from left)
154	
× 2	
308	
+ 1	Ninth digit (from left)

```
  309
×   2
  618
+   1      Tenth digit (from left)
  619      Decimal numeral
```

Note that the decimal numeral is multiplied by two nine times after adding the left-most digit; thus, that digit is ultimately multiplied by 2^9, or 512. The next 1 (fourth digit from the left) is multiplied by two six times; its value ends up being 2^6, or 64. Thus, the result is the same as in the first conversion algorithm.

The double-dabble algorithm is more complicated and involves a greater chance for error than simply adding the place values; consequently it is probably not a very good algorithm for use by people. However, since it involves performing the same sequence of simple steps repeatedly, it is an ideal algorithm for a computer. We will use a similar algorithm in chapter 10 to convert a string to its numeric value.

CONVERTING FROM DECIMAL TO BINARY

The easiest algorithm for converting a decimal numeral to binary is essentially the opposite of the double-dabble algorithm. Instead of repeatedly multiplying by two and adding the next digit, it involves repeatedly dividing by two and taking the remainder as the next digit. Consider the result of dividing a number by two. The quotient tells us how many twos are in the number while the remainder gives the number of ones; thus, the remainder (0 or 1) provides the right-most digit of the binary numeral.

If the quotient from the previous division is again divided by two, the resulting quotient is the number of fours in the original number while the remainder (again 0 or 1) is the number of twos or the second binary digit from the right. By repeating the division until the quotient becomes zero, we are able to construct the binary numeral, from right to left, from the remainders. In pseudocode, the conversion algorithm can be stated as follows:

```
Build the binary numeral from right to left, starting with
                                            the ones place
Repeat
      Divide the decimal numeral by two
            The remainder provides the next binary digit
                                    (from right to left)
            The quotient provides the decimal numeral for
                                    the next division
Until the decimal numeral equals zero
```

Following is an example, using the decimal numeral 173.

$$
\begin{array}{r}
86 \\ \hline
2\,)\,\overline{173}
\end{array}
\quad \text{R 1} \qquad \text{1s place} = 1
$$

$$
\begin{array}{r}
43 \\ \hline
2\,)\,\overline{86}
\end{array}
\quad \text{R 0} \qquad \text{2s place} = 0
$$

$$
\begin{array}{r}
21 \\ \hline
2\,)\,\overline{43}
\end{array}
\quad \text{R 1} \qquad \text{4s place} = 1
$$

$$
\begin{array}{r}
10 \\ \hline
2\,)\,\overline{21}
\end{array}
\quad \text{R 1} \qquad \text{8s place} = 1
$$

$$
\begin{array}{r}
5 \\ \hline
2\,)\,\overline{10}
\end{array}
\quad \text{R 0} \qquad \text{16s place} = 0
$$

$$
\begin{array}{r}
2 \\ \hline
2\,)\,\overline{5}
\end{array}
\quad \text{R 1} \qquad \text{32s place} = 1
$$

$$
\begin{array}{r}
1 \\ \hline
2\,)\,\overline{2}
\end{array}
\quad \text{R 0} \qquad \text{64s place} = 0
$$

$$
\begin{array}{r}
0 \\ \hline
2\,)\,\overline{1}
\end{array}
\quad \text{R 1} \qquad \text{128s place} = 1
$$

Thus, the decimal numeral 173 is equivalent to the binary numeral 10101101B. Like the double-dabble algorithm, this method also lends itself well to a computer solution since it involves repeating the same simple steps until some condition is met. We will use it in chapter 10 to convert a numeric value to a string.

Another algorithm that is often used to obtain the binary numeral for a number expressed in decimal is the reverse of our first method of converting from binary to decimal. It can be stated as follows:

```
Start on left side of binary numeral
Find the greatest binary place value LE decimal numeral
Repeat while place value is GE one
     If decimal numeral GE place value
          Next binary digit (from left to right) is one
          Subtract place value from decimal numeral
     Else (decimal numeral LT place value)
          Next binary digit (from left to right) is zero
     End if
     Divide place value by two
End repeat
```

Standard Pseudocode Abbreviations

The pseudocode above and throughout the rest of the text uses the following abbreviations for indicating relationships:

EQ - is equal to	GE - is greater than or equal to
NE - is not equal to	LT - is less than
GT - is greater than	LE - is less than or equal to

Following is an example using the same decimal numeral—173. First, the greatest binary place value that is less than or equal to 173 is 128.

```
   173
 - 128      Left-most digit (128s) = 1
    45
```

Next digit from left (64s place) = 0, since 45 LT 64

```
    45
 -  32      Next digit (32s place) = 1
    13
```

Next digit (16s place) = 0, since 13 LT 16

```
    13
 -   8      Next digit (8s place) = 1
     5

     5
 -   4      Next digit (4s place) = 1
     1
```

Next digit (2s place) = 0, since 1 LT 2

```
     1
 -   1      Last digit (1s place) = 1
     0
```

Again, the result is 10101101B.

BINARY ARITHMETIC

Not only does a computer store all data in binary, but the processor also performs all arithmetic (addition, subtraction, multiplication, and division) in binary. Consequently, we can enhance our own understanding of the machine by also learning how to compute in binary. You may be surprised to discover that binary arithmetic is really much simpler and less complicated than is decimal arithmetic; however, you will also discover that it is much more laborious and repetitious.

Binary Addition

First we will examine binary addition. Recall that binary numerals are similar to decimal numerals except that the place values are powers of two instead of powers of ten. Consequently, the algorithm for adding in binary is very similar to that used in decimal addition, with two differences. First, binary addition does not require a knowledge of all the sums that we had to memorize in order to add in decimal. Think back to the time when your teacher stopped allowing you to count on your fingers; you probably recall having some difficulty in remembering such sums as $5 + 7$, $8 + 6$, $9 + 4$, $9 + 9$, and so on. To add in binary, we need only to know the sums of $0 + 0$, $0 + 1$, $1 + 0$, and $1 + 1$.

The other difference is that, since 1 is the highest digit allowed in binary, we will have to carry any time a sum is greater than one; in decimal, we carry only when the sum is greater than nine. As an example of binary addition, we will add the numerals 100101101B and 001111110B. Just as in decimal addition, we should begin with the ones place (right-most digit): one plus zero equals one, so the ones place in the sum is 1. Then we move over to the twos place: zero plus one equals one, so the second digit in the sum is also 1.

```
  1 0 0 1 0 1 1 0 1 B
+ 0 0 1 1 1 1 1 1 0 B
                1 1 B
```

Adding in the next place (fours) generates a carry. One plus one equals two, but we cannot use 2 as a binary digit; in binary, two is written as 10B, which is a two-digit numeral. We handle it the same as a sum greater than nine in decimal addition: we carry the left-most digit (twos place).

```
            1
  1 0 0 1 0 1 1 0 1 B
+ 0 0 1 1 1 1 1 1 0 B
              0 1 1 B
```

Now we add the next place (eights): one (the carry) plus one plus one equals three, which is written in binary as 11B. Again, we must carry the left-most digit.

Actually, the processor does not add all three ones at a time. It adds the two digits, resulting in 0 with 1 to carry; then it adds the previous carry to the 0, resulting in 1.

```
        1 1
    1 0 0 1 0 1 1 0 1 B
+ 0 0 1 1 1 1 1 1 0 B
              1 0 1 1 B
```

Continuing the same process, right-to-left, we arrive at the sum 110101011B.

```
      1 1 1 1 1
    1 0 0 1 0 1 1 0 1 B
+ 0 0 1 1 1 1 1 1 0 B
  1 1 0 1 0 1 0 1 1 B
```

We can easily verify our results by converting to decimal, adding, and converting the sum back to binary: 100101101B = 301; 001111110B = 126; 301 + 126 = 427; 427 = 110101011B.

Binary Subtraction

Binary subtraction is similar to decimal subtraction, except that whenever we borrow one and bring it to the next place to the right it is worth two instead of ten. As an example, we will subtract 01010110B from 10001010B. Again, we begin with the right-most (ones) place: zero minus zero equals zero, so the right-most digit in the difference is 0. We then move over to the twos place: one minus one equals zero, so the twos place in the difference is also 0.

```
    1 0 0 0 1 0 1 0 B
 -  0 1 0 1 0 1 1 0 B
                0 0 B
```

The fours place requires borrowing, since we cannot subtract one from zero; we simply borrow one from the next place, just as we would in decimal subtraction. The difference is that the binary place values are powers of two instead of ten. Thus, we borrow one from the eights place, leaving zero; one eight is worth two fours, so we now have two in the fours place and can do the subtraction: two minus one equals one.

```
            0 2
    1 0 0 0 1̶ 0̶ 1 0 B
 -  0 1 0 1 0 1 1 0 B
              1 0 0 B
```

Moving on to the eights place: zero minus zero equals zero. We again have to borrow before subtracting in the 16s place; however, the next place over (32s) is zero. We have to move over to the left-most place before we are able to borrow; we then must work our way back across to the 16s place: borrow one from the 128s place, leaving zero 128s and giving two 64s; now, borrow one from the 64s place, leaving one 64 and giving two 32s; finally, borrow one from the 32s place, leaving one 32 and giving two 16s.

```
    1 1
  0 2 2 2 0 2
  1 0 0 0 1 0 1 0 B
- 0 1 0 1 0 1 1 0 B
          0 1 0 0 B
 128 64 32 16  8  4  2  0
```

We are now able to complete the subtraction, resulting in the difference: 00110100B.

```
    1 1
  0 2 2 2 0 2
  1 0 0 0 1 0 1 0 B
- 0 1 0 1 0 1 1 0 B
  0 0 1 1 0 1 0 0 B
```

Again, we can check our results by converting to decimal, subtracting, and converting back to binary: 10001010B = 138; 01010110B = 86; 138 − 86 = 52; 52 = 00110100B.

Twos-Complement Addition

We should note at this point that processors do not perform subtraction in the above manner; in fact, processors do not subtract at all! In order to keep the CPU circuitry as simple as possible, subtraction is performed as **twos-complement addition**. This actually coincides with your previous experience with math; recall from high school algebra that subtraction is defined as adding the opposite, where the opposite of a number is simply the number that must be added to it to get zero. Thus an expression such as 5 − 11 is rewritten as 5 + -11 (five plus negative eleven). In binary, the opposite of a number is represented as a twos-complement binary numeral.

To obtain the twos complement of a binary numeral, we first obtain its ones complement by inverting all the bits (change 1 to 0 and change 0 to 1). The twos complement may then be obtained by incrementing (adding one to) the ones complement. As an example, we obtain the twos complement of 01110010B as follows:

```
0 1 1 1 0 0 1 0 B      Numeral to start with
1 0 0 0 1 1 0 1 B      Ones complement (all bits inverted)
            + 1
1 0 0 0 1 1 1 0 B      Twos complement of 01110010B
```

We can verify that 10001110B is indeed the opposite of 01110010B by adding them; the sum of any number and its opposite is always zero.

```
1 1 1 1 1 1 1
  0 1 1 1 0 0 1 0 B
+ 1 0 0 0 1 1 1 0 B
  0 0 0 0 0 0 0 0 B
```

Notice that the result is zero *only* if we ignore the last carry. One of the rules of twos-complement addition is that the carry out of the high-order bit must be thrown away. Actually, we will learn later that the processor uses the last carry, or lack thereof, to control a bit within the Flags (or Program Status) register. For now, the last carry is to be ignored. With that in mind, we can now use twos-complement addition to perform the same subtraction as in the preceding binary subtraction example. Recall that we subtracted 01010110B from 10001010B. Rather than subtracting, we first obtain the twos complement of 01010110B:

```
0 1 0 1 0 1 1 0 B
1 0 1 0 1 0 0 1 B      Ones complement (reverse bits)
            + 1
1 0 1 0 1 0 1 0 B      Twos complement
```

Now, instead of subtracting, we simply add the twos complement:

```
1         1   1
  1 0 0 0 1 0 1 0 B
+ 1 0 1 0 1 0 1 0 B       Twos complement of 01010110B
  0 0 1 1 0 1 0 0 B
```

By throwing away the last carry, we obtain 00110100B, which is the same result we obtained earlier by subtraction. By reducing subtraction to reversing bits, incrementing, and then adding, the designers of the processor were able to avoid the need to build in extra circuitry to do subtraction; the result is a simpler design for the processor.

Binary Multiplication

Even better than addition or subtraction, multiplication demonstrates the beautiful simplicity of binary arithmetic. We need only to know the multiplication tables up to one times one!

To multiply in binary, begin with the ones place of the multiplier (bottom number), and multiply it times the multiplicand, right to left, writing the answer beginning just below the ones place. Then do the same with the twos place of the multiplier, writing the answer beginning under the twos place. Repeat the process for all digits in the multiplier. Finally, add the results of all the multiplications to obtain the product.

Since each digit of a binary multiplier is either zero or one, the multiplication is very easy: if it is one, simply copy the multiplicand; if it is zero, forget it, and go to the next digit, since zero times anything is zero. The following example computes the product of 10001010B and 1011B. First, multiply each digit in the multiplier times the multiplicand, ignoring the fours place since it is zero.

```
        1 0 0 0 1 0 1 0 B
    ×           1 0 1 1 B
        1 0 0 0 1 0 1 0
    1 0 0 0 1 0 1 0
1 0 0 0 1 0 1 0
```

Now add the results of each of the three multiplications, giving the product 10111101110B.

```
        1 0 0 0 1 0 1 0 B
    ×           1 0 1 1 B
        1 0 0 0 1 0 1 0
      1 0 0 0 1 0 1 0
  1 0 0 0 1 0 1 0
  1 0 1 1 1 1 0 1 1 1 0 B
```

Check it: 10001010B = 138; 1011B = 11; 11 * 138 = 1518; 1518 = 10111101110B.

Binary Division

Binary division is also very simple. We will use the example of 10001010B divided by 1010B. Just as in decimal division, we begin on the left of the dividend (10001010B) looking for the digit where we can begin dividing: 1B is less than the divisor; 10B is still too small; similarly, 100B and 1000B are still too small to divide by 1010B; finally, 10001B is big enough.

Now, we see why binary division is so simple. If we were dividing in decimal we would have to guess the digit (from 1 to 9) in the quotient; we would then write down our guess, multiply it times the divisor, and attempt to subtract, only to discover as often as not that our guess was too small or too big. In binary, we have no such problem; if a numeral is divisible at all by another numeral, then it is always divisible exactly one time. Thus, we write 1 for the first digit in the quotient, multiply it times the divisor (that is also easy), and subtract.

```
                1
1 0 1 0 B ) 1 0 0 0 1 0 1 0 B
          - 1 0 1 0
            1 1 1
```

After subtracting, we bring down the next digit just as in decimal division, and check to see if the result is divisible. 1110B is greater than the divisor, 1010B, so it is divisible one time. Again, we write 1, multiply back, and subtract.

```
                1 1
1 0 1 0 B ) 1 0 0 0 1 0 1 0 B
          - 1 0 1 0
              1 1 1 0
            - 1 0 1 0
              1 0 0
```

Bring down the next digit, 1, and check the result. 1001B is too small to divide by 1010B; more correctly, it is divisible zero times, so we write 0 above the digit that we just brought down.

```
                1 1 0
1 0 1 0 B ) 1 0 0 0 1 0 1 0 B
          - 1 0 1 0
              1 1 1 0
            - 1 0 1 0
              1 0 0 1
```

Now we can bring down the last digit. 10010B is larger than 1010B, so it is divisible one time. Write 1 for the last digit in the quotient, multiply back, and subtract.

```
                1 1 0 1 B   Remainder 1 0 0 0 B
1 0 1 0 B ) 1 0 0 0 1 0 1 0 B
          - 1 0 1 0
              1 1 1 0
            - 1 0 1 0
                1 0 0 1 0
              - 1 0 1 0
                1 0 0 0
```

The difference resulting from the last subtraction is not zero, so the division results in a remainder: quotient 1101B, remainder 1000B. As in decimal division, we must check to ensure that the remainder is less than the divisor; if not, we have made an error. The 8086/8088 microprocessor does division in much the same manner, resulting in an integer quotient with a remainder.

We could express our result as a fraction, 1101B 1000B/1010B. Alternately, if we were doing decimal division, we might write a decimal point and several zeros at the end of the dividend and carry it out as a decimal fraction. We can do the same thing in binary, except that the period is a **binary point** rather than a decimal point, and the result is a **binary fraction** rather than a decimal fraction. The place values to the right of the binary point are not tenths, hundredths, or thousandths; they are halves, fourths, eighths, sixteenths, and so on (2^{-1}, 2^{-2}, 2^{-3}, 2^{-4}, etc.).

```
                              1 1 0 1 . 1 1 0 0 1 1 0 0
                      ┌─────────────────────────────────
         1 0 1 0 B )  1 0 0 0 1 0 1 0 . 0 0 0 0 0 0 0 0
                      - 1 0 1 0
                          1 1 1 0
                        - 1 0 1 0
                            1 0 0 1 0
                          - 1 0 1 0
                              1 0 0 0   0
                            - 1 0 1   0
                                1 1     0 0
                              - 1 0     1 0
                                  1 0 0 0 0
                                - 1 0 1 0
                                    1 1 0 0
                                  - 1 0 1 0
                                      1 0 0 0
```

Notice that carrying the division out results in a repeating binary fraction (1100 repeats forever). This may seem strange since we divided by ten (1010B = 10). We know that division by 10 *never* results in a repeating decimal fraction; why did we get a repeating binary fraction? The answer lies in the place values; one tenth cannot be expressed exactly as a sum of the binary place values (halves, fourths, eighths, and so on). In binary division, any divisor that is not a power of two may result in a repeating binary fraction. It is this fact that causes the unexpected rounding errors that are sometimes produced by computer systems.

REPRESENTING SIGNED INTEGERS IN BINARY

All of our preceding discussion has dealt only with representing positive integers in binary form; we have assumed that the number is positive and used all available bits as binary digits. When all bits are interpreted as binary digits and the number is assumed to be positive, the binary numeral is referred to as an **unsigned integer**. Often, however, a computer must store negative as well as positive values; this is done by treating the high-order bit as a sign rather than as a binary digit. When the high bit is interpreted as a sign, we refer to the data as a **signed integer**.

In signed-integer storage a zero in the high bit indicates that the value is positive; the positive value is then represented in binary in the remaining bits. If the high bit is one in a signed integer, then the value is negative and is represented in the remaining bits in **twos-complement form**. The bit patterns 00000000B through 01111111B represent the positive integers +0 through +127; the patterns 10000000B through 11111111B represent the negative integers -128 through -1. Notice that zero is stored as a positive integer, contrary to what you learned in algebra (that zero is neither positive nor negative). Also notice that what looks like a negative zero (10000000B) is really -128.

Figure 2-3 indicates all the possible values that may be stored in one byte when interpreted as an unsigned integer and when interpreted as a signed integer (high bit = sign):

Figure 2-3   **Byte Values, Signed and Unsigned**

BIT Pattern	Unsigned	Signed
00000000B	0	+0
00000001B	1	+1
00000010B	2	+2
00000011B	3	+3
$\star$	$\star$	$\star$
$\star$	$\star$	$\star$
$\star$	$\star$	$\star$
01111101B	125	+125
01111110B	126	+126
01111111B	127	+127
10000000B	128	-128
10000001B	129	-127
10000010B	130	-126
$\star$	$\star$	$\star$
$\star$	$\star$	$\star$
$\star$	$\star$	$\star$
11111100B	252	-4
11111101B	253	-3
11111110B	254	-2
11111111B	255	-1

It is very important to understand at this point that the processor makes no distinction between unsigned and signed integers. To the processor, 00000011B

+ 10000010B = 10000101B. It is entirely up to the programmer to interpret the results as 3 + 130 = 133 (unsigned) or as +3 + -126 = -123 (signed). (Note that as a signed value 10000010B equals -126 since its twos complement is 01111110B, and 10000101B equals -123 since its twos complement is 01111011B.) Similarly, 00000001B + 11110000B is always 11110001B; it might represent either 1 + 240 = 241 (unsigned) or +1 + -16 = -15, depending on the programmer's intent. The processor neither knows nor cares whether a particular bit pattern represents a signed or an unsigned integer; that is up to the programmer.

RANGES OF VALUES: BIT, BYTE, WORD, DOUBLE-WORD, QUAD-WORD

We shall now examine the numeric values that may be stored in the various groupings of bits that were discussed earlier. A single bit can store a value that is either zero or one. From the table above, we see that a byte can store a range of values from 0 through 255 if it represents an unsigned integer; when used to store a signed integer, a single byte can store a value from negative 128 through positive 127. A word (sixteen bits) stores binary numerals from 0000000000000000B through 1111111111111111B; converting to decimal, we obtain the range for a word of 0 through 65,535 (as an unsigned integer), or from negative 32,768 through positive 32,767 (as a signed integer).

A double-word consists of thirty-two bits and can store an unsigned integer from 0 through 4,294,967,295 or a signed integer from negative 2,147,483,648 through positive 2,147,483,647. A quad-word (sixty-four bits) can store an unsigned integer from 0 through 18,446,744,073,709,551,615 or a signed integer from negative 9,223,372,036,854,775,808 to positive 9,223,372,036,854,775,807.

HEXADECIMAL NUMERAL SYSTEM

Hexadecimal comes from the Latin *hexas* (six) and *decimus* (ten), and means *base sixteen*. The **hexadecimal numeral system** uses sixteen characters to represent numbers: 0 through 9 and A through F; A is worth ten, B is worth eleven, C is twelve, D is thirteen, E is fourteen and F is fifteen. The place values are all powers of sixteen: 1, 16, 256, 4096, 65536, and so on (16^0, 16^1, 16^2, 16^3, 16^4, and so on). Following the assembler's convention, we will indicate all hexadecimal numerals with the letter H, as in 7FH, which is the number 127 (7 * 16 + 15 * 1).

A PAUSE IN THE ACTION

Why Hexadecimal Is Important

Although the binary numeral system is convenient for the computer, it is often inconvenient for people due to the number of digits required to represent a number of any size. As a result, most documentation uses numeral systems of a higher base; numbers are often represented in the hexadecimal numeral system. Hexadecimal serves as a sort of shorthand for binary, in order to reduce the number of digits required without completely losing sight of the binary bit patterns.

The use of decimal numerals also reduces the number of digits required to represent a given number, but we have already seen the difficulty in converting between binary and decimal; it is no simple process. It is very difficult to envision, without laborious conversion, the bit pattern (binary numeral) resulting from a number that has been represented in decimal. However, conversion between binary and hexadecimal is very quick and easy and can be done mentally, without pencil and paper. Consequently, hexadecimal provides a convenient means of abbreviating binary numerals whenever the binary bit pattern is important.

Since the hexadecimal numeral system is so commonly used in documentation, we need to become familiar with it.

BINARY/HEXADECIMAL NUMERAL CONVERSION

As mentioned earlier, conversion between binary and hexadecimal is very simple. This simplicity results from the fact that sixteen is a power of two ($16 = 2^4$). Consider the resulting hexadecimal and binary place values. The hexadecimal place values are 1, 16, 256, 4096, and so on. The binary place values are *1*, 2, 4, 8, *16*, 32, 64, 128, *256*, 512, 1024, 2048, *4096*, and so on. Every fourth binary place value is the same as the next hexadecimal place value.

In fact four binary digits are exactly equivalent to one hexadecimal digit. One hexadecimal digit can have a value from 0 through F, or zero through fifteen; this coincides exactly with the values that can be represented by four binary digits: 0000B through 1111B. Consequently, in order to convert from hexadecimal to binary, we merely expand each hexadecimal digit to four binary digits. For example:

```
FAH =      1111 1010B or 11111010B
80BCH =    1000 0000 1011 1100B or 1000000010111100B
74DH =     0111 0100 1101B or 11101001101B
```

To convert from binary to hexadecimal, simply break the binary numeral into groups of four digits, and convert each group into one hexadecimal digit.

10010110B is 1001 0110B = 96H
0101000100100011B is 0101 0001 0010 0011B = 5123H
101001001110B is 1010 0100 1110B = A4EH

Notice that eight bits (one byte) becomes exactly two hexadecimal digits; one word is exactly four hexadecimal digits. Each hexadecimal digit represents one nibble.

KEY TERMS TO REMEMBER

Twos-complement addition	Unsigned integer
Binary point	Twos-complement form
Binary fraction	Hexadecimal numeral system
Signed integer	

HEXADECIMAL/DECIMAL CONVERSION

Documentation may show numbers in hexadecimal or decimal. Sometimes it is necessary to convert not to binary but to another of those two bases in order to fully understand the documentation. Consequently, we will now discuss conversions between hexadecimal and decimal.

Converting from hexadecimal to decimal, is similar to converting from binary to decimal, except that the place values are different (1, 16, 256, 4096, and so on), and each digit may be any value from 0 through F (fifteen). Simply multiply each hexadecimal digit by its place value and add the results.

```
4FABH =    4  * 4096 = 16384
       + 15 *  256 =  3840
       + 10 *  16  =   160
       + 11 *  1   =    11
                      20395
```

The easiest method of converting from decimal to hexadecimal is to perform repeated division; divide repeatedly by sixteen, using the remainders as the hexadecimal digits. Remember that the remainders provide the digits from right to left; the remainder of the first division is the ones place. To convert decimal 4523 to hexadecimal do the following calculations:

```
       282 R 11 (B)
16 ) 4523
        17 R 10 (A)
16 ) 282
         1 R 1
16 ) 17
         0 R 1
16 ) 1
4523 = 11ABH
```

We can summarize the base conversions discussed in this chapter as follows:

S U M M A R Y O F Base Conversions

Decimal to any other base:

Divide repeatedly by the desired base. The remainders provide the digits from right to left.

Any other base to decimal:

Write down the place values. Multiply each digit by its place value and add up the results.

Hexadecimal to binary:

Convert each hexadecimal digit to four binary digits.

Binary to hexadecimal:

Break into groups of four binary digits, from right to left. Convert each group of four binary digits to a single hexadecimal digit.

SUMMARY

All data storage inside a computer is made up of a series of electronic switches, each of which can represent either zero or one. The processor has immediate access to two types of storage: registers, which are within the processor, and memory, which is external to the processor but directly connected to it by a series of conductors on the circuit board. There are two types of memory: RAM and ROM. The processor can alter the contents of RAM (random-access memory) as well as read its contents; thus it is often referred to as read/write memory. ROM is read-only memory; its contents cannot be altered. It is used because it is non-volatile.

In order to store numbers, each switch is used as a single binary (base two) digit or bit. In order to store numbers larger than one, bits must be grouped together into bytes, words, double-words, and/or quad-words. All arithmetic is performed in binary by the processor; the beautiful simplicity of the binary numeral system permits the simplest possible circuitry within the processor. The processor circuitry need only "know" the sums from 0 plus 0 up to 1 plus 1 and the products from 0 times 0 up to 1 times 1.

In order to save digits, computer documentation often uses hexadecimal numerals. Each hexadecimal digit is exactly equivalent to four binary digits. Consequently, the conversion between binary and hexadecimal is quick and simple. Converting between decimal and either binary or hexadecimal is not so simple. To convert any other base to decimal, multiply each digit of the numeral times its place value and add the results. To convert from decimal to any other base, divide repeatedly by the base; each remainder provides one digit working from right to left.

VOCABULARY

V2-1   In your own words, define each of the following terms:

a) Decimal numeral system	m) Read/write memory
b) Binary numeral system	n) Volatile
c) Hexadecimal numeral system	o) Nonvolatile
d) Bit	p) Number
e) Byte	q) Numeral
f) Word	r) Twos-complement addition
g) Double-word	s) Binary point
h) Quad-word	t) Binary fraction
i) Nibble	u) Unsigned integer
j) Register	v) Signed integer
k) RAM	w) Twos-complement form
l) ROM	

REVIEW QUESTIONS

Q2-1   List the first twenty-one binary place values beginning with the ones place (right to left).

Q2-2   List the first six hexadecimal place values (from right to left).

Q2-3   What is the range of values that can be represented in one byte, if interpreted as an unsigned integer? If interpreted as a signed integer?

Q2-4 What is the range of values that can be represented in one word, if interpreted as an unsigned integer? If interpreted as a signed integer?

Q2-5 What is the range of values that can be represented in a double-word, if interpreted as an unsigned integer? If interpreted as a signed integer?

Q2-6 How does the processor do subtraction? Does the CPU need to "know" how to borrow?

Q2-7 What does it mean when the high bit of a signed integer is 1?

Q2-8 Why do computers often produce results with unexpected rounding off errors?

Q2-9 Why is the hexadecimal numeral system often used in computer documentation?

Q2-10 Why is ROM memory often used in computers? Is it likely that a computer might use *only* ROM memory (no RAM)?

Q2-11 Which can the processor access most quickly, registers or memory?

Q2-12 How many bytes is one kilobyte? One megabyte? One gigabyte?

PROBLEMS

P2-1 Do the necessary base conversions to complete the following table:

Binary	Decimal	Hexadecimal
11011100B	_____	_____
_____	15435D	_____
_____	_____	1FD3H

P2-2 Do the necessary base conversions to complete the following table:

Binary	Decimal	Hexadecimal
10101111B	_____	_____
_____	23567D	_____
_____	_____	AC45H

P2-3 Add in binary; show carrying.

01110101B + 10111011B

P2-4 Add in binary; show carrying.

01111111B + 00110010B

P2-5 Subtract in binary; show borrowing.

11111110B - 00010011B

P2-6 Subtract in binary; show borrowing.

10000110B - 01100011B

P2-7   Use twos-complement addition to do the same subtraction as in P2-5; show all work.

11111110B - 00010011B

P2-8   Use twos-complement addition to do the same subtraction as in P2-6; show all work.

10000110B - 01100011B

P2-9   Multiply in binary; show all work.

10100101B * 00011101B

P2-10   Multiply in binary; show all work.

01111010B * 00100110B

P2-11   Do the following binary division; show all work.

0000010111100011B / 1011B

P2-12   Do the following binary division; show all work.

1001010111100011B / 00001011B

P2-13   Just for fun, try the following problems using hexadecimal arithmetic.

C1B5H + 28BFH
C1B5H - 28BFH
C1B5H * 0023H
C1B4H / 0BH

3

PC Operation and
System Software

INTRODUCTION

We need to gain some familiarity with the IBM PC and its system software before attempting to learn to program in assembly language. This chapter discusses some fundamentals of PC operation, the operating system (MS-DOS, PC-DOS, and others), BIOS (Basic Input/Output System), and DEBUG, which is a tool for the writing and/or debugging of assembly-language programs. We will also discuss SYMDEB and CodeView but have chosen to emphasize DEBUG for three reasons: it is always available (on the DOS diskette), it is quick and relatively easy to learn, and it provides commands which will enable us to learn quickly to write and save some simple assembly-language programs (a capability not provided by the more complex and more powerful CodeView).

Upon completion of the chapter, you should be familiar with the PC hardware, know how to "boot" the system, understand the most commonly used DOS commands, and have a beginning comprehension of the inner workings of the operating system and BIOS, and the manner in which they provide services to programs. In addition, you should be familiar with the use of DEBUG or SYMDEB for the creation, viewing, and testing of machine-language programs.

MAJOR HARDWARE COMPONENTS

All computers are made up of four functional types of hardware: **processing hardware**, **input hardware**, **output hardware**, and **auxiliary-storage hardware**. In addition, a system may contain a fifth type, **communications hardware**, to enable it to communicate with other computers. Figure 3-1 provides a schematic view of the interaction of the fundamental computer components.

Processing hardware is the nucleus of the system and is made up of the **Central Processing Unit** or **CPU**, **main storage** (memory, both RAM and ROM), and the necessary support circuitry. On the IBM PC, the processing hardware is contained within the CPU cabinet (refer to Figure 3-2) and utilizes an Intel 8088 mi-

Figure 3-1   Interaction of Computer Components

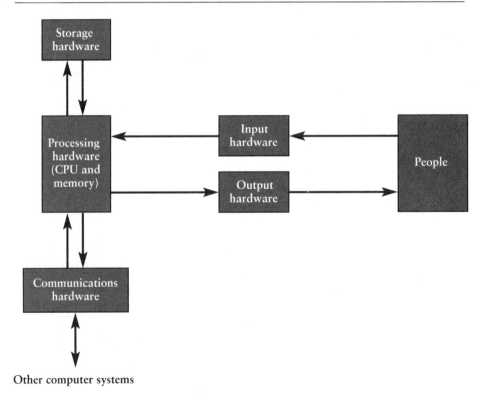

croprocessor. Compatible machines may use another microprocessor within the 8086/8088 family (8086, 8088, 80186, 80286, 80386, 80386SX, 80486, or 80586). The processor will be discussed more thoroughly in the next chapter.

Input hardware converts data or information from people-understandable form to electronic form for storage in memory and/or for processing by the CPU; it moves data in from a person to the processing hardware. The primary input hardware for a PC is the keyboard (see Figure 3-2). Whenever a key is pressed or released, the keyboard hardware converts it to a unique scan code (electronic form) and passes it to the CPU for interpretation and storage in memory. Some other input devices which are commonly used with the IBM PC are a mouse, barcode reader, light pen, digitizer pad, and touch-sensitive screen. The keyboard will be discussed more fully in chapter 9.

Output hardware serves the opposite function: it converts data from electronic form to a people-readable form, enabling the transfer of data out from the processor to a person. The most important output device used with a PC is the monitor (see Figure 3-2). Actually, the output is accomplished by two devices: the video adapter card and the monitor or CRT (Cathode Ray Tube) screen. The video adapter card is located within the CPU cabinet and converts the digital data in memory to a video signal which causes the monitor to display the correct images on the CRT. Video output will be discussed more fully in chapter 8. Some other common output devices are printer, tone generator ("beep" or "bell"), voice synthesizer, and plotter.

Auxiliary-storage hardware, sometimes called simply storage hardware, is used to permanently store large quantities of data in electronic form for later use by the processor. Auxiliary storage differs from primary storage or memory in that it is not directly addressable by the processor. Stored data must be copied into memory for access by the processor; any modified data must then be copied back to auxiliary storage. Confusing auxiliary storage with input/output hardware is a common error which should be avoided. The data is stored in electronic form, rather than people-readable form.

Most auxiliary-storage hardware uses magnetic media: magnetic tape or magnetic disk. Magnetic disk is most commonly used with the IBM PC, although magnetic tape is sometimes used for backup purposes. Magnetic-disk storage will be discussed thoroughly in chapters 11 and 12.

The IBM PC normally contains one or two 5¼-inch or 3 ½-inch flexible (floppy) disk drives and may also include one or more rigid or fixed disks. In most cases, the disk drives are located inside the CPU cabinet at the front of the unit; however, a system may contain one or more external drives connected to the CPU by cables.

The drives are assigned single letter names. A and B are always reserved for floppy drives. If a system only has one floppy drive, then the operating system treats it as two logical drives and allows the user to use two diskettes, A and B, prompting whenever it is necessary to swap them. Rigid or fixed disks are also assigned single letter names beginning with the letter immediately following that of the last floppy drive (C if the system includes either one or two floppy drives).

Figure 3-2   **IBM PC AND IBM PS/2 MODEL 90XP 486**

BOOTING THE SYSTEM

The term **boot** is short for **bootstrap**, which derives from the expression, "to lift oneself by one's bootstraps," meaning to work one's way up from meager beginnings. When a system is booted, a small amount of machine code located in ROM instructs the processor to load and execute the first sector (boot block) from the diskette in drive A, or from the first hard disk if there is no diskette in drive A or the drive door is open. The instructions in the boot block instruct the processor to load the files IBMBIO.COM, IBMDOS.COM, and COMMAND.COM from the disk and to begin execution of COMMAND.COM.

From that point on COMMAND.COM controls the processing, displaying the DOS prompt (A> or C>) to the screen, monitoring the keyboard, interpreting commands entered at the keyboard, and loading and executing applications or utility programs upon command. Upon completion, all application programs must transfer control back to COMMAND.COM.

There are two ways to boot a system. A **hardware boot** (also called **hard boot** or **cold boot**) occurs automatically when power is turned on to the machine. A **software boot** (**soft boot** or **warm boot***)* is generated when the <Alt>+<Ctrl>+<Del> key combination is entered at the keyboard of a machine that has already successfully booted. Additionally, some compatibles have a reset button, which generates a hard boot when pressed.

To hard boot a floppy-based system (with no hard disk), properly insert the DOS diskette into drive A and turn the power on. If power is already on and a hard boot is required, turn the power off for at least fifteen seconds before turning it back on. If power is already on to a compatible which has a reset button, press it instead of cycling the power switch.

To perform a soft boot on a floppy-based system which has previously been hard booted, ensure that the DOS diskette is in drive A and press <Alt>+<Ctrl>+<Del> (hold down the <Alt> and <Ctrl> keys and press and release the <Del> key).

To boot from the hard disk of a hard-disk system or to boot from the file server on a networked system, ensure that drive A is empty before turning the power on, pressing the reset button, or pressing <Alt>+<Ctrl>+<Del>. Since it is unable to read from drive A, the system will load the boot block and operating system from the hard disk or network file server. When booting from a file server, the network software will probably require that you log in by entering some sort of user name or ID and a password; see your instructor for your network log-in procedures.

If you are working with a system that is shared with others (as in a PC lab), we strongly recommend that you always perform a soft boot upon sitting down at a machine that is already on. This is to ensure a fresh start for the operating system in case the previous user has left the system in some abnormal state. Additionally, as you begin to program in assembly language there will be times when, due to programming errors, your program does not properly return control to DOS; the system locks up and will not respond to the keyboard. Whenever this occurs, you will need to reboot the system. First try a soft boot; if this fails, then perform a hard boot.

Upon either a soft or hard boot, the operating system may ask you for the current date and time. If so, enter the current date in the following format:

mm-dd-yyyy

In the format, *mm* is the current month from 1 through 12, *dd* is the current day of the month from 1 through 31, and *yyyy* is the current year; the first two digits of the year may be omitted if they are 19. The dashes ("-") must be entered to separate the three parts of the date.

Also if requested, enter the current time in the following format:

hh:mm:ss.xx

hh is the hour from 0 through 23 (0 = midnight, 12 = noon, 13 = 1 P.M., and so on), *mm* is the minutes past the hour from 0 through 59, *ss* is the seconds past the minute from 0 through 59, and *xx* is hundredths of a second from 00 through 99. Any of the parts that are zero may be omitted from the right. For example, 13:21 is the same as 13:21:0.0 (1:21 P.M.).

In any case, always ensure that the DOS prompt (A> or some other letter followed by >) appears on the screen after booting. A prompt of "Ok" indicates that DOS did not properly boot from the disk or file server and the system has instead entered the cassette BASIC interpreter located in ROM. Check that any diskette has been properly inserted and try again.

KEY TERMS TO REMEMBER

Processing hardware	CPU
Input hardware	Main storage
Output hardware	Boot, bootstrap
Auxiliary-storage hardware	Hard boot, cold boot
Communications hardware	Soft boot, warm boot

THE OPERATING SYSTEM

MS-DOS is an operating system that supports disk storage (DOS stands for Disk Operating System), developed by Microsoft Corporation and licensed to IBM and others for use in IBM PCs and other compatible PCs. The operating system is stored on the DOS disk in three files, two of which are hidden and so do not show up in a disk directory. The two hidden files are IBMBIO.COM and IBM-DOS.COM; on the DOS diskette supplied with some compatible machines, the two files may be named IOSYS.COM and MSDOS.COM. The third file, which is not hidden from directory searches, is the command interpreter, COMMAND.COM.

When the system is booted, the three system files are loaded into RAM and COMMAND.COM is executed; thereafter, all three files remain in memory until power is shut off or the machine is soft booted. Whenever the DOS prompt (A>) is displayed on the screen, the processor is executing the instructions of the command interpreter.

When the user enters something at the keyboard by pressing the <Enter> key, the command interpreter first checks to see if it recognizes the entry as an internal command. If so, it retains control of the processor and executes a procedure within itself to service the command. After performing the internal command, the command interpreter redisplays the DOS prompt and resumes monitoring the keyboard for the next command.

If the command interpreter does not recognize the entry as an internal command, it looks on the disk for a program file whose name matches the keyboard entry. In searching for program files the command interpreter looks first for a file with a primary name matching the command and an extension of .COM. If none is found, it looks for the file with an extension of .EXE. Finally, if neither a matching .COM or .EXE file is found, it looks for a file with an extension of .BAT. If a matching filename is not found with any of the three extensions, then the command interpreter displays the error message, "Bad command or file name," redisplays the DOS prompt, and retains control of the processor.

If a matching program file is found with an extension of either .COM or .EXE, the command interpreter loads the program file into memory and transfers control to it; the program is then responsible for returning processor control to the command interpreter when finished. Upon return from the program the command interpreter redisplays the prompt and resumes monitoring the keyboard for the next command.

If the matching file has an extension of .BAT then it is interpreted as a **batch file**, a sequence of DOS commands to be executed in order. The command interpreter retains control of the processor, reading one line at a time from the file. Each line of the batch file is interpreted as if it had been entered from the keyboard. After interpreting the last line of the batch file, the command interpreter resumes monitoring the keyboard for the next command.

In addition to the three operating system files, the DOS diskette also contains a number of utility program files with extensions of .COM and .EXE. Microsoft and IBM refer to these utility programs as external commands. In reality, they are not really commands at all, but are treated like all other program files by the command interpreter.

A PAUSE IN THE ACTION

Why DOS Is Important

All user interaction with a computer is accomplished through the operating system. Consequently, any PC user (including an assembly-language programmer) must understand the fundamentals of MS-DOS: terminology, file specifications, and a number of internal and external commands. Trying to program in assembly language without a fundamental knowledge of DOS is like trying to play a game of chess with no knowledge of the rules.

Before discussing operating system commands we must clarify several terms. The following terms will be used throughout our discussion of DOS commands.

DOS Prompt: The **DOS prompt** is used by the command interpreter to indicate that it is ready to receive a command. The standard form for this prompt is a drive specifier followed by the greater-than sign (A>, B>, C>). The prompt is displayed as the last line on the screen whenever the command interpreter is waiting for a command. Besides prompting for input, the DOS prompt also indicates the current default drive (see below).

Default Drive: With any reference to a disk file DOS needs to know on which drive to look for the file. The drive may be specified as part of the file specification (see below) or it may be omitted. DOS maintains a **default drive** to be used for any file specification in which the drive is omitted.

    The default drive always begins as the drive from which the system was booted but may be changed at any time by the user (See the *d:* system command below). This default drive is indicated by the drive specifier of the DOS prompt; for example, a prompt of C> indicates that any file specification that does not contain a drive specifier will be assumed by DOS to be on drive C.

File Specification:

    DOS organizes all disk data (including programs) into files. To access the disk, the user must provide DOS with a **file specification**, often abbreviated as **filespec**, to identify the desired data. DOS uses the filespec to find the data on the disk. In chapters 11 and 12 we will discuss the mechanisms by which DOS finds the data. For now we need only understand the rules to be followed when forming a filespec. A DOS file specification consists of three parts, in the following format:

    [d:]filename[.ext]

    No spaces are permitted within the filespec. The colon and period are required by DOS to separate the three parts of the filespec. Each of the three parts is interpreted by DOS as follows:

    d: A single-letter disk

    followed by a colon (A:, B:, etc.). The drive specifier (and colon) may be omitted if the desired drive is the same as the default drive indicated by the DOS prompt, A>, B>, etc.

    filename   The **primary filename** of a filespec consists of at least one and not more than eight characters. If more than eight characters are entered the command interpreter truncates the right-most characters, keeping only the first eight characters. Unlike many operating systems, DOS allows great flexibility in the choice of filename characters; any combination of the following characters may be used:

Letters	DOS makes no distinction between upper- and lowercase.
Numbers	The digits from 0 through 9
Others	The following special characters are also permitted within the filename: !, @, #, $, %, ^, &, (,), -, _, {, }, ~

.ext   The **file extension** consists of a period followed by zero to three characters. The permitted characters are the same as for the filename. The extension is optional. The period may be included or omitted if there is no extension. If more than three characters are entered, only the first three will be used by DOS; the rest will be ignored.

Some valid file specifications are MY_PROG.ASM, B:YOURPROG.EXE, A:DATAFILE, INV34.DAT, C:123_456.

Wild Cards: Some DOS commands recognize question mark (?) and asterisk (*) as **wild cards** (or **global filename characters**) in a filename or extension. The use of wild cards allows a filespec to refer to multiple files. "?" is used to mean any character in this position. "*" means any character(s) for this part (or the rest of this part) of the file specification. Wild cards may be used in the filename or extension only; a wild-card character may not be used as the drive specifier. Following are some examples of filespecs containing wild cards:

`A:*.*`	Refers to all files on drive A.
`*.ASM`	Refers to all files on the default drive with an extension of .ASM.
`B:PROG??.ASM`	Refers to all files on drive B with an extension of .ASM and a filename that has PROG as the first four characters, with anything for the fifth and sixth characters, and no seventh or eighth character.
`PROG*.EXE`	Refers to all files on the default drive with an extension of .EXE and a filename that has PROG as the first four characters and anything (or nothing) for the rest of the filename.

Standard I/O Device Names:

Certain names have been assigned to input and output devices and so may not be used for filenames. The following names are reserved for **standard I/O device names:**

`CON`	System console (keyboard and screen). CON indicates the screen when used for output, the keyboard when used for input. When used for input, the input is terminated by pressing <F6> (or <Ctrl>+<Z>) followed by <Enter>.

COM*n*   Asynchronous serial communications adapter. COM1 indicates the first serial port, COM2 is the second serial port, and so on. May be used for either input or output.

AUX   Auxiliary port, first serial communications adapter. AUX is a synonym for COM1.

LPT*n*   Parallel printer port. LPT1 indicates the first printer port; LPT2 is the second printer; LPT3, the third printer port. May be used for output only.

PRN   First parallel printer port. PRN is synonymous with LPT1.

NUL   Null device, "bit bucket." When used for input, an immediate end-of-file is generated; when used for output, all output is discarded.

External Command:

An **external command** is a DOS command that requires that the DOS diskette be in the disk drive or that DOS be available from a hard disk or network file server at the time the command is entered. It is not really a part of the operating system; rather it is a utility program included on the DOS diskette which must be loaded into memory by the command interpreter just prior to its execution. Since external commands are really utility programs, DOS must be able to find the program file with an extension of .COM or .EXE on the disk. The command is really a file specification without an extension; a drive specifier must be included if the utility program is not located on the default drive.

Internal Command:

Internal commands do not require that the DOS diskette be in the disk drive or available from a hard disk or network file server for execution. The code for executing the command is included as a part of the command interpreter (COMMAND.COM), which is loaded into memory when the system is booted, and which remains resident thereafter. Since internal commands are not program files, they must not be thought of as filespecs; an internal command should never be preceded by a drive specifier.

KEY TERMS TO REMEMBER

DOS prompt	Wild cards
Default drive	Global filename characters
Filespec	Standard I/O device names
Drive specifier	Internal command
Primary filename	External command
File extension	

System Commands

There are a number of important DOS commands which must be understood by any PC user regardless of the user's primary area of interest. Consequently, we have included here a listing with explanations of some commonly used DOS commands. For each we have indicated if it is an internal command or an external command (utility program). Since external commands are program files, any of the following external commands may be preceded by a drive specifier to indicate the disk drive where the utility program file is to be found.

The following list is by no means complete; for a complete list of DOS commands consult the DOS manual. Many DOS commands allow for optional parameters which may be included or omitted according to the user's desire. We have adopted the commonly used convention of enclosing any such optional parameters within square brackets ([and]).

The first seven commonly used commands involve disk storage but are not directly related to data files.

`d:` *Internal*

To change the DOS default drive, enter the drive specifier alone on a line. Examples:

`D:` Changes the default drive to D.

`A:` Changes the default drive to A.

FORMAT *d:* `[/1] [/8] [/V] [/S] [/B]` *External*

FORMAT prepares a new diskette for use by writing special markers (sector IDs) to the diskette. It also checks the diskette and identifies any bad sectors. All new diskettes must be formatted before use. Diskettes may be reformatted as many times as desired, but be careful: ***all data*** is destroyed whenever a disk is formatted!

Appending /1 to the command causes the disk to be formatted for use with single-sided disk drives; since only one side of the disk will subsequently be used by DOS, the diskette will only store half as much data as a double-sided diskette. Appending /8 causes DOS to format the disk with eight sectors per track instead of nine sectors per track; use it if the disk is to be used in a machine operating under DOS version one. Sectors and tracks will be thoroughly discussed in chapter 11.

To give a volume name to a disk, append /V to the command. Upon completion of the format, DOS prompts for a volume name of up to eleven characters. The volume name appears in all directories of the disk and is also displayed by the VOL command, described below. Note: version four DOS ignores /V; see "More Recent Versions of DOS" below. You should use /V to give your diskettes the volume names of WORKING and BACKUP.

/S causes DOS to copy the system files (IBMBIO.COM, IBMDOS.COM, and COMMAND.COM) to the disk after it is formatted. The new disk is now a "bootable" system disk.

WARNING

The system files are copyrighted software; you must not copy them unless you own the DOS license. *Never* use /S on a FORMAT command when working with a borrowed DOS diskette such as one in your school's PC lab.

/B causes the disk to be formatted with space allocated for the system files, IBMBIO.COM and IBMDOS.COM. It does not copy the system files to the diskette. Following is an example of the FORMAT command:

FORMAT A:/V   Formats the diskette in drive A and prompts for a volume name to be written to the disk.

CHKDSK [d:] [filename.ext] [/F] [/V]   *External*

CHKDSK (check disk) should be used periodically to verify the integrity of the data structures which DOS uses to keep track of and to allocate disk space. Those data structures (directory and File Allocation Table or FAT) will be discussed thoroughly in chapter 11. CHKDSK examines the disk allocation structures and reports information about the organization of the data on a disk. Optionally, CHKDSK will attempt to correct any problems detected in the allocation structures.

If no drive specifier is provided, the default drive is examined. After examining the directory and FAT, CHKDSK generates a report giving the total space on the disk, the number of files and the number of bytes used by those files, the number of bytes in bad disk sectors, and the number of bytes available for the storage of new data. Although the major function of CHKDSK is to examine disks, it also provides information about memory: the number of bytes of total memory in the machine and the number of bytes currently available for use (not used by DOS).

CHKDSK also reports any errors detected in the allocation structures. Such errors may be created by the failure of a program to close all files or by swapping diskettes in the middle of a program while files are open. If errors are found, CHKDSK asks if you want to correct them; enter "Y" or "N." Even with a Y response, errors will not be corrected unless the /F switch was specified in the command line. The /F switch must be used in order for CHKDSK to correct any disk errors.

If *filename.ext* is specified, then CHKDSK also provides a report of the fragmentation of the file (discussed in chapter 11); wild cards may be used to check several files. Use /V to instruct CHKDSK to report its progress as it checks the disk. Following are some examples of the use of CHKDSK:

CHKDSK B:/V   Checks the diskette in drive B, reporting the progress of the check.

CHKDSK C:/F	Checks drive C and allows the correction of any errors which are found.
CHKDSK *.ASM	Checks the default drive and reports any fragmentation of all files whose extension is .ASM.

DISKCOPY *d:* **[d:]**   *External*

DISKCOPY copies an entire diskette (all files, directories, FAT, and so on) to another diskette; the second diskette is an exact duplicate of the first. The first drive specifier (*d:*) is the diskette to copy from; the second specifier is the diskette to copy to. If the second drive specifier is omitted, the default drive will be used. When the command is entered, DOS prompts you to put the diskettes to copy from and to into the specified drives and then pauses. Insert the proper diskettes and press any key. Following is an example of the use of DISKCOPY:

DISKCOPY A: B: Duplicates drive A to drive B.

DISKCOPY provides a method of backing up your work by duplicating your WORKING diskette to your BACKUP diskette. It may be faster than using the COPY command with wild cards (see below) for the input specifier, but only if the diskette to be copied contains many files. Since DISKCOPY makes an exact copy of the diskette, files that are fragmented on the input diskette will also be fragmented on the new diskette. In most cases it is better to use "COPY A:*.* B:" for backing up diskettes.

WARNING

Since DISKCOPY is an external command, it requires that the DOS diskette be in the disk drive when the command is entered whenever working on a floppy-based machine. If you are using a "borrowed" DOS diskette, such as one in a school's PC lab, *make sure you replace it* with your own diskette when prompted to insert the disks. Failure to remove the DOS diskette from the input drive would result in your copying the operating system, which is *copyrighted software*!

DISKCOMP *d:* **[d:]**   *External*

DISKCOMP may be used to compare two diskettes to see if they are exactly the same. Two diskettes that contain identical files may not be organized in the same manner; their directories and File Allocation Tables may be different, and the data may be stored on different areas of the disk. Consequently, DISKCOMP may report differences even though the diskettes contain the exact same data. The drive specifiers (*d:*) determine the diskettes to be compared. If the second drive specifier is omitted, the default drive will be used.

When the command is entered, DOS prompts you to put the diskettes to be compared into the specified drives and then pauses. After inserting the proper diskettes, press any key. Any differences are reported by diskette side and track; if the diskettes are exactly identical, DISKCOMP reports "Diskettes compare OK."

VOL [d:]   *Internal*

VOL displays the volume name (if any) of the disk in the specified drive (default drive if none is specified).

VERIFY [ON] [OFF]   *Internal*

When the verify switch is ON, DOS verifies everything it writes to a disk. This makes writing to a file take longer but ensures that the data has been written properly. The VERIFY command can be used to find out the current status of the switch, or to turn it on or off. Examples:

VERIFY	Reports the current switch status: ON or OFF.
VERIFY ON	Turns the verify switch ON.
VERIFY OFF	Turns the verify switch OFF.

The following seven DOS commands are commonly used to access disk data files.

DIR [filespec] [/P] [/W]   *Internal*

DIR provides a directory of the names of all or some of the files on a disk with the size, date, and time of each file. If the filespec is omitted, the directory will include all files on the default drive. If only the drive specifier is provided, the directory will include all files on the specified drive. If a complete filespec is given, the directory will include all files that match the filespec. The filespec may include wild cards. If either the filename or extension is omitted, then DOS treats that part of the filespec as a wild card ("*").

/P appended to the command causes DOS to display one screen at a time, pausing when the screen is full; press any key for the next screen. /W causes DOS to list five filenames on each screen line; size, date, and time are not shown. Examples:

DIR	(Same as DIR *.*) Lists the names of all files on the default drive.
DIR P*/W	Lists all files on the default drive whose primary names begin with P. Lists the filenames only (no size, date, or time), five filenames per screen line.
DIR B:/P	Lists the names of all files on drive B. Lists one screen at a time, pausing after each screen.

DIR .ASM   (Same as DIR *.ASM) Lists the names of all files on the default drive that have .ASM as the file extension.

DEL *filespec*   *Internal*

The DEL command deletes the file(s) with the specified filespec. If wild cards are used in the filespec then all matching entries are deleted. If wild cards are used for both the filename and the extension (*.*), then DOS verifies that you really want to delete everything. However, if an asterisk is used for only one of the parts or if question marks are used instead of asterisks, DOS will ***not*** check before deleting all matching directory entries. Be careful with wild cards; you may delete more than you want to. Examples of the DEL command:

DEL GARBAGE.ASM   Deletes a file called GARBAGE.ASM from the default drive.

DEL B:*.ASM   Deletes all files with an extension of .ASM (all assembly-language source files) from the diskette in drive B. Be sure that is what you want to do.

DEL A:*.*   Deletes all files from drive A. DOS will first display the message "Are you sure (Y/N)" and wait for your response; enter "Y" to delete all files, "N" to cancel the command without deleting anything.

ERASE *filespec*   *Internal*

ERASE is a synonym for DEL (see above).

RENAME *filespec filespec*   *Internal*

RENAME (may be abbreviated as REN) is used to change the name of a disk file without copying or changing the contents of the file. Two file specifications are required. The first is the existing filename (to be renamed) and may include a drive specifier; the second is the new name to be given to the file and must not contain a drive specifier. The use of wild cards in the existing filespec results in the renaming of all matching directory entries. A wild card in the new filespec causes DOS to leave that part of the name unchanged. An error is generated if the existing file cannot be found or if a file already exists with the new name. Some examples are:

RENAME PROG1.ASM PROG2.*   Changes the name of a file on the default diskette from PROG1.ASM to PROG2.ASM.

REN B:*.DAT *.DTA   Renames all files on drive B which have an extension of .DAT. The existing primary file names are retained; the extensions are all changed to .DTA.

`COPY` *`filespec`*`[+`*`filespec`*`] [`*`filespec`*`][/V]`   *Internal*

The COPY command is used to copy the contents of one file to another file. Two file specifications are allowed; the first is the input file (to copy *from*), and the second is the output file (to copy *to*). The input file is never altered. If the output file already exists, it is replaced. Wild cards may be used in the input filespec to copy several files. If only the drive is specified for the output file or if wild cards are used, the output file will have the same name as the input file. If the output filespec is omitted then the output will be a file of the same name on the default drive.

If two or more filespecs separated by plus (+) signs are specified as input, the files are concatenated (joined together) into the output file. A standard I/O device name may be specified for either an input and/or output filespec. /V appended to any command causes DOS to verify the new file after the copy. Some examples of the COPY command are:

`COPY A:*.* B:`	Copies all files on drive A onto drive B, keeping the same filenames. This is the preferred way to back up your work (WORKING diskette in A, and BACK-UP diskette in drive B).
`COPY PROG3.ASM PROG3.BAK`	Copies PROG3.ASM to another file called PROG3.BAK, both on the default disk.
`COPY A:MYDATA.DAT B:`	Copies MYDATA.DAT on drive A to a file of the same name on drive B.
`COPY A:*.ASM B:`	Copies all files with an extension of .ASM from drive A onto drive B, with the same filenames. Could be used to back up all assembly-language source files.
`COPY FILE1.DAT+FILE2.DAT+FILE3.DAT FILE4.DAT`	
	Appends FILE2.DAT and FILE3.DAT onto the end of FILE1.DAT and copies the result into FILE4.DAT. FILE1.DAT, FILE2.DAT, and FILE3.DAT are not altered.
`COPY CON MYFIL`	Creates the file named MYFIL on the default drive and copies everything typed on the keyboard into it. To stop copying into the file, press <F6> or <Ctrl>+<Z> and then <Enter>.
`COPY MYFIL PRN`	Copies the contents of MYFIL to the first parallel printer port. This is one

way to obtain a hard copy printout of a file.

TYPE *filespec*   *Internal*

TYPE is used to display the contents of a file to the screen. Wild cards are not permitted in the filespec. If a nontext file (such as .COM or .EXE) is TYPED, the results will be unreadable. Following is an example of the use of the TYPE command:

TYPE C:PG1.ASM   Displays the contents of PG1.ASM on drive C.

COMP *[filespec] [filespec]*   *External*

Use the COMP (compare) command to compare the contents of two files, obtaining a report of any differences. Wild cards may be used to compare multiple pairs of files. For any differences between the two files, COMP reports the offset (in hexadecimal) from the beginnings of the files where the difference was detected and also displays (in hexadecimal) the value of the byte that occurs in each file at that offset.

Since COMP is an external command, it requires that the DOS diskette be in the disk drive at the time of execution on a floppy-based machine. If the filespecs are specified, COMP does not give you a chance to remove the DOS diskette, replacing it with your own diskette. To have an opportunity to exchange diskettes, enter the command without filespecs; COMP prompts for the two filespecs, at which time you may swap diskettes.

Following are four commonly used non-disk-related system commands.

DATE *[mm-dd-[yy]yy]*   *Internal*

The DATE command reports the current system date and/or changes the system date. If the date is omitted from the command, then DOS displays the current date and asks for a new date. Enter the new date in the format *mm-dd-[yy]yy*, where the first two digits of the year may be omitted if 19 is desired, or simply press <Enter> to leave the date unchanged. If the date parameter is entered on the command line, then DOS uses it as the new system date without displaying the previous system date. For example:

DATE 6-29-90   Sets the system date to June 29, 1990.

TIME *[hh:mm:ss.xx]*   *Internal*

TIME reports the current system time and/or allows you to change it; with the exception of the time format it works much like the DATE command described above. If desired, seconds and hundredths of a second may be omitted. The hour should be entered as a number from 0 to 23, where 0 is midnight, 13 is 1 P.M., and so on.

CLS   *Internal*

CLS (clear screen) does not allow parameters. It blanks the entire screen and positions the cursor to the upper-left corner of the screen.

VER   *Internal*

Use VER to display the version number of the DOS in use on the machine. No parameters are accepted. The version number consists of the single-digit major version number followed by a decimal point and a two-digit minor revision level.

Following is a brief summary of what are probably the six **most** frequently used of the above DOS commands:

MOST COMMONLY USED DOS Commands

FORMAT *d:*[/1][/8][/V][/S][/B]

External command. Formats a diskette. Prepares a diskette for use by DOS. Diskettes must be formatted before use.

DIR [*filespec*][/P][/W]

Internal command. Provides a directory listing.

TYPE *filespec*

Internal command. Displays a file's contents to the screen.

COPY *filespec*[+*filespec*] [*filespec*][/V]

Internal command. Creates a duplicate copy of a file or creates a new file which is the result of the concatenation of two or more files.

RENAME *filespec filespec*

Internal command. Renames a disk file. Changes the name without altering or copying the file contents.

DEL *filespec*

Internal command. Deletes or erases a disk file. Deletes multiple files if *filespec* contains wild cards.

Obtaining Hard Copy Output

As described earlier, the COPY command may be used to obtain a printed copy of a displayable text file by specifying PRN as the device to copy to. However, it is sometimes necessary to obtain a hard copy of data that is displayed on the screen but not stored in a text file. One example of such a requirement is the need to obtain a listing of a program that has been entered with DEBUG, discussed later in this chapter. Another example is the need for a hard copy of the screen output generated by a program. DOS provides two methods, both using the <PrtSc> key, of obtaining a printed copy of screen data.

A **screen dump** is obtained by typing <Shift>+<PrtSc> (hold down <Shift> and press <PrtSc>). On 101-key keyboards <Shift> is not required; merely press <PrtSc>. During a screen dump, DOS copies all data currently on the screen to the printer. Once the dump has been initiated, DOS does not respond to further commands until the entire screen has been printed. A screen dump has two major shortcomings. First, since it always dumps the entire screen, it is often difficult to obtain a listing without extraneous unwanted data. The second problem is that a screen dump prints only one screen at a time; a long listing must be broken into several screens, dumped one at a time. The result is often difficult to follow.

A second method, **screen-printer toggle**, usually produces much more satisfactory results than a screen dump. The key combination, <Ctrl>+<PrtSc>, acts as a toggle switch turning screen-to-printer output on or off. Typing it once activates the printer; typing it again deactivates it. When the printer is activated nothing is printed immediately; any data already on the screen is not printed. However, all data subsequently displayed to the screen is also sent by DOS to the printer. Once the printer has been activated it remains on, printing all screen output until <Crtl>+<PrtSc> is entered a second time to deactivate it.

To obtain any hard copy output with the screen-printer toggle, type <Crtl>+<PrtSc> once to activate the printer. Then enter the necessary commands to cause the desired output to be displayed on the screen; the screen output is simultaneously sent to the printer. Once the desired printout is obtained, type <Crtl>+<PrtSc> once more to deactivate the printer.

Before attempting a hard copy output by any method, you must first ensure that a printer is properly attached to the parallel printer port of your PC. In some situations, attempting printer output when no printer is attached may freeze up the system, forcing a reboot, and resulting in the loss of your work.

Some PC labs use a rotary switch to connect several PCs to one printer. In any such configuration, the switch must be set to the proper position prior to attempting printer output; if using the screen-printer toggle, the printer must be toggled off before changing the switch position to another PC. If your lab uses a local area network with a print spooler, you may have to enter a special spool command at the DOS command level prior to attempting any printer output. Consult your instructor for specific instructions for the use of the printer(s) in your school's lab.

DOS System Services

As described above, DOS remains in memory at all times after the system has been booted. Whenever DOS executes a program (either a utility program—external command—or an application program), it loads the program into memory above itself and then transfers control to the program. From that point on the program controls the processor. DOS is no longer in control; however, DOS is still present in memory and includes a number of routines, called system services, which can be used by the program. These services are all in the form of routines that may be accessed with the interrupt (INT) instruction, which will be explained in chapter 5. The various services provided by DOS will be discussed throughout the text as needed.

In general, to access a system service a program must set up values in registers as required for the particular service and then execute an INT instruction of the correct type. The INT instruction transfers control to the correct routine in DOS which examines the registers, performs the correct service, and then returns control back to the program.

BIOS (BASIC INPUT/OUTPUT SYSTEM

In addition to the system service routines included in DOS, the IBM PC also provides numerous fundamental input and output services through BIOS (Basic Input/Output System). Note that the term "Basic," as used here, means "fundamental" or "rudimentary" and has nothing to do with the programming language (Beginners All-purpose Symbolic Instruction Code). BIOS services differ from DOS system services in three major ways.

First, the DOS services are contained in the system files on the DOS diskette, while BIOS is stored in nonvolatile read-only memory (ROM). Consequently, BIOS is available immediately upon power-up of the machine and is the same for a given machine regardless of the version of DOS in use.

Second, as indicated by the word "Basic," BIOS routines provide fundamental rudimentary services. These services are usually less flexible and more difficult to use than the more sophisticated services provided by DOS. On the other hand, BIOS services tend to be simpler and more efficient for the machine and often allow the programmer to get closer to the hardware.

Third, BIOS services are often utilized by DOS services; whenever a program accesses a DOS system service, the DOS routine may often in turn use an INT instruction to access a BIOS service. The converse is not true; BIOS services *never* make use of DOS system services.

Most input/output by a program may be accomplished in one of three ways: 1) the program directly accesses the appropriate peripheral hardware, 2) the program uses a BIOS system service that handles the hardware access for it, or 3) the program uses a DOS system service, which then uses one or more BIOS system services for access to the hardware. Throughout most of this text, we will discuss all three methods of achieving input/output.

As a general rule, whenever given a choice of directly accessing hardware, using a BIOS system service, or using a DOS system service, the programmer

Figure 3-3   Relationship of Program, DOS, BIOS, Hardware

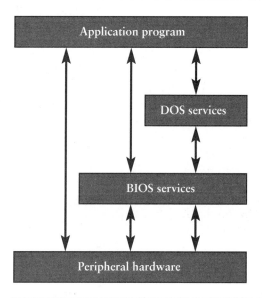

should use the DOS service unless speed of execution is extremely important. Figure 3-3 illustrates the relationship between the application program, DOS services, BIOS services, and peripheral hardware.

DEBUG.COM: A PROGRAMMING AND DEBUGGING TOOL

DEBUG is a utility program provided on the DOS diskette and also included on earlier versions of the macro assembler. Its major purpose is for the debugging of executable (.COM and .EXE) program files. It provides for the controlled execution of programs with the capability of monitoring and altering registers and memory during execution. It makes it possible to "read" machine-language code by disassembling it to its equivalent assembly-language mnemonics. In addition to DEBUG, we will also discuss the more advanced debugging utilities (SYMDEB and CodeView) at the end of this chapter.

To run the debugger, enter the following command at the DOS prompt:

```
DEBUG      [filespec]
```

The filespec is optional; if used, DEBUG immediately loads the specified file for debugging. Including a filespec in the command line is equivalent to using the Name and Load commands (discussed later).

Upon entry, DEBUG displays a dash (-) to prompt for a command. All commands consist of a single letter, either upper- or lowercase, sometimes followed by one or more parameters. We will discuss DEBUG parameters and commands shortly. For reference, we have provided a sample DEBUG session in Figure 3-4. For clarity, all keyboard input has been bolded as well as numbered (to the right).

Line 2 uses the Register command to display the values of all registers upon entry to DEBUG (note that BX and CX are both 0). Lines 3 through 12 use the Assemble command to write a simple program that finds the sum and difference of 4095 (0FFFH) and 255 (00FFH), storing the results into memory at [120] and [122]. Lines 13 through 16 use the Go and Trace commands to execute the program, watching its effects on the registers.

Line 17 Dumps memory to verify the results in memory at [120] through [123]. Line 18 disassembles the program (Unassemble command). Lines 19 through 24 use the Register, Name, and Write commands to save the program to a file called F3-4.COM on the default disk (A:). Line 25 Quits to DOS.

Lines 26 and 27 use DOS commands to verify that the program file has been created with the correct size and that it executes and properly returns to DOS. Note that the program generates no output. Lines 28 through 34 are a second DEBUG session in which the program is loaded, initial register values are displayed (note the value of CX), the program is disassembled and run, and memory is dumped to verify proper results.

Figure 3-4   Sample DEBUG Session

```
A> DEBUG                                                                    (1

-R                                                                          (2
AX=0000 BX=0000 CX=0000 DX=0000 SP=FFEE BP=0000 SI=0000 DI=0000
DS=1E82 ES=1E82 SS=1E82 CS=1E82 IP=0100 NV UP EI PL NZ NA PO NC
1E82:0100 01AF1DE8    ADD    [BX+E81D],BP          DS:E81D=0000

-A 100                                                                      (3
1E82:0100 MOV         AX,FFF                                                (4
1E82:0103 MOV         BX,AX                                                 (5
1E82:0105 MOV         CX,FF                                                 (6
1E82:0108 ADD         AX,CX                                                 (7
1E82:010A SUB         BX,CX                                                 (8
1E82:010C MOV         [120],AX                                             (9
1E82:010F MOV         [122],BX                                            (10
1E82:0113 INT         20                                                  (11
1E82:0115                                                                 (12

-G =100 103                                                               (13
AX=0FFF BX=0000 CX=0000 DX=0000 SP=FFEE BP=0000 SI=0000 DI=0000
DS=1E82 ES=1E82 SS=1E82 CS=1E82 IP=0103 NV UP EI PL NZ NA PO NC
1E82:0103 89C3        MOV    BX,AX
```

Figure 3-4:   (continued)

```
-T                                                                    (14

AX=0FFF BX=0FFF CX=0000 DX=0000 SP=FFEE BP=0000 SI=0000 DI=0000
DS=1E82 ES=1E82 SS=1E82 CS=1E82 IP=0105 NV UP EI PL NZ NA PO NC
1E82:0105 B9FF00        MOV     CX,00FF

-T 5                                                                  (15

AX=0FFF BX=0FFF CX=00FF DX=0000 SP=FFEE BP=0000 SI=0000 DI=0000
DS=1E82 ES=1E82 SS=1E82 CS=1E82 IP=0108 NV UP EI PL NZ NA PO NC
1E82:0108 01C8          ADD     AX,CX

AX=10FE BX=0FFF CX=00FF DX=0000 SP=FFEE BP=0000 SI=0000 DI=0000
DS=1E82 ES=1E82 SS=1E82 CS=1E82 IP=010A NV UP EI PL NZ AC PO NC
1E82:010A 29CB          SUB     BX,CX

AX=10FE BX=0F00 CX=00FF DX=0000 SP=FFEE BP=0000 SI=0000 DI=0000
DS=1E82 ES=1E82 SS=1E82 CS=1E82 IP=010C NV UP EI PL NZ NA PE NC
1E82:010C A32001        MOV     [0120],AX            DS:0120=200E

AX=10FE BX=0F00 CX=00FF DX=0000 SP=FFEE BP=0000 SI=0000 DI=0000
DS=1E82 ES=1E82 SS=1E82 CS=1E82 IP=010F NV UP EI PL NZ NA PE NC
1E82:010F 891E2201      MOV     [0122],BX            DS:0122=8901

AX=10FE BX=0F00 CX=00FF DX=0000 SP=FFEE BP=0000 SI=0000 DI=0000
DS=1E82 ES=1E82 SS=1E82 CS=1E82 IP=0113 NV UP EI PL NZ NA PE NC
1E82:0113 CD20          INT     20

-G                                                                    (16

Program terminated normally

-D 120 L4
                                                                      (17
1E82:0120 FE 10 00 0F                                          ....

-U 100
                                                                      (18
1E82:0100 B8FF0F        MOV     AX,0FFF
1E82:0103 89C3          MOV     BX,AX
1E82:0105 B9FF00        MOV     CX,00FF
1E82:0108 01C8          ADD     AX,CX
1E82:010A 29CB          SUB     BX,CX
1E82:010C A32001        MOV     [0120],AX
1E82:010F 891E2201      MOV     [0122],BX
1E82:0113 CD20          INT     20
1E82:0115 FB            STI
1E82:0116 8B0E2601      MOV     CX,[0126]
1E82:011A 03C8          ADD     CX,AX
1E82:011C 894FF7        MOV     [BX-09],CX
1E82:011F 8BFE          MOV     DI,SI
```

Figure 3-4:   (continued)
_____

```
-R BX                                                         (19
BX 0F00
:0                                                            (20


-R CX                                                         (21
CX 00FF
:15                                                           (22


-N F3-4.COM                                                  (23


-W                                                            (24
Writing 0015 bytes


-Q                                                            (25


A> DIR F3-4                                                  (26

Volume in drive A has no label
Directory of A:\

F3-4      COM       21 07-01-91    3:38p
          1 File(s)    356352 bytes free


A> F3-4                                                      (27


A> DEBUG F3-4.COM                                           (28


-R                                                            (29
AX=0000 BX=0000 CX=0015 DX=0000 SP=FFFE BP=0000 SI=0000 DI=0000
DS=1E9F ES=1E9F SS=1E9F CS=1E9F IP=0100 NV UP EI PL NZ NA PO NC
1E9F:0100 B8FF0F        MOV     AX,0FFF


-U 100 L15                                                   (30
1E9F:0100 B8FF0F          MOV       AX,0FFF
1E9F:0103 89C3            MOV       BX,AX
1E9F:0105 B9FF00          MOV       CX,00FF
1E9F:0108 01C8            ADD       AX,CX
1E9F:010A 29CB            SUB       BX,CX
1E9F:010C A32001          MOV       [0120],AX
1E9F:010F 891E2201        MOV       [0122],BX
1E9F:0113 CD20            INT       20


-D 120 L4                                                    (31
1E9F:0120 A1 B6 05 BB                                  ....


-G                                                            (32

Program terminated normally
```

Figure 3-4: (continued)

```
-D 120 L4                                                          (33
1E9F:0120 FE 10 00 0F                              . . . .

-Q                                                                 (34

A>
```

DEBUG Parameters

The format of all parameters used in DEBUG commands is very restrictive; little flexibility is allowed. Following is a discussion of DEBUG parameters:

filespec   A valid DOS file specification (*d:filename.ext*). If the file has an extension (usually .COM or .EXE), then it must be included in the filespec; DEBUG has no default extension. See lines 23 and 28 of Figure 3-4.

register_name

The name of a sixteen-bit 8088 register. Valid sixteen-bit register names for use with DEBUG commands are: AX, BX, CX, DX, SP, BP, SI, DI, DS, ES, SS, CS, IP (or PC), and F (flags register). The complete 8088 register set will be discussed in the next chapter. See lines 19 and 21 of Figure 3-4.

value   A hexadecimal numeral of up to four digits. Don't put an H on the end to indicate hexadecimal; DEBUG requires that all *value*s be in hex. Some valid *value*s are:
   3B
   F000
   3D4

byte_value   A hexadecimal numeral of up to two digits. Don't put an H on the end; DEBUG requires that all *byte_value*s be in hex. Following are some valid *byte_value*s:
   3F
   24
   B

string   A sequence of characters enclosed in quotation marks (either single or double). DEBUG converts the *string* to a *list* of *byte_value*s, each of which is the ASCII code for one character in the string. The ASCII character code will be discussed in chapter 8. Some examples of *string*s are:
   'TEST'   (Same as: 54 45 53 54)
   "Hi there."   (Same as: 48 69 20 74 68 65 72 65 2E)

list   A series of one or more *byte_value*s and/or *string*s, separated by spaces. Some valid *list*s are:

```
'Testing' D A A
41 42 'CDEFG' 48 49
```

address   A two-part memory address consisting of *segment:offset*; the colon is required to separate the two parts, unless the *segment* is omitted. *Segment* may be either a *value* or a segment *register_name* (CS, DS, SS, or ES). If the *segment* (and colon) are omitted from the *address*, the current value of DS is used for most commands; **G**o, **L**oad, **T**race, **U**nassemble, and **W**rite assume CS when the *segment* is omitted. Some valid *address*es are:

```
14AB
03C0:0120
CS:100
```

range   A range of *address*es specifying a section of memory. The *range* may be specified in either of two ways:

      *address*1 *address*2   Specifies the starting and ending *address*es of the block of memory; *address*2 must be offset only.

      or

      address L *value*   Specifies the starting *address* and length (number of bytes) of the memory block. See lines 17, 31, and 33 of Figure 3-4.

Some valid *range*s are:

```
3C0:120 13F        (both ranges
3C0:120 L 20       are equivalent)
```

A PAUSE IN THE ACTION

Why DEBUG Is Important

Since it is relatively quick and easy to learn, we will use DEBUG's Assemble command to write our first few assembly-language programs. In addition to its use as a programming tool, you need to understand DEBUG (or another debugger) in order to be able to debug your later programs, which will be written with a text editor and assembled and linked. Without the help of a debugging utility, it is often very difficult if not impossible to determine why a program does not work.

DEBUG Commands

Following is a list of DEBUG commands. Note that in each case the command is a *single letter*, sometimes followed by one or more parameters. DEBUG allows but does not require a space between the command and the first parameter; it does require spaces between parameters when there is more than one. For ease of reading, we have included a space between every command and its first parameter.

The following command is used to exit a DEBUG session.

Q *Quit*

Exit DEBUG and return to DOS. No parameters are permitted. See lines 25 and 34 of Figure 3-4.

The following three commands are all used to display the contents of registers or memory either as data or as code.

R *Register*

Examine register values. DEBUG displays the current values of all registers (in hexadecimal). See lines 2 and 29 of Figure 3-4. Also see below for another form of the **R**egister command, used to modify a register value.

D [*range*] *Dump*

Displays memory contents in hexadecimal; also displays the data as ASCII characters whenever possible. If *range* is omitted, the dump begins with the first address after the last dump (DS:100 if this is the first **D**ump command) and dumps 128 bytes. If only an *address* is used in place of *range*, 128 bytes are dumped beginning at *address*. See lines 17, 31, and 33 of Figure 3-4.

U [*range*] *Unassemble*

Disassembles memory contents from machine-language to 8088 assembly-language mnemonics. If *range* is omitted, the disassembly starts at the first address after the last disassembly (CS:IP the first time) and disassembles approximately twenty bytes. If *address* is used in place of *range*, approximately twenty bytes are disassembled, beginning at *address*. See lines 18 and 30 of Figure 3-4.

Four DEBUG commands are commonly used to alter the contents of registers or memory.

R [*register_name*] *Register*

Change register values. DEBUG displays the current value of the specified sixteen-bit register and allows for the modification of the value stored in the register. Press <Enter> to leave the register as is; enter a *value* to change the contents of the register. See lines 19 through 22 of Figure 3-4.

If F is entered for *register_name*, DEBUG displays a two-character code for the status of each flag in the flags register and allows the modification of any flag by the entry of a two-character code for the desired new status.

E address [list] *Enter*

Enters the *list* as a series of *byte_value*s into memory beginning at *address*. If *list* is omitted, DEBUG displays *address* and its current contents and allows you to change it or leave it the same. To leave the memory byte unchanged, press <Enter> or <Space Bar>; to change it, type a *byte_value* and press <Enter> or <Space Bar>. If <Space Bar> is pressed, DEBUG continues with the Enter command, advancing to the next higher memory address, displaying its contents, and allowing you to change it or leave it unchanged. Press <Enter> when ready to exit the Enter command.

F range list *Fill*

Fills the memory within the *range* with the *byte_value*s in the *list*. *List* is truncated on the right if too long for *range*; *list* is repeated as many times as necessary if shorter than *range*.

A [address] *Assemble*

Assembles 8086/8088 assembly-language mnemonics directly into memory. You enter assembly-language instructions, and DEBUG assembles them into machine language, storing the machine code into memory. The optional *address* specifies the memory address to start at; if omitted, the machine-language instructions are stored beginning at the address indicated by CS (Code Segment register) and IP (Instruction-Pointer register).

To quit assembling, press <Enter> (no instruction) when prompted for an instruction. The Assemble command may be used to write simple programs in assembly language or to modify existing machine-language programs. See lines 3 through 12 of Figure 3-4.

Two commands are commonly used for controlled execution of machine-language instructions stored in memory.

G [=address] [address [address [address ...]]] *Go*

Executes machine-language instructions stored in memory. Execution begins with the instruction at CS:IP or at =*address* if specified. Up to ten *address*es may be specified as **break points**. All break-point *address*es must be the first byte of an 8086/8088 instruction in RAM (random-access memory); break points cannot be set within ROM (read-only memory). When program execution encounters a break point, execution stops, control is passed back to DEBUG, and all registers are displayed. The Go command provides controlled execution for the debugging of machine-language programs.

DEBUG sets break points by temporarily storing two bytes of code from the break-point *address* and then replacing those two bytes with an INT 3 instruction. The type three interrupt, when executed during program execution, causes control to pass back to DEBUG. DEBUG then replaces every break point with its original two bytes of code before displaying the registers and the next instruction and returning control to the keyboard. Since DEBUG must modify the code to set a break point, break points may not be set in read-only memory. See lines 13, 16, and 32 of Figure 3-4.

T [=address] [value]   *Trace*

Executes and traces the number of instructions specified by *value*, beginning at =*address* if specified. If =*address* is not specified, then execution begins at CS:IP. DEBUG uses the processor's TRAP flag to regain control after each instruction. Before executing an instruction, DEBUG sets the TRAP flag; this causes the processor to automatically execute a type one interrupt immediately after the instruction, thus returning control to DEBUG.

Upon regaining control, DEBUG immediately displays the registers and the next instruction. If *value* has been specified, DEBUG then sets the TRAP flag again and executes the next instruction, continuing until *value* instructions have been executed before returning control to the keyboard. Since DEBUG does not have to modify the code, as with Go command break points, the Trace command may be used to step through ROM (read-only memory) as well as RAM. See lines 14 and 15 of Figure 3-4.

Three commands are used to read or write disk data files (usually executable, either .EXE or .COM files).

N filespec   *Name*

Defines the file to be used for any subsequent file-structured Load or Write commands. The extension (usually .COM or .EXE) must be included in *filespec*. See line 23 of Figure 3-4.

L [address]   *Load File*

Loads a file from disk into memory. The filename must have been previously defined with the Name command. *Address* may not be specified if the file has an extension of .COM or .EXE; DEBUG examines executable files and determines where and how to load them. For any other extension (data file, for example) the file is loaded into memory beginning at *address*; if *address* is omitted, nonexecutable files are loaded beginning at DS:0000H.

After loading the file, DEBUG sets the double-word BX:CX to the number of bytes loaded from the file. Usually (file size less then 65536) BX is zero, CX is the file length; if BX is not zero, then the file length is BX times 65536 plus·CX.

`W [address]`   *Write File*

Writes BX:CX bytes of data to a file from memory beginning at *address* or at CS:100 if *address* is omitted. The filename must have been previously specified with the **Name** command, and BX:CX (double-word) must have been set to the number of bytes to be written. Use the **Register** command discussed earlier. For fewer than 65536 bytes, set BX to zero, CX to the number of bytes; for more than 65535 bytes, set BX to the quotient and CX to the remainder of the number of bytes divided by 65536.

.EXE files cannot be written with DEBUG. The **Write** command is normally used to save .COM files to disk. See line 24 of Figure 3-4.

The **Load** and **Write** commands may also be used for non-file-structured disk access, to read from or write to specific disk sectors rather than data files. Be careful! Writing to specific disk sectors may destroy critical DOS structures and cause a loss of all data on the disk.

`L address byte_value value value`   *Load*

Loads disk sectors (non-file-structured) from disk into memory. With this form of the **Load** command, you specify the disk location instead of a filename; the load is not affected by any previous **Name** command. *Address* specifies the memory location into which to begin the load. The *byte_value* specifies the drive to read from: 0 for drive A, 1 for drive B, and so on. The first *value* specifies the logical sector number to begin reading; the second *value* specifies how many sectors to read. This form of the **Load** command is useful for examining the boot block, directory, and File Allocation Table of a disk.

`W address byte_value value value`   *Write*

Writes data from memory to disk sectors (non-file-structured). With this form of the **Write** command, you specify the disk location instead of a filename; the write is not affected by any previous **Name** command. *Address* specifies the memory location from which to begin the write. The *byte_value* specifies the drive to write to: 0 for drive A, 1 for drive B, and so on. The first *value* specifies the logical sector number to which to begin writing; the second *value* specifies how many sectors to write.

This form of the **Write** command is ***extremely dangerous*** but can be useful if it is necessary to modify the boot block, directory, or File Allocation Table of a disk.

Six more DEBUG commands are often used for the miscellaneous purposes described below.

H *value value*   *Hex*

Performs hexadecimal arithmetic; displays the sum and difference in hexadecimal of the two hexadecimal *value*s.

M *range address*   *Move*

Copies the block of memory specified by *range* into the memory locations beginning at *address*. Overlapping moves are handled properly, whether moving up or down in memory.

C *range address*   *Compare*

Compares the data stored in memory within the *range* to the data in memory (same length) beginning at *address*. Differences (if any) are displayed.

S *range list*   *Search*

Searches through memory within the *range* of addresses for any occurrences of the *list* of *byte_value*s and displays the address(es) of all occurrences.

I *value*   *Input*

Inputs and displays a byte through the I/O port specified by *value* (I/O ports will be discussed in a later chapter).

O *value byte_value*   *Output*

Outputs *byte_value* to the I/O port specified by *value* (I/O ports will be discussed in a later chapter).

Following is a brief summary of eleven of the most frequently used DEBUG commands:

MOST COMMONLY USED DEBUG Commands

Q

Quit. Exit DEBUG. Return to DOS.

R [*register_name*]

Register. Displays the current values of all registers or displays and alters the value in a single sixteen-bit register.

D [*range*]

Dump. Displays memory values in hexadecimal and ASCII (if displayable).

U [*range*]

Unassemble. Disassembles code from memory. Displays assembly-language instructions for the machine-language instructions stored in memory.

E *address* [*list*]

Enter. Allows the entry of data as hexadecimal byte values, storing the resulting binary values into memory.

A [*address*]

Assemble. Allows the entry of code as assembly-language instructions. Immediately assembles the instructions, storing the resulting machine code into memory.

G [*=address*] [*address* [*address* [*address* ...]]]

Go. Executes machine instructions stored in memory. Begins at the address specified by *=address*. Sets one or more break points at which to halt execution and return to DEBUG.

T [*=address*] [*value*]

Trace. Executes one or more machine instructions beginning at the address specified by *=address*.

N *filespec*

Name. Establishes the file specification to be used by any subsequent Load or Write commands.

L [*address*]

Load. Reads the file previously specified by the Name command into memory, beginning at *address*.

W [*address*]

Write. Writes from memory to the file previously specified by the Name command. Cannot be used to write .EXE files.

MORE RECENT VERSIONS OF DOS

All subsequent versions of DOS are compatible with version one. Each extends the capabilities of the operating system without significantly altering the commands and capabilities of previous versions.

The primary extension of version two is the provision for the better manage-ment of hard disks through subdirectories and paths (to be discussed in chapters 11 and 12).

Version three provides record-locking capabilities for the support of networks and also permits the usage of high-density 5¼-inch and 3½-inch disk drives. For compatibility, three new switches have been added to the FORMAT command to allow for the formatting of lower-density diskettes in high-capacity drives:

FORMAT   `d:[/4]`

or

FORMAT   `d:[/T:tracks/N:sectors]`

/4 is used in a machine with a high-capacity 5¼-inch disk drive (1.2M) to for-mat a diskette as double density (360K) so that it may also be used in a machine with a low-capacity drive.

/T:*tracks*/N:*sectors* specifies the number of tracks per side and sectors per track for a diskette. It is usually used with a high-capacity 3½-inch drive (1.44M) to format a diskette as quad-density (720K—80 tracks, 9 sectors per track) so that it may also be used in a low-capacity 3½-inch drive. The switches to format a 720K diskette are /T:80/N:9.

/T and /N may also be used to format a 360K diskette in a high-capacity 5¼-inch drive. /T:40/N:9 produces the same results as /4 discussed above.

The version of DEBUG included with DOS version three provides an addi-tional very useful command:

P `[=address] [value]`   *Proceed*

Proceed is almost the same as Trace, except that it executes as a single in-struction any subprocedure call, loop, or interrupt. Tracing a call instruction re-turns control to the user after one instruction, at the beginning of the subprocedure; Proceed returns control at the next instruction after the call, after execution of the entire subprocedure. Subprocedures, interrupts, and loop in-structions will be discussed in chapters 5 and 6.

Version four DOS supports hard disks larger than thirty-two megabytes. (Versions two and three require that large hard disks be partitioned into multiple logical drives, each less than or equal to thirty-two megabytes.) Additionally, the version four FORMAT command has been modified in three ways: (1) It *always* prompts for a volume name (the /V switch is allowed but has no effect), (2) it places a randomly generated serial number on each formatted diskette, and (3) it provides a simplified method of specifying diskette formats:

FORMAT `d:[/F:size]`

Size is the number of kilobytes for the disk. Possible values are: 160, 180, 320, 360, 720, 1200, or 1440. Use 360 to format a double-density diskette in a high-capacity 5¼-inch drive; use 720 to format a quad-density (often called double-density) diskette in a high-capacity 3½ -inch drive.

OS/2

OS/2 is Microsoft/IBM's answer to the challenge of Intel's 80286 processor. Previous to the release of OS/2, the PC AT, high-end PS/2s, and compatible machines utilizing the 80286 and later processors simply functioned as fast PCs or XTs; MS-DOS does not support the extended capabilities of the processor. OS/2 was designed to make full use of the 80286's capabilities: Protected mode, which allows for multitasking, the ability to directly address more than one megabyte of memory, and the use of magnetic disk as virtual memory.

In addition to fully supporting the 80286, OS/2 also provides for the dynamic linking of executable programs. Since it uses instructions that are not supported by the 8088, 8086, or 80186 processors, OS/2 requires a machine with an 80286 or later processor; it will not run on a PC, XT, or low-end PS/2 or compatible utilizing the 8086 or 8088 processor. Following is a brief discussion of each of OS/2's major added features.

Multitasking refers to the ability of an operating system to execute two or more application programs concurrently, with each program completely protected from any interference by the others. Note that the programs execute *concurrently*, not *simultaneously*. The 80286, like any other processor, is only capable of executing one instruction at a time; under multitasking, the processor executes several instructions for one task, then moves on to the next task to execute several instructions, then to the next task, and so on until it returns to the first task again to execute several more instructions.

OS/2 uses the 80286 processor's Protected mode to allow for multitasking. Before giving processor control to a program, the operating system first sets up a descriptor table in low memory defining (among other things) the memory limitations of each segment in that task. Each segment descriptor contains a three byte (twenty-four-bit) Segment Base specifying the lowest address of the segment, and a two-byte (sixteen-bit) Segment Limit specifying the size of the segment.

The segment descriptor table itself is within the memory limitations of the operating system, but outside the limitations of the task; thus, the task is not allowed to directly modify its own descriptor. As the task executes, any reference to memory is checked by the processor to ensure that it is within the task's memory limits; any attempt by a task to address memory outside its limits generates a protection exception interrupt which returns control to the operating system, which can then terminate the task. Thus, each task is limited by the hardware to its own memory space and cannot interfere with any memory belonging to another task or to the operating system.

The use of descriptor tables, set up by OS/2 and checked by the processor, also allows the processor to address more memory than is possible under DOS. Because of the manner in which the 8086/8088 family of processors specifies memory addresses (discussed in the next chapter), an instruction is limited to specifying memory addresses from 0 through FFFFFH, or one megabyte of memory. In Protected mode, however, the specified address is treated not as an absolute memory address but as an offset from the twenty-four-bit base memory address specified by the descriptor table. Thus, by the use of protected mode, OS/2 allows the addressing of more than one megabyte (up to sixteen megabytes) of memory.

There remains the dilemma of many tasks running on a machine that has only one screen and one keyboard. OS/2 solves the problem by allowing the user to designate tasks as foreground or background. Only one task at a time may be executed in the foreground; all other concurrent tasks execute in background. Whenever the foreground task generates screen output, that output immediately appears on the monitor; any screen output from a background task does not appear on the monitor but is saved in memory to appear later when the user designates that task as foreground. Only the foreground task can accept keyboard input; if a background task requires keyboard input, its execution is suspended until the user brings it to the foreground.

For compatibility, OS/2 provides a Real mode for execution of programs written for DOS. With a few minor exceptions, Real mode supports all commands and system services provided by DOS; thus, an OS/2 machine is still capable of running programs that were designed and written for DOS. The programming examples and problems in this text all require Real mode for execution under OS/2.

Dynamic linking of executable programs allows multiple programs to share the same subprocedures, stored separately from the mainline programs. This is an improvement over MS-DOS; in a DOS environment, a program may be written and assembled or compiled in several parts, but all the modules must then be linked into one executable program file prior to execution (linking modules will be discussed in chapters 6 and 7).

If two or more programs use the same subprocedure, then (under DOS) identical copies of that subprocedure are linked into all of the executable-program files, increasing each file's size; this wastes disk space, but more importantly it leads to maintenance problems. If such a shared subprocedure is modified in a DOS environment then every program that uses it must be relinked by the programmer. Forgetting to relink any program results in its using the old version of the subprocedure that was originally linked into it.

OS/2 permits the linking of modules at execution time, as the program is loaded for execution. A module that is shared by many programs may be placed in a dynamic-link library (DLL) rather than linking it into each of the executable programs that uses it. Each program that uses it simply contains a definition record telling OS/2 to link in the subprocedure as the program is loaded for execution. Consequently, the subprocedure module is stored only once rather than in every program file, saving disk space. More importantly, any modification of such a subprocedure automatically takes effect whenever any program that uses it is executed. Programs that share a DLL do not have to be relinked when the module is altered.

The last major innovation of OS/2 is the provision for virtual memory management; OS/2 uses magnetic disk to expand its virtual memory beyond the physical memory installed in the machine. Physical memory is limited to sixteen megabytes; in reality, most machines contain less than that maximum. Through virtual memory management, OS/2 makes it appear that a machine contains up to one gigabyte of memory. It accomplishes this by swapping code or data as necessary between memory and disk. If at any time the physical memory of the machine proves insufficient for the requirements of all the tasks running concurrently, the operating system finds a segment of memory whose code or data is not currently in use, copies the code or data to the disk, and frees up that segment of memory for use in meeting the current memory requirement.

When it swaps a segment to disk, OS/2 clears a bit (Present bit) within the descriptor table for the task to which the swapped segment belongs; any subsequent attempt by the task to address the code or data that has been swapped out (Present bit clear) causes the processor to generate a Not-Present interrupt, which returns control to OS/2. OS/2 then suspends the task until it has swapped the code or data back into memory, possibly to a different area of memory, and updated the descriptor table; execution of the suspended task is then resumed. Note that this swapping back in may necessitate the swapping out of some other segment.

SYMDEB, CODEVIEW, AND TURBO DEBUGGER

SYMDEB and **CodeView** are debugging tools that have replaced DEBUG on later versions of macro assembler diskettes. SYMDEB (SYMbolic DEBugger) is really an extension of DEBUG rather than a different program. It supports all the commands supported by DEBUG; our earlier discussion of DEBUG applies just as well to SYMDEB. All exercises in this text that specify the use of DEBUG may be completed with SYMDEB instead. The major extension of SYMDEB over DEBUG is that it allows the user to refer to memory addresses by the symbols that were defined in the source program, while DEBUG requires actual memory addresses.

CodeView is an entirely new program supplied with version five of the macro assembler and with many Microsoft compilers. It utilizes windows and menus to interact with the user instead of the rather cryptic commands of DEBUG and SYMDEB. CodeView can also simultaneously display source code, the resulting machine code, and register values during testing and execution of a program. The **Turbo Debugger**, supplied with Borland International's Turbo Assembler and compilers, is very similar to CodeView and provides much the same capability.

The use of either CodeView or the Turbo Debugger requires that the executable program must have been assembled and linked to include special debugging information. We will discuss the use of CodeView and the Turbo Debugger more thoroughly in chapter 8.

One major drawback of CodeView and the Turbo Debugger is that they can only be used for the debugging of programs that have been created with a text editor, an assembler, and a linker (to be discussed in chapter 6). They cannot be used to write and save simple programs as can DEBUG (Assemble, Name, and Write commands). It is primarily for this reason that we have discussed DEBUG in this chapter; it is a relatively easy-to-learn tool for our early exploration of assembly language.

SUMMARY

Every computer is made up of four functional types of hardware: processing, input, output, and auxiliary storage. To perform any function, the processing hardware must be controlled by an operating system (MS-DOS or PC-DOS for IBM PC's and compatibles). A system must be booted in order to load the operating system and begin its execution; a PC is booted by turning on the power switch (hard boot) or by typing the key combination <Alt>+<Ctrl>+<Del> (soft boot).

When a system is booted, COMMAND.COM assumes control of the processor. COMMAND.COM is capable of performing a number of services (internal commands) and of loading and executing programs from disk (external commands and application programs). All disk files are referred to by a file specification that is made up of three parts: drive specifier, primary filename, and filename extension. Programming assignment PA3-1 should help you familiarize yourself with the machine and the operating system.

DEBUG.COM is a tool for working with executable programs. It is supplied on the DOS diskette as well as on all early versions of the macro assembler diskette. It is quite restrictive in its command structure and allowed parameters, but is indispensable for any assembly-language programmer. The better you understand DEBUG, the more successful you will be in assembly language. Completion of programming exercise PA3-2 should give you at least a beginning familiarity with DEBUG. Do not hesitate to use DEBUG or another debugging utility whenever you have problems with any later programming assignments.

VOCABULARY

V3-1   In your own words, define each of the following terms.

a) Processing hardware
b) CPU
c) Input hardware
d) Output hardware
e) Auxiliary-storage hardware
f) Bootstrap
g) DOS prompt
h) Default drive
i) File specification

j) Drive specifier
k) Primary filename
l) Filename extension
m) Wild card (global filename character)
n) Internal command
o) External command
p) System service
q) BIOS

V3-2 In your own words, describe each of the following DEBUG parameters.

a) Filespec
b) Register_name
c) Value
d) Byte_value

e) String
f) List
g) Address
h) Range

REVIEW QUESTIONS

Q3-1 In your own words, describe the function of each of the following DOS commands. Indicate whether the command is internal or external; also describe any optional or required parameters.

a) CHKDSK
b) CLS
c) COMP
d) COPY
e) DATE

f) DEL
g) DIR
h) DISKCOMP
i) DISKCOPY
j) ERASE

k) FORMAT
l) REN
m) TIME
n) TYPE
o) VERIFY

p) VER
q) VOL

Q3-2 Which DOS command would you use to create a duplicate copy of a disk file?

Q3-3 Which DOS command would you use to change the name of a disk file?

Q3-4 Which DOS command would you use to view the contents of a disk file?

Q3-5 Which DOS command would you use to prepare a diskette for use?

Q3-6 Which DOS command would you use to get rid of an unwanted disk file?

Q3-7 Which DOS command would you use to obtain a listing of the names of the files on a disk?

Q3-8 In your own words, describe the function of each of the following DEBUG commands. Give the full name of the command and what it does, and describe any optional or required parameters.

a) A
b) C
c) D

d) E
e) F
f) G

g) H
h) I
i) L

j) M
k) N
l) O

m) Q
n) R
o) S

p) T
q) W

Q3-9   Which DEBUG command would you use to display the contents of all registers?

Q3-10   Which DEBUG command would you use to display the contents (as hexadecimal and ASCII values) of memory?

Q3-11   Which DEBUG command would you use to display the contents (as assembly-language instructions) of memory?

Q3-12   Which DEBUG command would you use to enter hexadecimal or ASCII data into memory?

Q3-13   Which DEBUG command would you use to enter machine instructions (typed as assembly-language instructions) into memory?

Q3-14   Which two DEBUG commands might you use to execute all or part of a program stored in memory?

Q3-15   Which two DEBUG commands would you use to read a file from disk into memory?

Q3-16   Which three DEBUG commands would you use to write data and/or instructions from memory to a disk file?

Q3-17   Which command would you use to exit DEBUG (back to DOS)?

Q3-18   What characteristic distinguishes input and output hardware from auxiliary-storage hardware?

Q3-19   Describe the difference between a hardware boot and a software boot.

Q3-20   Describe the three parts of a DOS file specification.

Q3-21   List the standard DOS I/O device names and the devices they denote.

Q3-22   In general, which type of DOS commands, internal or external, are most often used?

Q3-23   If you were to design an operating system, what two criteria would you use to decide if a particular command should be made internal or external?

Q3-24   What are the differences between DOS system services and BIOS services?

Q3-25   List the register names recognized by DEBUG.

Q3-26   What are the two parts of a memory address?

Q3-27   Which DEBUG command, G or T, could be used to step through BIOS code, one instruction at a time?

PROGRAMMING ASSIGNMENTS

PA3-1   In order to complete the following exercises, you need two diskettes of the proper size for your machine. Label each with your name and your instructor's name. In addition, label one as WORKING and the other as BACKUP. *Note*: Write the information on the labels **before** attaching them to the diskettes. If the labels are already attached, use only a felt-tipped marker with light pressure; do not use a ball-point pen or a pencil.

Complete the following exercises in order to become familiar with your machine and with DOS commands. Refer to the DOS commands discussed earlier in this chapter while doing the exercise. Write down your responses to any questions.

a) Boot the system following the appropriate procedures for your system. Ensure that the DOS prompt appears; if not, try booting again. After booting the system, properly insert your new blank WORKING diskette into drive A. Write down the DOS prompt that now appears on the screen. Use the VER command to determine the version of DOS you are using; write down the version number.

b) Try to do a directory of your WORKING diskette; write down the command you enter. What message did you get on the screen? Why do you think you got that message?

c) Try to verify the integrity of your WORKING diskette using CHKDSK; write down the command. Did it work? Why?

d) Now, format your WORKING diskette so you can use it. Be careful not to format the DOS diskette. You may be required to use one or more switches (/4, /T/N, or /F:) to avoid formatting at high density; check with your instructor. Write down the command you used.

e) Now do another directory of your WORKING diskette. Did you get the same results as in step b? Why? Write down the message.

f) Run CHKDSK again on your diskette; write down the command. Did it work this time? Why?

g) Format your WORKING diskette again, but this time, give it the volume name WORKING. Write down the command you entered at the DOS prompt.

h) Do another directory of your diskette. What has changed? Write down the message which now appears. Use the VOL command to check just the volume name of the diskette.

i) Repeat step g with your BACKUP diskette in drive A; enter BACKUP when asked for the volume name. What advantage do you see in giving volume names to diskettes?

j) Your screen now has a good deal of information on it; what command should you use to blank it all out so you can work with a fresh screen? Enter the command to blank the screen.

k) Check the system date and time, and correct them if necessary (you probably will not need to change them); write down the commands you used.

Now, insert your WORKING diskette in drive A and your BACKUP diskette in drive B. If you are working with a single drive system, you will use the single drive as both A and B. Put your WORKING diskette in the drive; insert your BACKUP diskette later, whenever prompted to insert the diskette for drive B.

l) Use the COPY command to create a file called TEST.TXT; copy from CON to A:TEST.TXT. Type in anything you like for the file data, but make it at least five lines long, pressing <Enter> after each line. When finished, press <F6> (or <Ctrl>+<Z>) and then <Enter>. Did the drive A light come on? Why?

m) Do a directory of drive A again. Is the message the same as the last time you did a DIR? Write down the message.

n) Use the TYPE command to take a look at the file you just created. Does it look like what you typed? Write down the command you used.

o) If your PC has a printer attached or if it is connected to a network with a print spooler, use three methods to obtain a hard copy of TEST.TXT. First, use the COPY command to copy the file to the printer (PRN). Then use the TYPE command to display the file to the screen, and do a screen dump. Finally, toggle the printer on, use the TYPE command to display the file to the screen (and printer), and then toggle the printer off.

p) Use the COPY command to copy your new file to TEST.TXT on your BACKUP diskette in drive B. Write down the command you used. Watch the lights on the disk drives. Describe what they did.

q) Use the COMP command to compare the file on your WORKING diskette with the one on your BACKUP diskette. Write down the command. Did they compare OK?

r) Now use the DISKCOMP command to compare your two diskettes. Write down the command. Why does DISKCOMP report a difference?

s) Now, try to create a second copy of the file on your WORKING diskette, with the same name. Enter:

```
COPY A:TEST.TXT A:TEST.TXT
```

Did it work? Why?

t) Try again. This time, copy it to another file with the name TEST2.TXT, on your WORKING diskette. Did that work? Do a directory to make sure you now have two files on your WORKING diskette.

u) Use the COPY command with wild cards (*) to back up your WORKING diskette to your BACKUP diskette. Do a directory of both diskettes; are they now the same?

v) Use RENAME to change the name of TEST2.TXT, on your WORKING diskette, to TEST3.TXT, then repeat step u. Are the two directories the same now? Why?

w) Use the ERASE or DEL command with wild cards to delete **all** files from your WORK-ING diskette; write down the command you used. Then do a directory of your WORKING diskette. Write down the message. What does it mean?

x) Now use the COPY command to restore your WORKING diskette from your BACK-UP diskette, just as you would if the data had been accidentally lost. Do a directory of your WORKING diskette; have you lost any data?

y) Delete all files from both your diskettes. If you are not yet comfortable with the machine, repeat these exercises from step g.

PA3-2 Complete the following exercises in order to become familiar with DEBUG (or SYMDEB). Refer to the DEBUG commands discussed earlier in this chapter, while doing the exercise. Write down your responses to any questions.

a) At the DOS prompt, enter the command to invoke DEBUG (or SYMDEB); include the DOS drive specifier, if it is not the default drive. What prompt now appears to indicate that DEBUG is ready for a command?

b) Use the **Register** command to examine the current values of all 8086/8088 registers; remember that the values displayed are in hexadecimal. Write down the values of all the registers.

c) Use the **Register** command to change the value in AX to 3F4CH (hexadecimal, do not enter the H); then change CX to FFFFH. Use the **Register** command again to examine all the registers. What has changed?

d) Use the **Hex** command to find the sum and difference of 3F19H and 1A4CH (3F19H +

1A4CH and 3F19H − 1A4CH); write down the results and check them by hand. Use the Hex command again to find the sum and difference of 1A4CH and 3F19H (1A4CH + 3F19H and 1A4CH − 3F19H). Write down the results; is the difference correct? Hint: Remember that negative numbers are stored in twos complement. Now find the sum and difference of FF19H and 1A4CH. Write down the results; is the sum correct? Why is the sum smaller than FF19H?

e) Enter the Dump command, without any parameters, to examine memory. Note that DEBUG shows the address (segment:offset) on the left side of the screen, the data in hexadecimal in the middle of the screen, and attempts to show the same data as ASCII characters to the right of the screen; a period (.) indicates that the byte of data is not displayable as an ASCII character. Also notice the address (segment:offset) where the dump began. Why did DEBUG use that segment? Why that offset? How many bytes were displayed? Enter the Dump command again, without parameters. Why did this dump begin at offset 0180?

f) Now dump only sixteen bytes, beginning at offset 100H (100H through 10FH), specify the range as *address address* (first and last offsets to dump). Write down the command and the results. Dump the same sixteen bytes again, but this time specify the range as *address Lvalue* (offset to start at and number of bytes, in hex, to dump). Write down your command; was there any difference in the results? If so, you did something wrong; try again.

g) Use the Enter command to store the string, "THIS IS A TEST!", into memory beginning at offset 100H; write down your command. Now, store the string, "THES AS A TEST.", into memory beginning at offset 110H. Dump all thirty-two bytes and look at DEBUG's ASCII display to ensure that you entered the data correctly. From the hexadecimal display, what is the ASCII code (in hex) for T? For H? For S?

h) Use the Compare command to compare the sixteen bytes beginning at offset 100H with the data beginning at 110H; write down your command. Where did DEBUG find differences? Is that correct?

i) Now use the Enter command with a list to enter the numeric (no quotes) values, 00H through 0FH, into offsets 120H through 12FH. Enter the same sixteen values into memory at 130H, but this time enter them one at a time instead of as a list. To do so, specify only the address (offset) with the Enter command. Then as DEBUG displays each byte, press <Space Bar> if it is already correct, or type the new value followed by <Space Bar>; press <Enter> after typing the **last** value.

j) Use the Dump command to examine memory from 120H through 13FH. Is 120H through 12FH the same as 130H through 13FH? They both should be 00H through 0FH; repeat step i if they are not correct. Now, tell DEBUG to compare 120H through 12FH with 130H through 13FH; write down the command. Were there any differences reported?

k) Now, use the Assemble command to assemble the following program into memory beginning at offset 100H:

```
MOV     AX, 1111
MOV     BX, AX
INC     BX
SUB     AX, BX
NEG     AX
DEC     AX
AND     BX, AX
INT     20
```

The instruction, INT 20, uses a DOS system service to cause the program to return to DEBUG (or DOS, if run from DOS) upon completion. Note that after you enter each instruction, DEBUG responds with the address where the next instruction will be stored. Are all the instructions the same length (same number of bytes)? After the program is entered, press <Enter> at the address after the last instruction. How many bytes long is your program?

l) Dump the program (D 100 LF). What you see is the machine-language instructions, represented by DEBUG in hexadecimal, which resulted from your assembly-language instructions. Now, Unassemble the program (U 100 LF); DEBUG shows the address where each instruction begins, shows the machine-language instruction in hexadecimal, and disassembles the instruction to its equivalent assembly-language instruction. Are the assembly-language instructions the same as what you entered? How many bytes long is the longest instruction in this program? The shortest?

If your PC has a printer available, obtain a hard copy listing of your program. Toggle the printer on, Unassemble the program again, then be sure to toggle the printer back off.

m) Execute the entire program (Go command) without break points. The DEBUG message, "Program terminated normally," indicates that the program successfully completed and returned to DEBUG. Which instruction caused control to return to DEBUG? Take a look at the register values displayed by DEBUG. Did they change? Does that make sense?

n) The results obtained in step m, above, are slightly misleading in that it appears that the program did not modify any register values. Actually, the register values *did* change; however, DEBUG restores all registers to their previous values when a program returns control (INT 20). Execute the program again, setting a break point at the offset of the INT 20 instruction; because of the break point, INT 20 does not execute, and DEBUG does not restore the registers. Now, have the register values been changed by the program? What offset is now in IP? If the Go command is entered again (without =*address*), at what offset will execution begin?

If your PC has a printer available, obtain a hard copy of the results of executing the program. Toggle the printer on, and execute the program again with a break point at INT 20 (you must use =*address* to cause execution to begin at offset 100H). Remember to toggle the printer back off.

o) Execute your program one instruction at a time, using the Trace command. *Important*: Do not use the Trace command to execute the last instruction (INT 20); use the Go command, without a break point, and control will return properly to DEBUG. Each Trace command executes the instruction pointed to by the IP register (or specified in the command by =*address*), displays the register values after execution of that instruction, and then displays the next instruction that has not yet been executed. Note the register values before and after each instruction and describe what each of these instructions does in the program:

```
MOV        AX, 1111
MOV        BX, AX (Does AX change?)
INC        BX
SUB        AX,BX
NEG        AX
DEC        AX
```

p) Now, step through the program again, but this time use the Go command with break point. Your first Go command will have to specify the address at which to begin execution (=*address*), since IP is no longer 100H. For each instruction, specify the offset of the very next instruction as the break point. When you get to the INT 20 instruction, do *not* specify a break point. Do the instructions have the same effect as in step o?

q) Save your program to a program file called PA3-2.COM, on your WORKING diskette. You must perform three steps to properly save the program:

1) First, you must use the **Register** command to set BX:CX to the number of bytes to be saved (set BX to zero, CX to the number of bytes in the program). To calculate the number of bytes in the program, subtract the starting offset (100H) from the offset after the last instruction (10FH, if you keyed the program exactly); what DEBUG command can be used to do the subtraction? The difference of the two offsets is the number of bytes in the program; set CX to that value. Do not forget to set BX to zero. Write down the two **Register** commands you used.

2) Next, use the **Name** command to provide DEBUG with the name to be used for your file. Include a drive specifier in the filespec, if your WORKING diskette is not in the default drive. Write down the command.

3) Finally, save the program using the **Write** command without parameters. Write down the command as entered. Did the diskette light come on?

r) Exit DEBUG and do a directory of your working diskette. Is the file there? Is it fifteen bytes long? If not, repeat this exercise and carefully save the program. Execute your program from DOS (enter PA3-2; d:PA3-2 if your WORKING diskette is not in the default drive). Did your program generate any output to the screen?

s) Execute DEBUG. Examine the registers; what values are in BX and CX? Now, load your program file (**Name**, then **Load**), and examine the registers again. What values are now in BX and CX? Why did CX change? Disassemble the program and ensure that it is correct and complete. Play with it; change some of the instructions using the **Assemble** command; step through the program two or three instructions at a time.

t) Exit DEBUG. If you are still not comfortable with DEBUG, repeat this exercise and spend time playing around; experimentation is the best way to learn. *Caution*: Do not use the **Write** command with the drive, logical-sector, and number-of-sectors parameters; writing to specific disk locations can be very dangerous.

4

8086/8088
Processor Fundamentals

INTRODUCTION

In this chapter we will discuss the inner workings of the processor and how it is programmed to perform a specific function. Upon completion of the chapter, you should know the functional parts of the processor (Execution Unit, Arithmetic and Logic Unit, Bus Interface Unit, register set) and how they interact, as well as the manner in which the processor communicates with other system hardware. You will also understand the general syntax of assembly-language instructions, the data addressing modes supported by the 8086/8088 processor (the various ways in which the programmer may specify the data to be used by instructions), and the concept of memory segmentation as implemented by the 8086/8088 processor. Finally, we will discuss the operation of the stack, which is used for temporary data storage.

8086/8088 MICROPROCESSOR ARCHITECTURE

A **microprocessor** is a processor that is contained on a single **IC** or **integrated circuit.** The integrated circuit is a very thin wafer or chip of silicon, about 1/4-inch square, the surface of which is embedded with minute patterns of metallic impurities that precisely control the flow of electrons through the silicon. The result is that an electronic circuit made up of many thousands of resistors, transistors, wires, and other components is compressed to fit on the single silicon chip. For protection and to permit its connection to other components, the fragile silicon chip is enclosed in plastic with conductors leading out through the plastic case to metal pins which can be plugged into a socket on a circuit board (See Figure 4-1).

At this point we should clarify the difference between the 8086 and 8088 processors. Most early microprocessors were **eight-bit processors;** they could only process one byte of data at a time. In order to add two words of data, an eight-bit processor requires two additions: first it must add the two low-order bytes and then add the two high-order bytes plus any carry from the sum of the low bytes. The 8086 was developed as a **sixteen-bit processor.** It is capable of dealing with a full word of data at a time; it can do a word addition in one instruction. This ability made the 8086 faster and more powerful than earlier eight-bit processors but also led to cost problems for machines built around it. Since sixteen-bit microprocessors were a relatively recent development, sixteen-bit peripheral hardware, such as memory circuitry, was still rather expensive when compared with eight-bit peripherals.

Intel solved this cost problem through the development of the 8088, a hybrid between a sixteen-bit processor and an eight-bit processor. Internally, the 8088

Figure 4-1   8088 Microprocessor

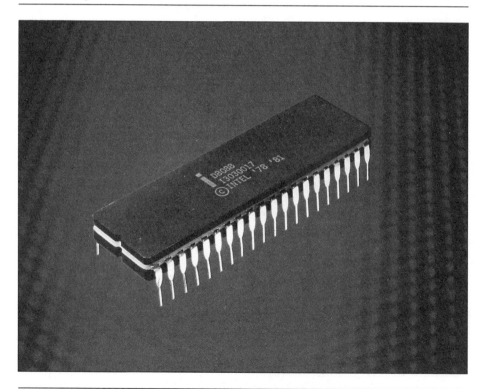

functions identically to the 8086; it processes sixteen bits at a time. Externally, however, the 8088 functions as an eight-bit processor; it accesses data from peripheral devices one byte at a time. For example, if the 8088 needs to read a word of data from memory, it does two reads of one byte each and then internally combines the two bytes into one word. Once the data is inside the processor, it is treated as a word, just as in the 8086. The result is that the 8088 functions as a sixteen-bit processor internally, but permits the use of less-expensive eight-bit peripheral devices.

The circuitry of most processors can be divided into three functional units: the **Execution Unit** or **EU** (sometimes called the **Control Unit** or **CU**), the **Arithmetic and Logic Unit** or **ALU**, and internal storage or **registers**. Unlike many other microprocessors the 8086/8088 has a fourth functional unit, the **Bus Interface Unit** or **BIU**. Remember that while these four circuits can be separated by function, they are all physically located on the same silicon wafer. In the following sections, we will discuss the purpose of each functional unit of the 8086/8088 processor. Figure 4-2 provides a graphic illustration of the interplay among the four circuits.

KEY TERMS TO REMEMBER

Microprocessor	EU, CU
IC	ALU
Eight-bit processor	Register set
Sixteen-bit processor	BIU

Execution Unit (EU)

The Execution Unit controls the activity within the processor. It is responsible for retrieving binary machine-language instructions from the **Instruction Queue** maintained by the Bus Interface Unit, deciphering them, and seeing to it that the correct steps are performed within the processor to carry out each instruction. If an instruction requires the use of data that is stored internally, in a register, then the Execution Unit retrieves the data from the correct register; if the instruction requires external data, from memory perhaps, then the EU requests the data from the Bus Interface Unit.

Whenever an instruction calls for an arithmetic or logical function, the EU passes the data to the Arithmetic and Logic Unit together with a command telling the ALU what to do with the data. The EU then accepts the resulting data from the ALU and sees to it that it is stored into the correct location (register or memory), as designated by the instruction.

Figure 4-2   Functional Schematic of 8086/8088 Microprocessor

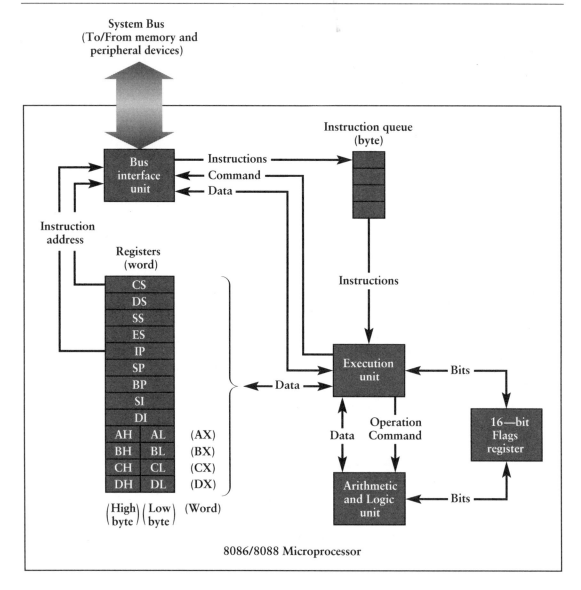

Arithmetic and Logic Unit (ALU)

While the EU controls activity within the processor, it is not capable of performing any arithmetic or logical manipulation of the data; that function is performed for it by the Arithmetic and Logic Unit. The ALU contains circuitry that is capable of generating the sum of two numbers (bytes or words), in much the same manner as we added binary numerals in chapter 2. In addition, its circuitry is also capable of incrementing (adding one to) a byte or word, decrementing (subtracting one from) a byte or word, and of shifting or rotating the bits in a byte or word to the left or to the right.

Finally, the ALU is able to perform bit-by-bit logical operations on bytes or words, inverting all the bits of a byte or word (NOT or ones complement) for example. Other instructions (AND, OR, XOR) cause the ALU to examine the corresponding pairs of bits in two bytes or two words and to follow a predefined rule for determining the corresponding bits of the result. By inverting bits, incrementing the result, and performing addition, the ALU also performs subtraction (as twos-complement addition) upon request by the Execution Unit. Another operation often listed as a function of the ALU is the comparing of data. Actually, as we will see when discussing the CMP instruction, the ALU uses subtraction (twos-complement addition) to do the comparison.

The ALU within the 8086/8088 can also combine some of these operations to perform multiplication and division. Recall from chapter 2 that we performed binary multiplication as a series of additions of the multiplicand, shifting it to the left each time. Recall also that we performed division as a series of subtractions, working our way to the right through the dividend (equivalent to shifting the dividend to the left). By combining its ability to shift bits and to add, the ALU is able to perform multiplication upon command; similarly, it implements division for the EU by performing a series of subtractions while shifting the dividend to the left. In each case, the Execution Unit simply requests multiplication or division; the ALU then performs all the necessary steps and returns the proper result (product or quotient and remainder) to the EU.

As the ALU completes a requested operation, it also controls individual bits within a special register called the Flags register (sometimes called the Program Status register). It sets (1) or clears (0) the correct bits to reflect specific characteristics of the result of the operation, such as whether the result was zero or nonzero, whether it was positive or negative, or if the result is too big (too many bits) to be stored in a byte or word. The Execution Unit checks the status of those Flag bits or Status bits whenever executing certain instructions, primarily conditional jumps.

Bus Interface Unit (BIU)

In most microprocessors, the Execution Unit is responsible for communicating with peripheral devices outside the processor. Whenever data stored in memory is called for as input to an instruction, the EU must directly request that data from the memory circuitry; the EU must also instruct memory circuitry to store the result of an operation whenever called for by the instruction. More importantly, the Execution Unit of most microprocessors, upon completion of one instruction, must request and wait for the next byte of machine code from memory. This waiting for the next instruction results in idle time for the processor. In the design of the 8086/8088 processor, Intel avoided much of this idle time through the introduction of the Bus Interface Unit and a pipelined design.

Besides storing or retrieving data as commanded by the Execution Unit, the BIU also operates somewhat autonomously to maintain a four-byte Instruction Queue within the processor. It constantly monitors the two registers (CS and IP) which point to the machine-language instructions in memory, reads the instructions from memory, and attempts to keep the Instruction Queue continually updated to contain the next four bytes of instructions. Consequently, as soon as the EU completes execution of one instruction, the next instruction is already waiting within the Instruction Queue. Thus most EU idle time is avoided. As will be discussed later, transfer-of-control instructions create an exception to this process.

It is in the BIU design that the 8088 differs from the 8086. In both processors, the EU and ALU can process a full word at a time. In both processors, when the EU needs a word of data from memory, it requests a word from the BIU. In the 8086, as long as the memory address is even, the BIU reads the entire word from memory, via a sixteen-bit data bus, and passes it to the Execution Unit. In the 8088, however, the BIU communicates with memory via an eight-bit data bus, first reading the low byte, then reading the high byte, then combining the two into one word to be passed to the EU. Because it has to do two reads, the 8088 takes longer to retrieve a word from memory than does the 8086. However, if the memory address happens to be odd, then the 8086 BIU functions in the same manner as the 8088 BIU, reading one byte at a time from the bus; thus the 8086 provides faster memory access than does the 8088 only if word data is kept at even memory addresses.

Internal Storage (Registers)

Storage of data within the processor is accomplished by a set of fourteen registers, each consisting of sixteen bits. Four of these word registers can each be addressed as two eight-bit registers (high byte and low byte). The registers can generally be categorized into four groups: Four **Segment registers**, three **Pointer registers**, two **Index registers**, and four **General-Purpose registers**, which can also be addressed a byte at a time. In addition to the thirteen registers listed above, the 8086/8088 contains one more sixteen-bit register, called the **Flags register**, which will be discussed below.

The Segment registers (**CS, DS, SS,** and **ES**) are always used to specify the segment half of a memory address. Memory segmentation will be discussed later in this chapter; for now, keep in mind that the processor always uses a sixteen-bit segment together with a sixteen-bit offset to specify memory addresses. The segment part of the address is always stored in one of the four Segment registers. Each of these registers is normally used to point to the beginning of a specific segment of memory. A particular memory location can then be addressed as an offset from the beginning of the appropriate segment.

CS, the **Code-Segment register**, points to the beginning of the code segment, the area of memory where the processor instructions are stored. The BIU always uses it as the segment half of the address from which to fetch instructions into the Instruction Queue. It is normally not explicitly modified by the programmer; since it controls from where the next instruction is fetched, modifying it is *very* dangerous.

DS, the **Data-Segment register**, normally points to the beginning of the segment of memory in which data is stored. It is used as the segment half of the address for most data storage or retrieval. Most instructions allow the programmer to specify a segment override, to be discussed later, to instruct the processor to use one of the other three Segment registers.

SS is the **Stack-Segment register**. It points to the area of memory in use as a stack and is used as the segment half of the memory address for all stack operations, which will be discussed later in this chapter. It is also used for other memory access, whenever the Base-Pointer register (BP) is used to specify the memory offset.

ES, the **Extra-Segment register,** is not normally used by the processor unless it has been explicitly specified by the programmer as a segment override. The exception to this rule is a group of special "string" instructions, which normally assume ES as the destination segment to receive the results of the operation. As implied by its name, it is provided in order to allow the programmer to set aside and access a segment of memory for some use other than as code, data, or stack.

The Pointer registers (**IP, SP,** and **BP**) are normally used to specify the offset half of a memory address. IP and SP are used by the processor for very specific purposes while the use of BP is left up to the programmer.

IP, the **Instruction-Pointer register,** is also sometimes called **PC** or the **Program Counter**. It is used by the BIU as the offset half of the memory address from which to fetch the next four bytes of instruction into the Instruction Queue; together with CS, IP controls which instruction is to be executed next. The Execution Unit automatically increments IP every time it extracts a byte from the Instruction Queue and modifies it during the execution of transfer-of-control instructions.

SP, the **Stack-Pointer register,** specifies the offset half of the memory address for all stack operations. The stack pointer may be directly modified, but the programmer must take great care when doing so. In chapter 7, we will discuss the direct modification of SP for the passing of parameters on the stack.

BP, the **Base-Pointer** register, is one of four registers that the programmer may explicitly use to address memory; when so used, it specifies the offset half of the memory address. However, unlike the other three registers that may be used as memory offsets, the use of BP causes the processor to use the Stack-Segment register rather than the Data-Segment register as the segment half of the address; BP points to the stack segment rather than to the data segment. Consequently, BP is often used to address parameters passed to a subroutine on the stack; in chapter 7 we will discuss the use of BP for parameter passing.

The programmer can also use the Index registers (**SI** and **DI**) to explicitly address memory, to specify the offset half of a memory address. Unless a segment override is specified or BP is used in conjunction with one of them, explicit use of SI or DI always addresses the data segment; the processor uses DS as the segment half of the address. In addition, the processor implicitly uses SI and DI for the offset half of the memory addresses for all "string" instructions. The programmer can also use SI and DI for general purposes to store any sixteen-bit value.

SI, the **Source-Index register,** is automatically used by the processor, with all "string" instructions, as the offset half of the source (from) memory address; DS is automatically used as the segment half of the source address. DI, or the **Destination-Index register,** always specifies the offset half of the destination (to) address for "string" instructions; ES is always used as the segment half of the address. We will discuss "string" instructions in chapter 10.

The General-Purpose registers (**AX, BX, CX,** and **DX**) are the only 8086/8088 registers that are addressable a byte at a time; each is divided into two addressable byte registers. Thus the General-Purpose registers can be named as four sixteen-bit registers or as eight eight-bit registers, **AH, AL, BH, BL, CH, CL, DH,** and **DL.** It is very important to remember that each byte register is really one half of the corresponding word register. Any modification of AH also modifies the high byte of AX, leaving the low byte of AX unchanged. Storing any value into DL also stores that value into the low eight bits of DX; the high eight bits of DX are left unchanged. Similarly, storing any value into BX destroys whatever data was previously stored in both BH and BL.

As the name implies, the General-Purpose registers are provided for the general use of the programmer. They may be used to store any byte or word values the programmer desires. In addition, each of the General-Purpose registers may be used for certain special purposes and are consequently sometimes given special names to reflect those purposes.

AX (word) and AL (byte) are often called the **Accumulator register;** the name is a throwback to earlier processors in which only the accumulator register could be used as a destination operand to receive the results of an arithmetic or logical operation. The 8086/8088 has no such restriction on destination operands; however, machine-language arithmetic and logical instructions, which have AX or AL as the destination operand and an immediate value (constant) as the source operand, are one byte shorter than those which use any other register as the destination operand. Additionally AX or AL are assumed by the processor as implicit operands for a number of instructions: input and output instructions, multiplication and division instructions, and instructions for adjusting during binary-coded-decimal arithmetic.

BX is referred to as the **Base register;** it is similar to BP, the Base-Pointer register, in that it may be used to address memory as the offset half of the memory address. The difference is that with BX as the offset the processor uses DS, the Data-Segment register, as the segment half of the address; if BP is used as the offset, the processor gets the segment from SS, the Stack-Segment register. Other than that major distinction, BX may be used in the same manner as BP. It is the *only* General-Purpose register that may be used to address memory.

CX, sometimes called the **Counter register,** is implicitly used by the processor, in conjunction with loop instructions and the repeat prefix for "string" instructions, to count the number of iterations. CL may be used explicitly, with shift and rotate instructions, to specify the number of bits to shift or rotate left or right.

DX, sometimes called the **Data register,** is the only register that may be used to specify the I/O port address for input and output instructions. Remember that the special uses for AX, BX, CX, and DX do not in any way restrict the programmer from using them for general purposes. In addition to the special uses described above, AX, BX, CX, and DX can be used to store *any* word value the programmer desires; AH, AL, BH, BL, CH, CL, DH, and DL may be used to store *any* byte values.

A PAUSE IN THE ACTION

Why Study the Processor?

There is a one-to-one correspondence between assembly language and the processor's instruction set. Assembly-language instructions often must reference the processor's registers by name and in the manner allowed by each register. Assembly-language instructions must also properly utilize the capabilities of the Control Unit, the Bus Interface Unit and the Arithmetic and Logic Unit.

Additionally, assembly language is most often used in situations where machine efficiency is necessary. Such machine efficiency cannot be achieved without an intimate understanding of the machine (processor). Consequently, in order to make effective use of assembly language, a programmer must become very familiar with the inner workings of the processor. That intimate understanding is the goal of this chapter.

Flags Register

The Flags register, sometimes called the **Program-Status register,** is a sixteen-bit register which is treated by the processor as a series of individual bits, each of which is always true (one) or false (zero). Only nine of these bits are accessible to the programmer; some of the other seven bits are used internally by the processor, but are invisible to the program and so will not be discussed here. Figure 4-3 illustrates the bit positions of the program-accessible flags. The flags can be divided into two groups: **Processor-Control flags** and arithmetic-and-logic **Result flags.** Following is a brief explanation of the meaning of each flag, beginning with the Processor-Control flags.

The Processor-Control flags (**DF, IF,** and **TF**) are normally controlled (set or cleared) explicitly by program instructions and affect the manner in which subsequent instructions are executed. During the execution of instructions, the Execution Unit checks the status of the flags and takes appropriate action.

DF, the **Direction flag,** is controlled entirely by the program with the instructions STD and CLD. It determines the direction of the "string" instructions. Specifically, the Execution Unit inspects DF upon execution of any "string" instruction to determine whether to increment or decrement the Index register(s) used by the instruction. Its status is reported by DEBUG as **UP** if DF is clear (zero) or **DN** (DowN) when it is set (one).

Figure 4-3   Flags Register Bits

Bit #

15	14	13	12	11	10	9	8	7	6	5	4	3	2	1	0
*	*	*	*	OF	DF	IF	TF	SF	ZF	*	AF	*	PF	*	CF

16-BIT
FLAGS REGISTER

* = Unused or used internally only

IF is the **Interrupt-Enable flag.** Its status determines whether the processor will respond to external interrupts from other hardware devices connected to the system bus; the processor will not respond to hardware interrupts unless IF is set. IF is set or cleared by the instructions STI and CLI and is also always cleared automatically when the processor executes an interrupt. Its status, as reported by DEBUG, is either **DI** (Disable Interrupts) if it is clear, or **EI** (Enable Interrupts) if it is set.

The **Trap flag,** TF, causes the processor to single-step through a program. The Execution Unit checks TF after *every* instruction; if it is set, then the processor clears it and immediately executes an interrupt type one. We will discuss interrupts in the next chapter. DEBUG uses the Trap flag to regain control after every program instruction in order to implement the Trace command; its status is not reported by DEBUG since it is always clear upon completion of an instruction.

The Result flags (**ZF, CF, AF, SF, OF,** and **PF**) are normally controlled automatically by the ALU to reflect attributes of the result of the last arithmetic or logical operation. The Result flags are checked by the Execution Unit in the execution of any Conditional jump; the current status of the flags determines whether the jump will take place. CF is the only Result flag that can be explicitly controlled by the program.

ZF, the **Zero flag,** is set by the ALU whenever any arithmetic or logic instruction results in a value of zero, when all bits in the result are zero; it is cleared any time a result is any value other than zero. Its status is reported by DEBUG as **ZR,** if it is set (the result was ZeRo), or **NZ,** if it is clear (result was Not Zero).

CF is the **Carry flag.** When set, it usually indicates that the result of an unsigned arithmetic operation is invalid, that the resulting value was too big to store correctly in a word, or for byte instructions, in a byte; for unsigned subtraction, it indicates that the result is less than zero. It is set or cleared by the ALU during arithmetic or logic operations to indicate whether the operation resulted in a carry out of the high bit. For most operations, it is set if there was a carry out and cleared if there was no carry out of the high bit. For subtraction instructions (SUB and SBC), however, it is controlled by the ALU in exactly the opposite manner; it is set whenever there was *not* a carry out of the high bit.

To understand why the function of the Carry flag must be reversed for subtraction, recall from chapter 2 that the ALU performs subtraction as twos-complement addition. Also recall that during twos-complement addition a carry out of the high bit is expected; the lack of a carry indicates that the result is less than zero and so cannot be stored properly as an unsigned value. Besides being automatically controlled by the ALU, the Carry flag is the only Result flag that the program can explicitly manipulate; it can be set, cleared, or complemented (STC, CLC, CMC). DEBUG reports its status as **CY** (CarrY) if set, or as **NC** (No Carry) if clear.

AF, or the **Auxiliary-Carry flag,** is set or cleared to indicate whether there was a carry out of the low nibble (low four bits). The programmer cannot use it directly since there are no instructions to directly modify it nor do any of the Conditional jumps test its status; the processor uses it when performing instructions for adjusting for binary-coded-decimal arithmetic. Its status is reported by DEBUG as **AC** (Auxiliary Carry) if set, or as **NA** (No Auxiliary carry) if clear.

SF, the **Sign flag,** is a reflection of the high bit of the result of the last arithmetic or logic operation. Recall from chapter 2 that signed integers use the high bit of the byte or word as the sign bit to indicate whether a number is positive or negative. A one in the high bit indicates that the number is negative and is stored in the remaining bits in twos-complement form; a high bit of zero indicates that the remaining bits represent a positive (or zero) number. Whenever any arithmetic or logic instruction is executed, the ALU copies the high bit of the result into the Sign flag. DEBUG reports the status of SF as **NG** (NeGative) if it is set, or as **PL** (PLus) if it is clear.

OF is the **Overflow flag;** its status indicates whether the result of the last operation was too big or too small to be stored as a signed integer. It serves the same purpose for signed arithmetic that the Carry flag serves for unsigned arithmetic: to indicate that the result is not to be trusted. Specifically, the ALU sets OF whenever the carry into the high bit is different from the carry out of the high bit. While this may seem strange, the important thing to remember is simply that OF is set whenever a result is too big or too small to be stored correctly as a signed integer. The status of OF is reported by DEBUG as **OV** (OVerflow) if set, or as **NV** (No oVerflow) if clear.

PF, or **Parity flag,** is the last Result flag for us to consider. It is used primarily in communication-control programs. The ALU counts the number of bits that are one, in the result of each arithmetic or logical operation. If the result contains an even number of ones, the ALU sets the Parity flag; it clears the Parity flag if there is an odd number of ones in the result. Note that PF does *not* indicate whether the number is odd or even; it indicates whether it has an even or odd number of ones in its binary representation. For example, the number 2 is even, but its parity is odd since there is an odd number (one) of ones in its binary representation (00000010B). DEBUG indicates the status of PF as **PE** (Parity Even) when it is set, and as **PO** (Parity Odd) when it is clear.

The functional parts of the processor can be summarized as follows. Take a moment to review.

SUMMARY OF **8086/8088 Processor**

Execution Unit (EU)

Decodes and executes machine instructions.

Arithmetic and Logic Unit (ALU)

Performs math and logical operations on command by the EU.

Bus Interface Unit (BIU)

Handles all communications with the "outside world" via the system bus. Maintains instruction queue.

Internal storage (registers)

Used for internal data storage. Five general types:
Segment registers
CS (Code Segment), DS (Data Segment), SS (Stack Segment), ES (Extra Segment)
Pointer registers
IP (Instruction Pointer), SP (Stack Pointer), BP (Base Pointer)
Index registers
SI (Source Index), DI (Destination Index)
General-Purpose registers
AX (AH, AL), BX (BH, BL), CX (CH, CL), DX (DH, DL)
Flags register
Sixteen-bit register, nine bits of which are used to indicate true/false conditions. Made up of two types:
Processor-control flags: DF, IF, TF
Result flags: ZF, CF, AF, SF, OF, PF

THE SYSTEM BUS AND PERIPHERAL HARDWARE

Thus far, our discussion has centered on the processor. We now need to discuss the means by which the processor communicates with the outside world. By "outside world" we mean all the other hardware devices that are separate from the processor but that are inside the CPU cabinet, plugged into the system board along with the processor. It should be noted that many of these devices are themselves very sophisticated microprocessors, which are designed to perform special functions. Some of the peripheral devices inside an IBM PC are

Memory

Up to one megabyte of system memory, including that which is on the system board, the video adapter card, and any add-on memory boards.

8253 Timer chip

Generates an external interrupt every fifty-five milliseconds to allow the PC to keep track of real time (system date and time).

8259 Interrupt Controller chip

Processes hardware (external) interrupts.

6845 CRT Controller

Located on the video adapter card. Controls the video signals to the monitor.

NEC D765 or Intel 8272 Floppy Disk Controller

Located on the disk adapter card. Acts as an interface between the processor and the disk drive.

Intel 8237 Direct Memory Access (DMA) Controller

Located on the system board. Used by the disk controller to transfer data between disk and memory.

8250 Asynchronous Communications Element or Universal Asynchronous Receiver/Transmitter (UART)

Located on each serial communications adapter card (COM1, COM2, and so on).

The processor communicates with all these devices through a series of conductive traces or signal lines on the system board, called the **System Bus**. If the processor is the brain of the computer then the System Bus is the spinal cord, allowing the brain to communicate with and control all the other parts of the system. The system board also includes a series of slots by which add-on cards may be connected directly into the bus for communication with the processor. The bus is made up of three functional parts, three groups of signal lines: the **Data Bus**, the **Address Bus**, and the **Control Bus**.

To read from memory, for example, the processor (Bus Interface Unit) puts the correct memory address onto the Address Bus and puts the command to read from memory onto the Control Bus. All devices connected to the bus see this address and command simultaneously, but only the memory-control circuitry on the system board, video adapter, and any add-on boards containing memory respond to it. The memory-control circuitry is then responsible for decoding the address, retrieving the data from the appropriate memory chips, and placing the data onto the Data Bus for retrieval by the BIU.

To write to memory, the BIU puts the memory address onto the Address Bus, the byte of data onto the Data Bus, and a command to write to memory onto the Control Bus. The memory-control circuitry decodes the command and the address, retrieves the data from the Data Bus, and stores it into the correct memory chips. All other circuitry simply ignores the command.

Communication with the many special-purpose microprocessors attached to the System Bus is accomplished through **I/O ports**. The term I/O is a bit misleading and should not be confused with the input/output hardware, discussed in the last chapter. I/O ports do not transfer data between the system and people, as I/O hardware does; they are used for the transfer of data between the 8086/8088 processor and the other support hardware within the system. The IN and OUT instructions tell the processor to input or output data through the I/O ports.

When executing an IN instruction, the BIU puts the I/O port address onto the Address Bus and puts the command to input data onto the Control Bus. The circuitry on some peripheral device attached to the bus recognizes the read command and decodes the I/O port as the address of some register within the peripheral device. It then retrieves the data from the register and places it onto the Data Bus from which it is retrieved by the BIU and fed to the Execution Unit within the processor.

To execute an OUT instruction, the BIU puts the command to output data onto the Control Bus, the I/O address onto the Address Bus, and the data to be output onto the Data Bus. The circuitry of a peripheral device is then responsible for recognizing the output command and the I/O address and for retrieving the data from the data bus.

Since the 8086/8088 is capable of addressing one megabyte of memory, it must be able to generate addresses from 00000H through FFFFFH. Consequently, in order to carry twenty-digit binary addresses, the Address Bus is made up of twenty signal lines. The size of the Data Bus depends on the processor. Since the 8088 addresses memory one byte at a time, the Data Bus is made up of eight signal lines. Any machine that utilizes the 8086 microprocessor requires a sixteen-bit data bus.

GENERAL INSTRUCTION FORMAT

All assembly-language instructions consist of at least an **operation code** or **opcode**, which tells the processor what to do. Many opcodes must be followed by one or two **operands**, specifying the immediate values, registers, or memory addresses to be used in the operation. Some opcodes allow no operands; others require one operand; still others require two operands. If an instruction has an operand, then it must be separated from the opcode by one or more spaces and/or tabs. A second parameter, if there is one, is separated from the first by a comma. Extra spaces and tabs, between two operands or between the opcode and first operand, are ignored and can be used to make the instruction more readable. Thus, we have the following general instruction format:

opcode   [*operand*[, *operand*]]

It may be helpful to think of instructions as imperative sentences. The opcode is the verb, telling the processor what to do; the operands, if any, act as direct and indirect objects, specifying what to perform the operation with and what to do it to. Since the instructions are always imperative commands, the subject is always understood to be the processor.

The rest of this chapter contains many examples of assembly-language instructions, many of which include numeric constants. In all such sample instructions, we have followed DEBUG's convention of representing all numeric constants as hexadecimal numerals, without the H suffix to indicate hexadecimal. Throughout the explanatory material, however, we have followed the usual convention of indicating a nondecimal numeral by appending a suffix of B for binary or H for hexadecimal. Some valid instructions and their English translations are listed below:

1) NOP   No operation. Do nothing.

2) HLT   Halt. Stop.

3) INC   AL   Increment (add one to) the AL register.

4) ADD   CL, [100]   Add the value stored in memory at offset 100H to CL.

5) SUB   [200], BH   Subtract contents of register BH from memory at offset 200H.

6) MOV   DX, 74   Store the value 74H into DX.

7) PUSH   CX   Put the value in CX onto the top of the stack.

8) POP   ES   Take the value from the top of the stack, storing it into ES.

9) INT   20   Execute an interrupt type 20H; terminate the program, returning control to DOS.

Notice that some of the operands in the above instructions are modified, while others are not. In the fourth instruction (ADD CL, [100]), CL is altered; its stored value is increased by the value stored in memory location 100H. The value in memory, however, is **not** modified; its value is simply read by the processor in order to know what to add to CL. In the fifth instruction (SUB [200], BH), a memory location is modified while the value in BH does not change. Similarly, the sixth instruction (MOV DX, 74) changes the value in DX, but does not change the other operand, the number 74H; indeed, a numeric value **cannot** be changed. The seventh instruction (PUSH CX) does not modify its operand, CX; however, the operand ES is modified in the eighth instruction (POP ES).

Instructions may contain two types of operands, **source operands** and **destination operands**. A source operand is one that is *not* modified or written to by the operation. It is used for input to the operation only. A destination operand is any operand whose value *is* modified; it receives the result of the operation.

Note that a destination operand may also be used as input to the operation. For example, in order to execute the fourth instruction above (ADD CL, [100]), the Execution Unit must first read both CL and memory location 100H and then pass the two values to the ALU with a command to add; the EU then receives the sum from the ALU and stores it into CL. Thus, CL is used for both input and output. The fact that it receives the output makes it a destination operand.

In each of the fourth (ADD CL, [100]) and fifth (SUB [200], BH) instructions above, one of the two operands is enclosed in brackets to indicate that it is a memory location rather than an immediate numeric value. Memory may be specified for either a source or a destination operand. However, if an instruction has two operands, they can never both be memory. Only one operand in a given instruction may refer to a memory location.

Also notice that in the above instructions, some operands (AL, CL and BH) are **byte operands** while others (DX, CX, and ES) are **word operands**. Most instructions have two forms or types in machine language, byte and word. An assembly-language instruction is assembled either as a byte instruction or as a word instruction, depending on the type of its operand(s). It must be one or the other; it cannot be both. Consequently, if an instruction has two operands, they must both be of the same type. The following instructions are invalid because the types of the operands do not match:

```
MOV     AL, DX     (Invalid - byte, word)
SUB     DI, CL     (Invalid - word, byte)
```

KEY TERMS TO REMEMBER

System Bus	Operand
Data Bus	Source operand
Address Bus	Destination operand
Control Bus	Byte operand
I/O port	Word operand
Opcode	

The type of a register is always easily determined by the register name, but the types of memory and immediate value operands may be ambiguous. Consider the following two instructions:

```
SUB        [200], BH        Subtract the value in BH from memory at offset 200H.
MOV        DX, 74           Store 74H into DX.
```

The [200] in the first instruction could refer to the byte at that memory location or it could refer to a word of memory (the two bytes at 200H and 201H). Similarly, the immediate value 74, in the second instruction, might mean the byte value 74H, or it could refer to the word value 0074H; the assembler and DEBUG do not assume that it is a byte value simply because it is small enough to be stored as a byte or because it has been written as two hexadecimal digits.

In these two examples, the ambiguity is no problem; it is resolved by the type of the other operand (BH in the first instruction, DX in the second). Since both operands must be of the same type, the type of the ambiguous operand is taken to be the same as that of the other operand (byte in the first instruction, word in the second). Sometimes, however, the assembler or DEBUG may need help in determining the type of an operand. Consider the following instructions:

```
INC        [200]            Increment (add one to) memory at offset 200H.
ADD        [200], 30        Add 30H to memory at offset 200H.
```

In both cases, it is impossible to determine the type of the operands; [200] might mean a word of memory or a byte of memory, and 30 might be the byte value, 30H, or the word value, 0030H. In each case, the assembler or DEBUG is unable to determine the type and so reports an error.

THE PTR OPERATOR

In any instruction in which the assembler or DEBUG cannot resolve type ambiguity, the programmer must remove the ambiguity by explicitly stating the type of an operand with the **PTR operator**. The operand must be preceded by WORD PTR or BYTE PTR to state its type. Note that PTR is not an instruction or part of an instruction; it is an operator which tells the assembler or DEBUG to assemble the instruction as a byte instruction or as a word instruction. We will learn later of some other uses for the PTR operator. If both of the above instructions, with ambiguous operands, are intended to operate on bytes, then they should be coded as shown below:

```
INC        BYTE PTR [200]          Increment the byte of memory at offset
                                   200H.

ADD        BYTE PTR [200], 30      Add 30H to the byte of memory at offset
                                   200H.
```

    or

```
ADD        [200], BYTE PTR 30
```
Add the byte value 30H to memory at offset 200H.

If the same two instructions are intended as word instructions, then they should be rewritten as:

```
INC        WORD PTR [200]
```
Increment the word of memory at offset 200H.

```
ADD        WORD PTR [200], 30
```
Add 0030H to the word of memory at offset 200H.

or

```
ADD        [200], WORD PTR 30
```
Add the word 0030H to memory at offset 200H.

Notice that the PTR operator is only required for one of two operands, whenever both would be ambiguous without it. As long as the type of one of the two operands is known, DEBUG or the assembler can easily determine whether to assemble it as a byte instruction or as a word instruction. The PTR operator may also be used in cases in which it is not required, but must be used carefully so as not to create a type mismatch in the operands. For example, the following three instructions, although redundant, are perfectly legal.

```
MOV        BX, WORD PTR FF              (OK - word, word)
SUB        BYTE PTR [100], CL           (OK - byte, byte)
ADD        BYTE PTR [100], BYTE PTR FF  (OK - byte, byte)
```

The following four instructions, however, are all invalid due to the misuse of the PTR operator. In the first three, the PTR operator creates a mismatch in the types of the operands. The fourth instruction attempts to declare a word register as a byte; AX is always a word.

```
MOV        BX, BYTE PTR FF              (No - word, byte)
SUB        WORD PTR [100], CL           (No - word, byte)
ADD        BYTE PTR [100], WORD PTR FF  (No - byte, word)
INC        BYTE PTR AX                  (No - AX cannot be byte)
```

The following example may or may not be accepted by your assembler. Although redundant, it is valid; however, some versions of the assembler do not permit you to explicitly state the type, even if correct, of any register.

```
INC        WORD PTR AX     (Assembler may not accept)
```

Much of the previous discussion of the general instruction format and the PTR operator can be summarized as the following set of rules which must always be observed in the formation of instructions:

Rules for Forming Instructions

1) If an instruction has both a source operand and a destination operand, the destination operand is always the left-most operand (to the left of the comma).

2) If an opcode requires two operands, they cannot both be memory (brackets); one of the two must be an immediate (numeric) value or a register.

3) If an instruction has two operands, they both must be of the same type; they must both be byte operands, or they must both be word operands.

4) If an operand's type is ambiguous and cannot be determined from the type of another operand, then its type must be explicitly stated with the PTR operator.

5) A source operand can be any of the three data addressing modes, discussed below: an immediate (constant) value, a register, or a memory location.

6) A destination operand, since it is to store the result of the operation, must be either a register or a memory location; a destination operand can never be an immediate value.

DATA ADDRESSING MODES

Thus far, we have referred, without much explanation, to operands that are immediate values, registers, or memory. We now need to further clarify the 8086/8088 processor's **Data Addressing modes**, the different ways in which the programmer may specify operands in instructions. As suggested by our previous discussions, the three fundamental addressing modes are **Immediate mode, Register mode,** and **Memory mode**; we will see shortly that memory addressing must be further broken down, because the 8086/8088 allows many ways to address memory. First, we will examine Immediate and Register modes, then we will look in detail at the many forms of Memory addressing.

Immediate-mode data addressing is analogous to constants in a high-level language program; the programmer specifies the actual data value to be used. It is called Immediate mode because, in the resulting machine language, the value is integrated into the instruction; it is stored as a part of the instruction, immediately following the opcode and the destination operand. In each of the following examples, the source operand 1A4C is Immediate mode.

MOV	AX, **1A4C**	Store 1A4CH into AX.
ADD	SI, **1A4C**	Add 1A4CH to SI.
SUB	WORD PTR [DI], **1A4C**	Subtract 1A4CH from the word of memory at the offset specified by DI.

```
AND        [1F20], WORD PTR 1A4C        Logical AND 1A4CH with memory
                                        at offset 1F20H.
```

Note that the PTR operator was required in the last two instructions in order to explicitly state the type of the operands. Also note that, in every instruction, 1A4C is the source operand, to the right of the comma. Since it is a constant value, which cannot be changed, Immediate mode can never be used for a destination operand. For example, the following instruction is illegal since it attempts to use Immediate-mode data addressing for the destination operand:

```
MOV        1A4C, AX        Invalid - Store the value from AX into the immediate
                           value 1A4CH ??
```

In **Register**-mode data addressing, the programmer supplies the name of a register (other than the Instruction pointer or a Segment register) from which data is to be read and/or to which the output of the operation is to be written. IP can never be used for Register-mode addressing. With three exceptions (PUSH, POP and MOV) to be discussed in the next chapter, the segment registers (CS, DS, SS, and ES) cannot be used for Register-mode addressing.

Since registers are storage and can be used to store the result of an operation as well as to supply input data for the operation, Register mode can be used for either the source operand or the destination operand or for both. Each of the following examples makes use of Register-mode data addressing for one or both operands:

```
MOV        [DI], BX        Store the value from register BX into memory at the
                           offset specified by DI.
MOV        AX, 1A4C        Store 1A4CH into register AX.
ADD        AH, AL          Add the value in register AL to register AH.
INC        SI              Increment the value in register SI.
NEG        BL              Negate (twos complement of) the value in register BL.
```

In the above examples, BX, AX, AH, AL, SI, and BL are all Register addressing mode. Note that [DI] is not Register mode; the mere presence of a register name does not always ensure that Register mode is in use. Any operand enclosed in brackets constitutes Memory addressing. A register name that is not enclosed in brackets refers to the data stored in that register and is Register-mode data addressing.

As mentioned above, the 8086/8088 provides many different forms of Memory addressing. They are similar in that the data is stored in memory, the programmer in one way or another supplies the offset half of the desired memory address, and the processor uses a Segment register for the segment half of the address. Except for two circumstances, when BP or a segment override is used (to be explained later), the processor always uses the value in DS as the segment for the memory address. As seen in the previous examples, Memory addressing is distinguished from Immediate and Register modes by enclosing the operand in brackets ([and]).

A PAUSE IN THE ACTION

Why Data Addressing Modes Are Important

Many processor instructions require that the programmer specify data to be used as input by the instruction as well as the location into which to store the resulting (output) value. Most instructions severely limit the manner in which the data values may be specified (data addressing modes).

Consequently, a thorough understanding of the various data addressing modes is an absolute prerequisite to an understanding of the instruction set discussed in the next chapter.

Since memory can be written to as well as read from, Memory-mode data addressing, like Register mode, can be used for either the destination operand or for the source operand in an instruction; however, it cannot be used for both. If an opcode requires two operands, they can never both be Memory mode; one of the two operands must always be Register or Immediate mode. The two fundamental modes of addressing memory are **Direct Memory mode** and **Indirect Memory mode**. We will see shortly that there are several forms of Indirect Memory addressing, but first we will look at Direct Memory addressing.

For Direct Memory addressing, the programmer provides the memory offset as an immediate value enclosed in brackets. The processor uses the value in DS as the segment half of the address. Following are some examples of instructions using Direct Memory addressing:

MOV	AX, **[1000]**	Store the word value from memory at offset 1000H into AX.
ADD	**[2B4]**, DL	Add the value in DL to the byte of memory at offset 2B4H.
SUB	**[F000]**, SI	Subtract the value in SI from the word of memory at F000H.
INC	BYTE PTR **[142]**	Increment the byte value in memory at offset 142H.

In the above examples, [1000], [2B4], [F000], and [142] are all Direct Memory mode operands. Be careful in your use of brackets in the forming of operands. Use brackets if and only if you intend to address memory. Note that the following two instructions, while they look much alike, produce vastly different results:

MOV	AX, 1000	Store 1000H into AX.
MOV	AX, [1000]	Store the word value in memory at offset 1000H into AX.

The first instruction stores an immediate value into AX; after its execution AX contains the value 1000H. The second instruction reads whatever value has previously been stored in memory at offset 1000H within the data segment and stores that value into AX. After execution, AX contains whatever value has been previously stored in memory at that address. Also keep in mind that two operands cannot both be memory; the following instruction is invalid since it attempts to use Memory mode for both operands:

```
MOV     WORD PTR [100], [200]     (Invalid - both memory)
```

The second means of addressing memory, Indirect Memory mode, uses registers to indirectly specify the offset. A register name is enclosed in brackets to cause the processor to read a memory *offset* from that register; the register is used to point to the memory location at which the data is stored. While the 8086/8088 rigidly restricts which registers may be used for Indirect Memory addressing, it does provide a good deal of flexibility in the way those registers may be combined to point to memory.

The simplest form of Indirect addressing is **Base-or-Index** Memory mode, in which the Base register (BX), Base-Pointer register (BP), or one of the two Index registers (SI or DI) is used to point to the desired memory location. The register name is enclosed in brackets to indicate Memory addressing rather than Register addressing. When the instruction executes, the processor uses the value currently stored in the register as the offset of the memory location where the data is stored. The following instructions make use of Base-or-Index addressing:

SUB	**[BX]**, CX	Subtract the value in CX from memory at the offset specified by BX.
OR	AL, **[BP]**	Logical OR with AL the value in memory at the offset from SS specified by BP.
DEC	WORD PTR **[SI]**	Decrement (subtract 1 from) the word at the offset specified by SI.
MOV	**[DI]**, BL	Store the value in BL into memory at the offset specified by DI.

The operands [BX], [BP], [SI], and [DI] all use a Base register or Index register to specify the memory offset, to point to the desired memory location. When executing the second instruction, the processor uses SS as the segment half of the address, since BP is used as the Base register; [BP] points to the stack segment. The other three instructions all point to memory within the data segment; the processor uses DS as the segment half of the address.

A second, more flexible form of Indirect memory addressing is **Base-or-Index-Plus-Displacement**. Again, the Base or Base-Pointer register or an Index register is used to help specify the offset. However, a displacement is also provided to be added to the value in the register in determining the memory offset. The displacement is treated as a signed integer within the range -32768 through +32767 and is stored as a part of the machine-language instruction. The following are examples of Base-or-Index-Plus-Displacement Memory addressing:

ADD	**[BX + 300A]**, CX	Add the contents of CX to the memory location whose offset is the value in BX plus 300AH.

SUB	AL, **[BP + 4]**	Subtract from AL the value stored in the memory location whose offset from SS is the value in BP plus 4.
INC	WORD PTR **[SI − 43]**	Increment the value in the memory location whose offset is the value in SI minus 43H.
MOV	**[DI − 1431]**, BL	Store the value in BL into the memory location whose offset is the value in DI minus 1431H.

In each instruction, the processor reads the value currently stored in the Base or Index register, adjusts it by adding the positive or negative displacement, and uses the result as the offset for a memory location. Since BP is used as the Base register in the second instruction, the processor uses SS as the segment half of the memory address. The other three examples all refer to memory within the data segment; the processor uses DS as the segment half of the address.

Base-or-Index-Plus-Displacement provides a handy means of addressing tables of data. To address a particular entry in a table, first calculate into a Base or Index register the distance from the beginning of the table to the desired table member by multiplying the member number times the length of each member. The desired table member is then addressed using Base-or-Index-Plus-Displacement mode where the displacement is the offset of the first member of the table.

There are two peculiarities of the resulting 8086/8088 machine code that we should discuss here. First, the processor has two forms of all Base-or-Index-Plus-Displacement addressing: byte displacement and word displacement. If the specified displacement is within the range of a signed byte, −128 through +127, the displacement is stored as a byte within the machine-language instruction. The resulting instruction is one byte longer than a similar instruction using Base or Index (without displacement) addressing.

If the specified displacement is outside the range of a byte, however, the assembler or DEBUG generates an instruction that stores the displacement as a word, resulting in an instruction two bytes longer than a similar instruction with no displacement. Since the choice of byte or word displacement is made by the assembler or DEBUG, you will not normally need to worry about the distinction unless you are working within very strict memory requirements where each byte is important.

The second oddity is that there is no actual machine code for Base or Index addressing (without a displacement) whenever BP is used as the Base register. Using BX, SI, or DI for Base or Index (without displacement) results in machine-language instructions with no displacement, making the instruction one byte shorter than with a displacement. BP, however, is always assembled with a displacement. Consequently, the following two assembly-language instructions result in exactly the same machine code; in both cases, the instruction is assembled with a byte displacement of zero:

MOV	**[BP]**, AX	(assembled as [BP + 0])
MOV	**[BP + 0]**, AX	

The third form of Indirect Memory addressing is **Base-Plus-Index** mode, in which the memory offset is specified as the sum of a Base register and an Index register. The processor adds the value in the Base register to the value stored in the Index register and uses the result as the offset for the memory location. If the Base register is BP, then the processor uses SS as the segment. If BX is used for the Base register, then DS is used as the segment. The following all use Base-Plus-Index Memory addressing mode:

INC	WORD PTR **[BX + SI]**	Increment the word of memory whose offset is the value in BX plus the value in SI.
ADD	**[BX + DI]**, CX	Add the value in CX to the word of memory whose offset is the value in BX plus the value in DI.
MOV	BYTE PTR **[BP + SI]**, 4C	Store 4CH into the byte of memory at offset BP + SI from SS.
SUB	DX, **[BP + DI]**	Store the word in memory, at offset BP + DI from SS, into DX.

Note that in each case, the offset is specified as the sum of a Base register and an Index register; the 8086/8088 does not allow the sum of the two Base registers or the sum of two Index registers. Consequently, the following instructions are invalid because they attempt to use both Base or both Index registers:

MOV	[BX + BP], AX	(Invalid - base + base)
MOV	AX, [SI + DI]	(Invalid - index + index)

At this point, you can probably predict the fourth and last memory mode. With **Base-Plus-Index-Plus-Displacement** Memory addressing mode, the processor adds the values of the specified Base and Index registers, then adds the positive or negative displacement, and uses the result as the offset of the memory address. Again, the displacement will be a byte if within the range −128 through +127; if the displacement is outside that range, the instruction will be assembled with a word displacement. In any case, the displacement is limited to the range −32768 through +32767. Following are some examples of Base-Plus-Index-Plus-Displacement Memory addressing:

ADD	AX, **[BX + SI + 23]**	Memory offset is value in BX plus value in SI plus 23H.
INC	BYTE PTR **[BX + DI + 1BC4]**	Offset is value in BX plus value in DI plus 1BC4H.
MOV	CL, **[BP + SI + 1]**	Offset from SS is BP plus SI plus 1.
MOV	**[BP + DI - 5]**, BYTE PTR 3	Offset from SS is BP plus DI minus 5.

Take some time to review the following summary of data-addressing modes.

SUMMARY OF Data-Addressing Modes

Immediate

Constant value specified by the programmer. Stored within the machine instruction immediately following the opcode.

Register

A register name *not* enclosed in brackets. Refers to the data stored in the register.

Memory

Indicated with brackets ([ ]). Refers to data stored in a memory location. Two fundamental modes:

Direct

An immediate value within brackets. Refers to the contents of the memory location whose offset is specified by the immediate value.

Indirect

Uses one or two registers (within brackets) to specify the offset of the memory location. The contents of the register(s) determine the memory location. Four types:

Base or Index

Uses a Base register (BX or BP) or Index register (SI or DI) to specify the memory offset.

Base or Index Plus Displacement

Uses a Base register (BX or BP) or Index register (SI or DI) plus an immediate-value displacement to specify the memory offset.

Base Plus Index

Uses the sum of a Base register (BX or BP) plus an Index register (SI or DI) to specify the memory offset.

Base Plus Index Plus Displacement

Uses the sum of a Base register (BX or BP) plus an Index register (SI or DI) plus an immediate-value displacement to specify the memory offset.

MEMORY SEGMENTATION

We have alluded to memory segmentation many times in our previous discussions. We shall now look at the topic in detail: how it works, why it is used, and the advantages it provides.

Twenty address bits are required in order to address one megabyte of memory. Recall that the System Address Bus consists of twenty signal lines and so can carry any address from zero to one megabyte minus one (00000H through FFFFFH). The 8086/8088 processor, however, does not have any twenty-bit registers; to achieve a twenty-bit address, it must use a combination of two registers, a segment register and a sixteen-bit offset.

Whenever putting an address onto the bus, the Bus Interface Unit effectively adds the offset to the value in a Segment register, shifted four bits to the left, and then puts the result directly onto the Address Bus:

$$
\begin{array}{ll}
\text{xxxxxxxxxxxxxxxx} & \text{16-bit offset} \\
+\ \underline{\text{xxxxxxxxxxxxxxxx}} & \text{16-bit segment} \\
\text{xxxxxxxxxxxxxxxxxxxx} & \text{20-bit address to bus}
\end{array}
$$

Since the segment is shifted left four onto the address bus, the resulting absolute address is sixteen times the value actually stored in the segment register. Looked at the other way, the value stored in the segment register must be one sixteenth the absolute address at which the segment begins. For example, a value of zero in a segment register causes that segment to begin at absolute address zero; a value of one in a segment register causes the segment to begin at absolute address 10H or 16; a value of two results in a segment beginning at absolute address 20H or 32; and so on. A segment must always begin at an address that is a multiple of sixteen, called a **paragraph boundary**.

Given a fixed value for a segment register, offsets can vary from zero to FFFFH, allowing the addressing of up to sixty-four kilobytes of memory within that segment. Note that 64K is the *maximum* segment size; offsets may be restricted to less than FFFFH within a particular program. Consequently, a segment may be, and often is, less than 64K.

Finally, a segment register with a value of 0000H together with an offset of 0000H result in an absolute address of 00000H, while a segment of F000H and an offset of FFFFH result in an absolute address of FFFFFH. Through segmentation, the processor can generate absolute addresses from 00000H through FFFFFH for one megabyte of total memory-addressing capability.

SEGMENT OVERRIDE PREFIX

As discussed earlier, the processor normally uses the value in DS as the segment for all Memory addressing unless BP is used as the Base register, in which case the processor uses SS for the segment. A **segment override prefix** allows the programmer to specify the use of some other Segment register. In assembly language, the override is specified by preceding the Memory mode operand with the name of the desired Segment register to be used, followed by a colon. Some examples of the use of segment overrides follow:

```
ADD      AL, ES:[BX + 5]          Absolute address is
                                   (ES * 16) + BX + 5.

INC      BYTE PTR DS:[BP + 3]     Absolute address is
                                   (DS * 16) + BP + 3

MOV      BYTE PTR CS:[100], 43    Absolute address is
                                   (CS * 16) + 100H
```

Note that the last instruction addresses memory within the code segment and so involves a program's rewriting of itself, a permitted but *very* dangerous practice. It should also be pointed out that the assembly-language syntax is a bit deceptive in that it makes it appear that the override comes in the middle of the instruction as a prefix to the operand. In reality, a segment override is assembled as a one-byte prefix to the instruction; it precedes the opcode and causes the processor to use the specified Segment register for the Memory operand on the single next instruction. Thus, the above three instructions are really assembled as follows:

```
ES:                               Segment override.
ADD      AL, [BX + 5]             Absolute address is
                                   (ES * 16) + BX + 5.

DS:                               Segment override.
INC      BYTE PTR [BP + 3]        Absolute address is
                                   (DS * 16) + BP + 3.

CS:                               Segment override.
MOV      BYTE PTR [100], 43       Absolute address is
                                   (CS * 16) + 100H.
```

The override prefix applies only to the Memory-mode operand in the ***next single instruction.*** There can be no confusion as to which operand the override is to apply, since no instruction can have more than one Memory-mode operand.

STACK OPERATIONS

As mentioned in our earlier discussion of the register set, the 8086/8088 processor allows for the setting aside of an area of memory that is addressed by the Stack Segment register (SS) and the Stack Pointer register (SP). Recall also that any use of the Base Pointer register (BP) for Memory-mode addressing, by default, addresses the stack segment; SS is used for the segment half of the address. This area of memory is called the **stack** and is used primarily for temporary data storage.

The term *stack* effectively describes the manner in which the stack operates. You can think of it as a stack of papers. Whenever you want to temporarily remember something, you simply write it on a piece of paper and put it on top of the stack. In order to retrieve some previously remembered data, you take the top paper from the stack. It is critical that you understand that such a stack operates as **Last-In-First-Out**, or LIFO; the last item stored is the first item retrieved, and the first item stored will be the last item retrieved. Thus, data must always be retrieved from the stack in the *opposite order* of its storage.

When a program is loaded for execution, DOS sets SS to point to the beginning (lowest address) of the stack segment and sets SP to the number of bytes that were set aside for the stack. As an example, suppose the stack is to use 100H bytes, beginning at absolute address 58A10H. Before giving control to the program, DOS stores the value 58A1H (absolute address divided by sixteen) into SS and stores 0100H into SP. Figure 4-4 illustrates stack memory upon execution of the program, when the stack has not yet been used. Notice that, for clarity, we have shown lower memory addresses toward the top of the page with higher memory address to the bottom.

Figure 4-4   **"Empty" Stack**

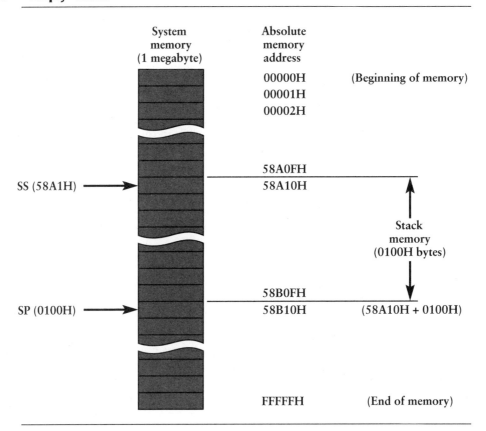

In order to push the value 1234H onto the stack, the processor first subtracts two from SP (0100H − 0002H = 00FEH) and then moves the word of data to the stack using SS (58A1H) for the segment and SP (00FEH) as the offset (absolute address = 58A10H + 00FEH = 58B0EH). The low byte, 34H, is stored at SS: [SP] (absolute address = 58B0EH) and the high byte, 12H, is stored at SS: [SP + 1] (absolute address = 58B0FH). Whenever any word of data is stored in memory, the low byte is always stored in the lower memory address.

Note that the programmer merely specifies what data is to be pushed; he or she does not specify where it is to be stored on the stack. The processor takes care of that automatically by always subtracting two from SP and then storing the data using SS: [SP]. To push a second word of data, 5678H for example, the processor again subtracts two from SP (00FEH − 0002H = 00FCH), and moves the word of data to SS: [SP] (absolute address = 58A10H + 00FCH = 58B0CH). Figure 4-5 illustrates the stack after the two pushes.

Figure 4-5   Stack after Two Pushes

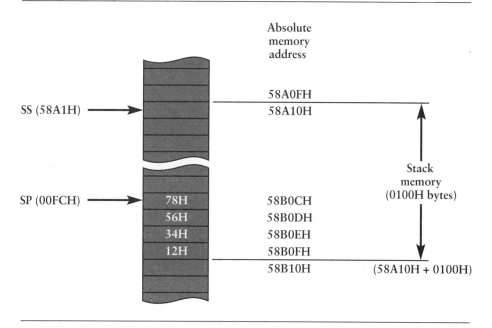

Notice that SS: [SP] now points to the word of data that was last pushed, 5678H. To pop the last word of data from the stack, the programmer specifies the destination operand into which it should be stored. The processor automatically moves from SS: [SP] to the specified destination operand, then adds two to SP (00FCH + 0002H = 00FDH). Thus the last value, 5678H, is popped from

Figure 4-6   Stack after Two Pushes, One Pop

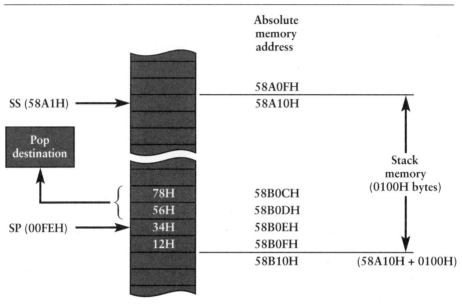

the stack, and SP is adjusted to point to the previously pushed value, 1234H. Figure 4-6 shows the stack after the last word of data has been popped.

Note that the value 5678H is still in stack memory; however, it is above the top of the stack, as determined by SP, and so cannot be retrieved by any future pop. Any future pushes will overwrite it; thus, it is effectively removed from the stack. The value 1234H is now at the top of the stack and so is next to be retrieved by a pop.

The processor instruction set includes instructions to explicitly push data onto the top of the stack (PUSH and PUSHF) and to pop data from the top of the stack (POP and POPF). Additionally, the processor automatically pushes data onto the stack or pops data from the stack during the execution of Branch-and-Return instructions (CALL, INT, RET, and IRET) or when responding to an external interrupt from a peripheral hardware device.

There are two very important points to keep in mind regarding stack operations. The first is that all stack operations operate on words; all stack operations push or pop data a word at a time. The second point is that the stack is, in essence, shared by the processor and the programmer. When executing a call or an interrupt, the processor automatically pushes the return address to the top of the stack. If that return address is no longer at the top of the stack when a subsequent return or interrupt return executes, the program will not return properly. If the programmer has pushed and failed to pop some value, then that value will be at the top of the stack when the return executes and so will be used as the "return" address, with disastrous results.

DESCENDANTS OF THE 8086 PROCESSOR

Like the 8086, the **80186** is a true sixteen-bit processor, utilizing a sixteen-bit data bus. Also like the 8086, it uses a twenty-bit address bus, giving it a maximum of one megabyte of addressable memory. In fact, it differs from the 8086 only in that its instruction set has been extended. We will briefly discuss some of its added instructions in the next chapter.

The **80286** is also a sixteen-bit processor that uses a sixteen-bit data bus. However, it uses a twenty-four-bit address bus, giving it a memory addressing capability of sixteen megabytes. It operates in two modes, Real and Protected. In Real mode the 80286 is functionally identical to the 80186. Absolute memory addresses are calculated as a sixteen-bit offset plus sixteen times a sixteen-bit segment; the result is a twenty-bit absolute address. Consequently, in Real mode the 80286 is limited to one megabyte of memory.

Only in Protected mode can the 80286 generate twenty-four-bit absolute memory addresses, and so address sixteen megabytes of memory. Recall from the last chapter that in Protected mode the 80286 uses a segment descriptor table set up by OS/2; among other things, each descriptor contains a twenty-four-bit Segment Base and a sixteen-bit Segment Limit.

Upon every memory access, the processor compares the twenty-bit address, resulting from the segment and offset, with the task's Segment Limit. If it is greater than the Segment Limit, the processor executes a special interrupt, returning control to the operating system for termination of the task. If the twenty-bit address is within the Segment Limit, then it is added to the twenty-four-bit Segment Base, resulting in a twenty-four-bit absolute address to the address bus.

The **80386** is a thirty-two-bit processor, with thirty-two-bit registers and requiring a thirty-two-bit data bus. It is capable of processing double words of data. It also uses a thirty-two-bit address bus, giving it a memory addressing capability of up to four gigabytes (one gigabyte equals 2 to the thirtieth power or 1024 to the third power). Like the 80286, it operates in both Real and Protected modes; in Real mode, it too is functionally equivalent to the 80186. However, in Protected mode, the 80386 provides three basic environments, Native, Segmented, and Virtual 86.

In Native environment, the 80386 supports protected multitasking, up to four gigabytes of physical memory, and up to sixty-four gigabytes of virtual memory. No currently available operating system takes advantage of Native mode. Segmented environment emulates the 80286 with up to sixteen megabytes of memory addressing. Virtual 86 allows multiple applications to run in separate one-megabyte memory partitions; in essence, it allows the 80386 to function as many 8086s.

The **80386SX** is a hybrid thirty-two-bit/sixteen-bit processor. Internally it is a thirty-two-bit processor like the 80386. However, it uses a sixteen-bit data bus. Whenever the Execution Unit requests a thirty-two-bit memory access, the Bus Interface Unit performs two sixteen-bit accesses much as the 8088 BIU performs two eight-bit memory accesses for each sixteen-bit memory request. The 80386SX executes the entire 80386 instruction set and supports the same modes and environments but accesses memory via a sixteen-bit data bus permitting the use of less-expensive sixteen-bit peripheral devices.

The **80486** has a built-in math coprocessor as well as memory caching. For each member of the 8086/8088 family up through the 80386SX, Intel has developed a math coprocessor (80x87) for the hardware processing of floating-point (real) and extended-precision (large integer) numbers. The general-purpose processor (8086, etc.) communicates with the math coprocessor (8087, etc.) via the system bus. The 80486, with the coprocessor built-in, can process floating-point and extended-precision numbers much more quickly.

As of this writing Intel is reportedly in the process of developing the **80586**, a sixty-four-bit processor. It will contain sixty-four-bit (eight-byte) registers and will use a sixty-four-bit data bus for memory access. Since standard IEEE format uses eight bytes for floating-point-number storage, the 80586 should be able to process real-numeric data very quickly; it will need only a single memory access to store or retrieve a floating-point value. It should be noted that there is currently very little off-the-shelf software utilizing the thirty-two-bit capability of the 80386; it may be a very long time before software developers catch up with the 80586.

SUMMARY

The IBM PC, XT, and compatibles use an Intel 8088 microprocessor; some compatibles use an 8086 microprocessor. The 8086 is a true sixteen-bit processor, while the 8088 is a hybrid. Internally, the 8088 can process an entire word of data at a time; however, it uses an eight-bit Data Bus to access external data a byte at a time. Since the 8086 and 8088 both share the same instruction set, they are often referred to as the 8086/8088 processor.

The four functional units of the 8086/8088 are the Execution Unit, the Arithmetic and Logic Unit, the Bus Interface Unit, and the register set or internal storage. The EU decodes binary instructions and controls the other units to cause the correct operation to be performed. All arithmetic or logic operations are performed for the EU by the ALU, which also automatically sets or clears Result flags to reflect the results of each operation. The BIU, upon command by the EU, handles all communications with external devices over the system bus. The BIU also automatically maintains a four-byte instruction queue so that the EU does not have to wait for the retrieval of instructions from memory.

The register set is made up of fourteen sixteen-bit registers: the Flags register, four Segment registers (CS, DS, SS, and ES), three Pointer registers (IP, SP, and BP), two Index registers (SI and DI), and four General-Purpose registers (AX, BX, CX, and DX), which are also addressable as eight eight-bit registers (AL, AH, BL, BH, CL, CH, DL, and DH). Although the Flags register is a sixteen-bit register, only nine of its bits are available to the program, each representing a true/false value. There are three Processor-Control flags (DF, IF, and TF) and six Result flags (ZF, CF, AF, SF, OF, and PF).

The 8086/8088 instruction syntax consists of an opcode, sometimes followed by one or two operands. Operands are of two types. A destination operand is any operand whose value is modified by the instruction; a source operand is one whose value is not modified by the instruction. Most instructions have two forms in the resulting machine language, byte or word, as determined by the type of the operand(s) in the assembly-language instruction. If an instruction has two operands, they must both be the same type. Whenever the type cannot be otherwise determined (no Register mode operand) the PTR operator is used to explicitly state the type of an operand.

There are three fundamental data addressing modes for operands: Immediate mode, Register mode, and Memory mode. An instruction can never have two Memory-mode operands. The two fundamental types of Memory-mode addressing are Direct Memory mode and Indirect Memory mode. Direct memory mode specifies the memory offset as an immediate value enclosed in brackets; Indirect Memory mode specifies the offset with a combination of a Base register and/or an Index register and, optionally, a displacement, inside brackets. The four types of Indirect Memory addressing are Base-or-Index, Base-or-Index-Plus-Displacement, Base-Plus-Index, and Base-Plus-Index-Plus-Displacement.

All memory addressing is composed of two parts, a sixteen-bit segment and a sixteen-bit offset. The segment value is always contained in one of the four segment registers, usually DS, while the offset is provided by an immediate value (Direct Memory addressing) and/or by the contents of a Base and/or an Index register (Indirect Memory addressing). In determining the absolute address to put onto the twenty-bit Address Bus, the BIU adds the offset to sixteen times the segment, resulting in a twenty-bit absolute address.

SS and SP are used as the segment and offset of an area of memory to be used as a stack, for temporary data storage. All stack operations involve the transfer of a word of data to or from the top of the stack, as indicated by SP. The EU automatically subtracts two from SP before pushing data onto the stack and automatically adds two after popping data from the top of the stack. Consequently, the stack operation is always Last-In-First-Out; the last item pushed will be the first to be popped. Data must always be popped from the stack in the opposite order of that in which it was pushed.

VOCABULARY

V4-1 In your own words, define each of the following terms:

a) Microprocessor

b) Integrated Circuit

c) Eight-bit Processor

d) Sixteen-bit Processor

e) Execution Unit

f) ALU

g) BIU

h) Instruction Queue

i) System Bus

j) Data Bus

k) Address Bus

l) Control Bus

m) I/O Port

n) Opcode

o) Operand

p) Source Operand

q) Destination Operand

r) PTR Operator

s) Paragraph Boundary

t) Segment Override Prefix

u) Stack

v) LIFO

REVIEW QUESTIONS

Q4-1 Briefly explain the difference between the 8086 and 8088 microprocessors. Which of the four functional units accounts for the difference?

Q4-2 List the four groups of registers (besides the Flags register) in the 8086/8088 processor's register set. Briefly explain the use of each register group.

Q4-3 For each register group that you listed above, list and explain the individual registers belonging to the group; give the full name and two-letter name for each register, and briefly explain its use.

Q4-4 How many bits is the Flags register? How many are accessible to the program?

Q4-5 What are the two types of flags contained in the Flags register? Which type is controlled only by explicit program instructions? Which type is controlled automatically by the ALU?

Q4-6 List the flags in each of the two groups and briefly explain its significance.

Q4-7 How many signal lines make up the Address Bus on the system board? How many make up the Data Bus (both 8088 and 8086)?

Q4-8 Describe the general syntax for all 8086/8088 instructions.

Q4-9 If an instruction has both a destination and a source operand, on which side of the comma does the source operand belong?

Q4-10 If an instruction has two operands, what restriction applies to the type of the two operands?

Q4-11 When is the PTR operator necessary in a statement?

Q4-12 What are the three fundamental data addressing modes of the 8086/8088? Which addressing mode cannot be used for a destination operand? Which addressing mode cannot be used for both operands in a two-operand instruction?

Q4-13 What are the two ways of addressing memory? What character(s) is/are used to indicate that an operand refers to memory?

Q4-14 What are the four types of Indirect Memory addressing? List the four registers that may be used to address memory. Which is the only General-Purpose register that may be used to address memory?

Q4-15 Describe the rule the processor uses to determine the segment half (which Segment register to use) of a memory address.

Q4-16 In assembly language, does a segment override prefix belong before the opcode or after the opcode and before an operand? What about the resulting machine-language instruction?

Q4-17 What is the restriction on the type of operands for all stack operations?

Q4-18 Will AX and BX be changed by the following four instructions? Explain why.

```
PUSH    AX
PUSH    BX
POP     AX
POP     BX
```

Q4-19 Which register is modified by the following single instruction?

```
PUSH    CX
```

Q4-20 For each of the following, indicate if the instruction is valid or invalid. If invalid, briefly explain why.

a)	MOV	AX, AL	l)	PUSH	[BP]
b)	ADD	3AB4, DX	m)	POP	DL
c)	ADD	DX, 3AB4	n)	ADD	DX, WORD PTR CH
d)	ADD	[3AB4], DX	o)	MOV	[BX + DI + 5], CL
e)	DEC	BYTE PTR SI	p)	MOV	CX, [BX + BP]
f)	DEC	BYTE PTR [SI]	q)	MOV	BL, [BX]
g)	MOV	AL, AL	r)	MOV	CL, [CX]
h)	INC	[BX]	s)	ADD	[1A], 1A
i)	INC	BYTE PTR [BX]	t)	INC	BYTE PTR [SI + DI]
j)	INC	WORD PTR [BX]	u)	DEC	WORD PTR [BP + SI]
k)	SUB	WORD PTR [DI], [14B]	v)	DEC	BYTE PTR [BP + SI]

PROGRAMMING ASSIGNMENTS

PA4-1 Manually trace through each of the following programs and predict the values that will be stored in the registers upon completion. List all registers (except IP and SP) that are modified, along with their resulting contents; also list the contents of any modified memory locations. Remember that all Immediate values are in hexadecimal and that all arithmetic should be performed in hexadecimal; your results should also be shown in hexadecimal.

```
a) MOV       SI, 3A4
   NOP
   ADD       SI, 10
   NOP
   INT       20

b) MOV       AX, 3F42
   MOV       BX, 112E
   ADD       AX, BX
   SUB       BX, AX
   INT       20

c) MOV       CX, 0
   MOV       DX, FFFF
   INC       DX
   SUB       CX, DX
   INT       20

d) MOV       SI, 1
   MOV       DI, SI
   INC       DI
   PUSH      SI
   PUSH      DI
   POP       SI
   POP       DI
   INT       20

e) MOV       AL, 41
   MOV       AH, 42
   MOV       [200], AX
   PUSH      AX
   PUSH      [200]
   MOV       BYTE PTR [200], 50
   MOV       AX,0
   POP       [200]
   POP       AX
   INT       20

f) MOV       DX, 807F
   PUSH      DX
   ADD       DH, DL
   MOV       [200], DH
   POP       DX
   SUB       DH, DL
   MOV       [201], DH
   INT       20

g) MOV       BX, 200
   MOV       SI, 20
   NOP
   MOV       BYTE PTR [BX + SI + 2], 11
   INC       SI
   MOV       BYTE PTR [BX + SI + 2], 22
   INT       20
```

PA4-2   Use DEBUG to check your predicted results in PA4-1 above. Using the Assemble command, key in each program. Then, execute the program using the Go command with a break point at the offset of the INT 20 instruction. Compare the resulting register values, as displayed by DEBUG, with the values that you predicted in PA4-1; also, use the Dump command to check any modified memory locations. If the results are not what you predicted, use the Trace command to step through the program again and determine where you went wrong in your trace.

PA4-3   Using DEBUG, write a program that finds the sum (+) and difference (−) of decimal 100 and decimal 75. Remember that DEBUG only accepts hexadecimal; you will have to do the conversions. At the end of the program, the sum should be in register CX, and the difference should be in register DX. Remember to terminate the program (return to DOS or DEBUG) with an interrupt type 20H. Save the program onto your diskette as PA4-3.COM. Don't forget to set BX and CX to the correct values before saving (See step q of PA3-2 in the last chapter). Use <Ctrl>+<PrtSc> together with the Unassemble and Go commands to obtain a hard copy of your program listing and of the results, when run.

PA4-4   Using DEBUG, write a program that calculates the sum and difference of decimal 120 and decimal 42 (both byte values) and stores the results in memory, the sum at offset 200H, the difference at offset 201H. The program should also store the sum plus one into offset 202H and the difference minus one into offset 203H. At the beginning of the program, push all registers to be used; pop the registers at the end of the program, so that upon completion all registers are restored to their original values. Terminate the program with an interrupt type 20H. Save the program as PA4-4.COM. Make sure BX and CX contain the correct values before saving (See step q of PA3-2 in the last chapter). Use <Ctrl>+<PrtSc> together with the Unassemble, Go, and Dump commands to obtain a hard copy of your program listing and of the results, when run.

5

8086/8088 Instruction Set

INTRODUCTION

In this chapter, we will discuss the core of the 8086/8088 instruction set, the most commonly used instructions. A number of more advanced and less commonly needed instructions will be saved for discussion later in the text as required. We have divided the instruction set into six fundamental groups: **Data-Transfer** instructions, **Arithmetic** instructions, **Logical** instructions, **Shift-and-Rotate** instructions, **Transfer-of-Control** instructions, and special **Processor-Control** instructions.

DATA-TRANSFER INSTRUCTIONS

Data-Transfer instructions are used to move or copy data to and/or from registers and/or memory. They are all performed by the Execution Unit, without the aid of the Arithmetic and Logic Unit. Whenever any source or destination operand involves memory access, the Bus Interface Unit retrieves or stores the data upon command by the Execution Unit. The fundamental Data-Transfer instructions are MOV, XCHG, PUSH, PUSHF, POP, and POPF. In the following paragraphs, we will discuss each instruction, its operands, and the effect of the instruction.

MOV   *dest, source*

> MOV (move) is probably the most commonly used instruction in assembly language. It stores data from *source* to *dest*. *Source* is **never** modified and may be any data addressing mode (Immediate, Register, or Memory). The *source* value is copied into *dest*, which must be either Register or Memory mode (**not** Immediate). The two operands cannot both be memory. Both operands must be the same type, word or byte.
>
> Unlike most other instructions (the other exceptions are PUSH and POP, below) MOV allows a Segment register as one of its two operands. However, if one operand is a Segment register, the other operand may not be Immediate mode or another Segment register; it must be either Memory mode or Register mode (other than a Segment register).

XCHG   *dest1, dest2*

> XCHG (exchange) swaps the values stored in the two operands. This is a simple but powerful capability; compare it with many high-level languages in which *three* statements are required to swap the values in two storage locations. Note that since both operands are destination operands (they are both modified), Immediate mode is not allowed. Since the two operands cannot both be Memory mode, at least one must always be Register mode; the other can be either Register or Memory mode. Both operands must be the same type, byte or word.

PUSH   *source*

> PUSH moves the value of *source* to the top of the stack. First the processor subtracts two from SP. Then the source-operand value is copied to the word of memory at SS:[SP]. PUSH places two limitations on the operand, not normally required of source operands. First, it must always be a word; byte values cannot be pushed. Second, unlike most source operands it cannot be Immediate mode; it must be either Register or Memory mode.
>
> Contrary to the general rule, PUSH (like MOV and POP) permits a Segment register as its source operand. Also note that in addition to the source operand PUSH also modifies the Stack Pointer and memory; it has two implicit (not stated) destination operands: SP and the word of memory at SS:[SP].

POP   *dest*

> POP takes the word value from the current top of the stack and stores it into *dest*. First the value in the word of memory at SS:[SP] is copied into *dest*. Then two is added to SP. As with PUSH, POP requires that the operand be a word. Otherwise, the operand has the normal restriction for a destination operand: it cannot be Immediate mode. SP is an implicit destination operand, and the word of memory at SS:[SP] is the implicit source operand. Besides MOV and PUSH, POP is the only instruction to allow a Segment register as its operand.

PUSHF

PUSHF (push flags) does not allow explicit operands. Its implicit source operand is the Flags register; it pushes the current contents of the sixteen-bit Flags register to the top of the stack. It is normally used to temporarily store the status of the flags for later retrieval. As with PUSH, PUSHF also has SP and the word of memory at SS:[SP] as implicit destination operands.

POPF

Like PUSHF, POPF (pop flags) allows no explicit operands. It pops the word value currently at the top of the stack into the Flags register. The Flags register and SP are implicit destination operands; the word of memory at SS:[SP] is the implicit source operand.

MOST COMMONLY USED Data-Transfer Instructions

```
MOV           dest, source
     Copy data from source to dest.

PUSH          source
     Push word value in source onto top of stack.

POP           dest
     Pop word value from top of stack into dest.
```

ARITHMETIC INSTRUCTIONS

All Arithmetic instructions involve the Arithmetic and Logic Unit as well as the Execution Unit. If any operand is Memory mode then the Bus Interface Unit performs the memory access for the EU. All Arithmetic instructions have the Flags register as an implicit destination operand; as it performs the required arithmetic operation, the ALU also sets or clears bits within the Flags register to reflect characteristics of the value resulting from the operation.

The most commonly used Arithmetic instructions are **ADD, INC, ADC, SUB, CMP, DEC, SBB,** and **NEG.** Four more instructions for multiplication and division will be discussed later in the text when needed. All Arithmetic instructions allow either byte or word operands, and all operands must follow the normal rules for data addressing modes.

ADD   *dest, source*

ADD causes the Execution Unit to pass the *dest* and *source* values to the ALU with a command to add. The ALU performs a binary addition and returns the result to the EU, which stores it into *dest*, overwriting the value previously stored there. The effect is to increase the value stored in *dest* by the *source* value. ADD also modifies all the Result flags (Carry, Parity, Auxiliary Carry, Zero, Sign, and Overflow) to reflect the results of the addition.

INC   *dest*

INC (increment) adds one to *dest*. It has the same effect on the destination operand as the instruction

```
ADD dest, 1
```

Although the effect on the destination operand is the same as adding one with the ADD instruction, there are two major differences: 1) INC is a shorter and faster machine-language instruction, and 2) INC does not modify the Carry flag.

Since one is an Immediate-mode source operand, it must be stored as part of the ADD *dest*, 1 instruction. This increases the size of the machine-language ADD instruction and also increases the time for its execution. INC has no source operand, resulting in a shorter and faster machine-language instruction.

Unlike ADD, INC does not modify the Carry flag. ADDing one to a byte value of FFH results in 00H with the Carry flag set; incrementing a byte value of FFH also results in 00H but does not alter the Carry flag from its previous value.

ADC   *dest, source*

ADC (add with carry) adds the *source* value to *dest* and increments the result if the Carry flag was set prior to its execution. It is identical to the ADD instruction except that it includes any carry from a previous addition.

ADC is used most often when adding values that are too big to be stored in a word. For example, a program might need to store an unsigned value greater than 65535. Such a large value could be stored in the double-word DX:AX, where the four low-order hexadecimal digits are stored in AX, and the four high-order digits are stored in DX. Using two word registers in this manner provides eight hexadecimal digits for the storage of values up to FFFFFFFFH (4294967295). For example, the hexadecimal value 1BC542H would be stored as 001BH in DX and C542H in AX.

A similar large value might be stored in the double-word BX:CX. Suppose then that it is necessary to add the double-word value in BX:CX to the double-word value in DX:AX and to store the result into DX:AX. We might show the desired operation as follows:

```
    DX:AX
+   BX:CX
    DX:AX
```

To perform the above addition, we first must add CX to AX; as we do so, the result may exceed 65535 and generate a carry. Next, we must add BX plus any carry from the previous addition to DX. The desired double-word addition can be performed by the following two instructions:

```
ADD         AX, CX
ADC         DX, BX
```

SUB   *dest, source*

SUB (subtract) subtracts the *source* value from *dest*. In addition to modifying the destination operand, it also modifies all Result flags. The subtraction is performed as twos-complement addition. Recall that performing subtraction as twos-complement addition normally results in a carry out of the high bit; the lack of a carry indicates that the result is less than zero.

For example, 2 minus 1 done as twos-complement addition results in a carry; 1 minus 2 as twos-complement addition does not generate a carry. In order to allow the Carry flag to be used to indicate borrowing, the ALU inverts the carry into the Carry flag; a carry out of the high bit clears the Carry flag while no carry out sets the Carry flag. Consequently, 2 minus 1 clears the Carry flag to indicate no borrow, while 1 minus 2 sets the Carry flag to indicate that a borrow has taken place.

CMP   *dest, source*

CMP (compare) performs a subtraction (discarding the result) in order to allow the comparison of two values without modifying either operand. *Dest* is not modified. The left-hand operand is shown as *dest* only because it is coded that way in the resulting machine-language instruction and consequently must follow the data-addressing rules for destination operands; it may not be Immediate mode. To understand the value of an instruction that performs subtraction but discards the result, consider the following:

```
CMP         AL, 41
```

The ALU subtracts 41H from the value currently in AL and sets or clears Result flags based on the result of the subtraction. The EU discards the result returned by the ALU, but that discarded result has already determined the status of the flags. The program can then use the flags to determine if the value in AL is less than 41H (Carry flag set), equal to 41H (Zero flag set), or greater than 41H (Carry flag and Zero flag both clear). Note that the Carry flag follows the same rule as in the SUB instruction. It is set if and only if the subtraction results in a borrow (the inverse of the carry out of the high bit during the twos-complement addition).

DEC   *dest*

DEC (decrement) is the opposite of INC. It subtracts one from *dest*. Like INC, it does not alter the Carry flag, but does control all other Result flags.

SBB   *dest, source*

SBB (subtract with borrow) is to subtraction as ADC is to addition. It subtracts the *source* value from *dest* and subtracts one more if the Carry flag was set when the instruction began execution. Note that whenever performing subtraction (or CMP) the Carry flag is set if and only if the subtraction results in a borrow (the source value is greater than the destination value). SBB is most commonly used to perform double-word subtraction. Consider the following desired subtraction:

```
      DX:AX
   −  BX:CX
      DX:AX
```

Such a double-word subtraction would be performed in assembly language as follows:

```
SUB        AX, CX
SBB        DX, BX
```

NEG   *dest*

NEG (negate) performs a twos-complement on *dest*. Since the twos-complement of a number is its opposite, NEG is used to convert a value to its opposite, to change the sign of the value.

MOST COMMONLY USED Arithmetic Instructions

```
ADD          dest, source
```
Add *source* value to *dest*.

```
INC          dest
```
Add 1 to *dest*.

```
SUB          dest, source
```
Subtract *source* value from *dest*.

DEC   *dest*

    Subtract 1 from *dest*.

CMP   *dest, source*

    Subtract *source* value from *dest* value, setting Result flags, discarding difference.

LOGICAL INSTRUCTIONS

Logical instructions are those which treat data not as binary numerals but as individual bits representing True or False. To a logical instruction a byte represents eight individual zeros (False) or ones (True). The logical operations are performed by the ALU, which returns the result to the Execution Unit for storage in the destination operand. The Logical instructions provided by the 8086/8088 are **AND, TEST, OR, XOR,** and **NOT.**

All Logical instructions accept either byte or word operands. All operands must follow the normal data-addressing-mode rules for source and destination operands. Logical instructions affect all the Result flags (Carry, Parity, Auxiliary Carry, Zero, Sign, and Overflow). However, since bits are treated individually there can never be a carry from one bit to the next. Consequently, the Carry flag, Auxiliary-Carry flag, and Overflow flag are always cleared by any Logical instruction. The only flags with any real meaning after a Logical instruction are Parity, Zero, and Sign.

AND   *dest, source*

AND performs a bit-by-bit logical AND of the *source* value with *dest*. Each bit in the destination result is one if and only if the corresponding bits in the destination and source input values are both one. If either bit is zero, then the corresponding bit in the result is zero. Following is an example of a logical AND:

```
      01101101B    (from dest)
AND   10111100B    (from source)
      00101100B    (result to dest)
```

A common use of AND is for **masking bits out** of a value, for forcing specific bits to zero while retaining the original value of other bits. Suppose we are using bit #5 in DH to indicate some True/False condition, and we need to make the condition False (force bit #5 to zero). We could use the following instruction:

```
AND         DH, DF
```

Note that DFH equals 11011111B; bit #5 is zero while all other bits are one. The instruction results in the following operation by the ALU:

```
    xxxxxxxB    (original value in DH)
AND 11011111B   (mask = DFH)
    xx0xxxxxB   (new value of DH)
```

Bit #5 is forced to False (zero) while all other bits in DH remain unchanged. AND is also sometimes used to mask out bits in numeric values. Suppose we have some value stored in AL but are interested only in the low-order nibble; the high nibble is meaningless in our application. We can force the high-nibble bits to zero with the following instruction:

```
AND         AL, 0F
```

That instruction has the following effect on the value in AL:

```
    xxxxxxxB    (original value in AL)
AND 00001111B   (mask = 0FH)
    0000xxxxB   (new value for AL)
```

TEST   *dest, source*

TEST is to AND as CMP is to SUB; the ALU performs an AND, setting and clearing flags in the same manner as the AND instruction. The Execution Unit discards the result; *dest* is not altered. As with CMP, the left-most operand has been designated as *dest* because it must follow the data-addressing rules for destination operands; it cannot be Immediate mode.

As its name implies, TEST is often used to test individual bits in the destination operand (to see if a particular bit is zero or one) without changing the value of either operand. A common usage is in checking to see if a particular bit is True (one) or False (zero). Suppose again that we are using bit #5 in DH as a flag to indicate a True/False condition. This time, however, we do not want to modify its value; we simply want to test its current status. We would use the instruction:

```
TEST        DH, 20
```

That instruction results in the following operation:

```
    xxxxxxxB    (value in DH)
AND 00100000B   (mask = 20H)
    00x00000B   (result is discarded)
```

After the operation, the Zero flag indicates whether bit #5 is True or False. If bit #5 is True (one), then the result is 00100000B, which clears the Zero flag; if bit #5 is False (zero), then the Zero flag is set since the result is 00000000B. In either case the result is discarded; DH is not modified in any way.

OR   *dest, source*

OR performs a bit-by-bit logical OR of the *source* value with *dest*. A bit in the result is one if either of the two corresponding bits in the input values is one (even if both are one); a result bit is zero if and only if both corresponding input bits are zero. The following is an example of an OR operation:

```
   01101001B    (from dest)
OR 10101100B    (from source)
   11101101B    (result to dest)
```

OR is often used for **masking bits in** to a value, for forcing specific bits to one while retaining the original value of other bits. Suppose again that bit #5 in DH represents a True/False flag. Also suppose that our program needs to set the flag, to make it True. We would use the following instruction:

```
OR          DH, 20
```

The instruction would result in the following operation, which forces bit #5 to True while leaving the other bits unchanged:

```
   xxxxxxxxB    (original value in DH)
OR 00100000B    (mask = 20H)
   xx1xxxxxB    (result to DH)
```

XOR   *dest, source*

XOR (exclusive or) examines corresponding bits in the input values and produces one in the corresponding result bit if one or the other, but not both, of the input bits is one. Stated differently, each result bit is one if and only if the corresponding input bits are different. Following is an example of a word XOR operation:

```
    011010011110001B    (from dest)
XOR 101011001010011B    (from source)
    110001010100010B    (result to dest)
```

XOR is often used to invert or complement selected bits in the destination operand (use NOT, described below, to invert all bits). For example, in order to invert a True/False flag in bit #5 of DH we might use the following instruction:

```
XOR          DH, 20
```

Note that 20H = 00100000B. Bit #5 is one; all other bits are zero. Bit #5 in the result will be one if and only if bit #5 in DH was different than one (it was zero) before the operation; thus, bit #5 is inverted. All other bits result in one if and only if the corresponding bit in DH was different than zero (was one) before the instruction; thus, all other bits in DH remain unchanged.

NOT   *dest*

NOT performs a ones complement on *dest*; it inverts all bits. It does not allow a source operand. The following is an example of a NOT operation on a byte value:

      NOT 11001001B   (from *dest*)
          00110110B   (result to *dest*)

MOST COMMONLY USED Logical Instructions

AND   *dest, source*

Each bit in *dest* result is one if and only if the corresponding bits in the *dest* and *source* input values are both one.

OR   *dest, source*

Each bit in *dest* result is one if and only if either of the corresponding bits in the *dest* and *source* input values is one.

TEST   *dest, source*

Performs an AND but discards the result. Only modifies Result flags.

SHIFT-AND-ROTATE INSTRUCTIONS

Besides the Logical instructions, the 8086/8088 also provides another group of instructions that treat data as individual bits, rather than as numeric data. Since they deal with bits, the Shift-and-Rotate instructions are very often grouped with the Logical instructions. We prefer to treat them as a separate group, however, because they have so much in common with each other and yet differ in so many ways from the Logical instructions.

As implied by the name, all Shift-and-Rotate instructions move the bits within the destination operand to the left or to the right. Shift instructions insert a zero or one to fill the "hole" created on one side of the operand and discard the bit that "falls off" the other side. Rotate instructions bring the bit that "falls off" around (either directly or through the Carry flag) to fill the "hole" created at the other end. In all cases, the bit that "falls off" is always copied into the Carry flag.

The 8086/8088 Shift instructions are **SHL**, **SHR**, and **SAR**. The assembler and DEBUG also allow another mnemonic, **SAL**, which is treated as a synonym for SHL; it generates the same machine-language instruction. The Rotate instructions allowed by the 8086/8088 are **ROL**, **ROR**, **RCL**, and **RCR**.

All Shift-and-Rotate instructions require two operands, destination and source. The destination operand must follow the usual addressing-mode rules for destination operands; it must be either Register or Memory. Unlike other op-codes, the types of the two operands do not necessarily match. The destination may be either a byte or a word, while the source operand must be either the immediate value, one, or the byte Counter register, CL; *nothing* else is allowed for the source operand.

The source operand determines how many times to move the bits to the left or right in the destination operand. A source operand of one causes the destination to be shifted or rotated once to the left or right. Alternatively, CL may be specified as the source, in which case the number of times to shift or rotate the destination operand is determined by the value in CL. Note that, if used, CL is a source operand; its value is not altered.

Also note that, even if the source operand is the immediate value, one, no Immediate-mode value is stored within the instruction; the machine-code instruction is the same length whether the source operand is CL or one. A single bit within the instruction tells the ALU whether to use one or to use CL; a zero in that bit causes the ALU to shift or rotate the destination by one bit, while one causes it to use the value in CL as the number of bits to shift or rotate.

The following paragraphs provide a list, with explanations, of all Shift-and-Rotate-instructions. Figure 5-1 provides a graphic representation of the results of each instruction. The effects of the instructions on the Flags register will be discussed shortly.

SHR   *dest*, 1

     or

SHR   *dest*, CL

SHR (shift right) shifts the bits in *dest* to the right. The left-most bit becomes zero, and the right-most bit is shifted out into the Carry flag. When the source operand is CL, the Carry flag is determined by the last bit to be shifted out. SHR is a quick way to divide a value by two since it shifts each bit to the next lower binary place. For example, 00001100B (twelve) when shifted right one results in 00000110B (six).

SHL   *dest*, **1**

> or

SHL   *dest*, **CL**

> SHL (shift left) shifts all bits to the left within *dest*. A zero is shifted into the right-most bit, and the left-most bit is shifted out into the Carry flag. If the source operand is CL, the Carry flag is determined by the last shift. Since it shifts each bit to the next higher binary place value, SHL is a quick way to multiply by two or by a power of two.

SAR   *dest*, **1**

> or

SAR   *dest*, **CL**

> SAR (shift arithmetic right) is provided for the shifting of signed integers in which the left-most bit represents the sign rather than a binary digit. Since SHR always shifts a zero into the high bit, it may produce improper results for signed integers. For example, 11110100B (-12), shifted right one by SHR, results in 01111010B (+122).
>
> In order to produce correct signed results, SAR copies the left-most bit back into itself, preserving the sign; otherwise, it is identical to SHR. 11110100B (-12) when shifted right one by SAR, results in 11111010B (-6), the expected result of division by two.

SAL   *dest*, **1**

> or

SAL   *dest*, **CL**

> SAL (shift arithmetic left) is merely a synonym for SHL, provided by the assembler and DEBUG. SHL and SAL both result in the same machine-language instruction.

Figure 5-1   **Shift-and-Rotate Instructions**

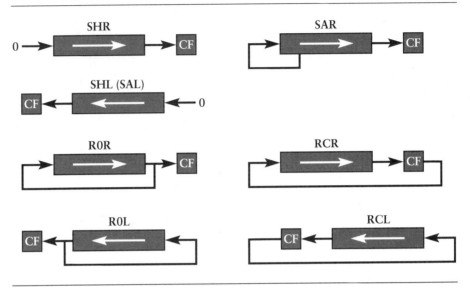

ROR   *dest*, 1

        or

ROR   *dest*, CL

Like SHR, ROR (rotate right) moves all bits to the right. However, instead of inserting zero into the high bit, the ALU rotates the low bit around and into the high bit as well as into the Carry flag. Rotating right by four (move four into CL; specify CL as source) is an easy way to exchange the high and low nibbles of a byte operand.

ROL   *dest*, 1

        or

ROL   *dest*, CL

ROL (rotate left) moves all bits to the left within *dest*; the high bit is copied into both the low bit and the Carry flag. Rotating left by four produces the same results as rotating right by four and may also be used to exchange the high and low nibbles of a byte operand.

RCR   *dest*, 1

>   or

RCR   *dest*, CL

RCR (rotate right through carry) is similar to ROR except that the Carry flag rather than the low bit is rotated into the high bit of *dest*; the high bit is determined by the previous status of the Carry flag. RCR is provided to allow for the shifting to the right of double-word values. For example, in order to shift the value in DX:AX right by one (divide by two) we would use the following two instructions:

```
SHR      DX, 1 ;(SAR if signed)
RCR      AX, 1
```

Note that as it shifts DX to the right the first instruction shifts the low bit into the Carry flag. The second instruction then rotates that bit from the Carry flag into the high bit of AX as it rotates AX to the right. The result is that the entire double-word value is shifted to the right (divided by two).

RCL   *dest*, 1

>   or

RCL   *dest*, CL

RCL (rotate left through carry) is similar to RCR. It moves all bits to the left, moves the previous value of the Carry flag into the low bit, and moves the high bit into the Carry flag. It is provided to allow for shifting double-word values to the left. The following instructions multiply the double-word value in DX:AX by two:

```
SHL      AX, 1
RCL      DX, 1
```

All Shift-and-Rotate instructions are performed by the ALU, which maintains the Result flags to indicate characteristics of the results of the operation. When CL is specified as the source operand, the status of all flags results from the bit movement during the last shift or rotate.

It is very important to correctly understand the effects on the flags of all instructions since virtually all program decisions are based on the status of Result flags. Unfortunately, the manner in which the Shift-and-Rotate instructions affect the flags is misstated in much documentation. After a good deal of experimentation, we have determined the following:

1) As discussed above, the Carry flag results from the last bit shifted or rotated out of the destination operand.

2) The Overflow flag is set or cleared to reflect any change in the high bit of

the destination operand. It is set if and only if the high bit changes as a result of a Shift or Rotate instruction.

3) The Rotate instructions affect only the Carry and Overflow flags; all
other Result flags (Sign, Zero, Parity, and Auxiliary Carry) are not altered by Rotate instructions. The rest of this discussion applies only to
Shift instructions.

4) The Sign flag is set or cleared to reflect the status of the high bit of the
destination operand after a Shift instruction. It is set if and only if the
high bit of the result is one.

5) The Zero flag is set or cleared to reflect the overall result of the destination
operand. It is set if and only if the result of the Shift instruction is zero.

6) The Parity flag is set or cleared to reflect the parity of the result of a Shift
instruction. It is set if and only if the result contains an even number of
ones in its binary digits.

7) The Auxiliary Carry flag is set by Shift instructions if and only if a one is
shifted to the left out of the low nibble of the destination operand (if and
only if the shift is to the left and the destination operand contains one in
bit #3 prior to execution of the instruction). In all other cases AF is
cleared by any Shift instruction.

8) Note that SHR and SAR always clear certain flags, regardless of the data
in the destination operand. The Auxiliary Carry flag is always cleared by
any shift to the right (SHR or SAR). Also, since SHR always fills the high
bit with zero, it also always clears the Sign flag. Finally, since SAR copies
the high bit back into itself, it always clears the Overflow flag.

Figure 5-2 summarizes the effect of the Shift-and-Rotate instructions on the
Result flags.

Figure 5-2   Effect on Flags of Shift-and-Rotate Instructions

	OF	SF	ZF	AF	PF	CF
SHR	x	0	x	0	x	x
SAR	0	x	x	0	x	x
SHL (SAL)	x	x	x	x	x	x
ROR	x					x
RCR	x					x
ROL	x					x
RCL	x					x

x = Altered (0 or 1, depending on the data).
0 = Always cleared.
　= Not altered, retains previous status.

TRANSFER-OF-CONTROL INSTRUCTIONS

Transfer-of-Control instructions cause the processor to execute instructions out of sequence, to continue execution at some point in memory other than the instruction immediately following the currently executing instruction. All transfer of control is accomplished by the Execution Unit's altering of the memory offset in the Instruction Pointer register; if it's a Far transfer of control (to another segment), then the segment address in the Code Segment register is also modified.

Recall that the Bus Interface Unit (BIU) uses CS and IP to point to memory from which to read instructions to constantly update the Instruction Queue, from which the Execution Unit (EU) draws instructions for execution. As it executes a Transfer-of-Control instruction the EU modifies IP (and CS if Far). The EU then must pause briefly while the BIU refreshes the Instruction Queue. Since IP has changed, the Queue does not contain the correct instructions and must be refreshed by the BIU before the EU can resume execution. This is the only time (immediately following a Transfer-of-Control instruction) that the Execution Unit has to wait for instructions to be fetched from memory.

The Transfer-of-Control instructions fall into four major groups: **Unconditional jumps, Conditional jumps, Branch-and-Return instructions,** and **Iteration instructions.**

Unconditional Jumps

Unconditional jumps always transfer control to another memory address. The general syntax for an Unconditional jump is as follows:

```
JMP          target
```

Target is a source operand that specifies the memory location from which to draw the next instruction. Since *target* is a source operand, it is never modified and may be any data addressing mode: Immediate, Register, or Memory. In an **Immediate-mode jump,** the target address is specified as an immediate value (or values). A **Register-mode jump** uses a sixteen-bit register to specify the target address; the value stored in the register specifies the offset of the next instruction to be executed. A **Memory-mode jump** uses any of the memory-addressing modes discussed earlier to specify a memory location from which to read the new value for IP (and for CS if Far).

Although it is somewhat transparent to the programmer, the 8086/8088 has three types of Immediate-mode jumps: **Short, Near,** and **Far.** Both Short and Near jumps modify only the Instruction Pointer, so control remains within the current code segment. A Far jump modifies **CS** as well as IP.

In machine language, a Short Immediate-mode jump is two bytes long and contains a **byte displacement** to be added to the Instruction Pointer. The displacement is measured from the offset of the next instruction and is treated as a signed integer from -128 through +127. Thus the maximum range for a Short Immediate-mode jump is 128 bytes backward through 127 bytes forward from the offset of the next instruction following the jump.

A Near Immediate-mode jump is a three-byte machine-language instruction, containing a **word displacement** to be added to IP as an unsigned integer. In order to jump backward, a large displacement is used to cause IP to "wrap around" from the end to the beginning of the segment. Consequently, a Near jump has no restriction on its range except that its target must be within the 64K code segment.

The distinction between Short and Near Immediate-mode jumps is somewhat transparent to the programmer since they both may be coded identically in assembly language. DEBUG or the assembler normally decides which machine-language instruction to use. We have discussed the distinction here for two reasons. First, as an assembly-language programmer, you should be aware that your jump instruction may result in either a two-byte or a three-byte instruction in the resulting executable program. Second, we will see shortly that all Conditional jumps are assembled with a byte displacement and so have the same range restrictions as a Short Immediate-mode jump.

Using the DEBUG Assemble command, the syntax for either a Short or a Near Immediate-mode jump is as follows:

```
JMP        target_offset
```

Target_offset is an immediate value from 0 through 65535 (0000H through FFFFH) specifying the offset of the instruction to which to transfer control. DEBUG determines the jump displacement by subtracting the offset of the next instruction from *target_offset*, and then determines whether to assemble the instruction as a Short jump or as a Near jump.

If the calculated displacement is within the range of a byte, -128 through +127 (128 bytes backward through 127 bytes forward), DEBUG assembles it as a two-byte Short Immediate-mode jump, the second byte of which is the byte displacement. When the displacement is outside the range of a byte, DEBUG assembles it as a three-byte Near Immediate-mode jump with a word displacement. A Short or Near Immediate-mode jump has the following effect, when executed:

```
ADD        IP, displacement
```

A Far Immediate-mode jump modifies both IP and the Code Segment register and so may transfer control to any memory address within the 8086/8088's one megabyte of memory addressing capability. By modifying CS as well as IP, Far jumps permit multiple code segments within the same program, allowing programs with more than 64K of code. Using the DEBUG Assemble command, a Far Immediate-mode jump is coded as follows:

```
JMP        target_segment:target_offset
```

Target_segment and *target_offset* are four-digit hexadecimal numerals specifying the memory address of the next instruction to be executed. The colon separating the segment and offset is required by DEBUG in order to indicate that a Far Immediate-mode jump is desired.

A machine-language Far Immediate-mode jump does not use a displacement to specify the target address. The five-byte machine-language instruction consists of a one-byte op-code followed by *target_offset* (word) and *target_segment* (word). During execution, the offset is copied into IP, and the segment is copied into CS. The effect of a Far Immediate-mode jump is as follows:

```
MOV         IP, target_offset ·
MOV         CS, target_segment
```

As mentioned earlier, the 8086/8088 also allows Register and Memory modes for the target address of an Unconditional jump. A Register-mode Unconditional jump takes the following form in assembly language:

```
JMP         register
```

Register is any word register except for IP or any of the Segment registers; SP, BP, SI, DI, AX, BX, CX, and DX are all valid. *Register* is a source operand; its value is not modified. A Register-mode Unconditional jump has the following effect when executed:

```
MOV         IP, register
```

Since *register* can contain any value from 0 through 65535, and since CS is not modified, a Register-mode jump is always a Near jump; its range is anywhere within the current code segment. However, unlike Near Immediate-mode jumps, the value in *register* is treated as the target offset rather than as a displacement; the value in *register* is copied into IP, not added to it.

Since the code offset in *register* might be calculated by the program based on data or on previous events, Register-mode Unconditional jumps are sometimes used to provide program decision-making capability. Such use can produce very efficient machine code. However, the use of Register-mode jumps also tends to make the program difficult to follow and maintain. Consequently, we discourage their use and recommend instead the use of Conditional jumps, to be discussed shortly.

A Memory-mode Unconditional jump uses data stored in a memory location as the target address of the jump. The target address is read by the processor from the specified memory location. Since either a single word (offset only) or two words (segment and offset) may be stored at the memory location, the jump may be either Near or Far. Using DEBUG's Assemble command, a Memory-mode Unconditional jump takes the following forms:

```
JMP         [memory]
```

or

```
JMP          FAR [memory]
```

Memory can be any of the memory data-addressing modes discussed earlier: Direct, Base-or-Index, Base-or-Index-Plus-Displacement, Base-Plus-Index, or Base-Plus-Index-Plus-Displacement. The effects of a Near and a Far (respectively) Memory-mode Unconditional jump are as follows:

```
MOV          IP, [memory]
```

or

```
MOV          IP, [memory]
MOV          CS, [memory + 2]
```

Note that the word of data at the memory location is copied into IP; if it is a Far jump, then the following word (at the memory location plus two) is also moved into CS, resulting in an intersegment jump. The use of Memory-mode Unconditional jumps provides the programmer with tremendous power and flexibility; however, the misuse or overuse of Memory-mode jumps can easily result in a program that is virtually impossible to maintain. Imagine trying to follow the logic of a program that contains the following instruction:

```
JMP          [BX + SI + 300]
```

It is extremely difficult to determine the target address of the jump in order to know where to continue with the program logic. First, the values in BX and SI (when execution reaches the jump) must somehow be determined. From those values the memory location can be determined. Then it is necessary to somehow determine what value is stored in that memory location when the jump executes.

The value in the memory location finally determines the target offset of the jump, where the logic trace may be continued. Should you ever use a Memory-mode jump, be sure to include ample, clear, well-thought-out internal documentation to explain why it is used and how to determine the target of the jump under all possible circumstances.

A PAUSE IN THE ACTION

Why Jump Instructions Are Important

In your high-level programming classes the use of any GOTO (or equivalent) statements has probably been discouraged or even prohibited. You might, therefore, wonder why we must spend so much time discussing jumps (the assembly-language equivalent of GOTO).

The processor's instruction set (and assembly language) contains none of the programming constructs used to control the logic flow in high-level languages. As we will discuss in the next two chapters, all logic constructs such as selection (select one of two alternatives, if . . . else), case (select one of many alternatives), and iteration (repeat while, repeat until, repeat with counter) must be constructed from Conditional and Unconditional jumps. Consequently, a thorough understanding of both Unconditional and Conditional jumps is critical to an assembly-language programmer.

Conditional Jumps

Most program decision making is implemented in assembly language through the use of Conditional jumps, which transfer control only if the proper condition has been met. With one exception (JCXZ), all Conditional jumps cause the Execution Unit to examine the Flags register in order to decide whether to do the jump. It is the status of the Result flags (except for the Auxiliary Carry flag) that determines if control is to be transferred to the target offset, or if the jump is to be ignored and execution continued with the instruction immediately following the Conditional jump.

All Conditional jumps are Short Immediate-mode jumps. The target offset must always be specified as an immediate value; neither Register mode nor Memory mode is permitted. The target offset is stored in the machine-language instruction as a byte displacement, with a range of -128 through +127, which is added to IP if the jump takes place. Consequently, Conditional jumps are always limited to the range of 128 bytes backward through 127 bytes forward from the offset immediately following the Conditional jump instruction.

The Conditional jumps supported by the 8086/8088 are JE (JZ), JNE (JNZ), JA (JNBE), JNA (JBE), JB (JNAE, JC), JNB (JAE, JNC), JG (JNLE), JNG (JLE), JL (JNGE), JNL (JGE), JO, JNO, JS, JNS, JP (JPE), JNP (JPO), and JCXZ. Following is an explanation of the entire set of 8086/8088 Conditional jump instructions.

JE	*target_offset*	(jump if equal)
JZ	*target_offset*	(jump if zero)

JE and JZ are synonyms for the same machine-language instruction. The status of the Zero flag determines if the jump will take place; the jump is executed if and only if the Zero flag is set (one). It is used with either signed or unsigned arithmetic to cause a transfer of control whenever the last Arithmetic or Logical instruction resulted in zero.

JNE	*target_offset*	(jump if not equal)
JNZ	*target_offset*	(jump if not zero)

JNE and JNZ are synonyms for the machine-language instruction that is the opposite of JE (JZ). The transfer of control takes place if and only if the Zero flag is clear. It is used when the data represents either signed or unsigned integers and jumps whenever the result of the last Arithmetic or Logical instruction was any value other than zero.

| JA | *target_offset* | (jump if above) |
| JNBE | *target_offset* | (jump if not below or equal) |

JA and JNBE are synonyms. The processor examines both the Carry flag and the Zero flag. The jump takes place if and only if the Carry flag and the Zero flag are both clear (zero); if either flag is set, the jump does not happen. JA or JNBE is used when performing unsigned arithmetic to cause a transfer of control whenever an operation results in an unsigned value greater than zero and within the range allowed by the type of the destination operand. The jump occurs if and only if the result of the last Arithmetic or Logical instruction was 1 through 255 for a byte instruction, or 1 through 65535 for a word instruction.

| JNA | *target_offset* | (jump if not above) |
| JBE | *target_offset* | (jump if below or equal) |

JNA and JBE are synonyms and are the opposite or complement of JA (JNBE). The jump takes place if and only if either the Carry flag or the Zero flag is set; the jump fails to take place only if both flags are clear. It is also used when working with unsigned values. The program jumps if the result is not above zero and within the unsigned range of the operand (not within the range 1 through 255 or 1 through 65535).

JB	*target_offset*	(jump if below)
JNAE	*target_offset*	(jump if not above or equal)
JC	*target_offset*	(jump if carry)

JB, JNAE, and JC all result in a machine-language instruction that checks the status of the Carry flag. The processor jumps to *target_offset* if and only if the Carry flag is set, if the result of the last Arithmetic or Logical instruction was outside the unsigned range for the operand (not within the range 0 through 255 or 0 through 65535).

JNB	*target_offset*	(jump if not below)
JAE	*target_offset*	(jump if above or equal)
JNC	*target_offset*	(jump if no carry)

JAE, JNB, and JNC are synonyms for the complement of JB (JNAE, and JC). The processor jumps if and only if the Carry flag is clear. Transfer of control takes place if the last Arithmetic or Logical result was within the range of unsigned values for the operand (0 through 255 or 0 through 65535).

Notice that the previous four instructions all check the Carry flag and so are useful only when performing unsigned arithmetic, when interpreting data as unsigned integers (0 through 255 for byte values, or 0 through 65535 for word values). The next four instructions check both the Overflow and Sign flags and should be used if and only if the data is to be treated as signed integers (-128 through +127 for byte values, or -32768 through +32767 for word values).

---

* * * * IMPORTANT * * * *

It is up to you, the programmer, to decide how the program should interpret the data and to choose instructions from the correct set of Conditional jumps. Choose instructions that use "A" or "B" (above or below) when performing unsigned arithmetic; choose instructions that use "L" or "G" (less than or greater than) when interpreting the data as signed values.

| JG | *target_offset* | (jump if greater than) |
| JNLE | *target_offset* | (jump if not less than or equal to) |

JG and JNLE check the Sign flag, the Overflow flag, and the Zero flag. The jump takes place if and only if the Zero flag is clear and either the Sign and Overflow flags are both clear or they are both set. In other words, the jump will take place if and only if the result is not zero (Zero flag clear) and not negative (Sign flag clear and correct with no overflow, or Sign flag set but incorrect due to an overflow). JG and JNLE are used when data is being interpreted as signed integers, and a transfer of control is necessary whenever the result is positive (greater than zero).

| JNG | *target_offset* | (jump if not greater than) |
| JLE | *target_offset* | (jump if less than or equal to) |

JNG and JLE are the complements of JG and JNLE. The Execution Unit performs the jump if and only if the Zero flag is set or the Sign flag is set with the Overflow flag clear or the Sign flag is clear with the Overflow flag set. The jump takes place if the result was zero (Zero set) or the result was negative (Sign set and correct with Overflow clear, or Sign clear but incorrect since Overflow is set). When performing signed arithmetic, use JNG or JLE to cause a jump when the result is not greater than zero.

| JL | *target_offset* | (jump if less than) |
| JNGE | *target_offset* | (jump if not greater than or equal to) |

JL and JNGE cause a jump if and only if either the Sign flag is set and the Overflow flag is clear, or the Sign flag is clear and the Overflow flag is set. The jump happens when the result is negative, that is when the Sign flag is set and correct (no Overflow) or it is clear but incorrect (Overflow set). Use JL or JNGE when data should be interpreted as signed integers, and it is necessary to transfer control if the result is negative (less than zero).

JNL	*target_offset*	(jump if not less than)
JGE	*target_offset*	(jump if greater than or equal to)

JNL and JGE are the complements of JL and JNGE and are used with signed arithmetic to cause a jump whenever the result is not negative. The jump occurs if and only if the Sign and Overflow flags are both clear or they are both set, when the Sign flag is clear and correct (no Overflow) or it is set but incorrect (Overflow).

Notice that each of the previous four instructions checks both the Sign flag and the Overflow flag to determine if a signed result is positive or negative. This is made necessary by the characteristics of twos-complement addition. The Sign flag is normally set if and only if a result is negative; however, if the result is too big or too small to fit in eight or sixteen bits, the Overflow flag is set to indicate that the status of the Sign flag is invalid (the opposite of what it should be). Normally one of the above instructions should always be used whenever checking the sign of a result.

Occasionally, however, it is desirable to check either the Sign flag or Overflow flag alone regardless of the other flag's status. The next four instructions provide that capability.

JO	*target_offset*	(jump if overflow)

JO is used to check if a result is valid or invalid as a signed integer and to jump if the result is outside the signed range of the operand (-128 through +127 or -32768 through +32767). The jump occurs if and only if the Overflow flag is set. When performing signed arithmetic, JO is used for much the same purpose as JC is used when performing unsigned arithmetic, to cause a jump if the last result was outside the range of the operand and consequently is not to be trusted.

JNO	*target_offset*	(jump if not overflow)

JNO is the complement of JO and also checks the validity of a result as a signed integer. It jumps if and only if the Overflow flag is clear, indicating that the result is valid as a signed integer.

JS	*target_offset*	(jump if sign)

JS checks only the Sign flag without verifying its validity. The jump takes place if and only if the Sign flag is set, if the high bit of the result is one. It is most often used to check the size of an unsigned result, to check if it is greater than 127 (byte) or 32767 (word). Since it does not check the Overflow flag, it should not normally be used to check the sign of the result when performing signed arithmetic.

JNS   *target_offset*   (jump if not sign)

JNS is the complement of JS. It causes a jump if and only if the Sign flag is clear.

The next two Conditional jumps check the Parity flag and are most commonly used in communications-control programs where the high bit of each byte is used as a parity bit for the validation of received data. Recall that the ALU counts the number of bits that are one in every result and controls the Parity flag, setting it if the number of ones is even and clearing it if there is an odd number of ones in the result.

JP   *target_offset*   (jump if parity)
JPE   *target_offset*   (jump if parity is even)

JP and JPE jump if and only if the Parity flag is set, indicating even parity (an even number of ones) in the result.

JNP   *target_offset*   (jump if no parity)
JPO   *target_offset*   (jump if parity is odd)

JNP and JPO transfer control if and only if the Parity bit is clear, indicating odd parity (an odd number of ones).

The final Conditional jump instruction is the "oddball". It is the only Conditional jump that does not test the flags to determine whether the jump should take place. It is also the only one that does not have a complementary (opposite) instruction; there is no such instruction as JCXNZ or JNCXZ. We will see why it was included by Intel in the 8086/8088 instruction set when we discuss the loop instructions.

JCXZ   *target_offset*   (jump if CX is zero)

JCXZ causes the Execution Unit to examine the value in the CX register to determine whether to do the jump. The jump occurs if and only if the value currently in CX is zero.

Branch-and-Return Instructions

Branch-and-Return instructions provide for the modularization of programs. The programmer is able to break the solution of the problem into a number of subprocedures or subroutines, each of which solves one part of the problem, and a mainline procedure, which uses the subprocedures to solve the entire problem. Whenever the mainline procedure transfers control to a subprocedure, it must do so in such a way that upon completion the subprocedure can return control back to the mainline for the next step in the solution. This is accomplished in assembly language through the use of the instructions **CALL**, **RET**, **INT**, and **IRET**.

MOST COMMONLY USED Jump Instructions

Unconditional Jump:

> JMP   *target_offset*
>
> > Continue execution at the immediate-value *target_offset*.

Conditional Jumps:

Unsigned arithmetic:

> JA (JNBE)   *target_offset*
>
> > Jump if above, if not below or equal.

> JNA (JBE)   *target_offset*
>
> > Jump if not above, if below or equal.

> JB (JNAE, JC) *target_offset*
>
> > Jump if below, if not above or equal, if carry.

> JNB (JAE, JNC) *target_offset*
>
> > Jump if not below, if above or equal, if no carry.

Signed arithmetic:

> JG (JNLE)   *target_offset*
>
> > Jump if greater than, if not less than or equal to.

> JNG (JLE)   *target_offset*
>
> > Jump if not greater than, if less than or equal to.

> JL (JNGE)   *target_offset*
>
> > Jump if less than, if not greater than or equal to.

> JNL (JGE)   *target_offset*
>
> > Jump if not less than, if greater than or equal to.

Other Conditional jumps:

> JE (JZ)   *target_offset*
>
> > Jump if equal, if zero flag set.

> JNE (JNZ)   *target_offset*
>
> > Jump if not equal, if zero flag not set.

> JCXZ   *target_offset*
>
> > Jump if CX is zero.

CALL causes the processor to push the value in the Instruction Pointer register onto the stack. As the call executes, the Instruction Pointer has already been incremented to the offset of the next instruction; consequently, the value pushed to the stack is the offset of the next instruction after the call. If it is a Far call, the processor first pushes the Code Segment register and then pushes IP. Once the return address has been pushed onto the stack, the processor jumps to the target address, which should be the beginning of a subprocedure that ends with a Return instruction.

When execution reaches the Return instruction (**RET**) at the end of the subprocedure, the processor pops the value currently at the top of the stack into IP; if it is a Far return, it also pops the next word from the stack into CS. The result is that IP (and CS, if it is a Far return) is restored to the value that was pushed by the call. Execution returns to the next instruction after the call. Note that a Far call pushes CS first and then pushes IP; a Far return pops them in the reverse order, IP first and then CS.

Also take warning that when the processor executes a return it has no way to verify that the value at the top of the stack is indeed the return address that was pushed by the call. A return always pops whatever value is currently at the top of the stack (whatever the Stack Pointer register points to) into IP. It is the programmers responsibility to ensure that SP points to the return address when execution reaches the Return instruction.

Consider the following scenario. The programmer pushes AX at the beginning of a subprocedure but carelessly forgets to pop it at the end, before the Return instruction. Consequently, the value at the top of the stack when the return executes is not the correct return address pushed by the Call instruction; it is whatever value happened to be in AX when it was pushed at the beginning of the subprocedure. The processor pops this "garbage" into IP and execution "returns" to the wrong memory address, which may not even contain instructions. The BIU reads whatever is stored at CS:[IP] even if it is data rather than instructions, and the Execution Unit executes it as instructions. The programmer most likely will have to reboot the machine in order to regain control. Be careful!

The correct assembly-language syntax for a Call instruction is:

```
CALL        address
```

Address is a source operand specifying the memory location to which to transfer control after pushing the return address. Since it is a source operand, *address* is never modified and can be any valid data-addressing mode. Consequently, there are three types of calls: Immediate-mode, Register-mode, and Memory-mode. With one exception, the data-addressing modes allowed for calls are identical to those allowed for Unconditional jumps!

The one exception is that there is no such thing as a Short Immediate-mode call (byte displacement). All Immediate-mode calls are assembled as either Near (word displacement) or Far (segment:offset). We should also point out that there are no conditional calls; all calls are unconditional. If it is necessary that a program perform a call only under certain conditions, then a Conditional jump must be used to branch around the call whenever it should not happen.

The syntax for a Near Immediate-mode call is as follows:

```
CALL        target_offset
```

Target_offset is the offset of the beginning of the subprocedure. The assembler or DEBUG calculates the word displacement by subtracting the current offset (of the next instruction) from *target_offset* and assembles the Near Call instruction with the word displacement. When the program is executed the Near Immediate-mode Call instruction has the following effect.

```
PUSH        IP
ADD         IP, displacement
```

A **Far** Immediate-mode call is coded within DEBUG as follows:

```
CALL        target_segment:target_offset
```

Target_segment and *target_offset* are immediate values from 0000H through FFFFH (0 through 65535) representing the segment and offset of the first instruction of the subprocedure to be called. The instruction is assembled as a five-byte machine-code instruction: the byte op-code followed by *target_offset* and *target_segment* (one word each). The effect of the Far Immediate-mode call is as follows:

```
PUSH        CS
PUSH        IP
MOV         CS, target_segment
MOV         IP, target_offset
```

A Register-mode call is always Near and is coded as follows:

```
CALL        register
```

Register is a sixteen-bit register name other than IP or any of the four Segment registers. The target offset of the call is determined by the value stored in *register* when the instruction executes. The effect of a Register-mode call is as follows:

```
PUSH        IP
MOV         IP, register
```

Memory-mode calls may be either Near or Far. The syntax within DEBUG is as follows:

```
CALL        [memory]
```

or

```
CALL        FAR [memory]
```

Memory may be any valid memory addressing mode. The target of the call is determined by the offset (and segment, if Far) stored in the memory location. The effect, upon execution, is as follows:

```
PUSH      IP
MOV       IP, [memory]
```

or

```
PUSH      CS
PUSH      IP
MOV       IP, [memory]
MOV       CS, [memory + 2]
```

Any subprocedure that receives control through a Call instruction must end with a return to transfer control back to the instruction immediately following the call. The Return instruction (Near and Far, respectively) is coded as follows with the DEBUG **A**ssemble command:

```
RET
```

or

```
RETF
```

Although we will learn later of a return operand that facilitates the passing of parameters to subprocedures, we will assume for the moment that no operands are allowed by a return. The effect of the Return instruction (Near and Far respectively) is as follows:

```
POP       IP
```

or

```
POP       IP
POP       CS
```

A PAUSE IN THE ACTION

Why Branch-and-Return Instructions Are Important

CALL and RET instructions are necessary for program modularization. By using CALL and RET, the programmer is able to break a large problem apart into smaller chunks, each of which is solved by a subprocedure. The overall problem is then solved by calling the subprocedures in the proper sequence from the mainline program. Effective program modularization, solving one part of the problem at a time, results in programs that are easier to test and debug and are much easier to maintain later.

Additionally, any task that must be performed more than once at different points within the program should be written as a subprocedure that is called repeatedly whenever necessary by the program. In chapter 7, we will learn to define building-block modules, which are written and tested once, and which may then be used at any point in any future program to perform commonly needed tasks such as input, output, and storage of data.

The final two Transfer-of-Control instructions, interrupt and interrupt-return, are in some ways similar to Call and Return but allow a great deal more flexibility. To see the need for this added flexibility, assume for a moment that you were designing an operating system. You need to provide a number of system services accessible to future programmers. You could conceivably implement those services in the form of Far subprocedures each ending with a Far return. In order to access a system service (to display a character for example), a future programmer would simply perform a Far call to the correct memory address. Upon completion (after display of the character), the Far return at the end of the service would return control back to the program. Many earlier microcomputer operating systems implemented system services in just this manner.

The problem with the scheme comes about when it is necessary to revise the operating system. When modifying an operating system it is often very difficult or even impossible to maintain the same addresses for all system-service routines. If the address of any system-service routine is changed, however, existing programs will no longer work with the new version of the operating system. In order to update to the new version of the operating system, users are required to modify the Far call addresses in any programs that use system services, or to purchase new versions of all such programs.

In the design of MS-DOS, Microsoft avoided this problem by implementing all system services via interrupt instructions rather than Far calls. Each system service is written as an **interrupt-service routine** ending with an Interrupt-return instruction. As the system boots, BIOS and DOS build an **interrupt-vector table** made up of 256 addresses called **interrupt vectors**. Each interrupt vector specifies the address of a system-service routine. This vector table resides in the first kilobyte (1024 bytes) of memory, and each interrupt vector is four bytes long consisting of the offset (word) followed by the segment (word) of the Far address at which the interrupt-service routine begins.

Once this table has been built, any program that needs to access a system service does so with an Interrupt instruction specifying the **interrupt type** as a byte value from 0 through 255. The processor uses the interrupt type to look up the desired interrupt vector in the vector table and to transfer control to the address specified by that vector. Using this scheme, a system-service routine need not reside at the same address in different versions of DOS; each version of DOS simply builds its vector table with the correct addresses for all system services in that version of DOS. As long as a program accesses system services with the Interrupt instruction, it will still run correctly with any later version of DOS.

We have already made frequent use of one such system service, the service for returning control back to DOS upon completion of a program. We have terminated all programs with INT 20. Interrupt type 20H causes the processor to transfer control to the address specified by the interrupt vector stored in the interrupt-vector table at address 0000H:0080H. Note that the vector is stored within segment 0000H, at an offset of four times the interrupt type. The vector that was stored by DOS at 0000H:0080H causes a transfer of control to the area of DOS responsible for recovering control of the processor upon completion of a program.

Another system service we will use repeatedly throughout this text is the DOS Function Call, which is accessed by interrupt type 21H, and which provides a great number of different services. To use the DOS Function Call, the programmer must put a function code into AH (telling DOS which service is desired), set up any other registers as required by the service, and then execute an interrupt type 21H. To display a character to the screen, for example, the program puts the function code to display a character (02H) into AH, puts the character (ASCII value of the character) into DL, and then executes an interrupt type 21H. The following code displays the character "A" to the screen:

```
MOV        AH, 2
MOV        DL, 41
INT        21
```

Interrupt type 21H causes the processor to transfer control to the DOS Function Call routine pointed to by the interrupt vector stored at [0000H:0084H]. The DOS Function Call code examines AH, determines that the character in DL is to be displayed, and transfers control to the DOS routine for displaying a character. The character in DL is displayed to the screen, and control is returned to the instruction immediately following the Interrupt instruction.

The Interrupt instruction is similar to a Far call in that it saves the return address (segment and offset) to the stack before transferring control; however there are several major differences. Besides obtaining the target address from the interrupt-vector table, the Interrupt instruction automatically pushes the flags register and clears the Interrupt-enable flag to disable any subsequent external (hardware) interrupts, prior to the transfer of control. The syntax for an Interrupt instruction is as follows:

```
INT        type
```

Type is an Immediate-mode byte value from 0 through 255 (00H through FFH). The Interrupt instruction has the following effect:

```
PUSHF
```

```
CLI
PUSH      CS
PUSH      IP
MOV       IP, [0:type * 4]
MOV       CS, [0:type * 4 + 2]
```

All interrupt-service routines (to which control is to be passed via an interrupt instruction) must terminate with an interrupt return to properly return control to the instruction immediately following the Interrupt instruction. The syntax for an interrupt return is as follows:

```
IRET
```

No parameters are allowed. The effect of IRET is as follows:

```
POP       IP
POP       CS
POPF
```

The result is to return to the address that was pushed by the Interrupt instruction and to restore the flags register to its status prior to the Interrupt instruction. Note that a program that needs to access a DOS or BIOS system service uses only the Interrupt instruction (INT). The Interrupt-return instruction (IRET) is built into DOS, at the end of the interrupt-service routine for handling the system service. Later in the text we will discuss the design and implementation of your own interrupt-service routines. Until then, you will not use IRET.

MOST COMMONLY USED **Branch-and-Return Instructions**

CALL   *target_offset*
   Push current value of IP then jump to the immediate-value *target_offset*.

RET
   Pop IP; return to next instruction after last CALL (as long as the stack has not been messed up).

INT   *type*
   PUSH the Flags register, CS and IP; clear Interrupt flag; jump to the address (offset and segment) specified by the interrupt vector stored at memory location [0:4*type]. Used to access BIOS and DOS system services.

Iteration Instructions

The 8086/8088 microprocessor does not provide any instructions that are equivalent to the high-level language WHILE or UNTIL statements or clauses. Such constructs must be built by the programmer from Conditional and Unconditional jumps. However, the processor does provide a loop instruction that allows for the repetition of a block of instructions a predetermined number of times. The CX (Counter) register is always used by the processor to count the number of iterations; CX is counted down to zero.

Additionally, two more instructions provide for exiting the loop early based on the status of the Zero flag. Like Conditional jumps, all three Loop instructions allow only Short Immediate mode and are assembled with a byte displacement. Consequently, Loop instructions allow a range of 128 bytes backward through 127 bytes forward. The syntax for **LOOP** is as follows:

```
LOOP            target_offset
```

Target_offset is normally the offset of the first instruction in the loop. The Loop instruction is normally placed at the end of the loop. Its effect is similar to the following:

```
DEC             CX
JCXNZ           target_offset
```

Note that JCXNZ (jump if CX not zero) is not a valid 8086/8088 instruction; it is used here for illustrative purposes only. Also note that the ALU does not alter any Result flags as it decrements CX during execution of the Loop instruction. The flag statuses are determined by previous instructions, not by the result in CX after decrementing. In particular, the Zero flag is not set or cleared by the Loop instruction.

To use the Loop instruction, CX must be initialized before the beginning of the loop to the number of times the loop is to be repeated. Each time the Loop instruction executes, it decrements CX; if CX is not yet zero then the loop is repeated. As a result, the loop repeats CX times. Upon completion of the loop, CX is always zero. As an example, the following code could be used to multiply the value in BX by the value in CX:

```
50E0:014C       MOV     AX, 0
50E0:014F       ADD     AX, BX
50E0:0151       LOOP    14F
50E0:0153
```

We will see later that the 8086/8088 provides a much better way to multiply (MUL). For now, the above section of code would work—or would it? Suppose first that we need to multiply three by seven. The program would move three into BX and seven into CX, prior to executing the section of code listed above.

The Move instruction at offset 14C initializes AX to zero, and execution enters the loop beginning at offset 14F. BX is added to AX, resulting in three in AX. The Loop instruction at 151 decrements CX from seven to six; since CX is not zero, the program loops back to offset 14F for the second pass through the loop, adding BX to AX again. Eventually on the seventh pass, CX is one; BX is added to AX for the seventh time, resulting in seven times three in AX. The Loop instruction decrements CX once more, resulting in zero; since CX is now zero the processor does not branch back to 14F but continues execution at offset 153. Upon completion of the loop, AX contains the product three times seven; the code works this time.

Suppose, however, that we need to multiply three by zero; if our code works, we should end up with zero in AX. To perform the multiplication, the program would move three into BX and zero into CX prior to executing our program section. The Move instruction at offset 14C initializes AX to zero as it should, but the processor then immediately enters the loop and executes the instruction at offset 14F, adding BX to AX, resulting in three in AX. Things get even worse when the Loop instruction executes. CX is decremented before the Execution Unit checks to see if it is zero. The result of decrementing zero in CX is 65535 (0000H − 0001H = FFFFH). Since CX is not now zero, the program loops back to 14F for another iteration. In fact, the program makes 65536 repetitions in all, adding BX to AX each time! Upon completion, AX is obviously not zero.

The processor has an instruction, JCXZ, which is intended for just this situation. Recall that JCXZ is the "oddball" among Conditional jumps; it differs from all other Conditional jumps in that it checks the value in CX, rather than checking the Flags register, to determine if the jump should happen. In order for our section of code to work properly in all cases, we should rewrite it as follows:

```
50E0:014C     MOV     AX, 0
50E0:014F     JCXZ    155
50E0:0151     ADD     AX, BX
50E0:0153     LOOP    151
50E0:0155
```

If CX is zero, the corrected program section skips around the loop executing it zero times and resulting in zero in AX. The engineers at Intel included JCXZ in the 8086/8088 instruction set for just this purpose. As a general rule, whenever you use a Loop instruction in a program, you should always include JCXZ immediately before the first instruction of the loop.

The final two iteration instructions (and two synonyms) allow a means of exiting a loop early, before it has repeated CX times. Like LOOP, they both decrement CX (without altering the Zero flag or any other Result flags) and check the resulting value in CX to help determine if the loop is to be repeated. Unlike LOOP, however, they also check the status of the Zero flag.

LOOPE (loop if equal) and its synonym **LOOPZ** (loop if zero) exit the loop early if the Zero flag is clear. The syntax is as follows:

```
        LOOPE          target_offset
```

or

```
        LOOPZ        target_offset
```

After decrementing CX, control is transferred to *target_offset* if and only if CX is not zero and the Zero flag is set (by a previous instruction). If the last Arithmetic or Logical instruction within the loop has cleared the Zero flag, then the loop quits early, before CX has been counted down to zero.

LOOPNE (loop if not equal) and its synonym **LOOPNZ** (loop if not zero) provide a complement for LOOPE (LOOPZ). The loop is exited early if the Zero flag is set. The syntax is as follows:

```
        LOOPNE         target_offset
```

or

```
        LOOPNZ        target_offset
```

CX is decremented (without modifying any flags), and the Execution Unit then checks both the Zero flag and the CX register. Control is transferred to *target_offset* if and only if CX is not zero and the Zero flag is clear.

M O S T   C O M M O N L Y   U S E D   Iteration Instruction

LOOP *target_offset*
> Decrement CX, then jump to the immediate-value *target_offset* if CX is not zero. Used at end of a loop to cause it to repeat CX times.

PROCESSOR-CONTROL INSTRUCTIONS

The last group of instructions to be considered in this chapter all have to do with controlling the behavior of the processor. **Processor-Control instructions** allow no operands and have no immediate effect on data, either in registers or in memory. However, they may affect the manner in which the processor executes subsequent instructions. The instructions we will consider are **NOP**, **HLT**, and a group of instructions for explicitly manipulating the Flags register: **STC**, **CLC**, **CMC**, **STD**, **CLD**, **STI**, and **CLI**.

NOP (non-op or no operation) is a single-byte instruction that requires three clock cycles for execution and tells the processor to do nothing! It allows the programmer to use up a byte of code without doing anything (to adjust the next instruction to an even memory address, for example) or to use up clock cycles during execution for timing purposes. In reality, NOP is simply a synonym for the instruction to exchange the AX register with itself. The following two instructions are synonymous, resulting in the same one-byte machine-language instruction, which uses three clock cycles but does not alter any data or flags:

```
NOP
XCHG        AX, AX
```

HLT (halt) stops the execution of a program until an external (hardware) interrupt is received by the processor. It is used whenever a program needs to wait for an interrupt from a peripheral device before continuing execution. If the Interrupt-Enable flag is clear (disable interrupts) when the halt executes, the processor does not recognize external interrupts and so will remain in a halt state indefinitely; a hardware boot will be necessary to regain control of the processor. If the Interrupt-Enable flag is set, the processor will continue execution with the first external interrupt.

Finally, there is a set of instructions for explicitly manipulating the Carry flag, Direction flag, and Interrupt-enable flag. The Carry flag is the only Result flag that may be explicitly manipulated. Three instructions are provided for explicitly controlling the Carry flag, STC (set Carry flag), CLC (clear Carry flag), and CMC (complement Carry flag). We will later learn the usefulness of STC and CLC for returning a Boolean (True/False) value from a subprocedure. CMC reverses the status of the Carry flag, changing one to zero or zero to one.

STD (set Direction flag) and CLD (clear Direction flag) are used to control the status of the Direction flag, which in turn controls the operation of the "String" instructions to be discussed later. STI (set Interrupt-enable flag) and CLI (clear Interrupt-enable flag) explicitly control the status of the Interrupt-enable flag; STI enables external interrupts, and CLI disables external interrupts.

MOST COMMONLY USED Processor-Control Instructions

NOP

    Non-op; do nothing.

STC

    Set (1) Carry flag.

CLC

    Clear (0) Carry flag.

Since the Direc-tion and Interrupt-enable flags are not Result flags, the ALU never modifies the status of either flag while performing arithmetic or logical operations. Their statuses are changed only when the Execution Unit executes one of the above instructions.

This completes our discussion of the processor instruction set. Remember that it is not necessary that you completely understand all the minute details of all instructions at this point. We will review instructions as needed throughout the rest of the text, and you will probably refer back to the above discussion frequently as you work in assembly language. At this point you should simply have a good feel for the kinds of operations the processor can be instructed to perform.

You should also be aware of some operations that are taken for granted by high-level language programmers but are not directly supported by the processor's instruction set. Most notably, there are no equivalents for the IF . . . THEN . . . ELSE BASIC statement, the COBOL UNTIL clause, or the Pascal or FORTRAN DO loops. In assembly language such programming logic must be implemented with Conditional jumps. We will discuss the implementation of structured-programming constructs in some detail in the following two chapters.

For now, Figure 5-3 provides an example program (written with DEBUG) that uses jumps to implement a general loop in order to find the double-word sum of a series of byte values beginning at offset 128H and terminated with a byte with a value of zero (at offset 13AH). The instructions at offsets 100H and 103H initialize DX and AX to zero (the sum will be accumulated in DX:AX). CH is initialized to zero at offset 105H (byte values will be moved into CL, and CX will be added to the accumulator). The instruction at 107H initializes BX (base register) to point to the series of byte values.

The instructions from offsets 10AH through 117H comprise a general loop to accumulate the total. The first two instructions in the loop (at 10AH and 10CH) move a byte value from memory into CL (CX) and increment BX to point to the next byte value for the next time around the loop. The next two instructions (at 10DH and 110H) test for termination of the loop, jumping to the next instruction after the end of the loop if the byte value in CL is zero.

Note that when first assembling the loop, we did not know exactly what address to jump to in order to exit the loop. We had to guess and so assembled the instruction at 110H to jump to 120H. After finishing assembly of the program, we then reassembled the instruction at 110H to jump to the correct offset immediately after the last instruction of the loop (119H).

The instructions at 112H and 114H accumulate the total into DX:AX by adding to AX and adding any carry to DX. The Jump instruction at 117H completes the loop by jumping back to 10AH to obtain the next byte value.

After completion of the loop, the Move instructions at 119H and 11CH store the double-word sum (low word first) into memory at 124H. Finally the interrupt instruction at 120H (INT 20H) effects a proper return to DOS or DEBUG.

Figure 5-3   Sample Program Written with DEBUG

```
-A
1E82:0100 MOV     AX,0
1E82:0103 MOV     DX,AX
1E82:0105 MOV     CH,AL
1E82:0107 MOV     BX,128
1E82:010A MOV     CL,[BX]
1E82:010C INC     BX
1E82:010D CMP     CL,0
1E82:0110 JE      120
1E82:0112 ADD     AX,CX
1E82:0114 ADC     DX,0
1E82:0117 JMP     10A
1E82:0119 MOV     [124],AX
1E82:011C MOV     [126],DX
1E82:0120 INT     20
1E82:0122


-A 110
1E82:0110 JE 119
1E82:0112


-U 100 L22
1E82:0100 B80000      MOV     AX,0000
1E82:0103 89C2        MOV     DX,AX
1E82:0105 88C5        MOV     CH,AL
1E82:0107 BB2801      MOV     BX,0128
1E82:010A 8A0F        MOV     CL,[BX]
1E82:010C 43          INC     BX
1E82:010D 80F900      CMP     CL,00
1E82:0110 7407        JZ      0119
1E82:0112 01C8        ADD     AX,CX
1E82:0114 83D200      ADC     DX,+00
1E82:0117 EBF1        JMP     010A
1E82:0119 A32401      MOV     [0124],AX
1E82:011C 89162601    MOV     [0126],DX
1E82:0120 CD20        INT     20

-E 128 1 5 23 AB 6C DF 3A B7 BC 89 41 DC CD FF 0F F0 AA 0

-D128 L20
1E82:0120                      01 05 23 AB 6C DF 3A B7          s..#.l.:.
1E82:0130  BC 89 41 DC CD FF 0F F0-AA 00 0E 16 01 E3 1A 26   ..A............&
1E82:0140  C5 B5 10 01 83 C7 04 8C-                          ........

-RBX
BX 0000
:0
```

Figure 5-3: (continued)

```
-RCX
CX 0000
:3B

-N F5-3.COM

-W

Writing 003B bytes

-D 124 14
1E9F:0120            4F F9 8B 0E                          O...

-G =100

Program terminated normally

-D 124 L4
1E9F:0120            E7 08 00 00                          ....

-Q
```

DESCENDANTS OF THE 8086 PROCESSOR

As mentioned in the last chapter, the 80186 instruction set is an extension of the 8086/8088 instruction set. One major addition is that all Shift-and-Rotate instructions allow any byte Immediate-mode value (from 1 through 255) for the source operand (for example, SHL BX, 5). Recall that the 8086/8088 allows only CL or an Immediate-mode value of one. Another extension is that the 80186 supports PUSH with an Immediate-mode source operand. The 80186 also includes two more Push instructions. PUSHA pushes all registers (AX, CX, DX, BX, SP, BP, SI, and DI), and POPA pops the same registers in the reverse order.

In Real mode, the 80286, 80386, 80386SX, and 80486 instruction sets are almost identical to that of the 80186 except that the 80386, 80386SX, and 80486 allow thirty-two bit register names (EAX, EBX, ECX, EDX, ESP, EBP, ESI, and EDI). In Protected mode, a number of other instructions are supported. Most of those instructions are available only to the operating system and so will not be discussed here. Note that if any of the extended instructions are used in a program, that program is limited to machines with an 80186 or later processor; it will not run on any machine that uses an 8088 or an 8086 processor.

SUMMARY

With a few exceptions, we have now discussed the entire set of instructions supported by the 8086/8088 processor. You should not worry too much if you do not feel totally comfortable with all the details of the instruction set; we will review instructions as needed throughout the rest of the text. You should at least have a good understanding of the big picture, the kinds of fundamental operations the processor can be commanded to perform and the six fundamental groups of instructions: Data-Transfer, Arithmetic, Logical, Shift-and-Rotate, Transfer-of-Control, and special Processor-Control instructions.

You should also be aware of some of the processor's limitations. No instructions are provided for the input of data from the keyboard or for the output of data to the screen. The input and output of data requires a number of instructions within the program as well as the use of many more instructions provided by DOS and BIOS system services.

VOCABULARY

V5-1   In your own words, describe the general purpose of each of the following groups of instructions:

a) Data-transfer instructions

b) Arithmetic instructions

c) Logical instructions

d) Shift-and-Rotate instructions

e) Transfer-of-Control instructions

f) Processor-Control instructions

V5-2   In your own words, define each of the following terms:

a) Immediate-mode jump

b) Register-mode jump

c) Memory-mode jump

d) Short jump

e) Near jump

f) Far jump

g) Byte displacement

h) Word displacement

i) Interrupt-service routine

j) Interrupt vector

k) Interrupt-vector table

l) Interrupt type

REVIEW QUESTIONS

Q5-1   List six Data-Transfer instructions, showing the correct syntax and briefly describing the effect of each.

Q5-2   List eight Arithmetic instructions, showing the correct syntax and briefly describing the effect of each.

Q5-3   List five Logical instructions, showing the correct syntax and briefly describing the effect of each.

Q5-4   List seven (no synonyms) Shift-and-Rotate instructions, showing the two possible forms of each and briefly describing the effect of each.

Q5-5   List the Shift instructions that always clear one or more Result flags and tell which flag(s) each one clears.

Q5-6   List the Result flags that are affected by the Rotate instructions.

Q5-7   Of the six general types of instructions, which ones involve the ALU?

Q5-8   What are the three types of Unconditional Immediate-mode jumps? What is the range of each?

Q5-9   Besides Immediate-mode, what are the other two addressing modes allowed by Unconditional jumps? What is the range of each?

Q5-10   What is the only data-addressing mode allowed by Conditional jumps? What is the range of all Conditional jumps?

Q5-11   Which Conditional jump does not check the Flags register to determine whether the jump should happen? Why was it included in the instruction set?

Q5-12   Which Conditional jumps are used for comparing unsigned values? Which are the equivalent Conditional jumps for comparing signed values?

Q5-13   List the four Branch-and-Return instructions, and describe the effect of each.

Q5-14   List the three Iteration instructions provided by the processor. What is the range of all Iteration instructions?

Q5-15   What instruction tells the processor to do nothing? What instruction is it a synonym for?

Q5-16   What instruction causes the processor to stop and wait for an external interrupt from some hardware device?

Q5-17   Which flags may be explicitly modified by the program? List and explain the instructions that modify each.

Q5-18   What is the only flag that can be explicitly modified, and whose new status can then be checked by a Conditional jump?

Q5-19   Which instructions throw away the result returned by the ALU? Since they throw away the result without modifying either operand, what use are they?

Q5-20   What is the only instruction that requires two destination operands?

Q5-21   Which groups of instructions cause the ALU to manipulate individual bits rather than binary numeric values?

Q5-22   List all instructions that explicitly or implicitly affect the stack.

Q5-23   Which instruction is commonly used to mask bits out (force selective bits to zero) of an operand?

Q5-24   Which instruction is commonly used to mask bits in (force selective bits to one) of an operand?

Q5-25   Which instruction is commonly used to complement (reverse) selective bits within an operand?

Q5-26   Which instruction complements (reverses) all bits within an operand?

Q5-27   Which instruction is commonly used to check the status of a bit within an operand?

PROGRAMMING ASSIGNMENTS

PA5-1   Manually trace through each of the following program listings and predict the values that will be stored in the registers upon completion. List all registers (except IP and SP) that are modified along with their resulting contents; also list the contents of any modified memory locations. Remember that all Immediate values are in hexadecimal and that all arithmetic should be performed in hexadecimal; your results should also be shown in hexadecimal. To trace any Logical or Shift-and-Rotate instruction, you will have to convert the value to binary, perform the operation, and then convert the binary result back to hexadecimal.

```
a) MOV     AX, 2D
   MOV     CL, 4
   SHL     AX, CL
   INT     20

b) MOV     DX, B4
   MOV     AX, A6
   SHR     DX, 1
   RCR     AX, 1
   INT     20

c) MOV     DX, B4
   MOV     AX, A6
   SAR     DX, 1
   RCR     AX, 1
   INT     20

d) SUB     DX, DX
   MOV     AX, A5
   ADD     AX, 5B
   ADC     DX, 1
   INT     20

e) xxxx:0100      MOV       BL, AA
   xxxx:0102      TEST      BL, 2
   xxxx:0105      JZ        109
   xxxx:0107         XOR       BL, BL
   xxxx:0109      TEST      BL, 80
   xxxx:010C      JNZ       110
   xxxx:010E         DEC    BL
   xxxx:0110      INT       20
```

```
f)  xxxx:0100    MOV        CX, 202
    xxxx:0103    MOV        DX,10F5
    xxxx:0106    CMP        CX, DX
    xxxx:0108    JNA        110
    xxxx:010A        MOV        [200], CX
    xxxx:010E    JMP        114
    xxxx:0110        MOV        [200], DX
    xxxx:0114    ROR        WORD PTR [200], CL
    xxxx:0118    INT        20

g)  xxxx:0100    MOV        AX, FF00
    xxxx:0103    CALL       120
    xxxx:0106    CALL       140
    xxxx:0109    INT        20

         .
         .
         .

    xxxx:0120    MOV        [200], AL
    xxxx:0123    MOV        [201], AL
    xxxx:0126    MOV        [202], AL
    xxxx:0129    MOV        [203], AH
    xxxx:012D    MOV        [204], AH
    xxxx:0131    MOV        [205], AH
    xxxx:0135    MOV        [206], AX
    xxxx:0138    MOV        [208], AX
    xxxx:013B    MOV        [20A], AX
    xxxx:013E    RET
    xxxx:013F    NOP
    xxxx:0140    NOT        BYTE PTR [201]
    xxxx:0144    NEG        BYTE PTR [202]
    xxxx:0148    NOT        BYTE PTR [204]
    xxxx:014C    NEG        BYTE PTR [205]
    xxxx:0150    NOT        WORD PTR [208]
    xxxx:0154    NEG        WORD PTR [20A]
    xxxx:0158    RET

h)  xxxx:0100    MOV        AX, F00F
    xxxx:0103    MOV        BX, D3D3
    xxxx:0106    CALL       120
    xxxx:0109    CALL       140
    xxxx:010C    INT        20

         .
         .
         .

    xxxx:0120    MOV        [200], BX
    xxxx:0124    MOV        [202], BX
    xxxx:0128    MOV        [204], BX
    xxxx:012C    MOV        [206], BX
    xxxx:0130    MOV        [208], BX
    xxxx:0134    MOV        [20A], BX
    xxxx:0138    RET
```

```
        .
        .
        .
xxxx:0140        AND        [200], AH
xxxx:0144        OR         [201], AH
xxxx:0148        XOR        [202], AH
xxxx:014C        AND        [203], AL
xxxx:0150        OR         [204], AL
xxxx:0154        XOR        [205], AL
xxxx:0158        AND        [206], AX
xxxx:015C        OR         [208], AX
xxxx:0160        XOR        [20A], AX
xxxx:0164        RET
```

PA5-2   Use DEBUG to check your predicted results in PA5-1 above. Using the Assemble command, key in each program. Then execute the program using the Go command with a break point at the offset of the interrupt type 20H instruction. Compare the resulting register values, as displayed by DEBUG, with the values you predicted in PA5-1; also, use the Dump command to check any modified memory locations. If the results are not what you predicted, use the Trace command to step through the program again and determine where you went wrong in your manual trace.

PA5-3   Using DEBUG, write a program that uses subprocedures to calculate and store the sum and difference of two numbers.

Write a subprocedure, starting at offset 110H, that finds the sum of AX and BX and stores the result into memory at offset 130H.

Write another subprocedure, starting at offset 120H, that finds the difference of AX and BX (AX minus BX), and stores the result into memory at offset 132H.

Each subprocedure should save and restore (PUSH and POP) any register(s) that is/are modified within the subprocedure. Each subprocedure must end with a RET instruction immediately after the POP(s).

Write the mainline procedure, starting at offset 100H. Store decimal 255 into AX, decimal 75 into BX. Then call the two subprocedures to calculate and store the sum and then the difference. Terminate the program with an interrupt type 20H (at end of mainline).

Save the program as PA5-3.COM (Name and Write commands). Remember to set up BX:CX (R BX and R CX) as the proper number of bytes to save the subprocedures, as well as the mainline.

PA5-4   Use DEBUG to write a program that displays a message from memory to the screen.

Use the Enter command to store the message into memory at offset 120H. Use the Null character (a byte with a value of zero) as a data trailer to mark the end of the message. For example:

```
E 120 'This is a test.', D, A, 0
```

Note: 0DH (13) and 0AH (10) are the ASCII codes for Carriage Return and Line Feed; 00H is the ASCII Null character, used as the data trailer.

Write a mainline procedure that uses a loop to retrieve the characters from memory and display them to the screen. The repetition should stop when the data trailer (Null character) is encountered; the trailer should not be displayed. Following is the logic for a possible solution to the problem:

```
Move the offset of the message into Msg_ptr (one of the word
                registers that may be used to address memory)
Repeat
    Move a byte from memory, using [Msg_ptr], into DL
    Increment Msg_ptr to the next character
Quit repeating when DL is 0
    Move 2 into AH (function code to display a character)
    Do a DOS function Call (INT 21H instruction)
End repeat
Return to DOS
```

Note: Do not try to use a Loop instruction to implement the repetition. Loop is useful only when repeating a sequence of instructions a fixed number of times. You should use a compare (CMP) and a Conditional jump to implement the loop exit (Quit repeating when DL is 0) as well as an Unconditional jump at the end of the loop (End repeat) to go back to the beginning of the loop.

Test your program (**Go** command with no break point) and make any necessary corrections. Save the program as PA5-4.COM. Make sure BX and CX are the correct values to save everything up to and including the data trailer, but no more. Then run the program from DOS to make sure that it is saved properly.

PA5-5 Using DEBUG, write a program that uses a subprocedure to display numeric values in binary to the screen.

Write the subprocedure, beginning at offset 120H, to display the numeric value in BX to the screen, in binary. The ASCII codes for the characters '0' and '1' are 30H and 31H, respectively. You may use the following logic for the subprocedure:

```
Save (push) any registers that will be modified
Repeat 16 times
    Shift BX left 1 (high bit into CF)
    If CF is set
        Move 31H into DL
    Else
        Move 30H into DL
    Endif
    Move 2 into AH (function code to display a character)
    Do a DOS Function Call (INT 21H instruction)
End repeat
Move 2 into AH (function code to display a character)
Move 42H ('B') into DL
Do DOS Function Call (INT 21H instruction)
Move 2 into AH
Move 0DH (CR) into DL
Do DOS Function Call
Move 2 into AH
```

```
Move 0AH (LF) into DL
Do DOS Function Call
Restore (pop) all registers that were saved
Return
```

Use LOOP to implement the repetition. Initialize CX to sixteen just before the beginning of the repetition (Repeat 16 times) and use a Loop instruction at the end (End repeat) to cause the loop to repeat.

Write the mainline procedure at offset 100H to use the subprocedure to display the values 14F3H, 25ABH, and 7CD8H in binary.

Use the Go command to test the program; verify that it displays the correct binary numerals and returns properly to DEBUG. Then save the program as PA5-5.COM, exit DEBUG, and run the program from DOS.

6

Using the
Macro Assembler

INTRODUCTION

Throughout the previous chapters, we have written all our assembly-language
programs using the Assemble command of DEBUG. We have done so because
DEBUG is relatively quick to learn and provides a simple tool for learning the ba-
sics of assembly language. It was also necessary that you become familiar with
DEBUG in order to use it to diagnose logic errors in later programs. However,
programming with DEBUG has some serious drawbacks; consequently, all future
programs will be written using a text editor, the macro assembler (MASM.EXE),
and the linker (LINK.EXE).

To understand the need for a more sophisticated assembler, recall that
DEBUG requires an address for all Immediate-mode Transfer-of-Control instructions. Any forward jump or call requires that the programmer estimate the target
address for the transfer instruction and then continue coding. Later, when the
correct address has been determined, the programmer must remember to go back
and correct the target address.

A second even more serious problem with programming in DEBUG is that
only the executable machine-language program may be saved to diskette (.COM
file). The source statements written by the programmer are discarded after assembly. This makes program maintenance virtually impossible. The executable
program contains no internal documentation (comments and/or remarks) to help
with future maintenance.

Also, since DEBUG discards the source program, maintenance requires the
disassembly of the executable program and then the assembly of any required

new instructions. If new instructions must be inserted into the program, or if a sequence of instructions must be replaced with a longer sequence, then the **Move** command must be used to move the rest of the program in order to provide room for the new instructions. However, Moving the rest of the program changes all subsequent addresses and therefore requires that all references to those addresses within the entire program must be altered.

A further disadvantage of DEBUG as a programming tool is that it can be used to create only .COM files, which are limited to a single segment. This means that programs created with DEBUG are limited to 64 kilobytes total length, cannot use Far Transfer-of-Control instructions, and cannot organize the data, stack, and code into separate segments. Thus, much of the power of the 8086/8088 processor is lost when programming with DEBUG. Using the macro assembler, we will create .EXE files, which are unlimited in length, allow us to separate the data, stack, and code, and allow for the use of Far Transfer-of-Control instructions.

Program development with the macro assembler is done in three stages, as illustrated in Figure 6-1. First a source file with an extension of .ASM is created using a text editor. Then the source file is **assembled** (translated into machine language) to create an object file with an extension of .OBJ. Finally, the object file is **linked** to create the executable program file with an extension of .EXE. Upon completion of this process, there are three versions to every program: the source file, the object file, and the executable file. When the program is run, the executable file (.EXE) is loaded by DOS and executed. Whenever the program requires modification, the programmer edits the source file and then reassembles it to create a new object file, which is then relinked to create the new executable program file.

In this chapter, we will discuss each of those three stages in detail. First we will discuss requirements of the source file, including the format of each source line, the use of symbolic names to simplify the addressing of both data and code and the use of a number of **directives** to provide the assembler with information about the manner in which to perform the assembly. Next, we will discuss the use of a text editor for the creation of the source file. Then, we will discuss the use of the assembler (MASM.EXE) to create the object version of the program. Finally, we will discuss the use of the linker (LINK.EXE) for the creation of the executable program file.

Figure 6-1   Program Development System Flowchart

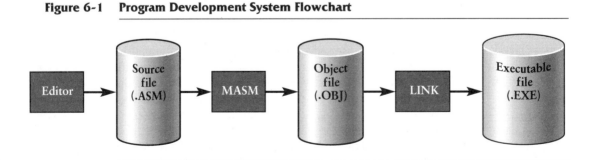

Although the processor's instruction set does not provide most of the structured-programming constructs taken for granted when working in high-level languages (Sequence, Iteration, Selection, and Case), it is very helpful to learn to think in terms of those constructs when designing the logic of a program. Consequently, we will discuss the implementation of the various forms of Iteration (repetition) in this chapter. Selection and Case will be discussed in the next chapter.

THE ASSEMBLER SOURCE FILE

An assembly-language source file is a text file with an extension of .ASM, which contains a sequence of assembly-language source lines. The primary filename is usually the same as the primary name desired for the executable program file. In addition to instructions that tell the processor what to do during program execution, the source file also contains directives or pseudo-ops that tell the assembler to take some action during assembly. The last line of every source file should contain an END directive to inform the assembler of the end of the file and to specify the entry point for the program, the address at which execution should begin.

Figure 6-2 illustrates a sample source file. We will refer back to this figure throughout the following discussion of the source line format and assembler directives. Note that the line numbers in the right-most columns are for reference only; they are not part of the source file.

SOURCE LINE FORMAT

Each line of assembly-language source code, whether an instruction or a directive, is made up of four fields: the **Name field**, the **Action field**, the **Expression field**, and the **Remark field**. The Name, Action, and Expression fields are separated by one or more <Space> and/or <Tab> characters; extra spaces and/or tabs are ignored by the assembler. The Remark field always begins with a semicolon (;) to separate it from the rest of the source line.

```
Name    Action Expression    ;Remark
```

Depending on the desired result, one or more source-line fields may be left blank. Although the assembler completely ignores the Remark field, good programming practice requires a Remark on virtually every source line. Otherwise, all fields are optional. Following is an explanation of the purpose and significance of each field.

Figure 6-2   Sample Source File
(Line numbers are for reference only)

```
              TITLE    PROGRAMMING ASSIGNMENT 6-1                    (1
              PAGE     55, 80                                        (2
                                                                    (3
COMMENT |     PROGRAM:      PA6-1.ASM                                (4
              PROGRAMMER:   Your name here                           (5
              DATE:         Date here                                (6
              CLASS:        Class name and number here               (7
              INSTRUCTOR:   Instructor's name here                   (8
                                                                    (9
         PROGRAM TO DISPLAY A MESSAGE TO THE SCREEN USING DOS        (10
         INTERRUPT 21H, FUNCTION 2 (DISPLAY CHARACTER IN DL)         (11
                                                                    (12
         INPUT PARAM'S:  NONE                                        (13
         OUTPUT PARAM'S: NONE                                        (14
                         RETURNS TO DOS, UPON COMPLETION             (15
         |                                                          (16
                                                                    (17
                                                                    (18
;STACK SEGMENT ===================================================== (19
                                                                    (20
STACK         SEGMENT PARA STACK 'STACK'       ;BEGIN STACK          (21
                                               ;   SEGMENT           (22
                                                                    (23
              DB      64 DUP ('*STACK* ')      ;DEFINE 512           (24
                                               ;   BYTE STACK        (25
                                                                    (26
STACK         ENDS                             ;END OF STACK SEGMENT (27
                                                                    (28
                                                                    (29
;DATA SEGMENT ====================================================== (30
                                                                    (31
DATA          SEGMENT PARA PUBLIC 'DATA'       ;BEGIN DATA           (32
                                               ;   SEGMENT           (33
                                                                    (34
         ;DEFINE A MESSAGE TERMINATED WITH A NUL-CHARACTER           (35
         ;   TRAILER (13 = CR, 10 = LF)                              (36
MY_MSG        DB      13, 10                                         (37
              DB      ' Hi there!', 13, 10, 10                       (38
              DB      'This is a test.', 13, 10, 0                   (39
                                                                    (40
DATA          ENDS                             ;END OF DATA SEGMENT  (41
                                                                    (42
                                                                    (43
;CODE SEGMENT ====================================================== (44
                                                                    (45
CODE          SEGMENT PARA PUBLIC 'CODE'       ;BEGIN CODE           (46
                                               ;   SEGMENT           (47
```

Figure 6-2   (continued)

```
                                                                     (48
              ASSUME  CS:CODE, SS:STACK                              (49
                                       ;ASSOCIATE CS AND SS          (50
                                       ;  WITH PROPER SGMENTS        (51
                                                                     (52
MAIN          PROC    FAR              ;BEGIN MAINLINE               (53
                                       ;  FAR PROCEDURE              (54
                                                                     (55
       ;INITIALIZATION (SAME FOR ALL PROGRAMS)                       (56
       ;FIRST, SET UP FOR RETURN TO DOS VIA PSP                      (57
              PUSH    DS               ;PUT RETURN SEG (PSP)         (58
                                       ;  TO STACK                   (59
              MOV     AX, 0            ;PUT ZERO RETURN              (60
              PUSH    AX               ;  OFFSET TO STACK            (61
       ;NOW, ADDRESS THE DATA SEGMENT WITH DS                        (62
              MOV     AX, DATA         ;POINT DS TO                  (63
              MOV     DS, AX           ;  DATA SEGMENT               (64
              ASSUME  DS:DATA          ;ASSOCIATE DS WITH            (65
                                       ;  DATA SEGMENT               (66
                                                                     (67
       ;BEGIN MAINLINE CODE                                          (68
       ;DISPLAY A MESSAGE                                            (69
              MOV     SI, OFFSET MY_MSG  ;POINT SI TO 1ST            (70
                                       ;  CHAR OF MESSAGE            (71
       ;USE A GENERAL LOOP TO DISPLAY THE MESSAGE                    (72
LP_BEG:       BEGIN GENERAL LOOP (QUIT WHEN DL EQ 0)                 (73
                  MOV   DL, [SI]       ;GET NEXT CHARACTER           (74
                  INC   SI             ;  OF DATA                    (75
              CMP     DL,0             ;EXIT LOOP WHEN               (76
              JE      LP_END           ;  CHAR IS TRAILER            (77
                  CALL    DSPLY_CHR    ;DISPLAY IT                   (78
                  JMP     LP_BEG       ;CONTINUE THE LOOP            (79
LP_END:       ;END OF LOOP                                           (80
                                                                     (81
       ;MAINLINE CODE ENDS HERE                                      (82
              RET                      ;FAR RETURN TO DOS VIA        (83
                                       ;  PSP                        (84
                                                                     (85
MAIN          ENDP                     ;END OF MAIN PROCEDURE        (86
                                                                     (87
;-------------------------------------------------------------------(88
;SUBPROCEDURE TO DISPLAY THE CHARACTER IN DL                         (89
                                                                     (90
DSPLY_CHR     PROC    NEAR             ;BEGIN NEAR PROCEDURE         (91
                                                                     (92
              PUSH    AX               ;SAVE MODIFIED REG            (93
              MOV     AH, 2            ;CODE TO DISPLAY A CHAR       (94
              INT     21H              ;DOS FUNCTION CALL            (95
              POP     AX               ;RESTORE IT                   (96
```

Figure 6-2   (continued)

				(97
	RET		;NEAR RETURN	(98
				(99
DSPLY_CHR	ENDP		;END OF PROCEDURE	(100
				(101
CODE	ENDS		;END OF CODE SEGMENT	(102
				(103
	END	MAIN	;END OF PA6-1.ASM	(104
			; ENTRY POINT = MAIN	(105

Name Field

The Name field, if present, is the first data in the source line. It begins in the first column of the source line and contains a symbolic name. The first character of a symbolic name must always be alphabetic, not numeric, in order to avoid confusion with a numeric constant. A name can be any length, but only the first thirty-one characters are significant. In practicality, you will not usually want to use more than ten to twelve characters for any name. Although the first character must be alphabetic, the remaining characters may be alphabetic and/or numeric. In Figure 6-2, the following lines all contain symbols in their Name fields: 21, 27, 32, 37, 41, 46, 53, 73, 80, 86, 91, 100, and 102.

Names are used for **Symbolic addressing**, to relieve the programmer of the need to code addresses within instructions. As the assembler assembles a source file, it counts the number of bytes used by each instruction or data definition and maintains a **Location counter** of the Offset address of the source line currently being assembled. Whenever it encounters a **symbol definition**, within the Name field of a source line, it assigns the current value of the Location counter to that symbol; thus, the symbol is assigned the offset, in memory, where the instruction or data resulting from the source line will be stored. Depending on the contents of the Action field, the name may also be assigned a **Type** (Near, Far, Byte, Word, etc.) by the assembler.

When the assembler encounters a **symbol reference** within the Expression field of a source line, it replaces the symbol with its offset (the offset of the source line in which the name was defined) and when appropriate its Type. Consequently, when using the assembler instead of DEBUG, we don't need to concern ourselves with real addresses. We address data and code symbolically by defining a symbolic name within the Name field of the source line to which we wish to refer. We may then refer to that source line by placing the same name in the Expression field of other source lines; the assembler determines the address of the defined symbolic name and replaces each name reference with that address.

Symbolic addressing makes initial programming easier by allowing the programmer to refer to addresses by name rather than by value; it also makes program maintenance much easier. Any removal, change, or addition of instructions within a source program necessarily changes the addresses of all subsequent instructions and/or data within the executable program. However, the programmer need not worry about the address changes, as would be necessary with DEBUG. When the source program is reassembled, the assembler calculates the new addresses for all symbols and automatically makes the appropriate replacements of the new addresses for all symbolic references.

There are many kinds of symbols, as determined by the Action field of the source line in which the symbol is defined: Variable names, Equated symbols, Segment names, Procedure names, Label names, Macro names, Record names, and Structure names. We will discuss Variables, Equates, Segments, Procedures, and Labels later in this chapter. Macros will be discussed in the next chapter. Structures will be discussed in chapter 12.

Action Field

The Action field of a source line follows the Name field and is separated from it by one or more <Space> and/or <Tab> characters. Although not required by the assembler, we recommend always beginning the Action field in the seventeenth column (two tabs from the left), except when indenting within a Selection, Case, or Iteration construct (refer to Figure 6-2). Lining up the Action fields and then indenting inside loops and selections makes the source program much easier to read and maintain. The Action field always contains either the opcode of a processor instruction or an assembler **directive** or **pseudo-op**.

It is important to understand the difference between instructions and directives. An instruction describes an action to be performed by the processor at execution time (when the program is executed, after assembly and linking); the assembler translates it into the appropriate machine-language instruction. A directive, on the other hand, does not result in a machine-language instruction; rather it specifies some action to be taken by the assembler at assembly time (while assembling the source program into machine language). While a directive does not, of itself, result in a machine-language instruction, it often does have an effect on the machine-language instructions that result from subsequent source instructions. Most of the 8086/8088 instruction set was discussed in the previous chapter; directives will be discussed more thoroughly later in this chapter.

KEY TERMS TO REMEMBER

Name field	Symbol definition
Action field	Symbol type
Expression field	Symbol reference
Remark field	Directive, pseudo-op
Symbolic addressing	

Expression Field

The Expression field follows the Action field, separated from it by one or more <Space> and/or <Tab> characters. We recommend a single tab between the Action and Expression fields. The Expression field may be empty or may contain one or more **operands**. If the Action field contains an instruction opcode, then the Expression field must contain the correct number of operands, separated by commas. Similarly, a directive in the Action field may require a specific number of operands within the Expression field. Since a directive specifies an action to be taken by the assembler while assembling the source, a directive operand must always represent a value that is known to the assembler at assembly time.

An operand within the Expression field may be a register name or may be composed of a combination of numeric constants, symbols, and **operators**. Any operators in an expression must be capable of evaluation at assembly time. Consequently, the values to be operated upon must be known to the assembler at assembly time. Assembler operators will be discussed later in this chapter.

Remark Field

The Remark field may begin in any column of the source line and is indicated to the assembler by a semicolon (;). All data in the source line following the semicolon is ignored by the assembler and is used by the programmer to provide **internal documentation** for the program. As a general rule, every line of source code should contain a Remark field, which explains the purpose of the instruction or directive. For readability, we suggest using the <Tab> key to line up all remarks in the same column, at about column 41 or 49.

It is important that you spend a great deal of time and thought in composing remarks. Even with good internal documentation, assembly language is very difficult to read and understand; without good remarks it is virtually impossible to maintain. In composing your remarks, try to explain not what the instruction does, but *why* it does it. Following is an example of some very *bad* internal documentation:

```
                MOV     AX, 0           ;MOVE ZERO INTO AX
                JCXZ    LOOP_END        ; JUMP TO LOOP_END IF CX
                                        ;  IS ZERO
LOOP_BEG:       ADD     AX, BX          ;ADD BX TO AX
                LOOP    LOOP_BEG        ;LOOP TO LOOP_BEG
LOOP_END:       MOV     BX, AX          ;MOVE AX INTO BX
```

The above remarks add nothing to the readability of the program; they simply restate the instructions. Following is the same code with *good* internal documentation. Notice that the remarks do not state what the instructions do; rather they explain the purpose of each instruction in terms of the solution to the problem.

```
;MULTIPLY CX TIMES BX, STORING THE PRODUCT BACK INTO BX
; USE REPEATED ADDITION TO ACCOMPLISH THE MULTIPLICATION
                MOV     AX, 0           ;START PRODUCT AT ZERO
                JCXZ    LOOP_END        ;DON'T EXECUTE LOOP IF
                                        ;  MULTIPLIER (CX)
                                        ;  IS ZERO
LOOP_BEG:       ;BEGIN LOOP CX TIMES
                   ADD     AX, BX  ; ADD THE MULTIPLICAND
                                        ;  TO THE PRODUCT
                LOOP    LOOP_BEG        ;REPEAT THE ADDITION, CX
                                        ;  (MULTIPLIER) TIMES
LOOP_END:       ;END LOOP CX TIMES
                MOV     BX, AX          ;STORE PRODUCT INTO BX
```

The worthlessness of the remarks in the first example above is so obvious that it may seem unnecessary and trivial to even discuss it here. Unfortunately, however, a great many assembly-language programs written by experienced programmers as well as beginners are full of just such inane and useless "documentation." It is important not only that you include a Remark field in each line of source code, but also that you ensure that each remark serves to *clarify* the code. As a general rule, you should put at least as much time and effort into composing good remarks as you spend determining the instructions and directives necessary for the problem solution.

TWO-PASS ASSEMBLY

At this point, we must discuss the manner in which the assembler determines the addresses of defined symbols. Consider the following statement at line 77 of Figure 6-2:

```
JE      LP_END
```

The instruction constitutes a forward transfer of control; LP_END is defined on a source line that occurs later in the program (line 80). Such a forward reference presents MASM with a problem similar to that faced by a programmer writing in DEBUG, without symbolic addressing: the address of LP_END is not yet known when the jump instruction is first encountered. How does the assembler know what target address to assemble in the jump instruction?

MASM is a **two-pass assembler;** it solves the problem of forward references by reading through the entire source file twice from start to end. During the first pass through the source, MASM does not attempt to generate machine-language instructions; it simply builds a table of the addresses of all symbols within the program. While it does not generate machine-language instructions during pass one, it does need to determine the length in bytes of the machine-language instruction that will eventually result from each source line.

For each source instruction, MASM determines the number of bytes that will be needed for the resulting machine-language instruction and adds that number to the Location counter in order to constantly keep track of the current Offset address. Every symbol defined in a Name field is then added to a **Symbol table** along with its Offset address (the current value of the Location counter) and its Type, determined by the Action field of the line on which it is defined. Upon completion of pass one, MASM has built a table containing all symbols defined within the program, the addresses at which they are defined, and their Types.

During pass two, MASM translates the source instructions into the appropriate machine-language instructions. As it does so, it replaces each reference to a symbol in an Expression field with the symbol's address from the Symbol table built in pass one and uses the symbol's Type to determine the type (Byte, Word, Near, Far, etc.) of the instruction. As it completes pass two, the assembler again maintains a Location counter in order to verify the addresses determined in pass one. Each time a symbol definition is encountered, the symbol's address from the Symbol table is compared with the current value of the Location counter.

Any difference between a symbol's address and the Location counter indicates that one or more previous instructions resulted in a machine-language instruction of a different length than that predicted during pass one; consequently, every previous reference to the symbol has been replaced with the incorrect address, resulting in incorrect object code. In such an instance, the assembler reports the error as "Phase error between passes." Never link an object file that has resulted in a Phase error; correct and reassemble the source file until no Phase error is generated before linking.

A Phase error is probably the most difficult of all assembler errors to debug; there are many causes for the error, and the source line at which the error is reported is never the line that actually caused the problem. To understand the error, keep in mind that it can occur only on a source line that contains a symbol definition in the Name field and that the line actually causing the error (the line that was interpreted differently during pass two than in pass one) occurs somewhere between the line at which the error is reported and the last preceding line containing a symbol definition in its Name field.

One method of identifying the offending source line is to edit the source file, entering symbols (such as TST1, TST2, TST3, etc.) on all source lines between the line at which the error was reported and the last line above it on which a symbol is already defined. Reassemble the source file and note the first line at which the error is now reported (it may also be reported on all subsequent lines with a Name field). The offending source line is the line *just previous to* the first line at which the Phase error is now reported.

The line causing a Phase error may also be identified without editing the source file, by using the assembler list file. Immediately reassemble the source file with the /D option and specifying a list file (See Creating an Object File—

MASM.EXE). The list file will then contain a listing for both pass one and pass two of the assembly. Compare the two pass listings, from the last previous symbol definition to the line at which the Phase error was reported, and find the source line that was interpreted differently between passes (pass one and pass two listings are different).

Once you have identified the offending line by either method, determine why it was interpreted differently in pass two than in pass one, correct it, and re-assemble the source file. Do not forget to remove any extra symbols that you may have inserted if you used the first method.

It should be understood that a two-pass assembler such as MASM does not entirely solve the problem of forward references; consider the CALL instruction at line 78 in Figure 6-2:

```
CALL    DSPLY_CHR
```

Its target, DSPLY_CHR, is defined as a Procedure name later in the program at line 91 (the PROC and ENDP directives are fully discussed later in this chapter). When the above instruction is encountered during pass one, MASM must determine the length in bytes of its resulting machine-language instruction. However, since DSPLY_CHR is a forward reference, its type (Near or Far) is not yet known. Consequently MASM does not know if the instruction should result in a Near call (a three-byte instruction) or a Far call (a five-byte instruction).

In such a case, the assembler assumes on pass one that it is a Near procedure and so adds three bytes to the Location counter. In our example, this is correct; DSPLY_CHR is later defined (at line 91) as a Near procedure. Had DSPLY_CHR been defined as a Far procedure, however, then MASM's three-byte guess would turn out to be wrong, and it would report the error, "Forward needs override or far." We would have to resolve the problem by using the PTR operator, discussed later in this chapter, to inform the assembler of the Far type of the procedure.

In order to resolve the problem of unknown Types of forward references, some assemblers (but not MASM) make three passes through the source file. During pass one, such a three-pass assembler merely determines the Type of each symbol. Addresses of all symbols are then determined during pass two, and machine-language instructions are generated during the third pass.

KEY TERMS TO REMEMBER

Operand	Two-pass assembler
Operator	Location counter
Internal documentation	Symbol table

NEAR CODE LABELS

Near Labels are normally defined within a code segment and are used for the symbolic specification of the target addresses of Transfer-of-Control instructions. Lines 73 and 80 of figure 6-2 contain Near Label definitions; lines 77 and 79 contain references to those Near Labels. The syntax to define a Near Label is as follows:

```
symbol:          [instruction or directive]
```

Notice that *symbol* must always be followed immediately by a colon (:) in the Near Label definition. The colon is not a part of the Label name; it simply tells the assembler that the symbol is a Near Label as opposed to any other kind of symbol. The Action and Expression fields of the line on which *symbol* is defined may contain an instruction (or, rarely, a directive), may be left blank, or may contain only a remark as in Figure 6-2.

Symbol is defined to the assembler as a Code Label with a Type of Near, and an offset equal to the current value of the Location counter. Any reference to *symbol* within an Expression field results in a Near transfer of control, and *symbol* is replaced with its offset. Consequently, any reference to a Near Label always constitutes an Immediate-mode jump, call, or loop.

Figure 6-2, lines 73 through 80, provides an example of the use of labels in a block of code to implement a General-loop construct:

```
LP_BEG:          ;BEGIN GENERAL LOOP TO DISPLAY THE MESSAGE
                 MOV      DL, [SI]   ;GET NEXT CHARACTER
                 INC      SI         ;  OF DATA
                 CMP      DL, 0      ;EXIT LOOP WHEN
                 JE       LP_END     ; CHAR IS TRAILER
                 CALL     DSPLY_CHR  ;DISPLAY IT
                 JMP      LP_BEG     ;CONTINUE THE LOOP
LP_END:          ;END OF LOOP
```

Note that the source code does not contain any real addresses; the two jump instructions use Near Label references to specify the target addresses. When the program in Figure 6-2 is assembled, the above block of code assembles as follows:

```
     Seg:Off     Instruction

xxxx:000D     MOV    DL, [SI]
xxxx:000F     INC    SI
xxxx:0010     CMP    DL, 0
xxxx:0013     JE     001A
xxxx:0015     CALL   001B
xxxx:0018     JMP    000D
xxxx:001A     ......
```

Note that each Label reference within the source code is automatically replaced by its offset, as an immediate value, during assembly. In the resulting machine-language instructions, the correct jump displacements are calculated by the assembler from the offsets of the Labels. Were we to find it necessary to modify the code, we would simply add, change, or delete instructions as necessary within the source file and reassemble. The assembler would calculate the new offsets of all Labels and automatically use those offsets as the targets of the jump instructions.

NUMERIC CONSTANTS

By default, MASM interprets all numeric constants as decimal numerals. 13 and 10 in lines 37 through 39 of Figure 6-2 are interpreted as decimal numerals, thirteen and ten. The base or radix of all numerals is assumed to be decimal or base ten. Thus, the following instruction is assembled to a machine-language instruction that moves one hundred into AL:

```
        MOV     AL,  100
```

Note that this is different from DEBUG. DEBUG would interpret 100 in the above instruction as a hexadecimal numeral, and so would assemble it to move **256** into AL. Although the assembler's default is to interpret numeric constants as decimal numerals, values may also be expressed in other numeral bases by appending a single-letter suffix, specifying the base of the numeral.

The base specifiers allowed by the assembler are **B** for a binary or base-two numeral, **O** or **Q** for an octal or base-eight numeral, **D** for a decimal numeral, and **H** for a hexadecimal or base-sixteen numeral. D (decimal) is necessary because the assembler provides a directive (see the .RADIX directive, later in this chapter) for changing the default numeral base to something other than decimal. The following instructions all result in exactly the same machine-language instruction, which moves the binary value, 01100100, into AL:

```
        MOV     AL,  100
        MOV     AL,  100D
        MOV     AL,  01100100B
        MOV     AL,  144Q
        MOV     AL,  64H
```

This flexibility in the specification of numeric constants leads to the possibility of misinterpretation by the assembler. Suppose we wish to move ten into AL, but we wish to use hexadecimal representation for the numeric constant, ten. We might code the following instruction, intending AH as the hexadecimal numeral for ten:

```
        MOV     AL,  AH
```

Although we intended AH to represent a hexadecimal numeral for the Immediate value ten, it would be interpreted by the assembler as Register-mode addressing and would be assembled as the instruction to move the contents of the AH register into AL. Further confusion is possible; consider the following instruction, which is intended to move the hexadecimal value F23 into the register BX:

```
MOV     BX,  F23H
```

F23H is valid as a symbol reference and would be interpreted as such by the assembler, probably resulting in an error since F23H has most likely not been defined as a symbol. To avoid any such confusion, all numeric constants must begin with a decimal digit from 0 through 9. Anything that begins with a digit from 0 through 9 is interpreted by the assembler as a numeric constant. Thus, to ensure interpretation as numeric constants, the two above instructions should be coded as follows:

```
MOV     AL,  0AH
```

and

```
MOV     BX,  0F23H
```

ASSEMBLER DIRECTIVES

As mentioned earlier, the Action and Expression fields of a source line may contain either an 8086/8088 instruction or an assembler directive. Also recall that a directive, often called a pseudo-op, describes some action to be taken by the assembler at assembly time while the source is being assembled. Following is a brief discussion of some of the more commonly used directives. Other directives will be discussed as needed later in the text.

Directives can be grouped into six major categories: Listing directives, Data directives, Memory directives, Macro directives, Conditional directives, and Other directives, which do not fit nicely into any other category. Macro directives and Conditional directives will be discussed in the next chapter.

Listing Directives

As we shall see later, MASM may be requested to create a special list file during assembly. The list file, if created, contains a listing of all source lines together with the resulting machine-language instructions and offsets. Listing directives affect the format of that list file, if requested; they never affect the resulting executable program. The three most often used Listing directives are **PAGE**, **TITLE**, and **SUBTTL**.

PAGE is used to tell the assembler the number of lines per page and the number of characters per line for the list file. The default, if no page length or line length is specified, is fifty-eight lines per page and eighty characters per line. The general syntax for the PAGE directive is as follows:

```
PAGE    [length, width]
```

The optional *length* and *width* parameters specify the number of lines per page and the number of characters per line for the list file. Line 2 of Figure 6-2 tells the assembler to list fifty-five lines per page with eighty characters per line:

```
PAGE    55, 80
```

If any list file line exceeds eighty characters, MASM will insert a <CR> + <LF> to cause a wraparound to the next line. After fifty-five lines on any page, the assembler inserts a Form-Feed (<FF>) character, causing the printer to eject and go to a new page during printing of the list file. PAGE may also be used without parameters to force a new page within the list file. The following source line causes MASM to insert a <FF> character at the current position within the list file.

```
PAGE
```

MASM always inserts a line at the top of each page of the list file with the system date and the name and version number of the assembler. Two other Listing directives, TITLE and SUBTTL, may be used to cause the assembler to insert one or two additional lines at the top of every page.

TITLE may be used only once in a source file to specify a title to be printed on the second line of each page of the listing. The syntax for the TITLE directive is as follows:

```
TITLE listing title
```

Listing title may be any combination of characters and is printed on the second line of all subsequent list file pages. Line 1 of Figure 6-2 directs the assembler to print "PROGRAMMING ASSIGNMENT 6-1" at the top of each listing page:

```
TITLE PROGRAMMING ASSIGNMENT 6-1
```

SUBTTL may be used as many times as desired to specify a subtitle to be printed on the third line of each subsequent page of the listing. The syntax for SUBTTL is as follows:

```
SUBTTL [listing subtitle]
```

The optional *listing subtitle* is printed on the third line of all subsequent list file pages. The following source line directs MASM to print the subtitle "CODE SEGMENT" on the third line of each subsequent list file page:

```
SUBTTL CODE SEGMENT
```

A SUBTTL directive alone, with nothing in the expression field, cancels any previous SUBTTL directives and causes the assembler to print no subtitles on subsequent pages:

```
SUBTTL
```

Data Directives and Variables

Data directives are used to define one or more memory locations, usually within the data segment and/or stack segment, to be used for the storage of data. Each allows for the definition of a **variable name** by which to symbolically refer to the data stored in the memory location. Data directives also permit the specification of **initial values**, values to be initially stored in the memory location(s) when the program is first loaded for execution.

Lines 37 through 39 of Figure 6-2 use the DB Data directive to define data within the program; line 37 also defines the variable MY_MSG. The general syntax for defining data is as follows:

```
[symbol]      Dx      list-of-values
```

Symbol is an optional variable name by which to symbolically refer to the data elsewhere within the program. If specified, any later reference to *symbol* within the expression field of a source line results in a direct-memory addressing operand ([offset]) with the Type determined by *x*.

List-of-values is a list of one or more values, of the appropriate type, separated by commas (,), to be initially stored in the defined memory. Note that the values will be contained in the defined memory locations within the executable program file. Thus, the values represent initial values for the variables when the program is loaded for execution; as the program executes, it may modify any variable by moving data into it, in which case the initial value is lost.

Five Define-data directives are provided: **DB, DW, DD, DQ,** and **DT.** DB defines one or more bytes of data and assigns a Type of Byte to the Variable, *symbol*, if present; DW defines one or more words of data and results in a Word Type for any variable in the Name field; DD defines a **double-word** (four bytes) and results in a Type of Dword; DQ defines a **quad-word** (four words, eight bytes) and results in a Type of Qword. DT defines ten bytes (used for packed binary-coded-decimal storage) and results in a Type of Tbyte. The following directive, within the data segment, would define one byte of data with an initial value of 255 (FFH):

```
MY_BYTE      DB      255
```

The above directive also defines MY_BYTE as a variable whose Type is Byte. Any later reference to MY_BYTE results in a direct-memory addressing of the defined byte of data. For example, the following two instructions might be used, within the code segment, to address the byte of defined data:

```
MOV     AL, MY_BYTE
MOV     MY_BYTE, 0
```

Each reference to the variable MY_BYTE results in a Byte move with direct-memory addressing. Thus, the two instructions would be assembled as follows where *offset* is the offset, from the beginning of the data segment, at which the DB directive occurs (the value in the Location counter):

```
MOV     AL, BYTE PTR [offset]
MOV     BYTE PTR [offset], 00
```

Notice that in each instruction *offset* is enclosed within brackets and so constitutes direct-memory addressing, not Immediate mode. Consequently, the first instruction would result in the copying of the value 255 from the memory location into AL; it would not move *offset* into AL. The second instruction would store a value of zero into MY_BYTE, thus replacing its initial value of 255.

As another example, the following directive defines seven bytes of data, with the initial values 65, 66, 67, 68, 13, 10, and 0 (41H, 42H, 43H, 44H, 0DH, 0AH, and 00H); the variable MSG_1 is defined as direct-memory addressing to the first byte of data (65), with a Type of Byte:

```
MSG_1        DB     65, 66, 67, 68, 13, 10, 0
```

The following seven directives are exactly equivalent to the above single directive; they produce exactly the same number of bytes of data and define the Variable, MSG_1, as the same offset and Type:

```
MSG_1        DB     65
             DB     66
             DB     67
             DB     68
             DB     13
             DB     10
             DB     0
```

DB also allows a string, within single or double quotes, for any of the values within the list. For each character within the string, the assembler defines one byte initialized to the ASCII code for the character. The ASCII code will be discussed more fully in chapter 8; for now, the ASCII code for A is 65, the code for B is 66, etc. Consequently, the following directive is exactly equivalent to the above directives; it results in the same seven bytes of data and the same offset and Type for the variable MSG_1:

```
MSG_1        DB     'ABCD', 13, 10, 0
```

A PAUSE IN THE ACTION

Significance of Data Directives

Data directives are somewhat analogous to the variable declarations required by such languages as C, Pascal, or FORTRAN or to the statements within the data division of a COBOL program. They cause the assembler to allocate memory for the storage of data and also provide a means of symbolically addressing the data storage by name rather than by address.

Unlike high-level language variable declarations, Data directives specify only the size of a variable and not the type of data to be stored there. Managing the data type (character, integer, or real, for example) is entirely the programmer's responsibility.

Note that any initial values specified with a Data directive behave like a COBOL value clause or like a C static variable; they do not behave like the initial values of an auto variable in C. That is to say the variables will contain the initial values immediately upon execution of the program but will not be automatically reinitialized during execution of the program. If any variable must be reinitialized upon reentry to a block of code, then it must be explicitly reinitialized with a MOV instruction at the beginning of the block of code.

The following Define-word directive defines two words (four bytes) of data; it also defines MY_WORD as a variable with the Type of Word:

```
MY_WORD        DW      255, 256
```

Recall that whenever a word value is stored in memory, the low (least significant) byte is stored first, followed by the high (most-significant) byte. Consequently, the above directive results in the definition of four bytes of memory initialized to the following four byte values:

```
FFH 00H 00H 01H
```

The above directive also defines the variable MY_WORD as direct-memory addressing to the offset of the first word (255, 00FFH), with a Type of Word. For example, the following two instructions might be coded within the code segment:

```
MOV     MY_WORD, 1
MOV     MY_WORD + 2, 2
```

Those instructions would assemble as follows, where *offset* is the offset of MY_WORD within the data segment, and *offset +2* is two greater than *offset*:

```
MOV     WORD PTR [offset], 1
MOV     WORD PTR [offset +2], 2
```

The first instruction moves the new value, 1, into the first word of MY_WORD, replacing its initial value of 255. The second instruction moves 2 into the second word, which had an initial value of 256.

DW also allows a two-byte string as a value. The ASCII value of the first character is the initial value for the high byte; the ASCII code of the second character is the initial value of the low byte of the word. Since the low byte of a word is always stored before the high byte, the two characters are reversed in memory. For example, the following two directives produce the same initial values for four bytes of memory.

```
DW      'AB', 'CD'
DB      'B', 'A', 'D', 'C'
```

DD defines a double-word (four bytes) of data. The low word is stored first in memory, followed by the high word. Since each word is stored with the low byte first, followed by the high byte, the result is that the lowest of the four bytes is stored first, followed by the next-to-lowest, followed by the next-to-highest, followed by the highest byte. For example, the following DD and DB directives produce the same initial values in memory:

```
DD      12345678H
DB      78H, 56H, 34H, 12H
```

DQ defines a quad-word (four words, eight bytes) of data. Again, the lowest-order byte is stored first, followed by the other seven bytes in ascending order; the eighth byte is the most significant byte. The following two directives produce the same eight bytes of initial memory values:

```
DQ      123456789ABCDEF0H
DB      0F0H, 0DEH, 0BCH, 9AH, 78H, 56H, 34H, 12H
```

Any value in the list of values for any of the above Define-data directives may be replaced with a question mark (?) to indicate that the memory does not need to be initialized, that its initial value is unimportant to the program. In such a case, the assembler initializes the memory to zero. For example, the following two instructions result in identical object code, one byte of memory containing an initial value of zero:

```
DB      0
DB      ?
```

Although the assembler does not distinguish between a value of zero and an uninitialized value (?), you should use whichever is appropriate to the problem in order to improve the readability of the program. For example, if a byte of memory is to be used as a counter and must contain an initial value of zero in order for the program to work properly, then it should be defined as follows with an initial value of zero.

```
MY_COUNT        DB      0
```

Defining MY_COUNT with an initial value of 0 rather than ? makes it clear to the next programmer that the program function depends on that initial value. On the other hand, if an instruction within the program moves zero into MY_COUNT, then its initial value upon loading of the program is not important; the program instruction initializes it. In that case, the data should be defined as follows in order to inform the next programmer that the program does not depend on an initial value of zero in MY_COUNT:

```
MY_COUNT        DB      ?
```

All Define-data directives allow the use of the **DUP** operator to repeat the definition of a value or list of values. The syntax for the DUP operator is as follows:

```
[symbol]        Dx      count DUP (list-of-values)
```

Dx may be any of the above Define-data directives. *Count* specifies the number of times to define the *list-of-values* within the required parentheses. As an example, the following two directives result in exactly the same object code: eight words of memory, with each word initialized to a value of five.

```
MY_VAR          DW      8 DUP (5)
MY_VAR          DW      5, 5, 5, 5, 5, 5, 5, 5
```

Also, since DUP allows the repetition of a list of values, the following two directives produce exactly the same results: twelve bytes of memory with initial values of 0, 1, and 2, repeated four times.

```
MY_LIST         DB      4 DUP (0, 1, 2)
MY_LIST         DB      0, 1, 2, 0, 1, 2, 0, 1, 2, 0, 1, 2
```

Similarly, since DB allows a string inside single quotes to specify the values, the following three directives all result in exactly the same object code: fifteen bytes of memory, with the ASCII values of T, E, S, T, and " " (space) repeated three times.

```
MY_STRING       DB      3 DUP ('TEST ')
MY_STRING       DB      'TEST ', 'TEST ', 'TEST '
MY_STRING       DB      'TEST TEST TEST '
```

Although the DUP operator produces the same results as a list of values for initialized variables, it produces rather different results for uninitialized variables. For example, the following two directives do not produce the same results:

```
                DB      ?, ?, ?, ?, ?
                DB      5 DUP (?)
```

As discussed earlier, the first directive results in five bytes of memory each with an initial value of zero. The second directive also produces five bytes of memory; however, the five bytes resulting from the second directive are truly uninitialized. The assembler does not set aside five bytes initialized to zero; instead, it simply directs the linker to skip over five bytes. Consequently, the initial values of the five bytes are undefined and may be anything from zero through 255.

Memory Directives

Memory directives are used to inform the assembler of the manner in which memory is to be used within the program. They may be used to organize the memory into segments and, within a code segment, into procedures. **SEGMENT** and **ENDS** designate the beginning and end of program segments. **PROC** and **ENDP** designate the beginning and end of procedures within a code segment. **AS-SUME** informs the assembler of the usage of segments, and **LABEL** allows the definition of Far Labels within a procedure.

SEGMENT and ENDS Directives. The SEGMENT directive is used to indicate the beginning of a segment. In Figure 6-2, lines 21, 32, and 46 provide examples of the SEGMENT directive. Its syntax is as follows:

```
Segname      SEGMENT [align] [combine] ['class']
```

Segname is required and defines the name of the segment. Although *segname* may be any valid symbol, it is a good practice to use symbols that suggest the usage of the segment, such as CODE, DATA, STACK or STAK, MAIN_CODE, SUB_CODE, INIT_DATA, COMMON_DATA, etc. The assembler replaces any later reference to *segname* with an Immediate-mode value of one-sixteenth the absolute address at which the segment begins. Thus, *segname* automatically refers to the segment half of the addresses of all variables or labels defined within the segment. Lines 63 and 64 of Figure 6-2 move the Segment address of DATA into AX and then into DS:

```
MOV     AX, DATA        ;POINT DS TO
MOV     DS, AX          ; DATA SEGMENT
```

Note that two moves are required because DATA evaluates as an Immediate-mode segment address. Recall that MOV allows a Segment register as one operand, but requires that the other operand not be Immediate mode or another Segment register. Consequently the single instruction that we would like to use, "MOV DS, DATA", is invalid.

The same Segment-name symbol may be used for multiple Segment directives. If two or more segments are given the same Segment name, the assembler may combine the segments into one, depending on the *combine* type. Multiple segments of the same name must all have the same *align* type, *combine* type, and '*class*'.

Align, *combine*, and '*class*' are all optional and instruct the assembler and linker as to the manner in which segments should be organized in memory. *Align* is the desired alignment type of the segment. It provides the assembler with information about the type of address on which to begin the segment. Five alignment types are permitted: **BYTE, WORD, DWORD, PARA,** and **PAGE.**

A BYTE alignment causes the segment to begin at the very next available absolute memory address. An alignment type of WORD causes the segment to begin on a word boundary, an even absolute memory address. If the next available memory address is odd, the assembler will skip over that memory address and begin the segment on the next (even) address. DWORD instructs MASM to begin the segment on a double-word boundary. Up to three bytes of memory will be skipped over in order to begin the segment at an address that is a multiple of four. PARA begins the segment on a paragraph boundary. A paragraph is sixteen bytes; thus MASM will skip over up to fifteen bytes in order to begin the segment on an absolute address that is a multiple of sixteen. PAGE begins the segment at the next available page (256 bytes). Up to 255 bytes of memory may be skipped over in order to begin the segment on an absolute address that is a multiple of 256.

If *align* is specified for a segment of the same *segname* as a previously defined segment, then it must be the same as the alignment type of the previously defined segment of the same Segment name. If *align* is omitted, it defaults to the alignment type of any previously defined segment of the same Segment name. If *align* is omitted and no segment of the same *segname* has been previously defined, then the alignment defaults to PARA.

Because of the manner in which absolute addresses are specified by the 8086/8088 processor (sixteen times a segment-register value plus an offset), all segments must begin on a paragraph (or page) boundary; the absolute address must be divisible by sixteen. Whenever several segments are to be combined, the first segment must always begin on a paragraph boundary. Subsequent segments to be combined with the first segment may begin on any boundary for the 8088 processor. For maximum efficiency during execution by a sixteen-bit (8086, 80186, or 80286) processor, subsequent segments should be aligned on word boundaries; segments that are to use the thirty-two bit capability of the 80386 processor are more efficient if aligned on a double-word boundary.

Combine specifies a combine type, instructing the assembler as to the manner in which to combine segments with the same Segment name. The allowed combine types are **PUBLIC, STACK, COMMON, MEMORY,** and **AT segaddress.** COMMON and AT combine types will be discussed in chapter 8.

A combine type of PUBLIC (lines 32 and 46 of Figure 6-2) causes the segment to be combined with all other segments of the same Segment name. All offsets within all PUBLIC segments of the same *segname* are calculated relative to the beginning of the first segment. In essence, the multiple PUBLIC segments, with the same Segment name, are treated by the assembler as consecutive parts of one segment. The length of the resulting segment is equal to the sum of the lengths of all the combined segments.

Consequently, it is possible to define a segment in sections, ending each section of the segment with ENDS, beginning each new section with the same *segname* as used previously, and giving all sections a PUBLIC combine type. In such a case, it is important to remember that, although the program contains multiple SEGMENT and ENDS directives for the same *segname*, only one segment has been defined.

If the program is to be linked with LINK.EXE, then MEMORY combine type is identical to PUBLIC; the two combine types are interchangeable. MEMORY combine type is provided in order to allow the use of other linkers that support the Intel definition of MEMORY combine type.

STACK combine type (line 21 of Figure 6-2) is similar to PUBLIC in that it also causes all segments of the same *segname* to be combined into one segment. However, a combine type of STACK also causes DOS to initialize the Stack-Segment and Stack-Pointer registers to that segment whenever the resulting executable program is loaded for execution. DOS initializes SS to one-sixteenth the absolute address at which the segment is loaded; DOS also initializes SP to the length of the segment ("bottom" of the stack). A program should have only one segment of STACK combine type; however, that single segment may be defined, if desired, with multiple SEGMENT and ENDS directives with the same Segment name. It is also possible to create a stack segment without using the STACK combine type. If this is done, however, DOS will not automatically initialize SS and SP; the program must contain instructions to initialize both SS and SP prior to any instructions that make use of the stack.

If multiple segments of the same Segment name are defined, they must all be given the same combine type. If *combine* is omitted and another segment of the same *segname* has been previously defined, then the combine type is the same as that of the previously defined segment. If *combine* is omitted and no other segment of the same *segname* has been previously defined, then the segment is **private**; private segments of the same *segname* are not combined. Each private segment is independent of the others; offsets within each segment are calculated relative to the beginning of that individual segment.

'Class' provides a class name, which controls the order in which segments are to be organized within the executable program. The class name must always be enclosed in single quotation marks ('). It may be any combination of alphanumeric characters; however, the assembler expects a class of 'CODE' or a class name that ends with 'CODE' ('A_CODE', for example) for any segment containing processor instructions. Good programming practice dictates the use of 'CODE', 'DATA', and 'STACK' (or 'STAK') for the appropriate class names.

Segments with the same class are loaded contiguously, one after another, even if the Segment names are different and regardless of their placement within the source program. However, unless the Segment names are the same, they are not combined into one segment. They are arranged contiguously, but offsets within each segment are still calculated relative to the beginning of that segment, independent of the other segments.

If multiple segments of the same *segname* are defined, then they all must have the same class name. If *'class'* is omitted, then a segment is given the null class name (same as '') unless a segment of the same *segname* has been previously defined, in which case the class will be the same as the class of the previously defined segment. All segments with a null class name are loaded contiguously.

M O S T   C O M M O N L Y   U S E D   Segment Directives

It is important to understand all the many possibilities for segment names, alignments, combine types, and classes. However, most mainline programs use only three segment directives for the definition of the code, data, and stack segments:

```
STACK      SEGMENT PARA STACK 'STACK'
DATA       SEGMENT PARA PUBLIC 'DATA'
CODE       SEGMENT PARA PUBLIC 'CODE'
```

ENDS is used to designate the end of a segment, which was begun with the SEGMENT directive. ENDS is used in Figure 6-2 at lines 27, 41, and 102. Its syntax is as follows:

```
segname        ENDS
```

Segname is the Segment name defined by the SEGMENT directive. ENDS does not automatically end the last segment opened with a Segment directive; it attempts to end the segment whose name is *segname*. Segments may be nested, one inside the other within the source file. However, they must be fully nested; they cannot overlap. For example, the following "nesting" of segments is not allowed since DATA is not entirely enclosed within CODE; an illegal overlapping of segments has been attempted.

```
CODE            SEGMENT
        .
        .
        .
DATA            SEGMENT
        .
        .
        .
CODE            ENDS
        .
        .
        .
DATA            ENDS
```

However, the following nesting is perfectly legal since it results in DATA being entirely enclosed within CODE:

```
CODE            SEGMENT
       .
       .
       .
DATA            SEGMENT
       .
       .
       .
DATA            ENDS
       .
       .
       .
CODE            ENDS
```

It should be understood that the nesting of segments is for programming convenience only; the segments are not nested within the resulting executable file. All instructions and/or directives within the inner segment are moved by the assembler outside the outer segment, arranged with any other segments of the same class, and combined with any other PUBLIC segments of the same *segname*.

ASSUME Directive. The ASSUME directive (lines 49 and 65 of Figure 6-2) is used to inform the assembler of the use of segments and of the manner in which to associate Segment registers with segments. The syntax is as follows:

```
ASSUME segreg:segname[,segreg:segname[, ... ]]
```

Segreg is the name of a Segment register: CS, DS, SS, or ES. *Segname* is the Segment name with which to associate the Segment register. Subsequent instructions, in which the processor assumes a Segment register for the referencing of data, are assembled with Segment overrides if necessary in order to cause the processor to use the correct Segment register. In essence, the ASSUME directive informs the assembler of the segment to which each Segment register will point during program execution; it is the programmer's responsibility to ensure that a Segment register really does address the segment with which it has been associated.

If desired, separate ASSUME directives may be used for each Segment register, or two or more Segment registers may be associated in one directive. A program may contain as many ASSUME directives as desired. The association of a Segment register with a segment may be changed as many times as desired with subsequent ASSUME directives; for proper program execution, a Segment register's segment association must be changed only when the value stored in the Segment register will have been changed by program instructions at execution time.

Any attempt to define a Near Label, when the CS register is not currently associated with the segment within which the Label is defined, results in the assembler error, "No or unreachable CS." To correct the error, edit the source to include an ASSUME directive associating CS with the segment, then reassemble.

If any data instruction references a variable that is defined within a segment that is associated with any Segment register other than DS (or SS, if the BP register is used for data addressing), then the assembler inserts a Segment override to cause the processor to use the correct Segment register. If an instruction references a variable within a segment that is not currently associated with any Segment register, then the assembler reports the severe error, "Can't reach with segment reg." In any such case, examine your code carefully to determine the Segment register that currently addresses the segment within which the variable is defined; then enter an ASSUME directive to associate that Segment register with the segment. As an example of the results of segment associations, consider the following:

```
SEG_1          SEGMENT
VBL_1          DB      ?
SEG_1          ENDS

SEG_2          SEGMENT
VBL_2          DB      ?
SEG_2          ENDS

SEG_3          SEGMENT
VBL_3          DB      ?
SEG_3          ENDS

SEG_4          SEGMENT
VBL_4          DB      ?
SEG_4          ENDS

               .
               .
               .

               ASSUME  SS:SEG_1, DS:SEG_2, ES:SEG_3

               MOV     VBL_1, AL
               MOV     VBL_2, AL
               MOV     VBL_3, AL

               MOV     [BP + VBL_1], AL
               MOV     [BP + VBL_2], AL
```

Without Segment overrides, the processor would automatically assume DS as the segment half of the destination memory address in each of the first three MOV instructions. Since VBL_2 is within the segment associated with DS, no override is necessary for the second MOV instruction. However, VBL_1 is within SEG_1, which is associated with SS, and VBL_3 is within a segment associated with **ES**; consequently, Segment overrides are necessary in order for the processor to use the correct Segment registers for the first and third instructions. The assembler automatically inserts the necessary Segment-override prefixes and assembles the first three MOV instructions as follows:

```
SS:
MOV     [0000], AL
MOV     [0000], AL
ES:
MOV     [0000], AL
```

Since the Base-Pointer register is used for addressing memory in each of the last two instructions, the processor (at execution time) would automatically assume **SS** as the Segment register in each instruction. The assembler, therefore, inserts a Segment override for any data that is not within the segment associated with SS. The fourth and fifth instructions are therefore assembled as follows:

```
MOV     [BP+0000], AL
DS:
MOV     [BP+0000], AL
```

Occasionally, it is necessary to change the Segment register associations within a program. Suppose that our program continued with the following instructions and directive:

```
PUSH    DS                      ;SWAP DS AND ES
PUSH    ES                      ;   (NOW DS POINTS
POP     DS                      ;    TO SEG_3;
POP     ES                      ;    ES TO SEG_2)

ASSUME DS:SEG_3, ES:SEG_2       ;REASSOCIATE DS & ES
MOV     VBL_2, AL
MOV     VBL_3, AL
```

During program execution, the PUSH and POP instructions will change the values in DS and ES. DS will now contain the Segment address for SEG_3 and ES will address SEG_2. In order to ensure proper data addressing in subsequent instructions, it is therefore necessary to use another ASSUME directive to inform the processor of the change in DS and ES, to reassociate DS and ES. As a result, the two MOV instructions are assembled as follows with the necessary Segment override for the first instruction, which addresses data within the segment now associated with ES:

```
ES:
MOV     [0000], AL
MOV     [0000], AL
```

It is crucial that any instructions that modify Segment registers be carefully coordinated with ASSUME directives, in order to ensure that each Segment register is always associated with the segment it currently addresses. In practice, most programs do not modify Segment registers once they have been initialized; consequently, most programs need only establish the Segment register associations once within the program. We will discuss the initialization of Segment registers later in this chapter.

As a final example of the effects of the ASSUME directive, consider the following instruction, which might be coded after the last instruction in our example above:

```
MOV    VBL_4, AL
```

VBL_4 is defined within SEG_4, which has not been associated with any Segment register. The assembler is unable to ensure correct data addressing by the processor. Consequently, the severe error "Can't reach with segment reg" is reported and the object file must not be linked.

A PAUSE IN THE ACTION

Most Common Use of ASSUME

Although the ASSUME directive should be used to reassociate any Segment register that is altered by the program, most programs contain only two such directives. The first is normally placed at the beginning of the code segment, as in line 49 of Figure 6-2, in order to associate CS and SS, which are automatically initialized by DOS:

```
ASSUME    CS:CODE, SS:STACK
```

The second ASSUME occurs immediately after the program initializes DS to point to the DATA segment, as in lines 63 through 65 of Figure 6-2:

```
MOV       AX, DATA
MOV       DS, AX
ASSUME    DS:DATA
```

PROC and ENDP Directives. PROC and ENDP (end procedure) are used to designate the beginning and end of procedures within a code segment and to provide the assembler with information about those procedures. The PROC directive is used in lines 53 and 91 of Figure 6-2. Its syntax is as follows:

```
name          PROC    [type]
```

Name is the name of the procedure. Its address is determined by the current value of the Location counter. Any future reference to *name*, as in "CALL *name*", is replaced by the assembler with the immediate-value offset (and segment, if it is a Far procedure) of the symbol, *name*.

Type may be either NEAR or FAR. Any CALL to the procedure, from anywhere within the source program, is automatically assembled as a Near or Far call instruction, depending on the *type* of the procedure. Any return within the procedure is automatically assembled as a Near or Far return as determined by *type*. Thus, the programmer usually need not directly specify the types of calls and returns; the assembler determines the type from the PROC and ENDP directives. If *type* is omitted, then it defaults to Near.

ENDP indicates the end of a procedure (lines 86 and 100 of Figure 6-2). Its syntax is as follows:

```
name          ENDP
```

Name is the same Procedure name as was used for the PROC directive. Every PROC directive requires a corresponding ENDP directive. Note that ENDP is a directive, not an instruction; it serves only to inform the assembler at assembly time of the end of a procedure for the purpose of determining the type (Near or Far) of any return within the procedure. ENDP does not result in a return from the procedure; a RET instruction is required before the ENDP directive to cause a return at execution time.

The assembler does not check for any return instruction(s) within a procedure; it is entirely up to the programmer to ensure that a procedure returns (RET instruction) at the correct point in the logic. The assembler permits multiple RET instructions at any point(s) within the procedure. However, good programming practice requires that, for ease of maintenance, every procedure have exactly one exit point, which normally should be the last instruction of the procedure. Consequently, the ENDP directive should always be immediately preceded by a return instruction, the only return instruction within the procedure.

Like segments, procedures may be nested. The nesting must be complete; overlapping of procedures is not permitted. Unlike nested segments, however, nested procedures result in the nesting of the instructions in the resulting executable program; the instructions within the inner procedure are not moved outside the outer procedure. Besides serving as documentation to improve the readability of a program, the PROC and ENDP directives of a procedure, which is nested inside another procedure, perform two functions. First, they inform the assembler of the type of call (Near or Far) to assemble for any call to the *name* of the nested (inner) procedure. Second, they inform the assembler of the type of return to assemble for any RET instruction within the inner procedure.

LABEL Directive. Recall from our earlier discussion that including a Name field followed by a colon on any source line defines a Near Label; any jump to that Label is assembled as a Near jump. The **LABEL** directive allows the definition of Far Labels within a code segment; any call or unconditional jump to a Far Label results in a Far call or Far jump. The syntax of the LABEL directive is as follows:

```
name            LABEL   type
```

Name is the Label name; *type* is the Label type, either NEAR or FAR. If *type* is NEAR, then the LABEL directive has the same effect as defining a Near label with a colon; the Label is defined as a Near Label. If *type* is FAR, then *name* is defined as a Far Label; any Transfer-of-Control instruction referencing *name* as its target is assembled as a Far transfer of control.

The LABEL directive is most often used to define a second, alternate entry point to a Far procedure. Good programming practice, however, dictates that every procedure have only one entry point, the first instruction of the procedure; the PROC directive provides that single entry point (the Procedure name). Consequently, we do not recommend the use of the LABEL directive; we have discussed it here only because it is often used (and misused) by other programmers and so may be encountered during program maintenance.

Other Directives

A few more commonly needed directives, which do not easily fit into any of our earlier categories, are **EQU, =, COMMENT, %OUT, .RADIX, END, EXTRN,** and **PUBLIC.** We will discuss EXTRN and PUBLIC in the next chapter.

EQU and = Directives. EQU and = are both used to provide a numeric definition for a symbol. The syntax for each is as follows:

```
symbol          EQU     expression
symbol          =       expression
```

The assembler evaluates *expression* and equates *symbol* with the resulting numeric value. All future references to *symbol* are replaced by the assembler with the numeric value of *expression*. A symbol that has been equated with = is redefinable; it may be equated again, to another value if desired, later in the program. EQU is nonredefinable; once a symbol has been defined with EQU, it may not be redefined. Otherwise, EQU and = may be used interchangeably. Following is an example of an equated symbol:

```
BIT_MSK         EQU     00001000B
```

The assembler evaluates the expression, 00001000, as a binary numeral and equates BIT_MSK with the result (eight). All later occurrences of the symbol BIT_MSK are then replaced with the numeric value, eight (00001000B). Thus the reference to BIT_MSK in the following instruction would be replaced by its definition:

```
                AND    AL, BIT_MSK
```

After replacement, the above instruction would be assembled as follows:

```
AND    AL, 8
```

COMMENT Directive. COMMENT is used to include a large block of internal documentation that must be ignored by the assembler; see lines 4 through 16 of Figure 6-2. The syntax for a COMMENT directive is as follows:

COMMENT *delim-char*
block of internal
documentation to be
ignored by the assembler
delim-char

Delim-char may be any character, except <Space> or <Tab>, that does not appear in the block of internal documentation (vertical slash <|> in Figure 6-2). After recognizing the COMMENT directive, the assembler uses the very next non-<Space>, non-<Tab> character as the comment delimiter character. The assembler then ignores all characters up to and including the next occurrence of the delimiter character. Be careful to use a delimiter character that does not occur within the body of the comment. Any attempt to use the delimiter character within the text of the block of internal documentation would be interpreted by the assembler as the end of the comment; the assembler would then attempt to assemble the rest of the documentation block, probably resulting in many errors. Also be careful to include the delimiter character at the end of the comment. Omitting the second delimiter may cause all the rest of the source file to be interpreted as comment and so ignored.

%OUT Directive. %OUT is used to cause the assembler to output a message to the standard output device (the screen, unless standard output has been redirected). Its syntax is as follows:

```
%OUT    message
```

Message is any message you wish the assembler to display during assembly of the source file. The following example, if placed at the beginning of the source file, would cause the assembler to report the beginning of each of its two passes through the source (IF1, a conditional directive, will be discussed in the next chapter):

```
IF1
    %OUT BEGINNING THE FIRST PASS
ELSE
    %OUT BEGINNING THE SECOND PASS
ENDIF
```

.RADIX Directive. .RADIX is used to change the default base for numeric constants that do not have a suffix (B, Q, O, D, or H) to specify the numeral base. Recall that the default radix is ten; numeric constants are interpreted as decimal numerals unless they end with a base specifier. .RADIX may be used to change that default to any value from two through sixteen. The syntax is as follows:

```
.RADIX expression
```

Expression must evaluate to a value from two through sixteen and specifies the new radix; any numeric constant in *expression* is always interpreted as a decimal numeral, regardless of the current radix. For example, consider the following:

```
MY_VAR1       DB        101
              .RADIX    2
MY_VAR2       DB        101
              .RADIX    16
MY_VAR3       DB        101
```

MY_VAR1 is initialized to one hundred and one since the numeric constant is interpreted as a decimal numeral. MY_VAR2 is initialized to five since the radix has been changed to 2. The radix is then changed to sixteen, so MY_VAR3 is initialized to two hundred and fifty seven. Note that 16 in the second .RADIX directive is interpreted as a decimal numeral even though the current radix at that point is two; *expression* is always interpreted as decimal.

Remember that the default radix applies only to numeric constants with no base specifier; any base specifier in a numeral overrides the default radix. This is true even when the default radix is sixteen and the base specifier might be valid as a hexadecimal digit. For example, consider the following:

```
              .RADIX    16
YOUR_VAR1     DB        11B
YOUR_VAR2     DB        11D
```

YOUR_VAR1 is initialized to three, not to two hundred and eighty three (256 + 16 + 11); B as the last character of the numeral is interpreted by the assembler as the binary base specifier rather than as a hexadecimal digit. Similarly, D, as the last character of a numeric constant, is always interpreted as the decimal base specifier, regardless of the current default radix. Consequently, YOUR_VAR2 is initialized to eleven; it is not initialized to two hundred and eighty five (256 + 16 + 13). In order for the above values to be interpreted as hexadecimal numerals they must use the H base specifier as follows, regardless of the fact that the default radix is sixteen:

```
              .RADIX    16
YOUR_VAR1     DB        11BH
YOUR_VAR2     DB        11DH
```

We have presented .RADIX here because you may encounter it in code written by others; however, we recommend that you do not use it. Your source code will be easier to maintain if you always leave the default radix at ten and use a base specifier for any numeric constant you wish to enter in any other base. Besides, we have worked with at least one early version of MASM that does not handle the .RADIX directive properly; it simply ignores it (the default radix remains ten), resulting in a great deal of confusion for the original programmer and for any subsequent programmer.

END Directive. The END directive (line 104 of Figure 6-2) serves two purposes in a source program. First, END informs the assembler of the end of the source file; consequently, every source program should contain an END directive as the last line of the source file. In addition, the END directive may be used to inform the assembler of the address at which program execution should begin. The syntax for the END directive is as follows:

```
END                                    [entrypoint]
```

Entrypoint is a symbol, usually a Procedure name, specifying the entry point for the program, the point at which execution is to begin. The assembler causes the linker to include information within a relocation header at the beginning of the executable file that will cause DOS to properly initialize CS and IP to *entrypoint* upon loading of the program for execution. DOS initializes CS to one-sixteenth the absolute address at which the segment containing *entrypoint* is loaded and initializes IP to the offset of *entrypoint*, within that segment. Thus, program execution begins at the desired entry point.

Every source program must be terminated with the END directive. For now, every END directive must specify the entry point for the program. We will learn in the next chapter that two or more object files (resulting from two or more source files) may be linked together to form one executable file; in such a case, only one END directive should specify an entry point. Otherwise, always specify an entry point with the END directive.

Before continuing, spend some time reviewing the following summary of the most commonly used assembler directives.

MOST COMMONLY USED Directives

Listing directives:
    Affect only the assembler list file, if created. No effect if list file is not created.

    PAGE   [length, width]
        Sets the page length and width of the list file.

    TITLE   listing title

Determines the title to be printed on the second line of every page in list file. One title directive per source file.

SUBTTL   [*listing subtitle*]

Determines the subtitle to be printed on the third line of each subsequent page in list file, until next SUBTTL.

Data directives:

[*symbol*]   Dx   *list-of-values*
or
[*symbol*]   Dx   *count* DUP (*list-of-values*)

D*x* is either DB, DW, DD, or DQ. Defines a Byte, Word, Double-word, or Quad-word of data for each value in *list-of-values*. Defines *symbol* as a variable of type Byte, Word, Double-word or Quad-word. If DUP operator is used, duplicates the definition *count* times.

Near code labels:

symbol: [instruction or directive]

Defines *symbol* as a near code label to be used as the target of jump or call instructions.

Memory directives:

Segname   SEGMENT *align combine 'class'*

Begins a segment named *segname* (usually DATA, CODE or STACK). *Align* is BYTE, WORD, PARA, or PAGE (normally PARA) and determines the type of address at which the segment begins.
Combine is PUBLIC, STACK, COMMON, MEMORY, or AT segaddress (usually PUBLIC or STACK) and determines whether segment is combined with others of the same name.
'*Class*' is any string of characters (usually 'DATA', 'CODE', or 'STACK') and determines the organization of segments in memory.

segname   ENDS

Ends the segment named *segname*.

ASSUME   *segreg*:*segname*

Associates *segreg* (CS, SS, DS, or SS) with *segname* (defined with segment directive). Tells the assembler where *segreg* points.

name   PROC [*type*]

Begins a *type* procedure named *name*. *Type* is either NEAR or FAR. All calls or jumps to *name* and any RET within the procedure are assembled as Near or Far as determined by *type*.

name   ENDP

Ends the procedure named *name*.

Other directives:

COMMENT   *delim-char* `block of internal documentation`
                 delim-char

Allows the definition of a large block of internal documentation. *Delim-char* is the first non-<Space> non-<Tab> character following the directive and may not be used in the block of documentation. The assembler ignores all text until the second occurrence of *delim-char*.

END   `[entrypoint]`

Marks the end of a source file. *Entrypoint*, if specified, is a label or procedure name and informs the assembler of the entry point for the program, the instruction at which execution should begin.

OPERATORS IN EXPRESSIONS

The assembler provides a number of operators that may be used to cause it to perform some calculation at assembly time or to alter the normal replacement for a symbol. The assembler must always be able to evaluate the operator at assembly time. The most commonly used assembler operators are **+, −, *, /, OFFSET, SEG, PTR, SHORT,** and **segment override.**

Arithmetic Operators

The four arithmetic operators (+, −, *, and /) may be used to cause the assembler to calculate the value of an Immediate-mode operand. In evaluating an expression with multiple operators, the assembler follows the usual algebraic order of operations. For example, the following five lines of source code all result in exactly the same machine-language instruction, which moves four into the AL register:

```
MOV     AL, 4

MOV     AL, 2 * 3 - 2

MOV     AL, (1 + 1) * 2

MOV     AL, 8 - 2 * 2

MOV     AL, 12 / 3
```

Two arithmetic operators, + and −, may also be used to perform arithmetic operations on symbolic addresses (direct-memory-mode operand). The following instruction causes the assembler to add three to the offset of the variable MY_BYTE, and to use the resulting offset for direct-memory addressing:

```
MOV   MY_BYTE + 3, 23
```

Assuming that MY_BYTE is at offset 0041H within the data segment and has a type of Byte, then the above instruction would be assembled as follows:

```
MOV   BYTE PTR [0044H], 23
```

PTR Operator

We have been using the **PTR** operator for some time now to specify the type (Byte or Word) of memory locations and numeric-constant immediate values. Actually, the PTR operator is a bit more flexible. In addition to BYTE and WORD, PTR may be used to specify three other types for memory or immediate values: **DWORD**, **QWORD**, and **TBYTE**. DWORD specifies a double-word (two words, four bytes); QWORD specifies a type of quad-word (four words, eight bytes); TBYTE specifies ten-byte (ten bytes) and is normally used for packed binary coded decimal.

The PTR operator may also be used to specify the type of a code Label (or Procedure name) as either **NEAR** or **FAR** in a Transfer-of-Control instruction. Normally, the assembler determines Label and Procedure-name types from directives as discussed earlier. However, when the transfer of control is forward, the assembler does not yet know the type of the Label or name and so assumes Near. Whenever the target of a forward transfer of control is a Far Label or Procedure name, the programmer must use the PTR directive to inform the assembler of the Label's type in order to avoid the "Forward needs override or far" error. For example, the following instruction performs a call to a Far Label or procedure that is defined later in the source program:

```
CALL   FAR PTR MY_FAR_PROC
```

If a forward reference is to a Near Label or procedure, then it is permitted but not necessary to use PTR to specify the type as Near.

SHORT Operator

The **SHORT** operator is used to cause the assembler to assemble an Unconditional Immediate-mode jump as Short rather than Near. Recall that there are two types of intrasegment Immediate-mode Unconditional jumps: Short and Near. A Short jump is assembled with a byte displacement and so is one byte shorter than a Near jump, which uses a word displacement. Whenever possible, the assembler checks the distance of any Unconditional Immediate-mode jump and assembles it as a Short jump if the displacement is within the range of −128 through +127 bytes.

However, if the jump is forward to a Label that is defined on a later source line, then the assembler does not yet know the displacement during pass one, and so always assembles it as a Near jump with a word displacement. In such a situation, the programmer may use the SHORT operator to cause the assembler to assemble the forward jump as Short, with a byte displacement. The following instruction results in a Short jump to the Label MY_LBL:

```
JMP     SHORT MY_LBL
```

You must take care in your use of the SHORT operator. If the displacement turns out to be greater than 127 bytes, then the instruction cannot be assembled as a Short jump and so results in the severe error, "Jump out of range," during assembly. In such a case, remove the SHORT operator from the source line and reassemble.

Segment-Override Operator

A Segment-override operator, also discussed previously, may be used to explicitly cause the assembler to precede an instruction with a Segment-override prefix. The Segment-override prefix then causes the processor to use a Segment register other than DS as the Segment address of the memory location. Any memory operand may be preceded by CS:, DS:, ES:, or SS: as a Segment override. For example, the following instruction uses direct-memory addressing to move a value into a variable that has been defined within the stack segment, rather than within the data segment:

```
MOV     SS:MY_STK_VRBL, 00H
```

Assuming that MY_STK_VRBL occurs at an offset of 004FH from the beginning of the Stack segment and has a Type of Byte, then the above instruction would be assembled as follows:

```
SS:
MOV     BYTE PTR[004FH], 00H
```

When executed, the Segment-override prefix causes the processor to use SS as the Segment address of the next instruction. Thus the absolute address of the memory location to which to move 00H is calculated as sixteen times the value in SS plus 004FH.

Note that if MY_STK_VRBL is defined within a segment that the program has previously associated with SS (with an ASSUME directive) then the above explicit Segment-override prefix is allowed but not necessary. Since MY_STK_VRBL's segment is associated with SS, the assembler would automatically insert the necessary Segment override. Explicitly stating the override, however, does not cause the insertion of two Segment-override prefixes.

OFFSET and SEG Operators

To understand the need for the remaining two commonly used operators, recall that references to variables automatically produce Direct-memory data addressing mode; the variable refers to the data stored within a memory address, rather than to the address itself. Sometimes it is desired to refer to the memory address as an Immediate-mode value, rather than to the data stored in the memory address. For example, line 70 of Figure 6-2 initializes SI to point to the message that has been defined as MY_MSG within the data segment:

```
MOV    SI, OFFSET MY_MSG
```

The OFFSET operator causes the assembler to assemble the instruction with the offset of MY_MSG as an Immediate-mode value, rather than as Direct-memory addressing. Consequently, MASM assembles the instruction as follows:

```
MOV    SI, WORD PTR 0000H
```

Notice that the Type of the immediate value 0000H is Word. The OFFSET operator always results in an immediate value whose Type is Word.

A similar need is filled by the **SEG** operator. It is sometimes necessary to initialize a word register to the Segment address of a symbol. It is usually preferable to do so by referencing the Segment name as in lines 63 and 64 of Figure 6-2:

```
MOV    AX, DATA        ;POINT DS TO
MOV    DS, AX          ;  DATA SEGMENT
```

It is possible, however, to accomplish the same initialization without referring directly to the Segment name; the SEG operator may be used in conjunction with a variable or label defined within the segment. Since MY_MSG is defined within DATA in Figure 6-2, the following two instructions would accomplish the same initialization of DS:

```
MOV    AX, SEG MY_MSG    ;POINT DS TO
MOV    DS, AX            ;  DATA SEGMENT
```

Like OFFSET, the SEG operator always returns a Word immediate value. The immediate value is equal to the Segment address of the symbol, one-sixteenth the absolute address of the beginning of the segment within which the symbol is defined.

MOST COMMONLY USED **Operators**

Arithmetic:

$+, -, *, /$

Used in Immediate-mode expression

$+, -$

Used in Direct-memory-mode expression.

OFFSET

Modifies a variable name to its offset as a word immediate value.

PTR

Modifies the type of a memory reference or label. Allowed types are: Memory:

```
BYTE, WORD, DWORD, QWORD, TBYTE
```

Label:

```
NEAR, FAR
```

SHORT

Causes a forward jump to assemble as Short (byte displacement).

Segment override

CS:, DS:, SS:, or ES:. Precedes a memory-mode operand to cause the assembler to insert a segment-override prefix before the instruction. Causes the processor to use the specified segment register as the segment half of the address.

ENSURING A PROPER RETURN TO DOS

Upon completion, every program must return control of the processor to DOS or DEBUG. In order to facilitate the return, DOS or DEBUG includes the necessary INT 20H instruction at offset zero within the **Program Segment Prefix**. The PSP will be discussed in detail later in the text; for now, it is a 256-byte (100H) block of memory that DOS sets up as it loads a program for execution. Any program may return control to DOS by executing a Far return to offset zero within the PSP. To inform the program of the location of the PSP, DOS initializes the DS register to contain the Segment address of the PSP.

To accomplish the Far return to the PSP, the mainline procedure of every program must properly initialize the stack; the first few instructions of every program must place the PSP Segment address (DS) and an Offset address of zero onto the stack. The mainline procedure of every program should begin as does Figure 6-2 (lines 58 through 61):

```
              Stack Initialization (in Every Program)

   PUSH     DS                 ;PUT RETURN SEG (of PSP)
                               ; TO STACK
   MOV      AX,0               ;PUT ZERO RETURN
   PUSH     AX                 ; OFFSET TO STACK
```

In addition, every mainline procedure should terminate with a return instruction and should be defined as a Far procedure. The resulting Far return at the end of the program pops the offset of zero into IP and the PSP's segment address into CS. Control is then transferred to the INT 20H instruction at offset zero of the PSP. The INT 20H instruction causes the a proper return to DOS.

INITIALIZING REGISTERS

Recall that the ASSUME directive informs the assembler of the segment to which each Segment register will point during program execution; the assembler then calculates offsets relative to those segments. In order for the program to execute properly, CS, SS, DS, and ES (if associated with a segment) must all be initialized to point to the segment associated with each by the ASSUME directive(s). In addition, IP and SP must also be properly initialized.

Provided that an *entrypoint* has been specified by the END directive within the source file, DOS automatically initializes CS and IP. The linker includes the segment and offset of *entrypoint* within the relocation header at the beginning of the executable file. Upon loading of the program, DOS initializes CS to the Segment address and IP to the Offset address of the first instruction to be executed, as specified by *entrypoint*. For example, line 104 of Figure 6-2 causes DOS to initialize CS to the Segment address of CODE and IP to the offset of the procedure MAIN:

```
          END     MAIN
```

Normally, DOS also automatically initializes SS and SP in a similar manner, using a Segment address and Offset address placed in the relocation header by the linker. SS is initialized to the Segment address of the segment that has been defined within the source file with a combine type of STACK; SP is initialized to the length of the segment. When the executable program resulting from Figure 6-2 is loaded, DOS initializes SS to the Segment address of STACK and initializes SP to 512 (refer to lines 21 through 27).

If a program contains no segment with a combine type of STACK, then SS and SP are not automatically initialized by DOS; in such a case, the program must include instructions to initialize SS and SP prior to any instructions that make use of the stack.

Initialization of DS (in Every Program)

```
MOV     AX, DATA          ;POINT DS TO
MOV     DS, AX            ;DATA SEGMENT
ASSUME  DS:DATA           ;ASSOCIATE DS WITH
                          ; DATA SEGMENT
```

DS is not initialized by DOS to the data segment; rather, it is initialized to the Program Segment Prefix, as discussed above. For proper addressing of data, DS must always be initialized by program instructions at execution time. Every program must contain instructions, at or soon after the entry point, to initialize DS to the data segment. Every program must contain instructions similar to those in lines 63 through 66 in Figure 6-2:

If an ASSUME directive is used to associate ES with any segment, then similar instructions must be included to initialize ES to the segment with which it has been associated. If a program includes instructions to modify any Segment register after initialization, then those instructions must be immediately followed by another ASSUME directive to reassociate the Segment register.

CREATING A SOURCE FILE—TEXT EDITOR

Assembly-language source files may be created with the Microsoft editor (supplied with version five of the Macro assembler), the Turbo editor (supplied with the Turbo assembler and other Borland products), WordStar, WordPerfect, or almost any other text editor or word processor. However, some precautions must be observed.

Most word processors and some specialized text editors insert special "invisible" characters within a document in order to facilitate automatic word wrap, reformatting of paragraphs, automatic paging, or special commands for a particular compiler. If a source file contains such special characters, it will not assemble. The special characters are meaningful only to the word processor program or to the compiler with which a specialized text editor is intended to be used and will not be understood by MASM.

Whenever using any word processor you must use only nondocument, text, or program mode. With some word processors, which do not have a nondocument mode, you must use the appropriate command to save your work into a plain text or ASCII file. Any word processor that does not have a nondocument mode or a command to save as pure text is not suitable for creating assembler source files.

Despite the preceding cautions, most text editors and word processors will work fine for the creation of assembly-language source files. To get a rough idea of whether a particular word processor or text editor is suitable, use it to create a text file and then exit to DOS. Use the DOS TYPE command to display the file to the screen. If the file is unreadable on the screen, or if it contains any graphics characters, then the text editor or word processor is not compatible with the assembler.

CREATING AN OBJECT FILE—MASM.EXE

Once you have written your source file using a text editor or word processor, you must use the macro assembler to convert it to machine language in an object file. To assemble a program, enter the command

```
MASM
```

Or, if MASM.EXE is on any drive other than the default drive, enter

```
d:MASM
```

The drive specifier *d:* is the disk drive on which MASM.EXE is stored. Upon loading and execution by DOS, MASM displays a copyright message and then prompts for the name of the source file:

```
Source filename [.ASM]:
```

Enter the name of the source file, including a drive specifier if your source file is not on the default drive. You need not include an extension unless you have created the source file with an extension other than .ASM.

Then MASM prompts for the name to be used for the resulting object file:

```
Object filename [filename.OBJ]:
```

The default *filename* is the same as the source filename entered at the first prompt. If *filename* is correct and you desire that it be created on the default drive, simply press <Enter>. If *filename* is correct, but you wish to create it on other than the default drive, enter the drive specifier only. If you wish to use a different name, enter the full name (with a drive specifier unless you wish to use the default drive); you need not include an extension unless you want to use an extension other than .OBJ.

MASM then prompts for the name to be assigned to an assembler list file:

```
Source listing [NUL.LST]:
```

Recall that NUL is DOS's null device name (bit bucket); if no list file is desired, simply press <Enter>. Otherwise, enter the name of a file, including the drive specifier if you want the file created on other than the default drive; the assembler then creates a list file showing your source code along with the resulting machine language and any errors that occurred during assembly. If no extension is specified, MASM will give the list file a default extension of .LST.

Finally, MASM prompts for the name to be used for a cross-reference file:

```
Cross reference [NUL.CRF]:
```

A cross reference file can be used with the cross-reference utility CREF.EXE to obtain a listing of all occurrences of every symbol used in the source program. Press <Enter> if you do not wish to create a cross reference file, or enter the name of the desired file. Include a drive specifier if anything other than the default drive is desired; .CRF is the default extension used by MASM if no extension is specified.

At any of the above prompts, you may end your response with a semicolon (;) to cause MASM to skip over all remaining prompts, automatically using the defaults. The effect is the same as pressing <Enter> for all remaining prompts.

If MASM is unable to find the source file or unable to create any specified output file, it reports the error and returns immediately to DOS. Otherwise, it begins the assembly. Any syntax errors in the source file are reported by listing the line where the error was found followed by an error message, explaining what is wrong with the source line. If no list file was specified, errors are listed to the screen; otherwise, errors are listed within the list file. Upon completion of the assembly, MASM always reports the number of errors to the screen as follows:

```
Warning    Severe
Errors     Errors
  m          n
```

Never try to link an object file from an assembly that reports any severe errors. Also, as a general rule, do not try to use any object file that resulted in any warning errors. Use an editor to correct the errors in the source file and then assemble it again.

Following is an example of the assembly of a source file called PA6-1.ASM to create the object file PA6-1.OBJ and the list file PA6-1.LST, but no cross-reference file:

Sample Assembly (PA6-1.ASM to PA6-1.OBJ and PA6-1.LST)

```
A>B:MASM

The Microsoft MACRO Assembler, Version 1.27
(C) Copyright Microsoft Corp 1981,1984

Source filename [.ASM]: PA6-1
Object filename [PA6-1.OBJ]:
Source listing  [NUL.LST]: PA6-1
Cross reference [NUL.CRF]:

Warning   Severe
Errors    Errors
0         0

A>
```

Optionally, MASM parameters may be specified on the DOS command line
rather than in response to prompts. The syntax of the command line, with parameters, is as follows:

```
[d:]MASM srcfile[,[objfile][,[lstfile][,[crffile]]]][;]
```

Srcfile, *objfile*, *lstfile*, and *crffile* are the names of the source file, object file,
list file, and cross-reference files, respectively. One or more of the filenames may
be specified on the command line. Commas must be entered in order to accept
the default for one file while specifying a nondefault name for a subsequent file.
If fewer than four files are specified, MASM prompts normally for all remaining
files except that a semicolon (;) may be entered at the end of the command line to
cause MASM to use the defaults for all remaining files without prompting. The
following command might be used to accomplish the same assembly as in the example above:

```
A>B:MASM PA6-1,,PA6-1;
```

During assembly, the assembler translates the source code into the appropriate instructions and data, storing the result into an object file. It also creates a list
and/or cross-reference file, if specified; assembly is faster if no list or cross-reference has been requested.

Although the resulting object file contains machine-language instructions, it is
not executable. It consists of a series of variable-length records in a format recog-
nizable only by the linker. Some records contain machine instructions; others contain information about the alignment and combining of segments, the necessary
initialization of segment and pointer registers, references to external symbols, and

other information needed by the linker in order to create an executable file. The object file must now be linked to create an executable program (.EXE) file.

CREATING AN EXECUTABLE FILE—LINK.EXE

The Microsoft linker (LINK.EXE) is responsible for reading one or more object files and creating an executable file that is ready to be loaded and executed. To link an object file, enter the command:

```
LINK
```

Or, if LINK.EXE is on a disk drive other than the default drive, enter:

```
d:LINK
```

The drive specifier *d:* is the name of the drive on which LINK.EXE is stored. LINK displays a copyright message and then prompts for the name of the object file(s) to be linked:

```
Object Modules [.OBJ]:
```

Enter the name(s) of one or more object files. If multiple object files are to be linked together, list them all separated by spaces or plus (+) signs, i.e., MY-MAIN+MYSUB. Include the drive specifier in the name of each and every object file that is not on the default drive. You need not include extensions unless an object file has an extension other than .OBJ (some other extension was specified to the assembler).

LINK then prompts for the name to use for the executable program file:

```
Run File [filename.EXE]:
```

The default *filename* is the primary name of the object file specified at the first prompt (the first object file, if multiple object files are being linked). Press <Enter> to create an executable file on the default disk with the default name. Enter a drive specifier to create the executable file, with the default name, on other than the default disk. Enter a filename to create the executable file with a name other than that of the object file.

Next, LINK prompts for the name, if any, to be assigned to a map file:

```
List File [NUL.MAP]:
```

A map file is a listing of the addresses of all segments in a program and, optionally, all public symbols within the object file(s); we will discuss public symbols in the next chapter. If no map file is desired, press <Enter>. To create a map file, enter the full filename to be used. Include the extension; it does not default to .MAP. To cause LINK to include the list of public symbols within the map file, you must add the switch, /MAP to the end of your response, i.e., MYPROG.MAP/**MAP**.

Finally, LINK asks for the name of any object libraries to be searched for external symbols, during the link:

```
Libraries [.LIB]:
```

We will discuss object libraries in the next chapter; for now, just press <Enter>. LINK then reads from the object file(s) and creates the executable file. If any errors occur, LINK reports them to the screen; otherwise, LINK simply returns to DOS with no further messages. Following is an example of the linkage of a single object file called PA6-1.OBJ to create an executable file PA6-1.EXE with no map file and no object library:

Sample Link (PA6-1.OBJ to PA6-1.EXE)

```
A>B:LINK

Microsoft 8086 Object Linker
Version 2.44 (C) Copyright Microsoft Corp 1983

Object Modules [.OBJ]: PA6-1
Run File [PA6-1.EXE]:
List File [NUL.MAP]:
Libraries [.LIB]:

A>
```

As with MASM, LINK parameters may be specified on the command line. The syntax of the command line, with parameters, is as follows:

```
[d:]LINK objfile(s)[,[runfile][,[mapfile][,[libfile(s)]]]][;]
```

Objfile(s), *runfile*, *mapfile*, and *libfile(s)* are the names for the object file(s), executable file, map file, and library file(s), respectively. As with MASM, one or more of the filenames may be specified on the command line. Commas must be entered in order to accept the default for one file while specifying a nondefault name for a subsequent file. If fewer than four files are specified, LINK prompts normally for all remaining files except that a semicolon (;) may be used to cause LINK to use the defaults for all remaining files without prompting. The following command performs the same link as in the above example.

```
A>B:LINK PA6-1;
```

TASM (TURBO ASSEMBLER) AND LATER VERSIONS OF MASM

At the time of this writing, Microsoft is currently up to version five of the macro assembler. This text is intended to work with all versions of MASM, from version one on. Except for a few minor quirks, all later versions of the assembler are compatible with version one; the capabilities of the assembler have been extended but not significantly altered in later versions.

The major extensions added to later versions are the support of processors developed subsequent to the 8086/8088 and the addition of predefined macros for the passing of parameters between an assembly-language routine and the various compilers produced by Microsoft. Version five can support the full instruction sets of the entire Intel family of processors up to the 80386. By default, it supports only the 8086/8088 instruction set; any attempt to assemble an instruction supported only by a later processor results in an error. The following three directives have been added in order to selectively enable the assembly of instructions supported by later processors:

```
.186
.286
.386
```

The three above directives instruct a version five assembler to support the full instruction set for the 80186, 80286, or 80386 processors, respectively. It is important to remember that any program that contains instructions for later processors will not execute properly on any machine based on either the 8086 or 8088 processor. For this reason, the above directives should never be included in any program unless the program is intended only for use with the specified processor or a later processor.

The addition of predefined macros in version five resulted in a number of reserved words (TEST and OUT, for example), which should not be used as symbols. Any use of a reserved word as a symbol results in the warning error "Reserved word used as symbol" whenever the source is assembled with version five of MASM. In such a case, simply change every occurrence of the symbol within the program, and then reassemble.

The Turbo assembler from Borland is compatible with version five of the Microsoft Macro assembler and may be used for all programming assignments in this text. The assembler and linker are named TASM.EXE and TLINK.EXE, and both require that all parameters be specified on the command line. Otherwise, the syntax for each is the same as the syntax for assembly and linkage with MASM and LINK:

```
TASM srcfile[,[objfile][,[lstfile][,[crffile]]]][;]
TLINK objfile(s)[,[runfile][,[mapfile][,[libfile(s)]]]][;]
```

Another major difference is that TASM is a **single-pass assembler**; it reads the source file only once during assembly. Consequently, any conditional directives (discussed in the next chapter) that are pass-dependent may be handled differently. Most notably, IF1 always evaluates as True, and IF2 is always False. TASM produces warning errors for any such pass-dependent directives.

The last major difference is that TASM treats STACK as a reserved word (alignment type). Any use of STACK as a symbol results in a warning error. To avoid such a warning error when using TASM, line 21 of Figure 6-2 should be rewritten as follows:

```
STAK          SEGMENT PARA STACK 'STACK'          ;BEGIN STACK
```

IMPLEMENTING STRUCTURED-PROGRAMMING CONSTRUCTS

As you may have learned in previous classes in programming in high-level languages, three structured-programming constructs are necessary for the solving of all problems. Those necessary programming constructs, **Sequence**, **Selection** (or **Alternation**), and **Repetition** (or **Iteration**), are provided by the syntax of most modern high-level language compilers or interpreters. An additional construct, **Case**, is provided by many languages. It is the presence of these constructs in the language syntax that makes structured programming possible. With the exception of Sequence and one form of Repetition, 8086/8088 assembly language does not automatically provide those necessary constructs; they must be designed by the programmer using the instructions supported by the processor.

Unfortunately, assembly-language programmers often do not think in terms of programming constructs. Much too often programmers who enforce good structure upon themselves while working in high-level languages completely forget about structure when programming in assembly language! The result is often unstructured "spaghetti-code" programs that are not only extremely difficult to maintain but are also often less efficient for the machine than a well-structured program.

Before attempting to write any assembly-language code for the solution of a problem, you should carefully work out the logic of the problem solution in pseudocode, making use of structured-programming constructs. Only after you have completely designed a solution in pseudocode are you ready to begin implementing that solution in assembly language. Following this advice will result in programs that are easier to maintain and are often more efficient for the machine as well. As an added bonus, most programmers find that planning program logic in terms of structured-programming constructs saves initial development time. The program may take a little longer to design and write, but it takes much less time to test and debug.

The Selection and Case constructs will be discussed in the next chapter. Following is a discussion of the implementation of the Sequence and Repetition constructs.

Sequence Construct

The Sequence construct simply requires that any programming language must provide some means for the programmer to specify the sequence or order in which statements or instructions are to be executed. In machine language, the sequence is automatically provided by the Execution Unit, which increments the Instruction-Pointer register every time it retrieves a byte of code from the Instruction Queue. Consequently, machine-language instructions are executed in the sequence in which they are stored in memory.

Since the assembler assembles source instructions in sequence, the order of execution of instructions is determined by the order of the assembly-language source instructions. Thus the Sequence construct is automatically provided in assembly language. Simply arrange the source instructions in the order in which you wish them to be executed.

Repetition (Iteration) Construct

In addition to sequence, many problem solutions require a **loop**, the repetition or iteration of a sequence of steps. In fact there are many different types of repetition as distinguished by the manner in which the loop is terminated, how the program determines when to stop the repetition. The syntaxes of various high-level languages often directly support four types of Iteration constructs: **Repeat n times, Repeat with counter, Repeat while**, and **Repeat until**. In addition, many high-level languages allow the programmer to build **General loops** through the use of Conditional and Unconditional branching. In the following section we will discuss the implementation in assembly language of each type of iteration.

Unfortunately, many high-level language syntaxes do not directly support the Repeat-n-times construct. Programmers often must use the more complex Repeat-with-counter construct, even though the counter may not be used by the program except to terminate the loop after the correct number of iterations. This usually results in code that is both less efficient for the machine and less understandable for people. Fortunately for us, 8086/8088 assembly language does directly support Repeat n times with the LOOP and JCXZ instructions. Consider the following desired iteration:

```
Repeat DX times
     Perform some process
End repeat
```

That construct can be easily implemented in assembly language as follows (note the use of indentation to make the iteration construct easier to see):

```
        MOV      CX, DX               ;LOOP USES CX AS COUNTER
        JCXZ     LP_END               ;SKIP LOOP IF COUNT IS 0
LP_BEG: ;BEGIN REPEAT CX TIMES
            CALL     PROCESS          ;PERFORM THE REPEATED
                                      ;  PROCESS PROCEDURE
            LOOP     LP_BEG           ;CONTINUE LOOP
LP_END:  ;END REPEAT
```

Although the processor directly supports the Repeat-n-times construct with the LOOP instruction, it does not really maintain a count of the iterations; CX counts down to zero rather than up to the desired number of iterations. Sometimes it is necessary not only to repeat a process but also to maintain a continuous count of the number of repetitions completed thus far. In such cases a Repeat-with-counter construct is called for. In pseudocode, such a construct might be expressed as follows:

```
Repeat varying AX from SI to DI
    Display the value in AX
End repeat
```

In most high-level languages, repeat with counter is implemented with the test for termination at the end of the loop. In such an implementation, the loop always executes at least once regardless of the start and stop values. Such a Repeat-with-counter construct can be implemented in assembly language as follows (note the use of indentation):

```
        MOV      AX, SI               ;INITIALIZE COUNTER TO
                                      ;  START VALUE
LP_BEG: ;BEGIN REPEAT VARYING AX FROM SI TO DI
            CALL     DSP_AX           ;DISPLAY VALUE IN AX
            INC      AX               ;NEXT COUNTER VALUE
        CMP      AX, DI               ;TEST FOR CONTINUATION
        JBE      LP_BEG               ;  OF THE LOOP
        ;END REPEAT
```

Some compilers and interpreters implement the Repeat-with-counter construct with the test at the beginning. If the start value is already past the stop value, the loop terminates immediately without executing the body. The same Repeat-with-counter (with the test at the beginning) would be implemented as follows (again, note the indentation):

```
        MOV      AX, SI               ;INITIALIZE COUNTER TO
                                      ;  START VALUE
LP_BEG: ;REPEAT VARYING AX FROM SI TO DI
        CMP      AX, DI               ;TEST FOR TERMINATION
        JA       LP_END               ;  OF THE LOOP
```

```
                CALL       DSP_AX          ;DISPLAY VALUE IN AX
                INC        AX              ;NEXT COUNTER VALUE
                JMP        LP_BEG          ;CONTINUE THE LOOP
LP_END:   ;END REPEAT
```

The Repeat-while and Repeat-until constructs, though similar in that they both use a True/False condition to terminate the loop, differ in two very important ways. The first is implied by the key words, "while" and "until." A Repeat-while loop continues as long as the condition is True and terminates when the condition becomes False; a Repeat-until loop continues as long as the condition is False and terminates when it becomes True. The other less obvious difference is that Repeat while tests the condition before the body of the loop, and Repeat until performs the test after the loop body. Consequently, the body of a Repeat-until loop always executes at least once. A Repeat-while loop may not execute at all (if the condition is already False when the loop is encountered).

Because it always executes at least once, the Repeat-until construct can be difficult to use since it does not easily handle a very common problem of processing variable amounts of data with some sort of trailer used to mark the end of the data. As an example, suppose the problem involves retrieving and processing bytes of data from memory. Before the loop begins execution, SI points to the first byte of data. The number of bytes of data is not known. Instead, a zero is used as a **data trailer** to mark the end of the data. Zero is the trailer indicating when to terminate the loop; it is not part of the data and so should not be processed. Following is an attempt to solve the problem with a Repeat-until construct in both pseudocode and its assembly-language implementation (note the indentation of the loop body in both pseudocode and assembly language):

```
Repeat
     Move a byte into AL from [SI]
     Increment SI to next byte of data
     Process the byte in AL
Until AL EQ 0

LP_BEG: ;REPEAT UNTIL AL EQ 0
                MOV        AL, [SI]        ;GET NEXT BYTE
                INC        SI              ; OF DATA
                CALL       PROC_AL         ;PROCESS THE BYTE IN AL
        CMP        AL, 0                    ;TEST FOR CONTINUATION
        JNE        LP_BEG                   ; OF THE LOOP
        ;END REPEAT
```

Trace through the above code and notice the problem. Since it does not check the condition until after the body of the loop, it attempts to process the trailer as if it were data. Occasionally (but not in this case) the processing of the trailer is desired. In such cases, a Repeat-until loop should be used.

Much more often, however, processing the trailer produces unsatisfactory results, as in our example. Consequently, most high-level languages do not even provide a true Repeat-until loop with the test at the end. The most notable exceptions are PASCAL and C, which do indeed implement a true Repeat-until loop. Note that the COBOL UNTIL clause performs the test before the loop and so is not a true Repeat until; rather it is a Repeat while not.

The problem attempted above can be solved more satisfactorily with a Repeat-while construct. However, a Repeat-while loop requires that the programmer use a priming read/trailing read structure. Since Repeat while checks the condition immediately before the loop body, the program must obtain the first data item before the beginning of the loop (priming read). In order to process a different item of data for each iteration, the program must obtain the next data item at the end of the body of the loop (trailing read). Following is the pseudocode and assembly language for solving the above problem with a Repeat-while construct (note the indentation of the loop body):

```
Move a byte into AL from [SI]    (priming
Increment SI to next byte of data    read)
Repeat while AL NE zero
      Process the byte in AL
      Move a byte into AL from [SI]    (trailing
      Increment SI to next byte of data    read)
End repeat
```

```
          MOV      AL, [SI]               ;GET A BYTE OF DATA
          INC      SI                     ; (PRIMING READ)
LP_BEG:   ;REPEAT WHILE AL NE 0
          CMP      AL, 0                  ;TEST FOR TERMINATION
          JE       LP_END                 ; OF THE LOOP
              CALL     PROC_AL            ;PROCESS THE BYTE IN AL
              MOV      AL, [SI]           ;GET NEXT BYTE OF DATA
              INC      SI                 ; (TRAILING READ)
              JMP      LP_BEG             ;CONTINUE THE LOOP
LP_END:   ;END REPEAT
```

Note that the same two instructions for reading a byte of data must appear twice in the code in order to make the Repeat-while construct function properly (priming read and trailing read). In our example, the requirement for both a priming and a trailing read only adds three bytes to the executable program. Sometimes, however, each read may require many instructions to obtain an item of data, adding greatly to the size of the resulting program.

In high-level languages, such inefficiency is tolerated in order to take advantage of the ease of maintenance of the Repeat-while construct built into the syntax of the language. The only alternative in most high-level languages is to build a General loop with branching (GOTO), which results in code that is more difficult to maintain.

Since even the Repeat-while construct must be built using jumps in assembly language, a General-loop construct is often more easily maintained as well as more efficient for the machine. A General loop contains two parts to the loop body, with the test of the condition occurring in the middle of the loop rather than at the beginning or end. Usually the first part of the loop body obtains the data, and the second part (following the test) processes the data. Structuring the loop in this manner provides all the advantages of a Repeat-while construct without the need for both a priming and a trailing read. Below is a General-loop solution to the same problem as above (note the indentation of both parts of the loop body in both pseudocode and assembly language):

```
Repeat
     Move a byte into AL from [SI]
     Increment SI to next byte of data
Quit repeating when AL EQ 0
     Process the byte in AL
End repeat
```

```
LP_BEG:  ;GENERAL LOOP (QUIT WHEN AL EQ 0)
                 MOV       AL, [SI]        ;GET NEXT BYTE
                 INC       SI              ; OF DATA
         CMP       AL, 0                   ;TEST FOR TERMINATION
         JE        LP_END                  ; OF THE LOOP
                 CALL      PROC_AL         ;PROCESS THE BYTE IN AL
                 JMP       LP_BEG          ;CONTINUE THE LOOP
LP_END:  ;END OF LOOP
```

A well-structured General loop is often the most efficient for the machine as well as the most easily maintained Repetition construct in assembly language. As you work in assembly language, you will probably find yourself using the General-loop construct more often than any other form of iteration.

SUMMARY OF Structured-Programming Constructs

Sequence

Specify the sequence of operations. Determined by the order of source lines.

Repetition (Iteration)

Repeat a sequence of instructions (loop); must provide some means of determining when to stop repeating. There are five types of iteration:

Repeat n times
Implemented with JCXZ and LOOP instructions.

Repeat with counter
Initialize counter before loop; increment each time around loop; quit when counter exceeds stop value.
Repeat while
Test for termination at beginning of loop; quit when condition becomes False.
Repeat until
Test for termination at end of loop; quit when condition becomes True.
General loop
Test for termination in middle of loop.

Selection (Alternation)

Causes the program to choose one of two alternatives. Discussed in the next chapter.

Case

Causes the program to choose one of many alternatives. Discussed in the next chapter.

SUMMARY

Programming in DEBUG (using the Assemble command) is severely limited; serious assembly-language programming requires the use of the macro assembler (MASM). Using the assembler, programs are developed in three stages and result in three versions of the program. First, a source file is created with text editor; then MASM reads the source file and translates it into machine language, creating an object file; finally LINK is used to read the object file and create the finished executable version of the program. Whenever the program is run, the executable file is loaded and executed by DOS. Whenever the program must be modified, the necessary changes are made to the source file, which must then be reassembled and relinked in order to create a new executable file.

In addition to 8086/8088 instructions, the source file may also contain directives instructing the assembler as to the manner in which to perform the assembly. It is very important to distinguish between instructions and directives. Directives are performed by the assembler, at assembly time; instructions are merely translated by the assembler and are performed by the processor, at execution time.

Since the processor's instruction set does not provide the structured-programming constructs supported by most high-level languages, it is necessary to construct them with the jump instructions that are provided. The various iteration constructs (Repeat n times, Repeat with counter, Repeat until, Repeat while, and General loop) were discussed in this chapter. The Selection and Case constructs will be discussed in the next chapter.

It is very important that you train yourself to think in terms of structured-programming constructs when designing a solution to a problem. Do not think in terms of jumps. Design the solution in structured pseudocode first; then translate your pseudocode to assembly language using only those jumps that are necessary to implement the structured pseudocode. The result is programs that are easier to maintain and often more efficient for the machine, and which usually require less total time to develop (programming time plus testing/debugging time).

VOCABULARY

V6-1   In your own words, define each of the following terms:

a) Name field	k) Procedure name
b) Action field	l) Location counter
c) Expression field	m) Symbol table
d) Remark field	n) Directive
e) Symbolic addressing	o) Pseudo-op
f) Symbol definition	p) Operand
g) Symbol reference	q) Operator
h) Variable name	r) Double-word
i) Label	s) Quad-word
j) Segment name	t) Two-pass assembler, single-pass assembler

V6-2   In your own words, define each of the following terms:

a) Sequence construct	e) Repeat-until construct
b) Repetition (iteration) construct	f) Repeat-while construct
c) Repeat-n-times construct	g) General-loop construct
d) Repeat-with-counter construct	h) Data trailer

REVIEW QUESTIONS

Q6-1   Explain the function of each of the following assembler operators:

a) +	e) OFFSET	h) SHORT
b) −	f) SEG	i) Segment-override
c) *	g) PTR	j) DUP
d) /		

Q6-2   List the five data (variable) types, and give the size, in bytes, of each.

Q6-3   List the two label types and explain the effect that each label type has on a Transfer-of-Control instruction.

Q6-4   List and explain the three listing directives discussed in this chapter.

Q6-5   List and explain the four data-definition directives discussed in this chapter.

Q6-6   Explain the differences, if any, in the results of the following two directives:

```
DB ?, ?, ?, ?, ?, ?, ?, ?
DB 8 DUP (?)
```

Q6-7   Explain the purpose of the SEGMENT and ENDS directives.

Q6-8   What is the purpose of the Alignment parameter in a SEGMENT directive? List and explain the five possible Alignment types. What Alignment is used by the assembler, as a default, if none is specified in the directive?

Q6-9   Explain the purpose of the Combine parameter in a Segment directive. List and explain the three Combine types discussed in this chapter. What is the default Combine type, if none is specified?

Q6-10   What is the purpose of the Class parameter in a SEGMENT directive?

Q6-11   What are the PROC and ENDP directives used for? What is the purpose of the Type parameter in a PROC directive? What are the two allowed Types?

Q6-12   Explain the purpose of the ASSUME directive.

Q6-13   What directive may be used to allow the entry of many lines of remark, without using any semicolons (;)?

Q6-14   What directive may be used to cause the assembler to print a message to the screen during assembly?

Q6-15   What directive causes the assembler to interpret numeric constants as numerals of some base other than decimal?

Q6-16   Which structured-programming construct allows the program to execute a block of instructions more than one time? List and explain its various forms.

PROGRAMMING ASSIGNMENTS

PA6-1   Use a text editor or nondocument mode of a word processor to enter the source program in Figure 6-2 into a file called PA6-1.ASM. Do not enter the line numbers in the rightmost columns of Figure 6-2; they have been included in the figure for reference purposes only.

Assemble the source file to create PA6-1.OBJ. Then link it to obtain PA6-1.EXE. To test your program, enter

```
· PA6-1
```

at the DOS prompt. If it doesn't execute properly and return to DOS, use DEBUG to find the problem.

PA6-2   Use a text editor or word processor to create a source file called PA6-2.ASM. Pattern it after Figure 6-2 (without the line numbers in the right-most columns), but use a Repeat-while construct (in place of the General loop) to display the message.

Assemble the source file to create PA6-2.OBJ. Then link it to obtain PA6-2.EXE. To test your program, enter

```
PA6-2
```

at the DOS prompt. If it doesn't execute properly and return to DOS, use DEBUG to find the problem.

PA6-3   Use a text editor or word processor to create a source file called PA6-3.ASM, patterned after Figure 6-2 (without the line numbers in the right-most columns).

Define several messages in the data segment (MSG_1, MSG_2, etc.), and terminate each with a NUL character (0).

Add another subprocedure, DSPLY_MSG, which uses a loop for displaying a string addressed by SI and terminated with a NUL trailer. It should save (PUSH) and restore (POP) any registers it modifies, just as DSPLY_CHR saves and restores AX.

The mainline should not contain a loop. In order to display each message, it should merely initialize SI to the offset of the message and call DSPLY_MSG.

Assemble the source file to create PA6-3.OBJ. Then link it to obtain PA6-3.EXE. To test your program, enter

```
PA6-3
```

at the DOS prompt. If it doesn't execute properly and return to DOS, use DEBUG to find the problem.

PA6-4   Do programming assignment PA6-1, PA6-2, or PA6-3. Then use DEBUG to load and examine your executable program (.EXE). Use the **R**egister command to see all registers; notice that, unlike our earlier .COM files, the segment registers are not all the same. Notice the values in SP and IP. Use the **U**nassemble command to disassemble your code; notice that there are no comments or remarks. Use the **T**race command and/or the **G**o command with breakpoints to step through the program. Play around with it.

7

The Building-Block Approach

INTRODUCTION

If you were going to build an adobe house, you would undoubtedly begin by making bricks. Not until a large number of bricks had been mixed, formed, sun-baked, and inspected, would you even consider beginning the construction of the house itself. Unfortunately, too few programmers approach problems in this manner; putting the house before the bricks is the single most common cause of failure and discouragement among beginning assembly-language programmers.

Typically, the programmer is presented with some problem and then immediately sets about attempting to solve the problem in assembly language. Within a short time he or she gets thoroughly bogged down in all the details of outputing characters to the screen or printer, getting characters from the keyboard, converting between numeric and character data, accessing disk files, and so on. The original problem becomes hopelessly lost in the confusion of detail; the programmer then typically throws up his or her hands in helpless defeat, gives up on the problem, and resolves henceforth to abandon assembly-language programming to the gurus, the experts, the masters.

The fact is that most of those "gurus" are mere mortals like the rest of us, but with one major difference: they have learned to get the details out of the way first before attempting to solve any specific problem. Successful assembly-language programmers usually use a **building-block** approach (often called a tool-box approach). They start by building up libraries (or toolboxes) of easy-to-use routines that perform commonly needed tasks such as screen output, keyboard input, and disk access. Once these libraries have been completed and tested, the programmer no longer has to worry about the details of input and output while solving a specific problem.

This approach is necessary because, unlike most high-level languages, assembly language provides no easy-to-use input/output statements such as the BASIC statements PRINT and INPUT. Assembly-language programming requires the development by the programmer of a number of nonspecific, very general modules for performing such common tasks as keyboard input and screen output.

The modular concept is borrowed to some extent from top-down design, which you may have discussed in a high-level language programming class. Unlike the modules developed through top-down design, however, building-block modules are not developed in response to a particular problem; rather they are developed before attempting to tackle any specific problem. Only after many such building blocks have been designed, written, and tested does the programmer attempt to design and implement a solution to a specific problem in assembly language.

In designing and writing building blocks, we should bear in mind that they will be used repeatedly in a wide variety of programs. This leads us to two sometimes contradictory considerations. First, since they may be used many times in any given program, they should be made as efficient as possible for the machine, in terms of memory usage and speed of execution. Actually, since most of our building blocks will be used for input and output of data, speed is much less important than memory size. Most input and output need only be as fast as the person at the keyboard. However, a typical program needs to input or display data many times; if a large amount of memory is used each time one character is input or displayed, then the result will be a very large program.

The second major consideration is that the building blocks should be as easy to use as possible. The whole purpose of this approach is to decrease the complexity of programs; if our building blocks are complicated and clumsy to use, then we have not accomplished that goal. These two goals, machine efficiency and programmer efficiency, do not always go hand in hand; in fact they are often in direct conflict. The trick is to try to satisfy both criteria and, whenever that is impossible, to find a satisfactory compromise. Whenever a compromise is necessary, it is usually better to lean toward programmer efficiency rather than machine efficiency.

Just as the idea of building blocks is borrowed with modification from the concept of top-down design, we can also borrow some other rules of structured programming. First, each module should perform only one function. We should look carefully at the purpose of each proposed building block; if it is to serve more than one purpose, even if closely related, then we should separate the functions and write a separate building block for each.

Next, modules should maintain data isolation. A module should not alter the data stored in any memory location or register except when necessary to return some output value back to the program that uses it. Whenever a register or memory area is to be altered, it must be clearly indicated as an output parameter. This requirement should be clear when you consider that we want the building blocks to be easy to use in a wide variety of programs. Use of the module would be complicated indeed if we constantly had to worry about inadvertently modifying registers in which we may be storing values critical to the proper function of the calling program.

Last, each module should have exactly one entry point and exactly one exit point. There must be one point within a module, usually the first instruction, to which control is passed every time the module is used by any program. Also, there must be one point, usually the last instruction, at which the module returns control back to the calling program. We will see that in order to maintain data isolation our modules will push registers upon entry and pop them just prior to returning control. Pushes and pops must be carefully matched. This is very difficult to maintain if calling programs are to enter the module at different points or if the module is to return control from more than one point.

Any time you find yourself wanting to allow more than one entry or exit point, look closely at the module function; chances are that it is actually two or more separate but related functions. Separate the functions and design one building block for each.

The above discussion can be stated in six formal rules to be followed in the design and implementation of our building blocks:

Rules for the Development of Building Blocks

1) Each building block should perform only one function.

2) Building blocks should maintain data isolation.

3) Each building block should have exactly one entry point and one exit point.

4) For programmer efficiency, building blocks should be as simple and easy to use as possible.

5) For machine efficiency, building blocks should use as little memory as possible.

6) Whenever rules four and five conflict, compromise in favor of rule four.

In this chapter, we will learn how to develop such building blocks. Before we can do so, however, we must discuss some new directives: MACRO, ENDM, and a number of Conditional directives for controlling assembly.

MACRO AND ENDM DIRECTIVES

MASM provides two directives, **MACRO** and **ENDM**, that allow for the definition of macros. In fact, it is precisely because the assembler supports macros that it is called MASM, short for macro assembler. A **macro definition** is a set of instructions and/or directives with a name assigned to it. Thereafter, each time we code the macro name into the program (called a **macro invocation**), MASM recognizes it and replaces the macro name with its definition; this process of replacing the macro name with its definition is referred to as a **macro expansion**.

The ability to "abbreviate" an entire set of instructions and/or directives with a single-word macro name is in itself a powerful tool. However, if every invocation of a macro expanded to exactly the same instructions as every other invocation of the same macro then its use would be severely limited. The real power of macros comes from our ability to alter the expansion slightly each time we invoke the macro.

This ability to control the macro expansion is provided through the use of "dummy" and "real" parameters. A macro definition may include a list of **dummy parameters**; the dummy parameters may then be referenced by the instructions making up the body of the macro definition. When the macro is invoked later in the program, a list of **real parameters** is supplied by the programmer. As the macro is expanded, MASM replaces the dummy parameters in the definition with the real parameters supplied with the macro invocation.

A macro definition is begun with the **MACRO** directive and must be ended with the **ENDM** directive. The syntax for a macro definition is as follows:

```
name        MACRO       [list of dummy parameters]


            Body of the
            macro definition,
            referencing the
            dummy parameters.


            ENDM                            ; name
```

The remark, "*;name*", on the last line (ENDM) is purely for documentation; since it is a remark, it is ignored by the assembler. Note that the macro definition must appear in the program *before* any attempt to invoke it; MASM does not look ahead for macro definitions. Also note that the macro definition does not generate any code; it is not assembled. Only when the macro is invoked is it expanded and assembled.

Once it has been defined, the macro may be invoked as many times as necessary, as follows:

```
            name        [list of real parameters]
```

The assembler expands the single-line macro invocation to include all instructions and/or directives within its definition. During the expansion, every occurrence of a dummy parameter within the definition is replaced by the corresponding real parameter from the invocation. The above invocation is expanded to

```
Body of the
macro definition,
with the dummy parameters
replaced by the real parameters
```

As an example, we might define the following macro with two dummy parameters (PRM_1 and PRM_2):

```
MY_TEST     MACRO     PRM_1, PRM_2

            MOV       AX, PRM_1
            MOV       BX, PRM_2
            CALL      TEST_PROC

            ENDM                      ;MY_TEST
```

Remember that the above macro definition generates no code; the macro definition is not assembled. Later in the program, we might invoke the above macro a number of times, supplying different real parameters with each invocation:

```
MY_TEST   345, 676

MY_TEST   CX, SI

MY_TEST   27, DI
```

Each of the above macro invocations is expanded by the assembler to include all the instructions within the macro definition. During the expansion, however, all references to dummy parameters within the definition are replaced with the real parameters supplied by the invocation. Consequently, the above three lines are expanded and assembled as follows:

```
MOV       AX, 345
MOV       BX, 676
CALL      TEST_PROC

MOV       AX, CX
MOV       BX, SI
CALL      TEST_PROC

MOV       AX, 27
MOV       BX, DI
CALL      TEST_PROC
```

Thus, while the macro definition generates no code, each macro invocation adds three instructions to the program. Later in this chapter we will develop a macro for positioning the cursor on the screen.

SUMMARY OF Macro-Related Directives

> *name*   MACRO   [*list of dummy parameters*]
>
> Begins the definition of a macro. Provides a list of dummy parameters to be replaced by real parameters during expansion.
>
> **ENDM**   ;*name*
>
> Ends a macro definition.
>
> *name*   *list of real parameters*
>
> Macro invocation. Expanded by the assembler to the macro definition, *name*. Provides a list of real parameters to replace the dummy parameters during expansion.

CONDITIONAL DIRECTIVES

Conditional directives are used to cause MASM to evaluate a condition as True or False and to make a decision as to how to assemble the source code. Since they are directives for the assembler (not instructions for the processor) all conditions to be evaluated must involve only values known to the assembler at assembly time. Also, Conditional directives may be used only to control the manner in which the program is assembled; they may never be used to cause the processor to make decisions at execution time.

All execution-time decisions to be made by the processor must be constructed with Conditional jumps. Later in this chapter, we will discuss the use of Conditional jumps for the implementation of the Selection and Case programming constructs to enable the program to make decisions at execution time.

The Conditional directives provided by MASM are **IF, IFE, IF1, IF2, IFB, IFNB, IFIDN, IFDIF, IFDEF, IFNDEF, ELSE,** and **ENDIF.** The general syntax for all Conditional directives is as follows:

```
IF condition
      Block of statements
      and/or directives
      to assemble if the
      condition is True
[ELSE
      Block of statements
      and/or directives
      to assemble if the
      condition is False]
ENDIF
```

Every Conditional directive requires an ENDIF directive to inform the assembler of the end of the conditional assembly. The ELSE directive is optional and may be used with any condition to provide a block to be assembled if the condition is False. The assembler evaluates the IF*condition* as either True or False. If it is True, then the true block is assembled; any False block (following an ELSE directive) is ignored. If the condition evaluates to False, then the True block is ignored, and the False block (if any) is assembled.

IF (if True, if not zero) and **IFE** (if equal to zero, if False) are complementary conditions and require the following syntax:

```
IF          expression
IFE         expression
```

IF evaluates as True if and only if the value of *expression* is True (nonzero). IFE is True if and only if *expression* is False (zero). In either case, *expression* must have a constant value, known to the assembler at assembly time, and may not contain forward references.

IF1 (if pass one) and **IF2** (if pass two) are used to cause instructions and/or directives to be assembled only on the first or second pass of the assembler. The syntax is:

```
IF1
IF2
```

Recall that MASM is a two-pass assembler; it reads through the source file twice, from beginning to end, calculating addresses for all symbols on pass one and generating the object file on pass two. IF1 evaluates as True during the first pass through the source file and as False during the second pass. IF2 is False during the first pass and True throughout the second pass.

IFB (if blank) and **IFNB** (if not blank) are also complementary and are used within macro definitions to test the existence or nonexistence of real parameters in a macro invocation. The syntax is as follows:

```
IFB         <dumyparam>
IFNB        <dumyparam>
```

Dumyparam is one of the parameters in the dummy parameter list of a macro definition and must always be enclosed within angle brackets (<>). When a macro invocation is expanded, *dumyparam* is replaced by the corresponding real parameter from the real parameter list supplied with the invocation. Thus IFB and IFNB actually test for the existence of a real parameter. IFB evaluates as True if and only if the real parameter, corresponding to *dumyparam*, was omitted from the parameter list in the macro invocation. IFNB is True if and only if the real parameter was not omitted.

IFB and IFNB are usually used to allow for default parameter values, to cause the assembly of some default instruction or directive whenever a parameter is left blank in an invocation. We will use IFB to provide for default parameter values in our locate-cursor building block developed later in this chapter.

IFIDN (if identical) and **IFDIF** (if different) are also used primarily to test parameters within a macro definition. The required syntax is as follows:

```
IFIDN     <dumyparam1>,<dumyparam2>
IFDIF     <dumyparam1>,<dumyparam2>
```

or

```
IFIDN     <dumyparam1>,<stringconst>
IFDIF     <dumyparam1>,<stringconst>
```

Dumyparam1 and *dumyparam2* are parameters within the dummy parameter list of a macro definition and must be enclosed in angle brackets (<>). *Stringconst* is a string constant, which is not enclosed in quotation marks, but which must be enclosed in angle brackets. As with IFB and IFNB, IFIDN and IFDIF are evaluated after the dummy parameters have been replaced by the real parameters provided with the macro invocation. Thus, they actually compare two real parameters or compare one real parameter with a string constant. IFIDN evaluates as True if and only if the two parameters, or the parameter and the string constant, are exactly identical. IFDIF results in a value of True if and only if the two parameters, or parameter and string constant, are not identical.

IFDEF (if defined) and **IFNDEF** (if not defined) are used to test whether a symbol has been previously defined in the Name field of a source line within a program. The syntax is as follows:

```
IFDEF     symbol
IFNDEF    symbol
```

IFDEF is True if and only if *symbol* has been previously defined. Conversely, IFNDEF evaluates as True if and only if *symbol* has not been previously defined.

Be careful in your use of IFDEF and IFNDEF. If *symbol* constitutes a forward reference to a symbol defined later in the program, then *symbol* will not be defined on the first pass but will be defined on the second pass. Thus, IFDEF or IFNDEF will evaluate differently on the two passes, resulting in the block of instructions and/or directives assembling during pass one but not during pass two. If the block contains instructions or directives that use memory, then the addresses of all subsequent symbols will be different during the second pass than what was calculated for them during the first pass. The assembler reports such an occurrence as "Phase error between passes," and the resulting object file should not be linked since all symbol references may have been replaced with incorrect addresses.

Remember that Conditional directives may **never** be used to attempt to cause a program decision at execution time. Conditional directives cause the assembler to make a decision as to the instructions to be included in the executable program; any program decisions must be accomplished by building a Selection or Case construct using one or more Conditional jump instructions. Before continuing, review the following summary of the most commonly used Conditional directives.

SUMMARY OF **Conditional Directives**

Conditional directives cause the assembler to make decisions during assembly; they can never be used to cause the program to make decisions during execution. A block of instructions and/or directives is assembled only if the condition evaluates to True; if ELSE is used, a second block is assembled only if the condition evaluates to false.

IF1

> True during pass 1.

IF2

> True during pass 2.

IFB   *<dumyparam>*

> True if the real parameter replacement for *dumyparam* is blank (omitted).

IFNB   *<dumyparam>*

> Complement of IFB. True if the real parameter replacement for *dumyparam* is not blank (not omitted).

IFIDN   *<dumyparam1>,<stringconst>*

> True if the real parameter replacement for *dumyparam* is exactly identical to *stringconst*.

IFDIF   *<dumyparam1>,<stringconst>*

> Complement of IFIDN. True if the real parameter replacement for *dumyparam* is not exactly identical to *stringconst*.

IFDEF   *symbol*

> True if *symbol* has been previously defined.

IFNDEF   *symbol*

> Complement of IFDEF. True if *symbol* has not been previously defined.

ELSE

> Optional. If used, the following block is assembled only if the previous Conditional directive evaluates to False.

ENDIF

> Marks the end of a Conditional directive. Every Conditional directive must be terminated with ENDIF.

LOCATE-CURSOR BUILDING BLOCK

We are now ready to design and implement our first building block. The rest of this section consists of an attempt to develop, in a very short time, many of the ideas and techniques an experienced assembly-language programmer may have evolved over many months or even years of trial and error. Consequently, we will do things many different "wrong" ways before we finally find a "right" way; that is the way ideas evolve. Try not to become discouraged or impatient; you must resist the temptation to skip past all the "mistakes" to the final resolution of the problem. Each "mistake" contains lessons to be learned, ideas and techniques to be understood.

As an example of a building block, we will use the problem of positioning the cursor on the screen. We will utilize BIOS video services to do the bulk of the work; our responsibility will be to provide BIOS with the information it needs to do the job. We will discuss video output in detail in the next chapter; for now, in order to position the cursor on the screen we must

```
Put the desired screen location into DX
     Row (0 through 24) into DH
     Column (0 through 79) into DL
Put 02H into AH
Put 00H into BH
Execute an interrupt type 10H (INT 10H)
```

The interrupt instruction transfers control to BIOS video services in read-only memory (ROM); the BIOS code locates the cursor as specified by the DX register and then returns program control to the next instruction following the interrupt. Thus to locate the cursor to the upper-left corner of the screen, we might code the following five instructions:

```
MOV      DH, 0        ;ROW #
MOV      DL, 0        ;COL #
MOV      AH, 02H      ;OPERATION CODE
MOV      BH, 00H      ;PAGE # (SEE CH 8)
INT      10H          ;TO BIOS VIDEO SVCS
```

Later in the program, to locate the cursor to the center of the screen, we could code as follows:

```
MOV      DH, 12       ;ROW #
MOV      DL, 40       ;COL #
MOV      AH, 02H      ;OPERATION CODE
MOV      BH, 00H      ;PAGE # (SEE CH 8)
INT      10H          ;TO BIOS VIDEO SVCS
```

This is unsatisfactory. Every positioning of the cursor requires that we code five instructions; we must remember the correct values for AH and BH and be very careful to type them correctly; we must remember in which registers to put the row and column, and we must not get the two mixed up; we must also remember to execute the proper interrupt type each time (10H). In addition, if the program uses AX, BX, or DX to store some values that must not be lost, then we must be very careful to push the used registers before altering them and to pop them in reverse order when finished. This is just the type of picky detail we would like to avoid. What we need is a building block that will allow us to code

```
          LOCATE     0, 0
```

or

```
          LOCATE     12, 40
```

or even

```
          LOCATE     AL, BL
```

where the desired row is stored in AL, and the column is in BL.

The MACRO and ENDM directives, discussed earlier, allow us to define just such a macro for positioning the cursor. The macro name will be LOCATE, and we need two dummy parameters (ROW and COL) for the row and column at which to position the cursor. The first line of our macro definition is

```
LOCATE     MACRO     ROW, COL
```

We then write the body of the macro definition using the dummy parameters, spelled exactly, wherever we want the assembler to substitute the real parameters and ending the macro definition with the ENDM directive. The result is as follows:

```
LOCATE     MACRO     ROW, COL

           MOV       DH, ROW     ;ROW #
           MOV       DL, COL     ;COL #
           MOV       AH, 02H     ;OPERATION CODE
           MOV       BH, 0       ;PAGE # 0
           INT       10H         ;TO BIOS VIDEO SVCS
           ENDM                  ;LOCATE
```

Once the macro has been defined in a program, we may use it as often as we like to position the cursor anywhere on the screen. For example, to locate the cursor to the upper-left corner of the screen, we simply code

```
          LOCATE     0, 0
```

MASM recognizes LOCATE as a previously defined macro and so expands it to its definition, replacing the dummy parameters with the real parameters, which were supplied in the macro invocation. Our single-line macro invocation results in:

```
+          MOV    DH, 0       ;ROW #
+          MOV    DL, 0       ;COL #
+          MOV    AH, 02H     ;OPERATION CODE
+          MOV    BH, 0       ;PAGE # 0
+          INT    10H         ;TO BIOS VIDEO SVCS
```

Note: The plus signs (+) to the left of each line are not part of the source code. We have shown them here only to emphasize that the indicated lines of code are the result of a macro expansion.

Observe that the dummy parameters, ROW and COL, in the macro definition have been replaced in the expansion by the real parameters, 0 and 0; otherwise, the expansion is identical to the definition. The five instructions resulting from the macro expansion are assembled into machine language, which causes BIOS to position the cursor to row 0, column 0 when the program is executed.

Similarly, to locate the cursor to the center of the screen, we might invoke the macro as follows:

```
LOCATE    12, 40
```

The assembler expands the macro invocation to:

```
+          MOV    DH, 12      ;ROW #
+          MOV    DL, 40      ;COL #
+          MOV    AH, 02H     ;OPERATION CODE
+          MOV    BH, 0       ;PAGE # 0
+          INT    10H         ;TO BIOS VIDEO SVCS
```

The result of the macro expansion is to cause BIOS to position the cursor to row 12, column 40.

We still have a number of problems with our macro, however. First, the macro modifies a number of registers in violation of our rule number two for building blocks (data isolation). We will defer the solution of that problem until later; for now, we have a much more serious problem. Suppose the desired row and column are register values rather than immediate values. Perhaps the desired row has been previously stored into DL, and the desired column is stored in DH; then we would invoke the macro as follows:

```
LOCATE    DL, DH
```

Remember, DL contains the desired row, and DH contains the desired column. During the expansion, MASM substitutes DL for ROW and DH for COL. The resulting expansion is as follows:

```
+              MOV      DH, DL        ;ROW #
+              MOV      DL, DH        ;COL #
+              MOV      AH, 02H       ;OPERATION CODE
+              MOV      BH, 0         ;PAGE # 0
+              INT      10H           ;TO BIOS VIDEO SVCS
```

Would this result in the proper location of the cursor? No. The desired column was stored in DH, but that value was overwritten in the first line of the expansion by the row value in DL. Thus if the row value in DL were 24 and the column value in DH were 40, for example, the cursor would be positioned to row 24, column 24 instead of row 24, column 40, as desired. With only two parameters, we might conceivably solve the problem through the very careful use of the IFIDN conditional directive. However, if there were more than two parameters, six or seven for example, attempting to protect all the parameter values with IFIDN directives would become extremely complicated.

The only suitable solution is to first move the parameter values one by one into some temporary storage area in memory; once all parameters have been safely stored, we can move the values one by one from the temporary storage into the desired registers. The 8086/8088 provides us with just such a temporary storage area, the stack.

The temporary storage and retrieval of values on the stack is usually accomplished with the PUSH and POP instructions. However, PUSH and POP place two restrictions on their operands that make them unsatisfactory for our present needs. Our parameters, ROW and COL, are both byte values; PUSH and POP require word operands. Also, we wish to allow immediate-mode real parameters for ROW and COL; PUSH and POP do not allow immediate-mode operands. We need another way to address the stack.

The Base-Pointer register (BP) provides just such an alternate method of addressing the stack. Recall that whenever BP is used in any form of indirect-memory addressing, the processor uses SS as the segment half of the address. Consequently, we can use Base-Pointer-plus-Index memory addressing to MOV parameters to and from the stack.

Before we can safely store values on the stack using BP, however, we must create a two-byte "hole" or safe area in the stack for our parameters, and we must point BP to the stack hole. We can do so by subtracting two from the stack pointer and moving its resulting value into BP. Consider the effect of the following instructions:

```
SUB      SP, 2
MOV      BP, SP
```

Figure 7-1 illustrates the creation of a stack hole by the above instructions.

**Figure 7-1   Stack after: SUB SP, 2
                              MOV BP, SP**

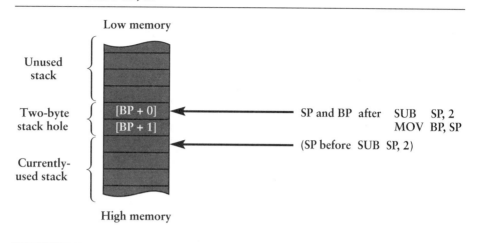

As illustrated by Figure 7-1, we now have two bytes of safe stack area in which to store our parameter values ([BP+0] and [BP+1]). Any subsequently pushed data will now go onto the stack above that two-byte stack hole (toward low memory). Of course SP now no longer points to the last value pushed; once we are through, we must add two to SP to close the hole. Our macro definition now looks like the following:

```
LOCATE      MACRO       ROW, COL

            SUB         SP, 2           ;MAKE 2-BYTE STACK HOLE
            MOV         BP, SP          ;POINT BP TO STACK HOLE
            MOV         [BP+0], ROW     ;SAVE PARAMS TO
            MOV         [BP+1], COL     ;   STACK HOLE
            MOV         DH, [BP+0]      ;ROW FROM STACK
            MOV         DL, [BP+1]      ;COL FROM STACK
            MOV         AH, 02H         ;OPERATION CODE
            MOV         BH, 0           ;PAGE # 0
            INT         10H             ;TO BIOS VIDEO SVCS
            ADD         SP, 2           ;CLOSE STACK HOLE
            ENDM                        ;LOCATE
```

We are getting close, but our macro still has problems. We want to allow ourselves the option of using either immediate or register addressing mode for the real parameters when invoking the macro (we will see shortly that we may not use any form of memory addressing). As written, the macro does not allow immediate mode. Consider what happens if we invoke the macro as follows:

```
LOCATE   12, 40
```

The expansion contains the following two instructions:

```
+        MOV      [BP+0], 12      ;SAVE PARAMETERS
+        MOV      [BP+1], 40      ;  INTO STACK HOLE
```

MASM cannot determine whether to assemble each instruction as a byte move or as a word move, since both operands are ambiguous. The destination operand, [BP+0], addresses memory and so might refer either to the byte at that location or to the word at that location, and 12 is an immediate value that might mean either 0CH (byte) or 000CH (word). The ambiguity must be resolved by explicitly stating the operand size with the PTR operator. To make our macro work for immediate-mode real parameters, we must then change those two instructions as follows:

```
MOV      BYTE PTR [BP+0], ROW     ;PARAM'S TO
MOV      BYTE PTR [BP+1], COL     ;  STACK HOLE
```

These are the only instructions in the macro that require the PTR operator. In every other case, MASM can tell the size of the instruction from one or the other of the operands. As a general rule, PTR will be required in all our future macros, but only in the instructions that move the dummy parameters to and from the stack.

One more problem still remains in our macro; it modifies several registers: BP, DX, AX, and BX. SP is also modified, but we were careful to restore it to its original value by adding two immediately before the end of the macro. Modifying the values of the other registers within the macro violates our second rule of designing building blocks (data isolation) and would make the macro very dangerous to use. Thus, we need to make one more change; we must push all used registers at the beginning of the macro and pop them at the end in order to restore them to their original values. We now have the following macro definition:

LOCATE Building Block as a Macro Only

```
LOCATE      MACRO     ROW, COL

            PUSH      AX                        ;SAVE
            PUSH      BX                        ;  ALL
            PUSH      DX                        ;  USED
            PUSH      BP                        ;  REGISTERS
            SUB       SP, 2                     ;MAKE 2-BYTE STACK HOLE
            MOV       BP, SP                    ;POINT BP TO STACK HOLE
            MOV       BYTE PTR [BP+0], ROW ;PARAMS
            MOV       BYTE PTR [BP+1], COL ;  TO STACK HOLE
```

```
          MOV      DH, [BP+0]          ;ROW FROM STACK
          MOV      DL, [BP+1]          ;COL FROM STACK
          MOV      AH, 02H             ;OPERATION CODE
          MOV      BH, 0               ;PAGE # 0
          INT      10H                 ;TO BIOS VIDEO SVCS
          ADD      SP, 2               ;CLOSE STACK HOLE
          POP      BP                  ;RESTORE
          POP      DX                  ;   ALL
          POP      BX                  ;   USED
          POP      AX                  ;   REGISTERS

          ENDM                         ;LOCATE
```

We have now arrived at a workable macro for locating the cursor to any position on the screen. It can easily be used in almost any situation. In terms of ease of use for the programmer, its one limitation is that the real parameters used in the macro invocation must be either immediate or register addressing mode; they cannot be memory. To understand why, consider the following situation. Suppose we were to use the DB directive in the data segment to set up two bytes of memory to store the desired row and column:

```
DATA          SEGMENT     PARA PUBLIC "DATA"

SCRN_ROW      DB          12
SCRN_COL      DB          40

DATA          ENDS
```

Then, within the code segment, we invoke the locate macro as follows:

```
          LOCATE     SCRN_ROW, SCRN_COL
```

The macro expansion with SCRN_ROW and SCRN_COL substituted for the dummy parameters contains the following two instructions:

```
+         MOV      [BP+0], SCRN_ROW    ;SAVE PARAMETERS
+         MOV      [BP+1], SCRN_COL    ; INTO STACK HOLE
```

[BP+0] and SCRN_ROW are both memory addressing modes as are [BP+1] and SCRN_COL. Thus the two instructions attempt to move from memory to memory, which the 8086/8088 processor cannot do; the source operand and destination operand may not both be memory. We will simply have to live with this limitation. Whenever we wish to locate to row and column values that are stored in memory, we must first move the values into byte registers, which we then use as the real parameters; we may use any available registers. Thus, we could accomplish the above locate as follows:

```
        MOV         AH, SCRN_ROW        ;OR ANY BYTE REG
        MOV         AL, SCRN_COL        ;OR ANY BYTE REG
        LOCATE      AH, AL
```

The LOCATE macro we have now developed follows most of our six rules for developing building blocks: 1) it performs only one function; 2) it maintains data isolation; 3) it has one entry point (the first instruction) and one exit point (the ENDM directive); and 4) it is easy to use in a wide variety of situations. But what about rule five? Are we making efficient use of memory? Every time the macro is invoked within a program, it is expanded out to its full definition. Thus, each invocation adds eighteen instructions to the program. When assembled, those instructions add from thirty-four to thirty-six bytes of machine code (thirty-four bytes if both parameters are registers; thirty-six bytes if both are immediate mode).

Thirty-six bytes may not seem like much, but suppose the macro is used one hundred times in the program; that amounts to about three and a half kilobytes. We need to examine the building block to see if we can decrease the memory required for each invocation. In doing so we should be careful, however; remember that rule six says in effect that programmer efficiency takes precedence over machine efficiency in most cases. We need to find a way to shrink the macro without jeopardizing its ease of use.

SUBPROCEDURES

We can greatly decrease the amount of code that is repeated with every macro invocation through the use of a **subprocedure**. Whereas a macro is fully expanded on every invocation, repeating much the same code, the subprocedure code will exist only once in the executable program but will be used repeatedly by each macro expansion. The subprocedure will be defined using the PROC and ENDP directives discussed in the last chapter; we will use Near subprocedures for all building blocks.

Each macro expansion will access the subprocedure at execution time with a CALL instruction, and the subprocedure will end with a RET instruction to return control to the calling macro expansion. Much of the code currently in our macro can be moved to such a subprocedure. Its form should be something like

```
$LOCATE     PROC    NEAR            ;NEAR SUBPROCEDURE TO
                                    ;  LOCATE THE CURSOR


            body
            of the
            subprocedure
```

```
            RET                              ;NEAR RETURN TO MACRO
                                             ;  EXPANSION

$LOCATE     ENDP                             ;END OF SUBPROCEDURE
```

We could have used any valid symbol for the subprocedure name. $LOCATE was chosen for several reasons. First, we could not have used LOCATE; that would have matched the macro name and confused the assembler. Second, we want to ensure that we do not accidentally use the same name as a symbol in any subsequent program in which we invoke the macro. Third, it is helpful to use a naming convention that enables us to determine later that this subprocedure is used by the LOCATE macro. $LOCATE satisfies all those requirements. The $ as the first character has no special meaning to the assembler; it is simply treated as one of the characters in the subprocedure name. By using it, we can ensure that we never use it as a symbol in any subsequent program; we will never use $ as the first character of a symbol, except for our building-block subprocedure names.

Now, we need to look closely at our macro to determine which instructions might be taken out of the macro and placed in the subprocedure. Any such instructions, in a subprocedure, will add to program size only once regardless of how many times we invoke the macro. Actually, rather than looking for instructions to remove from the macro, it is much easier to first determine which instructions may not be removed to the subprocedure. Whatever does not have to remain in the macro, we may then remove to the subprocedure.

In examining the macro, we notice the two instructions that put the parameters onto the stack:

```
    MOV       BYTE PTR [BP+0], ROW    ;PARAMS TO
    MOV       BYTE PTR [BP+1], COL    ;  STACK HOLE
```

Each makes reference to a dummy parameter that is to be replaced by a real parameter as the macro is expanded. Those two instructions must be left in the macro. Also, in order for those instructions to work properly, we must keep the instructions that create a stack hole with BP pointing to it. Since the macro will modify BP to point to the stack hole, we must also retain the instruction that saves its value so it can be restored. Therefore, we must also retain the following three instructions within the macro:

```
    PUSH      BP                       ;SAVE IT
    SUB       SP, 2                    ;MAKE 2-BYTE STACK HOLE
    MOV       BP, SP                   ;POINT BP TO STACK HOLE
```

The other pushes and pops do not have to be retained in the macro, since the macro no longer modifies those registers; the subprocedure will modify them, so the subprocedure will push them and pop them. After execution of the above five instructions, the macro may then call the subprocedure:

```
          CALL        $LOCATE
```

The subprocedure code must retrieve the parameter values from the stack into the correct registers, set up AH and BH properly, interrupt to BIOS to position the cursor, and then return to the macro expansion just after the CALL instruction. The macro then needs to do some house cleaning. It must close the stack hole and then restore BP to its previous value:

```
          ADD         SP, 2           ;CLOSE STACK HOLE
          POP         BP              ;RESTORE
```

The body of the macro definition may then be shortened to the following eight instructions:

```
LOCATE    MACRO       ROW, COL

          PUSH        BP              ;SAVE IT
          SUB         SP, 2           ;MAKE 2-BYTE STACK HOLE
          MOV         BP, SP          ;POINT BP TO STACK HOLE

          MOV         BYTE PTR [BP+0], ROW ;PARAMS TO
          MOV         BYTE PTR [BP+1], COL ; STACK HOLE

          CALL        $LOCATE         ;SUBPROC POSITIONS
                                      ;   THE CURSOR

          ADD         SP, 2           ;CLOSE STACK HOLE
          POP         BP              ;RESTORE IT

          ENDM                        ;LOCATE
```

All the remaining instructions should be made a part of the subprocedure, which then becomes the following:

```
$LOCATE    PROC       NEAR

          ;SAVE ALL USED REGISTERS
          PUSH        AX              ;REGISTERS
          PUSH        BX              ;   USED IN
          PUSH        DX              ;   SUBPROCEDURE

          ;GET PARAMETERS FROM STACK, SET UP OTHER REGISTERS,
          ;   AND INTERRUPT TO BIOS VIDEO SERVICES
          MOV         DH, [BP+0]      ;ROW # FROM STACK
          MOV         DL, [BP+1]      ;COL # FROM STACK
          MOV         AH, 02H         ;OPERATION CODE
```

```
        MOV       BH, 0           ;PAGE # 0
        INT       10H             ;TO BIOS VIDEO SVCS

;RESTORE REGISTERS AND RETURN TO MACRO
        POP       DX              ;RESTORE ALL
        POP       BX              ;  REGISTERS TO
        POP       AX              ;  ORIGINAL VALUES

        RET                       ;NEAR RETURN TO
                                  ;  MACRO

$LOCATE    ENDP
```

Notice that the macro pushes BP with its very first instruction and pops BP as its very last instruction. Also notice that in the procedure all pushes are located at the very beginning and all pops are located immediately before the RET. This is important in ensuring a match of pushes and pops. Always push all used registers at the beginning of a module and pop them in reverse order at the very end. Any violation of this rule makes the module difficult to maintain and increases the risk of a push/pop mismatch.

Now let us examine what happens when we invoke the LOCATE macro in a program. Suppose we want to locate to a column within line 24 at the bottom of the screen. Also assume that the program has somehow previously determined the desired column and stored it into CL. We would invoke the macro as follows:

```
        LOCATE    24, CL
```

The macro is expanded by the assembler and results in the following eight instructions in the assembled program:

```
+       PUSH      BP                      ;SAVE IT
+       SUB       SP, 2                   ;MAKE 2-BYTE
+                                         ;  STACK HOLE
+       MOV       BP, SP                  ;POINT BP TO
+                                         ;  STACK HOLE
+       MOV       BYTE PTR [BP+0], 24 ;PARAMS TO
+       MOV       BYTE PTR [BP+1], CL ; STACK HOLE
+
+       CALL      $LOCATE                 ;SUBPROC POSITIONS
+                                         ;  THE CURSOR
+       ADD       SP, 2                   ;CLOSE STACK HOLE
+       POP       BP                      ;RESTORE IT
```

The first five instructions result in a two-byte stack hole containing the values of the real parameters, 24 and the column value contained in CL. At this time, BP and SP both point to the parameter values on the stack. The CALL instruction then causes the processor to push the return address (the offset of the next instruction, ADD SP, 2) onto the stack and transfer control to the beginning of the subprocedure. The next instruction to be executed therefore will be the first instruction of the subprocedure:

```
PUSH      AX
PUSH      BX
PUSH      DX
MOV       DH, [BP+0]
MOV       DL, [BP+1]
MOV       AH, 02H
MOV       BH, 0
INT       10H
POP       DX
POP       BX
POP       AX
RET
```

Although SP has been modified by the CALL and is further modified by the three pushes, BP remains pointing directly to the parameter values. Thus BP can be used by the next two instructions to retrieve the parameter values into DH and DL, as required by BIOS.

The subprocedure then sets up AH and BH and executes an interrupt type 10H. This transfers control to the BIOS-video-services code, which positions the cursor to the row in DH and the column in DL and then returns to the subprocedure at the next instruction following the interrupt. The subprocedure then pops the saved register values, which results in SP pointing once again to the return offset. The RET instruction properly returns control to the macro expansion at the instruction ADD SP, 2.

After adding two to SP to close the stack hole, the macro expansion pops the original value of BP from the stack. At this point, the cursor has been located to the desired position and all registers are back to their original values. The invoking program then continues execution with the instruction following the macro invocation.

A PAUSE IN THE ACTION

Be Patient

As mentioned earlier, our intent in this section is to illustrate a number of ideas and concepts that most often are evolved over many months or years of trial and error. Consequently, we have developed (and still must develop) many interim solutions before we finally arrive at the ultimate solution to the locate-cursor building block.

Since the concepts developed in this section are crucial to successful assembly-language programming, it is critical that you resist any temptation to skip ahead to the final solution. Each interim solution illustrates vital concepts that are necessary to your understanding of the final building block.

Our building block will work as written thus far; however, we can make two more improvements. First, note the order of execution of the instructions RET and ADD SP, 2. Although RET is in the subprocedure, and ADD SP, 2 is in the macro expansion, they are always executed consecutively. That is, ADD SP, 2 is always executed immediately following RET.

This fact enables us to remove the ADD instruction from the macro. RET allows us to specify a value to be added to the stack pointer during the return. The instruction

```
        RET         n
```

has the effect of

```
        POP         IP
        ADD         SP, n
```

Notice that the return offset is popped from the stack into IP first, then the stack is adjusted. Once again, the fact that such a capability is included in the processor's instruction set is no accident. The engineers at Intel anticipated our use of a stack hole for parameter passing and wanted to make the job easier. We can take advantage of their thoughtfulness by changing the last instruction of the subprocedure to:

```
        RET         2               ;BACK TO THE MACRO
                                    ;  CLOSING STACK
```

Since the subprocedure now closes the stack hole as it returns, we must remove the ADD instruction from the macro. We should remove the following from the macro definition:

```
        ADD         SP, 2           ;CLOSE STACK HOLE
```

For clarity and ease of maintenance, we should also make it clear within the macro that the procedure closes the stack hole. We should modify the remark on the macro's CALL instruction to read

```
        CALL        $LOCATE         ;SUBPROC POSITIONS
                                    ;  CURSOR AND CLOSES
                                    ;  2-BYTE STACK HOLE
```

The stack adjustment adds two bytes to the RET instruction within the subprocedure; removing the ADD instruction shortens the macro definition by three bytes of machine code. Thus, we have saved three bytes on every macro invocation and paid for it with two bytes added to the subprocedure, which appears only once in the program.

DEFAULT PARAMETER VALUES

The next improvement we will make affects only the macro definition; we will use a Conditional directive to allow for **default parameter** values. In designing screen output, it is very often necessary to locate the cursor to the upper-left corner of the screen, more often than to any other position. It would be very useful, therefore, if we could invoke our macro without parameters as follows:

```
LOCATE
```

The macro should then default to the upper-left corner of the screen, to row 0 and column 0. We can allow for such default parameter values through the use of IFB or IFNB directives. Recall that IFB and IFNB are Conditional directives that may be used to control the manner in which a program is assembled. We can use IFB to provide default values for ROW and COL by modifying the following two statements in the macro definition:

```
MOV      BYTE PTR [BP+0], ROW      ;PARAM'S TO
MOV      BYTE PTR [BP+1], COL      ;  STACK HOLE
```

To cause ROW and COL to default to zero when left blank in the macro invocation, replace the above two lines with the following:

```
IFB      <ROW>                         ;ROW TO STACK
    MOV          BYTE PTR [BP+0], 0    ;  DEFAULT ROW
ELSE
    MOV          BYTE PTR [BP+0], ROW  ;  ROW
ENDIF

IFB      <COL>                         ;COL TO STACK
    MOV          BYTE PTR [BP+1], 0    ;  DEFAULT COL
ELSE
    MOV          BYTE PTR [BP+1], COL  ;  COLUMN
ENDIF
```

With the above changes to the macro definition, the macro still works properly when invoked with real parameters:

```
LOCATE   BL, CL
```

The above invocation results in both IFB directives evaluating as False since neither real parameter was left blank. The following two instructions would therefore be assembled into the macro expansion:

```
+            MOV         BYTE PTR [BP+0], BL        ; ROW
+
+            MOV         BYTE PTR [BP+1], CL        ; COLUMN
```

The macro may now also be invoked without parameters as follows:

```
LOCATE
```

Invoking the macro without parameters results in True for both IFB directives and so generates the following two instructions in the expansion:

```
+            MOV         BYTE PTR [BP+0], 0         ; DEFAULT ROW
+
+            MOV         BYTE PTR [BP+1], 0         ; DEFAULT COL
```

Thus, the cursor position defaults to the upper-left corner of the screen. The macro definition also allows us to specify one of the real parameters while leaving the other blank as follows:

```
LOCATE    24
LOCATE    , 20
```

The first invocation leaves only COL blank and so would position the cursor to column 0 of row 24. The second invocation leaves ROW blank and so positions the cursor to column 20 of row 0.

INTERNAL DOCUMENTATION

In writing our LOCATE building block, we have been careful to include remarks explaining each instruction. Such **internal documentation** is essential for maintainability of the building block. However, we also need documentation aimed at building-block use as well as maintenance. Such documentation should not include details of how the building block does its job, but simply what it does and how we can use it. We would prefer not to have to examine the entire building block in order to figure out how to use it; thus, internal documentation for the use of a building block should be placed at the beginning of the module, clearly set aside from the body of the module.

We will satisfy this requirement for further documentation by including a header at the beginning of each macro and another header at the beginning of each subprocedure. The macro header should provide only the information necessary for using the macro; it should not confuse matters with information about the procedure. It should provide the name of the macro and what it does and should describe all parameters: purpose, size, addressing modes allowed, and default values, if applicable. In addition, we will see shortly that many macros will be included in the same file; therefore, the header should include a means for quickly identifying where one macro ends and the next one begins. The following would make a good header for our LOCATE macro:

```
COMMENT     | LOCATE MACRO ===============================

            POSITIONS THE CURSOR ON THE SCREEN
            USES $LOCATE SUBPROCEDURE IN CONSOLE.LIB

            INPUT PARAMETERS:
                    ROW =       ROW TO POSITION TO (0 - 24)
                                SIZE: BYTE
                                ADDRESSING MODES: REGISTER OR
                                        IMMEDIATE
                                DEFAULT: 0
                    COL =       COLUMN TO POSITION TO (0 - 79)
                                SIZE: BYTE
                                ADDRESSING MODES: REGISTER OR
                                        IMMEDIATE
                                DEFAULT: 0


            OUTPUT PARAMETERS:
                    NONE
        |
```

We now need to write a similar header for our $LOCATE subprocedure. We should be careful to remember that we are no longer documenting the macro; we are documenting the use of the subprocedure. Therefore, our header should explain how to use the subprocedure alone; it should contain information needed by a programmer to use the subprocedure directly from a program or to write his or her own macro to use the subprocedure. Specifically, the subprocedure header should not refer to addressing modes or default values since they apply only to the macro.

We will learn shortly that our subprocedure will be written as a separate module, in its own .ASM file; therefore, we need to identify the name of the file and the name of the programmer within the header. We must also explain what the subprocedure does and how to use it. We need to explain the parameters passed to and/or from the subprocedure: the purpose of the parameter, its size, and its location on the stack. The following header would serve those needs:

```
COMMENT     |                       $LOCATE.ASM

            Yourname here

            SUBPROCEDURE TO POSITION THE CURSOR WITHIN PAGE
            0 OF THE SCREEN
```

```
USES INT 10H (BIOS VIDEO SERVICES), OPERATION
     02H

INPUT PARAMETERS:
     ROW TO POSITION TO
          SIZE:     BYTE
          LOCATION: [BP+0]
     COLUMN TO POSITION TO
          SIZE:     BYTE
          LOCATION: [BP+1]


OUTPUT PARAMETERS:
     NONE
```

BUILDING A MACRO LIBRARY

The building block we have just written can now be used in any future program that needs to position the cursor. Remember, however, that the macro must be defined within the source program and prior to any invocation. The macro definition must therefore be included at the beginning of every future program that needs to use it. There are a number of ways of accomplishing this. One would be to type the macro definition in every program we write. This would not be satisfactory. Aside from the extra typing required, there would be a high probability of introducing typographical errors during typing. Slightly better would be to use the cut-and-paste capability of a text editor to put the macro definition into each program.

An even better method is to use the INCLUDE directive provided by MASM. The required syntax is

```
INCLUDE   filespec
```

The effect of the INCLUDE directive is to cause MASM to open the indicated file and to read its contents into the file currently being assembled. In effect, the INCLUDE directive is replaced by the exact contents of the file; the result is the same as if the entire contents of the included file had been typed in place of the INCLUDE directive.

To avoid having to include many different macro files, one for each building block used in a program, we will organize all macros into one file that must be included in any program that uses them. Such a file containing many macro definitions is called a **macro library** and is usually given an extension of .MLB. A macro library is nothing more than a source file that contains a number of macro definitions.

   We could combine all macros into one library; however, it is usually more practical to group the macros into several libraries, according to function: CONSOLE.MLB—all macros for keyboard input or screen output; PRINTER.MLB—macros for printer output; and DISK.MLB—macros for disk I/O. We will discuss printer and disk I/O later in the text.

   CONSOLE.MLB will be a source file containing our LOCATE macro definition as well as the definitions of all other screen and keyboard macros we develop later. Whenever writing any program that involves keyboard input and/or screen output, we simply include the macro library early in the program with the following directive:

```
INCLUDE   CONSOLE.MLB
```

   The single INCLUDE directive defines all console-related macros. Remember, however, that no code is added to the program by a macro definition. Only those macros that are invoked are expanded, adding code to the program. Thus, including the entire library of macros (many of which may not be used) has no adverse effect on the size or speed of the resulting executable program.

   Including the macro library does, however, increase the time it takes for MASM to assemble the program. We can make one more slight improvement, which will decrease the extra time required for assembly. Recall that MASM is a two-pass assembler; it reads through the source program twice from beginning to end. All macro invocations are expanded on the first pass, while MASM is calculating the addresses of all symbols.

   Upon completion of the first pass, no macro invocations remain in the program since they have already been expanded. To save assembly time, we should include the macro library only on pass one, when working with MASM. Recall that the Conditional directive IF1 evaluates as True only while MASM is making its first pass through the source program. To cause MASM to read the macro library only on its first pass, we should use the following directives:

```
IF1
    INCLUDE   CONSOLE.MLB
ENDIF
```

   Note that the IF1 and ENDIF directives should be used if working with MASM, but should be omitted when working with the Turbo assembler. Recall that TASM is a single-pass assembler. IF1 has no effect, since it always evaluates as True; use of IF1 with TASM does however result in a "Pass dependent" warning error. Consequently, IF1 should be omitted when working with TASM in order to avoid the bothersome warning error.

   We now have an easy method of ensuring that all macros are defined at assembly time, prior to any macro invocation. Recall, however, that our macro calls a subprocedure, $LOCATE; therefore, we must also ensure that, at execution time, the subprocedure code exists within the code segment of the executable program.

We might approach the problem in the same manner we used for our macro definitions; that is, we might combine all our subprocedures into one file, CONSOLE.PLB (procedure library), for example, and include that file in every program. To do so, however, would result in a great deal of unnecessary code in the resulting executable program since the assembler would generate machine-language instructions for all the subprocedures, including those which are never used in the program. We need to explore a way to easily include only the necessary subprocedures in an executable program.

EXTERNAL SUBPROCEDURES

Recall that one of the major functions of LINK is to link several object modules together into one executable program. We can take advantage of this function by writing and assembling our building-block subprocedures as **external subprocedures**. An external subprocedure is a subprocedure that is not defined within the program that calls it. Instead, it is written as a separate source file and is then assembled to obtain an object file; the program that calls it is also assembled to obtain an object file. Then the two object files are linked together into one executable program. The subprocedure code is combined with the mainline code by LINK rather than by MASM. This process requires the use of two new directives:

```
EXTRN      symbol:type
```

and

```
PUBLIC     symbol
```

Symbol is any symbol that has been defined in the name field of a source line within the file that contains the PUBLIC directive, and is referenced by an instruction within the file that contains the EXTRN directive. *Type* is the type of the symbol: NEAR, FAR, BYTE, WORD, DWORD, etc.

The EXTRN directive is used in the calling module to inform the assembler that an undefined symbol will be defined in another object module. It causes the assembler to defer resolution of the symbol's address until link time. The PUBLIC directive is used in the external module to enable LINK to find the symbol at link time.

Consider what happens during assembly of a program that uses our LOCATE macro, but does not contain the $LOCATE subprocedure. In each macro expansion, MASM encounters the instruction, CALL $LOCATE. The symbol $LOCATE must be converted to an address, but since the subprocedure is not defined within the mainline module the assembler does not know its address.

Without the EXTRN directive, MASM would report it as an "Undefined symbol" and would not be able to successfully assemble the program.

However, if $LOCATE has been defined as external then MASM does not attempt to replace the symbol with its address. Instead, it inserts a special record, called an **external reference**, into the object file telling the linker to determine the symbol address at link time. The job of resolving the symbol to its address is turned over to the linker.

In addition to informing the assembler that $LOCATE is external, the EXTRN directive must also notify the assembler that it is a Near procedure. Thus, to use $LOCATE as an external subprocedure, the CALL instruction must be preceded by the following directive:

```
EXTRN      $LOCATE:NEAR
```

Warning to TASM users: If :NEAR is omitted, TASM defaults to a Type of Word instead of generating an error as it should. Consequently, the later instruction, CALL $LOCATE, assembles as a Near Memory-mode call rather than as an Immediate-mode call. Instead of transferring control to $LOCATE, the processor uses the first word of memory (first two bytes of code) of the subprocedure as the target address for the call, probably locking up the machine. Don't forget the type of NEAR.

The EXTRN directive must appear in the program before the CALL instruction. Furthermore, we must take care to include an EXTRN directive for every subprocedure used by any macro that is invoked within the program; omitting any external subprocedure results in a "Symbol not defined" error during assembly. At the same time, we must be careful to declare as external only those subprocedures whose macros are invoked by the program; if a subprocedure has been declared as external, then its object code is linked into the executable program, even if it is never called.

We can ensure that the subprocedure is declared as external if and only if its macro is invoked by making the EXTRN directive a part of the macro definition, before the CALL instruction. If a macro is never invoked in a program, then it is not expanded, and there is no EXTRN directive. If the macro is invoked, on the other hand, then the EXTRN directive appears within its expansion. Consider, however, that the macro may be invoked many times within a program. The EXTRN directive should not be repeated in every expansion; it should appear only in the first expansion. Again, we should use a conditional directive.

```
IFNDEF     symbol
```

Recall that IFNDEF evaluates as True if and only if *symbol* has not yet been defined within the source file being assembled. We can use IFNDEF to cause the assembly of an EXTRN directive only upon the first invocation of a macro:

```
IFNDEF     $LOCATE
    EXTRN      $LOCATE:NEAR
ENDIF
```

The first time the macro is expanded, $LOCATE is undefined and the EXTRN directive is assembled resulting in the definition of $LOCATE as an external Near procedure name. In all subsequent macro expansions the IFNDEF directive is evaluated as False, and the EXTRN directive is ignored by the assembler.

We can now finalize our LOCATE macro definition. Remember that it will be written as one of many macro definitions within the macro library, CONSOLE.MLB. Since CONSOLE.MLB will eventually contain a number of macros, it will be very helpful to include a header at the beginning of the macro library file, explaining its use and listing the macros it contains. The file should begin with the header shown in Figure 7-2.

Figure 7-2   Macro Library Header

```
COMMENT |          CONSOLE.MLB

        Yourname here

        MACRO LIBRARY FOR CONSOLE I/O (KEYBOARD AND SCREEN)

        TO USE:
                INCLUDE CONSOLE.MLB AT THE BEGINNING OF THE MAINLINE
                        PROGRAM.
                SPECIFY CONSOLE.LIB AS THE LIBRARY FILE DURING LINK.

        MACROS INCLUDED IN THIS LIBRARY:
                LOCATE ROW, COL


        |
```

Immediately following the library file header, we should include our first macro. Our final macro definition for a locate-cursor building block is shown in Figure 7-3.

Figure 7-3   Macro for Locate-Cursor Building Block

```
COMMENT | LOCATE MACRO ==============================================

        POSITIONS THE CURSOR ON THE SCREEN
        USES $LOCATE SUBPROCEDURE IN CONSOLE.LIB

        INPUT PARAMETERS:
            ROW =       ROW TO POSITION TO (0 - 24)
                        SIZE: BYTE
                        ADDRESSING MODES: REGISTER OR IMMEDIATE
                        DEFAULT: 0
            COL =       COLUMN TO POSITION TO (0 - 79)
                        SIZE: BYTE
                        ADDRESSING MODES: REGISTER OR IMMEDIATE
                        DEFAULT: 0
```

Figure 7-3: (continued)

```
        OUTPUT PARAMETERS:
            NONE
          |

LOCATE      MACRO       ROW, COL

            IFNDEF      $LOCATE
                EXTRN       $LOCATE:NEAR
            ENDIF

            PUSH        BP              ;SAVE IT
            SUB         SP, 2           ;MAKE 2-BYTE
                                        ;  STACK HOLE
            MOV         BP, SP          ;POINT BP TO
                                        ;  STACK HOLE

            IFB         <ROW>           ;ROW TO STACK
                MOV         BYTE PTR [BP+0], 0  ;  DEFAULT ROW
            ELSE
                MOV         BYTE PTR [BP+0], ROW;  ROW
            ENDIF

            IFB         <COL>                   ;COL TO STACK
                MOV         BYTE PTR [BP+1], 0  ;  DEFAULT COL
            ELSE
                MOV         BYTE PTR [BP+1], COL ;  COLUMN
            ENDIF

            CALL        $LOCATE         ;SUBPROC POSITIONS
                                        ;  CURSOR AND CLOSES
                                        ;  2-BYTE STACK HOLE

            POP         BP              ;RESTORE IT

            ENDM                        ;LOCATE
```

We now must make some additions to our $LOCATE subprocedure to allow its use as an external subprocedure. We will write it as a separate source file called $LOCATE.ASM; then we will assemble it separately to obtain an object file, $LOCATE.OBJ. This object file will then be linked with the calling program's object file to create the executable program.

Since $LOCATE is defined as external in the calling program, the assembler makes it an external reference to be resolved by the linker. LINK must be able to determine the address of the symbol so that it can substitute that address for the external references within the calling program's object file. However, once $LO-CATE.ASM has been assembled, all symbols will have been replaced by their addresses; $LOCATE.OBJ contains no symbols to which LINK can refer, unless we tell MASM otherwise. We must declare it as a **public symbol**; we use the PUBLIC directive to instruct the assembler to put a record within the object file, providing

LINK with the address of the symbol we have declared external in another module. Thus, we must include the following statement in the file $LOCATE.ASM:

```
PUBLIC     $LOCATE              ;WILL BE CALLED FROM
                                ;  OUTSIDE THIS MODULE
```

Also, since $LOCATE.ASM is to be written and assembled as a separate module, it requires several more directives. We may want to obtain an assembler listing when we assemble it, so we should include two listing directives:

```
TITLE     $LOCATE.ASM     ;TITLE OF LISTING
PAGE      55, 80          ;LINES, WIDTH
```

We must also declare a code segment since $LOCATE is to be assembled alone rather than being assembled within the code segment of another program. We must declare the code segment as PUBLIC combine type with the name CODE and a class of 'CODE', so that it will be combined with the code segment of the calling program; otherwise it would be linked into a separate segment and would not be reachable by a Near call. Since it is to be combined with the calling program's code segment, it need not begin on a paragraph (sixteen byte) boundary; a byte boundary will suffice. We also need to use an ASSUME directive to inform the assembler of the name of the code segment. Thus we will need the following:

```
CODE         SEGMENT     BYTE PUBLIC 'CODE'

             ASSUME      CS: CODE

$LOCATE      PROC        NEAR

             PUBLIC      $LOCATE
             *
             *
             *
$LOCATE      ENDP

CODE         ENDS
```

It is also good practice to include a data segment within all modules, even those which have no data; in fact, we will later write and use a macro that requires that a data segment be defined in any module that uses it. Since it will be combined with the data segment within the mainline, it need not begin on a paragraph boundary. However, it is a good idea to try to keep data on even memory addresses to allow for sixteen-bit memory access by the 8086. We will use Word alignment. Thus, we need

```
DATA         SEGMENT     WORD PUBLIC 'DATA'

             ASSUME      DS:DATA
       ;DEFINE AN EMPTY DATA SEGMENT

DATA         ENDS
```

Finally, we need to mark the end of the source file with an END directive. We do not want to specify an entry point, since that will be specified by the END directive in the mainline program that is linked to the subprocedure. The last line of the source program must then be:

```
            END                             ;END OF FILE, $LOCATE.ASM
```

Putting all that together with our previously defined subprocedure, we end up with the final version of the $LOCATE subprocedure. The source file $LO-CATE.ASM should include the code indicated in Figure 7-4.

Figure 7-4   Procedure for Locate-Cursor Building Block

```
COMMENT |  $LOCATE.ASM

        Yourname here

        SUBPROCEDURE TO POSITION THE CURSOR WITHIN PAGE 0
        OF THE SCREEN
        USES INT 10H (BIOS VIDEO SERVICES), OPERATION 02H

        INPUT PARAMETERS:
               ROW TO POSITION TO
                    SIZE: BYTE
                    LOCATION: [BP+0]
               COLUMN TO POSITION TO
                    SIZE: BYTE
                    LOCATION: [BP+1]

        OUTPUT PARAMETERS:
               NONE


           |


               TITLE    $LOCATE.ASM
               PAGE     55, 80              ;LINES, WIDTH

DATA           SEGMENT  WORD PUBLIC 'DATA'

               ASSUME   DS:DATA
        ;DEFINE AN EMPTY DATA SEGMENT

DATA           ENDS

CODE           SEGMENT  BYTE PUBLIC 'CODE'

               ASSUME   CS:CODE

$LOCATE        PROC     NEAR

               PUBLIC   $LOCATE
```

Figure 7-4:   (continued)

```
        ;SAVE ALL    USED REGISTERS
              PUSH    AX                      ;SAVE REGISTERS
              PUSH    BX                      ;  USED IN
              PUSH    DX                      ;   SUBPROCEDURE

        ;GET PARAMETERS FROM STACK, SET UP OTHER REGISTERS,
        ; AND INTERRUPT TO BIOS VIDEO SERVICES
              MOV     DH, [BP+0]              ;ROW # FROM STACK
              MOV     DL, [BP+1]              ;COL # FROM STACK
              MOV     AH, 02H                 ;OPERATION CODE
              MOV     BH, 0                   ;PAGE # 0
              INT     10H                     ;TO BIOS VIDEO SVCS

        ;RESTORE REGISTERS AND RETURN TO MACRO
              POP     DX                      ;RESTORE ALL
              POP     BX                      ;  REGISTERS TO
              POP     AX                      ;   ORIGINAL VALUES

              RET     2                       ;BACK TO THE MACRO
                                              ;  CLOSING STACK

$LOCATE       ENDP

CODE          ENDS

              END                             ;END OF FILE, $LOCATE.ASM
```

Once the subprocedure has been entered into the source file, $LOCATE.ASM must be assembled to create the object file, $LOCATE.OBJ, which contains the public symbol $LOCATE. Thereafter, any program that uses the LOCATE macro must INCLUDE CONSOLE.MLB and must be linked to $LOCATE.OBJ. Figure 7-5 is a skeletal example of a mainline program that uses the LOCATE building block. Notice the INCLUDE directive immediately after the program header.

Figure 7-5   Example Program Using LOCATE Building Block

```
              TITLE F7-5.ASM
              PAGE  55, 80

COMMENT |     PROGRAM:      F7-5.ASM
              PROGRAMMER:   Your name here
              DATE:         Date here
              CLASS:        Class name and number here
              INSTRUCTOR:   Instructor's name here
```

Figure 7-5: (continued)

```
                SAMPLE PROGRAM USING LOCATE BUILDING BLOCK
                INPUT PARAM'S:  NONE
                OUTPUT PARAM'S: NONE
                            RETURNS TO DOS, UPON COMPLETION
                |

                INCLUDE    CONSOLE.MLB

;STACK SEGMENT =====================================================

STACK         SEGMENT    PARA STACK 'STACK'       ;BEGIN STACK

              DB         64 DUP ('*STACK* ')      ;DEFINE 512
                                                  ;  BYTE STACK

STACK         ENDS                                ;END OF STACK

;DATA SEGMENT ======================================================

DATA          SEGMENT    PARA PUBLIC 'DATA'       ;BEGIN DATA

DATA          ENDS                                ;END OF DATA

;CODE SEGMENT ======================================================

CODE          SEGMENT    PARA PUBLIC 'CODE'       ;BEGIN CODE

              ASSUME     CS:CODE, SS:STACK

MAIN          PROC       FAR                ;BEGIN MAINLINE

       ;INITIALIZATION (SAME FOR ALL PROGRAMS)
       ;FIRST, SET UP FOR RETURN TO DOS VIA PSP
              PUSH       DS                  ;PUT RETURN SEG (PSP)
                                             ;  TO STACK
              MOV        AX, 0               ;PUT ZERO RETURN
              PUSH       AX                  ;  OFFSET TO STACK
       ;NOW, ADDRESS THE DATA SEGMENT WITH DS
              MOV        AX, DATA            ;POINT DS TO
              MOV        DS, AX              ;  DATA SEGMENT
              ASSUME     DS:DATA             ;ASSOCIATE DS WITH DATA

       ;BEGIN MAINLINE CODE
                 .
                 .
                 .

              LOCATE                         ;CURSOR TO UPPER-LEFT
                                             ;  CORNER OF SCREEN

                 .
                 .
                 .
```

Figure 7-5: (continued)

```
              LOCATE    24, 79          ;CURSOR TO LOWER-RIGHT
                                        ;  CORNER OF SCREEN
                .
                .
                .
              MOV       BH, 12          ;CURSOR TO
              MOV       BL, 40          ;  MIDDLE
              LOCATE    BH, BL          ;  OF SCREEN
                .
                .
                .

          ;MAIN-LINE CODE ENDS HERE
              RET                       ;FAR RETURN TO DOS VIA
                                        ;  PSP

MAIN          ENDP                      ;END OF MAIN PROCEDURE

CODE          ENDS                      ;END OF CODE SEGMENT

              END       MAIN            ;END OF F7-5.ASM
                                        ;  ENTRY POINT = MAIN
```

To create an executable program, we must assemble the program (F7-5.ASM) in Figure 7-5, resulting in an object file that contains the macro expansion for each invocation and an external reference to the symbol $LOCATE. Finally, we must link the two object modules (F7-5.OBJ and $LOCATE.OBJ) together. In response to the LINK "Object Modules" prompt, we must enter the names of both object modules, separated by a plus (+) sign:

Object Modules [.OBJ]: **F7-5+$LOCATE**

When it encounters the external reference to $LOCATE within F7-5.OBJ, LINK looks up its address within the list of public symbols in $LOCATE.OBJ and replaces the external reference with the symbol's address. After completion of the link, F7-5.EXE contains the machine-language instructions from both F7-5.OBJ and $LOCATE.OBJ, and the call has been fixed to refer to the address of the first instruction within $LOCATE.OBJ.

BUILDING AN OBJECT LIBRARY

We still have one difficulty in using our building block. Whenever linking any future program, we must remember to link in the object modules required by all macros that were invoked within the program; if we forget one, the linker is unable to find the symbol that was declared as external and so reports the symbol as an unresolved external and is unable to complete the link. On the other hand, we must be careful not to link in any object module whose macro is not used within the program; to do so would result in machine-language code within the program that is never executed, thus increasing the size of the executable program unnecessarily.

We need something analogous to our macro library; we need a file that contains the object code for all subprocedures, but from which LINK draws only those object modules necessary for the resolution of the external references created by macro invocations. Such a file is called an **object library** and is made possible by the library manager program, **LIB.EXE**.

An object library is in some ways analogous to our macro library, but is also very different. A macro library is a source file, which we create with an editor, and which contains only macro definitions. An object library is a special file that can only be created or modified by the library manager program (LIB) and that contains a number of object modules along with an index to help LINK find the appropriate module within which each public symbol is defined. Since it contains object code, it cannot be created or altered with an editor. Only LINK and LIB can read and understand an object library file.

To create an object library, we first must write one or more external subprocedures and assemble each one separately to create object files. We then must run LIB and tell it to create the object library and to read from the appropriate object files, adding them as object modules to the library. LIB must also be used to later remove any unwanted object modules from the library or to replace any modules we have altered. Only LIB can modify an object library file.

Once an object library has been created and all building-block subprocedures added to it, we link all subsequent programs to it. To link to an object library, we enter only the name of the mainline program, F7-5 for example, in response to the LINK "Object Modules" prompt:

```
Object Modules [.OBJ]: F7-5
```

We then enter the name of the object library, CONSOLE for example, in response to the "Libraries" prompt:

```
Libraries [.LIB]: CONSOLE
```

Whenever LINK encounters an external reference within F7-5.OBJ, it looks up the symbol within the index in CONSOLE.LIB. From the index, LINK determines the name and location of the object module (subprocedure) within which the symbol is defined as public; it then copies the appropriate object module from the library and links it into the executable program. An object module is linked into the program only when necessary to resolve an external reference. The effect is that whenever a macro is invoked within the program, its subprocedure is linked into the executable program; if any macro is not invoked anywhere within the program, then its subprocedure is not linked into the program. LINK automatically links in only those subprocedures which are necessary.

KEY TERMS TO REMEMBER

Subprocedure	Default parameter
Macro library	External subprocedure
External reference	Public symbol
Object library	

Figure 7-6 illustrates the system flowchart for the development of programs using a macro library and object library of building blocks.

USING LIB.EXE

To use the library manager, insert the assembler diskette into drive B, your working diskette in drive A, and enter "B:LIB" at the DOS prompt. After displaying a copyright message, LIB prompts for the name of the library file:

```
Library name:
```

Enter the name of an existing object library or the name desired for a new object library. It is not necessary to enter the extension; it will default to .LIB. Another extension may be specified if desired; however, most versions of LINK will not recognize an object library file with any extension other than .LIB.

If LIB does not find an existing object library file of the name specified, it asks if you want to create a new object library:

```
Library does not exist. Create?
```

Enter "Y" if you are creating a new object library; enter "N" if you are attempting to modify an existing library but entered the name incorrectly.

LIB then asks for the operations to be performed on the object library file:

```
Operations:
```

Enter one or more desired operations all in one continuous line, with no spaces. The following are valid operations:

Figure 7-6: **Program-Development System Flowchart**

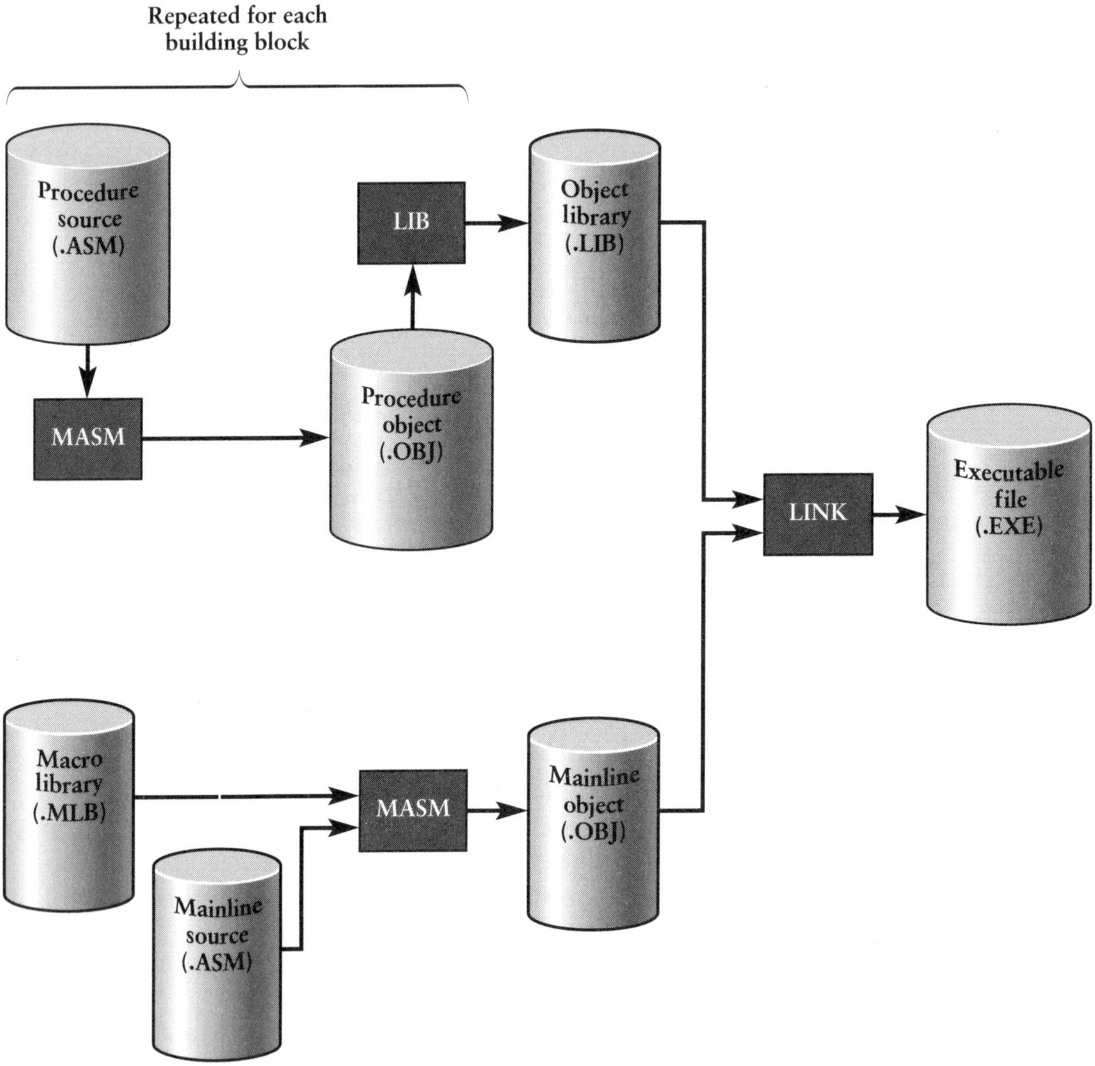

Plus sign   "+File_name" adds an object module to the library. LIB reads from an object file and adds it to the library as an object module with the primary filename as the module name. If the object file is not on the default drive diskette, then the drive must be specified (B:$LOCATE, for example). If the object file has any extension other than .OBJ, the extension must be specified.

Minus sign   "−Module_name" removes an object module from the library file. No drive or extension may be specified since Module_name refers to an object module within the library file, not to a separate object file.

Asterisk   "*Module_name" copies an object module from the library into a separate object file. The module is not removed from the library. The object file is always written to the default drive with an extension of .OBJ; LIB uses the module name as the primary filename.

Ampersand   "&" at the end of a line of operations causes LIB to repeat the "Operations:" prompt on the next line to allow for the entry of more operations. Use whenever the list of operations is too long to fit on one line.

To replace a module with a modified object file, you must remove it as well as add it. Enter either of the following in the list of operations (the order of removing and adding does not matter):

```
−Module_name+File_name
```

or

```
+File_name−Module_name
```

After the desired operations have been entered, LIB prompts for the name of a list file:

```
List file:
```

If you desire a listing of all public symbols and object modules within the library, specify the name of a file or device; if no listing is desired, press <Enter>.

If you are modifying an existing object library file, then LIB prompts for the name of the new library file:

```
Output library:
```

To keep the old library as is and create another library file with the operations performed on it, enter the name for the new library; the default extension is again .LIB. To make the changes to the existing library file, simply press <Enter>; after completion, the old library is preserved in a file with .BAK as its extension, and the .LIB file has the operations performed on it.

Following is a sample run of LIB in which the object library file, CONSOLE.LIB, is created and the single object module, $LOCATE, is added to it; no list file is obtained.

```
          Sample LIB Session (Create CONSOLE.LIB, add $LOCATE.OBJ)

       A>B:LIB

       Microsoft (R) Library Manager Version 3.10
       Copyright (C) Microsoft Corp 1983-1988. All rights
       reserved.

       Library name: CONSOLE
       Library does not exist. Create? Y
       Operations: +$LOCATE
       List file:

       A>
```

In order to modify a subprocedure, first modify the source (.ASM) file, then assemble it to obtain a modified object (.OBJ) file; finally replace the object module in the object library file. Following is a sample run of LIB in which the object module, $LOCATE, in CONSOLE.LIB is replaced with a modified object file, $LOCATE.OBJ. Again no list file is obtained.

```
          Sample LIB Session (replace $LOCATE.OBJ in CONSOLE.LIB)

       A>B:LIB

       Microsoft (R) Library Manager Version 3.10
       Copyright (C) Microsoft Corp 1983-1988. All rights
       reserved.

       Library name: CONSOLE
       Operations: -$LOCATE+$LOCATE
       List file:
       Output library:

       A>
```

To obtain a listing of all public symbols and object modules in a library, specify the name of a file or device (CON or PRN, for example) in response to the "List file:" prompt; you can obtain a listing without modifying the library file by pressing <Enter> at the "Operations:" prompt. Following is a sample run of LIB in which a listing of the completed CONSOLE object library is obtained; in the example, the listing is output to the screen (CON) but could just as well have been sent to the printer or to a disk file:

Sample LIB Session (Listing of CONSOLE.LIB)

```
A>B:LIB
Microsoft (R) Library Manager Version 3.10
Copyright (C) Microsoft Corp 1983-1988. All rights
reserved.

Library name: CONSOLE
Operations:
List file: CON

$DSPLY_CHR........ $DSP_CHR    $DSPLY_STR........ $DSP_STR
$INKEY............ $INKEY      $INPUT_CHR........ $INP_CHR
$INPUT_STR........ $INP_STR    $LOCATE........... $LOCATE
$SCROLL........... $SCROLL     $SCROLL_DOWN...... $SCROL_D

$DSP_CHR    Offset: 00000200H Code and data size: EH
  $DSPLY_CHR


$LOCATE     Offset: 00000400H Code and data size: 15H
  $LOCATE


$DSP_STR    Offset: 00000600H Code and data size: 21H
  $DSPLY_STR


$INP_CHR    Offset: 00000800H Code and data size: 19H
  $INPUT_CHR


$INP_STR    Offset: 00000A00H Code and data size: 83H
  $INPUT_STR


$SCROLL     Offset: 00000C00H Code and data size: 20H
  $SCROLL


$SCROL_D    Offset: 00000E00H Code and data size: 20H
  $SCROLL_DOWN


$INKEY      Offset: 00001000H Code and data size: 14H
  $INKEY

A>
```

Notice that the listing is in two parts. The first part is an alphabetical listing, in two columns, of all public symbols and the object modules in which they are defined. Each entry is in the following format:

```
Symbol...........Module
```

The second part of the listing is a list of all object modules, in the order in which they occur within the library. For each module, the listing gives the module name, the offset (from the beginning of the library file) at which the module is located, and the size in bytes of the module. Following each module name is a list of all public symbols defined within the module.

As with MASM and LINK, LIB also permits the specification of parameters on the command line. The syntax is as follows:

```
[d:]LIB libfile[,[operations][,[lstfile][,[newlib]]]][;]
```

For example, the following command performs the same operations as the second example above, replacing the $LOCATE object module in CONSOLE.LIB with a new version:

```
A>B:LIB CONSOLE, -$LOCATE+$LOCATE;
```

ANOTHER BUILDING BLOCK—DISPLAY A CHARACTER

As an example of another building block, let us consider the problem of displaying a character to the screen. Video output will be discussed fully in the next chapter; for now, to display a character the building block must

```
Put the character into DL.
Put the function code, 2, into AH.
Execute an interrupt type 21H.
```

Note that only one parameter is necessary, the character to be displayed. To create the building block, we should add a macro definition, DSPLY_CHR, to CONSOLE.MLB; if we have not already created CONSOLE.MLB, then we should create it and begin it with a macro library header as in Figure 7-2. The new macro to display a character should begin with a header similar to the one used for LOCATE. In addition to explaining the function of the macro, it should explain the purpose, size, and allowed addressing modes of the single parameter. The macro definition itself should begin with

```
DSPLY_CHR   MACRO    CHAR
```

The macro definition should also be very similar to the LOCATE macro, except that it only needs a one-byte stack hole for CHAR and does not need to allow any default parameters. Figure 7-7 provides a description of the required logic for the macro.

Figure 7-7   Macro Logic for Display-Character Building Block

```
Declare $DSPLY_CHR as external if not already defined.

Save the value in BP.
Create a 1-byte stack hole.
Point BP to the stack hole.
Move CHAR into the stack hole at [BP+0].
Call $DSPLY_CHR to display the character, close stack hole.
Restore BP to its original value.
```

Once the macro is completed in CONSOLE.MLB, we should write the source file for the procedure, $DSP_CHR.ASM. It should begin with a procedure header similar to the one in $LOCATE.ASM. The header should explain the function of the subprocedure as well as the purpose, size, and location (on the stack) of the parameter. The procedure itself should begin with the following PROC directive:

```
$DSPLY_CHR PROC      NEAR
```

Figure 7-8 summarizes the logic for the body of the procedure.

Figure 7-8   Procedure Logic for Display-Character Building Block

```
Declare $DSPLY_CHR as public.
Save all used registers.
Get the character from the stack into DL.
Put 2 into AH (function code to display character in DL).
Execute an interrupt type 21H (DOS function call).
Restore all saved registers.
Return, closing the one-byte stack hole.
```

Once $DSP_CHR.ASM is written, we should assemble it to obtain the object file, $DSP_CHR.OBJ, and then use LIB to add $DSP_CHR to the object library, CONSOLE.LIB; if CONSOLE.LIB has not been previously created, we should tell LIB to create it. The new building block could then be used in any future programs by including CONSOLE.MLB in the source file and then linking the resulting object file to the object library, CONSOLE.LIB. Within the source file, we would invoke the macro as follows in order to display characters to the screen:

```
DSPLY_CHR   'A'          ;DISPLAY AN "A"
DSPLY_CHR   13           ;DO A CARRIAGE RETURN
DSPLY_CHR   AL           ;DISPLAY THE CHARACTER
                         ;  STORED IN AL
```

INCLUDELIB DIRECTIVE AND TLIB

MASM version five and TASM provide an additional directive for the specification of a default object library. Its syntax is as follows:

```
INCLUDELIB libfile
```

Libfile is the filename of the object library to which the module is to be linked. The file extension need not be specified; it defaults to .LIB. Note that *libfile* is a file name only; it may not include a drive specifier or path. INCLUDELIB causes MASM (version five) or TASM to include a comment record within the object file, providing LINK or TLINK with the name of the default object library file to be used at link time. It eliminates the need to specify the object library name when linking.

If you are using TASM or version five or greater of MASM, you may simplify linking by adding the following directive to CONSOLE.MLB, immediately following the library comment header (after the delimiter character) in Figure 7-2:

```
INCLUDELIB CONSOLE
```

If you include such a directive in the macro library file then you need not specify an object library file when linking.

The library manager supplied with the Turbo assembler is called TLIB.EXE, rather than LIB.EXE. It is entirely compatible with LIB except that it requires that all parameters be specified on the command line:

```
[d:]TLIB libfile[,[operations][,[lstfile][,[newlib]]]][;]
```

SELECTION (ALTERNATION) CONSTRUCT

Many of your future programming assignments will require that the program make decisions at execution time. You may be tempted to implement such decisions with Conditional directives; do **not** attempt to do so. Conditional directives (since they are directives) cause the assembler to make a decision during program assembly. Conditional directives can **never** be used to cause the processor to make a decision at execution time.

All program decisions must be implemented with either a **Selection construct** (often called **Alternation construct**) or a **Case construct**. Selection causes the program to choose one of two possible alternatives and is implemented in high-level languages with If . . . Else . . . Endif or If . . . Then . . . Else. In pseudocode, a Selection construct is usually coded as follows:

```
If condition
      Block of statements
      to execute if
      condition is True
[Else
      Block of statements
      to execute if
      condition is False]
End if
```

Exactly one of the two blocks of instructions will be executed. If *condition* is True, then the first block is executed and the second block is skipped; if *condition* is False, then execution skips around the first block and only the second block is executed. The Else clause is optional. If it is omitted, then the two alternatives are to do the True block or to do nothing. The block of statements is executed only if *condition* is True; if it is False then execution skips around the entire block of statements.

Assembly language does not directly provide the Selection construct. It must be implemented through the use of Conditional jumps. As an example of implementing a Selection construct in assembly language, consider the problem of finding the absolute value (into CX) of the difference of two values, currently in AX and BX. One possible solution to the problem can be stated in pseudocode, as follows:

```
If AX GE BX
      Copy the value from AX into CX
      Subtract the value in BX from CX
Else
      Copy the value from BX into CX
      Subtract the value in AX from CX
End if
```

Note that if AX is greater than or equal to BX, then the resulting value in CX is AX − BX; otherwise, the result in CX is BX − AX. Thus the result in CX is the absolute value (always positive) of the difference between AX and BX. The following assembly-language code implements that logic:

```
               ;IF AX GE BX
               CMP     AX, BX           ;SKIP TRUE CLAUSE IF
               JNAE    AX_LESS          ;  AX LT BX
                   MOV     CX, AX       ;SUBTRACT BX FROM
                   SUB     CX, BX       ;  VALUE IN AX
                   JMP     SHORT CONT   ;GO ON
AX_LESS:       ;ELSE
                   MOV     CX, BX       ;SUBTRACT AX FROM
                   SUB     CX, AX       ;  VALUE IN BX
CONT:          ;ENDIF
```

The selection begins with a comparison and jump around the True block to the False block if the condition (AX GE BX) is not True. Note that JNAE was used because the data in AX and BX are to be treated as unsigned values; JNGE would have been used had we wanted to treat the data as signed values. Also note that the True clause must end with an Unconditional jump in order to avoid falling through and accidentally executing the False clause. As long as the False clause is short (under 127 bytes) the SHORT operator may be used to cause a Short Unconditional jump (byte displacement). If the assembler reports a "Jump out of range" error, then the SHORT operator must be removed to allow the assembly of a Near Unconditional jump (word displacement).

A selection that does not have a false clause, which involves taking action only when a condition is True, requires only a Conditional jump to branch around the block of statements when the condition is False. Consider the following logic:

```
If AL GT the ASCII character '9'
      Add 7 to AL
End if
```

We will require just such logic much later in the text when converting numeric data to characters for display. The logic could be implemented in assembly language as follows:

```
            ;IF AL GT '9'
            CMP     AL, '9'
            JNA     CONT
                ADD     AL, 7
CONT:       ;END IF
```

The limited range of Conditional jumps occasionally causes problems when implementing programming constructs. Recall that Conditional jumps are always Short, with a maximum range of 128 bytes backward through 127 bytes forward. Suppose we need to perform a selection in which the True clause consists of many instructions such as the following:

```
            ;IF AX GE BX
            CMP     AX, BX
            JNAE    CONT
                Block of many
                instructions
                to execute if
                AX GE BX
CONT:       ;END IF
```

If the block of instructions is very long, it may exceed the range of the Conditional jump (more than 127 bytes). If so, the assembler reports the severe error, "Jump out of range," and the resulting object file must not be linked. The selection must be rewritten using a Conditional jump around an Unconditional jump:

```
            ;IF AX GE BX
            CMP     AX, BX
            JAE     CONT_1
            JMP     CONT_2
CONT_1:             Block of many
                    instructions
                    to execute if
                    AX GE BX
CONT_2:     ;END IF
```

Note that JAE CONT_1 jumps to the block of statements if the condition (AX GE BX) is True. It is followed by an Unconditional jump (assembled as a Near jump with no range limit) around the block of statements. Thus, the block of statements executes only if the condition is True. Also note that the resulting code is less straightforward than it would be with just a Conditional jump (if that were possible). Use a Conditional jump around an Unconditional jump only when necessary, when the displacement is outside the range of a Conditional jump.

Sometimes it is necessary to implement a Selection construct in which the condition is a compound logical expression containing a logical operator, AND or OR. Consider the following logic to take some action if the data in AL is a capital letter from A through Z:

```
If AL GE 'A' and AL LE 'Z'
     Block
     of
     instructions
End if
```

Implementation in assembly language requires two comparisons and Conditional jumps as follows:

```
            ;IF AL GE 'A' AND AL LE 'Z'
            CMP     AL, 'A'
            JNAE    CONT
            CMP     AL, 'Z'
            JNBE    CONT
                Block
                of
                instructions
CONT:       ;END IF
```

The block of instructions executes if and only if both parts of the condition are True; execution jumps around the block of instructions if either part is False. Finally, consider the following selection in which the condition is a compound logical expression with OR as the logical operator:

```
If BL EQ 5 or BL EQ 15
     Block
```

```
        of
        instructions
End if
```

The block of instructions should be executed if either condition is True (or if both are True). It can be implemented as follows:

```
            ;IF BL EQ 5 OR BL EQ 15
            CMP    BL, 5
            JE     CONT_1
            CMP    BL, 15
            JNE    CONT_2
CONT_1:            Block
                   of
                   instructions
CONT_2:     ;END IF
```

A PAUSE IN THE ACTION

Importance of Structured-Programming Constructs

Since assembly language does not directly support structured-programming constructs, there is a tendency by assembly-language programmers to design problem solutions in terms of Conditional and Unconditional jumps. This tendency should be resisted as it most often results in "spaghetti-code" programs with convoluted logic and an excess of jumps.

Do not think in terms of jumps when designing programs. Design the logic with pseudocode, making use of structured-programming constructs and avoiding any use of "go to" or "branch to."

Once the structured logic has been designed, then implement it in assembly language using only those jumps which are necessary to implement programming constructs such as Iteration, Selection, and Case.

CASE CONSTRUCT

Occasionally a program must choose not one out of two alternatives, but one out of many alternatives. Such a decision requires a Case construct (CASE in Pascal, SWITCH in C, EVALUATE in COBOL). One common use of the Case construct is to service a menu choice from the user. If the user's choice has been input as a character into AL, then we might process the choice with the following logic:

```
Case of AL
      Case 1: AL = 'A'
```

```
          Do procedure 1
Case 2: AL = 'D'
          Do Procedure 2
Case 3: AL = 'F'
          Do procedure 3
Case 4: AL = 'M'
          Do procedure 4
Else
          Print error message
End case
```

The above Case construct can be implemented in assembly language as follows (note that each case ends with an Unconditional jump in order to avoid falling through and accidentally executing the else case):

```
              ;CASE OF AL
C_1:          ;CASE 1: AL = 'A'
        CMP       AL, 'A'
        JNE       C_2
              CALL       PROC_1
              JMP        SHORT C_END
C_2:          ;CASE 2: AL = 'D'
        CMP       AL, 'D'
        JNE       C_3
              CALL       PROC_2
              JMP        SHORT C_END
C_3:          ;CASE 3: AL = 'F'
        CMP       AL, 'F'
        JNE       C_4
              CALL       PROC_3
              JMP        SHORT C_END
C_4:          ;CASE 4: AL = 'M'
        CMP       AL, 'M'
        JNE       C_5
              CALL       PROC_4
              JMP        SHORT C_END
C_5:          ;ELSE
              CALL       PRINT_ERR
C_END:        ;END CASE
```

SUMMARY

Assembly language does not provide many of the input/output and data manipulation functions that we take for granted in high-level languages. In order to solve problems in assembly language, we first need to develop a library (toolbox) of easy-to-use building blocks (tools) to provide those basic functions. In fact, we create two types of libraries: The macro library is a source file, created with an editor, and contains a number of macro definitions; each macro places the parameters onto the stack and calls a subprocedure. The object library is created and managed using the object library manager program, LIB, and contains an object module for each subprocedure required by a macro; each subprocedure takes the parameters from the stack, performs the desired function, and returns to the macro.

To use the libraries, we INCLUDE the macro library into the source file of a program and then invoke the macros to perform the desired basic functions. During assembly, the assembler expands each macro invocation to its definition, substituting the real parameters for the dummy parameters in the definition. Once the program is assembled, we must link it to the object library by specifying the object library name during the link. LINK then extracts any used modules from the library and links them into the executable program.

All program decisions require the use of Conditional and Unconditional jumps for the implementation of the Selection and/or Case programming constructs. The Selection construct is used whenever the program must choose between two alternative sequences of instructions. The Case construct is used to allow the program to choose one of many possible alternatives.

You should get into the habit of using structured pseudocode for program design. Never think in terms of jumps when designing the solution to a problem. Rather you should think in terms of the structured-programming constructs discussed here and in the last chapter. When writing the program (once the design is complete), use only those jumps which are necessary in order to implement the programming constructs utilized in the pseudocode. The use of structured program design results in programs that use minimal branching and consequently are easier to test and debug, are much easier to maintain, and are often more efficient for the machine as well.

VOCABULARY

V7-1   In your own words, define each of the following terms:

a) Building block
b) Macro definition
c) Macro invocation
d) Macro expansion
e) Dummy parameters
f) Real parameters
g) Conditional directives
h) Subprocedure
i) Default parameter

j) Internal documentation
k) Macro library
l) External subprocedure
m) External reference
n) Public symbol
o) Object library
p) LIB.EXE, TLIB.EXE
q) Selection (alternation) construct
r) Case construct

REVIEW QUESTIONS

Q7-1   In your own words, describe the function of each of the following assembler directives:

    a) MACRO   d) EXTRN

    b) ENDM   e) PUBLIC

    c) INCLUDE   f) INCLUDELIB

Q7-2   What type of directives may be used to cause the assembler to make decisions about the manner in which to assemble the source?

Q7-3   Explain the use of the directives IF and IFE.

Q7-4   Explain the use of the directives IF1 and IF2.

Q7-5   Explain the use of the directives IFB and IFNB.

Q7-6   Explain the use of the directives IFIDN and IFDIF.

Q7-7   Explain the use of the directives IFDEF and IFNDEF.

Q7-8   Explain the use of the ELSE directive.

Q7-9   Explain the use of the ENDIF directive.

Q7-10   Suppose a program needs to check the value in BX to decide what value to move into AL. If BX is zero, it needs to move zero into AL; otherwise, it needs to move 255 into AL. Would the following block of code accomplish that task? If not, explain why, and rewrite the code to work properly.

```
IFIDN <BX>, <0>
    MOV    AL, 0
ELSE
    MOV    AL, 255
ENDIF
```

Q7-11   What value would be stored into AH by the following block of code?

```
MOV    AL, ' '
IFB    <AL>
    MOV    AH, 1
ELSE
    MOV    AH, 2
ENDIF
```

Q7-12   Would the following block of code move 1 into AH? If not, explain why.

```
MOV    AL, ''
IFB    <AL>
    MOV    AH, 1
ELSE
    MOV    AH, 2
ENDIF
```

Q7-13   Why does our LOCATE building block use the stack, rather than registers, for the passing of parameters?

Q7-14   What instruction is used in our LOCATE macro to create the stack hole for parameter passing?

Q7-15   Why was it desirable to move as much code as possible from our LOCATE macro to the $LOCATE subprocedure?

Q7-16   What directives are used to allow default parameters in a macro?

Q7-17   List the information that should be included in a macro header.

Q7-18   List the information that should be included in a procedure file header.

Q7-19   What directive must be used at the beginning of a mainline program that is to make use of building blocks?

Q7-20   What directive was necessary in our macro definition in order to allow it to call a procedure that is defined separately?

Q7-21   What directive was necessary in our procedure file in order to allow it to be called by the macro that is defined separately?

Q7-22   What is an object library?

Q7-23   Which is made up of source code, a macro library or an object library?

Q7-24   What is the purpose of LIB.EXE (or TLIB.EXE)?

Q7-25   List and describe the effect of each of the operators allowed by LIB (or TLIB).

Q7-26   Assume you have already used a text editor to create the following source files:

TEST.ASM	A mainline program that invokes both LOCATE and DSPLY_CHR macros.
CONSOLE.MLB	A macro library containing the macro definitions, LOCATE and DSPLY_CHR.
$LOCATE.ASM	The source file for the $LOCATE procedure.
$DSP_CHR.ASM	The source file for the $DSPLY_CHR procedure.

Describe the required sequence of steps using MASM, LINK, and LIB (or TASM, TLINK, and TLIB) to create the executable program, TEST.EXE. You may wish to refer to Figure 7-6.

Q7-27   After completing Q7-26, you modify the mainline procedure in TEST.ASM. What steps are necessary in order to create the new TEST.EXE?

Q7-28   After completing Q7-26, you modify the $LOCATE procedure in $LOCATE.ASM. What steps are necessary in order to create the new TEST.EXE?

Q7-29   After completing Q7-26, you modify the DSPLY_CHR macro in CONSOLE.MLB. What steps are necessary in order to create the new TEST.EXE?

Q7-30   Which two structured-programming constructs allow the program to make decisions? Explain the difference between the two constructs.

PROGRAMMING ASSIGNMENTS

PA7-1 Create a console library (CONSOLE.MLB and CONSOLE.LIB), and add a DSPLY_CHR building block. Refer to the discussion earlier in this chapter of the necessary macro and procedure. You may also want to refer to Figures 7-3 and 7-4 (macro and procedure for the LOCATE building block).

To test your building block, write a mainline program, PA7-1.ASM, to display several messages. It should be similar to PA6-1.ASM in the last chapter, except that it will use your building block to display characters. Immediately after the program header, you must INCLUDE CONSOLE.MLB; then use the DSPLY_CHR macro for any desired screen output. For example:

```
DSPLY_CHR     'T'      ;DISPLAY 'T' TO SCREEN
or
DSPLY_CHR     13       ;DISPLAY CR
or
DSPLY_CHR     AL       ;DISPLAY CHARACTER IN AL
```

Display any messages you like. After writing PA7-1.ASM, assemble it to obtain the object file PA7-1.OBJ. Then LINK it, specifying CONSOLE as the object library; the resulting PA7-1.EXE should display your messages to the screen and then return to the DOS prompt.

PA7-2 Create CONSOLE.MLB and CONSOLE.LIB, if you have not already done so. Then add a LOCATE building block to your library; refer to Figures 7-3 and 7-4. Write a test program, PA7-2, to test it: include several messages, positioning the cursor to a different location before displaying each message. In the next chapter, we will discuss a clear-screen building block; for now, use the DOS CLS command to clear the screen before running the program.

PA7-3 Do programming assignment PA7-1 or PA7-2. Then use DEBUG to load and examine your executable program. Disassemble the code. Note that each macro invocation has been replaced by its expansion; notice also that all dummy parameters have been replaced by real parameters. Macro expansions can be easily identified; they always begin with PUSH BP and end with POP BP.

Step through the program paying particular attention to register values before and after each macro expansion (before PUSH BP and after POP BP). Ensure that the macro expansions do not modify any register values, including SP.

Trace through a macro expansion and the subprocedure which it calls. Notice the sequence in which the instructions are executed and the manner in which the macro passes real parameters to the subprocedure.

8

Video and Printer Output

INTRODUCTION

Our exposure to video output in the last chapter was minimal, just enough to be able to develop two simple building blocks. In this chapter, we will thoroughly discuss both video and printer output. First we will examine the ASCII character code. Then we will discuss the video and printer hardware, BIOS video and printer services, and video and printer output through the DOS function call. Prior to our discussion of printer hardware, we must discuss the processor's input/output instructions, which allow it to communicate with the printer adapters and other peripheral hardware.

We will then examine some more useful building blocks for character output to the screen and printer via BIOS and DOS. After our discussion of single-character output, we will examine the different methods of storing and handling strings of characters, and we will discuss the building blocks for displaying and printing character strings. Finally, we will discuss recursion as an alternative to iteration, and we'll apply it to the problem of outputting a character string.

THE ASCII CHARACTER CODE

Much of the power of computers stems from the fact that they are capable of receiving, storing, manipulating, and conveying character data as well as numeric data. The ability of computers to process character data is achieved by assigning a numeric value from zero through 255 (or zero through 127) for each character to be stored. Such a one-to-one correspondence between characters and byte numeric values is called a **character code**. All commonly used character codes require a byte for the storage of one character.

The two most commonly used character codes are **ASCII** (American Standard Code for Information Interchange) and **EBCDIC** (Extended Binary Coded Decimal Interchange Code). EBCDIC is used on IBM mainframe computers as well as some minicomputers. Most minicomputers and virtually all microcomputers, including the IBM PC, represent characters in ASCII. Since we are working with the IBM PC, we will concentrate on the ASCII code. Figure 8-1 illustrates the correspondence between characters and their numeric values in ASCII.

Figure 8-1 **American Standard Code for Information Interchange (ASCII)**

Dec	Hex	Char	Dec	Hex	Char	Dec	Hex	Char
0	00	NUL	43	2B	+	86	56	V
1	01	SOH	44	2C	, (comma)	87	57	W
2	02	STX	45	2D	− (minus)	88	58	X
3	03	ETX	46	2E	. (period)	89	59	Y
4	04	EOT	47	2F	/	90	5A	Z
5	05	ENQ	48	30	0	91	5B	[
6	06	ACK	49	31	1	92	5C	\
7	07	BEL	50	32	2	93	5D	[
8	08	BS	51	33	3	94	5E	^
9	09	HT	52	34	4	95	5F	_ (underscore)
10	0A	LF	53	35	5	96	60	`
11	0B	VT	54	36	6	97	61	a
12	0C	FF	55	37	7	98	62	b
13	0D	CR	56	38	8	99	63	c
14	0E	SO	57	39	9	100	64	d
15	0F	SI	58	3A	:	101	65	e
16	10	DLE	59	3B	;	102	66	f
17	11	DC1	60	3C	<	103	67	g
18	12	DC2	61	3D	=	104	68	h
19	13	DC3	62	3E	>	105	69	i
20	14	DC4	63	3F	?	106	6A	j
21	15	NAK	64	40	@	107	6B	k
22	16	SYN	65	41	A	108	6C	l
23	17	ETB	66	42	B	109	6D	m
24	18	CAN	67	43	C	110	6E	n
25	19	EM	68	44	D	111	6F	o
26	1A	SUB	69	45	E	112	70	p
27	1B	ESC	70	46	F	113	71	q
28	1C	FS	71	47	G	114	72	r
29	1D	GS	72	48	H	115	73	s

30	1E	RS	73	49	I	116	74	t
31	1F	US	74	4A	J	117	75	u
32	20	(Space)	75	4B	K	118	76	v
33	21	!	76	4C	L	119	77	w
34	22	"	77	4D	M	120	78	x
35	23	#	78	4E	N	121	79	y
36	24	$	79	4F	O	122	7A	z
37	25	%	80	50	P	123	7B	{
38	26	&	81	51	Q	124	7C	|
39	27	'	82	52	R	125	7D	}
40	28	(	83	53	S	126	7E	~
41	29	)	84	54	T	127	7F	DEL
42	2A	*	85	55	U			

NOTE: ASCII uses only seven bits to represent the character; the high-order bit is reserved for use as a parity bit for error checking by telecommunications software and hardware. The same characters (NUL through DEL) are repeated for the codes 128 through 255 (80H - FFH).

It is very important to realize that there is no difference between the storage of characters and the storage of numbers within the computer. The same bit pattern (01000001B) that represents a byte numeric value of sixty-five also represents the letter A. The two are stored identically; the program is responsible for interpreting the stored value either as a number or as a character.

Note that ASCII defines all values from zero through 255. The codes zero through 31 as well as 127 are **control characters**; they are assigned specific purposes for communications control. Control characters are also often referred to as "nondisplayable" or "invisible" characters since they do not, by ASCII definition, result in a readable character on an output device. Similarly, standard ASCII defines the values from 128 through 255 as a repetition of the same characters as assigned for the values from zero through 127. These control characters and codes above 127 should not be confused with the extended keyboard characters to be discussed in the next chapter; extended keyboard characters apply only to keyboard input and have nothing to do with the ASCII code.

The IBM PC video hardware uses a **modified ASCII**; the codes above 127 and some of the control codes below 32 result in "funny" characters (happy face, foreign language symbols, graphics characters, etc.) when displayed to the screen. Refer to the PC BASIC reference manual for specific screen characters resulting from the codes. This modification to ASCII is nonstandard and applies only to IBM PC and compatible video hardware. Although the IBM Graphics printer (as well as many other dot-matrix printers) also prints special characters for the control codes and for the codes above 127, the characters assigned are entirely different; output of such codes to the printer will produce very different results than will their output to the screen. Refer to the specific printer manual to determine the modified ASCII character assignments for that printer.

COMMON AND AT COMBINE TYPES

Recall from our discussion in chapter 6 that the syntax for a segment directive is as follows:

```
Segname    SEGMENT   [align] [combine] ['class']
```

Also recall that the allowed *combine* types are PUBLIC, STACK, MEMORY, COMMON, AT segaddress, and private (default). We previously discussed PUBLIC, STACK, MEMORY, and private and deferred the discussion of both COMMON and AT segadress. Since COMMON combine type is sometimes useful and since AT segadress is especially useful in addressing video memory as well as the I/O port address table (useful for hardware access to the printer adapters), we will discuss them here.

COMMON combine type is used to redefine a segment of memory; its effect is much like the REDEFINES clause in COBOL. All segments with the same *segname* and a combine type of COMMON are begun at the same absolute address and so occupy the same memory addresses. The length of the resulting segment is equal to the length of the longest individual segment. Since the combined segments all occupy the same memory locations, only one initial value may be stored at each memory offset; consequently, if data is initialized in more than one of the COMMON segments, then only the initial values in the last COMMON segment are meaningful.

Recall that the assembler handles uninitialized data (?) differently with the DUP directive than without it. If data is initialized in a COMMON segment and then defined again as uninitialized data in a later COMMON segment, then its true initial value depends on whether DUP is used for the definition in the later segment. Consider the following example:

```
COMM_DATA   SEGMENT   PARA COMMON 'DATA'
TST_VAR1    DB        'TEST'
                      .
                      .
                      .
COMM_DATA   ENDS
                      .
                      .
                      .
COMM_DATA   SEGMENT   PARA COMMON 'DATA'
TST_VAR2    DB        ?, ?, ?, ?
                      .
                      .
                      .
COMM_DATA   ENDS
```

The assembler initializes the "uninitialized" values in TST_VAR2 to zero. Since TST_VAR2 occupies the same memory as TST_VAR1, the initial values of 'TEST' for TST_VAR1 are lost; both TST_VAR1 and TST_VAR2 are initialized to all zeros. In order to keep the initial values defined for TST_VAR1, TST_VAR2 must be defined in the second COMMON segment using the DUP operator, as follows:

```
TST_VAR2    DB 4    DUP (?)
```

Now the four bytes of TST_VAR2 in the second COMMON segment are truly uninitialized; the linker simply skips over four bytes for TST_VAR2. Consequently, the initial values supplied for TST_VAR1 in the first COMMON segment are preserved; the memory location occupied by both TST_VAR1 and TST_VAR2 contains the initial values of 'TEST'.

A combine type of **AT segaddress** is used to create a template for addressing a segment of memory outside the program. *Segaddress* is two-byte Segment address (one-sixteenth the absolute memory address at which the memory segment begins). The assembler does not generate any instructions or data for the segment; all instructions and initialized data are ignored except that the Location counter is updated by the number of bytes required by the instruction or data directive.

The segment adds nothing to the executable program. It merely provides a template of a segment of memory outside the program and is normally used to simplify the addressing of an area of system memory such as the screen, the interrupt vector table, or the I/O-port address table. This chapter contains two examples of the use of a segment with a combine type of AT *segaddress*: one to simplify addressing of video memory (Figures 8-4 and 8-5) and another to address the I/O-port address table contained in system memory (Figure 8-7).

KEY TERMS TO REMEMBER

Character code	Modified ASCII
ASCII	COMMON combine type
EBCDIC	AT segaddress combine type
Control character	

VIDEO ADAPTER HARDWARE

The IBM PC/XT uses **memory-mapped video**. A block of memory addresses is assigned to the screen; any data stored in this block of memory is automatically converted into a screen image. The amount of memory utilized and the addresses it occupies depend on the video adapter card in the machine. Many display adapters are currently used with the IBM PC family of computers.

Some of the most commonly used are: **Monochrome Display Adapter (MDA), Color/Graphics Adapter (CGA), Enhanced Graphics Adapter (EGA), Multi-Color Graphics Array (MCGA)** and **Video Graphics Array (VGA).** The MDA can display only text data and can drive only a monochrome monitor. The CGA can display either text data or graphics and is capable of outputting the proper electronic signal to drive a color monitor. The EGA, MCGA, and VGA all produce higher-resolution color/graphics than is possible with the CGA.

In an introductory text such as this it is not possible or appropriate to discuss the hardware details of all the various video adapters; such a discussion would require an entire text. However, we do feel that an understanding of the general principles involved is important. Consequently, we shall discuss one adapter, the CGA, in some detail.

The Color/Graphics Adapter contains a 6845 CRT Controller chip, or CRTC, and sixteen kilobytes of dual-ported video memory. The 6845 is a specialized microprocessor that reads the contents of the video memory and converts them to a video signal to create the correct image on the screen. The dual-ported memory can be accessed by both the 6845 CRTC and the system (8086/8088) processor. To display something, the system processor simply puts the correct data into the correct location in the screen memory; the 6845 then reads the data in memory and generates the correct signal to the monitor to cause the data to appear on the CRT.

The CRTC is capable of two very different interpretations of the data in screen memory. In **graphics video mode** the data in screen memory is interpreted as bits that indicate to the CRTC the manner in which to display the appropriate dot (**picture element** or **pixel**) on the screen.

In **text video mode** the data is interpreted as byte values containing the ASCII codes for the characters to be displayed. Two bytes are used for each character; the first byte contains the ASCII code for the character, and the second byte contains the **display attribute,** the manner in which the character is to be displayed.

The attribute byte contains the combination of colors for both the foreground (the character) and the background (the "box" around the character), as well as the intensity for the colors and whether the foreground should blink. Each color (foreground and background) is a combination of three colors (red, green, and blue), which are either on (bit = 1) or off (bit = 0). All three colors on results in white; all three off produces black. The normal display attribute is a black background with a white foreground; a white background and black foreground produces reverse video. Figure 8-2 illustrates the meaning of each bit of the display-attribute byte.

Because text mode uses two bytes for each character, and the screen is normally 80 columns by 25 lines, text mode requires 4,000 bytes for the entire screen (2 * 80 * 25). In 40-by-25 mode (double-wide characters), 2,000 bytes are required for one full screen of text data (2 * 40 * 25).

Figure 8-2   Display-Attribute Byte (Text Video Mode Only)

Bit #	Bit value	Result
0	0	Blue is off in foreground
	1	Blue is on in foreground
1	0	Green is off in foreground
	1	Green is on in foreground
2	0	Red is off in foreground
	1	Red is on in foreground
3	0	Normal intensity
	1	High intensity (bright)
4	0	Blue is off in background
	1	Blue is on in background
5	0	Green is off in background
	1	Green is on in background
6	0	Red is off in background
	1	Red is on in background
7	0	Normal - no blink
	1	Foreground blinks

Note: Bit 0 is the least-significant bit (right-most).

In graphics video mode screen memory is interpreted as individual bits indicating the status of the pixels. There are two possible graphics mode resolutions. Both resolutions allow 200 rows or **scan lines** of pixels; the difference is in the number of pixels per scan line and the number of bits used to represent a single pixel.

In 640/200 resolution, there are 640 pixels per row with each pixel either on or off as determined by a single bit of video memory. In 320/200 resolution, each scan line contains only 320 pixels; however, each pixel may be any one of four colors in the current **color palate**. Thus, since two bits are required to represent each pixel, as a value from zero through three, 320/200 resolution also requires 640 bits per scan line. Consequently, the total video memory required for either graphics mode is 16,000 bytes: 80 bytes per row (640 bits divided by 8) times 200 rows.

Although 16,000 bytes are required by graphics mode, the CGA actually contains sixteen kilobytes (16,384 bytes) with 384 bytes unused; the 384 bytes that are not used depends on the current mode of the adapter (80/25 text, 40/25 text, or graphics). The CGA memory is mapped to the absolute addresses, B8000H through BBFFFH or, as segment:offset, B800H:0000H through B800H:3FFFH.

When in 80/25 text mode, the CGA needs only 4,000 bytes of its sixteen kilobytes of memory in order to store a full screen of characters. Rather than wasting the other twelve-plus kilobytes, the designers cleverly divided the memory into pages of four kilobytes each (two kilobytes when in 40/25 text mode). It is possible to simultaneously store four full screens of text characters (eight in 40/25 text mode). The pages are numbered as zero through three (or zero through seven in 40/25 text mode).

When in 80/25 text mode, 4,000 (0FA0H) bytes are used for each page with 96 (0060H) unused bytes at the end of each page. A similar paging scheme is used in 40/25 text mode, except that each page is 2,000 (07D0H) bytes followed by 48 (0030H) unused bytes. Figure 8-3 illustrates the use of CGA memory in both 80/25 and 40/25 text modes.

Of course, only one page of 2,000 characters (1,000 if in 40/25 text mode) may be displayed on the screen at any given moment. The page that is currently displayed is called the **active page**; the active page is normally page zero but may be changed using BIOS video services discussed later.

Figure 8-4 illustrates the code to display a character directly to the adapter hardware in text mode. Note the use of AT segaddress combine type to define the video-memory segment.

Figure 8-3   CGA Memory Usage In Text Modes

```
80/25 Text Mode (4 pages)
B800H:0000H - 0F9FH      Page 0
       0FA0H - 0FFFH          (Not used)
       1000H - 1F9FH      Page 1
       1FA0H - 1FFFH          (Not used)
       2000H - 2F9FH      Page 2
       2FA0H - 2FFFH          (Not used)
       3000H - 3F9FH      Page 3
       3FA0H - 3FFFH          (Not used)
40/25 Text Mode (8 pages)
B800H:0000H - 07CFH      Page 0
       07D0H - 07FFH          (Not used)
       O800H - 0FCFH      Page 1
       0FD0H - 0FFFH          (Not used)
       1000H - 17CFH      Page 2
       17D0H - 17FFH          (Not used)
       1800H - 1FCFH      Page 3
       1FD0H - 1FFFH          (Not used)
       2000H - 27CFH      Page 4
       27D0H - 27FFH          (Not used)
       2800H - 2FCFH      Page 5
       2FD0H - 2FFFH          (Not used)
       3000H - 37CFH      Page 6
       37D0H - 37FFH          (Not used)
       3800H - 3FCFH      Page 7
       3FD0H - 3FFFH          (Not used)
```

Figure 8-4 **Display a Character Directly to Video Hardware (CGA)**

```
SCRN_SEG       SEGMENT     AT 0B800H         ;SEGMENT ADDRESS OF CGA

SCRN_MEM       DB          4000H DUP(?)      ;16 KBYTES OF SCREEN MEMORY

SCRN_SEG       ENDS
               .
               .
               .
CODE           SEGMENT     PARA PUBLIC 'CODE'
               .
               .
               .
       ;ADDRESS SCREEN MEMORY WITH ES
               MOV         AX, SCRN_SEG      ;POINT ES TO VIDEO
               MOV         ES, AX            ; MEMORY SEGMENT
               ASSUME      ES:SCRN_SEG       ;ASSOCIATE ES WITH SCREEN

       ;POINT DI TO OFFSET OF PAGE FOR DISPLAY
               MOV         AX, page          ;0 - 3 OR 0 - 7 FOR 40/25
               MOV         DX, 1000H         ;4 KBYTES PER PAGE
                                             ; (USE 800H FOR 40/25)
               MUL         DX                ;page TIMES BYTES/PAGE
               MOV         DI, AX            ;DI POINTS TO START OF PAGE

       ;ADJUST DI TO OFFSET OF LINE (WITHIN PAGE) FOR DISPLAY
               MOV         AX, line    ;0 - 24
               MOV         DX, 160           ;BYTES PER LINE (USE 80 FOR 40/25)
               MUL         DX                ;line TIMES BYTES/LINE
               ADD         DI, AX            ;DI POINTS TO START OF LINE IN PAGE

       ;ADJUST DI TO COLUMN (WITHIN PAGE AND LINE) FOR DISPLAY
               MOV         AX, column        ;0 - 79 (0 - 39 for 40/25)
               SHL         AX, 1             ;MULTIPLY column TIMES 2
               ADD         DI, AX            ;DI POINTS TO CORRECT BYTE IN
                                             ; VIDEO RAM

       ;STORE CHARACTER AND ATTRIBUTE INTO VIDEO MEMORY
               MOV         [SCRN_MEM+DI], character    ;DISPLAY IT
               MOV         [SCRN_MEM+DI+1], attribute ; WITH ATTRIBUTE
```

Note: Replace *page*, *line*, *column*, *character* and *attribute* with the appropriate immediate values, register names, or memory locations.

It should be noted that directly accessing the video hardware is hardware dependent and much more difficult than using BIOS or DOS video services. In any case, DOS cannot redirect standard output from any program that produces its output by directly accessing video hardware; similarly, <Ctrl>+<PrtSc> does not work properly with any program that directly accesses the video adapter. Video hardware should be directly accessed only when absolutely necessary (to provide extremely fast output, for example).

KEY TERMS TO REMEMBER

Memory-mapped video	Graphics video mode
MDA, CGA, EGA, MCGA, VGA	Pixel
Text video mode	Scan lines
Display attribute	Color palate
Active page	

In graphics mode (either 640/200 or 320/200), 16,000 bytes are required to represent a full screen of pixels. However, the memory is not organized quite as might be expected. One might expect that the first 16,000 bytes would be used for the pixels, leaving the last 384 bytes unused; this is not the case. The first 8,000 bytes (offsets 0000H through 1F4FH) are used for the even-numbered scan lines, the following 192 bytes (1F50H through 1FFFH) are unused, the next 8,000 bytes (2000H through 3F4FH) are used for the odd-numbered scan lines, and the last 192 bytes (3F50H through 3FFFH) are unused.

This memory usage actually makes sense when you consider the manner in which the monitor paints the screen. The monitor does not paint the full 200 scan lines at once from top to bottom; the scan lines are interlaced. The even numbered lines (0, 2, 4, ..., 198) are traced first, from top to bottom, then the odd lines (1, 3, ..., 199) are painted, from top to bottom, between the previously traced even scan lines. Such an interlaced scheme results in less screen flickering. The video memory is organized to allow the CRTC to use the first 8,000 contiguous bytes while painting the even-numbered scan lines and then to use the 8,000 contiguous bytes, beginning at offset 2000H, while painting the odd-numbered scan lines.

Although this organization makes the CRTC's job easier, it makes the programmer's job more difficult. Whenever manipulating pixels in graphics mode, you must remember that the even and odd scan lines are stored separately. For example, scan line zero is stored in offsets 0000H through 004FH; scan line one is at 2000H through 204FH; scan line two is at 0050H - 009FH; scan line three is at 2050H - 209FH. Figure 8-5 provides an example of the code to set, clear, or reverse (complement) a pixel in 640/200 graphics mode.

Figure 8-5   Manipulate a Pixel Directly to Video Hardware (CGA)

```
SCRN_SEG       SEGMENT    AT 0B800H           ;SEGMENT ADDRESS OF CGA

SCRN_MEM       DB         4000H DUP(?)         ;16 KBYTES SCREEN MEMORY

SCRN_SEG       ENDS
               .
               .
               .
CODE           SEGMENT    PARA PUBLIC 'CODE'
               .
               .
               .
       ;ADDRESS SCREEN MEMORY WITH ES
               MOV        AX, SCRN_SEG         ;POINT ES TO VIDEO
               MOV        ES, AX               ;   MEMORY SEGMENT
               ASSUME     ES:SCRN_SEG          ;ASSOCIATE ES WITH SCREEN

       ;POINT DI TO BEGINNING OF SCAN LINE
               MOV        AX, row              ;row = SCAN LINE (0 - 199)
               MOV        CL, 2                ;WILL SEPARATE EVEN & ODD SCAN
                                               ;   LINES
               DIV        CL                   ;AX / CL, QUOT TO AL, REM TO
                                               ;   AH (AH=0 => EVEN SCAN LINE,
                                               ;   AH=1 => ODD LINE)
               MOV        CH, AH               ;SAVE IT (EVEN OR ODD)
               MOV        CL, 80               ;BYTES/SCAN LINE (640 / 8)
               MUL        CL                   ;AL * CL, PRODUCT TO AX
       ;IF CH NE 0 (IF ODD SCAN LINE)
               CMP        CH, 0                ;SCAN LINE EVEN IF
               JE         EVN_SCN              ;   CH = 0
                   ADD        AX, 2000H        ;ADJUST ODD SCAN LINE TO
                                               ;   SECOND 8000 BYTES
EVN_SCN:       ;END IF
               MOV        DI, AX               ;DI POINTS TO BEGINNING OF
                                               ;   SCAN LINE

       ;ADJUST DI TO BYTE FOR PIXEL, DL TO BIT # WITHIN BYTE
               MOV        CL, 8                ;BITS PER BYTE
               MOV        AX, column           ;0 - 639
               DIV        CL                   ;AX / CL, QUOT TO AL, REM TO
                                               ;   AH (AL = BYTE NUMBER IN
                                               ;   SCAN LINE; AH IS BIT
                                               ;   NUMBER, FROM LEFT, OF
                                               ;   PIXEL: 0 = HIGH BIT,
                                               ;   7 = LOW BIT)
               MOV        CL, AH               ;SAVE BIT NUMBER OF PIXEL,
                                               ;   WILL USE FOR SHIFT, BELOW
               SUB        AH, AH               ;ZERO IT, NOW AX = BYTE NUMBER
               ADD        DI, AX               ;DI => OFFSET OF BYTE OF PIXEL
```

Figure 8-5: (continued)

```
;SET (OR CLEAR OR REVERSE) THE PIXEL
        MOV     AH, 80H             ;(10000000B) TO SET PIXEL
                                    ;TO CLEAR, USE 7FH (01111111B)
                                    ;TO REVERSE, ALSO USE 80H
        SHR     AH, CL              ;SHIFT THE 1 (OR 0) BIT TO
                                    ; CORRECT BIT FOR THE PIXEL
        MOV     AL, [SCRN_MEM + DI] ;GET THE EXISTING BYTE
        OR      AL, AH              ;SET THE CORRECT BIT FOR PIXEL
                                    ;TO CLEAR, USE "AND AL, AH")
                                    ;TO REVERSE, "XOR AL, AH")
        MOV     [SCRN_MEM + DI], AL ;PUT BYTE BACK INTO
                                    ;  SCREEN MEM, PIXEL IS
                                    ;  NOW SET (OR CLEARED
                                    ;  OR REVERSED)
```

Note: Replace *row* and *column* with the appropriate immediate values, register names, or memory locations.

INPUT/OUTPUT INSTRUCTIONS

Before addressing printer hardware, we must discuss two new processor instructions, **IN** and **OUT**, which allow the processor to move data to and from non-memory devices attached to the system bus. It is important not to confuse the I/O instructions with input and output to and from people. The processor alone cannot communicate in people-readable form; that is the responsibility of peripheral devices (such as printer adapter cards), which are attached to the system bus. Although the I/O instructions do not directly provide input/output to and from people, the processor often uses them to communicate with the device adapter cards, which then create the appropriate signals to drive the printer, keyboard, and other peripheral devices.

Only the AL (or AX) register may be specified as the destination operand for IN or as the source operand for OUT. The I/O port address may be specified either as a byte Immediate value (from zero through 255) or as the word value (zero through 65535) in the DX register. If the port address is specified as an Immediate value, then it is limited to zero through 255; any port address greater than 255 must be specified with DX as Register-mode addressing. Each instruction allows four possible combinations of operands. The four possible forms of the IN instruction are as follows:

```
IN      AL, byte_immed
IN      AL, DX
IN      AX, byte_immed
IN      AX, DX
```

The first form of the IN instruction inputs a byte value into AL from the I/O port specified as an Immediate value from zero through 255; the port address is stored as a byte Immediate value within the resulting machine-language instruction. Upon execution, the Bus Interface Unit places the I/O port address onto the low eight bits of the address bus, clears the high twelve address bits to zero, and places a command to input a byte onto the command bus. Since the command is to input data, rather than to read memory, the command and address are ignored by the memory control circuitry attached to the bus. The circuitry in some other peripheral device recognizes the input command and port address and retrieves the appropriate byte from a register within the peripheral device, placing it onto the data bus from which it is retrieved by the BIU.

The second form is identical to the first except that the BIU places the contents of the DX register onto the low sixteen bits of the address bus and clears the high four bits to zero. Consequently, the second form allows the addressing of I/O port addresses from zero through 65535. The last two forms are identical to the first two except that they input a word of data from a peripheral device and store it into AX.

The four allowed forms of the OUT instruction are as follows:

```
OUT     byte_immed, AL
OUT     DX, AL
OUT     byte_immed, AX
OUT     DX, AX
```

The OUT instruction causes the processor to output the byte value in AL or the word value in AX to the peripheral device that responds to the I/O port specified by a byte Immediate value or by the contents of the DX register. As with IN, the DX register must be used to specify any I/O port address greater than 255.

Note that although the processor's IN and OUT instructions support word values, none of the standard peripheral devices in the IBM PC/XT or compatibles is capable of responding to word input or output commands. Consequently, the word forms (using AX) are of little use on the IBM PC, unless communicating with some nonstandard adapter card that is capable of responding to word I/O requests.

PARALLEL PRINTER ADAPTER HARDWARE

The IBM PC may contain up to three parallel printer adapters. One is included on the IBM MDA video adapter (and on the CGA video adapter of some compatibles). The IBM parallel printer adapter is often included in machines that utilize an IBM CGA, which does not contain a parallel printer adapter.

Additionally, many other vendors sell multipurpose cards that contain one or more parallel printer adapters.

Communication by the processor with a printer adapter is entirely different than with a video adapter. A parallel printer adapter is not memory mapped; it does not contain any dual-ported memory that the processor can access. Instead, all communication between the processor and the adapter is through I/O ports via the IN and OUT instructions.

Every parallel printer adapter contains three registers that are accessible through I/O ports and are used for all communications between the CPU and the adapter: the **Data register** receives the character to be sent to the printer, the **Status register** contains bits reporting the current status of the printer, and the **Control register** is used by the CPU to control the operation of the adapter and printer. Figure 8-6 summarizes the I/O ports normally assigned to the three registers by various adapters; note, however, that many third-party adapters allow a choice of I/O ports through the use of DIP switches or jumpers.

As the PC boots, BIOS checks for an adapter at each of the above I/O port addresses, in order from top to bottom (3BCH first, then 378H, then 278H), and builds a port address table in RAM beginning at address 0040H:0008H. The port address of the data register of the first adapter found is stored at offset 0008H; that adapter is then treated by DOS and BIOS as LPT1 (PRN). The port address of the second adapter found (treated as LPT2) is stored as a word at offset 000AH; 000CH contains the port address of the third adapter, LPT3. A value of zero at any of the three offsets indicates that no more adapters were found.

Since the I/O ports for the printers may vary between machines depending on the adapters installed, any program that must output directly to a particular printer port (LPT1, LPT2, or LPT3) should obtain the Data register port address from the port address table. The I/O port for the Data register of the adapter for LPT1 may be obtained into DX as indicated in Figure 8-7. Note the use of AT segadress combine type to simplify addressing of the I/O port address table.

Figure 8-6   **Parallel Printer Adapter I/O Port Addresses**

	Data register	Status register	Control register
IBM MDA	3BCH	3BDH	3BEH
IBM printer adapter	378H	379H	37AH
3rd party printer adapters	278H	279H	27AH
Direction (input/output)	Out	In	Out/In

Figure 8-7   Initialize DX to Printer Adapter I/O Ports

```
PORT_TBL     SEGMENT   AT 40H                ;SEGMENT OF PORT TABLE

             DW        4 DUP(?)              ;SKIP OVER 8 BYTES
LPT1_PORT    DW        ?                     ;DEFINE VARIABLES FOR
LPT2_PORT    DW        ?                     ; THE THREE PRINTER
LPT3_PORT    DW        ?                     ; PORT ADDRESSES

PORT_TBL     ENDS
               .
               .
               .
CODE         SEGMENT   PARA PUBLIC 'CODE'
               .
               .
               .
             MOV       AX, PORT_TBL          ;ADDRESS I/O
             MOV       ES, AX                ; PORT TABLE
             ASSUME    ES:PORT_TBL           ; WITH ES
               .
               .
               .
             MOV       DX, LPT1_PORT         ;LPT1 PORT ADDRESS TO DX
                                             ; (or LPT2_PORT
                                             ; or LPT3_PORT)
```

Upon completion of the code in Figure 8-7, DX contains the I/O port address of the Data register of the desired adapter (LPT1, LPT2, or LPT3). The Data register (I/O port 3BCH, 378H, or 278H) is used to output a character from the CPU to the adapter. The Status register's I/O port is the Data register's port plus one (3BDH, 379H, or 279H). It is used as input to the processor in order to obtain the current status of the printer. Figure 8-8 illustrates the significance of each bit of the Status register.

The I/O port address of the Control register (3BEH, 37AH, or 27AH) may be obtained by adding two to the Data register I/O port. The Control register is normally used as output from the CPU to the printer adapter in order to control the function of the printer and adapter. If required, the current Control register value also may be input from the printer adapter to the CPU. The effect on the printer and adapter of each Control register bit is summarized in Figure 8-9.

**Figure 8-8   Parallel Printer Adapter Status Register
Input from adapter to CPU**

Bit #	Meaning
0 – 2	Unused, always 1
3	Error
	0 = printer error
	1 = normal
4	Select
	0 = printer not online
	1 = printer online
5	Paper
	0 = normal
	1 = printer out of paper
6	Acknowledge
	0 = acknowledge pulse
	1 = normal
7	Busy
	0 = printer is busy; do not send data
	1 = normal; ready for data

Note: Bit 0 is the least-significant bit (right-most).

**Figure 8-9   Parallel Printer Adapter Control Register
Output from CPU to adapter (may also be input)**

Bit #	Effect
0	Strobe
	0 = normal
	1 = pulse to output character
1	Auto line feed
	0 = normal, no auto line feed
	1 = auto line feed
2	Initialize
	0 = pulse to initialize printer
	1 = normal
3	Select
	Should always be 1
4	Enable interrupt
	0 = printer interrupt disabled
	1 = IRQ7 enabled on printer acknowledge
5 - 7	Unused - Always 1

Note: Bit 0 is the least-significant bit (right-most).

To print a character, first output it to the Data register. Then check the Busy bit of the Status register; keep checking until the printer is not busy. Finally, when the printer is not busy, cycle the Strobe bit of the Control register to one, then back to zero. The character in the Data register is sent to the printer when the Strobe bit cycles from one to zero. The necessary code to print a character through the parallel printer adapter, assuming that DX has already been initialized to the appropriate Data register I/O port address (3BCH, 378H, or 278H), is illustrated in Figure 8-10.

VIDEO OUTPUT THROUGH BIOS

BIOS video services provide a number of services for screen output, all accessed via interrupt type 10H (16). As with direct access to the adapter hardware discussed earlier, no BIOS services support redirection of standard output or the <Ctrl>+<PrtSc> printer toggle; any attempt to redirect standard output via the DOS command line or to obtain hard copy output through <Ctrl>+<PrtSc> will fail if the program utilizes BIOS video services for its screen output.

Figure 8-10   **Print a Character through Parallel Printer Adapter**

DX = Data register I/O port address
AL = Character to print

```
        ;OUTPUT THE CHARACTER TO THE ADAPTER
            OUT        DX, AL          ;CHARACTER TO DATA REG
                                       ; (I/O PORT 3BCH, 378H,
                                       ; OR 278H)
        ;WAIT UNTIL PRINTER IS NOT BUSY
            INC        DX              ; TO STATUS-REG I/O PORT
                                       ; (3BDH, 379H, OR 279H)
WAIT:       ;REPEAT UNTIL READY BIT SET IN STATUS REG
                IN        AL, DX       ;GET PRINTER STATUS REG
            TEST       AL, 80H         ;CONTINUE LOOP
            JZ         WAIT            ; UNTIL READY
            ;END REPEAT

        ;STROBE THE PRINTER ADAPTER TO SEND CHARACTER TO PRINTER
            INC        DX              ;TO CONTROL-REG PORT
                                       ; (3BEH, 37AH OR 27AH)
            IN         AL, DX          ;GET CURRENT VALUE
            OR         AL, 1           ;SET STROBE BIT (#0) TO 1
            OUT        DX, AL          ;STROBE THE PRINTER ADAPTER
            DEC        AL              ;CLEAR STROBE BIT (#0)
            OUT        DX, AL          ;TURN STROBE OFF TO PRINT
                                       ; THE CHARACTER
```

To use INT 10H (BIOS video services), place the appropriate operation code into AH; set up any other registers as indicated for the specific operation; and execute an interrupt type 10H. Following is a discussion of each of the BIOS video services.

00H - Set video mode:

To select the mode of a video adapter, put 00H into AH, put the desired mode (see Figure 8-11) into AL, and execute an interrupt type 10H. BIOS clears the screen and sets the video mode as indicated by AL.

Note from Figure 8-11 that modes 00H, 02H, and 05H are identical to modes 01H, 03H, and 04H except for the color burst signal. The color burst signal is required only for composite video monitors; it is not required for RGB monitors.

01H - Set cursor lines:

To customize the appearance of the cursor, put 01H into AH, put the desired cursor start and stop lines into CX, and execute an interrupt type 10H. Use operation 01H to change the cursor configuration (block, underscore, etc.).

CH = Start line of cursor (0 - 12 for MDA, 0 - 7 for others)
CL = Stop line of cursor (0 - 12 for MDA, 0 - 7 for others)

Figure 8-11   Video Modes (AL Register)

Mode (AL)	Reso- lution	Colors	Text/ Graphics	Adapters
00H	40/25 Color burst off	16	Text	CGA, EGA, MCGA, VGA
01H	40/25	16	Text	CGA, EGA, MCGA, VGA
02H	80/25 Color burst off	16	Text	CGA, EGA, MCGA, VGA
03H	80/25	16	Text	CGA, EGA, MCGA, VGA
04H	320/200	4	Graphics	CGA, EGA, MCGA, VGA
05H	320/200 Color burst off	4	Graphics	CGA, EGA, MCGA, VGA
06H	640/200	2	Graphics	CGA, EGA, MCGA, VGA
07H	80/25	2*	Text	MDA, EGA, VGA
0DH	320/200	16	Graphics	EGA, VGA
0EH	640/200	16	Graphics	EGA, VGA
0FH	640/350	2*	Graphics	EGA, VGA
10H	640/350	16	Graphics	EGA, VGA
11H	640/480	2	Graphics	MCGA, VGA
12H	640/480	16	Graphics	VGA
13H	320/200	256	Graphics	MCGA, VGA

* = Monochrome monitor only

BIOS sets the cursor scan lines according to CH and CL. The cursor lines determine the appearance of the cursor as it is displayed within the active page. In text mode with a CGA, each text line contains eight scan lines, numbered from zero through seven, top to bottom. A normal cursor starts on line six and stops on line seven. A block cursor starts on line zero and stops on line seven. If the start line is greater than the stop line, then the cursor includes the start line through line seven and "wraps" to lines zero through the stop line; the affect is a cursor made up of two parts, one above the other.

02H - Set cursor position:

To position the cursor within a screen page, put 02H into AH, page number into BH, desired position into DX, and perform an interrupt type 10H. This is the BIOS video service we used in the last chapter for the LOCATE building block.

    BH = Page
    DH = Row for cursor
    DL = Column for cursor

BIOS locates the cursor to the position specified by DH and DL within the page specified by BH. The new location determines where the cursor will appear if the page is active. Any subsequent output to that page will be located at the new cursor position, whether the page is active or not. Note that, in text mode, BIOS maintains a cursor position for all pages, not just for the active page.

03H - Read cursor position and cursor lines:

To read the current cursor configuration and location within any page, put 03H into AH, page number into BH, and execute an interrupt type 10H.

BIOS returns the position of the cursor within the page specified by BH, as well as the cursor lines. The position is returned in DX, with the cursor lines in CX.

    CH = Start line of cursor
    CL = Stop line of cursor
    DH = Row of cursor
    DL = Column of cursor

04H - Read light pen position:

To read the current position of a light pen for either text or graphics modes, put 04H into AH and execute INT 10H. BIOS returns light pen information as follows, in AH, BX, CX, and DX.

    AH = 0 Light pen not triggered—ignore rest of registers
    AH = 1 Valid values in registers, as described below
    DH = Text row of light pen
    DL = Text column of light pen
    CH = Pixel row of light pen (video modes 04H - 06H)
    CX = Pixel row of light pen (video modes 0DH - 13H)
    BX = Pixel column of light pen

05H - Select active page:

To select which text page is to be displayed to the screen, put 05H into AH, put the new active page number into AL, and execute INT 10H.

BIOS sets the active page to that specified by AL; the data within the new active page is immediately displayed on the screen.

06H - Scroll window up in active page:

To scroll all or part of the active page up, put 06H into AH, the number of lines to scroll into AL (0 to clear screen), the upper-left corner of window into CX (0, 0 for entire screen), the lower-right corner into DX, the attribute to use on the blank line(s) into BH, and do an interrupt type 10H.

AL = 0: Clear the screen window
AL = other: Number of lines to scroll up
CH = Row of upper-left corner
CL = Column of upper-left corner
DH = Row of lower-right corner
DL = Column of lower-right corner
BH = Attribute for fill line (entire window if AL = 0)

BIOS scrolls up the window, defined by CX and DX, the number of lines specified by AL; the bottom line(s) of the window is/are filled with blanks, using the display attribute in BH. If AL is zero, the entire window is cleared (filled with spaces) with the attribute in BH. Only the active page may be scrolled or cleared.

07H - Scroll window down in active page:

To scroll a screen window down, put 07H into AH, the number of lines into AL, upper-left corner of window into CX, lower-right corner into DX, the attribute to use on the blank line(s) into BH, and do an interrupt type 10H.

BIOS scrolls down all or part of active screen and fills the top line(s) with blanks, using the attribute in BH. Operation 07H is identical to operation 06H, above, except that it scrolls down instead of up.

08H - Read character and attribute at current cursor position:

To obtain the character and attribute at the current cursor position within any page, put 08H into AH, page number into BH, and do an interrupt type 10H.

BIOS reads the character and attribute at the current cursor position and returns them in AX.

AL = Character at the cursor
AH = Attribute of the character

09H - Write character and attribute at current cursor position:

To output a character with an attribute to any screen page, put 09H into AH, page into BH, character into AL, attribute into BL, number of times to repeat the character into CX, and do an interrupt type 10H.

BH = Page
AL = Character to display
BL = Display attribute for character
CX = Number of times to repeat the character

BIOS displays the character and attribute CX times, beginning at the current cursor position within the specified page. The cursor is not advanced after display! It remains at the position at which the character (or first character) is displayed. Control characters (BS, CR, LF, BEL, TAB, etc.) are not handled properly! They are displayed as graphics characters, musical notes, and so on.

0AH – Write a character only at current cursor position:

To display a character only, put 0AH into AH, page into BH, character into AL, number of times to repeat the character into CX, and do an interrupt type 10H.

BH = Page
AL = Character to display
CX = Number of times to repeat the character

BIOS displays the character with whatever attribute(s) is/are currently at the screen location(s). Otherwise, operation 0AH is identical to operation 09H above.

0CH – Write a dot (pixel):

Graphics modes only

To write a pixel, put 0CH into AH, page number into BH, pixel location into DX and CX, color ID into AL, and do an interrupt type 10H.

BH = Page (ignored for modes that support only one page)
DX = Row number of pixel
CX = Column of pixel
AL bits 0 through 6 = Pixel value
AL bit 7 =   0: Write the pixel value
                       1: XOR pixel value with current pixel contents

If bit seven of AL is zero, BIOS sets the pixel to the specified value. If bit seven is one, BIOS performs an Exclusive-OR of the specified pixel value on the value currently stored in the pixel location.

0DH – Read a dot (pixel):

Graphics modes only

To read the current color ID of a pixel, put 0DH into AH, page number into BH, pixel location into DX and CX, and do an interrupt type 10H.

BH = Page (ignored for modes that support only one page)
DX = Row number of pixel
CX = Column of pixel

BIOS returns the value of the specified pixel, in AL.

0EH - Write character and advance cursor (teletype):

To display a character and advance the cursor, put 0EH to AH, character to AL, page to BH, foreground color (graphics only) to BL, and do an interrupt type 10H.

AL = Character to display
BL = Foreground color for graphics modes
BH = Page for text modes

BIOS displays a single character and advances the cursor (teletype mode). BIOS does not alter the attribute byte currently in screen memory; the character is displayed with whatever attribute is currently at the screen location. The control characters BS, BEL, CR, and LF are handled properly. TAB is not properly handled!

0FH - Read current video status:

To determine the current video mode, active page, and character columns, put 0FH to AH, and execute INT 10H. BIOS returns the video mode, the active page, and the number of screen columns, as follows:

AL = Mode (see Figure 8-11)
BH = Active display page
AH = Number of character columns on screen

PRINTER OUTPUT THROUGH BIOS

Output to the parallel printer ports can be accomplished through **BIOS printer services**, accessed via interrupt type 17H and allowing access to any printer adapter by the printer number (LPT1, LPT2, or LPT3) regardless of the I/O ports of the actual adapters installed. To access a BIOS printer service, set AH to the desired operation code (0, 1, or 2), set DX to the desired printer (0 = LPT1, 1 = LPT2, 2 = LPT3), and set up any other registers as indicated below; then execute an interrupt type 17H. Following is a discussion of the three available BIOS printer services.

00H - Print a character to desired printer:

To print a character through any adapter, put 00H into AH, printer number into DX (0, 1, or 2), character into AL, and execute INT 17H.

AL = Character to print
DX = Printer (0 = LPT1, 1 = LPT2, 2 = LPT3)

BIOS looks up the printer adapter I/O port address, outputs the character to the adapter, waits until the printer is not busy, and strobes the adapter to send the character to the printer. Upon return, bit three of AH indicates the success or failure of the print operation.

AH bit 3 = 0: Normal; character was output successfully

AH bit 3 = 1: Time-out error; printer remained busy and BIOS was unable to print the character

01H - Initialize (reset) a printer:

To reset a printer to its initial power-up status, put 01H into AH, printer number into DX, and execute INT 17H.

BIOS strobes the Initialize bit in the Control register of the appropriate adapter to cause initialization (reset) of the printer. Upon return, bit three of AH indicates the success or failure of the reset operation.

AH bit 3 = 0: Normal; printer was initialized successfully

AH bit 3 = 1: Time-out error; printer did not respond; it is probably turned off

02H - Check printer status:

To check the status of a printer, put 02H into AH, printer number into DX, and execute INT 17H.

BIOS inputs the Status register from the appropriate adapter and returns it in AH, except that bits one through three and bit six are inverted by BIOS, and bit zero is used to indicate a printer time-out (no response from the printer adapter). The result in AH should be interpreted as follows:

Bit #	Meaning
0	Time-out
	0 = normal
	1 = time-out
1, 2	Unused, always 0
3	I/O error
	0 = normal
	1 = printer error
4	Select
	0 = printer not online
	1 = printer online
5	Paper
	0 = normal
	1 = printer out of paper
6	Acknowledge
	0 = normal
	1 = acknowledge pulse
7	Busy
	0 = printer is busy; do not send data
	1 = normal; ready for data

VIDEO OUTPUT THROUGH DOS

DOS provides three services for video output, all accessed through the DOS function call (INT 21H). The DOS function call also provides many other services besides video output. To access any DOS function call, place the appropriate function code into AH, set up other registers as required for the specific function, and execute an interrupt type 21H.

Video output through DOS has three major advantages over video output through BIOS or directly through the hardware. The first is that it is less likely to fail on partially compatible machines. The second advantage is that DOS video output can be redirected via the command line when the program is run, while video output through BIOS or through direct hardware manipulation cannot. Finally, functions 02H and 09H both check for <Ctrl>+<PrtSc>. If the <Ctrl>+<PrtSc> toggle is ON, then the output is also sent to the printer (LPT1).

Following is an explanation of the three DOS function calls for video output.

02H – Display a character:

To display a character via the DOS function call, put 02H (the function code) into AH and the character into DL, and execute INT 21H. This video service was used in the last chapter for the DSPLY_CHR building block.

DOS outputs the character to the screen at the current cursor position and advances the cursor. If the cursor is already at column 79, DOS automatically wraps it around; the cursor moves to the beginning of the next screen line. If the cursor is at column 79 of row 24, DOS scrolls the screen up, blanks the bottom line, and moves the cursor to the beginning of the new (bottom) screen line. Video-related control characters (BS, CR, LF, BEL, TAB, etc.) are properly displayed. If <Ctrl>+<PrtSc> is ON, the character is also output to PRN (LPT1).

06H – Direct console I/O:

Function 06H may be used to perform either output to the screen or input from the keyboard. To output to the screen, move 06H into AH, move the character (other than FFH) into DL, and execute an interrupt type 21H.

The character in DL is displayed to the screen as in function 02H above, except that DOS does not check for <Ctrl>+<PrtSc>. If DL contains FFH, as discussed in the next chapter, then function 06H performs keyboard input rather than video output.

09H – Display a string of characters:

To display a string of characters stored in memory with a single DOS function call, put 09H into AH; point DS:DX to the first byte of the string, and execute INT 21H. The string must be stored in memory and must use a dollar sign ($) as a trailer to mark the end of the string.

DS = Segment address of the string
DX = Offset of the first byte of the string

DOS begins displaying with the character at DS:[DX] and continues displaying all subsequent characters until it encounters $. $ is not displayed; it is used by DOS as a trailer to indicate where the string of characters ends. If <Ctrl>+<PrtSc> is ON, the string is also output to PRN (LPT1).

Since $ is required as the trailer, function call 09H may not be used to display any string that contains a dollar sign. We will discuss better means of handling character strings a little later in this chapter.

PRINTER OUTPUT THROUGH DOS

The DOS function call (INT 21H) also provides one function for printer output. As with all DOS function calls, it is accessed by putting the appropriate function code into AH, setting up other registers as required by the particular function, and executing an interrupt type 21H. Following is an explanation of the DOS function for printer output.

05H – Print a character to PRN (LPT1):

The DOS function call may be used for printer output to LPT1 (PRN) only. To print a single character to LPT1, put 05H into AH, put the character into DL, and execute INT 21H. DOS checks the printer status, waits until it is ready, and then prints the character to LPT1.

CAUTION

DOS does not return control to the program until it has successfully printed the character. If the printer is busy or offline or, worse yet, no printer is attached to the parallel printer port of the adapter, the system will lock up; if no printer is attached, the user may be required to reboot in order to regain control. If the printer is out of paper, DOS displays the following error message:

```
No paper error writing device PRN
Abort, Retry, Ignore?
```

The message appears two lines below the current cursor position; the screen scrolls up, if necessary. If the user presses "R," then DOS retries the print; the error will recur unless the user has corrected the problem (put paper into the printer). Pressing "I" causes DOS to ignore the out-of-paper error and attempt to print the character anyhow; this may lock up some printers and require the user to cycle the printer power off and on. If the user presses "A," then the program is aborted! Pressing "A" returns to the DOS prompt; any work the user has not saved to disk is lost!

Following is a brief summary of the most commonly used system services for video and printer output.

MOST COMMONLY USED Output System Services

```
INT 10H (BIOS video), operation 00H
```
Set video mode. AL = Mode.

```
INT 10H (BIOS video), operation 06H
```
Scroll window up in Active Page. AL = Lines (0 to clear screen), CX = Upper-left corner, DX = Lower-right corner, BH = Attribute.

```
INT 10H (BIOS video), operation 09H
```
Write a character and attribute to screen at current cursor position. BL = Color (Graphics mode), BH = Page (Text mode, normally 0), AL = Char, BL = Attribute, CX = Number of times to repeat.

```
INT 10H (BIOS video), operation 0EH
```
Write character to screen and advance cursor (teletype). AL = Char, BH = Page.

```
INT 17H (BIOS printer), operation 00H
```
Print a character to desired printer. AL = Char, DX = Printer (0 = LPT1, etc).

```
INT 17H (BIOS printer), operation 01H
```
Initialize (reset) a printer. DX = Printer.

```
INT 21H (DOS), function 02H
```
Display a character to screen. DL = Char.

```
INT 21H (DOS), function 05H
```
Print a character to PRN (LPT1). DL = Char.

BUILDING BLOCKS FOR VIDEO DISPLAY

In addition to LOCATE and DSPLY_CHR, a large number of other building blocks should be suggested by the above discussions of video output through hardware, BIOS, and DOS. Following is a brief discussion of several possible building blocks to be added to CONSOLE.MLB and CONSOLE.LIB.

Display a character and attribute, through BIOS:

```
BDSPLY_CHR      MACRO    CHAR, ATT, PAGE
```

CHAR (character), ATT (attribute), and PAGE are all byte input parameters allowing either register or immediate addressing mode. The macro should use an IFB or IFNB directive to default the page number (PAGE) to zero; it should also default the display attribute (ATT) to 07H (normal video—white on black). In addition, the building block will be much easier to use if it includes IFIDN directives to allow codes for the most common attributes. For example, it might include the following nested conditional directives:

```
IFB  <PAGE>                                  ;DEFAULT
    MOV BYTE PTR [BP+0], 0                    ; PAGE
ELSE                                         ; NUMBER
    MOV BYTE PTR [BP+0], PAGE                 ; TO
ENDIF                                        ; ZERO

IFB  <ATT>                                   ;DEFAULT ATT
    MOV BYTE PTR [BP+1], 07H                  ; IS NORMAL
ELSE
    IFIDN   <ATT>, <N>                        ;N ALSO RESULTS
        MOV BYTE PTR [BP+1], 07H              ; IN NORMAL
    ELSE
        IFIDN    <ATT>, <R>                   ;R RESULTS IN
            MOV BYTE PTR [BP+1], 70H          ; REVERSE VIDEO
        ELSE
            IFIDN    <ATT>, <B>               ;B RESULTS IN
                MOV BYTE PTR [BP+1], 87H      ; BLINK
            ELSE
                IFIDN    <ATT>, <H>           ;H = HI
                    MOV BYTE PTR [BP+1], 0FH  ; INTENS
                ELSE                          ;ELSE USE
                    MOV BYTE PTR [BP+1], ATT  ; ATT AS
                                              ; CODED
                ENDIF
            ENDIF
        ENDIF
    ENDIF
ENDIF
```

The procedure $BDSPLY_CHR should use BIOS video services (INT 10H) operation 09H to display the character with the desired attribute. Recall, however, that operation 09H does not advance the cursor after displaying the character, nor does it properly handle control characters. The easiest way to overcome this problem is by using a combination of BIOS video operations 09H (display character and attribute) and 0EH (display teletype).

The procedure should examine the character to determine if it is a video-related control character (BS, CR, LF, BEL, or TAB). If it's not a control character, then the subroutine should use BIOS video services operation 09H to display a space with the desired attribute (the cursor will remain at the same location). The subroutine then always uses BIOS video operation 0EH to display the character (control or otherwise) and to advance the cursor. The building block will not display TAB properly but will correctly handle all other characters.

Select the active video page:

```
SELECT_PAGE    MACRO    PAGE
```

PAGE is a byte input parameter specifying the video page to be displayed on the screen. The macro should put PAGE onto the stack and call the procedure $SEL_PAGE. The procedure should then use BIOS video services, operation 05H, to select the active page to be currently displayed to the screen.

Scroll a screen window up:

```
SCROLL  MACRO    LINES, UL_ROW, UL_COL, LR_ROW, LR_COL, ATT
```

All parameters are byte input parameters allowing either register or immediate mode. LINES is the number of lines to scroll the screen window up; the macro should allow a default of one. UL_ROW, UL_COL, LR_ROW, and LR_COL are the upper-left row, upper-left column, lower-right row, and lower-right column, respectively, of the screen window to be scrolled; they should default to the entire screen (0, 0, 24, and 79, respectively). ATT is the attribute for the blank line that will be created at the bottom of the screen; it should default to normal attribute (07H) and should allow the same attribute codes as in BDSPLY_CHR.

The macro should put the parameters (or defaults) into a stack hole and call the procedure $SCROLL. The procedure should retrieve the parameters from the stack into the proper registers and use BIOS video services, operation 06H, to scroll the screen window up.

Scroll a screen window down:

```
SCROLL_DN  MACRO    LINES, UL_ROW, UL_COL, LR_ROW, LR_COL, ATT
```

The macro should be identical to SCROLL, except that it must call a different procedure, $SCROLL_DN, which uses operation 07H to scroll down.

Clear a window of the screen:

```
CLS    MACRO    UL_ROW, UL_COL, LR_ROW, LR_COL, ATT
```

Recall that BIOS video services, operation 06H, clears the screen window if the number of lines in AL is zero. We can take advantage of that fact to create a clear-screen building block. Only a macro is necessary; the macro merely invokes the SCROLL macro, specifying zero for LINES and passing all other parameters through. To avoid confusion, in case CLS is invoked with any parameter that contains spaces, each of the parameters should be enclosed in angle brackets in the SCROLL invocation, as follows:

```
SCROLL    0, <UL_ROW>, <UL_COL>, <LR_ROW>, <LR_COL>, <ATT>
```

The result is that any invocation of CLS simply results in an expansion of SCROLL, with zero (0) as the real parameter for LINES. The IFB and IFIDN directives in SCROLL automatically provide the same defaults and attribute codes. If CLS is invoked without parameters, then its expansion results in an invocation of the SCROLL macro with all parameters blank except for LINES. The result is that the entire screen is cleared and filled with normal attribute spaces.

If you want the CLS macro to behave more like the DOS CLS command, then the cursor can be located to the upper-left corner of the screen (or screen window) after it is cleared. You might wish to also include an invocation of the LOCATE macro as follows:

```
LOCATE    <UL_ROW>, <UL_COL>
```

Set video mode:

```
SET_VID_MODE    MACRO    MODE
```

Since a program must sometimes change the video mode, it is helpful to develop a building block to change it. The procedure should use BIOS video services, operation 00H. MODE is a byte input parameter specifying the desired video mode. The macro header should include a list of the allowed modes similar to Figure 8-11.

Get video status:

```
GET_VID_STAT    MACRO    MODE, PAGE, COLS
```

Any program that modifies the video mode may need to first obtain and save the existing mode in order to restore it upon completion. Additionally, a program may need to determine the current active page or the number of character columns in the current mode. GET_VID_STAT will provide any or all of that information. The macro header should include a list of the allowed modes similar to Figure 8-11 or should refer to the list of modes in SET_VID_MODE.

MODE, PAGE, and COLS are optional byte output parameters to receive the video status information returned by BIOS. The macro should allow the omission of one or more of the parameters to allow the return of selective information. Since they are output parameters, register is the only allowed addressing mode for each parameter. The macro should not move any of the parameters onto the stack before calling the procedure; it should merely open a three-byte stack hole, point BP to the hole, and then call the procedure.

The procedure should use BIOS video services, operation 0FH, to obtain the video status information. It should put the status information onto the stack and return without closing the stack hole.

Upon return from the procedure, the macro should move the video information from the stack hole into each output parameter, unless the parameter is blank (use IFNB). After retrieving the status information, the macro must close the stack hole. Output parameters will be discussed more thoroughly in the next chapter. For now, Figures 8-12 and 8-13 illustrate the GET_VID_STAT macro and procedure.

Figure 8-12   Macro for Get-Video-Status Building Block

```
COMMENT | GET_VID_STAT MACRO ====================================

        OBTAINS THE CURRENT VIDEO MODE, ACTIVE PAGE, AND
        CHARACTER COLUMNS FROM BIOS.
        USES $GET_VID_STAT PROCEDURE IN CONSOLE.LIB

        INPUT PARAMETERS:
             NONE

        OUTPUT PARAMETERS:
             MODE = CURRENT VIDEO MODE
                   OPTIONAL PARAMETER
                   SIZE: BYTE
                   ADDRESSING MODES: REGISTER ONLY
             PAGE = ACTIVE PAGE
                   OPTIONAL PARAMETER
                   SIZE: BYTE
                   ADDRESSING MODES: REGISTER ONLY
             COLS = CHARACTER COLUMNS ON SCREEN
                   OPTIONAL PARAMETER
                   SIZE: BYTE
                   ADDRESSING MODES: REGISTER ONLY
        SEE SET_VID_MODE FOR A LIST OF VIDEO MODES
          |

GET_VID_STAT    MACRO   MODE, PAGE, COLS

                IFNDEF $GET_VID_STAT
                    EXTRN  $GET_VID_STAT:NEAR
                ENDIF

                PUSH    BP              ;SAVE IT
                SUB     SP, 3           ;MAKE 3-BYTE
                                        ; STACK HOLE
                MOV     BP, SP          ;POINT BP TO
                                        ; STACK HOLE
                CALL    $GET_VID_STAT   ;SUB-PROC DOES NOT
                                        ; CLOSE STACK HOLE
```

Figure 8-12:   (continued)

```
                IFNB    <MODE>              ;RETURN VIDEO
                    MOV     MODE, [BP+0]    ; MODE IF
                ENDIF                       ; NOT BLANK
                IFNB    <PAGE>              ;RETURN ACTIVE
                    MOV     PAGE, [BP+1]    ; PAGE IF
                ENDIF                       ; NOT BLANK
                IFNB    <COLS>              ;RETURN CHARACTER
                    MOV     COLS, [BP+2]    ; COLUMNS IF
                ENDIF                       ; NOT BLANK
                ADD     SP, 3               ;CLOSE STACK HOLE
                POP     BP                  ;RESTORE IT

                ENDM                        ;GET_VID_STAT
```

Figure 8-13   Procedure for Get-Video-Status Building Block

```
COMMENT |  $GET_VS.ASM

        Your name here

        SUBPROCEDURE TO OBTAIN CURRENT VIDEO STATUS
        INFORMATION
        USES INT 10H (BIOS VIDEO SERVICES), OPERATION 0FH

        INPUT PARAMETERS:
                NONE

        OUTPUT PARAMETERS:
                CURRENT VIDEO MODE
                        SIZE: BYTE
                        LOCATION: [BP+0]
                ACTIVE PAGE
                        SIZE: BYTE
                        LOCATION: [BP+1]
                CHARACTER COLUMNS
                        SIZE: BYTE
                        LOCATION: [BP+2]
        |

                TITLE $GET_VS.ASM         ;TITLE OF LISTING
                PAGE 55, 80               ;LINES, WIDTH

DATA            SEGMENT WORD PUBLIC 'DATA'

                ASSUME  DS:DATA
        ;DEFINE AN EMPTY DATA SEGMENT

DATA            ENDS
```

Figure 8-13:   (continued)

```
CODE                 SEGMENT BYTE PUBLIC 'CODE'

                     ASSUME  CS:CODE

$GET_VID_STAT        PROC    NEAR
                     PUBLIC  $GET_VID_STAT

            ;SAVE ALL USED REGISTERS
                     PUSH    AX                ;SAVE MODIFIED
                     PUSH    BX                ; REGISTERS
            ;SET UP REGISTERS AND INTERRUPT TO BIOS VIDEO SERVICES
                     MOV     AH, 0FH           ;OPERATION CODE
                     INT     10H               ;TO BIOS VIDEO SVCS
            ;RETURN VIDEO INFORMATION ON STACK
                     MOV     [BP+0], AL        ;RETURN MODE,
                     MOV     [BP+1], BH        ; ACTIVE PAGE,
                     MOV     [BP+2], AH        ; AND COLUMNS
            ;RESTORE REGISTERS AND RETURN TO MACRO
                     POP     BX                ;RESTORE MODIFIED
                     POP     AX                ; REGISTERS
                     RET                       ;NEAR RETURN TO MACRO;
                                               ; LEAVE STACK HOLE OPEN

$GET_VID_STAT        ENDP

CODE                 ENDS

                     END                       ;END OF FILE, $GET_VS.ASM
```

Figure 8-14 provides an example of a mainline program that uses both GET_VID_STAT and SET_VID_MODE building blocks. It sets the video mode to forty columns wide, displays a message, pauses, and then restores the original video mode before returning to DOS. The resulting program, F8-14.EXE, requires a CGA, MCGA, EGA, or VGA video adapter; it will not work with an MDA adapter.

Figure 8-14   **Example Program Using GET-VID-STAT, SET-VID-MODE, and DSPLY__CHR Building Blocks**

```
                     TITLE   F8-14.ASM
                     PAGE    55, 80

COMMENT |            PROGRAM: F8-14.ASM
                     PROGRAMMER:     Your name here
                     DATE:           Date here
                     CLASS:          Class name and number here
                     INSTRUCTOR:     Instructor's name here
```

Figure 8-14:   (continued)

```
                    SAMPLE PROGRAM USING GET_VID_STAT, SET_VID_MODE, AND
                    DSPLY_CHR BUILDING BLOCKS.

                    REQUIRES CGA, MCGA, EGA, OR VGA VIDEO ADAPTER.

                    INPUT PARAM'S:   NONE
                    OUTPUT PARAM'S:  NONE
                                     RETURNS TO DOS, UPON COMPLETION
                    |

                         INCLUDE CONSOLE.MLB


;STACK SEGMENT ============================================================

STACK            SEGMENT PARA STACK 'STACK'        ;BEGIN STACK

                 DB      64 DUP ('*STACK* ')       ;DEFINE 512
                                                   ; BYTE STACK

STACK            ENDS                              ;END OF STACK


;DATA SEGMENT =============================================================

DATA             SEGMENT PARA PUBLIC 'DATA'        ;BEGIN DATA

V_MODE           DB      ?

DATA             ENDS                              ;END OF DATA


;CODE SEGMENT =============================================================

CODE             SEGMENT PARA PUBLIC 'CODE'        ;BEGIN CODE

                 ASSUME  CS:CODE, SS:STACK

MAIN             PROC    FAR               ;BEGIN MAINLINE

        ;INITIALIZATION (SAME FOR ALL PROGRAMS)
        ;FIRST, SET UP FOR RETURN TO DOS VIA PSP
                 PUSH    DS                ;PUT RETURN SEG (PSP)
                                           ; TO STACK
                 MOV     AX, 0             ;PUT ZERO RETURN
                 PUSH    AX                ; OFFSET TO STACK
        ;NOW, ADDRESS THE DATA SEGMENT WITH DS
                 MOV     AX, DATA          ;POINT DS TO
                 MOV     DS, AX            ; DATA SEGMENT
                 ASSUME  DS:DATA           ;ASSOCIATE DS WITH DATA
```

Figure 8-14: (continued)

```
                    ;BEGIN MAIN-LINE CODE
                    ;SET VIDEO MODE TO 40/25, 16 COLOR, TEXT
                            GET_VID_STAT     DL       ;GET AND SAVE
                            MOV     V_MODE, DL        ; CURRENT VIDEO MODE
                            SET_VID_MODE     01H      ;SET NEW MODE
                    ;DISPLAY A MESSAGE TO THE SCREEN
                            DSPLY_CHR         'T'
                            DSPLY_CHR         'e'
                            DSPLY_CHR         's'
                            DSPLY_CHR         't'
                            DSPLY_CHR         'i'
                            DSPLY_CHR         'n'
                            DSPLY_CHR         'g'
                            DSPLY_CHR         ' '
                            DSPLY_CHR         '4'
                            DSPLY_CHR         '0'
                            DSPLY_CHR         '/'
                            DSPLY_CHR         '2'
                            DSPLY_CHR         '5'
                    ;PAUSE A MOMENT
                            CALL     STALL
                    ;RESTORE ORIGINAL VIDEO MODE
                            MOV     CH, V_MODE        ;GET MODE
                            SET_VID_MODE     CH       ;SET IT
                    ;MAIN-LINE CODE ENDS HERE
                            RET                        ;FAR RETURN TO DOS VIA
                                                       ; PSP

MAIN                ENDP                              ;END OF MAIN PROCEDURE


;-----------------------------------------------------------------
;PROCEDURE TO DELAY EXECUTION MOMENTARILY

STALL               PROC     NEAR

                            PUSH     CX               ;SAVE IT
                    ;USE NESTED REPEAT N TIMES LOOPS TO PAUSE
                            MOV     CX, 0             ;WILL LOOP 65536 TIMES
LP1_BEG:                    ;REPEAT 65536 TIMES
                                PUSH     CX           ;SAVE OUTER LOOP COUNT
                                MOV     CX, 100
LP2_BEG:                        ;REPEAT 100 TIMES
                                    LOOP   LP2_BEG  ;CONTINUE LOOP
LP2_END:                        ;END REPEAT 100 TIMES
                                POP     CX           ;RESTORE OUTER LOOP COUNT
                                LOOP   LP1_BEG        ;CONTINUE LOOP
LP1_END:                    ;END OF REPEAT 65536 TIMES
```

Figure 8-14:   (continued)

```
                POP     CX                  ;RESTORE IT
                RET                         ;RETURN

STALL           ENDP

CODE            ENDS                        ;END OF CODE SEGMENT

                END     MAIN                ;END OF F8-14.ASM
                                            ; ENTRY POINT = MAIN
```

Write a pixel in graphics mode:

```
        WRITE_PIXEL    MACRO    ROW, COL, PIXEL_VALUE
```

ROW and COL are word input parameters specifying the row and column of the desired pixel. PIXEL_VALUE is a byte input parameter specifying the desired value for the pixel as described earlier under BIOS video services, operation 0CH. The procedure should use BIOS operation 0CH to write the pixel at the appropriate row and column.

Read a pixel in graphics mode:

```
        READ_PIXEL    MACRO    ROW, COL, PIXEL_VALUE
```

ROW and COL are word input parameters specifying the row and column of the desired pixel. PIXEL_VALUE is a byte output parameter to receive the color returned by BIOS. The macro should open a four-byte stack hole, put the two input parameters onto the stack, and call the procedure. The procedure should use BIOS operation 0DH to read the pixel at the appropriate row and column, put the pixel value into the bottom of the stack hole (at [BP+3]), and return, closing three bytes of the stack hole. Upon return from the procedure, the macro should move the pixel value from the stack hole into PIXEL_VALUE and then close the last byte of the stack hole. Output parameters will be discussed more thoroughly in the next chapter.

BUILDING BLOCKS FOR PRINTER OUTPUT

Our discussion of printer output should also suggest a number of possible building blocks to facilitate output to printers.

Print a character to PRN (LPT1) through DOS:

```
        PRINT_CHR    MACRO    CHAR
```

The PRINT_CHR macro should be identical to DSPLY_CHR, except that it should call a different procedure, $PRINT_CHR. The procedure should be identical to $DSPLY_CHR except that it should use DOS function 05H instead of function 02H. Thus, DOS will print the character to LPT1 instead of displaying it to the screen.

Print a character to any printer through BIOS:

```
BPRINT_CHR    MACRO    CHAR, PRINTER
```

The procedure to output a character to any printer should use BIOS printer services (INT 17H), operation 00H, to print the character to the desired printer. Since BIOS requires the printer number as a word in DX, PRINTER should be a word input parameter. Alternatively, the building block may be written with PRINTER as a byte parameter. In that case, the procedure must retrieve the byte printer number into DL and zero out DH before executing INT 17H. The macro should use IFB and IFIDN directives to allow PRINTER to default to LPT1 (0) and to allow the use of standard device names (PRN, LPT1, LPT2, and LPT3) for PRINTER in the macro invocation.

Initialize a printer:

```
RESET_PRINTER  MACRO    PRINTER
```

The procedure uses operation 01H to initialize the printer. The macro should allow the same printer default and standard device names as BPRINT_CHR.

Get the status of a printer:

```
GET_PRT_STAT   MACRO    STAT, PRINTER
```

The macro should put PRINTER onto the stack as in BPRINT_CHR and then call the procedure. STAT is a byte output parameter to receive the status returned by BIOS. Since STAT is an output parameter, the macro should not place it onto the stack before calling the procedure. The procedure should use BIOS printer services, operation 02H, to get the status, returned by BIOS in AH. The procedure must then return the status by placing AH into the stack hole and returning without closing the stack hole. Immediately after the CALL, the macro must move the status from the stack into STAT. The proper handling of output parameters will be discussed more thoroughly in the next chapter.

CHARACTER STRING HANDLING

Thus far, with the exception of DOS function 09H, our discussion of screen and printer output has involved the output of single characters. Just as high-level languages allow for the storage and output of strings of characters, so do we need to discuss the handling of character strings. One characteristic of strings, which presents some new problems with which we have not yet dealt in our building blocks, is that character strings may be of varying lengths; character strings are **variable-length data structures.**

The fact that strings are variable in length results in two special considerations that we must take into account when passing parameters to any routine that must access a string. First, strings require a different method of parameter passing than what we have used thus far. Recall that, in order to display a single character, the macro placed the character itself onto the stack; the subprocedure then retrieved the character from the stack and displayed it. This is called **parameter passing by value;** the actual value to be used is placed onto the stack to be retrieved by the called subprocedure. This is also the default method of parameter passing used by some high-level languages, most notably PASCAL and C.

Since a string may be many characters, it may not be passed by value; it is not feasible to attempt to place the entire string onto the stack. Instead, the string is stored in memory, and the offset at which it is located is placed onto the stack by the macro. The subprocedure then retrieves the string offset from the stack into a base or index register (BX, SI, or DI) and uses that register as a pointer to the string characters in memory. This method of storing the data in memory and passing the offset of the data, rather than the data itself, to the subprocedure is referred to as **parameter passing by reference** or **by pointer.** This is the standard parameter-passing technique used by most high-level language compilers other than PASCAL and C. Some BASIC compilers, however, allow the specification of **"BY VALUE"** for subprogram parameters. For such compilers the default parameter-passing method is by reference, but the programmer may override the default to pass one or more parameters by value.

The need to pass parameters by reference, rather than by value, presents some special problems. Suppose that we define a macro for displaying a string of characters. The macro definition might begin as follows:

```
DSPLY_STR     MACRO     STR_OFF, TRAILER
```

The dummy parameter, STR_OFF, represents the offset of the string and will be placed onto the stack to be retrieved by the subprocedure that the macro calls; TRAILER might represent a character used to mark the end of the string. Whenever invoking the macro, we must be careful to specify a string offset as the real parameter for STR_OFF; TRAILER is a single byte and so may be passed by value, but the string must be passed by reference. Suppose then that we have defined a string in memory within the data segment, as follows:

```
MY_MSG        DB        'This is a test string', 13, 10, 0
```

It would be tempting to invoke the macro as follows:

```
DSPLY_STR        MY_MSG, 0
```

Recall however that the variable name, MY_MSG, is assembled as direct-memory addressing and refers not to the offset of the string but rather to the byte of data ('T') stored at that offset. The OFFSET operator must be used to force the assembler to assemble instructions with the offset of the data rather than the data itself. Thus, we might attempt to invoke the macro as follows:

```
DSPLY_STR        OFFSET MY_MSG, 0
```

However, this creates another problem. The assembler uses both commas and spaces to delimit the real parameters in a macro invocation. Consequently, the assembler would interpret the above invocation as specifying three real parameters where OFFSET is the first parameter to replace STR_OFF, MY_MSG is the second parameter to replace TRAILER, and 0 is a third real parameter, which has no corresponding dummy parameter and so is ignored by the assembler. To force the assembler to treat OFFSET MY_MSG as a single parameter, we must enclose it in angle brackets (< >). The angle brackets cause the assembler to treat the two "words" as a single parameter during the macro expansion. Thus the correct way to invoke the macro is as follows:

```
DSPLY_STR        <OFFSET MY_MSG>, 0
```

The second parameter-passing consideration for dealing with character strings is that the description of a string requires more than just its location. A string description also requires specifying a means of determining where the string ends; any routine that needs to access the string must know not only where the string begins in memory but also where it ends. Describing where a string ends is usually done either by specifying its length in bytes or, as above, by specifying a trailer character that marks the end of the string (and is not used as a character within the string). Figure 8-15 describes some common methods for storing and describing character strings.

A subroutine to display a string using method one, in Figure 8-15, needs to receive two parameters: the offset where the string begins and the number of characters in the string. The subprocedure retrieves the length from the stack and uses it as n in a repeat-n-times construct to display the characters of the string. If the length of the string is changed during program maintenance, then the real parameter for length must be changed in every invocation of the macro to display the string. This can lead to extreme difficulty during program maintenance; consequently it is not recommended.

If method two is used, a subroutine to display the string needs only one parameter: the offset of the first byte (length). The subprocedure uses the offset to retrieve the length byte, and again uses a repeat-n-times construct for displaying the string. If the number of string characters changes during maintenance, then the length need be changed in only one place (the length byte, stored as the first byte of the string); all references to the string will then use the new length.

Figure 8-15 **String Handling Methods**

1) Store the string characters only:

```
MY_MSG          DB      'This is a test.', 13, 10
```

Describe the string as a location and a length:

```
                DSPLY_STR      <OFFSET MY_MSG>, 17
```

2) Store the length as the first byte of the string:

```
MY_MSG          DB      17, 'This is a test.', 13, 10
```

Describe the string as a location only:

```
                DSPLY_STR      <OFFSET MY_MSG>
```

3) Store the string with a trailer character:

```
MY_MSG          DB      'This is a test.', 13, 10, 0
```

Describe the string as a location and a trailer character:

```
                DSPLY_STR      <OFFSET MY_MSG>, 0
```

4) Maintain a four-byte string descriptor block containing the offset and length of the string, stored at a fixed location and separately from the string data:

```
MY_MSG_DSC      DW      OFFSET MY_MSG, 17
                .
                .
                .
MY_MSG          DB      'This is a test.', 13, 10
```

Describe the string as the location of the descriptor block:

```
                DSPLY_STR      <OFFSET MY_MSG_DSC>
```

Since the length is stored as a byte, the string may not contain more than 255 characters; alternatively, the length might be stored as the first word at the string offset, in which case the string length could be up to 65525. In such a case, the subprocedure must be written to use the entire first word as the string length.

Using the third method in Figure 8-15, a subroutine to display a string needs two parameters: the offset at which the string begins and the character used as a trailer to mark the end of the string. The subprocedure then uses a Repeat-while or General-loop construct to retrieve and display consecutive characters of the string, terminating when it encounters the trailer character.

Alternatively, some predetermined character, such as the NUL character, might always be used as a trailer. In that case, a routine to display the string need only receive one parameter, the string offset; it would be designed to terminate the loop whenever it encounters the predetermined trailer. With such a design, the predetermined trailer character can never be used as a character within any string. A good compromise is to pass the trailer as a parameter but to write the macro so as to use a predetermined default trailer whenever the trailer parameter is omitted from a macro invocation.

The subprocedure to display a string using the fourth method would use the descriptor-block offset to retrieve both the offset and the length of the string data. It would then use a repeat-n-times construct to retrieve and display the string data.

Although more complex than any of the first three string-handling methods, the use of string descriptor blocks allows for **dynamic string storage**. In each of the first three methods, the string location must be predetermined at the time the program is written. With dynamic string storage, only the location of the fixed-length descriptor blocks must be predetermined; the location of the string data itself may be determined dynamically during program execution.

The programmer can allocate a large block of memory to be used for the dynamic storage of string data, as well as a table of descriptor blocks with uninitialized offsets and lengths. The program may then be written to keep track of used and unused string memory. Whenever the program needs to store a string, it uses any currently available (unused) string memory locations to store the character data. To make the string data addressable elsewhere in the program, it also updates the offset and length within the appropriate string descriptor block to describe the memory locations at which it has dynamically stored the string data.

BASIC interpreters and compilers use string descriptor blocks to provide dynamic string storage. Most assembly-language applications, however, do not require the flexibility (and resulting complexity) of dynamic string storage. Consequently, we will concentrate the rest of our string handling discussion on the second and third methods: storing the length as the first byte of the string and storing the string with a trailer character.

BUILDING BLOCKS TO DISPLAY AND PRINT CHARACTER STRINGS

A macro that uses the DOS function call (DSPLY_CHR building block) to display a string that has been stored with a trailer character, as in method three of Figure 8-15, needs two dummy parameters: the string offset and the trailer. In most applications, the NUL character will be used as a trailer; consequently, the macro should provide the NUL character as a default trailer whenever no trailer parameter is specified in the macro invocation. Figure 8-16 provides the necessary logic for the macro.

The procedure must retrieve the string offset from the stack, using it as a pointer to retrieve and display characters. It must compare each character to the trailer (on the stack) to determine when to stop displaying characters. It should display each character by invoking the DSPLY_CHR building block developed in the last chapter. Figures 8-17 and 8-18 illustrate the procedure logic utilizing a General-loop construct and Repeat-while construct, respectively, for the display of the string characters.

Figure 8-16   Macro to Display a String with Trailer

```
DSPLY_STR    MACRO STR_OFF, TRAILER

             Save BP
             Create a three-byte stack hole
             Point BP to stack hole
             Put STR_OFF into the stack hole at [BP+0]
             If TRAILER is blank
                  Put 0 (NUL character) into stack hole, at [BP+2]
             Else
                  Put TRAILER into stack hole at [BP+2]
             End if
             Call $DSPLY_STR
             Restore BP
```

Figure 8-17   Procedure to Display String with Trailer (General Loop)

```
$DSPLY_STR    PROC NEAR

              Save all registers to be modified
              Move the string offset from the stack, at [BP+0], into
                                        Str_ptr (BX, SI or DI)
              Repeat
                   Move a string byte (from [Str_ptr]) into Char
                                          (a byte register)
              Quit repeat when Char EQ TRAILER (at [BP+2])
                   Use DSPLY_CHR macro to display Char
                   Increment Str_ptr to next string character
              End repeat
              Restore all saved registers
              Return, closing stack hole
```

Figure 8-18   Procedure to Display String with Trailer (Repeat While)

```
$DSPLY_STR    PROC NEAR

              Save all registers to be modified
              Move the string offset from the stack, at [BP+0], into
                                          Str_ptr (BX, SI or DI)
              Move a string byte (from [Str_ptr]) into Char (a byte
                                                        register)
              Repeat while Char NE TRAILER (at [BP+2])
                   Use DSPLY_CHR macro to display Char
                   Increment Str_ptr to next string character
                   Move a string byte (from [Str_ptr]) into Char (a
                                                        byte register)
              End repeat
              Restore all saved registers
              Return, closing stack hole
```

The macro and procedure to print a string with a trailer should be identical to the DSPLY_STR building block, except that the macro (PRINT_STR) should call a different procedure ($PRINT_STR), which should use the PRINT_CHR building block to print each character rather than displaying it to the screen.

The building block to display a string with attribute, through BIOS video service (using BDSPLY_CHR), would be similar except that it would have two more input parameters, the display attribute and page number. The macro definition should begin as follows:

```
BDSPLY_STR    MACRO    STR_OFF, TRAILER, ATT, PAGE
```

The macro should default PAGE to zero and ATT to normal (07H) as in BDSPLY_CHR, discussed earlier. The procedure ($BDSPLY_STR) should move the page and attribute from the stack hole into byte registers. In order to display each character, it should invoke BDSPLY_CHR specifying those byte registers as the real parameters for PAGE and ATT. Otherwise, both the macro and procedure should be very similar to DSPLY_STR.

Similarly, a building block to print a string with a trailer through BIOS printer services would require a third parameter (PRINTER) for the printer number.

```
BPRINT_STR    MACRO    STR_OFF, TRAILER, PRINTER
```

The macro should allow the same default and device names as BPRINT_CHR, discussed earlier. The procedure ($BPRINT_STR) must move the printer number from the stack into a word (or byte) register. In order to print each character, it should then invoke BPRINT_CHR specifying that register as the real parameter for PRINTER.

The macro to display a string in which the length has been stored as the first byte of the string, as in method two in figure 8-15, needs only one dummy parameter, the string offset. Figure 8-19 illustrates the necessary logic for the macro.

The procedure ($DSPLY_STRL), called by the macro in Figure 8-19, must retrieve the string offset from the stack and use it to retrieve the string length and then the characters to be displayed. Figure 8-20 illustrates the necessary logic for the procedure.

The necessary logic for a PRINT_STRL macro to print a string with a length byte is identical to that of DSPLY_STRL except that it must call a different sub-procedure, $PRINT_STRL. The procedure, $PRINT_STRL, should be identical to $DSPLY_STRL in Figure 8-20, except that it should use PRINT_CHR, instead of DSPLY_CHR, to print each character rather than displaying it to the screen.

Figure 8-19   **Macro to Display a String with Length Byte**

```
DSPLY_STRL   MACRO STR_OFF

             Save BP
             Create a two-byte stack hole
             Point BP to stack hole
             Put STR_OFF into the stack hole at [BP+0]
             Call $DSPLY_STR
             Restore BP
```

Figure 8-20   **Procedure to Display a String with Length Byte**

```
$DSPLY_STRL   PROC NEAR

              Save all registers to be modified
              Move STR_OFF from the stack (at [BP+0]) into Str_ptr
                                          (use BX, SI or DI)
              Use Str_ptr to obtain the string length into CX (move
                                  [Str_ptr] into CL, 0 into CH)
              Repeat CX times
                  Increment Str_ptr to next character in string
                  Move a string byte (from [Str_ptr]) into Char (a
                                          byte register)
                  Use DSPLY_CHR macro to display Char
              End repeat
              Restore all saved registers
              Return, closing stack hole
```

DSPLY_STRL can also be modified to use BIOS video and printer services (use BDSPLY_CHR and BPRINT_CHR in the procedure) to output the string. BDSPLY_STRL and BPRINT_STRL each require modifications similar to those discussed earlier for BDSPLY_STR and BPRINT_STR.

RECURSION—AN ALTERNATIVE TO ITERATION

Recursion is a technique that is often used in lieu of iteration or repetition when programming in assembly language or in some high-level languages, most notably PASCAL and C. Recursion involves a subprocedure calling itself either directly or by invoking the macro that calls it. The idea is that, rather than having the subprocedure repeat a sequence of steps until the problem is solved, the subprocedure solves one step of the problem and then calls or invokes itself to solve the rest of the problem.

Instead of iteration (repetition), a recursive procedure uses selection (alternation) to determine if the problem solution is complete. If the solution is not complete, it performs one step in the solution and then invokes itself to complete the solution; if the solution is complete, it returns. Just as it is important to ensure that a loop has a means of terminating, it is also critical to ensure that a recursive procedure eventually detect that the problem solution is complete and so return instead of invoking itself again. Failure to detect the completion of the problem solution results in the procedure's repeatedly invoking itself, storing parameters and pushing return addresses and register values each time, until the stack pointer eventually wraps past zero and back to 65535. The result then is that important data or code is overwritten by subsequent pushes, and the system probably has to be rebooted.

The desire to allow recursive use of a subprocedure places some constraints on the design of the code. When a subprocedure invokes itself, the same code is executed a second time before the first execution of the code is complete. Similarly, the second execution may invoke itself again, in which case the second execution of the code does not complete until after the third execution has completed and returned. The result is that the beginning of the subprocedure is executed many times until the last execution finally returns, at which time each execution is finally completed. The first execution to begin is the last one to be completed.

Consequently, two restrictions are placed on the design of the recursive subprocedure. First, it must maintain data isolation; it must save and restore all modified registers. Otherwise, registers in use by the first invocation of the code would have their values destroyed, before the first invocation has completed, by subsequent executions of the same code. The second restriction is that parameters must be passed on the stack, so that when the subprocedure passes parameters to itself for another execution, it does not destroy the parameters that were passed in to it.

It is at least in part because of our desire to allow recursion that we have been careful to observe both considerations in the design of our building blocks; we have used the stack for all parameter passing, and we have maintained data isolation, pushing and popping all registers used by any building block. We will now use the problem of displaying a string of characters, terminated with a trailer character, as an example of a recursive procedure.

KEY TERMS TO REMEMBER

Variable-length data structure	Parameter passing by pointer
Parameter passing by value	Dynamic string storage
Parameter passing by reference	Recursion

BUILDING BLOCKS TO DISPLAY AND PRINT STRINGS RECURSIVELY

Figure 8-21 illustrates the logic for a procedure that uses recursion to display a string that has been stored with a trailer. The macro is the same as the one in Figure 8-16. Notice that the procedure begins by retrieving the string offset and trailer into registers, just as in Figures 8-17 and 8-18. However, the new procedure handles the display of the string characters in a very different manner.

Rather than using a loop to display the string, the procedure in Figure 8-21 obtains the first character of the string and compares it with the trailer. If the character is equal to the trailer, the procedure simply restores registers and returns; otherwise, it displays the single character, increments Str_ptr to the next character, and then invokes itself in order to display the rest of the string.

Note that the preceding presentation of recursion should not be interpreted as an indication that recursion is in any way superior to iteration. We have presented recursion here because it is often used by assembly-language programmers and so must be understood. However, it is this author's belief that recursion is often overused in situations where iteration would result in code that is both easier to maintain and more efficient for the machine. Specifically, our previous $DSPLY_STR procedures (Figures 8-17 and 8-18), using iteration, are probably superior to a recursive solution (Figure 8-21).

Figure 8-21   Recursive Procedure to Display String with Trailer

```
$DSPLY_STR    PROC NEAR
              Save all registers to be modified
              Move the string offset from the stack, at [BP+0], into
                                        Str_ptr (BX, SI or DI)
              Move TRAILER (from [BP+2]) into Trlr (a byte register)
              Move a string byte (from [Str_ptr]) into Char (a byte
                                                    register)
              If Char NE Trlr
                   Use DSPLY_CHR macro to display Char
                   Increment Str_ptr to next string character
                   Display the rest of the string by invoking DSPLY_STR
                        macro (with Str_ptr for STR_OFF, Trlr for TRAILER)
              End if
              Restore all saved registers
              Return, closing stack hole
```

Although recursion is a beautifully elegant concept much akin to proof by induction in mathematics, it usually results in code that is less straightforward and more difficult to maintain than does a Repeat-while or General-loop construct. In addition, while a recursive problem solution may appear on the surface to be more machine-efficient than an iterative solution, the opposite is often true.

While the source code of a recursive subprocedure is usually shorter than that of an equivalent iterative subprocedure, the resulting executable program is often larger due to the expansion of the macro invocation to call itself. More seriously, each step in a recursive solution requires the reexecution of the parameter-passing code within the macro expansion and of the instructions to save and restore registers and retrieve parameters within the procedure. Consequently, a recursive problem solution often results in slower code than does an equivalent iterative solution.

DEBUGGING HINTS

Up to now most of our programming assignments have involved relatively simple logic. Your major concern has been learning the processor's instruction set and the syntax required by the assembler. Most of the problems that you have encountered have probably been syntactical and have resulted in assembler or linker error messages that point directly to a specific offending line of code.

The programming assignments in this and later chapters require much more complex logic than those in previous chapters. Consequently, you will probably find yourself making fewer syntactical errors and more logic errors in your programs. More and more often, your programs will assemble and link without errors but will then lock up the machine or produce incorrect results when run. Such logic errors are much more difficult to identify than syntactical errors and require the development of debugging skills.

The debugging of programs is an art requiring intuition, imagination, creativity, and analytical skills that are developed through experience. We can give no simple straightforward algorithm that will always work. Every program is different and every bug is different; each situation requires the invention of its own unique debugging process. However, there are a few simple steps, often neglected by beginning programmers, that can make program debugging easier.

Debugging Logic Errors

1) Clearly define the bug. A bug is the difference between what a program should do and what it actually does.

   a) Know what the program is supposed to do. Make sure you understand the problem thoroughly. Many a "bug" has turned out to be nothing more than a UM (User Malfunction).

   b) Determine exactly what the program actually does. Run the program several times and determine exactly what it does differently than it should. "It doesn't work" is not very helpful. If it does not do what it should do, then exactly what does it do?

2) Determine the point during execution when the program misbehaves. Perhaps the answer to step 1b is that the system locks up and must be rebooted. If so, when does it lock up? Before displaying anything? After displaying one character? After an entire message but before the next message? After it has completed its job but before returning to DOS?

3) Determine the exact circumstances that produce the undesirable results. If the program accepts keyboard input (discussed in the next chapter), run it many times with different input values. What input produces incorrect results? What input, if any, produces correct results? Look for the pattern in any incorrect results!

4) Desk check the source code that executes under the circumstances determined in step 2 or 3. Look for obvious errors or omissions. Manually trace through the source code looking for the cause of any pattern noticed in step 3. Ensure that pushes and pops are matched and that all subprocedures end with a return.

Debugging Logic Errors (continued)

5) If necessary, use a debugging utility to trace through the executable code that executes under the conditions determined in steps 2 and 3. Only after completing steps 1 through 4 should you use a debugger. Disassemble the machine code, comparing it with what you expected to see. Trace through the code, watching registers and memory and comparing them with what you would expect. If the program locks up the system, pay special attention to the Stack Pointer (SP); write down its value upon entry to any building block and ensure that it still has the same value upon exit. See if any other registers are inadvertently modified by a building block.

Hint: When disassembling the mainline, building-block macro expansions may be easily identified; they all begin with PUSH BP and end with POP BP. Use Go with a break point at the offset of PUSH BP. Note all registers. Then, use Go again with a break point at the offset of the instruction immediately after POP BP. Did the building block do its job properly? Have any registers been inadvertently modified? Has SP changed?

6) See your instructor. You should ask for help only after completing the above five steps. Your instructor may even refuse to help unless you can demonstrate your own efforts by explaining exactly what the problem is, when it occurs, and what you have been able to determine with a debugger. Once you have made a genuine unsuccessful effort, however, do not hesitate to seek help. Do not let your ego get in the way! Very few students can learn to program in assembly language without some assistance now and then.

DEBUGGING UTILITIES—DEBUG, SYMDEB, CODEVIEW, TURBO DEBUGGER

Step 5 in the debugging process requires the use of a debugging utility: either DEBUG, SYMDEB, CodeView, or the Turbo Debugger. DEBUG was thoroughly discussed in chapter 3. While a text such as this cannot discuss all the available debuggers in great detail, there are a number of hints we can provide for the use of each.

It is always helpful to have an assembler list file of the mainline program as well as of the procedures for any building blocks. You may want to edit the source files first, declaring all symbols as public so they will show up in the map file. You may also want to insert new public symbols at strategic points in order to assist in debugging. To obtain a source listing, reassemble the mainline and each subprocedure, specifying a list file. To obtain a source listing of TEST.ASM for example, enter

```
MASM TEST,,TEST;
```

or

```
TASM TEST,,TEST;
```

You will also need a map file with a listing of all public symbols and their addresses. Since the linker determines the actual addresses of external references, the assembler list file will not always contain the correct addresses. Relink the program with the switch /M to generate a map file with a listing of public symbols. To obtain TEST.MAP (a map file of TEST.EXE) for example, enter

```
LINK TEST/M,,,CONSOLE
```

or

```
TLINK TEST/M,,,CONSOLE
```

Use the list file and map file to determine instruction and data offsets in order to correlate the source code with the resulting executable code being debugged.

In order to use the symbolic-debugging capabilities of SYMDEB, you must first use MAPSYM.EXE to create a symbol file from the map file. A symbol file contains the map file's list of public symbols in a special binary format that SYMDEB can read. To create TEST.SYM for example, enter

```
MAPSYM TEST
```

Once a symbol file has been created, enable symbolic debugging by including the symbol filename in the command line that invokes SYMDEB. To debug TEST.EXE for example, enter

```
SYMDEB TEST.SYM TEST.EXE
```

When disassembling machine code in symbolic debugging mode, SYMDEB shows all public symbols in line with the disassembled code. Additionally, public symbols may be used to specify addresses in all SYMDEB commands that require addresses. For example, the following command executes the program beginning at the entry point (MAIN) with a break point set at the beginning of the $DSPLY_CHR subprocedure:

```
G =MAIN $DSPLY_CHR
```

To use either CodeView or the Turbo Debugger, you must prepare a special version of the executable program with debugging information included. Reassemble the mainline and all building-block subprocedures with the switch /ZI within the command line to instruct MASM or TASM to include debugging information within each object file:

```
MASM TEST/ZI,,TEST;
```

or

```
TASM TEST/ZI,,TEST;
```

After creating the object files, the program must be relinked with a switch to cause LINK or TLINK to include the debugging information in the executable file. For LINK the switch is /CO; TLINK requires /V:

```
LINK TEST/CO/M,,,CONSOLE
```

or

```
TLINK TEST/V/M,,,CONSOLE
```

Once the special executable file has been created, invoke CodeView or the Turbo Debugger to debug the program:

```
CV TEST    (for CodeView)
```

or

```
TD TEST    (for Turbo Debugger)
```

Important: The use of debugging switches greatly increases the size of the resulting .OBJ and .EXE files and slows the execution of the program. They should be used only for debugging. Once the program has been successfully debugged it should be reassembled and relinked without the debugging switches.

SUMMARY

Output to either the screen or printer may be accomplished in any of three ways: (1) by directly accessing the video or printer adapter hardware, (2) through BIOS video and printer services (interrupt types 10H and 17H, respectively) or (3) via the DOS function call (interrupt type 21H). While it is generally preferable to perform input and output through DOS rather than through BIOS or by directly accessing the hardware, both video and printer output via the DOS function call have some disadvantages.

Video output through DOS does not permit the specification of a display attribute; all video output through the DOS function call displays the data with a normal attribute. Printer output through DOS has two disadvantages. First, DOS always outputs to LPT1; in order to output to a second or third printer, the programmer must first swap the printer port addresses in the port-address table. Second, DOS printer output is very inflexible in the handling of errors; it may result in the infamous "Abort, Retry or Ignore" error or, even worse, may lock up the system if no printer is attached to the parallel port of the adapter.

While DOS provides a function (09H) for displaying a string of characters, it is very inflexible in that it always requires a dollar sign ("$") as a trailer for the string. It is desirable to develop one or more building blocks to provide a more flexible means of displaying character strings. Since a string is a variable-length data structure, it may not be passed by value to a subprocedure. Rather it must be passed by reference; the offset of the beginning of the string must be placed on the stack. In addition, the subprocedure must have some means of determining the end of the string; it must be provided either with the length of the string or with a special trailer character that has been used to delimit the string.

Recursion is an alternative to iteration for the solution of problems that require the repetition of a series of steps. In a recursive problem solution, the procedure performs one step in the solution and then calls itself, usually through a macro invocation, to complete the solution. Recursion requires that the procedure maintain data isolation and that parameters be passed on the stack. While it is an elegant concept, recursion should not be overused.

VOCABULARY

V8-1   In your own words, define each of the following terms:

a) Character code

b) ASCII

c) Control characters

d) Modified ASCII

e) COMMON combine type

f) AT segaddress combine type

g) Memory-mapped video

h) Graphics video mode

i) Pixel

j) Scan line

k) Color palate

l) Text video mode

m) Display attribute

n) Active page

o) Variable-length data structure

p) Parameter passing by value

q) Parameter passing by reference

r) String descriptor block

s) Dynamic string storage

t) Recursion

REVIEW QUESTIONS

Q8-1   How many bytes of program memory will be occupied by MYDATA in the following example?

```
MYDATA    SEGMENT PARA PUBLIC 'DATA'
VAR1      DB 10 DUP ('*')
```

```
MYDATA          ENDS
                ·
                ·
                ·
MYDATA          SEGMENT
VAR2            DB 5 DUP (?)
MYDATA          ENDS
```

Q8-2 How many bytes of program memory will be occupied by MYDATA in the following example?

```
MYDATA          SEGMENT PARA COMMON 'DATA'
VAR1            DB 10 DUP ('*')
MYDATA          ENDS
                ·
                ·
                ·
MYDATA          SEGMENT
VAR2            DB 5 DUP (?)
MYDATA          ENDS
```

Q8-3 How many bytes of program memory will be occupied by MYDATA in the following example?

```
MYDATA          SEGMENT PARA AT B000H 'DATA'
VAR1            DB 10 DUP ('*')
MYDATA          ENDS
                ·
                ·
                ·
MYDATA          SEGMENT
VAR2            DB 5 DUP (?)
MYDATA          ENDS
```

Q8-4 Explain the amount of memory and the memory addresses assigned to a Color/Graphics video adapter.

Q8-5 In 80/25 text mode, how many video pages are supported by the CGA?

Q8-6 In 40/25 text mode, how many video pages are supported by the CGA?

Q8-7 List the two input/output instructions, showing the four allowed forms of each, and briefly describing the effect of each.

Q8-8 Explain the differences between the way data is output to the screen and the way it is output to a printer when directly accessing the adapter hardware.

Q8-9 Explain the use of each of the three parallel-printer adapter registers: Data, Status, and Control.

Q8-10 What instruction is used to access BIOS video services?

Q8-11 What instruction is used to access BIOS printer services?

Q8-12 What instruction is used to access the DOS function call for either video or printer output?

Q8-13   Explain the difference between parameter passing by value and by reference. Which must be used for variable-length parameters?

Q8-14   What string management method is used by BASIC in order to provide dynamic string storage?

PROGRAMMING ASSIGNMENTS

Important Note:

Each of the following problems, as well as most problems in subsequent chapters, involves additions to your library. For each assignment, you will add one or more macros to CONSOLE.MLB and one or more procedures to CONSOLE.LIB, or you will create or add to a new library, PRINTER.MLB and PRINTER.LIB. For each macro definition, be sure to include a header giving the details of how to use the macro: the name of the macro, what it does, the names of input parameters and output parameters (if any), and so on. For each parameter, tell its size, the addressing modes allowed, and its default value (if appropriate).

At the beginning of the file for each subprocedure, be sure to include a header giving details of how to use the subprocedure: the name of the subprocedure, what it does, what input parameters it expects, their sizes, and where they are located within the stack hole. If there are any output parameters to be returned by the procedure, you should also explain what they are and how they are returned (where they are placed on the stack).

In each case, after writing any subprocedure, you must first assemble it and then use the library manager (LIB) to add the resulting object file to your object library, CONSOLE.LIB or PRINTER.LIB.

For each problem, you will also create a mainline procedure to thoroughly test the building block(s). Use the problem name as the filename for the mainline procedure (PA8-1.ASM, PA8-2.ASM, PA8-3.ASM, etc.). After creating the mainline file, assemble it to create an object file (PA8-1.OBJ, PA8-2.OBJ, etc.), then link the mainline to CONSOLE.LIB and/or PRINTER.LIB to create the executable program (PA8-1.EXE, PA8-2.EXE, etc.). When linking, specify only the mainline (PA8-1, etc.) for object module(s). Specify CONSOLE.LIB and/or PRINTER.LIB for the library. The linker will link in only those object modules within the object library (or libraries) that are necessary in order to resolve external references.

If the resulting executable program does not execute properly, follow the debugging hints at the end of this chapter. If necessary use DEBUG, SYMDEB, CodeView, or Turbo Debugger to examine and step through the code in search of the error. Even if the program executes properly, use a debugging utility to examine the resulting machine code. Notice that labels and variables have been replaced with offsets and that each macro invocation has resulted in its expansion to the macro definition. Use the fact that all our macros begin with PUSH BP and end with POP BP to easily determine the beginning and end of each macro expansion.

PA8-1   If you did not do PA7-1 in the last chapter, do it before attempting this problem. Add a new building block to your library (CONSOLE.MLB and CONSOLE.LIB) to display a string with a trailer. Add a macro to CONSOLE.MLB:

```
DSPLY_STR MACRO STR_OFF, TRAILER
```

Allow a default of the NUL character (0, not "0") for TRAILER. The macro should put the parameters onto the stack and call a procedure, $DSPLY_STR, to display the message.

Write the procedure, $DSPLY_STR, to be called by the macro; call the file $DSP_STR.ASM (the filename must be abbreviated to eight characters). Use iteration (either Repeat-while or General-loop) to display the string.

Write a mainline module, PA8-1.ASM, to test the DSPLY_STR macro by displaying the message, "This is a test message." plus at least two more messages of your own. The three (or more) messages should be defined within the data segment with DB directives; every message must be defined with a trailer.

Use 0 (NUL character) as the trailer on at least two of the messages; use something else as the trailer on at least one message. When you invoke the DSPLY_STR macro within the code segment, use the default TRAILER (leave it blank) at least once.

PA8-2 Write a macro and mainline identical to PA8-1 except that the procedure uses recursion instead of iteration to display the string. Other than the name of the mainline (PA8-2.ASM) and the use of recursion in the procedure, this problem is identical to PA8-1.

PA8-3 Add a building block to your library to display a string that has been stored with its length as its first byte. Define the macro in CONSOLE.MLB as

```
DSPLY_STRL MACRO STR_OFF
```

Call the procedure $DSPLY_STRL in a file called $DSP_STL.ASM.

The mainline, PA8-3.ASM, should display the message, "This is a test message." plus at least two more messages. Each message must be defined within the data segment with its length as the first byte.

PA8-4 Create a new library (PRINTER.MLB and PRINTER.LIB) and add two building blocks: one to print a single character to PRN (LPT1) and another to print a string with a **trailer**. Define the macros as

```
PRINT_CHR MACRO CHAR
```

and

```
PRINT_STR MACRO STR_OFF, TRAILER
```

Call the procedures $PRINT_CHR and $PRINT_STR in separate files called $PRT_CHR and $PRT_STR. Use iteration within $PRINT_STR to print the string characters. The mainline program (PA8-4.ASM) should be identical to PA8-1 except that it invokes PRINT_STR instead of DSPLY_STR to output to the printer; refer to PA8-1 for details.

PA8-5 Create the same library and add the same building blocks as in PA8-4. However, use recursion rather than iteration within $PRINT_STR to print the string. This problem is identical to PA8-4 except that it uses recursion.

PA8-6 If you have not done PA8-4 or PA8-5, create the printer library and add a building block to print a single character to (PRN) as described in PA8-4. Add another building block to your library to print a string that has been stored with its length as its first byte. Define the macro in PRINTER.MLB as

```
PRINT_STRL MACRO STR_OFF
```

Call the procedure $PRINT_STRL in a file called $PRT_STL.ASM; call the mainline PA8-6.ASM. Refer to PA8-3 for details.

PA8-7 Add BDSPLY_CHR and BDSPLY_STR to your console library. Both should include parameters for the page number and attribute. The procedure $BDSPLY_CHR should use BIOS video services (operations 09H and 0EH) to display the character to the specified page with the desired attribute; see the earlier discussion of BDSPLY_CHR for details.

   BDSPLY_STR should display a string that is terminated by a trailer; it should be similar to DSPLY_STR discussed in PA8-1 except for the additional input parameters. Allow the defaults for PAGE and ATT, discussed earlier in the text.

   The mainline (PA8-7.ASM) should be similar to that of PA8-1 except that it should display at least two strings with normal attribute (using the default for one and specifying 07H for the other) and at least one string each with reverse video and blink for attributes. Display all strings to page zero; accept the default page on at least one invocation and specify the page (0) on at least one invocation.

PA8-8 Add BDSPLY_CHR and BDSPLY_STR to your console library, as in PA8-7. Also add SELECT_PAGE to change the active video page. Write a mainline program (PA8-8.ASM) similar to PA8-7 except that it displays all strings to page one. It should then select page one as the active page and pause for a moment. After the pause, the program should change the active page back to page zero before returning to DOS. The following code, or something similar, may be used to generate the pause; to change the length of the pause, modify the immediate value in the first MOV instruction:

```
                MOV     CX, 30
LOOP_1:         PUSH    CX
                MOV     CX, 0
LOOP_2:         LOOP    LOOP_2
                POP     CX
                LOOP    LOOP_1
```

   Note: This program requires a CGA, EGA, MCGA, or VGA adapter; it will not work on any PC with an MDA video adapter.

PA8-9 Create a printer library (PRINTER.MLB and PRINTER.LIB), unless you have already done so, and add two building blocks: BPRINT_CHR, which uses BIOS printer services to print a single character to any printer, and BPRINT_STR, which uses BPRINT_CHR to print a string with a trailer to any printer. The procedure, $BPRINT_STR, should use iteration.

   Other than invoking BPRINT_STR instead of PRINT_STR and the requisite need to specify the printer on each invocation, the mainline should be identical to PA8-4. Specify the printer in at least three different ways: take the default (PRN) on at least one invocation, specify the printer by device name at least once, and specify the BIOS printer number (0, 1, or 2) at least once. If your PC has more than one printer available, specify each of the printers in at least one invocation.

PA8-10 Create the same library (if necessary) and add the same building blocks as in PA8-9. However, use recursion rather than iteration, within $BPRINT_STR, to print the string. Other than the use of recursion, this problem is identical to PA8-9.

PA8-11 If you have not done PA8-9 or PA8-10, then create the printer library and add the building block to use BIOS printer services to print a single character to any printer as described in PA8-9. Add another building block (BPRINT_STRL) to print a string (to any printer) that has been stored with its length as its first byte. The procedure, $BPRINT_STRL, should invoke BPRINT_CHR to print each string character.

PA8-12 Add two new building blocks for handling graphics to your CONSOLE library: SET_VID_MODE and WRITE PIXEL. The mainline should first set the video mode to 640/200 graphics (mode 06H), then use WRITE_PIXEL to draw a rectangle with its upper-left corner at row 20, column 40 and its lower-right corner at row 179, column 599.

After drawing the rectangle, use DSPLY_STR or DSPLY_STRL (PA8-1, PA8-2, or PA8-3) to display some text inside the rectangle; note that DOS is capable of displaying text data while the screen is in graphics mode. The program should then pause for a few seconds (see PA8-8) and then change the video mode back to 80/25 text (mode 03H).

Note: This program requires a CGA, EGA, MCGA, or VGA adapter; it will not work on any PC with an MDA adapter.

9

Keyboard Input

INTRODUCTION

Almost every useful program must be capable of accepting user input from the keyboard as well as generating output to the screen or printer. In this chapter we will discuss keyboard input. First we will discuss the keyboard hardware and the manner in which it converts user input to electronic form for use by the processor. We will learn that the keyboard does not generate ASCII codes for the keys; rather it generates a unique number, called a scan code, whenever any key is depressed and another unique scan code when the key is released.

BIOS is then responsible for converting the scan codes from the keyboard to the appropriate characters, which are then stored in a buffer from which application programs obtain keyboard input. A program can retrieve keyboard input from the buffer either through BIOS keyboard services or through the DOS function call.

After discussing both BIOS keyboard services and DOS keyboard functions, we will discuss a number of keyboard-input building blocks. We will explore the necessary logic for building blocks that input a single character and that input a string of characters.

KEYBOARD HARDWARE

Each key cap on the keyboard is connected to a switch directly below the key cap. The keyboard also contains a specialized microprocessor that constantly scans the key switches to detect any change in state, from up to down or down to up, of any key. The keyboard microprocessor is connected via the keyboard cable to an 8255 Programmable Peripheral Interface chip on the system board inside the CPU cabinet. The 8255 is in turn connected to Interrupt Request line one (IRQ1) of the 8259 Interrupt Controller chip, also on the system board. We will discuss the 8255 and 8259 in depth in chapter 14.

Whenever any key (including the shift and toggle keys) changes state, the keyboard microprocessor, through the 8255 and 8259 chips, generates a hardware interrupt type 09H to the processor. In addition, the keyboard processor passes a unique byte value, called a **scan code**, to the 8255. Upon receipt of the type nine interrupt, the processor executes a keyboard interrupt service routine within BIOS, which retrieves the scan code from the 8255 and generates an acknowledgment to the keyboard indicating that the character has been received and processed.

The scan code, generated by the keyboard, indicates the key that has changed state as well as its new state. The low-order seven bits (bit zero through bit six) contain a number from one through eighty-three, identifying the key; the high-order bit (bit seven) indicates the new state of the key. If the key has just been depressed, bit seven is zero; bit seven set (one) indicates that the key has been released. Figure 9-1 lists the scan codes resulting when each of the keys is depressed; the release of any key results in the indicated scan code plus 128. For example, when the <Esc> key is pressed, the keyboard generates a scan code of one; when <Esc> is released, a scan code of 129 (81H) is generated.

Notice that the scan codes have nothing to do with the ASCII codes for the key characters; the scan code for <A> and the scan code for <B> are not consecutive, as one might expect. Notice also that the shift keys (<Left shift>, <Right shift>, <Alt>, and <Ctrl>), which we think of as doing nothing unless held down in conjunction with another key, also generate scan codes each time they are depressed or released. In fact, <Left shift> and <Right shift>, though we interpret them as synonymous, generate their own distinct scan codes. Note also that while we think of the keys as generating characters only when pressed, each key generates an interrupt type nine and accompanying scan code both when it is pressed and again when it is released.

Although the keyboard scan codes are completely unrelated to our own interpretation of the keys, there is a definite logic to them. The pattern derives from the key's location on the keyboard rather than from its meaning to us. The main (typewriter) section of the keyboard is assigned scan codes from one through fifty-eight, in a left-to-right, top-to-bottom fashion. One through fourteen are assigned, left-to-right, to the top row of keys, fifteen through twenty-eight are assigned to the next row of keys, and so forth to the bottom row (<Alt>, <Space> and <Caps lock>), which generate scan codes of fifty-six through fifty-eight.

The ten function keys generate scan codes from fifty-nine through sixty-eight, again in a left-to-right, top-to-bottom pattern. The keypad (right) section of the keyboard produces scan codes from sixty-nine through eighty-three, again following the same left-to-right, top-to-bottom pattern.

Figure 9-1   Keyboard Scan Codes (Key Depressed)

Main Keyboard

Key	Scan Code Dec	Hex	Key	Scan Code Dec	Hex
<Esc>	1	01	<A>	30	1E
<1> (!)	2	02	<S>	31	1F
<2> (@)	3	03	<D>	32	20
<3> (#)	4	04	<F>	33	21
<4> ($)	5	05	<G>	34	22
<5> (%)	6	06	<H>	35	23
<6> (^)	7	07	<J>	36	24
<7> (&)	8	08	<K>	37	25
<8> (*)	9	09	<L>	38	26
<9> (()	10	0A	<;> (:)	39	27
<0> ())	11	0B	<'> (")	40	28
<-> (_)	12	0C	<`> (~)	41	29
<=> (+)	13	0D	<Left shift>	42	2A
<Backspace>	14	0E	<\> (|)	43	2B
<Tab>	15	0F	<Z>	44	2C
<Q>	16	10	<X>	45	2D
<W>	17	11	<C>	46	2E
<E>	18	12	<V>	47	2F
<R>	19	13	<B>	48	30
<T>	20	14	<N>	49	31
<Y>	21	15	<M>	50	32
<U>	22	16	<,> (<)	51	33
<I>	23	17	<.> (>)	52	34
<O>	24	18	</> (?)	53	35
<P>	25	19	<Right shift>	54	36
<[> ({)	26	1A	<*>(PrtSc)	55	37
<]> (})	27	1B	<Alt>	56	38
<Enter>	28	1C	<Space>	57	39
<Ctrl>	29	1D	<Caps lock>	58	3A

Function Keys

Key	Scan Code Dec	Hex	Key	Scan Code Dec	Hex
<F1>	59	3B	<F6>	64	40
<F2>	60	3C	<F7>	65	41
<F3>	61	3D	<F8>	66	42
<F4>	62	3E	<F9>	67	43
<F5>	63	3F	<F10>	68	44

Numeric Keypad

Key	Scan Code Dec	Hex	Key	Scan Code Dec	Hex
<Num lock>	69	45	<6> (Curs right)	77	4D
<Scroll lock>	70	46	<+>	78	4E

<7> (Home)	71	47	<1> (End)	79	4F
<8> (Curs up)	72	48	<2> (Curs down)	80	50
<9> (Pg up)	73	49	<3> (Pg dn)	81	51
<->	74	4A	<0> (Ins)	82	52
<4>(Curs left)	75	4B	<.> (Del)	83	53
<5>	76	4C			

BIOS KEYBOARD INTERRUPT-SERVICE ROUTINE

Each time any key is pressed or released, the keyboard (through the 8255 and 8259 chips) generates a hardware interrupt type nine. During boot up, the type 09H interrupt vector has been initialized to point to a **keyboard interrupt-service routine** within BIOS. The keyboard interrupt-service routine, after saving registers, retrieves the scan code from the keyboard (through the 8255 chip), interprets it, and stores the appropriate character into the **keyboard buffer**. The keyboard buffer is a thirty-byte **queue** within system memory; since, as we will see shortly, each keyboard character is stored as two bytes, the keyboard buffer is capable of storing up to fifteen type-ahead characters. If the buffer is full when the user presses a key, BIOS beeps to indicate that the keystroke is lost.

The term "queue," as used above, refers to a temporary storage area, which is used in a first-in-first-out (FIFO) manner as opposed to the last-in-first-out (LIFO) operation of a stack. Whenever a program requests a keyboard character, BIOS returns the oldest character from the keyboard buffer or queue. Thus a program can retrieve characters from the buffer in the same order that the keys were pressed by the user.

Eight keys, seven of which do not directly result in characters being stored in the keyboard buffer, are treated by BIOS as **shift keys** and **toggle keys**. Four keys, <Left shift>, <Right shift>, <Alt>, and <Ctrl>, are treated as shift keys by BIOS. Nothing is stored into the keyboard buffer when the key is pressed or released; rather, BIOS simply keeps track of the current status of the key (depressed or released). BIOS then checks the current status of the shift keys in order to determine the manner in which to interpret other keystrokes.

Four other keys, <Caps lock>, <Num lock>, <Scroll lock>, and <Ins>, are treated by BIOS as toggle keys. BIOS maintains a one-bit toggle switch associated with each key. Each toggle switch is initialized to OFF at boot time; then, every time a toggle key is pressed, BIOS toggles the status of its associated switch, from ON to OFF or from OFF to ON. The status of the switch, rather than the status of the key, is then used by BIOS to determine the manner in which to interpret subsequent keys. With the exception of <Ins>, nothing is stored in the keyboard buffer when a toggle key is pressed; when <Ins> is pressed, BIOS not only toggles its associated switch, but also places a character into the keyboard buffer.

For all other keys, BIOS stores a character into the buffer when the key is pressed, when it receives the scan code with zero for bit seven. If the key is held down, the keyboard hardware repeats the interrupt and scan code until it is released; each time BIOS receives the interrupt and scan code, it stores the same character into the buffer. Each character is stored as two bytes within the keyboard buffer. The values of the two bytes depend on the type of key that has been pressed.

If the key is an alphabetic or punctuation key on the center keyboard and <Alt> is not depressed, or if the key is on the numeric keypad and the <Num lock> toggle is ON, then BIOS stores the appropriate ASCII character followed by the scan code of the key. As we will discuss shortly, BIOS's interpretation of keystrokes also allows for the entry of a second type of character, called an extended-keyboard character. Before discussing extended-keyboard characters, however, we will examine the manner in which ASCII control characters may be entered from the keyboard.

KEY TERMS TO REMEMBER

Scan code	Queue
Keyboard interrupt-service routine	Shift key
Keyboard buffer	Toggle key

ENTERING ASCII CONTROL CHARACTERS

BIOS interprets scan codes in a manner that allows for the entry of the entire ASCII code from the keyboard. Recall that the ASCII code includes all possible byte values from 0 through 255. In addition to the displayable characters from thirty-two (space) through 126 (tilde), 127 (DEL) and the values from zero (NUL) through thirty-one (US) are all defined by ASCII as control characters. BIOS allows the entry of **ASCII control characters** via special keys (<Enter>, <Backspace>, etc.) as well as through the use of the <Ctrl> key in conjunction with other keys. Figure 9-2 lists the key combinations that BIOS interprets as ASCII control characters.

Note that the key combinations listed in Figure 9-2 all result in ASCII characters; they are not extended-keyboard characters, which will be discussed shortly. Each listed key or key combination results in two bytes in the keyboard buffer, the first of which is the ASCII character indicated, and the second of which is the scan code of the key pressed alone or in conjunction with the <Ctrl> key to generate the ASCII control character. Also notice the general pattern: an alphabetic or punctuation key pressed in conjunction with the <Ctrl> key results in the ASCII character whose code is sixty-four less than the character that results from the same key pressed in conjunction with either <Shift> key.

Figure 9-2   Entering ASCII Control Characters

Key combination	Dec	Hex	Char name	Key combination	Dec	Hex	Char name
<Ctrl>+<@>	0	00	NUL	<Ctrl>+<O>	15	0F	SI
<Ctrl>+<A>	1	01	SOH	<Ctrl>+<P>	16	10	DLE
<Ctrl>+<B>	2	02	STX	<Ctrl>+<Q>	17	11	DC1
<Ctrl>+<C>	3	03	ETX	<Ctrl>+<R>	18	12	DC2
<Ctrl>+<D>	4	04	EOT	<Ctrl>+<S>	19	13	DC3
<Ctrl>+<E>	5	05	ENQ	<Ctrl>+<T>	20	14	DC4
<Ctrl>+<F>	6	06	ACK	<Ctrl>+<U>	21	15	NAK
<Ctrl>+<G>	7	07	BEL	<Ctrl>+<V>	22	16	SYN
<Backspace>	8	08	BS	<Ctrl>+<W>	23	17	ETB
<Ctrl>+<H>	8	08	BS *	<Ctrl>+<X>	24	18	CAN
<Tab>	9	09	HT	<Ctrl>+<Y>	25	19	EM
<Ctrl>+<I>	9	09	HT *	<Ctrl>+<Z>	26	1A	SUB
<Ctrl>+<Enter>	10	0A	LF	<Esc>	27	1B	ESC
<Ctrl>+<J>	10	0A	LF *	<Ctrl>+<[>	27	1B	ESC*
<Ctrl>+<K>	11	0B	VT	<Ctrl>+<\>	28	1C	FS
<Ctrl>+<L>	12	0C	FF	<Ctrl>+<]>	29	1D	GS
<Enter>	13	0D	CR	<Ctrl>+<6>	30	1E	RS
<Ctrl>+<M>	13	0D	CR *	<Ctrl>+<->	31	1F	US
<Ctrl>+<N>	14	0E	SO	<Ctrl>+<BS>	127	7F	DEL

* = Alternate key combination

Alternatively, the <Alt> key may be used in conjunction with the numeric keypad to enter any ASCII character from 1 through 255 (01H through FFH). To enter any ASCII character other than NUL (00H), hold down the <Alt> key and enter the code in decimal for the desired ASCII character on the numeric keypad. Upon release of the <Alt> key, BIOS evaluates the number typed on the keypad and stores it in the keyboard buffer as a single ASCII character. The ASCII code, from 1 through 255, is stored as the first byte in the buffer; the second byte (normally the key scan code) of a character, entered through the <Alt> key and numeric keypad, is always zero.

EXTENDED-KEYBOARD CHARACTERS

As mentioned earlier, BIOS allows for the entry of a second type of character in addition to ASCII characters, called **extended-keyboard characters**. If the key pressed is a function key, either alone or in conjunction with a shift key, or if it is an alphabetic or punctuation key in conjunction with the <Alt> key, or if it is a numeric-keypad key while the <Num lock> toggle is OFF, then it is interpreted and stored by BIOS as an extended-keyboard character; the first byte is zero and the second byte is the extended-keyboard character, often (but not always) the scan code of the key.

Note that the term **extended-ASCII characters** is often used to refer to such keystrokes. This terminology is very misleading. Such characters have nothing whatsoever to do with ASCII; they are simply BIOS's way of reflecting key-strokes that are totally unrelated to the American Standard Code for Information Interchange. They are meaningful only as input from the keyboard and are used by most programs for the entry of commands to the program rather than as character data. Consequently, we have adopted the term "extended-keyboard characters," which we will use throughout this text. Figure 9-3 lists the keystrokes and key combinations that are interpreted by BIOS as extended-keyboard characters.

Note that extended-keyboard characters, like ASCII characters, are stored by BIOS as two bytes within the keyboard buffer. However, the first byte of an extended-keyboard character is always zero; the second byte is the value indicated by Figure 9-3. Also remember that extended-keyboard characters are meaningful only as input from the keyboard and then only as commands, never as character data. They should never be interpreted as displayable characters; any attempt to display an extended-keyboard character will simply result in the display of the ASCII character of the same code (0 through 255), probably with very confusing results.

At this point, we should point out that the manner in which BIOS stores extended-keyboard characters results in some confusion. Recall from Figure 9-2 that the <Ctrl>+<@> (<Ctrl>+<2>) key combination results in an ASCII NUL

Figure 9-3   Extended-Keyboard Character Set

Main Keyboard

Key(s)	Ext-Kbrd-Char Dec	Hex	Key(s)	Ext-Kbrd-Char Dec	Hex
<Shift>+<TAB>	15	0F	<Alt>+<Z>	44	2C
<Alt>+<Q>	16	10	<Alt>+<X>	45	2D
<Alt>+<W>	17	11	<Alt>+<C>	46	2E
<Alt>+<E>	18	12	<Alt>+<V>	47	2F
<Alt>+<R>	19	13	<Alt>+<B>	48	30
<Alt>+<T>	20	14	<Alt>+<N>	49	31
<Alt>+<Y>	21	15	<Alt>+<M>	50	32
<Alt>+<U>	22	16	<Alt>+<1>	120	78
<Alt>+<I>	23	17	<Alt>+<2>	121	79
<Alt>+<O>	24	18	<Alt>+<3>	122	7A
<Alt>+<P>	25	19	<Alt>+<4>	123	7B
<Alt>+<A>	30	1E	<Alt>+<5>	124	7C
<Alt>+<S>	31	1F	<Alt>+<6>	125	7D
<Alt>+<D>	32	20	<Alt>+<7>	126	7E
<Alt>+<F>	33	21	<Alt>+<8>	127	7F
<Alt>+<G>	34	22	<Alt>+<9>	128	80
<Alt>+<H>	35	23	<Alt>+<0>	129	81
<Alt>+<J>	36	24	<Alt>+<->	130	82
<Alt>+<K>	37	25	<Alt>+<=>	131	83
<Alt>+<L>	38	26			

Function Keys

Key(s)	Ext-Kbrd-Char		Key(s)	Ext-Kbrd-Char	
	Dec	Hex		Dec	Hex
`<F1>`	59	3B	`<Ctrl>+<F1>`	94	5E
`<F2>`	60	3C	`<Ctrl>+<F2>`	95	5F
`<F3>`	61	3D	`<Ctrl>+<F3>`	96	60
`<F4>`	62	3E	`<Ctrl>+<F4>`	97	61
`<F5>`	63	3F	`<Ctrl>+<F5>`	98	62
`<F6>`	64	40	`<Ctrl>+<F6>`	99	63
`<F7>`	65	41	`<Ctrl>+<F7>`	100	64
`<F8>`	66	42	`<Ctrl>+<F8>`	101	65
`<F9>`	67	43	`<Ctrl>+<F9>`	102	66
`<F10>`	68	44	`<Ctrl>+<F10>`	103	67
`<Shift>+<F1>`	84	54	`<Alt>+<F1>`	104	68
`<Shift>+<F2>`	85	55	`<Alt>+<F2>`	105	69
`<Shift>+<F3>`	86	56	`<Alt>+<F3>`	106	6A
`<Shift>+<F4>`	87	57	`<Alt>+<F4>`	107	6B
`<Shift>+<F5>`	88	58	`<Alt>+<F5>`	108	6C
`<Shift>+<F6>`	89	59	`<Alt>+<F6>`	109	6D
`<Shift>+<F7>`	90	5A	`<Alt>+<F7>`	110	6E
`<Shift>+<F8>`	91	5B	`<Alt>+<F8>`	111	6F
`<Shift>+<F9>`	92	5C	`<Alt>+<F9>`	112	70
`<Shift>+<F10>`	93	5D	`<Alt>+<F10>`	113	71

Numeric Keypad (`<Num lock>` Toggle OFF)

Key(s)	Ext-Kbrd-Char		Key(s)	Ext-Kbrd-Char	
	Dec	Hex		Dec	Hex
`<Home>`	71	47	`<Del>`	83	53
`<Curs up>`	72	48	`<Ctrl>+<PrtSc>`	114	72
`<Pg up>`	73	49	`<Ctrl>+<Curs left>`	115	73
`<Curs left>`	75	4B	`<Ctrl>+<Curs right>`	116	74
`<Curs right>`	77	4D	`<Ctrl>+<End>`	117	75
`<End>`	79	4F	`<Ctrl>+<Pg dn>`	118	76
`<Curs down>`	80	50	`<Ctrl>+<Home>`	119	77
`<Pg dn>`	81	51	`<Ctrl>+<Pg up>`	132	84
`<Ins>`	82	52			

character; this is in agreement with virtually all ASCII keyboards and terminals and also follows the pattern that <Ctrl> key combinations produce ASCII codes that are sixty-four less than the ASCII code for the same key in conjunction with either <Shift> key (the ASCII code for "@" is sixty-four). Since <Ctrl>+<@> is interpreted as an ASCII character, BIOS stores it as the ASCII code for the NUL character (zero) followed by the scan code of the key (three). The result is that, although it is an ASCII character, the NUL character appears to be an extended-keyboard character when stored in the buffer. Unless handled properly, as we will discuss later, this confusion often results in the misinterpretation by many programs of the <Ctrl>+<@> key combination.

KEYBOARD INPUT THROUGH BIOS

Any program that requires keyboard input can obtain it from **BIOS keyboard services**, through an interrupt type 16H. It is very important not to confuse BIOS keyboard services with the keyboard interrupt-service routine. Execution of the interrupt-service routine is initiated by an **asynchronous event**, an interrupt type 09H from the keyboard hardware. The term "asynchronous" means that execution of the interrupt service routine is not within program control; it is controlled by an external event, the depression or release of a key by the user, the timing of which cannot be predicted when a program is written. When a key is pressed or released, the keyboard interrupt-service routine obtains the scan code from the keyboard, interprets it, and maintains the keyboard buffer as well as the status of the shift and toggle keys.

The execution of BIOS keyboard services is a **synchronous event**. It is controlled by program instructions; the timing of the execution of BIOS keyboard services is controlled by the programmer. Specifically, the BIOS keyboard services routine is executed whenever the processor executes an interrupt type 16H instruction. Its purpose is to provide a program with information about the keyboard buffer or the status of the shift and toggle keys.

KEY TERMS TO REMEMBER

ASCII control character	BIOS keyboard services
Extended-keyboard character	Asynchronous event
Extended-ASCII character	Synchronous event

To use BIOS keyboard services, a program should place the appropriate operation code into AH and execute an interrupt type 16H; no other registers besides AH need to be initialized. Information is returned by BIOS as indicated below. BIOS provides the following three keyboard services:

00H - Input a character:

To obtain the next character from the keyboard buffer, put the operation code (00H) into AH, and execute an interrupt type 16H.

BIOS retrieves the next (oldest) character from the keyboard buffer. If the buffer is empty, BIOS waits for a key to be typed; control does not return to the program until a character is available. The first byte of the character is returned in AL, the second byte in AH. Thus, AL and AH should be interpreted as follows:

If AL is not zero, or if AL is zero and AH is three, then it is an ASCII character; the ASCII code for the character is in AL, and the scan code of the key is in AH.

If AL is zero and AH is any value other than three, then AH contains an extended-keyboard character.

Note that a value of zero in AL does not always indicate an extended-keyboard character; if AL is zero and AH is three, then the zero in AL represents an ASCII NUL character and should be interpreted as such.

Note also that BIOS allows several ways to enter many ASCII characters; the scan code in AH may be used to determine the manner in which the character has been entered. For example, an ASCII plus sign (+) may be entered in any of the following three ways: pressing the <+> key at the upper-right corner of the main keyboard, pressing the <+> key on the numeric keypad, or holding down the <Alt> key while typing "43" on the numeric keypad (forty-three is the ASCII code for "+"). In all three cases, AL contains a value of forty-three (2BH). However, the scan code in AH is different in each case; the scan code in AH will be thirteen (0DH), seventy-eight (4EH), or zero (00H), respectively, for each of the three methods of entering the character.

01H – Check keyboard buffer:

To determine if the keyboard buffer contains any characters, put 01H into AH and execute an interrupt type 16H.

BIOS sets the Zero flag (ZR) if no character is available in the keyboard buffer. Otherwise, if one or more characters are available, BIOS clears the Zero flag (NZ) and returns the next character in AL and AH, as described above (operation 00H). However, the character is not removed from the keyboard buffer; it will be returned again by the next operation 00H. Operation 01H allows a program to "peek ahead" to determine the next character in the buffer, if any, without actually reading it from the buffer.

02H – Check status of shift and toggle keys:

To determine the current status of the shift keys and toggle key switches, move 02H into AH and execute an interrupt type 16H.

BIOS returns the current status of the shift keys and toggle key switches in AL, as follows:

Bit #	Key
0	<Right shift>
1	<Left shift>
2	<Ctrl>
3	<Alt>
4	<Scroll lock> toggle
5	<Num lock> toggle
6	<Caps lock> toggle
7	<Ins> toggle

Note: Bit 0 is the least-significant bit.

For the toggle keys (bits four through seven of AL), zero (bit clear) means the toggle switch is currently OFF (initial state); one (bit set) means the toggle is ON. For the shift keys (bits zero through three of AL), zero (clear) indicates that the key is not currently depressed; one (set) means the key is depressed.

KEYBOARD INPUT THROUGH DOS

In addition to BIOS keyboard services, a program may obtain input from the keyboard buffer through the DOS function call. As with previously discussed function calls, keyboard function calls are initiated by placing the appropriate function code into AH, setting up any other registers as indicated for the specific function, and executing an interrupt type 21H. Obtaining keyboard input through DOS, rather than through BIOS, provides two major advantages. The first is that the resulting code is more likely to work on partially compatible machines. The second advantage is that keyboard input through DOS may be redirected by the command line; if a program obtains its input through BIOS, then its input cannot be redirected. DOS provides the following seven function calls for keyboard input:

01H - Standard keyboard input:

To input a single character from the keyboard buffer, with echo and <Ctrl>+<Break> checking, put 01H into AH, and execute an interrupt type 21H.

If the keyboard buffer is empty, DOS waits for a character to be typed; control does not return to the program until the user presses a key that results in a character in the buffer. DOS performs a <Ctrl>+<Break> check; if <Ctrl>+<Break> has been entered since the last keyboard input, or if the current character is <Ctrl>+<C> (ASCII three, ETX), then DOS executes an interrupt 23H, aborting the program. Otherwise, DOS echoes the character to the screen and returns it in AL.

If, upon return, AL is any value other than zero, then it is an ASCII character. If AL is zero, then it is the first byte of an extended-keyboard character (or what DOS thinks is an extended-keyboard character); the program must do another DOS function call to read the second byte of the character. The extended-keyboard character is returned in AL on the second DOS function call.

Recall, however, that BIOS stores the ASCII NUL character (<Ctrl>+<@>) in the buffer as zero followed by a scan code of three. Since the first byte is zero, DOS misinterprets it and returns it as an extended-keyboard character. Consequently, a value of three in AL, after the second DOS function call, should be interpreted by the program as an ASCII NUL character rather than as an extended-keyboard character.

Also, in order to properly handle an ASCII NUL, the program must use another function, which does not perform a <Ctrl>+<Break> check, for the second function call after receiving zero in AL on the first function call. Otherwise DOS interprets the second byte of the NUL character (three) as a <Ctrl>+<C> and aborts the program.

Finally, because of the manner in which it echoes characters, function 01H is not recommended unless it is known that the user will never type an extended-keyboard character or <Ctrl>+<@>. For example, <F7> is echoed by function 01H as two characters (resulting from the two function calls), the first having a value of zero and the second a value of sixty-five. Consequently, <F7> is echoed as " A" (space A), producing very confusing results on the screen.

06H – Direct console I/O:

Recall from the last chapter that function 06H can be used for either video output or keyboard input. To input a character from the keyboard, move 06H into AH, move FFH into DL, and execute an interrupt type 21H.

If a character is available, DOS clears the Zero flag (NZ) and returns the next keyboard-buffer character in AL, as described above for function 01H. If no character is available, DOS does not wait for a character; the Zero flag is set (ZR), and control immediately returns to the program. DOS does not do a <Ctrl>+<Break> check and does not echo the character.

07H – Keyboard input without echo or <Ctrl>+<Break> checking:

To input a character from the keyboard without echo and without <Ctrl>+<Break> checking, put 07H into AH and perform an interrupt type 21H.

DOS waits for a character and returns it in AL as described earlier for function 01H. DOS does not echo the character to the screen and does not do a <Ctrl>+<Break> check. Function 07H is identical to function 01H (standard keyboard input), except for the lack of echo and <Ctrl>+<Break> checking.

Since it does not echo and does not check for <Ctrl>+<Break>, function 07H is recommended for the second function call, to obtain the second byte of an extended-keyboard character.

08H – Keyboard input without echo:

To input a character with <Ctrl>+<Break> checking but without echo, move 08H into AH and do an interrupt type 21H.

DOS waits for a character and returns it in AL as described earlier for function 01H. DOS does not echo the character to the screen but does perform a <Ctrl>+<Break> check. Function 08H is identical to function 01H (standard keyboard input), except that the character is not echoed to the screen.

Since it performs a <Ctrl>+<Break> check but does not echo the character, function 08H is recommended, in most cases, for obtaining keyboard input.

0AH - Buffered keyboard input:

Function 0AH may be used to input an entire string of characters into an input buffer within the program. To input into a buffer, move 0AH into AH, move the offset of the input buffer defined within the data segment into DX, initialize the first byte of the buffer (at DS:[DX]) to the total buffer length minus two (number of characters to allow the user to type before <Enter>), and execute an interrupt type 21H.

DOS copies characters from the BIOS keyboard buffer into the program input buffer, starting with the third byte (at DS:[DX+2]), until <Enter> is encountered. If the program input buffer becomes full before <Enter> is encountered, all keys except <Enter> and <Backspace> are ignored. When <Enter> is encountered, DOS stops the transfer of characters and places the number of characters copied, not counting <Enter>, into the second byte of the program input buffer (at DS:[DX+1]). Upon completion, the buffer (beginning with the second byte at DS:[DX+1]) contains the string entered at the keyboard with the string length stored as the first byte.

Function 0AH was intended by Microsoft as the complement of function 09H (display a string of characters), discussed in the previous chapter; however, the two functions were implemented in such a manner as to be completely incompatible. Recall that function 09H requires that the string be stored with a trailer ("$"). Function 0AH uses a length byte instead of a trailer. It seems that some of Microsoft's software engineers do not talk to each other.

0BH - Check keyboard buffer:

To determine if any input is available in the keyboard buffer, put 0BH into AH and execute an interrupt 21H.

DOS checks the keyboard buffer and reports its status in AL as either 00H or FFH. A value of zero (00H) in AL indicates that the keyboard buffer is empty; no keyboard input is currently available. A value of 255 (FFH) indicates that the keyboard buffer currently contains at least one character.

0CH - Flush keyboard buffer:

Function 0CH may be used to flush the BIOS keyboard buffer, to discard any "type ahead" entered by the user; optionally, any of the above functions, except 0BH, may be performed following the buffer flush. To flush the keyboard buffer, move 0CH into AH, move another function code (or a value other than a function code) into AL, and perform an interrupt type 21H.

The keyboard buffer is flushed; all previously typed characters, which have not yet been read from the buffer, are discarded. If AL is 01H, 06H, 07H, 08H, or 0AH, then the appropriate function is performed, as if it were in AH, following the buffer flush. If AL is any other value, nothing else is done after the flush.

Following is a summary of the most commonly used system services for keyboard input.

M O S T   C O M M O N L Y   U S E D **Keyboard System Services**

INT 16H (BIOS keyboard), operation 00H

Input a character into AX (first byte in AL, second byte in AH).

INT 16H (BIOS keyboard), operation 01H

Check keyboard buffer. ZF set if keyboard buffer is empty; otherwise, ZF clear and character in AX. Character remains in buffer.

INT 21H (DOS), function 07H

Keyboard input without echo or <Ctrl>+<Break> checking. Returns character in AL (0 if extended keyboard).

INT 21H (DOS), function 08H

Keyboard input without echo. Same as above, but checks for <Ctrl>+<Break>.

INT 21H (DOS), function 0BH

Check keyboard buffer. Returns 0 in AL if buffer empty; returns FFH if character available.

OUTPUT PARAMETERS IN BUILDING BLOCKS

Thus far, all our building blocks have had **input parameters** only. We have had to pass values from the mainline program in through a macro to a procedure in order to control the manner in which the procedure does its job. For example, we had to pass the character to be displayed into the DSPLY_CHR building block. None of our previous building blocks has had to pass resulting values back out to the mainline.

The writing of building blocks for keyboard input will require the use of **output parameters**. Do not let the terminology confuse you. The terms "input" and "output," when referring to parameters, must be distinguished from input from or output to the user. "Input" and "output" in reference to parameters indicate whether the value is passed in from the mainline to the building block or out from the building block to the mainline. It just happens that any building block that obtains input from the user requires an output parameter to pass the value out from the building block to the mainline program.

Just as we have passed input parameters on the stack, so we will also use the stack for output parameters, but with several significant new considerations. The major difference is that, while values are moved from input parameters to the stack by the macro and retrieved from the stack by the procedure, output values are be placed onto the stack by the procedure and are moved from the stack into output parameters by the macro. Also, while a macro places input parameters onto the stack before calling a procedure, a macro that uses output parameters will call the procedure first and then move the output value(s) from the stack into the output parameter(s) after the call instruction.

Although it does not place parameter values onto the stack, the macro still must open a stack hole with BP pointing to it prior to calling the procedure. Since the stack hole is used to pass a parameter out from the procedure to the macro, the procedure must not close the stack hole as it returns. The macro must close the stack hole after it has moved the output value from the stack into the output parameter.

Finally, since an output parameter must be capable of receiving and storing the value returned by the building block, it may never be Immediate mode. And since the macro must move the output value from the stack (memory) into the output parameter after calling the procedure, the parameter may never be Memory addressing mode. Consequently, output parameters allow only Register addressing mode. Although output parameters are always limited to Register mode, good programming practice dictates that we so state in the header of every macro that uses output parameters.

We will now use the problem of inputting a character from the keyboard, through DOS, as a specific example of a building block with an output parameter.

BUILDING BLOCK TO INPUT A CHARACTER THROUGH DOS

In designing a building block for keyboard input, we should make it as easy to use as possible; we should attempt to overcome any shortcomings in the manner in which DOS returns the keyboard character. Specifically, we do not want to require that future programs check the character and do a second input, if it is zero, in order to input an extended-keyboard character. Also, future programs should not have to check an extended-keyboard character to determine if it is really an ASCII NUL (<Ctrl>+<@>) that has been misinterpreted by DOS. Those problems should be handled by the building block so that future programs may be kept as simple as possible.

The building block should have one output parameter, CHAR, to receive the character, either ASCII or extended keyboard. CHAR should be an optional parameter; we should be able to invoke the building block, without parameters, to simply stall a program until any key is struck. <Ctrl>+<@>, returned by DOS as an extended-keyboard character with a value of three, should be returned by the building block as an ASCII character with a value of zero (ASCII NUL). Since both ASCII and extended-keyboard characters will be returned in the same output parameter, there remains the problem of somehow specifying to the mainline which type has been returned. The Flags register provides an easy means of so specifying.

Recall that the processor provides two instructions, STC and CLC, for setting and clearing the Carry flag and that the mainline program can use Conditional jumps (JC, JNC) to test the Carry flag following the invocation of the building block. Consequently, our building block can use the Carry flag to distinguish between ASCII and extended-keyboard characters. It should clear the Carry flag when returning an ASCII character and set the Carry flag when returning an extended-keyboard character.

The macro should begin with a header explaining what the building block does and how to use it. An explanation of parameters must be included in the header:

```
PARAMETERS:
    INPUT:  NONE
    OUTPUT: CHAR  = CHARACTER INPUT FROM KEYBOARD
                    SIZE: BYTE
                    ADDRESSING MODES: REGISTER ONLY
                    OPTIONAL PARAMETER - MAY BE OMITTED
            CARRY FLAG = INDICATES IF ASCII OR EXTENDED
                    CLEAR (NC) IF ASCII CHARACTER
                    SET (CY) IF EXTENDED-KEYBOARD CHARACTER
```

As with our other building blocks, the macro should only pass parameters and call the procedure. The procedure should do the body of the work: inputting the character through DOS, doing a second function call if necessary, returning <Ctrl>+<@> as an ASCII NUL, setting or clearing the Carry flag, and so on. The macro should create a one-byte stack hole with BP pointing to it, call the procedure, move the character from the stack into the parameter (unless the parameter is omitted), and close the stack hole.

While closing the stack hole, the macro must not alter the Carry flag, which has been set or cleared by the procedure. Recall that INC and DEC, although they modify all other flags, are the only two arithmetic instructions that do not alter the Carry flag. Consequently, the macro must use INC (not ADD) to close the stack hole. Figure 9-4 illustrates the logic of the macro.

Figure 9-4   INPUT_CHR Macro

```
INPUT_CHR    MACRO       CHAR

             Save BP
             Create one-byte stack hole (to receive character)
             Point BP to stack hole
             Call $INPUT_CHR
             If CHAR is not blank
                 Move character from stack (at [BP+0]) into CHAR
             Endif
             Close stack hole (Use INC, not ADD; must not alter
                                                Carry flag)

             Restore BP
```

The procedure must obtain the character from DOS, using function 08H so as to perform <Ctrl>+<Break> checking but not to echo the character. If the character is zero, then the procedure must do another DOS function call, this time using function 07H in order to avoid <Ctrl>+<Break> checking. If the second byte is three, then the procedure must return it as the ASCII NUL character, rather than as an extended-keyboard character.

The procedure must then put the character (either ASCII or extended keyboard) into the stack hole and set or clear the Carry flag; it should clear the Carry flag if returning an ASCII character and set it if returning an extended-keyboard character. The procedure must not close the stack hole as it returns. Figure 9-5 illustrates the logic for the $INPUT_CHR subprocedure.

OTHER BUILDING BLOCKS FOR KEYBOARD INPUT

Our earlier discussion of BIOS keyboard services and keyboard-related DOS function calls should suggest a number of building blocks in addition to INPUT_CHR. Following is a brief discussion of several building blocks that you may wish to add to your console library.

Figure 9-5   **$INPUT_CHR Procedure**

```
$INPUT_CHR    PROC         NEAR

              Save any registers to be used
              Use DOS function 08H to get the character into AL
              If AL NE 0
                   Clear the Carry flag (ASCII char)
              Else
                   Use DOS function 07H to get the second byte
                                                      into AL
                   If AL EQ 3 (<Ctrl>+<@>)
                        Move 0 into AL ("null" character)
                        Clear Carry flag (ASCII char)
                   Else
                        Set the Carry flag (extended-kbrd char)
                   Endif
              Endif
              Move AL into stack hole (at [BP+0])
              Restore any saved registers
              Return (do not close stack hole)
```

Input a character through BIOS:

```
BINPUT_CHR    MACRO    CHAR, SCAN
```

CHAR and SCAN are both optional byte output parameters allowing only register addressing mode. CHAR should receive the character returned by BIOS, either ASCII or extended keyboard. SCAN should receive the scan code of the character, if it is ASCII; if CHAR receives an extended-keyboard character, then SCAN should be 255 (FFH). The building block should clear or set the Carry flag to indicate the type of character.

If parameters are returned, as described, then a mainline program has the option of invoking the building block with no parameters for a keyboard stall, invoking it with a parameter for CHAR only and using the Carry flag to determine the type of character, or supplying both parameters in the macro invocation. If both parameters are supplied, then the mainline procedure may use either the Carry flag or the Byte register, SCAN, to determine the type of character; 255 (FFH) implies an extended-keyboard character, while any other value for SCAN indicates an ASCII character. Additionally, the program may, if necessary, use the value in scan to determine the exact manner in which an ASCII character has been entered.

The BINPUT_CHR macro definition should be very similar to the INPUT_CHR macro, discussed earlier, except that it must call a different procedure, $BINPUT_CHR, and must receive two optional output parameters, opening and closing a two-byte stack hole.

The procedure, $BINPUT_CHR, should use logic similar to the following:

```
Save any registers to be used
Use BIOS keyboard services, operation 00H, to input the
                               character into AL and AH
If AL NE 0 or AH EQ 3
     Clear the Carry flag (normal ASCII)
Else
     Set the Carry flag (extended-kbrd char)
     Move AH to AL (ext-kbrd char to AL)
     Move 255 to AH (ext-kbrd SCAN = 255)
Endif
Move AL (CHAR) and AH (SCAN) into the stack hole
Restore any saved registers
Return (don't close stack hole)
```

Check the keyboard buffer:

```
CHECK_KBRD     MACRO     STATUS
```

STATUS is a byte output parameter to receive the value indicating if a character is available in the keyboard buffer. Zero indicates that no character is available; FFH indicates that at least one character is available. The procedure should use either DOS function 0BH or BIOS keyboard services, operation 01H, to check the buffer. Optionally, the building block might be developed, with no parameters, to use the Carry or Zero flag to indicate the buffer status.

Check shift and toggle keys:

```
CHECK_KEYS     MACRO     KEYS
```

KEYS is a byte output parameter to receive the status of the shift and toggle keys. The procedure uses BIOS keyboard services, operation 02H, to obtain the status of the shift and toggle keys. The macro header explains the significance of the bits, which key is represented by each bit. Figures 9-6 and 9-7 provide the source code for the macro and procedure for the CHECK_KEYS building block.

Figure 9-6   Macro for Check-Key-Status Building Block

```
COMMENT | CHECK_KEYS MACRO =================================

GETS CURRENT STATUS OF SHIFT AND TOGGLE KEYS
USES $CHECK_KEYS SUBPROCEDURE IN CONSOLE.LIB

INPUT PARAMETERS:
        NONE
OUTPUT PARAMETERS:
        KEYS =  KEY STATUS
                SIZE: BYTE
                ADDRESSING MODES: REGISTER ONLY

                BIT #   KEY             MEANING
                0       <RIGHT SHIFT>   1 = DEPRESSED
                1       <LEFT SHIFT>    1 = DEPRESSED
                2       <CTRL>          1 = DEPRESSED
                3       <ALT>           1 = DEPRESSED
                4       <SCROLL LOCK>   1 = TOGGLE ON
                5       <NUM LOCK>      1 = TOGGLE ON
                6       <CAPS LOCK>     1 = TOGGLE ON
                7       <INS>           1 = TOGGLE ON

        |

CHECK_KEYS      MACRO   KEYS

                IFNDEF  $CHECK_KEYS
                    EXTRN       $CHECK_KEYS:NEAR
                ENDIF

                PUSH    BP                      ;SAVE IT
                DEC     SP                      ;MAKE 1-BYTE
                                                ;   STACK HOLE
                MOV     BP, SP                  ;POINT BP TO
                                                ;   STACK HOLE
                CALL    $CHECK_KEYS             ;SUBPROC GETS KEY STATS
                                                ;   DOES NOT CLOSE STACK
                MOV     KEYS, BYTE PTR [BP+0]    ;KEY STATUS  FROM STACK
                INC     SP                      ;CLOSE STACK HOLE
                POP     BP                      ;RESTORE IT

                ENDM                            ;CHECK_KEYS
```

Figure 9-7   Procedure for Check-Key-Status Building Block

```
COMMENT |                          $CHK_KYS.ASM

        Your name here

        SUBPROCEDURE TO CHECK CURRENT STATUS OF SHIFT AND TOGGLE KEYS
        USES INT 16H (BIOS KEYBOARD SERVICES), OPERATION 02H

        INPUT PARAMETERS:
                NONE

        OUTPUT PARAMETERS:
                KEY STATUS BYTE
                        SIZE: BYTE
                        LOCATION: [BP+0]


                TITLE    $CHK_KYS.ASM        ;TITLE OF LISTING
                PAGE     55, 80             ;LINES, WIDTH

DATA            SEGMENT  WORD PUBLIC 'DATA'

                ASSUME   DS:DATA
        ;DEFINE AN EMPTY DATA SEGMENT

DATA            ENDS

CODE            SEGMENT  BYTE PUBLIC 'CODE'

                ASSUME   CS:CODE

$CHECK_KEYS     PROC     NEAR

                PUBLIC   $CHECK_KEYS

        ;SAVE ALL USED REGISTERS
                PUSH     AX                 ;SAVE IT
        ;SET UP AH AND INTERRUPT TO BIOS KEYBOARD SERVICES
                MOV      AH, 02H            ;OPERATION CODE
                INT      16H                ;TO BIOS KEYBOARD SVCS
        ;RETURN STATUS, RESTORE REGISTERS AND RETURN TO MACRO
                MOV      [BP+0], AL         ;KEY STATUS TO STACK
                POP      AX                 ;RESTORE IT
                RET                         ;NEAR RETURN TO MACRO;
                                            ;  LEAVE STACK HOLE OPEN

$CHECK_KEYS     ENDP

CODE            ENDS

                END                         ;END OF $CHK_KYS.ASM
```

Figure 9-8 illustrates a sample program that uses the CHECK_KEYS building block. It gets the shift and toggle key status byte and uses a repeat-n-times loop to display the status of each of the eight bits.

Figure 9-8   Example Program Using CHECK__KEYS Building Block

```
              TITLE    F9-8.ASM
              PAGE     55, 80

COMMENT |     PROGRAM:         F9-8.ASM
              PROGRAMMER:      Your name here
              DATE:            Date here
              CLASS:           Class name and number here
              INSTRUCTOR:      Instructor's name here

          SAMPLE PROGRAM USING CHECK_KEYS AND DSPLY_CHR
          BUILDING BLOCKS.

          INPUT PARAM'S:  NONE
          OUTPUT PARAM'S: NONE
                          RETURNS TO DOS, UPON COMPLETION
              |

              INCLUDE CONSOLE.MLB

;STACK SEGMENT ===================================================

STACK              SEGMENT PARA STACK 'STACK'        ;BEGIN STACK

                   DB      64 DUP ('*STACK* ')       ;DEFINE 512
                                                     ; BYTE STACK

STACK              ENDS                              ;END OF STACK

;DATA SEGMENT ====================================================

DATA               SEGMENT PARA PUBLIC 'DATA'        ;BEGIN DATA

STAT_MSG           DB      13, 10, 'Shift and toggle keys: '

DATA               ENDS                              ;END OF DATA

;CODE SEGMENT ====================================================

CODE               SEGMENT PARA PUBLIC 'CODE'        ;BEGIN CODE

                   ASSUME  CS:CODE, SS:STACK

MAIN               PROC    FAR                       ;BEGIN MAINLINE
```

Figure 9-8:   (continued)

```
        ;INITIALIZATION (SAME FOR ALL PROGRAMS)
        ;FIRST, SET UP FOR RETURN TO DOS VIA PSP
                PUSH     DS                          ;PUT RETURN SEG (PSP)
                                                     ;  TO STACK
                MOV      AX, 0                        ;PUT ZERO RETURN
                PUSH     AX                           ;  OFFSET TO STACK
        ;NOW, ADDRESS THE DATA SEGMENT WITH DS
                MOV      AX, DATA                     ;POINT DS TO
                MOV      DS, AX                       ;  DATA SEGMENT
                ASSUME   DS:DATA                      ;ASSOCIATE DS WITH DATA


        ;BEGIN MAINLINE CODE
        ;GET THE SHIFT AND TOGGLE KEYS
                CHECK_KEYS          AL
                DSPLY_STR           <OFFSET STAT_MSG>
                                                     ;EXPLANATION TO USER
        ;USE A REPEAT-N-TIMES LOOP TO DISPLAY THE BITS
                MOV      CX, 8                        ;COUNT FOR LOOP
LP_BEG:         ;REPEAT 8 TIMES (8 BITS IN BYTE)
                    SHL      AL, 1                    ;SHIFT HIGH BIT INTO
                                                     ;  CARRY FLAG
                    CALL     DSPLY_CRY                ;  AND DISPLAY IT
                    LOOP     LP_BEG                   ;CONTINUE LOOP
LP_END:         ;END REPEAT 8 TIMES

        ;MAINLINE CODE ENDS HERE
                RET                                  ;FAR RETURN TO DOS VIA
                                                     ;  PSP

MAIN            ENDP                                 ;END OF MAIN PROCEDURE


;-----------------------------------------------------------------------
;PROCEDURE TO DISPLAY CARRY FLAG AS '0' OR '1'

DSPLY_CRY       PROC     NEAR

                PUSH  AX                             ;SAVE IT
                JNC   NO_CRY                         ;CHECK CARRY FLAG
                ;IF CARRY SET
                    MOV      AL, '1'                 ;WILL DISPLAY IT
                    JMP      SHORT IF_ND             ;CONTINUE
NO_CRY:         ;ELSE
                    MOV      AL, '0'                 ;WILL DISPLAY IT
IF_ND:          ;END IF
                DSPLY_CHR           AL               ;DISPLAY '1' OR '0'
                DSPLY_CHR           ' '              ;  AND A SPACE
                POP   AX                             ;RESTORE IT
                RET                                  ;RETURN
```

Figure 9-8:   (continued)

```
DSPLY_CRY          ENDP

CODE               ENDS                             ;END OF CODE SEGMENT

                   END    MAIN                      ;END OF F9-8.ASM
                                                    ;  ENTRY POINT = MAIN
```

Flush keyboard buffer:

```
          FLUSH_KBRD        MACRO
```

Since it has no parameters, the macro should not save and restore BP or create or close a stack hole; it should merely call the procedure, $FLUSH_KBRD. The procedure should use DOS function 0CH to flush the buffer; the procedure must initialize AL to a value other than a valid keyboard function (00H, for example) before doing the DOS function call.

BUILDING BLOCK TO DISPLAY AN IMMEDIATE STRING

Logically, the next topic for our discussion should be that of inputting a string of characters from the keyboard. However, as we shall see, any building block that inputs a string must also be capable of printing strings of characters. While this can be done using the building blocks discussed in the last chapter (DSPLY_STR or repeatedly invoking DSPLY_CHR), we can simplify things by developing a building block to display an immediate string. Consider the following two BASIC statements:

```
PRINT MSG$
PRINT "This is a test message."
```

The first statement requires that a string value first be stored (assigned) into the string variable, MSG$; the output statement then prints (displays) the characters stored in the variable. This is somewhat analogous to our own DSPLY_STR, in which the string must first be defined (stored) within the data segment; one input parameter to DSPLY_STR, then, is the location (offset) at which the string is stored.

The second BASIC statement allows the specification of the characters to be displayed, as a string constant, within the output statement itself. It would be helpful if we had an analogous building block with which we could specify the characters to be displayed as an Immediate-mode string, as follows:

```
DSPLY_IMMED_STR        'This is a test message.'
```

Such a building block is actually very simple. We merely need to develop a macro that stores the string into the data segment and then invokes our previously developed DSPLY_STR to display it. The only problem is determining a way to store the string into the data segment, since the DSPLY_IMMED_STR macro will always be invoked within the code segment. We can solve the problem by creating a nested segment.

Recall from our discussion of the SEGMENT and ENDS directives in chapter 6 that segments may be nested, one inside the other. Recall also, that when a segment is nested within another segment the assembler in effect moves the inner segment outside the outer segment and combines it with any other segments of the same name. We can write a macro whose invocation and expansion creates a data segment nested inside the code segment, within which the macro is invoked. The string will then be defined within that nested data segment. After ending the nested data segment, the macro then merely invokes DSPLY_STR in order to display the string. Figure 9-9 provides the entire macro definition.

Since DSPLY_IMMED_STR will be invoked within the code segment, the directives DATA SEGMENT and DATA ENDS will result in the nesting of segments within each macro expansion. The assembler effectively moves each resulting data segment outside the code segment and combines it with the previously defined segment with the name of DATA. Consequently, each expansion results in the definition of the string and trailer within the data segment, with a variable name of STR_BFR. The macro then invokes the previously defined building block, DSPLY_STR, to display the string stored at STR_BFR.

Notice that the macro definition includes a directive, LOCAL, which we have not yet discussed. The **LOCAL directive**, on the line immediately following the MACRO directive, is made necessary by the fact that the macro definition includes a variable name, STR_BFR, as well as by our need to be able to invoke the macro more than once within the same source program. Without the LOCAL directive, each macro invocation and resulting expansion would result in the definition of the variable called STR_BFR. The second and subsequent invocations would produce a "Redefinition of symbol" error by the assembler.

The LOCAL directive causes the assembler to replace each occurrence of the symbol STR_BFR with another symbol name that is unique to each macro expansion. Within the first macro expansion, both occurrences of STR_BFR (variable definition and variable reference in the DSPLY_STR invocation) are replaced by the assembler with the symbol ??0001; within the second expansion, both occurrences of the variable name are replaced with the assembler-generated symbol ??0002; the third expansion results in the symbol ??0003, and so forth. Consequently, each macro invocation results in a variable name that is different from all other invocations of the macro, thus avoiding the redefinition of the symbol.

MASM is very particular about the placement of the LOCAL directive. It must be on the very next line after the MACRO directive. No blank lines are permitted between the two directives. Furthermore, the line on which the MACRO directive occurs may not contain a remark. Nothing may occur between the MACRO directive and the LOCAL directive except for the list of dummy parameters and a single <Enter>.

Figure 9-9   Macro to Display an Immediate-Mode String

```
COMMENT | DSPLY_IMMED_STR MACRO =====================================

             DISPLAYS AN IMMEDIATE STRING
             USES DSPLY_STR MACRO
             INVOKING PROGRAM MUST CONTAIN A SEGMENT NAMED DATA
                  FOR EXAMPLE:
                       DATA        SEGMENT align combine 'class'
             INPUT PARAMETERS:
                  STRING =  STRING TO DISPLAY
                            IMMEDIATE VALUE, CHARACTERS IN
                                QUOTES AND/OR BYTE VALUES
                                ENCLOSED IN ANGLE BRACKETS
                  TRAILER = CHARACTER TO BE USED AS TRAILER TO MARK
                                                   END OF STRING
                            SIZE: BYTE
                            ADDRESSING MODES: REGISTER OR IMMEDIATE
             OUTPUT PARAMETERS:
                  NONE
                  NO REGISTERS MODIFIED


                  |


DSPLY_IMMED_STR        MACRO     STRING, TRAILER
                       LOCAL     STR_BFR

DATA                   SEGMENT                    ;DATA SEG MUST BE DEFINED
                                                  ; EARLIER IN PROGRAM

STR_BFR                DB        STRING           ;DEFINE STRING IN DATA
                                                  ; SEGMENT
                       IFB       <TRAILER>        ;DEFINE TRAILER IN DATA
                           DB    0                ; SEGMENT
                       ELSE                       ; (DEFAULT IS NUL)
                           DB        TRAILER
                       ENDIF

DATA                   ENDS                       ;BACK TO CODE SEGMENT

                       DSPLY_STR      <OFFSET STR_BFR>, <TRAILER>
                                                  ;INVOKE DSPLY_STR TO
                                                  ; DISPLAY IT
                       ENDM                       ;DSPLY_IMMED_STR
```

Once the DSPLY_IMMED_STR macro has been added to CONSOLE.MLB, each of the following macro invocations then becomes possible:

```
DSPLY_IMMED_STR        'Enter your first name '
DSPLY_IMMED_STR        <'Number too big', 7, 13, 10>
DSPLY_IMMED_STR        <8, ' ', 8>
```

The first example above would simply print the text within quotes and would leave the cursor at the end of the message. The second example would print the text of the message, followed by a BEL character to get the user's attention, followed by a CR and LF to move the cursor to the beginning of the next line. The third example would print a BS, followed by a space, followed by another BS. The result of the third example is to erase the character just to the left of the cursor from the screen; we will have just such a need within the procedure for our INPUT_STR building block.

A similar macro, BDSPLY_IMMED_STR, might be defined to display an immediate string with an attribute through BIOS. It would require an additional input parameter, ATT, for the attribute to use on the display. It would then be identical to Figure 9-9 except that it would invoke BDSPLY_STR to display the string, passing the additional parameter, <ATT>.

BUILDING BLOCKS TO INPUT CHARACTER STRINGS

Just as we found it necessary in the last chapter to construct building blocks to display character strings, it is also necessary to construct building blocks to input strings of characters. In doing so, we should ensure that any building block that inputs a character string stores it in a manner that is consistent and compatible with our building blocks that display strings. In the last chapter we concentrated on the display of strings that have been stored with a trailer to mark the end of the string, and strings that have been stored with the string length as the first byte. Similarly we will now discuss building blocks that input a string and store it in each of the two ways, appending a trailer to mark the end and inserting a length byte at the beginning.

The major difference between the building blocks for the two approaches comes at the end, after the string has been input. The code for inputting the string characters is much the same for both approaches. To begin with, any program that needs to do keyboard input must first define an area within the data segment as a buffer to store the input; the building block must then be provided with the location of that buffer. Consequently, the building block must have an input parameter for the offset of the buffer in which to store the string.

The building block must also limit the number of characters that it allows the user to enter; otherwise, the user might enter a string that is longer than the buffer, overwriting any data or code defined following the buffer. Thus, the building block must have another input parameter specifying the maximum number of characters the user can enter. Since keyboard input is usually limited to one screen line, it would make sense to default the maximum string length to eighty characters.

The buffer offset and the maximum number of characters to allow are necessary parameters for either approach to string storage. If the string is to be stored with a trailer, then the building block needs one additional input parameter specifying the trailer character to store onto the end of the string. To be consistent with our building blocks for displaying a string with a trailer, the building block should provide the NUL character as the default trailer. Figure 9-10 illustrates the required logic for the macro of a building block to input a string with a trailer.

The macro, INPUT_STRL, to input a string with a length byte would be identical to that illustrated in Figure 9-10 except that TRAILER is not necessary. The macro need only open a three-byte stack hole and pass BUFF_OFF and MAX_LEN.

The procedure, $INPUT_STR, called by the macro in Figure 9-10 is a good deal more complex than might seem necessary on the surface. First it needs to initialize a register to be used to point to the buffer; it must move the buffer offset from the stack hole into a register that can be used to address memory (BX, SI, or DI). Since it must count characters as they are entered, in order to limit the length of the string to the maximum length allowed, it also must initialize a Byte register to zero to be used to count characters as they are stored in the buffer.

The procedure then needs to loop, inputting characters from the keyboard (using INPUT_CHR) and storing the characters in successive byte memory locations within the buffer. As it loops, it should ignore any extended-keyboard characters, properly handle the <Backspace> key as a delete key, limit the number of characters the user may enter, and watch for the <Enter> key. When the user presses <Enter> it must quit the loop, retrieve the TRAILER character from the stack, store it into the buffer immediately following the last string character, and display CR and LF to move the cursor to the beginning of the next screen line; it must then return, closing the stack hole.

Figure 9-10   Macro to Input a String with Trailer

```
INPUT_STR    MACRO    BUFF_OFF, MAX_LEN, TRAILER

             Save BP
             Create a four-byte stack hole
             Point BP to stack hole
             Move BUFF_OFF (word) to stack hole (at [BP+0])
             If MAX_LEN is omitted
                 Move 80 (byte) to stack hole (at [BP+2])
             Else
                 Move MAX_LEN (byte) to stack hole (at [BP+2])
             Endif
             If TRAILER is omitted (blank)
                 Move 0 (byte) to stack hole (at [BP+3])
             Else
                 Move TRAILER (byte) to stack hole (at [BP+3])
             End if
             Call $INPUT_STR
             Restore BP
```

To ignore an extended-keyboard character, the procedure should simply beep at the user to indicate an error and then repeat the loop. If the character is an ASCII character, then the procedure must check to see if it is BS. If so, then it must properly delete the last character typed by the user. Deleting a character is, in itself, fairly complex. First the procedure must check the character count to see if there is anything to be deleted. If no characters have yet been entered, then it should simply beep at the user to indicate the error and repeat the loop to obtain the next character from the keyboard.

If one or more characters have been stored and counted, then it should delete the last character and repeat the loop. To delete the last character from the buffer, it simply needs to decrement the pointer register to back up by one in the buffer, and also decrement the character count since there is now one less character in the buffer. In addition, the character must be deleted from the screen. To do so, the procedure must display a BS (8) to back up on the screen, a space (32) to blank out the character, and another BS to back up again.

If the character is not CR, an extended-keyboard character, or BS, then the procedure must check the maximum length before storing the character. It should compare the character count with the maximum string length (on the stack). If the character count is greater than or equal to the maximum allowed length, then the procedure should simply beep to indicate the error and repeat the loop to try again. Note that the procedure should not terminate the loop when the maximum length is reached; it must continue the loop in order to allow the user to enter BS or CR.

If the maximum length has not yet been reached, then the procedure should store the character, echo it, and repeat the loop. To store the character, the procedure must move it to the memory location addressed by the buffer-pointer register. The buffer pointer and the character counter must then be incremented to point to the next byte of the buffer and to count one more character. The character must then be displayed, in order to echo it to the screen, before repeating the loop. Figure 9-11 summarizes the logic for the input of a string with trailer.

Note that the buffer must be at least one byte longer than the number of characters allowed the user (MAX_LEN). Whenever INPUT_STR is invoked, MAX_LEN must always be less than the number of bytes defined for the buffer. The macro header should include just such a caution for the next programmer.

A procedure, $INPUT_STRL, to store the string with a length byte would be very similar to the logic depicted in Figure 9-11 with three notable exceptions. First, it must store the characters beginning with the second byte of the buffer; it should increment Buff_ptr (BX, SI, or DI) immediately after moving BUFF_OFF from the stack into it. Second, after completing the loop, it must store the string length into the first byte of the buffer instead of storing TRAILER onto the end of the string; it should retrieve BUFF_OFF from the stack into Buff_ptr again and use it to store Char_count into the first byte of the buffer. Finally, since the macro opened only a three-byte stack hole, the procedure should close only three bytes on the return.

Figure 9-11   Procedure to Input a String with Trailer

```
$INPUT_STR PROC NEAR

    Save any registers to be used
    Move BUFF_OFF from stack (at [BP+0]) into Buff_ptr (base or index
                                                        register)
    Initialize Char_count (byte register) to 0
    Repeat (Quit when Char EQ CR)
        Repeat (Quit when Char is ASCII)
            Use INPUT_CHR to input a character into Char (byte
                                                        register)
        Quit repeat when Char is ASCII (not extended keyboard; Carry
                                                            clear)
            DSPLY_CHR 7 (beep)
        End repeat
    Quit repeat when Char EQ CR (13)
        If Char EQ BS (8)
            If Char_count EQ 0
                DSPLY_CHR 7 (beep; can't delete)
            Else
                DSPLY_IMMED_STR <8,' ',8> (erase last char from scrn)
                Decrement Buff_ptr (back up one in buffer)
                Decrement Char_count (one less char in buffer)
            End if
        Else      (Char is not BS)
            If Char_count AE MAX_LEN (MAX_LEN is on stack at [BP+2])
                DSPLY_CHR 7 (beep; can't accept it)
            Else
                Store Char into buffer (at [Buff_ptr])
                Increment Buff_ptr (to next unused byte of buffer)
                Increment Char_count (count one more char)
                DSPLY_CHR Char (echo it)
            Endif
        Endif
    End repeat
    Move TRAILER from stack (at [BP+3]) into buffer (at [Buff_ptr]);
                                                requires 2 moves
    DSPLY_IMMED_STR <13, 10> (CR + LF; cursor to beginning of next
                                                screen line)
    Restore any saved registers
    Return, closing four-byte stack hole
```

A building block, BINPUT_STR, to input a string using BIOS services should be similar, except that the procedure would use BINPUT_CHR to obtain keyboard characters and should probably use BDSPLY_CHR and BDSPLY_IMMED_STR to echo the characters and for other video output. Consequently, it requires two additional parameters: ECHO_ATT, the attribute to be used for the echo, and ECHO_PAGE, the video page in which to echo. The macro must, therefore, open two additional bytes of stack hole in which to pass the echo attribute and page. When passing ECHO_ATT, the macro must allow the same default and the same attribute codes as discussed in the last chapter for BDSPLY_CHR and BDSPLY_STR. The macro should default ECHO_PAGE to zero.

ENHANCED (101-KEY) KEYBOARD

Many modern PCs use an enhanced keyboard (101 keys) in place of the standard (83 keys) keyboard. Such a keyboard includes eighteen extra keys. With the exception of <F11> and <F12>, each duplicates the function of a key (or combination of keys) present on the standard keyboard. An enhanced keyboard is accessed through DOS in the same manner as a standard keyboard. The only difference is the possibility of receiving six new extended-keyboard characters:

```
<F11>          = 85H        <F12>          = 86H
<SHIFT>+<F11>  = 87H        <SHIFT>+<F12>  = 88H
<CTRL>+<F11>   = 89H        <CTRL>+<F12>   = 8AH
```

The BIOS keyboard operations discussed earlier (00H, 01H, and 02H) do not recognize <F11> or <F12>. Consequently, the BIOS on machines with enhanced keyboards provides the following three additional keyboard operations.

10H - Input a character from enhanced keyboard:

Operation 10H is identical to operation 00H except that it recognizes <F11> and <F12>, and it distinguishes between the standard and added cursor-control keys by returning E0H instead of 00H in AL. If <F11> or <F12> is pressed, BIOS returns with 0 in AL and the appropriate extended-keyboard character (listed above) in AH. If one of the added cursor-control keys has been pressed, AL contains E0H (instead of 00H), and AH contains the extended-keyboard character of the corresponding standard cursor-control key (see Figure 9-3). All standard keys are returned in the same manner as by operation 00H.

11H - Check enhanced keyboard buffer:

Operation 11H is identical to operation 01H except that it recognizes <F11> and <F12> and returns enhanced-keyboard characters as described above for operation 10H.

12H - Check status of enhanced keyboard shift and toggle keys:

Operation 12H is similar to operation 02H except that it uses AH, as well as AL, to return additional information about the shift and toggle keys. AL is the same as for operation 02H; AH should be interpreted as follows:

Bit #	Meaning if set
0	\<Left ctrl\> is down
1	\<Left alt\> is down
2	\<Right ctrl\> is down
3	\<Right alt\> is down
4	\<Scroll\> is down
5	\<Num lock\> is down
6	\<Caps lock\> is down
7	\<SysRq\> is down (added \<Print screen\>)

Note: Bit 0 is the **least**-significant bit.

Hardware access to an enhanced keyboard is a bit more complicated. With the exception of \<F11\> and \<F12\>, which simply generate new scan codes, all other added keys generate two or more scan codes when pressed and two or more scan codes when released. Pressing or releasing one of the added keys generates several type 09H interrupts with accompanying scan codes.

In some cases, the new key simply generates a scan code of E0H followed by the scan code of the equivalent standard key. For example, the standard \<Ctrl\> key generates a scan code of 1DH when pressed, and 9DH when released. The added \<Ctrl\> key (on the right side of the keyboard) generates two interrupts and scan codes (E0H followed by 1DH) when pressed and two scan codes (E0H followed by 9DH) when released.

Other added keys generate a sequence of several scan codes similar to the equivalent standard key in conjunction with the \<Left shift\> key. For example, pressing the extra \<Delete\> key generates four interrupts and scan codes (E0H, 2AH, E0H, and 53H), which is similar to pressing and holding \<Left shift\> (2AH) followed by the standard \<Del\> (53H). Releasing the added \<Delete\> generates a sequence of four scan codes (E0H, D3H, E0H, and AAH), which is similar to releasing the standard \<Del\> (D3H) and then releasing \<Left shift\> (AAH). Figure 9-12 lists the extra keys and the scan code sequences they generate when pressed and when released.

SUMMARY

Every time a key is depressed or released, the keyboard hardware generates an interrupt type 09H to the processor. The processor immediately stops whatever it is doing, saves the flags and the address of the next instruction, and transfers control to the BIOS keyboard interrupt-service routine. BIOS obtains a scan code identifying the key and indicating whether it has been depressed or released. The scan code is independent of the key's meaning; instead it is based on the physical location of the key. BIOS interprets the scan code, keeps track of the status of shift keys and toggle switches (related to the toggle keys) and stores input characters within the keyboard buffer.

Each character is interpreted either as an ASCII character or as an extended-keyboard character. In either case, two bytes are stored within the keyboard buffer. If it is an ASCII character, then it is stored as the ASCII code followed by the scan code of the key; an extended-keyboard character is stored as a byte with a value of zero followed by the extended-keyboard character code, often the scan code of the key. BIOS interprets the <Ctrl> key in combination with alphabetic and punctuation keys as ASCII control characters. In addition, the <Alt> key, when used in conjunction with the numeric keypad, is interpreted as ASCII characters, thus allowing for the entry of any ASCII character (from one through 255) from the keyboard.

The manner in which BIOS stores characters leads to confusion whenever the user enters an ASCII NUL from the keyboard. <Ctrl>+<@> is properly interpreted by the keyboard interrupt-service routine and is stored as an ASCII NUL character (zero) followed by the scan code of the <@> key (three). Unfortunately, this combination is later misinterpreted by the DOS function call as an extended character with a code of three. Consequently, any building block that obtains keyboard input should translate an extended-keyboard three to an ASCII zero (NUL).

Figure 9-12   Extra Scan Codes, Enhanced Keyboard

Extra key	Scan code sequence when pressed	Scan code sequence when released
<F11>	57H	D7H
<F12>	58H	D8H
<Alt>	E0H 38H	E0H B8H
<Ctrl>	E0H 1DH	E0H 9DH
</>	E0H 35H	E0H B5H
<Enter>	E0H 1CH	E0H 9CH
<Pause>	E1H 1DH 45H E1H 9DH C5H	**Nothing**
<Print screen>	E0H 2AH E0H 37H	E0H B7H E0H AAH
<Insert>	E0H 2AH E0H 52H	E0H D2H E0H AAH
<Home>	E0H 2AH E0H 47H	E0H C7H E0H AAH
<Page up>	E0H 2AH E0H 49H	E0H C9H E0H AAH
<Delete>	E0H 2AH E0H 53H	E0H D3H E0H AAH
<End>	E0H 2AH E0H 4FH	E0H CFH E0H AAH
<Page down>	E0H 2AH E0H 51H	E0H D1H E0H AAH
<Up arrow>	E0H 2AH E0H 48H	E0H C8H E0H AAH
<Left arrow>	E0H 2AH E0H 4BH	E0H CBH E0H AAH
<Right arrow>	E0H 2AH E0H 4DH	E0H CDH E0H AAH
<Down arrow>	E0H 2AH E0H 50H	E0H D0H E0H AAH

Input may be obtained from the keyboard buffer either by invoking BIOS keyboard services (INT 16H) or through the DOS function call (INT 21H). BIOS keyboard services, operation zero, returns both bytes of the next character, the first byte in AL and the second byte in AH. The DOS functions for keyboard input return only one byte, always in AL; if AL is zero, then the program must always execute a second DOS function call to obtain the second byte.

In order to input character strings, a program must define an input buffer within the data segment; the offset of the buffer must be supplied as an input parameter to any building block that inputs a character string. In addition, the program must ensure that any input does not exceed the buffer length. Consequently, the building block requires an input parameter specifying the maximum number of characters to allow the user to enter; in order to leave room in the buffer for the trailer or length byte, any program using the building block must specify a maximum string length that is at least one less than the length of the buffer. If the building block is to store the string with a trailer, then an additional parameter is required to specify the character to be used as the trailer.

VOCABULARY

V9-1 In your own words, define each of the following terms:

a) Keyboard scan code

b) Keyboard interrupt-service routine

c) Keyboard buffer

d) Queue

e) Shift key

f) Toggle key

g) ASCII control character

h) Extended-keyboard character

i) Extended-ASCII character

j) BIOS keyboard services

k) Asynchronous event

l) Synchronous event

m) Input parameter

n) Output parameter

REVIEW QUESTIONS

Q9-1 Explain the pattern of the assignment of scan codes to the keys.

Q9-2 Which is an asynchronous routine, the BIOS keyboard interrupt-service routine or BIOS keyboard services?

Q9-3 How long, in bytes, is the keyboard buffer? How many characters can it store?

Q9-4 How many shift keys are on the standard eighty-three-key keyboard? List them.

Q9-5 How many toggle keys are on the standard eighty-three-key keyboard? List them.

Q9-6 Which of the following causes shift and toggle keys to "behave" differently than the other keys: the keyboard hardware, the BIOS keyboard interrupt-service routine, or BIOS keyboard services?

Q9-7   Explain the manner in which BIOS stores ASCII characters in the keyboard buffer.

Q9-8   Explain the manner in which BIOS stores extended-keyboard characters in the keyboard buffer.

Q9-9   Which ASCII character is easily misinterpreted as an extended-keyboard character as a result of the manner in which BIOS stores characters in the keyboard buffer? What key combination generates the character?

Q9-10 Describe three possible ways to enter the ASCII character, 4, from the keyboard. Describe the two-bytes that are stored in the keyboard buffer in each case.

Q9-11 What instruction must a program execute in order to access BIOS keyboard services? What instruction can be used to access a DOS keyboard function?

Q9-12 When a program executes BIOS keyboard services, operation zero, does BIOS get the character to return directly from the keyboard or from the keyboard buffer?

Q9-13 With our method of parameter passing, what data addressing mode(s) is/are allowed for input parameters? What about output parameters?

Q9-14 In our building blocks to input a character, why did we use the Carry flag, rather than some other flag, to indicate the type of character?

Q9-15 Explain the LOCAL directive. When is its use necessary? Where does the assembler allow it? What does it cause the assembler to do?

PROGRAMMING ASSIGNMENTS

PA9-1 Add a new building block, INPUT_CHR, to your console library to input a character via the DOS function call. The macro should have one optional byte output parameter, CHAR, to receive the keyboard character. Use the Carry flag to indicate whether it is an ASCII or extended-keyboard character. Be sure to return <Ctrl>+<@> as an ASCII NUL character, rather than as an extended-keyboard character.

The procedure, $INPUT_CHR, in a file called $INP_CHR.ASM, should use DOS function 08H to get the character. If AL is zero, then use function 07H to get the extended-keyboard character.

Write a mainline program, PA9-1.ASM, to test your building block. Use the following logic in the code segment:

```
Repeat
     Input character into CL using INPUT_CHR
Quit repeat when character is extended (Carry flag set)
     Use DSPLY_CHR to display the character in CL
End repeat
Display "Press any key to return to DOS"
Use INPUT_CHR with no parameters to stall until any key is pressed
```

Run your program and press a number of keys to ensure that your building block is functioning properly. To terminate the program, press any key or key combination that generates an extended-keyboard character; nothing should be echoed to the screen for the extended-keyboard character. Notice what happens when you press <Enter>; also notice what happens when you press <Ctrl>+<Enter>. Be sure to try entering ASCII control characters, including <Ctrl>+<@>; the ASCII NUL should display as a space. Also verify that the program aborts whenever you type <Ctrl>+<Break> or <Ctrl>+<C> and that it does **not** abort when you type <Ctrl>+<@>.

PA9-2   Add a building block, BINPUT_CHR, to your library to use BIOS keyboard services to input a character from the keyboard. Provide two optional byte output parameters: CHAR, to receive the character, and SCAN, to receive the scan code if the character is ASCII, or 255 if it is an extended-keyboard character. Also use the Carry flag to indicate the type of character as in PA9-1. Return <Ctrl>+<@> as an ASCII NUL character rather than as an extended-keyboard character.

To test your building block, write a mainline program, PA9-2.ASM, similar to that in PA9-1. Use the keyboard scan code to determine the manner in which the character was entered. Use the following logic in the code segment:

```
Repeat
    Use BINPUT_CHR to input a character into BH, scan code into BL
Quit repeat when character is extended (Carry flag set)
    Use DSPLY_CHR to display the character in BH
    If BL EQ zero
        Display "(<Alt> + numeric keypad) "
    Else
        If BL below 59
            Display "(Main keyboard) "
        Else
            Display "(Numeric keypad) "
        End if
    End if
End repeat
Display "Press any key to return to DOS"
Use BINPUT_CHR with no parameters to stall until any key is pressed
```

Run your program and test it as in PA9-1. Also, enter several characters by each of the three possible methods to ensure that the program reports the proper method in each case.

PA9-3   Do PA9-1 or PA9-2. Then write a building block, CHECK_KBRD, to check the keyboard buffer and determine if it contains any input. It should have a single byte output parameter, STATUS, indicating the status of the buffer: 0 if the buffer is empty, 255 (FFH) if the buffer contains characters.

Write a mainline procedure, PA9-3.ASM, to test the building block. Use logic similar to the following:

```
Repeat
    Repeat
        Use CHECK_KBRD to get the keyboard status into DH
    Quit repeat when DH NE zero
        Display "No " (no CR+LF)
    End repeat
    Use INPUT_CHR (or BINPUT_CHR) to get the character into DH
Quit repeat when character is extended (Carry set)
```

```
        Display the character followed by CR and LF
    End repeat
```

PA9-4   Do PA9-1 or PA9-2. Then write a building block, CHECK_KEYS, to check the status of all shift and toggle keys (Refer to Figures 9-6 and 9-7).

Write a mainline procedure, PA9-4.ASM, that tests your building block. Display a message telling the user to press one or more toggle keys and/or hold down one or more shift keys and then press any other key. Use INPUT_CHR or BINPUT_CHR with no parameters to stall until the user presses a character-generating key. Then use CHECK_KEYS to obtain the status of the shift and toggle keys and use a series of TST and JZ or JNZ instructions to check the appropriate bits and report the status of all shift and toggle keys. Report the shift keys as either UP or DOWN and report the toggle keys as ON or OFF; report <Left shift> and <Right shift> individually.

PA9-5   Do PA9-1 or PA9-2 and then add a building block, FLUSH_KBRD, to flush the keyboard buffer. The building block should have no parameters; it should use DOS function 00H, with zero in AL, to empty the keyboard buffer.

Write a mainline program, PA9-5.ASM, to test the building block. The mainline program should flush the buffer and then use INPUT_CHR or BINPUT_CHR to obtain a character from the keyboard. When running the program, quickly press any key several times, immediately after entering the command to execute the program. Verify that the characters are discarded and that the program then waits for another character from the keyboard.

PA9-6   Do PA9-1 and then add another building block, INPUT_STR, to input a string from the keyboard, using INPUT_CHR, and store it with a trailer character. You will need three input parameters: BUFF_OFF (word) for the offset of the buffer within the data segment, MAX_LEN (byte) for the maximum number of characters to allow, and TRAILER (byte) for the character to be used as the trailer for the string. MAX_LEN should default to eighty and TRAILER should default to zero (NUL character).

The procedure $INPUT_STR should use INPUT_CHR to obtain each character from the keyboard buffer. It should ignore any extended-keyboard characters, properly handle <Backspace> as a delete key, restrict the number of characters to the maximum length specified, and terminate the input when the user presses <Enter>. Upon termination, it should display CR and LF to move the cursor to the beginning of the next line; it should then store the trailer character onto the end of the string.

Write a mainline program, PA9-6.ASM, to test the building block. Define an eighty-one-byte buffer, IO_BFR, within the data segment. Use at least the following logic within the code segment (you may add more):

```
    Input a string into IO_BFR, limiting the length to ten bytes and
                        specifying '#' as the trailer character.
    Use DSPLY_STR to display the string in IO_BFR
    Display CR+LF+LF to skip a line on the screen

    Input another string into IO_BFR; this time, accept the default
                        values for MAX_LEN and TRAILER
    Use DSPLY_STR to display the string in IO_BFR
```

PA9-7   Do PA9-1 and write a building block, INPUT_STRL, to input a string using INPUT_CHR and store it with a length byte. The building block should have two input parameters: BUFF_OFF (word), for the offset of the buffer within the data segment, and MAX_LEN (byte), for the maximum number of characters to allow.

The procedure $INPUT_STRL should use INPUT_CHR to obtain each character from the keyboard buffer; it should begin storing characters into the second byte of the buffer, ignoring any extended-keyboard characters, properly handling <Backspace> as a delete key, restricting the number of characters to the maximum length specified, and terminating the input when the user presses <Enter>. Upon termination, it should display CR and LF to move the cursor to the beginning of the next line; it should then store the string length into the first byte of the buffer.

Write a mainline program, PA9-7.ASM, to test the building block. Define an eighty-one-byte buffer, IO_BFR, within the data segment. Use at least the following logic within the code segment (you may add more):

```
Input a string into IO_BFR, limiting the length to ten bytes
Use DSPLY_STRL to display the string in IO_BFR
Display CR+LF+LF to skip a line on the screen

Input another string into IO_BFR; this time, accept the default
                                              value for MAX_LEN
Use DSPLY_STRL to display the string in IO_BFR
```

PA9-8   Do PA9-2, and add another building block, BINPUT_STR, to input a string using BIN-PUT_CHR, storing it with a trailer. The building block should be identical to that described in PA9-6 except that it requires two additional parameters: ECHO_ATT, for the attribute to use when echoing characters, and ECHO_PAGE, the video page in which to echo the characters. ECHO_ATT should allow the same default and attribute codes as allowed by BDSPLY_CHR and BDSPLY_STR, discussed in the last chapter. ECHO_PAGE should default to zero.

Write a mainline program, PA9-8.ASM, to test the building block. The mainline should be identical to that in PA9-6 except that it should specify normal video for the echo attribute on the first input and reverse video on the second input. It should also use BDSPLY_STR to display the string after each input.

PA9-9   Do PA9-2 and add another building block, BINPUT_STRL, to input a string using BIN-PUT_CHR, storing it with a length byte. The building block should be identical to that described in PA9-7 except that it requires two additional parameters: ECHO_ATT, for the attribute to use when echoing characters, and ECHO_PAGE, the video page in which to echo the characters. ECHO_ATT should allow the same default and attribute codes as allowed by BDSPLY_CHR and BDSPLY_STR, discussed in the last chapter. ECHO_PAGE should default to zero.

Write a mainline program, PA9-9.ASM, to test the building block. The mainline should be identical to that in PA9-7 except that it should specify normal video for the echo attribute on the first input and reverse video on the second input. It should also use BDSPLY_STRL to display the string after each input.

10

Input and Output
of Numeric Data

INTRODUCTION

Recall that our building blocks to display a character require the ASCII code of the character as an input parameter; the building blocks to display a string require a string of ASCII codes stored in memory. Similarly, our building blocks to input a single character or a string of characters from the keyboard have returned the ASCII codes, or extended-keyboard codes, of the depressed keys. Thus far all input and output has been of the ASCII codes for character data. We do not yet have the capability of inputting or outputting numeric data.

Suppose that a program has calculated a value, 16,682 for example, into the BX register. That numeric value, sixteen thousand six hundred and eighty-two, is stored in the register as a word binary value: 01000001 00101010. We might be tempted to use DSPLY_CHR to try to display the result; for example, we might display BH first, then display BL. The resulting output would be "A*" (01000001B = 65 = "A"; 00101010B = 42 = "*"). That is certainly not the output we desire!

In order to display a numeric value to the screen, our DSPLY_STR building block requires a **numeric string**; a string of ASCII characters representing the numeral whose value is the desired number. For the above numeric value, DSPLY_STR requires a five-byte string, "16682", followed by a trailer. If we use a NUL as the trailer, then the string must consist of six bytes with the following numeric values: forty-nine (31H), fifty-four (36H), fifty-four (36H), fifty-six (38H), fifty (32H), and zero (00H).

Similarly, if we use INPUT_STR to input from the keyboard, and the user enters "39", the value input into the buffer is not the number thirty-nine. Rather it is a numeric string, "39", consisting of the following three byte values: fifty-one (33H), fifty-seven (39H) and zero (00H). Any attempt to interpret the string as a numeric value, by moving the first byte into CH and the second byte into CL, for example, results in a complete misinterpretation of the data. The result in CX would be a numeric value of 3339H or 13,113.

It should now be clear that we need to develop some new building blocks to allow for the input and output of numeric data. However, rather than developing building blocks to display and input numeric data, we will obtain greater flexibility by developing building blocks that convert between numeric strings and numeric data. In order to output numeric data, we will first convert it to a numeric string and then use an existing building block to display or print the resulting string. Similarly, in order to input numeric data from the keyboard, we will use an existing building block to input it as a numeric string; we will then use our new building block to convert the numeric string to numeric data into a register.

The algorithms that we will use to convert between numeric data and the corresponding numeric strings are similar to the algorithms discussed in chapter 2 for converting between bases. The difference is that the computer stores numeric data in binary rather than decimal; the processor's native numeral system is base two, rather than base ten. Consequently, converting from numeric data (binary) to a numeric string (a numeral in any base) is analogous to our conversion from decimal to some other base. Similarly, converting from a numeric string (numeral, any base) to the corresponding numeric value (in binary) is analogous to our conversion to decimal from some other base.

The value of a numeric string depends on the numeral base in which it is represented. "101" represents the number five, if it is interpreted as base two; if interpreted as base ten, then it represents a value of one hundred and one. "101" represents still different values if interpreted as octal, hexadecimal, or any other base. Our conversion routines will be much more flexible if they are capable of converting to and from a numeral (numeric string) in any base. Consequently, the base to be used during the conversion needs to be one of the input parameters.

NUMERIC-TO-STRING CONVERSION ALGORITHM

In order to convert a number to a numeric string to be displayed or printed, the processor must convert from its native base (two) to some other base. The problem of conversion from numeric to string data, then, is very similar to the problem in chapter 2 of converting from base ten (our native numeral system) to some other base. Consequently, we will use an algorithm that is very similar to the algorithm we used to convert from base ten to other bases. Recall that we used repeated division by the new base to perform the conversion. Specifically, we used the following algorithm in order to convert from decimal (our native numeral base) to binary:

```
Build the binary numeral from right to left, starting with
                                    the ones place
Repeat
        Divide the decimal numeral by two
            The remainder provides the next binary digit (from
                                          right to left)
            The quotient provides the decimal numeral for the
                                          next division
Until the decimal numeral equals zero
```

A similar algorithm may be used to convert numeric data (in binary) to a numeric string (in any base) for display purposes. However, for maximum flexibility, we should be able to convert to a string in any base. Consequently, the repeated division should be by the desired base.

One problem with the repeated-division algorithm, however, is that it determines the digits from right to left rather than from left to right; the remainder of the first division provides the digit for the ones place, the second division provides the next higher place, and so on. Since we need to store digits into the buffer from left to right, beginning with the highest-value digit and ending with the ones place, we must somehow reverse the order of the digits when storing them into the buffer. The stack provides a convenient method of reversing the order of the digits, because it operates in last-in-first-out manner. We simply push the digits as they are determined; after all digits have been determined and pushed onto the stack, we then pop the digits off the stack, in reverse order, storing them into the string buffer from left to right. In order to ensure that we perform the same number of pops and pushes, we must count the digits as they are pushed and ensure that we pop all digits from the stack.

Another problem is that the remainder of each division yields the numeric value of the next digit, rather than the ASCII code for the character. It is necessary to convert each digit from its numeric value to the appropriate ASCII character before storing it into the buffer. If the remainder is zero through nine, then adding the ASCII code for "0" is sufficient. Consider the following examples:

Remainder	Plus "0" (48)	Resulting ASCII character
0	48	"0"
1	49	"1"
2	50	"2"
.	.	.
.	.	.
.	.	.
9	57	"9"

However, when converting to any base greater than ten (hexadecimal, for example), the remainder may be greater than nine. For example, during a conversion to a hexadecimal numeral (division by sixteen) a remainder of ten may result; the resulting hexadecimal digit should be "A". However, adding "0" (48) to ten results in 58, which is the ASCII code for ":" (colon). Whenever the result of adding "0" (48) is greater than "9" (57), we need to add seven in order to adjust to the correct hexadecimal digit (58 + 7 = 65 = "A"). Adding seven whenever the sum of the remainder and "0" is greater than "9" (57) produces the following results:

Remainder	Plus "0" (48)	Plus 7 (if > "9")	ASCII character
0	48		"0"
1	49		"1"
.	.		.
.	.		.
.	.		.
9	57		"9"
10	58	65	"A"
11	59	66	"B"
12	60	67	"C"
.	.	.	.
.	.	.	.
.	.	.	.

Keeping the above discussion in mind, we can arrive at an algorithm for converting any numeric value to the equivalent numeric string in any base. Note that the loop that performs repeated division should always execute at least once; we always want at least one digit in the numeric string. Consequently, we need to use a repeat-until construct, which performs the test for completion after the body of the loop. Figure 10-1 illustrates the logic for converting a number to a numeric string.

Figure 10-1   Convert a Number to a Numeric String

```
Initialize a Digit Counter to zero
Repeat
     Divide Number by Base, quotient to Number, remainder to Digit
     Add "0" to Digit (convert to ASCII)
     If Digit GT "9" (alphabetic digit)
          Add 7 to Digit
     End if
     Push Digit to stack (to reverse the order)
     Increment Digit Counter
Until Number EQ zero
```

Figure 10-1: (continued)

```
Repeat Digit Counter times
    Pop Digit from stack (reverse order)
    Store Digit into buffer (working from left to right)
End repeat
```

STRING-TO-NUMERIC CONVERSION ALGORITHM

The problem of converting a numeric string (in any base) to its numeric value (in binary) is similar to the problem discussed in chapter 2 of converting to decimal from some other base. Recall that we discussed an algorithm ("double-dabble") for converting from binary to decimal, which was essentially the inverse of the algorithm to convert from decimal to any other base. We did not recommend it in chapter 2, but it lends itself perfectly to a computer solution since it involves the repetition of a few relatively simple steps. Recall that it involved the use of repeated multiplication by the base (two):

```
Start with zero for the decimal numeral
Get the first binary digit (left-most)
Repeat while you have a digit
    Double the decimal numeral
    Add the binary digit (0 or 1) to the decimal numeral
    Get the next binary digit, if any (from left to right)
End repeat
```

We will use a similar algorithm to convert a numeric string into a number in a register. For maximum flexibility, we should be able to interpret the numeric string as a numeral in any base. Consequently, the repeated multiplication should be by the desired base. Recall that, when converting from a number to a string, it was necessary to convert numeric remainders to ASCII characters; similarly, when converting a string to a number, we must convert each character in the string to its numeric digit value before adding it to the number. With one exception, the problem of converting a character to its numeric value is just the opposite of the previous problem of converting the numeric remainder to the digit as an ASCII character.

The exception is that we should allow either uppercase or lowercase for alphabetic digits; if converting from base sixteen, we should interpret either "1a" or "1A" as twenty-six. Refer to Figure 8-1 (ASCII code), and notice that the ASCII code for each lowercase letter is exactly thirty-two (20H) greater than the code for the corresponding uppercase letter. Consequently, we can easily convert lowercase alphabetic characters to uppercase by simply subtracting thirty-two. Thus, we end up with the following algorithm for converting a digit from the ASCII character to its numeric value:

ASCII-to-Numeric Conversion

```
If Digit GE "a" and Digit LE "z" (if lowercase)
     Subtract 32 from Digit (convert to uppercase)
End if
If Digit GT "9" (if it is alphabetic)
     Subtract 7 from digit
End if
Subtract "0" (48, 30H) from the digit (from ASCII to
                                              numeric)
```

An additional problem we face when converting from a string to a number is that the string may not be a valid numeral. As we do the conversion, we must check for validity, and we must have some means of reporting the error when unable to convert the string. There are three major reasons why a string might not be a valid numeral:

Invalid Numeric String

1) It contains an invalid character (less than "0" or between "9" and "A" or greater than "Z".

2) A digit's numeric value is greater than or equal to the base; in any valid numeral, all digits must be less than the base.

3) The resulting numeric value is too big to store in the number of bits used to accumulate the number.

Note that letters above "F" are not necessarily invalid, if the base is sufficiently large. By allowing the digits "0" through "9" and "A" through "Z", we are able to convert numeric strings of any base up to thirty-six.

In order to avoid illogical results, we must carefully check for each of the three errors listed above during the conversion. We must check each digit before converting it to its numeric value to ensure that it is a valid character ("0" through "9" or "A" through "Z"). After converting to its numeric value, we must check to ensure that it is less than the base in use. Every time we increase the value of the resulting number, we must check the Carry flag to ensure that it did not become too big to be stored properly. Figure 10-2 illustrates the algorithm for converting from a numeric string to the number it represents.

Figure 10-2   Convert a Numeric String to a Number

```
Initialize Number to zero (will accumulate it)
Get first (left-most) Digit from string
Repeat while not at end of string
    If Digit GE "a" and Digit LE "z" (lowercase)
        Subtract 32 from Digit (to uppercase)
    End if
    If Digit LT "0" or Digit GT "Z"
                      or (Digit GT "9" and Digit LT "A")
        Abort conversion, reporting error
    End if
    If Digit GT "9" (alphabetic)
        Subtract 7 from Digit
    End if
    Subtract '0' from Digit (from ASCII to numeric)
    If Digit GE Base
        Abort conversion, reporting error
    End if
    Multiply Number by Base
    If multiplication resulted in carry (Number is too big)
        Abort conversion, reporting error
    End if
    Add Digit to Number
    If addition resulted in carry (Number is too big)
        Abort conversion, reporting error
    End if
    Get next Digit from string (left to right)
End repeat
```

MULTIPLICATION AND DIVISION INSTRUCTIONS

Since our algorithms for converting between numbers and numeric strings require multiplication and division, we now must discuss the multiplication and division instructions provided by the 8086/8088. We should first note that the instruction sets of many microprocessors do not provide such instructions; the ALUs of many microprocessors are limited to addition and subtraction. In order to do multiplication on such a processor, the programmer must write a building block to do the multiplication, either through repeated addition or by using an algorithm for binary multiplication similar to that discussed in chapter 2. Similarly, division on such a processor requires a set of instructions to perform repeated subtraction or to execute an algorithm similar to that discussed in chapter 2 for binary division.

The 8086/8088 processor, on the other hand, provides a group of four instructions for commanding the ALU to perform multiplication and division. The four instructions provided are **MUL**, **DIV**, **IMUL**, and **IDIV**. Each instruction may be coded in either of two forms, byte or word, as determined by the size of the source operand; a byte source operand results in byte multiplication or division and a word source operand results in word multiplication or division. All multiplication and division instructions are much less flexible than the more fundamental arithmetic instructions.

The destination operand of a byte multiplication or division is always the Accumulator register (AX); in a word multiplication or division, the destination is always the two Word registers, DX and AX. Since the destination is always AX (or DX and AX), only the source operand (to multiply or divide by) is specified in the assembly-language instruction and consequently encoded into the resulting machine-language instruction. A further limitation on operands is that the source operand may not be immediate data-addressing mode; only register and memory modes are permitted for the source operand. One further restriction of multiplication and division instructions is in their handling of the flags. They all modify all the Result flags (Overflow, Sign, Zero, Auxiliary Carry, Parity, and Carry). However, the flag results are all undefined for division, and only the Carry and Overflow flags are meaningful after a multiplication; all other Result flags are meaningless.

Two of the instructions, MUL and DIV, perform unsigned arithmetic; all bits in both the source and the destination are treated as binary digits. The other two instructions, IMUL and IDIV, perform signed arithmetic; the high bits of both the source and destination are treated as sign bits and are handled according to the standard algebraic rules for the multiplication and division of signed values. Following is an explanation of each of the instructions:

MUL   *source*

MUL causes the ALU to perform a binary multiplication by the source operand, which must be either Register or Memory addressing mode; it may not be Immediate mode. The destination operand is determined by the size of the source operand. If the source is a byte, then it is multiplied by the byte value in AL, and the word result is stored into AX. Note that multiplying a byte value (in AL) by another byte value (source operand) results in a word value (in AX). Note also that AH is always modified, even when the result is small enough (less than 256) to fit in a byte; if the result is less than 256, then AH is zero after the multiplication.

Both the source operand and AL are interpreted as unsigned values, resulting in an unsigned value in AX. All Result flags are modified. However, only the Carry flag and Overflow flag are meaningful; all other Result flags are undefined. The Carry and Overflow flags are both set if and only if the result is greater than 255, if there was a carry out of the low byte of the result into the high byte. In other words, both flags are set if and only if the high byte of the result (in AH) is not zero. Following is an example of an instruction with a byte operand and the arithmetic operation that results:

```
                              AL
        MUL      DH       ×  DH
                             AX
```

Since the source operand (DH) is a byte, its value is multiplied by the byte value in AL, and the resulting word value is stored into AX. DH is not modified. The Carry and Overflow flags both reflect the resulting value in AH; they are both set if and only if AH is not zero after execution.

If the source operand of the MUL instruction is a word, then the processor multiplies it by the word value in AX. The result of a word multiplied by a word is a double-word (thirty-two bit) value, requiring two word registers for storage. The high (most-significant) word of the result is stored in DX with the low (least-significant) word in AX. Note that DX is always modified by a word multiplication, even when the result is small enough (less than 65536) to be stored in AX; if the result is less than 65536, then zero is stored into DX.

As in a byte multiplication, all Result flags may be modified. However, only the Carry and Overflow flags are meaningful; all others should be ignored. Both the Carry flag and the Overflow flag are set if and only if there was a carry out of AX into DX, if and only if the resulting value in DX is not zero. Following is an example of a word multiplication instruction and the arithmetic operation that results:

```
                              AX
        MUL      CX       ×  CX
                            DX:AX
```

Since the source operand (CX) is a word value, it is multiplied by the word value in AX, resulting in a double-word value that is stored into DX:AX. CX is not modified. The Carry and Overflow flags reflect the resulting value in DX; they are both set if and only if the high word of the result, in DX, is not zero (the result is greater than 65,535).

DIV   *source*

DIV causes the processor to perform an unsigned integer division by the source operand, resulting in a quotient and remainder. Like MUL, DIV modifies all Result flags. However, the result for all flags is undefined; none of the Result flags contains any meaningful information after a DIV instruction.

Also as with MUL, the source operand must be either Register or Memory addressing mode, and the destination operand is determined by the size of the source operand. If the source operand is a byte, then the word value in AX is divided by the byte source value; the quotient is stored into AL and the remainder is stored into **AH**. Note that AH is always modified, even if the division is even; if the value in AX is evenly divisible by the source value, then a remainder of zero is stored in AH.

Also note that the result of the division may be too big to store in a byte (AL); for example 8000H / 2 = 4000H, which is too big to be stored in AL. Whenever the result of a byte division is bigger than 255, the processor does not modify either AL or AH; instead it executes an interrupt type 00H, which results in the aborting of the program with a "Divide overflow" error reported by DOS. Following is an example of a byte division and the arithmetic operation that results:

```
                              AL   R   AH
     DIV        BL        BL )‾A‾X‾‾‾‾‾‾‾‾
```

The word value in AX is divided by the byte value in BL, and the result is stored in AX, the quotient in AL, and the remainder in AH. BL is not modified. All Result flags are undefined. If the result is too big to be stored in AL (greater than 255), then the processor executes an interrupt type 00H (divide overflow) without modifying either AH or AL.

If the source operand is a word, then the double-word value in DX:AX is divided by the source; AX receives the quotient, and DX receives the remainder. DX is always modified; if the division is even, then the remainder, zero, is stored into DX. Note also that the dividend is always the double-word, DX:AX; if the intent is to divide the value in AX (less than 65536) by a word divisor, then the program must ensure that DX is zero before doing the division. If the resulting quotient is greater than 65,535, the processor executes an interrupt type 00H without modifying AX or DX. Following is an example of a word division as well as the resulting arithmetic operation:

```
                              AX   R   DX
     DIV        BX        BX )‾D‾X‾:‾A‾X‾‾‾
```

Since the source (divisor) is a word, the double-word in DX:AX is divided by the source; any value in DX is interpreted as 65,536 times the value. Upon completion, the quotient is stored into AX, the remainder into DX. BX is not modified. If the resulting quotient is too big to be stored in AX, then neither AX nor DX is modified; instead, the processor executes an interrupt type 00H, which results in a "Divide overflow" error from DOS.

IMUL   **source**

IMUL is identical to MUL except that it is used to perform signed multiplication; the ALU interprets the high bits of the source and destination values as signs rather than as binary digits. Recall that with addition and subtraction the interpretation of the data as signed or unsigned does not matter to the processor. The same is not true for multiplication; the processor must perform multiplication differently for signed values than for unsigned values. Consequently, we have been provided with the IMUL instruction for performing signed multiplication.

When executing an IMUL instruction, the ALU negates (NEG) any negative (high bit is one) source or destination (AL or AX) value before performing the multiplication. The multiplication is then always performed on positive values. After the multiplication is completed, the ALU XORs the two original sign bits to determine the sign of the result; the sign of the result is negative (sign bit is one) if and only if the signs of the multiplier and multiplicand were different. If the sign of the result is negative, then the processor negates the product in AX or in DX:AX.

Consequently, IMUL produces the correct results when the values being multiplied are interpreted as signed values. It should never be used when the values are to be interpreted as unsigned; MUL should be used to multiply unsigned values. Except for producing proper results for signed (rather than unsigned) multiplication, IMUL is identical to MUL.

IDIV   **source**

IDIV performs division on signed values; it interprets the high bits of the values as signs rather than as binary digits. Other than interpreting the high bits as sign bits, IDIV is identical to DIV.

To perform an IDIV, the ALU first negates any negative source or destination (AX or DX:AX) values, before performing the division; thus the division is always performed on positive values. The ALU must then determine the signs of both the quotient and the remainder. The sign of the quotient is determined in the same manner that IMUL determines the sign of a product, by the XOR of the signs of the divisor and dividend; the quotient is negated if its sign is negative. The sign of the remainder is always the same as the sign of the dividend (AX or DX:AX) regardless of the sign of the divisor (source); the remainder is negated if the dividend's sign was negative. Note that a negative value divided by a negative value, for example, results in a positive quotient with a negative remainder.

IDIV should always be used to perform division whenever the values are to be interpreted as signed. It should never be used when interpreting values as unsigned; DIV should be used if the values are unsigned.

S U M M A R Y   O F   Multiplication and Division Instructions

MUL

    AL * byte, product to AX

    or

    AX * word, product to DX:AX

IMUL

    Same as MUL, except treats high bit as sign

DIV

    AX / byte, quotient to AL, remainder to AH

    or

    DX:AX / word, quotient to AX, remainder to DX

IDIV

    Same as DIV, except treats high bit as sign

"STRING" INSTRUCTIONS

The 8086/8088 processor also provides another group of instructions, not usually implemented by microprocessors, which we have not yet discussed. Although this group of data-movement and logical instructions is commonly referred to as the **"string" instructions**, its use is not limited to the manipulation of string data. The "string" instructions make up a set of very powerful, but also very restrictive, instructions that may be used to manipulate any large blocks of data, string or otherwise.

Five fundamental "string" instructions are provided, three data-movement instructions and two arithmetic (comparison) instructions. The data-movement "string" instructions are **MOVS** (Move String: move data from memory to memory), **LODS** (Load String: move data from memory into the Accumulator register, AL or AX) and **STOS** (Store String: move data from the Accumulator register, AL or AX, into memory). The arithmetic "string" instructions are **CMPS** (Compare String: compare data in memory to other data in memory) and **SCAS** (Scan String: compare data in memory to data in the Accumulator register, AL or AX).

Note that two of the "string" instructions are exceptions to the rule that the source and destination operands of an instruction cannot both be memory mode; both operands of MOVS and CMPS are memory. All "string" instructions are very restrictive of the data-addressing modes allowed. Operands are predetermined by each instruction as either memory or the Accumulator register (AL or AX); Immediate-mode data addressing is not supported, nor is any register other than AL or AX.

Furthermore, memory addressing always uses predetermined Index and Segment registers; Memory-mode source operands are automatically addressed by **DS:[SI]**, and Memory-mode destination operands are always addressed by **ES:[DI]**. Since both source and destination operands are predetermined by each instruction, "string" instructions are normally coded without operands, and no operands are encoded into the resulting machine-language instructions. Consequently, all "string" instructions are one-byte machine-language instructions. Also, since the memory addressing is predetermined, the programmer must be very careful to ensure that the appropriate Segment and Index registers have been properly initialized to address the desired Memory-mode data before executing any "string" instruction.

Although there are only five fundamental "string" instructions, there are ten such machine-language instructions; each instruction allows two forms or types, byte and word. In order to specify the desired type of a "string" instruction, the programmer appends either B or W to the fundamental instruction name; for example, MOVSB moves one byte of data from DS:[SI] to ES:[DI], while MOVSW moves the word of data stored at DS:[SI] to the word of memory at ES:[DI]. For all "string" instructions in which one of the operands is the Accumulator register, AL is used in the byte instruction and AX is used in the word instruction. For example, STOSB stores the byte of data in AL into the byte memory location at ES:[DI]; STOSW stores the word in AX to the word of memory at ES:[DI].

Aside from the fact that "string" instructions are all one-byte instructions and so produce very memory-efficient code, their other major advantage stems from two further characteristics: first, each instruction automatically either increments or decrements any used Index register upon completion of the specified operation; second, each instruction allows a repeat prefix to cause the processor to repeat the instruction CX times. We will discuss the repeat prefixes shortly, after we have discussed the individual instructions.

Whether the Index registers are incremented or decremented during execution of the instruction is determined by the status of the Direction flag. If DF is clear (CLD; DEBUG reports as UP), any used Index register is incremented; if DF is set (STD; DEBUG reports as DN), any used Index register is decremented. As a consequence of the automatic incrementing or decrementing of Index registers, the processor is always ready to process the next (or previous) byte or word immediately after processing one byte or word of data. Following is an explanation of each "string" instruction.

MOVS

Move string is coded as either MOVSB or MOVSW. When executed, the processor copies the byte or word of data in memory at DS:[SI] to the byte or word of memory at ES:[DI]. After the data is copied, both SI and DI are incremented or decremented; the word form of the instruction increments or decrements both SI and DI twice in order to point to the next or previous word of data. MOVSB is logically equivalent to the following three instructions:

```
                 MOV      BYTE PTR ES:[DI], DS:[SI]
   MOVSB    =    INC      SI              ;or DEC SI
                 INC      DI              ;   DEC DI
```

If the Direction flag is clear (UP), then SI and DI are incremented, as shown; if it is set (DN), then MOVSB performs the same move but decrements both SI and DI. MOVSW is similar except that it copies a word of data from the source to the destination and increments or decrements SI and DI twice:

```
                 MOV      WORD PTR ES:[SI], DS:[SI]
                 INC      SI              ;or DEC SI
   MOVSW    =    INC      SI              ;   DEC SI
                 INC      DI              ;   DEC DI
                 INC      DI              ;   DEC DI
```

MOVS is often used to copy large blocks of data from one area of memory to another. It is a single-byte instruction that performs virtually the same function as several non-"string" instructions. Upon completion of the first move, the Index registers have already been automatically adjusted to be ready for the next move. When combined with a repeat prefix, to be discussed shortly, MOVS provides a very efficient means of copying large blocks of data.

LODS

Load string is a one-byte instruction, coded as either LODSB or LODSW. It copies a byte or word of data from the source memory location, at DS:[SI], into the Accumulator register, AL or AX. Since DI is not used by the instruction, it is not modified; only SI is incremented or decremented. The two forms of the instruction and the operations they perform are as follows:

```
LODSB    =       MOV        AL, DS:[SI]
                 INC        SI              ;or DEC SI

                 MOV        AX, DS:[SI]
LODSW    =       INC        SI              ;or DEC SI
                 INC        SI              ;   DEC SI
```

LODS is very useful when using iteration to process blocks of data stored in memory. After copying a byte or word of data from memory into the Accumulator for processing, the Source Index register is automatically incremented to point to the next byte or word to be processed the next time around the loop. A good example of a use for LODS is in our procedures for displaying character strings; in fact, you may want to go back and rewrite your display string building block procedures to use the single-byte LODS instead of MOV and INC for obtaining each character of the string.

STOS

Store string, coded as either STOSB or STOSW, is a single-byte instruction that is the complement of LODS. It copies the byte or word of data from the Accumulator register, AL or AX, into the destination memory location, at ES:[DI]. Since SI is not used by the instruction, it is not modified; only DI is incremented or decremented. The result of the two forms of the instruction may be thought of as follows:

```
STOSB    =       MOV        ES:[DI], AL
                 INC        DI              ;or DEC DI

                 MOV        ES:[DI], AX
STOSW    =       INC        DI              ;or DEC DI
                 INC        DI              ;   DEC DI
```

STOS is useful for storing blocks of data into memory. When used in conjunction with a repeat prefix, discussed later, LODS provides a very efficient means of initializing several bytes or words of memory all to the same value. STOS is also very useful, without a repeat prefix, for iteratively processing and storing data into memory. After each byte or word of data has been processed and made ready in AL or AX, it may be stored into memory using the single-byte STOS instruction. After copying the data into memory, the processor automatically adjusts DI to point to the location at which the next byte or word is to be stored. Our procedures for inputting character strings (and storing them into a memory buffer) provide an excellent use for STOS; you may wish to rewrite your input string building blocks to take advantage of the efficiency of STOS.

CMPS

Compare string, CMPSB or CMPSW, is a one-byte instruction that compares the data at the destination memory location (ES:[DI]) with the data at the source memory location (DS:[SI]). Recall that in order to do a comparison (CMP instruction) the processor performs a subtraction, setting and clearing the Result flags, but discarding the results of the subtraction. Neither operand is modified; only the Result flags are affected. Since SI and DI are both used by the instruction, they are both incremented or decremented after the comparison. Each of the two forms of the instruction produces the following results:

```
                    CMP      BYTE PTR DS:[SI], ES:[DI]
CMPSB    =          INC      SI              ;or DEC SI
                    INC      DI              ;   DEC DI


                    CMP      WORD PTR DS:[SI], ES:[DI]
                    INC      SI              ;or DEC SI
CMPSW    =          INC      SI              ;   DEC SI
                    INC      DI              ;   DEC DI
                    INC      DI              ;   DEC DI
```

Note that the comparison of the source with the destination memory address is done in a manner that is exactly the reverse of what you would expect. The value at the destination memory address is subtracted from the value at the source memory address, setting and clearing flags to reflect the result. Keep the order of the subtraction in mind whenever using a Conditional jump after CMPS to determine which is the larger of two memory values. JA or JG will transfer control if and only if the source value is greater than the destination value.

SCAS

Scan string is coded as either SCASB or SCASW. It compares the byte or word of data at the destination memory location, ES:[DI], with the data in the Accumulator register, AL or AX. Since SI is not used by the instruction, it is not modified; only DI is incremented or decremented. The two forms of the instruction and their results are as follows:

```
SCASB    =          CMP      AL, ES:[DI]
                    INC      DI              ;or DEC DI


                    CMP      AX, ES:[DI]
SCASW    =          INC      DI              ;or DEC DI
                    INC      DI              ;   DEC DI
```

As with CMPS, SCAS performs the subtraction in a manner that is the opposite of what you would expect; the value of the destination memory location is subtracted from the value in the Accumulator register in order to set and clear the Result flags. Usually this quirk of the processor presents no problem, since SCAS is most often used to determine only if the memory value is equal to or not equal to the Accumulator value; in determining equality or inequality, the order of the subtraction is not important. You must be careful, however, if you wish to use SCAS to determine which value is greater; the resulting Overflow, Carry, and Sign flags are exactly the opposite of the reasonable expectation.

Like all the other "string" instructions, SCAS is a one-byte instruction. Its most common use is in searching through a block of memory for a particular value. When combined with a repeat-if-not-equal prefix (see below), it can be used to search for a given character within a string as in the BASIC INSTR( ) function.

SUMMARY OF "String" Instructions

MOVS

    Move DS:[SI] to ES:[DI], adjust SI and DI.

LODS

    Move DS:[SI] to AL or AX, adjust SI.

STOS

    Move AL or AX to ES:[DI], adjust DI.

CMPS

    Compare ES:[DI] with DS:[SI], adjust SI and DI.

SCAS

    Compare ES:[DI] with AL or AX, adjust DI.

Although source and destination memory addressing is predetermined by all "string" instructions as DS:[SI] and ES:[DI], the processor does allow a segment override for the source segment register (DS) only. The Index registers and the Destination Segment register (ES) cannot be overriden. Since STOS and SCAS address only the destination memory location, they are not altered by any attempted segment override.

We will very shortly discuss the manner in which to override the source segment when working with the assembler. Whenever using the **Assemble** command of DEBUG, you can override the source segment for LODS, MOVS, or CMPS by immediately preceding the "string" instruction with a segment override prefix instruction. For example, the following two instructions move a byte of data from CS:[SI] to ES:[DI], incrementing or decrementing both SI and DI.

```
CS:
MOVSB
```

As mentioned earlier, no parameters are encoded into any machine-language "string" instruction; also, in machine language, each "string" instruction is either a byte or a word instruction. However, the assembler allows the coding of "string" instructions with operands (memory variables only) and without explicitly stating the type, byte (B) or word (W). For example, the following instruction is legal to the assembler:

```
MOVS       DST_VAR, SRC_VAR
```

It is critical to understand that the above assembly-language instruction does not automatically result in the movement of data from SRC_VAR to DST_VAR. The instruction is assembled as either MOVSB or MOVSW; upon execution, the processor moves data from DS:[SI] to ES:[DI], producing the correct results only if DS, SI, ES, and DI have been properly initialized. The assembler does not produce code to initialize the Segment and Index registers, nor does it verify that the programmer has included any such instructions.

Other than providing programmer documentation, the variable operands in the above instruction serve only two functions: to enable the assembler to determine the necessary type of instruction, byte or word, and to provide the assembler a means of determining if the variables are within the proper segments (associated with DS and ES). In the above instruction, the size of DST_VAR and SRC_VAR determine which instruction, MOVSB or MOVSW, is assembled. If the sizes of the two operands do not agree, the assembler reports the error, "Operand types must match," and is unable to assemble the instruction. If they are both byte variables, then MOVSB is assembled; if they are both word variables, then the instruction is assembled as MOVSW.

The assembler also checks the segments within which SRC_VAR and DST_VAR have been defined and verifies that the appropriate Segment register has been associated with each segment, by the ASSUME directive. Recall that the processor allows an override for the source segment but not for the destination segment. If ES has not been associated with the segment within which DST_VAR is defined, the assembler cannot assemble the instruction and so reports the error, "Cannot override ES for destination."

If DS has not been associated with the segment within which SRC_VAR is defined, then the assembler inserts a segment override prefix, if possible, to the Segment register that has been associated with the segment. If no Segment register has been associated with the segment within which SRC_VAR is defined, the assembler reports the error, "Cannot address with segment register."

The assembler also allows the coding of the other "string" instructions in a manner similar to the above discussion for MOVS (without size and with operands). The following instructions are all valid to the assembler:

```
LODS    SRC_VAR
STOS    DST_VAR
CMPS    SRC_VAR, DST_VAR
SCAS    DST_VAR
```

In each instruction, the assembler again uses the operand(s) only to determine the type (byte or word) of the instruction and to verify the correct association of Segment registers, inserting a source-segment override prefix whenever necessary and possible. The programmer is responsible for ensuring that the Segment and Index registers have been properly initialized to address SRC_VAR and/or DST_VAR.

"STRING"-INSTRUCTION REPEAT PREFIXES

The 8086/8088 provides two **repeat-prefix instructions** for use with any of the above "string" instructions. Note that the assembler allows synonyms for each prefix, resulting in five assembly-language prefixes, each of which is assembled to one of the two machine-language prefix instructions. The repeat prefixes provided by the assembler for use with "string" instructions are **REP**, **REPE**, and **REPZ** (synonymous) and **REPNE** and **REPNZ** (synonymous). In assembly language, repeat prefixes are coded on the same line as the "string" instruction; for example:

```
REP MOVSB
```

The repeat prefix is assembled in the resulting machine code as a one-byte prefix instruction immediately preceding the "string" instruction. For example, the above instruction, when assembled and later unassembled in DEBUG, results in the following (the given segment:offset is provided only to show the lengths of the instructions):

```
3FB4:1032 F3            REPZ
3FB4:1033 A4            MOVSB
3FB4:1034 ........
```

Note that repeat prefixes are supported only for "string" instructions; any attempt to use a repeat prefix with an instruction other than a "string" instruction generates an error from the assembler. DEBUG's Assemble command allows repeat prefix instructions anywhere in the program, but any repeat prefix that does not immediately precede a "string" instruction is ignored by the processor during execution. Following is a detailed explanation of each repeat prefix:

REP, REPE, or REPZ

REP, REPE, and REPZ are synonymous, resulting in the same one-byte machine-language prefix instruction, F3H. They cause the processor to repeat the immediately following "string" instruction CX times or until the "string" instruction clears the Zero flag (NZ), whichever occurs first. The following pseudocode illustrates the logic of the repeat:

```
Repeat while CX NE zero
        Perform the "string" instruction (and INC or DEC
                                        SI and/or DI)
        DEC CX
Quit repeat if the Zero flag was cleared by the
                        "string" instruction
End repeat
```

Note that the processor checks CX before executing the "string" instruction (repeat while); if CX is already zero, the "string" instruction will not be executed at all. Note also that CX is always decremented and SI and DI are always incremented or decremented, regardless of the instruction's effect on the Zero flag; the processor does not check the instruction's effect on the Zero flag until after it has decremented CX and incremented or decremented SI and/or DI.

Finally, notice that the exit from the loop based on the Zero flag occurs when the "string" instruction clears the Zero flag. If the "string" instruction does not modify the Zero flag, then the loop will always execute CX times, regardless of the status of the Zero flag. Consequently, the REPE and REPZ synonyms are not very meaningful with any of the data-movement instructions, MOVS, LODS, or STOS, since they never modify Result flags.

REPNE or REPNZ

REPNE and REPNZ result in the same one-byte machine-language prefix instruction, F2H; the processor repeats the immediately following "string" instruction CX times or until the "string" instruction sets the Zero flag (ZR). The repetition is the same as for REP (REPE, REPZ) except that the alternative exit from the loop occurs when the Zero flag is set by the "string" instruction.

Consequently, although it is a different machine-language instruction, REPNE (REPNZ) has exactly the same effect as REP (REPE, REPZ) when used with any of the data-movement instructions (MOVS, LODS, or STOS); the "string" instruction always executes CX times, since data-movement instructions never modify the Zero flag. However, the use of REPNE or REPNZ with a data-movement instruction produces confusing code; for clarity, only REP should be used with MOVS, LODS, or STOS.

Following are some examples of the use of "string" instructions with repeat prefixes to perform some common tasks.

Copy (or move) a block of data

When combined with REP, MOVS provides an efficient means of copying a block of data to a new memory location; DEBUG's Move command uses MOVSB. To copy a block of data from one memory location to another memory location:

```
Ensure that DS and SI point to the first byte of the
                                block to copy from
Ensure that ES and DI point to the first byte of the
                                block to copy to
Initialize CX to the number of bytes to be copied
CLD (Direction = UP)
REP MOVSB
```

If the block of memory is an even number of bytes, it can be copied a word at a time. Initialize CX to the number of words to be copied and use MOVSW, in place of MOVSB.

If data is to be moved to an overlapping block of memory, the above algorithm may not produce the proper results. The problem occurs when the beginning of the destination block is within the source block. When the destination block begins at an address that is higher than the first byte of the source block and lower than the address of the last byte of the source block, the above algorithm fails. The first several bytes to be moved will overwrite the last several bytes of the source block before they have been moved to the destination.

In such a case, the block of memory must be copied backward, beginning with the last byte of the source block, so that the end of the source block will have already been copied by the time it is overwritten. To do so, the above algorithm must be rewritten slightly, as follows:

```
Ensure that DS and SI point to the last byte of the
                                block to copy from
Ensure that ES and DI point to the last byte of the
                                block to copy to
Initialize CX to the number of bytes to be moved
STD (DN)
REP MOVSB
```

Initialize a block of data

As mentioned earlier, REP STOS is valuable when initializing an entire block of memory to some value; the DEBUG Fill command uses STOSB. To very quickly initialize a block of memory:

```
Ensure that ES and DI point to the first byte of the
                                block to initialize
Initialize AL to the value to which the block is to be
                                initialized
```

```
Initialize CX to the number of bytes to be initialized
CLD (Direction = UP)
REP STOSB
```

Compare two blocks of data

REPE CMPS may be used to compare two blocks of data, determining if they are identical and, if different, at which byte (or word) they first differ as well as which differing byte is greater. As the name implies, the comparison is often between two character strings, but it may be between blocks of numeric values as well. DEBUG uses CMPSB to implement the Compare command. The following logic compares two blocks of data:

```
Ensure that DS and SI point to the first byte of the
                              first block to compare
Ensure that ES and DI point to the first byte of the
                              second block to compare
Initialize CX to the number of bytes to be compared
CLD  (UP)
REPE CMPSB
```

Upon completion, the Zero flag indicates the result of the comparison. If set (ZR) then the two blocks of data are identical; otherwise (NZ), the two blocks of data are different. If they are different, then SI and DI point to the byte following the first nonidentical byte; since they were automatically incremented by the last execution of CMPSB, SI and DI must be decremented in order to point to the nonmatching characters.

If the blocks are different, a Conditional jump, JA or JB (JG or JL for a signed comparison), may be used to determine the inequality. JA (or JG) will cause a transfer of control if and only if the character in the source block (DS:[SI]) is greater than the corresponding byte in the destination block (ES:[DI]); JB (or JL) will cause a transfer of control if and only if the character in the source block is the lesser of the two.

To compare the data a word at a time, initialize CX to the number of words to compare, and change CMPSB to CMPSW. To find the first matching byte in two blocks of memory that you expect to be different, simply change the repeat prefix from REPE to REPNE. Upon execution, the Zero flag will be clear (NZ) if no match was found; if it is set (ZR), a match was found (DS:[SI-1] matches ES:[DI-1]).

Search for a value

REPNE SCAS provides a very efficient means of searching a block of data for a particular value, much like the INSTR (instring) function in BASIC. DEBUG implements the Search command with CMPSB. You can use the following process to locate the first occurrence of a byte value within a block of memory:

```
Ensure that ES and DI point to the first byte of the
                                        block to search
Initialize AL to the value for which to search
Initialize CX to the number of bytes in the block
CLD (UP)
REPNE SCASB
```

Upon completion, you can use the Zero flag to determine whether the value was found. The Zero flag set (ZR) indicates that it was found; Zero flag clear (NZ) indicates that the value in AL does not occur within the block of memory. If it was found (ZR), then ES:[DI] is the next byte after the matching byte; decrement DI to obtain the address at which the matching value occurs.

Alternatively, subtract the offset of the first byte of the block (initial value of DI) from the resulting value in DI to obtain the displacement within the block (number of bytes from the beginning) at which the value occurs. Such a process may be used to determine the length of a string that has been stored with a trailer (similar to the BASIC LEN function). Upon completion of the following, DI contains the length of the string:

```
Ensure that ES and DI point to the first byte of the
    string (ES to data segment, DI to string offset)
Initialize AL to the value of the trailer character
Initialize CX to 65,535
CLD (UP)
REPNE SCASB
DEC DI
Subtract string offset from DI
```

Notice that we have provided no examples of LODS with a repeat prefix. Although a repeat prefix is permitted with LODS, the result is simply to move the last byte or word of the block into AL or AX; all previous data is overwritten by the last byte or word. Repeat prefixes, though allowed, are not at all useful with LODS.

S U M M A R Y O F Repeat-Prefix Instructions

Valid only for single "string" instruction immediately following repeat prefix.

```
REP, REPE, REPZ
```
  Repeat following "string" instruction CX times unless it clears ZF.

```
REPNE, REPNZ
```
  Repeat following "string" instruction CX times unless it sets ZF.

BUILDING BLOCKS FOR NUMERIC-TO-STRING CONVERSION

We shall now discuss some possible building blocks for conversion from numeric data to a character string for output. We will first deal with unsigned integers in which the high bit is treated as a binary digit rather than as a sign bit; such an unsigned word integer has a value range of zero through 65,535. Later, we will discuss a building block to convert signed integers to strings. Also, we will at first limit ourselves to the storage of the resulting string with a trailer character.

In designing the building block, we should first consider the necessary parameters. The building block will require four input parameters: BFR_OFF, UNS_INT, BASE, and TRAILER. BFR_OFF is the offset (word) of the buffer in which to store the resulting numeric string. UNS_INT (word) is the unsigned-integer numeric value to be converted to a string in the buffer. BASE (byte) specifies the base for the resulting numeric string. Finally, TRAILER (byte) is the trailer character to be appended to the resulting string. The building block requires no output parameters, since no values need be returned to the mainline program. Figure 10-3 partially illustrates the necessary logic for the macro.

The procedure, $CNV_UNS_STR, should follow an algorithm much like that described in Figure 10-1. Although the procedure must follow the general logic of Figure 10-1, which you should review now, you must keep several specific considerations in mind in the procedure design. First, since we need to repeatedly divide the unsigned integer by the base, the procedure must move the unsigned integer from the stack hole into AX. The Accumulator register is always the destination operand of the DIV instruction; consequently, only AX may be used to store the unsigned integer for conversion.

A second consideration, which might not be at all obvious, is that the division we perform must be a word division. Recall that a byte DIV attempts to store the quotient as a byte in AL, producing a "Division overflow" interrupt (type 00H) if it does not fit. The result of our division by the base will often result in a new quotient that is greater than 255. If converting 65,000 to a decimal string, for example, the first division by ten would produce a quotient of 6,500, which requires a word for storage. Consequently, we must perform a word division so that the quotient will be stored in AX, rather than AL. This produces three more important considerations for our building-block procedure.

Figure 10-3   **Unsigned-Integer-to-String Conversion Macro**

```
CNV_UNS_STR     MACRO     BFR_OFF, UNS_INT, BASE, TRAILER

                Create stack hole
                Put parameters into stack hole; default BASE
                     (byte) to 10, TRAILER (byte) to NUL (0)
                Call $CNV_UNS_STR procedure
```

The first is that, since we must divide by a word, the base must be moved from the stack into a word register. However, note that in Figure 10-3 the macro puts BASE onto the stack as a byte, since it is never greater than 255. The procedure must, therefore, move the base into the low byte of a General-Purpose register and then move zero into the high byte of the register. Zeroing out the high byte results in a Word register containing the value of the base.

The second crucial consideration resulting from the need to do a word division is that DX must be zeroed immediately before the division. The unsigned integer is in AX and the base is in a word register, but the processor divides DX:AX by the word register (base). Consequently, DX must be zero when the DIV instruction executes. Furthermore, since DX is modified by each division, it must be reinitialized to zero each time around the loop, immediately before the DIV instruction.

The third consideration, resulting from the word division, is that the remainder (numeric value for the next digit) will be in DX, a word register after each execution of the DIV. However, since the base may never be greater than 255, the remainder will never be greater than 254. Thus, after the division, DH will always be zero and DL will contain the remainder to be converted into the ASCII character for the digit, as described in Figure 10-1. When pushing the digit to the stack in the conversion loop (first loop in Figure 10-1), the procedure will have to push the entire DX register even though the character is in DL; PUSH requires a word operand.

After the completion of the conversion loop, the procedure must move the buffer offset into a Base or Index register to be used to address the buffer during the storage loop (second loop in Figure 10-1). Since we have just studied the "string" instructions, it is suggested that you use DI and point ES to the data segment (do not forget to save and restore ES along with the other registers); the storage loop should then pop the digit (as a word) into AX and use STOSB to store it into the buffer.

Finally, after completion of the storage loop, the building-block procedure must store the trailer onto the end of the resulting string in the buffer. It should move the trailer from the stack into AL and then use STOSB to store it.

A building block to convert an unsigned integer to a string with a length byte should be very similar to the above discussion, but with some important differences. The macro, CNV_UNS_STRL, should be similar to CNV_UNS_STR in Figure 10-3, except that it must call a different procedure, $CNV_UNS_STRL, and it only needs three input parameters: BFR_OFF, UNS_INT, and BASE. It should consequently open and close only five bytes of stack hole.

The procedure, $CNV_UNS_STRL, to convert to a string with a length byte should also be similar to the above discussion, except that it must store the length byte into the first byte of the buffer instead of storing the trailer onto the end of the string. The easiest way to do so is to use STOSB to store the counter into the buffer immediately before beginning the storage loop; note that STOS always stores the Accumulator register to memory, so the count will probably have to be moved into AL first.

The problem of converting a signed integer with a value range of $-32,768$ through $+32,767$ to a string is also very similar. The macro, CNV_INT_STR or CNV_INT_STRL, should be identical to the macros discussed above, except for the procedure called. The procedure, $CNV_INT_STR or $CNV_INT_STRL, is also very similar, with one major exception. Our conversion algorithm (Figure 10-1) only works for positive values. Consequently, a procedure to convert a signed integer to a string must check the sign of the integer first. If the integer is negative, it must be negated, to make it positive; the procedure must then ensure that the resulting string begins with a minus sign (−). The following logic must be included immediately before the conversion loop:

```
If Integer LT 0 (use CMP and JG or JL, not JA or JB)
    Negate Integer (make it positive)
    Move '−' into Sign (a Byte register)
Else
    Move '+' into Sign
End if
```

Immediately before the storage loop, the procedure must check the sign and store "−" into the buffer if it is negative. The following logic must be included immediately before the storage loop:

```
If Sign EQ '−'
    Move Sign into AL
    Use STOSB to store it into first byte of buffer
End if
```

BUILDING BLOCKS FOR STRING-TO-NUMERIC CONVERSION

In discussing building blocks for conversion from a character string to a number, we will again deal first with unsigned integers; the numeric string to be converted may not contain a sign, and the resulting value is an unsigned integer, from zero through 65,535, in which the high bit is treated as another binary digit rather than as a sign. Later we will discuss a building block to convert a string with an optional leading sign to a signed integer. Also, we will at first limit ourselves to the conversion of strings that have been stored with a trailer character.

The macro requires three input parameters, STR_OFF, BASE, and TRAILER, and one output parameter, UNS_INT. STR_OFF (word) is the offset of the string to be converted. BASE (byte) is the base of the numeric string. TRAILER (byte) is the character that has been used as the trailer of the string. UNS_INT is the output parameter (word register) to receive the resulting unsigned-integer numeric value. Notice that the macro requires both input and output parameters.

When a building block requires both input and output parameters, the programmer has a choice of the manner in which to pass the parameters. One option is to open a stack hole big enough to hold all the parameters simultaneously; in our case, a six-byte stack hole. The other possibility is to open the smallest possible stack hole. In our current case, a four-byte stack hole is sufficient since we have four bytes of input parameters and two bytes of output parameter. In placing the output value onto the stack, the procedure reuses two bytes of the stack hole that were used for input values.

In either case, the procedure may close all but two bytes of the stack hole upon returning, or it may leave the closing of the stack hole entirely to the macro. If the procedure closes all but two bytes (RET 2, for a four-byte hole, or RET 4 for a six-byte hole), then the output value must have been placed at the bottom of the stack hole, at [BP+2] for a four-byte stack hole, or at [BP+4] for a six-byte hole.

Our procedure will use the Carry flag to indicate success or failure of the conversion, setting it (CY) if the string contains an invalid digit or if the value of the unsigned integer becomes greater than 65,535, and clearing it (NC) if the conversion has been successful. Consequently, in closing the stack hole (either the entire hole or just the last two bytes), the macro must not alter the Carry flag. To avoid altering the Carry flag, the macro must use INC instructions (not ADD) to close the stack hole. Figure 10-4 partially illustrates the logic for the macro.

To perform the conversion, the procedure should use an algorithm much like that illustrated in Figure 10-2; review Figure 10-2 before proceeding. Since the algorithm requires repeated multiplication, the code must be designed to accommodate the limitations of the MUL instruction. Since the destination of MUL is always the Accumulator register, we must use AX to accumulate the unsigned integer. Also, we must use a word multiplication; otherwise, the base would be multiplied by AL only, rather than by the entire unsigned integer being accumulated in AX.

Consequently, as in the conversion from an unsigned integer to a string, the base must be moved from the stack into a word register (base into low byte, zero into high byte). Unlike the previous conversion, however, there is no need to initialize DX to zero before the multiplication, as MUL multiplies AX by the source, storing the result into DX:AX. Immediately after the multiplication, the procedure must either verify the value in DX or check the Carry flag; if DX is not zero or if the Carry flag is set (CY), the unsigned integer has become greater than 65,535.

Since the unsigned integer is in AX, a Word register, the digit to be added must also be in a Word register. The procedure should obtain the ASCII character of each digit into the low byte of a General-Purpose register, convert it to its numeric value as a byte, and then move zero into the high byte of the register before adding it to the unsigned integer in AX.

Figure 10-4   String-to-Unsigned-Integer Conversion Macro

```
CNV_STR_UNS     MACRO     STR_OFF, UNS_INT, BASE, TRAILER

                Create stack hole
                Put input parameters into stack hole; default BASE
                         (byte) to 10, TRAILER (byte) to NUL (0)
                Call $CNV_STR_UNS (closes all but two bytes of
                                             stack hole)
                Move output value (word) from stack hole into INT
                Close stack hole (INC, not ADD)
```

Since we have just studied the "string" instructions, it would be nice to use LODSB to obtain each ASCII digit from the string. However, you must be careful if you do so. LODSB copies a byte value from the source memory location into AL, the low byte of the AX register, which we are using to accumulate the unsigned integer. Using LODSB requires some extra moving of values between registers and/or the pushing and popping of AX in order to protect the previously accumulated unsigned integer value.

Finally, the procedure needs a means of reporting an unsuccessful conversion when the string contains invalid digits or the resulting unsigned integer exceeds 65,535. The Carry flag provides a convenient means of doing so. The procedure should clear the Carry flag (NC) if the conversion has been successful. It should set the Carry flag (CY) to indicate an unsuccessful conversion. In addition, if the conversion is unsuccessful, the procedure should not put the value in AX onto the stack since it is invalid; when aborting the conversion, the procedure should set the Carry flag and return zero on the stack.

A building block to convert a string with a length byte to an unsigned integer should be very similar to that discussed above, with some modifications. The macro, CNV_STRL_UNS, should be similar to CNV_STR_UNS in Figure 10-4, except that it must call a different procedure, $CNV_STRL_UNS, and it only needs two input parameters: STR_OFF and BASE. It should consequently open only three (or five) bytes of stack hole.

The procedure, $CNV_STRL_UNS, to convert to an unsigned integer from a string with a length byte, should also be similar to the one discussed above. However, since the string has been stored with a length byte rather than with a trailer, the procedure must first obtain the length byte, ensuring that the Base or Index register used to address the string characters is incremented. The procedure should then use a repeat-n-times construct, rather than repeat while, to do the conversion. Note that the length is a byte; it must be moved into CL, and zero must be moved into CH. Do not forget a JCXZ immediately before the loop. Review the repeat-n-times construct in chapter 6, if necessary.

Figure 10-5 illustrates an example program that inputs and outputs numeric values. Note that it uses building blocks that handle strings with a length byte rather than with a trailer (INPUT_STRL, DSPLY_STRL, CNV_STRL_UNS, CNV_UNS_STRL). With minor modifications, it could easily be rewritten to handle strings with a trailer.

Figure 10-5   Example Program Using CNV_STRL_UNS and CNV_UNS_STRL Building Blocks

```
TITLE F10-5.ASM
PAGE 55, 80
```

Figure 10-5   (continued)

```
COMMENT |          PROGRAM:       F10-5.ASM
                   PROGRAMMER:    Your name here
                   DATE:          Date here
                   CLASS:         Class name and number here
                   INSTRUCTOR:    Instructor's name here

            SAMPLE PROGRAM USING CNV_STRL_UNS, CNV_UNS_STRL,
            INPUT_STRL, AND DSPLY_STRL BUILDING BLOCKS.

            CONVERTS FROM DECIMAL TO HEXADECIMAL.

            INPUT PARAM'S:  NONE
            OUTPUT PARAM'S: NONE
                            RETURNS TO DOS, UPON COMPLETION
            |

                   INCLUDE CONSOLE.MLB

;STACK SEGMENT =========================================================

STACK              SEGMENT  PARA STACK 'STACK'         ;BEGIN STACK

                   DB       64 DUP ('*STACK* ')        ;DEFINE 512

                                                       ;   BYTE STACK

STACK              ENDS                                ;END OF STACK

;DATA SEGMENT ==========================================================

DATA               SEGMENT  PARA PUBLIC 'DATA'         ;BEGIN DATA

PRMPT_MSG          DB       OFFSET ERR_MSG - OFFSET PRMPT_MSG - 1
                   DB       13, 10, 10, 'Enter a decimal numeral '
                   DB       '(0 to quit) '
ERR_MSG            DB       OFFSET HEX_MSG - OFFSET ERR_MSG - 1
                   DB       7, 'Invalid decimal numeral!'
HEX_MSG            DB       OFFSET IO_BFR - OFFSET HEX_MSG - 1
                   DB       'Hexadecimal equivalent: '
IO_BFR             DB       6 DUP ('*')

DATA               ENDS                                ;END OF DATA

;CODE SEGMENT ==========================================================
CODE               SEGMENT  PARA PUBLIC 'CODE'         ;BEGIN CODE

                   ASSUME   CS:CODE, SS:STACK
```

Figure 10-5 (continued)

```
MAIN                PROC    FAR             ;BEGIN MAINLINE

            ;INITIALIZATION (SAME FOR ALL PROGRAMS)
            ;FIRST, SET UP FOR RETURN TO DOS VIA PSP
                    PUSH    DS              ;PUT RETURN SEG (PSP)
                                            ;  TO STACK
                    MOV     AX, 0           ;PUT ZERO RETURN
                    PUSH    AX              ;  OFFSET TO STACK
            ;NOW, ADDRESS THE DATA SEGMENT WITH DS
                    MOV     AX, DATA        ;POINT DS TO
                    MOV     DS, AX          ;  DATA SEGMENT
                    ASSUME  DS:DATA         ;ASSOCIATE DS WITH DATA

            ;BEGIN MAINLINE CODE
            ;CONTINUE GETTING DECIMAL NUMERAL AND CONVERTING TO
            ;  HEXADECIMAL UNTIL USER ENTERS ZERO
LP1_BEG:            ;BEGIN GENERAL LOOP (QUIT WHEN USER ENTERS 0)
LP2_BEG:               ;BEGIN GENERAL LOOP (QUIT WHEN INPUT IS
                       ;  VALID)
                       DSPLY_STRL    <OFFSET PRMPT_MSG>
                                           ;PROMPT FOR DEC NUMERAL
                       INPUT_STRL    <OFFSET IO_BFR>, 5
                                           ;GET DEC NUMERAL
                       CNV_STRL_UNS  <OFFSET IO_BFR>, DX
                                           ;CONVERT DEC NUMERAL
                                           ;  TO NUMBER IN DX
                    JNC     LP2_END         ;QUIT LOOP WHEN NUMERAL
                                            ;  IS VALID
                       DSPLY_STRL    <OFFSET ERR_MSG>
                                           ;DISPLAY ERROR MESSAGE
                    JMP     LP2_BEG  ;CONTINUE INNER LOOP
LP2_END:               ;END GENERAL LOOP (NUMERAL IS VALID)
                    CMP     DX, 0           ;QUIT LOOP WHEN USER
                    JE      LP1_END         ;  ENTERS ZERO
                    CNV_UNS_STRL  <OFFSET IO_BFR>, DX, 16
                                            ;CONVERT TO HEX NUMERAL
                    DSPLY_STRL    <OFFSET HEX_MSG>
                    DSPLY_STRL    <OFFSET IO_BFR>
                                            ;DISPLAY HEX NUMERAL
                    JMP     LP1_BEG         ;CONTINUE OUTER LOOP
LP1_END:            ;END GENERAL LOOP (USER ENTERED 0)

            ;MAINLINE CODE ENDS HERE
                    RET                     ;FAR RETURN VIA PSP

MAIN                ENDP                    ;END OF MAIN PROCEDURE

CODE                ENDS                    ;END OF CODE SEGMENT

                    END     MAIN            ;END OF F10-5.ASM
                                            ;  ENTRY POINT = MAIN
```

The problem of converting a string with a leading sign to a signed integer with a value range of $-32,768$ through $+32,767$ is also very similar. The macro, CNV_STR_INT or CNV_STRL_INT, should be identical to those discussed above, except for the procedure called. The procedure, $CNV_STR_INT or $CNV_STRL_INT, is also very similar, with one major difference. The conversion algorithm in Figure 10-2 only converts strings without signs to unsigned integers. This procedure, therefore, must check the first character of the string to see if it is a sign. If so, the procedure must skip over it; after the conversion, the procedure must negate the result if the string began with a minus sign ($-$). Logic such as the following must precede the conversion loop:

```
If the first character EQ '-' or '+'
     Move it into Sign (Byte register), incrementing buffer
                                              pointer register
Else
     Move '+' into Sign
End if
```

Upon completion of the conversion, the signed integer in AX must be negated if the string had a leading minus sign ($-$). Before negating AX, however, the procedure must check its value to verify that it will be within the range for a signed integer, negative 32,768 through positive 32,767. After the conversion, and before placing the signed integer onto the stack, the procedure must include logic such as the following:

```
If Sign EQ '+'
     If AX GT (Above) 32767
          Abort conversion, reporting error
     End if
Else (Sign EQ '-')
     If AX GT (Above) 32768
          Abort conversion, reporting error
     Else
          Negate AX
     End if
End if
```

SUMMARY

Our previous input and output building blocks have all been for character data only. Some new building blocks are required to allow for the entry of numeric data from the keyboard and for the output of numeric data to the screen. Building blocks are needed for converting between strings and signed-integer numeric data as well as between strings and unsigned-integer data. Rather than limiting the building blocks to keyboard and screen I/O, we have chosen a more general approach, the development of building blocks for the conversion between numeric data and string data. This approach allows a great deal of flexibility.

After converting any numeric data to a string, the string may then be output to either the screen or to the printer using previously developed building blocks. Similarly, if we should later develop any new building blocks for character input (from the serial port, for example), we do not need to develop any additional building blocks for numeric-data input from the new device. We simply use the new input building block in conjunction with our existing building block (conversion from string to numeric data) in order to allow the input of numeric data from the new device.

The algorithms used to convert between numeric and string data are very similar to the algorithms, discussed in chapter 2, for the conversions between decimal numerals and numerals of other bases. An important point to remember is that while our "native" numeral system is decimal, the processor's "native" numeral system is binary. Thus the problem of enabling the processor to convert numeric data (stored in its "native" binary) to a numeric string (in any base) is quite similar to our own problem of converting a decimal (our "native" numeral system) to a numeral in any other base. The conversion is accomplished through repeated division by the desired base, where the remainder of each division provides the next digit (from right to left) for the numeric string. Since the first division provides the digit for the ones place (right-most digit of the resulting string), the digits must be stored in the string buffer in the opposite order of that in which they are obtained; the stack provides a convenient means of reversing the order of the resulting digits.

Similarly, the processor's conversion of a string (in any base) to numeric data (stored in binary) is very similar to the problem of our converting from a numeral in some other base to a decimal numeral, as discussed in chapter 2. One algorithm we discussed in chapter 2 (the "double-dabble" method), lends itself nicely to a computer implementation since it involves the repetition of a few relatively simple steps. That algorithm involves beginning with a value of zero and accumulating the numeric value by repeatedly multiplying the value by the base and adding the next digit. Most of the complexity of our building block results, not from the conversion itself, but from the need to verify the validity of the numeric string.

In order to implement the conversion algorithms, we found it necessary to discuss the processor's multiplication and division instructions. The 8086/8088 instruction set includes four multiplication and division instructions: MUL, DIV, IMUL, and IDIV. The 8086/8088 implementation of all multiplication and division instructions places severe restrictions on the permitted data addressing modes; the destination is always AX (and DX, in the word form of each), and the source must be either Register or Memory, never Immediate addressing mode. These data-addressing restrictions may sometimes lead to frustration; however, we should keep in mind that many microprocessors do not implement multiplication or division at all.

When executing multiplication and division instructions, the ALU follows algorithms much like the binary multiplication and division algorithms discussed in chapter 2. The exception is that the processor implements two of the instructions, IMUL and IDIV, to properly handle the high bit of each operand as a sign bit rather than as a binary digit.

In this chapter we also introduced a group of instructions, called "string" instructions, provided by the 8086/8088. Although often very useful when manipulating string data, they may be used for working with byte or word numeric data as well. The source and destination operands are both predetermined by each instruction. The source operand is always either the Accumulator register or the memory location at DS:[SI]; the destination operand is always either the Accumulator register or memory at ES:[DI].

Although the assembler allows variable operands with "string" instructions, they are used only for documentation and to enable the assembler to determine the type (byte or word) of the instruction and to verify that the variables are defined within segments that are associated with the appropriate Segment registers, inserting a segment-override prefix if necessary for the source memory operand. Operands are never encoded into the resulting machine-language instruction.

The three data-movement "string" instructions are MOVS (copy a byte or word from the source memory address to the destination memory address), LODS (copy a byte or word from the source memory address into AL or AX), and STOS (copy the byte or word from AL or AX into the destination memory address). Two arithmetic "string" instructions are provided for comparing data, CMPS (compare the byte or word at the destination memory address with the byte or word at the source memory address) and SCAS (compare the byte or word at the destination memory address with the data in AL or AX).

The great power of "string" instructions derives from the fact that each instruction automatically increments or decrements any used Index register after performing the appropriate operation and from the provision for a repeat prefix before any "string" instruction. REP, REPE, and REPZ are all synonyms for the same machine-language repeat prefix that causes the immediately following "string" instruction to be repeated CX times or until the "string" instruction clears the Zero flag, whichever occurs first. REPNE and REPNZ are synonyms for a prefix instruction that causes the following "string" instruction to repeat CX times or until the "string" instruction sets the Zero flag. Repeat prefixes are valid only with "string" instructions.

REVIEW QUESTIONS

Q10-1   What is meant by the term "numeric string"?

Q10-2   List and explain the operation of each of the 8086/8088 multiplication and division instructions.

Q10-3   List and explain the operation of each of the five "string" instructions provided by the 8086/8088.

Q10-4   List and explain the "string"-instruction repeat prefixes provided by the 8086/8088.

Q10-5 In order to convert from a number (stored in binary) to a numeric string (in decimal) we used an algorithm very similar to the one we used in chapter 2 to convert from a decimal numeral to a binary numeral. Why? Why didn't we use the algorithm for converting from binary to decimal?

PROGRAMMING ASSIGNMENTS

PA10-1 Add a new building block, CNV_UNS_STR, to your console library; if you prefer, create a new library, MATH.MLB and MATH.LIB, to hold the building block. The building block should convert an unsigned integer to a numeric string with a trailer.

You will need four parameters, all input: BFR_OFF (the offset within the data segment at which to store the resulting string), UNS_INT (the word unsigned integer value to be converted), BASE (the numeral base, as a byte, for the resulting string), and TRAILER (the byte character to use as the trailer on the resulting string). BASE should default to ten and TRAILER should default to zero (NUL character). In the macro header, explain the parameters, and caution the user to ensure that the buffer is at least one byte longer than the maximum possible string length (seventeen, if base is two).

Write a mainline program, PA10-1.ASM, to test the building block. Use DB DUP to define IO_BUF in the DATA segment (at least seventeen bytes long). Use the following mainline logic:

```
Display CR, LF, 'Decimal 43690 = Binary '
Convert the immediate value, 43690, to a binary string in
                      IO_BUF with '*' for a trailer
Display the string in IO_BUF (trailer is '*')

Display CR, LF, 'Decimal 36408 = Octal '
Move 36408 into DI
Convert the value in DI to an octal string in IO_BUF, with the
                                    default trailer
Display the string in IO_BUF (default trailer)

Display CR, LF, 'Hex F09C = Decimal '
Convert the immediate value, 0F09CH, to a string in IO_BUF,
                  accepting the default base and trailer
Display the string in IO_BUF (default trailer)

Display CR, LF, 'Decimal 61596 = Hex '
Move 16 into CL
Move 61596 into BX
Convert the value in BX to a string in IO_BUF with the base
                              specified as CL
Display the string in IO_BUF
```

PA10-2 Add a new building block, CNV_INT_STR, to your console or math library. The building block should be identical to that described in PA10-1, except that it should convert a signed integer to a numeric string with a trailer. It also requires four input parameters: BFR_OFF, BASE, and TRAILER are identical to CNV_UNS_STR in PA10-1; INT is the signed-integer numeric value to be converted to the string, with a leading minus (−) if negative. In the macro header, explain the parameters and caution the user to ensure that the buffer is at least one byte longer than the maximum possible string length (eighteen, if base is two).

Write a mainline program, PA10-2.ASM, to test the building block. Use DB DUP to define IO_BUF in the DATA segment (at least eighteen bytes long). Use the following mainline logic:

```
Display CR, LF, 'Decimal 32767 = Binary '
Convert the immediate signed value, +32767, to a signed binary
                        string in IO_BUF with '*' for a trailer
Display the string in IO_BUF (trailer is '*')

Display CR, LF, 'Decimal −14312 = Octal '
Move −14312 into DI
Convert the signed value in DI to an octal string in IO_BUF, with
                                        the default trailer
Display the string in IO_BUF (default trailer)

Display CR, LF, 'Unsigned-hex F09C = Signed-decimal '
Convert the immediate value, 0F09CH, to a signed string in IO_BUF,
                        accepting the default base and trailer
Display the string in IO_BUF (default trailer)

Display CR, LF, 'Decimal −31596 = Hex '
Move 16 into CL
Move −31596 into BX
Convert the signed value in BX to a string in IO_BUF with the base
                                        specified as CL
Display the string in IO_BUF

Display CR, LF, 'Octal 17652 = Hex '
Move 16 into CL
Move 17652Q into BX
Convert the signed value in BX to a string in IO_BUF,
                        specifying CL as the base
Display the string in IO_BUF
```

PA10-3   Add a new building block, CNV_UNS_STRL, to your console library; if you prefer, create a new library, MATH.MLB and MATH.LIB, to hold the building block. The building block should convert an unsigned integer to a numeric string stored with a length byte.

You will need three parameters, all input: BFR_OFF (the offset within the data segment at which to store the resulting string), UNS_INT (the word unsigned integer value to be converted), and BASE (the numeral base, as a byte, for the resulting string). BASE should default to ten. In the macro header, explain the parameters and caution the user to ensure that the buffer is at least one byte longer than the maximum possible string length (seventeen, if base is two).

Write a mainline program, PA10-3.ASM, to test the building block. Use DB DUP to define IO_BUF in the DATA segment (at least seventeen bytes long). Use the following mainline logic:

```
Display CR, LF, 'Decimal 43690 = Binary '
Convert the immediate value, 43690, to a binary string
                                        in IO_BUF
Display the string in IO_BUF

Display CR, LF, 'Decimal 36408 = Octal '
Move 36408 into DI
Convert the value in DI to an octal string in IO_BUF
Display the string in IO_BUF

Display CR, LF, 'Hex F09C = Decimal '
Convert the immediate value, 0F09CH, to a string in IO_BUF,
                                 accepting the default base
Display the string in IO_BUF (default trailer)

Display CR, LF, 'Decimal 61596 = Hex '
Move 16 into CL
Move 61596 into BX
Convert the value in BX to a string in IO_BUF with the base
                                        specified as CL
Display the string in IO_BUF
```

PA10-4   Add a new building block, CNV_INT_STRL, to your console or math library. The building block should be identical to that described in PA10-3, except that it should convert a signed integer to a numeric string with a length byte. It also requires three input parameters. BFR_OFF and BASE are identical to CNV_UNS_STRL in PA10-3; INT is the signed-integer numeric value to be converted to the string, with a leading minus (−) if negative. In the macro header, explain the parameters and caution the user to ensure that the buffer is at least one byte longer than the maximum possible string length (eighteen, if base is two).

Write a mainline program, PA10-4.ASM, to test the building block. Use DB DUP to define IO_BUF in the DATA segment (at least eighteen bytes long). Use the following mainline logic:

```
Display CR, LF, 'Decimal 32767 = Binary '
Convert the immediate signed value, +32767, to a signed binary
                                        string in IO_BUF
Display the string in IO_BUF
      `
Display CR, LF, 'Decimal -14312 = Octal '
Move -14312 into DI
Convert the signed value in DI to an octal string in IO_BUF
Display the string in IO_BUF

Display CR, LF, 'Unsigned-hex F09C = Signed-decimal '
Convert the immediate value, 0F09CH, to a signed string
                in IO_BUF, accepting the default base
Display the string in IO_BUF (default trailer)

Display CR, LF, 'Decimal −31596 = Hex '
Move 16 into CL
```

```
Move -31596 into BX
Convert the signed value in BX to a string in IO_BUF with the
                                        base specified as CL
Display the string in IO_BUF
```

PA10-5 Do PA10-1, then add a new building block, CNV_STR_UNS, to your console or math library. The building block should convert from a numeric string, with no leading sign and stored with a trailer, to an unsigned integer. It requires three input parameters: STR_OFF (the offset within the data segment of the string to be converted), BASE (the numeral base of the string), and TRAILER (the character that has been used as the trailer in the string). BASE should default to ten, and TRAILER should default to zero (NUL character).

One output parameter is required: UNS_INT (a Word register to receive the unsigned integer resulting from the conversion). In addition, the building block should use the Carry flag as output to indicate the success or failure of the conversion; CF should be set (CY) to indicate an invalid numeric string or cleared (NC) for a successful conversion. If the conversion is unsuccessful (CF set), then zero should be returned in UNS_INT. In the macro header, explain the parameters and the use of the Carry flag to indicate an error in conversion.

Write the mainline, PA10-5.ASM, to test the new building block. Use DB DUP to define IO_BUF in the DATA segment. Use the following mainline logic.

```
Repeat
    Display 'unsigned base 16 numeral? '
    Input a string into IO_BUF with "%" as the trailer,
                            limiting the length to 6
    Convert the string in IO_BUF to unsigned integer into
                CX; specify 16 as base, "%" as trailer
Quit repeat when conversion is successful (NC)
    Display BEL, 'Invalid - Try again', CR, LF, LF
End repeat

Convert the unsigned value in CX to a base ten (default)
                                    string in IO_BUF
Display IO_BUF
Display ' in base 10', CR, LF, LF

Repeat
    Display 'Unsigned base 8 numeral? '
    Input a string into IO_BUF, default trailer, maximum
                                        length of 7
    Move 8 into BL
    Convert the string in IO_BUF to unsigned integer in SI;
                    specify BL as base, default trailer
Quit repeat when conversion is successful (NC)
    Display BEL, 'Invalid - Try again', CR, LF, LF
End repeat

Convert the unsigned value in SI to a base ten (default)
                                    string in IO_BUF
Display IO_BUF
Display ' in base 10', CR, LF, LF
```

PA10-6 Do PA10-2, then add a new building block, CNV_STR_INT, to your console or math library. The building block should be identical to that described in PA10-5, except that it should allow a leading sign on the string, with a trailer, and convert it to a signed integer. STR_OFF, BASE, and TRAILER are identical to PA10-5.

One output parameter is required: INT (a word register to receive the signed integer resulting from the conversion). As with CNV_STR_UNS (PA10-5), the building block should use the Carry flag to indicate the success or failure of the conversion and return zero in INT if unsuccessful.

Write a mainline program, PA10-6.ASM, to test the building block. The logic should be identical to that of PA10-5.ASM, except that it should ask the user for signed numerals, allow string lengths of seven for the hexadecimal numeral and eight for the octal numeral, and use CNV_STR_INT and CNV_INT_STR for the string/signed-integer conversions.

PA10-7 Do PA10-3, then add a new building block, CNV_STRL_UNS, to your console or math library. The building block should convert from a numeric string, with no leading sign and stored with a length byte, to an unsigned integer. It requires two input parameters: STR_OFF (the offset within the data segment of the string to be converted) and BASE (the numeral base of the string). BASE should default to ten.

One output parameter is required: UNS_INT (a word register to receive the unsigned integer resulting from the conversion). In addition, the building block should use the Carry flag as output to indicate the success or failure of the conversion; CF should be set (CY) to indicate an invalid numeric string or cleared (NC) for a successful conversion. If the conversion is unsuccessful (CF set), then zero should be returned in UNS_INT. In the macro header, explain the parameters and the use of the Carry flag to indicate an error in conversion.

Write the mainline, PA10-7.ASM, to test the new building block. Use DB DUP to define IO_BUF in DATA segment. Use the following mainline logic.

```
Repeat
    Display 'unsigned base 16 numeral? '
    Input a string into IO_BUF, limiting the length to 6
    Convert the string in IO_BUF to unsigned integer into
                            CX, specifying 16 as base
Quit repeat when conversion is successful (NC)
    Display BEL, 'Invalid - Try again', CR, LF, LF
End repeat

Convert the unsigned value in CX to a base ten (default) string
                            in IO_BUF

Display IO_BUF
Display ' in base 10', CR, LF, LF

Repeat
    Display 'Unsigned base 8 numeral? '
    Input a string into IO_BUF, maximum length of 7
    Move 8 into BL
    Convert the string in IO_BUF to unsigned integer in SI,
                            specifying BL as base
Quit repeat when conversion is successful (NC)
```

```
        Display BEL, 'Invalid - Try again', CR, LF, LF
    End repeat

    Convert the unsigned value in SI to a base ten (default) string
                                                    in IO_BUF
    Display IO_BUF
    Display ' in base 10', CR, LF, LF
```

PA10-8   Do PA10-4, then add a new building block, CNV_STRL_INT, to your console or math library. The building block should be identical to that described in PA10-7, except that it should allow a leading sign on the string, with length byte, and convert it to a signed integer. STR_OFF and BASE are identical to PA10-7.

One output parameter is required: INT (a word register to receive the signed integer resulting from the conversion). As with CNV_STRL_UNS (PA10-7), the building block should use the Carry flag to indicate the success or failure of the conversion and return zero in INT if unsuccessful.

Write a mainline program, PA10-8.ASM, to test the building block. The logic should be identical to that of PA10-7.ASM, except that it should ask the user for signed numerals, allow string lengths of seven for the hexadecimal numeral and eight for the octal numeral, and use CNV_STRL_INT and CNV_INT_STRL for the string/signed-integer conversions.

PA10-9   Do PA10-1 and PA10-5 or PA10-3 and PA10-7 and then write an unsigned integer base-conversion program, PA10-9.ASM. Ask the user for the input base (to convert from) and convert it as a decimal numeral to a number in a word register. Then ask for the output base (to convert to) and convert it as a decimal numeral into another word register. In each case, if the user enters an invalid numeral, display an error message, and try again.

After obtaining the input and output base, begin a loop that asks the user for an unsigned numeral in the input base, telling the user to enter zero to quit. Convert the numeral (numeric string) to a number, using the input base; if the numeral is invalid, display an error message and try again. Exit the loop if the resulting number is zero; if it is not zero, then convert it back to a numeral (numeric string) using the output base. Display the resulting string, with a message indicating its base, and repeat the loop.

PA10-10   Do PA10-2 and PA10-6 or PA10-4 and PA10-8 and then write a signed integer base-conversion program, PA10-10.ASM. The program should be identical to PA10-9, except that within the loop it should ask the user for a signed numeral (leading sign allowed) in the input base and use the string/signed-integer building blocks to do the conversions.

PA10-11   Do PA10-1 or PA10-2. Then write a program called PA10-11.ASM, which inputs a string from the user, stores it with a trailer, and tells the user the length of the string. After inputting the string, use SCAS with a repeat prefix to search for the trailer and determine the string length. Then convert the length to a numeric string, and display it with a message explaining that it is the string length. If desired, develop a building block, GET_STR_LEN, to determine the string length.

PA10-12   Write a program that inputs a string into one buffer, uses MOVS with a repeat prefix to move it to another buffer, and displays the second buffer. If you have developed your input and display building blocks to store strings with a trailer, then you will have to use SCAS to determine the length of the string before moving it. You must move one more byte than the string length in order to include the length byte or trailer.

11

Magnetic Disk
Data Storage

INTRODUCTION

Magnetic disk is the most important form of auxiliary storage used by modern personal computers as well as by mini and mainframe computers. The principles of disk storage are important, not only for assembly-language programmers, but also for anyone who works extensively with computers of any type. However, most high-level languages isolate the programmer from the actual physical operation of the disk; the data is simply stored and retrieved somehow, as if by magic. Since we believe that the removal of the mystery and magic of computers is one of the more beneficial results of the study of assembly-language programming, we have dedicated this chapter to the technical aspects of data storage on magnetic disk.

We shall discuss the fundamental concepts of magnetic data storage, the physical organization of the data on magnetic disk (both flexible and rigid), and the services provided by BIOS for non-file-structured disk access. We will learn that disk access through BIOS differs radically from the file-structured disk access provided by high-level languages. BIOS disk services require that all disk data be accessed by actual physical location, rather than by filename.

We shall then discuss the manner in which DOS logically organizes the disk data in order to provide file-structured disk access. We will learn that any operating system must maintain at least two disk-allocation data structures—a file directory and an allocation table—in order to provide access to data by filename rather than by physical location. We will discuss, in some detail, the manner in which MS-DOS implements those two necessary allocation structures.

Finally, we will discuss the two fundamental methods of accessing file data (sequential and direct) as well as the fundamental data-file organizations (fixed-length record or structured, stream or unstructured, and variable-length record or terminal format). In the following chapter, we will discuss the manner in which the programmer accesses the file-structured disk services provided by DOS.

MAGNETIC DATA STORAGE

To understand magnetic data storage, we must first understand some basic principles of electricity and magnetism. First, any time an electrical current flows through a wire, or any other electroconductive material, it generates a directional magnetic flux or field around itself. Furthermore, if the wire is spiraled into a coil, the flux generated by each wrap of the coil augments the flux generated by the other wraps, resulting in a more powerful magnetic field. This property is called **electromagnetism**, and such a coil is often referred to as an **electromagnet**.

The direction of the magnetic field depends on the direction of current flow through the coil. If one end of the coil is connected to electrical ground, as is usually the case, then the direction of the magnetic field depends on the voltage applied to the coil; a positive voltage results in a magnetic field of one direction, and a negative voltage results in a field of the opposite direction. Figure 11-1 illustrates the magnetic flux resulting from applying a positive and negative voltage to a coil.

The second basic magnetic principle is essentially the complement of the first. If an electroconductive material (a wire, for example) is passed through a magnetic field, an electrical voltage is induced. This process is called **magnetic induction**. If the wire is shaped into a coil, then the voltage induced in each wrap adds to the voltage induced in the other wraps, resulting in a greater total voltage.

The polarity of the induced voltage, positive or negative, is a function of the direction of the magnetic field as well as the direction of movement of the coil through the field. If the direction of movement is kept the same, then a positive voltage results from one direction of the magnetic field, while the opposite direction of the field induces a negative voltage. Figure 11-2 illustrates the magnetic induction of a voltage.

The third basic magnetic principle is that certain materials have the capability of retaining a magnetic field; this property is called **permanent magnetism**. When exposed to a magnetic field, the atoms of some metals (primarily iron and chromium) align themselves with that field; the atoms then remain so aligned unless exposed to another magnetic field. Each atom generates a minute magnetic field due to the "flow" of electrons around the nucleus. When all the atoms have been aligned, the sum of their minute magnetic fields forms a measurable magnetic field. Subsequently, that material is permanently magnetized, as in a child's toy magnet. The direction of the resulting permanent magnetic field depends on the direction of the original magnetic field to which it was exposed.

Figure 11-1   Magnetic Field Resulting from Electron Flow

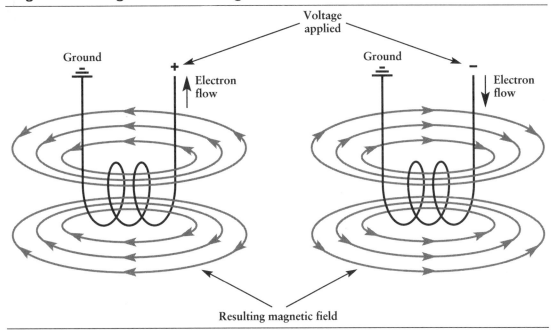

Figure 11-2   Voltage Induced by Magnetic Field

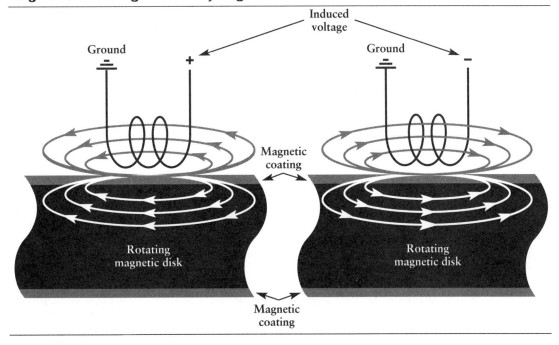

These three principles, electromagnetism, magnetic induction, and permanent magnetism, are utilized by all magnetic-media storage devices. A surface comprised of a nonmagnetic material (such as aluminum or plastic) is coated with minute particles of a magnetic material (such as iron or chromium oxide), firmly bonded to the surface. That surface is then passed in a fixed direction past a coil of wire in a **read/write head**.

To write or record data, spots of the magnetic material are magnetized by applying a voltage across the coil as the surface of the medium passes beneath it. The resulting current flow through the coil creates a magnetic field (electromagnetism), which then magnetizes the surface of the medium (permanent magnetism). The direction of magnetization depends on the voltage applied to the coil. A positive voltage magnetizes the surface in one direction; a negative voltage magnetizes it in the opposite direction. One direction stands for zero while the other direction stands for one. Thus, binary digits (or bits) of data are written to the medium.

To later read the data, the medium is again moved in the same direction past the coil in the read/write head. Instead of imposing a voltage on the coil, however, the hardware monitors the voltage across the coil. As the medium passes beneath the read/write head, the magnetic fields recorded earlier pass through the coil of wire, inducing a voltage within the coil (magnetic induction). Since the direction of movement is always the same, the polarity (positive or negative) of this voltage depends on the direction of the magnetic field, which itself is a result of the voltage applied when the data was written. Thus, by monitoring this voltage, the hardware is able to read back the bits of data that were previously written.

Note that this reading of the data is nondestructive; that is, reading the data does not remove the data from the magnetic medium. Once stored, the data remains until the atoms in the magnetic coating are realigned as a result of the writing of new data or by exposure of the medium to some other magnetic field. Of course the data will also be lost if the magnetic coating is removed or damaged by some physical trauma.

KEY TERMS TO REMEMBER

Electromagnetism	Magnetic induction
Permanent magnetism	Read/write head

DATA ORGANIZATION

Two types of magnetic disk media are commonly used by IBM-compatible PCs: **flexible disks** and **rigid disks**. Flexible disks are also commonly called **floppies** or simply **diskettes**. Rigid disks are often called **hard disks**, **conventional disks**, or

fixed disks. A floppy disk is made of flexible plastic with a magnetic coating bonded to it. This plastic disk is enclosed in a square jacket for protection. There are holes in the jacket to allow access to the disk surface by the drive hub, which rotates the disk inside the jacket, and by the read/write heads.

A hard disk is constructed of a nonmagnetic metal such as magnesium/aluminum alloy to which a magnetic coating is applied. Some hard disk drives allow for the removal and replacement of the disk surface(s); however, the hard drives commonly used with IBM-compatible PCs do not permit such removal. The disk surfaces, read/write heads, and drive mechanism are all sealed inside a plastic or metal case. It is because the disk surfaces are fixed (not removable) that disk drives are often called fixed disks.

Aside from the materials used for the disk, there is one other important difference between flexible-disk and rigid-disk technology. When a floppy drive door is closed, the read/write heads close against the disk surface; as the disk rotates the heads constantly rub the surface. In a rigid disk drive the read/write heads never quite touch the surface while the disk is rotating. Consequently, rigid disks can be made to rotate much faster than floppies and to rotate constantly as long as power is on, whereas floppy disk drives, in order to minimize wearing of the disk surface, rotate only when necessary. The light on a floppy drive indicates whether the disk is rotating; a fixed disk always rotates whenever power is on, and the light indicates when data is currently being read or written.

In either type of disk drive the disk is rotated within the drive with the read/write head(s) positioned against or very close to the disk surface. With a read/write head held in one position, the data written by that head forms a circle on the rotating disk. If the read/write head is moved to another position, nearer the center or nearer the perimeter of the disk, any data subsequently recorded forms another circle on the disk. These circles all have the same center, the hub of the disk, and so are referred to as "concentric." Thus the data on a disk is organized into **concentric circles**, called **tracks**.

Each track on a disk is capable of storing a very large amount of data, more than we would usually want to transfer into or out of memory at one time. Consequently, the hardware must be able to find and access smaller amounts of data within a particular track. This is accomplished by breaking each track into parts called **sectors**. The number of sectors per track and the size of each sector, measured in bytes, varies between disk drives; later, we will discuss the standards for IBM PCs. Figure 11-3 illustrates the manner in which data is organized on a disk.

A disk drive often contains more than one disk surface; a double-sided floppy disk has two surfaces while a hard disk typically has more. There is one read/write head for each surface. All of the read/write heads are linked together; when one moves they all move. Thus, when the read/write heads are held in one position, the disk drive may access data from a collection of tracks all the same distance from the center or hub. This collection or group of tracks, which can all be read with one positioning of the heads, is called a **cylinder**. The number of tracks per cylinder is equal to the number of disk surfaces and read/write heads in the disk drive.

Figure 11-3   Magnetic Disk Data Organization

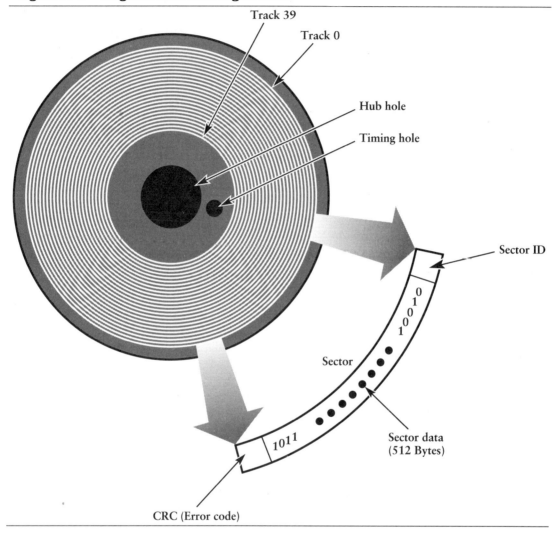

Just as it is helpful to group tracks into cylinders, it is also helpful to refer to groups of sectors. As we will discuss more fully at the end of this chapter, an operating system must be capable of keeping track of which areas of the disk are already used and what they are used for, and which areas have not yet been used and so are available for the storage of new data. This could be done by keeping track of individual sectors; in the case of large-capacity fixed-disk drives, however, the number of total sectors on the disk may be so great as to make this difficult. Also, accounting by individual sectors tends to make it difficult for an operating system to allow for disk drives of differing capacities.

Therefore, most operating systems account for the disk area in groups of sectors rather than by individual sectors. A group of consecutive sectors kept track of as a unit is called a **cluster**. The number of sectors thus grouped together by the operating system is called **cluster size**. In some cases the cluster size may be predetermined by the operating system; in other cases it may be built into the hardware or firmware of the storage device itself. More commonly, however, the cluster size of a device is written as data onto the disk itself and then is read and used by the operating system. In this manner, a particular operating system allows for the use of different storage devices each with a different cluster size; also, a particular storage device can be made compatible with different operating systems by using different cluster sizes.

KEY TERMS TO REMEMBER

Flexible disk	Fixed disk
Rigid disk	Track
Floppy	Sector
Diskette	Cylinder
Hard disk	Cluster
Conventional disk	Cluster size

The above discussion applies to all disk storage devices; now we shall discuss the disk drives normally used in IBM-compatible PCs. A standard, double-sided, 360K floppy diskette has forty tracks per side for a total of eighty tracks; stated another way, there are forty cylinders, two tracks per cylinder. Each of these tracks contains nine sectors. Each sector holds 512 bytes of data. Cluster size for a double-sided diskette is normally two. Note that two (sides per diskette) times forty (tracks per side) times nine (sectors per track) times 512 (bytes per sector) yields 368,640 or 360K, the total diskette capacity.

MS-DOS allows some flexibility in the way diskettes are formatted. If a diskette has been formatted for single-sided use with the "/1" switch, then only one surface is usable. This is because FORMAT writes sector IDs on only one side of the diskette. The diskette contains only forty usable tracks instead of eighty, each cylinder contains only one track, and the cluster size is one instead of two. If the diskette has been formatted for use by version one of DOS with "/8," then DOS uses only eight sectors in each track. Physically there are still nine sectors per track, and all nine sectors are accessible through BIOS, but DOS will use only eight.

The specifics of fixed-disk data organization (number of surfaces, tracks per surface, and so on) is harder to pin down since it depends on the particular hardware. For purposes of discussion we will consider a "typical" twenty-megabyte hard disk drive. Such a drive might have 4 disk surfaces with 615 tracks per surface (615 cylinders with 4 tracks per cylinder). Each track might contain 17 sectors. Sector size is always 512 bytes, the same as a floppy diskette. Such a typical hard disk might have a cluster size of 16. Remember, with the exception of sector size, which is always 512 bytes, all these numbers vary with different hard disk drives.

Most of the rest of our discussion of disk storage will concentrate on 5¼-inch double-density floppy diskettes. Before continuing, you should review the following diskette statistics.

Floppy Diskette Organization:

1 or more diskette drives per machine
2 sides per diskette
40 tracks per side
9 sectors per track
512 bytes per sector
2 * 40 * 9 * 512 = 360K

BIOS DISK SERVICES

Most of your previous exposure to disks has probably been with disk **files**. MASM.EXE, LINK.EXE, LIB.EXE, and DEBUG.COM are all stored in files on the assembler disk; all the programs you have written thus far have been stored on your disk in files; most high-level programming languages allow disk storage in data files. You have never had to worry about where on the disk your data is stored; you supplied a filename and let the system find the data for you. At the end of this chapter we will discuss how MS-DOS keeps track of data to allow access by files.

Unlike your previous experience, BIOS disk access is **non-file-structured**. BIOS knows nothing about filenames; it does not keep track of where data is stored; all BIOS disk access is by actual physical location. The programmer tells BIOS the exact physical location on the disk where he or she wants to read or write data.

This can be *very dangerous*! Later in this chapter, we will discuss the allocation structures that DOS maintains on any disk; without these data structures DOS cannot locate file data. If you accidentally tell BIOS to write to a disk area that is used by DOS to store one of these allocation structures, BIOS will indeed write to that area. DOS's critical data will be destroyed, and you can expect to lose access to all data on that disk.

As with most assembly-language programming, the question is not really *if* you will accidentally destroy a diskful of data, but *when* you will accidentally do so. Consequently, you should make sure when testing your programs that no diskette in the machine contains any data you want to keep. We also recommend that you do not test your programs on any machine with a hard disk; if you must do so, be absolutely sure that you have backed up recently.

In chapter 1 we recommended that you purchase at least four diskettes. So far you have used only two: one for your working diskette and one for a backup; you now have a use for the others. Before running any program that uses BIOS disk access, copy the executable program file along with any needed data files to one of your extra diskettes; use only this expendable diskette while testing your program. Remove ALL other disks from the machine! Use the fourth diskette whenever testing any program that requires two diskettes.

As mentioned above, BIOS requires that you specify the exact disk area to be accessed; you must specify the drive, side, track, and sector. All access is by sector; BIOS always reads or writes one or more full sectors of 512 bytes each.

All non-file-structured disk access is accomplished through interrupt type 13H, BIOS disk services. The general procedure is to put the code for the desired operation into AH, set up any other registers as required by that operation, and then execute the instruction, INT 13H. Following the disk access, the program should usually check the status returned by BIOS to determine success or failure. If an operation was successful, BIOS clears the Carry flag (NC) and returns 00H in AH; for an unsuccessful operation, BIOS sets the Carry flag (CY) and returns an error code in AH, specifying the reason for the failure.

The easiest way to check for success or failure of an operation is with a Conditional jump based on the Carry flag (JC or JNC). If the operation failed (Carry flag set), then the program may determine the cause of the failure by examining the value in AH. Figure 11-4 lists the possible error codes, returned in AH, with an explanation of each.

Following is a list of the most commonly used operations supported by BIOS disk services:

00H – Reset disk

Resets the disk controller chip on the floppy-disk-controller adapter card. This chip is automatically reset during boot up but should be reset again after any failed read or write operation. BIOS does not automatically wait for a drive to come up to speed before attempting a requested read or write; an extraneous error may result if the drive motor is off when the operation is requested. In the event of a read/write error, the program should reset the disk controller and retry the operation three more times before assuming that the error is real. To reset the controller chip:

```
Move 00H into AH.
Move the drive number into DL:
    00H - 7FH = floppy drive (00H = A, 01H = B);
    80H - FFH = hard disk (80H = 1st hard drive).
INT 13H.
```

BIOS resets the controller, setting or clearing the Carry flag and returning the status in AH as described above.

Figure 11-4   **BIOS Disk Services Error Codes**

00H = Successful; no error. This status is returned if and only if the Carry flag is clear (NC).

01H = Unknown operation code. The operation code in AH was not recognized by BIOS.

02H = Sector ID error (bad address mark). The disk is severely damaged or, more likely, not formatted.

03H = Write protect error. A write operation was attempted, and the write-protect tab is in place on the diskette, or the diskette is inserted upside down.

04H = Sector not found. A nonexistent sector or track was specified. For a diskette, the track was greater than thirty-nine (27H) or the sector was greater than nine. Another possibility is that the disk was formatted with improper sector IDs.

06H = Floppy disk removed. Diskette has been swapped since last accessed.

08H = DMA (direct memory access) overrun. The disk controller was unable to store the data into memory as quickly as it was read from the disk; one or more bytes of data were lost. Should never occur.

09H = Attempt to cross 64K boundary on read or write. The offset of the memory location for storage of the data would have exceeded 65,535. The buffer offset plus 512 times the number of sectors is greater than 65,535.

10H = Bad CRC (Cyclic Redundancy Check code) or ECC (Error Checking and Correcting code). The error check stored with the data on the disk does not compare correctly with the data itself; the disk is bad.

20H = NEC disk drive controller failure. Indicates a hardware failure of the disk controller adapter card.

40H = Seek operation failure. Indicates a mechanical or electrical failure of the disk drive.

80H = Time-out; disk failed to respond. Usually indicates that the drive door is open, no diskette is in the drive, or the diskette is inserted upside down.

01H - Get status

Operation 01H provides a second chance to check the status of a previous disk operation. The status is meaningful only if some disk operation has previously been performed. To obtain the last status:

```
Move 01H into AH.
Move the drive number into DL:
     00H — 7FH = floppy drive (00H = A, 01H = B);
     80H — FFH = hard disk (80H = 1st hard drive).
INT 13H.
```

The status of the last disk operation is returned by BIOS in AL; the value in AL is the same as that which was returned in AH by the last disk operation. Since operation 01H cannot fail, it always clears the Carry flag and returns zero (successful) in AH as its own status.

02H - Read sector(s)

Operation 02H reads one or more sectors from the disk into memory. In order to perform the read, BIOS must know three things: the exact physical location on the disk of the sector(s) to read, how many sectors to read, and the exact memory location at which to store the data. The memory location is specified in two parts: segment and offset. The disk location is specified in four parts: drive (00H through 7FH for floppy drives, 80H through FFH for hard disks), side (zero or one for a double-sided diskette), track (zero through thirty-nine for a double-density 5¼-inch diskette), and sector (one through nine for a nine-sector-per-track diskette). Note that track zero is the track nearest the perimeter of the diskette; track thirty-nine is nearest the center. Also note the inconsistency; the sector numbering starts at one, while numbering of the drive, side, and track begins at zero.

The BIOS disk service routine instructs the disk controller to copy the data directly from the disk into memory. The data does not pass through the processor; the disk controller puts it directly into memory. This process is called **direct memory access** or **DMA**.

It is the programmer's responsibility to ensure that he or she has set aside enough memory (buffer) to receive all the data without overwriting other data, the stack, or the code. Since a sector is 512 bytes, 512 is obviously the minimum size for the buffer. If more than one sector is to be read, the buffer must be large enough to receive that many sectors of data (512 times the number of sectors). To read one or more sectors from disk:

```
Move 02H into AH.
Move the drive number into DL:
     00H — 7FH = floppy drive (00H = A, 01H = B);
     80H — FFH = hard disk (80H = 1st hard drive).
Move the side into DH (0 = 1st side).
Move the track number into CH (0 = 1st track).
Move the sector number into CL (1 = 1st sector).
Move the number of sectors to be read into AL.
     Note: Attempting to read past the end of a track results
           in a time-out error (80H).
```

```
ES must point to the segment of the buffer.
Move the offset of the buffer into BX.
INT 13H.
```

BIOS causes the disk controller to copy the data in the designated sector(s) from the disk into the memory buffer (beginning at ES:[BX]). BIOS sets or clears the Carry flag and returns the status in AH as described above.

03H - Write sector(s)

One or more sectors are written from memory to the disk. As with operation 02H, read sector(s), BIOS must know the physical location of the sector(s) to write to, how many sectors to write, and the memory location (buffer) from which to get the data.

The BIOS disk service routine instructs the disk controller to make a DMA transfer directly from memory to the disk. The data does not pass through the processor; the disk controller takes it directly from memory.

The appropriate number of bytes, 512 times the number of sectors specified, will be copied from memory (beginning at the specified segment and offset) to the disk. If an insufficient number of bytes has been prepared in memory, "garbage" will be written to the disk. It is the programmer's responsibility to ensure that the data is properly prepared before executing the write operation. To write one or more sectors to disk:

```
Move 03H into AH.
Set up all other registers as in operation 02H above.
INT 13H.
```

BIOS causes the disk controller to copy the data from the buffer (beginning at ES:[BX]) to the designated sector(s) on the disk. BIOS sets or clears the Carry flag and returns the status in AH as described above.

04H - Verify sector(s) - Check if data can be read

Operation 04H verifies the integrity of the disk. BIOS causes the disk controller to locate the specified sector(s) and read the data, checking the CRC(s) or ECC(s), without transferring the data into memory (See Figure 11-4, error code 10H, bad CRC or ECC).

Operation 04H is identical to operation 02H except that the data is not stored into memory. To verify one or more disk sectors, move 04H into AH, set up all other registers (except for ES and BX) as in operation 02H above, and execute an interrupt type 13H. Since no data is transferred, BIOS does not use ES or BX.

BIOS instructs the disk controller to verify the specified sector(s). No data is transferred to or from disk; no memory is altered. The status is returned as described above.

Take a few moments to review the most commonly used BIOS disk operations.

S U M M A R Y   O F **BIOS Disk Operations**

```
INT 13H, operation 00H
```
> Reset disk. DL = drive (00H − 7FH = floppy, 80H − FFH = hard disk).

```
INT 13H, operation 01H
```
> Get disk status. DL = drive. Returns last status in AL.

```
INT 13H, operation 02H
```
> Read sector(s). DL = drive, DH = side, CH = track, CL = sector, AL = number of sectors, ES:[BX] = buffer.

```
INT 13H, operation 03H
```
> Write sector(s). DL = drive, DH = side, CH = track, CL = sector, AL = number of sectors, ES:[BX] = buffer.

```
INT 13H, operation 04H
```
> Verify sector(s). DL = drive, DH = side, CH = track, CL = sector, AL = number of sectors.

BUILDING BLOCKS FOR NON-FILE-STRUCTURED DISK ACCESS

The above discussion of BIOS disk services suggests a number of building blocks for providing non-file-structured disk access. Following is a discussion of several building blocks that you might add to a disk I/O library (DISK.MLB and DISK.LIB):

Reset the disk controller:

```
RESET_DISK    MACRO    DRV, STAT
```

DRV is a byte input parameter specifying the drive to reset and should default to drive A (0). STAT is an optional byte output parameter to receive the status from BIOS. The Carry flag should also indicate success or failure. The procedure uses BIOS disk services operation 00H to reset the disk controller. Invoke RESET_DISK after any failed read operation (READ_SCTR or VERIFY_SCTR below).

Get status of last disk operation:

```
GET_STATUS    MACRO    DRV, LAST_STAT
```

DRV is a byte input parameter specifying the desired drive and should allow the same default as in RESET_DISK. LAST_STAT is a byte output parameter to receive the status returned by BIOS. The procedure uses operation 01H to get the status of the last BIOS disk operation. Since operation 01H is always successful, there is no need to return the current status or to preserve the Carry flag.

Read one or more disk sectors:

```
READ_SCTR    MACRO DRV, SIDE, TRAK, SCTR, NBR, BUFF_OFF, STAT
```

DRV, SIDE, TRAK, and SCTR are all byte input parameters specifying the physical disk location from which to read (drive, side, track, and sector). DRV should default to drive A (0), if omitted.

NBR is a byte input parameter specifying the number of sectors to read. It should default to one. BUFF_OFF is a word input parameter specifying the offset within the data segment of the buffer to receive the data. STAT is an optional byte output parameter to receive the status returned by BIOS. Additionally, the Carry flag should indicate the success or failure of the read, as upon return from BIOS.

The procedure, $READ_SCTR, should use operation 02H to read one or more sectors from disk into the buffer set aside by the program. The value in DS should be used as the segment for the buffer; it must be moved into ES before the INT 13H instruction. Alternatively, another parameter, BUFF_SEG, might be used to allow the buffer in any segment. Both the procedure and the macro must be careful not to alter the Carry flag after the return from BIOS.

The macro header should explain parameters including the purpose, the size, the allowed addressing modes, any defaults, if optional, and so on for each parameter. In addition, it should explain the significance of the Carry flag upon exit from the building block. The macro header should also warn the next programmer to ensure that the buffer is at least NBR * 512 bytes long, and that SCTR + NBR should not exceed the number of sectors per track.

Write one or more disk sectors:

```
WRITE_SCTR    MACRO DRV, SIDE, TRAK, SCTR, NBR, BUFF_OFF, STAT
```

All parameters are the same as in READ_SCTR discussed above; the macro should allow the same defaults and provide the same explanations and cautions. It should warn the user that NBR * 512 bytes of data must be prepared before the invocation. The procedure, $WRITE_SCTR, should use operation 03H to write the sector(s) to the disk from the buffer at DS:[BUFF_OFF] (or BUFF_SEG:[BUFF_OFF]).

Verify one or more disk sectors:

```
VERIFY_SCTR    MACRO DRV, SIDE, TRAK, SCTR, NBR, STAT
```

DRV, SIDE, TRAK, SCTR, NBR, and STAT are the same as for READ_SCTR; BUFF_OFF is unnecessary since no data is copied into memory.

The procedure, $VERIFY_SCTR, uses operation 04H to verify the disk controller's ability to read one or more sectors of a disk. The macro and procedure should both be very similar to READ_SCTR above.

KEY TERMS TO REMEMBER

Direct Memory Access (DMA)   Non-file-structured disk access
File

DOS DISK ALLOCATION

Note: It is not recommended that you use the following information to circumvent DOS in manipulating files. On the contrary, it is strongly recommended that you manage DOS files using the function calls described in chapter 12. We have included this discussion of DOS disk allocation so that as an assembly-language programmer you will understand how the operating system does its job. Furthermore, it is possible that at some time in the future you may be required to write a device driver or some other system program that requires interpreting DOS's allocation structures.

In any case, we wish to emphasize that attempting to directly manipulate DOS's allocation structures not only requires a great deal of extra work and skill on the part of the programmer, but also involves extreme risk!

As discussed earlier, most operating systems, MS-DOS included, provide **file-structured** disk access. The term "file-structured" means that the application programmer is relieved of the need to know the physical location of his or her data on the disk; the programmer provides a filename by which to refer to the data, and the operating system keeps track of the physical location of the data.

Keeping track of the data by filename places three requirements on the operating system. First, it must maintain a **file directory**, a list of the names of all data files currently on the disk. It must be capable of adding filenames to the directory as files are created and removing names as files are deleted. Second, it must keep a record of which areas of the disk have been allocated to each data file. Third, it must be capable of finding unused disk areas for allocation to new or expanding data files. Remember from our earlier discussion that allocation of disk space is usually done in groups of consecutive sectors, called clusters, rather than by individual sectors.

Unlike some operating systems in which disk space must be preallocated by operations personnel, MS-DOS provides for **dynamic disk allocation**. An application program can direct the operating system to create, extend, truncate, or delete files at execution time without the intervention of operations personnel.

When MS-DOS creates a file for an application program, it allocates no space to the file. As data is added to the file, MS-DOS automatically allocates clusters of space as needed to hold the new data. Similarly, if a file shrinks in size or is deleted entirely, MS-DOS automatically deallocates that space, freeing it up for allocation to other files.

In order to provide dynamic disk allocation, MS-DOS must be able to find unused clusters for allocation to growing files very quickly. Since disk allocation occurs frequently and automatically during execution of application programs, needed disk space must be identified almost instantaneously. Any delay in allocation would result in a serious degradation of performance.

MS-DOS keeps track of the allocation of disk space through a combination of the directory and a **File Allocation Table**, or **FAT**. Each twelve-bit FAT entry corresponds to one cluster within the **data area** of the disk—the area in which all file data is stored. Each directory entry contains a starting cluster number that provides entry into a **linked list** of cluster entries within the FAT. The term "linked list" means that each FAT entry contains the number of the next FAT entry for that file, which then contains the cluster number of the next entry.

KEY TERMS TO REMEMBER

File-structured disk access	FAT (File Allocation Table)
File directory	Data area
Dynamic disk allocation	Linked list

Microsoft calls such a linked list an **allocation chain**. Given the first cluster number (obtained from the directory entry), MS-DOS can trace through the linked list of FAT entries to determine all the clusters currently allocated to the file. A series of values (FF8H through FFFH) has been reserved for the last FAT entry for a file, to designate the end of an allocation chain. In addition, another value (000H) is reserved for use in a FAT entry to indicate that its corresponding cluster is currently unused. By searching the FAT for this value, MS-DOS can quickly identify such unused clusters for dynamic allocation to expanding files.

When a disk is formatted, FORMAT writes a one-sector **boot record** to the first sector of the disk (side zero/track zero/sector one). This boot record is loaded and executed by BIOS upon power-up or <Alt>+<Ctrl>+<Del>; it contains the instructions necessary to control the loading and execution of the rest of the operating system.

Following the boot record, FORMAT creates two identical copies of the File Allocation Table, beginning at side zero/track zero/sector two. The duplicate copy of the FAT is stored, ostensibly, for verification of integrity; however, it has been this programmer's experience that DOS often uses the first copy without detecting any discrepancy between the two copies. In any case, two copies of the FAT are stored on the disk. On diskettes formatted by DOS version one or by version two with the "/8" switch (eight sectors per track), each copy of the FAT takes up one sector of disk space; DOS versions two and above (nine sectors per track) use two sectors for each copy of the FAT.

Disk Directory

Immediately following the two copies of the FAT, FORMAT builds the **root directory** for the disk. For diskettes formatted as eight sectors per track, the directory begins at side zero/track zero/sector four; on nine-sector-per-track diskettes, it begins at side zero/track zero/sector six. If the diskette has been formatted with the "/1" switch (single-sided), four sectors are used for the root directory; on double-sided diskettes, the root directory is seven sectors long.

Note that DOS versions two and above allow for subdirectories, to be discussed more thoroughly in the next chapter; subdirectories are actually special data files and so may be any length. With the exception of size limitations, the following description applies to subdirectories as well as to the root directory.

The directory is made up of a series of 32-byte entries. Sixteen directory entries can fit in one sector (512 divided by 32); thus, a single-sided diskette allows a maximum of 64 root-directory entries (4 times 16), and a double-sided diskette has room for 112 entries (7 times 16). Figure 11-5 illustrates the layout of each directory entry in either the root directory or a subdirectory file.

FAT (File Allocation Table)

As discussed earlier, DOS uses the FAT for two purposes. First, it is used to quickly find unallocated clusters on the disk. Second, it is used to record which disk clusters have been allocated to a particular file. The directory entry indicates only the starting cluster of the file; DOS uses that as a starting point into a linked list or chain of allocation entries from which it determines every cluster used by the file. To accomplish these two purposes, the FAT must have one entry for every cluster within the data area of the disk; the data area is all the remaining disk area following the root directory and is used to store the data for all files. Also, in order to build allocation chains, each entry must be large enough (have enough bits) to specify the next **logical cluster** number; the designers of DOS chose to use twelve bits (1½ bytes) for each entry.

The first two entries (number zero and number one) of the FAT do not represent clusters within the data area, but instead contain information about the format of the disk. The two entries comprise the first three bytes of the FAT, but only the first byte is meaningful; the second and third bytes are always FFFFH. The first byte indicates the format of the disk; Figure 11-6 lists the possible values and the indicated formats.

Figure 11-5   **Disk Directory Entry**

Byte	Purpose - Meaning

0–7   File Name. The primary filename, padded on the right with spaces (20H). The first byte of the File-Name field (byte number zero) indicates the status of the directory entry as follows:

00H   This entry has never been used since the disk was formatted. Used by DOS to limit directory searches; as soon as DOS sees a 00H entry, it terminates any directory search.

E5H   This entry has been used, but is currently deleted. When DOS creates a new file, it uses the first available entry (00H or E5H).

2EH (".")   This is one of the first two entries in a subdirectory. The first entry begins with a single period followed by ten spaces (20H); the second entry begins with two periods (2E2EH) followed by nine spaces. The subdirectory bit is set in the Attribute byte of both entries. The Starting-Cluster field of the first entry contains the starting logical cluster number of this subdirectory file. The Starting-Cluster field of the second entry holds the starting logical cluster number of this subdirectory's parent directory (0000H if the parent is the root directory).

Any other value indicates that this is an entry for an active file. This byte is the first character in the filename.

8–10   File Extension. The filename extension, padded on the right with spaces (20H).

11   Attribute byte. A one byte value indicating any special characteristics of the file. Each bit has the following meaning:

Bits	Meaning if bit is set

0   File is flagged as read only. Any attempt to open it for output results in an error.

1   Flagged as a hidden file. It is excluded from normal directory searches.

2   The file is a system file. It is also excluded from normal directory searches.

3   The entry is a volume label. Bytes zero through ten contain the eleven-character volume label for the disk instead of a filename and extension; the rest of the entry contains no other meaningful information. Used only in root directory.

4   The file is a subdirectory.

5   Archive bit. This bit is set on by DOS when the file is created or modified; it is set off when the file is backed up with the BACKUP utility. Used by BACKUP and RESTORE to determine if the file has changed since last backed up.

6–7   Not currently used.

12–21   Reserved.

22–23   File Time. The system time of the creation or last update of the file. The time is stored in the following format:

Figure 11-5 (continued)

Bits	Meaning
0–4	One half the seconds (0 through 29)
5–10	Minutes in binary (0 through 59)
11–15	Hour in binary (0 through 23)

24–25   File Date. The system date of the creation or last update of the file. The date is stored in the following format:

Bits	Meaning
0–4	Day in binary (1 through 31)
5–8	Month in binary (1 through 12)
9–15	Years in binary, since 1980 (0 through 119 = 1980 through 2099)

26–27   Starting Cluster. The logical cluster number of the first cluster of the file; see the discussions of the FAT and the data area, below, for explanation of logical cluster number. Also, the entry number of the first entry within the FAT of the allocation chain for this file. 0000H if the file has no space allocated to it (no allocation chain in the FAT).

28–31   File Size. The size of the file, in bytes. Space is allocated to files in clusters; however, the last cluster is usually not completely full. This field gives the number of bytes actually used by the file. The least-significant word of the file size is stored in bytes twenty-eight and twenty-nine; bytes thirty and thirty-one store the most significant word.

Figure 11-6   **First Byte of FAT**

Value	Meaning
F8H	A hard disk.
FCH	A 5¼-inch diskette formatted as single-sided, nine sectors per track.
FDH	A 5¼-inch diskette formatted as double-sided, nine sectors per track.
FEH	A 5¼-inch diskette, single-sided, eight sectors per track.
FFH	A 5¼-inch diskette, double-sided, eight sectors per track.

The first entry that actually maps the data area is entry number two; the first cluster within the data area is therefore assigned logical cluster number two. Also, two is the lowest number contained in the Starting-Cluster-Number field of any directory entry, except that 0000H is used to indicate that the directory entry has no space allocated to it. Figure 11-7 lists the possible values and significance of each FAT entry from number two on.

Figure 11-7   FAT Entries (number two and above)

Value	Meaning
000H	Indicates that the corresponding logical cluster is currently unallocated; it is free for allocation to any new or expanding files.
FF8H–FFFH	This is the last cluster in an allocation chain; no more clusters have been allocated to the file whose chain led to this entry. DOS normally uses FFFH.
FF0H–FF7H	If part of an allocation chain, then the value represents the logical cluster number of the next cluster in the chain. If not part of an allocation chain, then this cluster is reserved and will not subsequently be allocated. FORMAT flags bad clusters with FF7H.

Any other value represents the logical cluster number of the next cluster in an allocation chain.

Note that the size of each FAT entry (twelve bits) places some constraints on the maximum number of clusters allowed on a disk. In twelve bits DOS can store a number from zero through FFFH (4095). Logical cluster numbering begins with two, and the values FF8H through FFFH are reserved for use in marking the end of an allocation chain. Thus, the possible values for an entry used to indicate the next cluster in an allocation chain are 2 through FF7H (4087). Even if the FAT were to be made longer (more than two sectors), it still would be limited to the mapping of 4086 clusters of data area.

This limitation should clarify the need, discussed at the beginning of this chapter, for allocating disk space in clusters rather than as individual sectors. If each FAT entry represented only one sector, then only 4,086 sectors of disk space would be addressable by the FAT. That would limit a hard disk to 2.043 megabytes of data area (4,086 times 512). Programmers who are accustomed to working with thirty- or forty-megabyte hard disk systems will appreciate the restrictions that such a limit would place on the user.

To continue, each twelve bit (1½ byte) entry in the FAT represents a cluster within the data area of the disk. Three bytes are used to hold every two FAT entries. With that in mind, Figure 11-8 illustrates an algorithm for finding a FAT entry, given a logical cluster number.

To trace an allocation chain for a file, first take the starting cluster number (word) from bytes twenty-six and twenty-seven of the directory entry; if it is 0000H, then there is no allocation chain; no space is allocated to the file. Otherwise, it is the logical cluster number of the first cluster in the file. Perform the algorithm described in Figure 11-8 to find and retrieve the first FAT entry. If this entry is any value less than 0FF8H, then it is the logical cluster number of the next cluster of the file. Repeat the above algorithm on it to find the second FAT entry. Continue with this process until the FAT entry is 0FF8H or greater; the resulting list of logical cluster numbers may then be used to retrieve the data from the data area of the disk.

Figure 11-8   Locating a FAT Entry from a Logical Cluster Number

---

1) Multiply the logical cluster number by three.

2) Divide the result of step one by two. (The quotient provides an offset into the FAT where the cluster's entry is located; the remainder indicates whether the entry is the high twelve bits or the low twelve bits of the two bytes at that offset.)

3) Move the word (two bytes) located at the offset obtained in step two into a word register.

4) If step two resulted in a zero remainder, then proceed to step five; otherwise shift the word register right four. (This shifts the entry in the twelve high-order bits to the twelve low-order bits.)

5) AND the word register with 0FFFH. (This masks out all but the twelve low-order bits, which contain the entry.)

6) The resulting value in the word register is the FAT entry.

Data Area

For maximum performance, DOS allocates all disk space by cylinders; all space in a given cylinder is allocated before going to the next cylinder. This means that on a double-sided diskette, after allocating all sectors in a track on side zero, DOS allocates sectors in the same track on side one; when that track is completely allocated, DOS moves to the next higher track on side zero, and so forth. On a hard disk with four surfaces, DOS would allocate all sectors in a track on side zero; then all sectors in the same track on side one; then side two, same track; then side three, same track; finally, DOS would begin allocating the next higher track back on side zero.

For convenience, sectors are assigned a **logical sector** number following the same pattern. Side zero/track zero/sector one is logical sector number zero. Side zero/track zero/sector two is logical sector number one. On a diskette with nine sectors per track, side zero/track zero contains logical sectors number zero through number eight. If it is single-sided, then logical sector number nine is side zero/track one/sector one; if it is double-sided, then logical sector number nine is side one/track zero/sector one. These are the same logical sector numbers used by the DEBUG Load and Write commands.

Do not confuse logical sector numbers with logical cluster numbers used within the directory and the FAT! Logical cluster numbers apply only to the data area of the disk and are numbered relative to the beginning of the data area, after the root directory; logical sector numbers apply to the entire disk and are relative to side zero/track zero/sector one.

KEY TERMS TO REMEMBER

Allocation chain	Logical cluster number
Boot record	Logical sector number
Root directory	

The data area of a disk begins immediately after the root directory and continues to the last logical sector of the disk. Since the lengths of both the FAT and the root directory vary with the format of the diskette, the location of the beginning of the data area is also dependent on the diskette format. Figure 11-9 summarizes the logical sectors of the various areas of the diskette as it is organized by DOS.

Figure 11-9 **Diskette Organization**
Logical Sectors Occupied by FAT, Directory, and Data

Format: sides, sectors /track	FAT #1	FAT #2	Root directory	Data area
1, 8	1	2	3– 6	7–319
2, 8	1	2	3– 9	10–639
1, 9	1–2	3–4	5– 8	9–359
2, 9	1–2	3–4	5–11	12–719

Note: In all formats, logical sector 0 is the boot block

Recall that the data area of the disk is mapped by the FAT as logical clusters. Also, recall that the first two FAT entries, number zero and number one, are used to hold information about the format of the disk; specifically, the first byte indicates the format, and the other two are always FFFFH. This first byte can be used in conjunction with the information in Figure 11-9 to determine the beginning of the data area.

FAT entry number two is the first entry used to map the data area. For consistency, the first cluster within the data area is assigned logical cluster number two to match the number of its FAT entry. The rest of the disk is assigned consecutive logical cluster numbers, following the pattern of assigning numbers to all the clusters within a cylinder before going to side zero of the next cylinder. There remains, then, the problem of finding the data indicated by a logical cluster number obtained from a directory entry or a FAT entry. Given a logical cluster number, the algorithm illustrated in Figure 11-10 will yield the physical location of the data sector.

Figure 11-10   Locating a Data Sector from a Logical Cluster Number

First, calculate the logical sector number:

1) Subtract two from the logical cluster number.

2) Multiply the result from step one by the cluster size of the disk (one for single-sided diskettes, two for double-sided diskettes).

3) To the result from step two add the logical sector number of the beginning of the data area.

4) The result of step three is the logical sector number of the first sector of the cluster.

The physical location of the data can now be calculated from the logical sector number as follows:

1) Divide the logical sector number by the number of sectors per track (eight or nine).

2) Add one to the remainder from step one; the result is the sector number within the track determined in step four below.

3) Divide the quotient from step one by the number of sides to the disk (one or two).

4) The remainder from step three is the side; the quotient from step three is the track number.

FILE-STRUCTURED DISK ACCESS

By making use of the allocation structures discussed above, DOS is able to provide a number of file-related services to users and to application programs. Some of the services necessary for file-structured disk access are:

- Providing for file management:
  Provide a listing of filenames (directory).
  Create a file.
  Rename a file.
  Delete or erase a file.

- Providing access to file data:
  Open a file.
  Read data from an open file.
  Write data to an open file.
  Close a file.

The next chapter will discuss the function calls through which a program may gain access to DOS's file-related services. In the following paragraphs, we will examine the manner in which DOS uses the directory and File Allocation Table in order to provide the services.

PROVIDING FOR FILE MANAGEMENT

When a user enters the DIR command or a program requests a directory search, DOS must be able to determine the names of all disk files. To do so DOS needs only to examine the directory entries. If the first byte of an entry is 00H, then it has never been used. Since DOS always uses directory entries in sequence, this indicates that there are no more used entries in the directory; DOS terminates the directory search without going further. If the first byte of an entry is E5H, then it has been deleted, and so DOS ignores it and goes on to the next entry. If the first byte is neither of these values, then it is an active file. DOS then checks the Attribute byte. If it indicates that the file is hidden or is a system file or volume label, DOS ignores it and goes on to the next entry; otherwise DOS takes the filename and extension from the first eleven bytes of the directory entry and displays them to the user or returns them to the program.

When requested to rename a file from an old name to a new name, DOS again needs only to use the directory. It searches the directory looking for an already existing file with the requested new name; if it finds a matching entry, DOS reports an error and terminates the request. Otherwise, it searches the directory for an entry that matches the old name; if it encounters a 00H entry before finding a match, it terminates the request returning an error. Otherwise (if it finds a matching entry), DOS replaces the first eleven bytes of the directory entry with the new name and extension.

Creating a new file always requires the use of the directory; if a file of the same name already exists, then DOS must also manipulate the FAT. First DOS searches the directory for an entry that matches the filename; if it finds no match, then it looks for an unused or deleted entry (discussed in the following paragraph). If it finds a match, then DOS uses the entry; it updates the File-Date and File-Time fields to the current system date and time, updates the Attribute byte, and sets the File-Size field to zero. Next, DOS deallocates all disk space previously used by the file. To do this it uses the directory entry's Starting-Cluster field to find the first FAT entry in the old allocation chain. Then it proceeds through the allocation chain changing each entry to 000H to deallocate the cluster. Finally, DOS stores 0000H into the directory entry's Starting-Cluster field. Thus, the existing file is truncated to zero bytes with no allocated disk space.

If a matching directory entry was not found on a create request, then DOS searches the directory for the first entry beginning with either 00H (unused) or E5H (deleted); if no such entry is found, the directory is full, and DOS terminates the request with an error. Otherwise, DOS puts the filename and extension into the first eleven bytes of the directory entry, sets up the Attribute byte, puts the system date and time into the File-Date and File-Time fields, and initializes the File-Size field to zero. Then DOS puts 0000H into the Starting-Cluster field of the directory entry to indicate that the entry has no allocation chain. The file has now been created with no space allocated to it. DOS then makes the file immediately available for access by the program; see the discussion below of access to existing files.

To delete a file, DOS first searches the directory for a matching entry; if no match is found, DOS terminates the request and returns an error. If a match is found, DOS changes the first byte of the entry to E5H to flag it as deleted; nothing else is changed in the directory entry. The file has now been deleted, but disk space is still allocated to it. To deallocate the disk space, DOS gets the first logical cluster number from the Starting-Cluster field of the deleted directory entry and proceeds through the allocation chain within the FAT, replacing each entry with 000H to flag it as unused.

PROVIDING ACCESS TO FILE DATA

Allowing access to the data within an existing or newly created file is much more complex than any of the above services. In order to discuss it, we need to introduce some new terms. The term **relative sector** refers to the sectors within a file, relative to the first sector allocated to that file, and unrelated to the actual physical location on disk. Relative sector number zero is the first sector in the first cluster allocated to the file, regardless of its location on the disk. Relative sector number one is the second sector allocated to the file. Relative sector number two is the third sector allocated to the file and need not be physically located anywhere near relative sectors zero or one (unless the cluster size is three or greater).

The term **physical record** refers to the data contained in one relative sector. Although it is often used synonymously with relative sector, its proper meaning is slightly different. A relative sector is a sector on the disk. A physical record is the data that can be physically stored in one sector though it may be currently stored in memory. Since it is made up of all the data contained in a sector, a physical record is always exactly 512 bytes.

In order to provide for the transfer of physical records between disk and memory, DOS sets aside an area of memory for each open file, called a **file buffer**. The terms **physical read** and **physical write** or, collectively, **physical disk access**, refer to the physical transfer of data between disk and memory. A physical read results in a DMA transfer of a physical record from a specified relative sector on disk to the file buffer that DOS has set aside for that file. A physical write copies the physical record stored in the file buffer to the appropriate relative sector of the disk file. DOS uses BIOS disk services (INT 13H), operation 02H (Read sector) or 03H (Write sector), to perform any necessary physical read or physical write.

KEY TERMS TO REMEMBER

Relative sector	File buffer
Physical record	Physical disk access

The terms logical record and relative record refer, not to the manner in which the data is physically stored on disk, but to the logical organization of the data, the manner in which the application program wishes to access the data. A **logical record** is one unit of data, of whatever length is necessary for the program's logical interpretation of the data. For example, a file containing data about employees might be organized such that eighty bytes are used to store all the necessary information about each employee. The application program would then specify to DOS a logical record length of eighty for that file.

Subsequently, DOS provides the program with access to the file data in units of eighty bytes (one logical record) at a time. The term **relative record** refers to the position of logical records, relative to the beginning of the file. The first logical record in the file (the first eighty bytes) is relative record number zero; relative record number one is the second logical record in the file (the next eighty bytes).

In order to access the file data by logical record, the application program must allocate an area of memory, called a **record buffer**. Do not confuse the terms record buffer and file buffer; a file buffer is automatically set up by DOS, is always 512 bytes long, and is used by DOS to receive or prepare physical records; a record buffer is defined within the application program, usually within the data segment, and is used for the receipt or preparation of logical records. The record buffer must be at least as long as the logical record length specified to DOS.

Three more terms are necessary in order to understand the manner in which DOS provides access to file data: **logical read** and **logical write** or, collectively, **logical disk access**. A logical disk access results in the copying of data, by DOS, between the file buffer and the record buffer. When performing a logical read, DOS copies a logical record from the file buffer to the program's record buffer. A logical write copies data from the record buffer to the file buffer. As will be discussed shortly, any logical read or logical write may or may not require that DOS do a physical read (and possibly a physical write) prior to the copying of data between the record buffer and the file buffer.

A program asks to be allowed to access an existing file by requesting that DOS open the file. DOS searches the directory for a matching filename; if a match is not found, DOS returns an error and terminates the request. Otherwise, DOS associates the file with a file buffer for the storage of physical records. DOS then examines the Starting-Cluster field of the directory entry, calculates the physical location on the disk, and reads the first sector of the file (relative sector number zero) into the file buffer.

The application program has defined a record buffer, usually within the data segment. It must either inform DOS of the address of the record buffer and of the desired logical record length prior to any access to the data (traditional functions), or it must specify the record buffer location and logical record length on every subsequent disk access (extended functions). Once the file has been opened, the program may then begin accessing the data stored in the file. All subsequent access to the file by the program consists of logical reads and writes. Each logical disk access results in the transfer of a logical record between the program's record buffer and DOS's file buffer.

When the program requests a logical disk access, either read or write, DOS multiplies the desired relative record number by the logical record length and then divides by 512 to calculate the relative sector within which the desired relative record is stored. DOS then compares this relative sector number with that of the physical record that is currently in the file buffer. If the correct physical record (from correct relative sector) is already in the file buffer, then DOS immediately transfers the correct number of bytes of data (logical record) between the record buffer and the file buffer (from the record buffer to the file buffer for a logical write, from the file buffer to the record buffer for a logical read). If the file buffer already contains the correct physical record, then no physical read or write is performed.

However, if the desired logical record is not contained within the physical record currently in the file buffer (if the physical record is from the wrong relative sector of the file), then DOS must perform at least a physical read and, possibly, a physical write before performing the logical read or write. If the physical record, currently in the file buffer, has been modified (if a logical write has been performed) since it was read from the disk, then DOS must perform a physical write to copy the modified physical record back to the relative sector from which it was originally read; if the physical record, currently in the file buffer has not been modified, then no physical write is performed.

After performing the physical write (if necessary), DOS does a physical read to transfer the required physical record (from the correct relative sector) into the file buffer. Finally, DOS performs the logical read or write for the program, transferring the appropriate logical record between the program's record buffer and the file buffer. Remember that a logical disk access does not always result in a physical disk access; the physical record containing the desired logical record is often already in the file buffer when the request for a logical read or write occurs.

Whenever performing a physical read to obtain the needed physical record into the file buffer, DOS uses the file's allocation chain within the FAT to determine the logical clusters allocated to the file, from which it then calculates the physical location of the relative sector to be read. When servicing a logical write request, the relative sector number of the physical record needed in the file buffer may be beyond the total number of sectors in all the clusters allocated to the file; if so, DOS must allocate additional space to the file.

To allocate additional space, DOS examines the FAT for the first unused entry (000H); if none is found, then the disk is full, and DOS returns an error and terminates the logical write request without transferring any data. Otherwise, DOS puts the logical cluster number of the currently unused cluster into the FAT entry that previously marked the end of the chain; then DOS puts FFFH into the new FAT entry making it the new end of the chain. Once the new cluster has been allocated, DOS continues with the physical read as described above and then services the logical write.

When the program is finished accessing the file, it must notify DOS by requesting that DOS close the file. First, DOS flushes the file buffer; if the physical record currently in the file buffer has been modified, DOS physically writes it to the correct relative sector of the file. Then DOS stores the system date and time, as of the last modification to the file, into the File-Date and File-Time fields of the directory entry and updates the File-Size field to reflect any change in the file size.

It is critical that any file to which a program has logically written data be closed. Failure to do so will result in the loss of file data; the last physical record will not be written to the disk. Even more seriously, the failure to close a file may result in the loss of available disk storage. DOS updates the FAT immediately upon allocating new disk space to the file, thereby making that logical cluster unavailable for future allocation, but does not update the directory entry until the file is closed. Failure to close the file and update the directory entry may result in "lost" clusters of disk space.

FILE FRAGMENTATION

Recall from chapter 3 the discussion of the differences between the DISKCOPY and COPY *.* commands. Reference was made in that discussion to **file fragmentation**; specifically, it was stated that DISKCOPY perpetuates file fragmentation onto the new disk, while COPY *.* copies the data into **contiguous** files on the new disk. We are now in a position to fully understand that statement.

Consider the following scenario. We begin with a newly formatted disk; no disk space has yet been allocated, so the FAT consists entirely of 000H entries (with the exception of the first two entries). We create a file, FILE_1, and write a small amount of data to it. The first available FAT entry is number two, so DOS allocates logical cluster two to the file. Then we create another file, FILE_2, and write a small amount of data to it. DOS allocates the first available logical cluster, which is number three. Now we modify FILE_1 adding additional data; we eventually fill up logical cluster number two, requiring DOS to allocate new space to the file. The first available cluster is number four since logical cluster three is already allocated to FILE_2. FILE_1 is now fragmented; it is not contiguous since it occupies logical clusters number two and number four, skipping over logical cluster number three (See Figure 11-11).

Figure 11-11   Fragmentation of FILE1

	Data area			
Cluster # 2	3	4	5	
FILE_1 (1st cluster)	FILE_2	FILE_1 (2nd cluster)		

Such fragmentation can become even worse. Suppose we now delete FILE_2. Its directory entry is flagged as deleted (E5H), and logical cluster number three is deallocated; DOS changes FAT entry number three to 000H. Now we again write additional data to FILE_1, eventually filling up logical cluster four. When DOS allocates more disk space to the file, it uses the first available logical cluster, which happens to be number three. Consequently, FILE_1 now begins in cluster two, continues in cluster number four, then jumps backward to logical cluster number three. As FILE_1 continues to grow, the next logical cluster allocated to it will be number five. The resulting fragmentation is illustrated in Figure 11-12.

Figure 11-12   Further Fragmentation of FILE1

Data area

Cluster #	2	3	4	5	
	FILE_1 (1st cluster)	FILE_1 (3rd cluster)	FILE_1 (2nd cluster)	FILE_1 (4th cluster)	

Over the life of a disk, such file fragmentation or scattering of the data can become quite severe. In one sense, this is not a problem, since DOS is able to follow the allocation chain and find the file data in the correct order. However, such fragmentation does result in greater movement of the read/write heads back and forth across the disk than would be required if the data were contiguous. This extra head movement slows down access to the disk data, degrading overall system performance.

Now, to return to DISKCOPY versus COPY *.*. DISKCOPY copies sector by sector from the source disk to the target disk, duplicating the directory and the FAT and retaining any file fragmentation. COPY *.* on the other hand copies file-by-file, allocating space and building a new directory and FAT on the target disk as it does so. As long as the destination disk was empty to start with (newly formatted or all files deleted), then all clusters are free for allocation. Thus; as DOS looks for unallocated space on the target disk, the next free cluster is always the very next logical cluster; consequently, the files are written contiguously to the new disk.

The resulting disk, since its files are contiguous, requires less head movement to access the data and so provides better system performance. Of course, as it is used and its files are modified it will also eventually become fragmented. File fragmentation is a price we must pay for dynamic disk allocation.

KEY TERMS TO REMEMBER

Logical record	Logical disk access
Relative record	File fragmentation
Record buffer	Contiguous

FILE ACCESS METHODS

Data files are typically accessed in one of two ways, sequentially or directly. **Sequential access** allows the reading or writing of records in sequential order only. The file records are processed in order, beginning with the first record of the file and proceeding through the entire file record by record. Each read or write automatically accesses the next record after the last one accessed. In order to read the twentieth record, for example, the program must first read through the first nineteen records.

Sequential access does not allow the modification of the data within a file since it does not permit the rewriting of a modified record back to its original location in the file. In fact, when accessing a file sequentially, most programs either read from the file or write to the file, but not both. In order to update file data, the entire file is copied to a new file, modifying the desired records as they are copied; the program reads from the old version of the file and writes to the new version. Consequently, programs that use sequential access cannot quickly and immediately make minor changes to the file data.

Direct access (called **random access** by IBM and Microsoft) allows a program to directly access any desired record within a file without accessing the preceding records. When using direct access the program does not automatically access the next record on each read or write. Rather, the program is required to specify the relative record number of the desired record for each file access. The program can directly access the twentieth record in the file, without accessing the first nineteen records, by doing a direct-access read or write and specifying nineteen as the relative record number (remember that the first record in the file is relative record number zero).

Through direct access, a program can quickly and immediately update data within a file, without the need to copy the file. The program directly reads the desired record specifying its relative record number, modifies it within the record buffer, and then rewrites it to the same location in the file by specifying the same relative record number. DOS provides direct access as well as sequential access to file data.

DATA FILE ORGANIZATION

Most data files store the file data in one of three fundamental file organizations: fixed-length record, stream, or variable-length record. The data in a **fixed-length record file** (often called a **structured file**) is organized into records, all of the same length. Each record is made up of a group of fixed-length fields (name, address, and social security number, for example) and stores all the needed data about one person or thing; the file, made up of a collection of records, stores all the data about a group of people or things. Many traditional high-level languages, such as COBOL and RPG, store data in fixed-length record files.

The data to be stored in one record is often of a different length than that to be stored in another record; the name Joe Doe, for example, is much shorter than the name Alexandrovitch Dimitropoulos. However, when stored in the file, the records must all be of the same length. The data in each field of each record is padded, usually with spaces, to make it the same length as the same field in all other records.

Fixed-length record or structured file organization provides two major advantages. First, it allows the data to be accessed in units that are logical to the solution of the particular problem. Each disk access reads or writes all the information about one person or thing; the next read or write accesses another complete person or thing. The other advantage is that fixed-length record organization allows both sequential and direct access by person or thing. The reading of relative record number ten, for example, provides access to all the data about the eleventh person or thing in the file. The program can directly modify the data for any one of the people or things stored in the file by reading the appropriate record, modifying it within the record buffer, and rewriting it to the same file location.

The major disadvantage of fixed-length record organization is that real-world data is not always so neatly structured. Text, for example, does not lend itself to fixed-length records. While this textbook may be well-organized, it is not the sort of organization that lends itself to storage as fixed-length records made up of fixed-length fields. Consequently, the word processor on which this text was written stores documents in **stream files** or **unstructured files** rather than fixed-length record files.

A stream or unstructured file consists of a continuous stream of characters that are not organized into logical records. Looked at from another perspective, the logical record length of a stream file is always one, since the file is accessed as individual characters rather than as fixed-length records. The data can be accessed either sequentially, one character after another, in order, from beginning to end, or it can be accessed directly. However, direct access to a stream file is by **relative character** number, rather than by relative record number. C and PASCAL are examples of modern high-level languages that provide stream-file data storage.

The advantage of stream-file data storage is that it is so free-form. No particular organization is imposed on the data by the operating system or compiler; the application program determines the structure (or lack thereof) of the data. If appropriate to the application, the program may access the data as a stream of individual characters with no particular organization. If the problem lends itself to fixed-length records, then the application program can impose such an organization by always reading or writing the same number of characters (one logical record) from or to the data stream. Either way, any structure or organization of the data is imposed by the application program, as appropriate to the particular application, rather than by the operating system or high-level language.

The major disadvantage of stream-file storage is that accessing the data as fixed-length records may require some extra complexity in the application program. Sequential access by fixed-length record is fairly straightforward; the programmer merely must be careful to specify the same number of characters (logical record length) for each read or write. However, if the application requires direct access by fixed-length records, the program is made more complex by the fact that stream-file organization provides direct access by relative character number rather than by relative record number. Prior to each direct access, the application program must calculate the necessary relative character number by multiplying the desired relative record number by the logical record length. Of course this extra complexity can be greatly reduced by including the calculation within a building block.

All versions of DOS provide a group of file-related functions (called **traditional functions**), which access files as fixed-length records. Since they do not provide for paths (discussed in the next chapter) and consequently do not support hard disks very well, they are seldom used by modern programmers. Another group of file-related functions (called **extended functions**) provide much better hard-disk support and so are much more commonly used. The extended functions (to be discussed in the next chapter) directly support only stream-file storage and access. The program can, however, derive both sequential and direct access by fixed-length records, as described in the previous paragraph.

A **variable-length record file** is a special type of stream file in which the data is organized into logical records of varying lengths. Some high-level languages (COBOL, for example) implement variable-length records by beginning each record with a byte or word specifying the length of the record. A more common scheme, when working in assembly language, is to delimit the records with a CR+LF sequence as a trailer.

Such a file is often called a **terminal-format file** and is similar to the sequential files supported by BASIC (and accessed with PRINT # and INPUT # statements). In a terminal-format file, the stream of characters is organized into records (often referred to as lines) by appending a CR+LF sequence (13, 10) to mark the end of each record. Additionally, an ASCII SUB (26) is usually used as a trailer, after the last record, to mark the end of the file.

To read from a terminal-format file, a program reads one character at a time from the stream, saving the characters into a buffer, until the CR+LF sequence or SUB is encountered. Once the CR+LF or SUB is encountered (end of record or end of file) the program returns the data that has been saved into the buffer (without the CR+LF or SUB) as the next record or line from the file. To write to a terminal-format file, the program writes the entire variable-length record (line) followed by the CR and LF characters. After writing the last record and before closing the file, the program writes a SUB (26) as an end-of-file trailer.

Such files are called terminal format because they are handled in much the same manner as a terminal (or console) made up of a keyboard and video screen. Data is stored into the file just as it would be transmitted to the screen of a terminal. Data is read from the file in much the same manner as data is input from the keyboard. The similarity is even more evident when the BASIC statements are compared: PRINT and INPUT for terminal access; PRINT # and INPUT # for terminal-format file access.

An advantage of terminal-format storage is that it permits variable-length records. It provides for the organization of the data into records without imposing any organization or structure on each record. Variable-length data does not have to be padded with spaces, and each record is completely free-form with no predetermined structure. Such a file lends itself extremely well to the storage of text; most text editors, such as EDLIN or the Turbo editor, store text in terminal-format files.

The major disadvantage of terminal-format file organization is that it does not permit direct access by record. Since the records are not of a fixed length, it is impossible to calculate the relative character number from a given relative record number. In order to find the beginning of the tenth record, for example, the program must read through the first nine records, counting the CR+LF end-of-record markers. Consequently, terminal-format files provide sequential access only.

KEY TERMS TO REMEMBER

Sequential access	Stream file
Direct access	Unstructured file
Random access	Relative character
Fixed-length record file	Variable-length record file
Structured file	Terminal-format file

NEW DISKETTE FORMATS

The IBM PC, PC/XT, and most compatibles use double-sided double-density (DSDD) 5¼-inch diskette drives, capable of storing up to 360 kilobytes. Our preceding discussion has concentrated on such drives. Other types of diskette drives have gained common usage in more recent machines. The IBM AT and some XT and AT compatibles use double-sided high-density (DSHD) 5¼-inch diskettes capable of storing 1.2 megabytes. The PS/2 and some XT and AT compatibles use 3½-inch diskettes, either quad density (DSQD, 720K) or high density (DSHD, 1.44MB). The number of tracks per side and sectors per track differs with each of the newer drive types. Figure 11-13 summarizes the more recent diskette formats.

Theoretically, it should be possible to use operation 02H, 03H, or 04H to read, write, or verify an entire track on a high-density diskette (more than nine sectors per track). However, many high-density drives are unable to maintain proper timing for more than nine sectors. Whenever reading, writing, or verifying an entire track on a high-density diskette, it is advisable to read or write the first nine sectors and then read or write the rest of the track.

Besides differing in the number of tracks per side, sectors per track, and capacities, the newer diskette formats also organize DOS's data structures slightly differently. Figure 11-14 summarizes the DOS organization of diskettes other than 5¼-inch double-density.

Figure 11-13   **Summary of Diskette Formats**

Disk size	Format	Capacity	Tracks per side	Sectors per track	Cluster size	1st byte of FAT
5¼	DSHD	1.2MB	80	15	1	F9H
3½	DSQD	720K	80	9	2	F9H
3½	DSHD	1.44MB	80	18	1	F0H

Figure 11-14   **Summary of Diskette Organizations Logical sectors occupied by FAT, directory, and data**

Disk size	Capacity	FAT #1	FAT #2	Root directory	Data area
5¼	1.2MB	1–7	8–14	15–28	29–2399
3½	720K	1–3	4–6	7–13	14–1439
3½	1.44MB	1–9	10–18	19–32	33–2879

Note: In all cases, logical sector 0 is the boot block

PC/ATs, PS/2s, and other machines that support diskettes other than double-density 5¼-inch provide an additional BIOS disk services operation:

08H - Get Drive Parameters

Operation 08H is valid for a hard disk drive on any system containing a hard disk. For floppy disk drives it is valid only on PC/ATs, PS/2s, and compatibles; it is not valid for floppy drives on the PC or PC/XT. To obtain the parameters of a disk drive:

```
Move 08H into AH.
Move the drive number into DL:
     00H — 7FH = floppy drive (PC/AT and PS/2 only —
                            00H = A, 01H = B, etc.);
     80H — FFH = hard disk (80H = 1st hard drive).
INT 13H.
```

If unsuccessful, BIOS sets the Carry flag and returns the status in AH. 01H (Unknown operation code) is returned if the operation is attempted on a PC or PC/XT floppy drive. Otherwise, BIOS returns the drive parameters as follows:

BL =   Drive type (valid only for floppy drive on PC/AT or PS/2):

01H = 5¼-inch, double-density (360K).

02H = 5¼-inch, high-density (1.2MB).

03H = 3½-inch, quad-density (720K).

04H = 3½-inch, high-density (1.44MB).

CL = Sectors; high bits of tracks − 1.

Bits 0–5 = number of sectors per track.

Bits 6–7 = high two bits of one less than number of tracks per side.

CH = Low eight bits of one less than number of tracks per side.

DH = One less than number of sides.

DL = Number of physical drives attached to the controller.

ES:[DI] = Segment:offset of disk-drive parameter table.

Note that operation 08H returns the parameters of a disk drive; it does not return the format of the diskette in a floppy drive. The diskette format must still be determined by examining the first byte of the FAT. However, operation 08H does enable us to distinguish between 5¼-inch high-density and 3½-inch quad-density diskettes, both of which contain F9H as the first byte of the FAT (see Figure 11-13). If operation 08H returns an error status of 01H or a successful status with a type of 01H or 02H, then the diskette is 5¼ inch; otherwise, it is a 3½-inch diskette and should be interpreted accordingly.

The preceding discussion suggests another building block that we should add to our library in order to provide easy access to BIOS disk services, operation 08H:

Get disk drive parameters:

```
GET_PRMS    MACRO DRV, TYPE, SIDES, TRAKS, SCTRS, NO_DRVS, STAT
```

DRV is a byte input parameter specifying the desired drive and should default to 0 (drive A). TYPE, SIDES, TRAKS, SCTRS, NO_DRVS, and STAT are all optional output parameters. TYPE is a byte parameter to receive the floppy drive type. SIDES, also a byte, receives the number of sides. TRAKS is a word to receive the ten-bit number of tracks per side. SCTRS is a byte parameter to receive the number of sectors per track. NO_DRVS, also a byte, returns the number of floppy drives. STAT is as described for the previous building blocks.

The procedure uses operation 08H to obtain the drive parameters. It should properly interpret the values returned in CX as the number of tracks per side and sectors per track. Whenever necessary, it should increment the returned parameters before returning them on the stack. In addition to any explicitly used registers, the procedure must save and restore both ES and DI since operation 08H alters them.

Figure 11-15 illustrates one use of the READ_SCTR and RESET_DISK building blocks. It reads the first sector of the FAT of a diskette and reports the first byte (format byte) in hexadecimal.

Figure 11-15   Example Program Using READ_SCTR and RESET_DISK Building Blocks

```
                    TITLE    F11-15.ASM
                    PAGE     55, 80

COMMENT  |          PROGRAM:        F11-15.ASM
                    PROGRAMMER:     Your name here
                    DATE:           Date here
                    CLASS:          Class name and number here
                    INSTRUCTOR:     Instructor's name here
            REPORTS THE FORMAT (FIRST BYTE OF FAT) OF A DISKETTE

            USES INPUT_STR, CNV_STR_UNS, CNV_UNS_STR, DSPLY_STR,
            READ_SCTR, AND RESET_DISK BUILDING BLOCKS

            INPUT PARAM'S:  NONE
            OUTPUT PARAM'S: NONE
                            RETURNS TO DOS, UPON COMPLETION
            |

                    IF1
                        INCLUDE CONSOLE.MLB
                        INCLUDE DISK.MLB
                    ENDIF

;STACK SEGMENT ================================================================

STACK               SEGMENT PARA STACK 'STACK'        ;BEGIN STACK
                                                      ;  SEGMENT

                    DB      64 DUP ('*STACK* ')       ;DEFINE 512
                                                      ;  BYTE STACK

STACK               ENDS                              ;END OF STACK SEGMENT

;DATA SEGMENT =================================================================

DATA                SEGMENT PARA PUBLIC 'DATA'        ;BEGIN DATA
                                                      ;  SEGMENT
                ;DEFINE BUFFERS AND ERROR MESSAGES
IO_BUF              DB      5 DUP('*')
D_BUF               DB      512 DUP('#')   ;BUFFER FOR 1 SECTOR
PRMPT_MSG           DB      'Floppy drive number (0 - 127)? ', 0
INV_DRV             DB      7, 'Invalid drive - Try again'
                    DB      13, 10, 10, 0
READ_ERR            DB      13, 10, 7, 'Unable to read FAT - '
                    DB      'Status: ', 0
FMT_MSG             DB      13, 10, 'Diskette format '
                    DB      '(1st byte of FAT): ', 0
HEX_MSG             DB      'H', 13, 10, 10, 0
```

Figure 11-15 (continued)

```
DATA            ENDS                              ;END OF DATA SEGMENT

;CODE SEGMENT ===================================================================

CODE            SEGMENT PARA PUBLIC 'CODE'        ;BEGIN CODE
                                                  ;  SEGMENT

                ASSUME   CS:CODE, SS:STACK        ;ASSOCIATE CS AND SS
                                                  ;  WITH PROPER SEGMENTS

MAIN            PROC    FAR                        ;BEGIN MAINLINE
                                                  ;  FAR PROCEDURE

        ;INITIALIZATION (SAME FOR ALL PROGRAMS)
        ;FIRST, SET UP FOR RETURN TO DOS VIA PSP
                PUSH     DS                        ;PUT RETURN SEG (PSP)
                                                  ;  TO STACK
                MOV      AX, 0                     ;PUT ZERO RETURN
                PUSH     AX                        ;  OFFSET TO STACK
        ;NOW, ADDRESS THE DATA SEGMENT WITH DS
                MOV      AX, DATA                  ;POINT DS TO
                MOV      DS, AX                    ;  DATA SEGMENT
                ASSUME   DS:DATA                   ;ASSOCIATE DS WITH
                                                  ;  DATA SEGMENT


        ;BEGIN MAINLINE CODE
                CLS                                ;CLEAR SCREEN
                LOCATE                             ;GO TO U-L CORNER
        ;GET VALID FLOPPY DRIVE NUMBER
LP1_BEG:        ;BEGIN GENERAL LOOP (QUIT WHEN DRIVE IS VALID)
                DSPLY_STR       <OFFSET PRMPT_MSG>
                                                  ;PROMPT USER
                INPUT_STR       <OFFSET IO_BUF>, 3
                                                  ;GET DRIVE #
                CNV_STR_UNS     <OFFSET IO_BUF>, BX
                                                  ;CONVERT TO NUMERIC
                JC       LP1_CNT                   ;CONTINUE LOOP IF INPUT
                                                  ;  IS NOT NUMERIC
                CMP      BX, 80H                   ;QUIT LOOP WHEN VALID
                JB       LP1_END                   ;  FLOPPY DRIVE
LP1_CNT:        DSPLY_STR       <OFFSET INV_DRV>
                                                  ;DISPLAY ERROR MESSAGE
                JMP      LP1_BEG                   ;CONTINUE LOOP
LP1_END:       ;END GENERAL LOOP (AL IS VALID FLOPPY DRIVE)
        ;READ 1ST SECTOR OF FAT (SIDE 0, TRACK 0, SECTOR 2).
        ;  TRY FOUR TIMES IF NECESSARY.
                MOV      CX, 4                     ;MAX TRIES
```

Figure 11-15   (continued)

```
        LP2_BEG:            ;REPEAT UNTIL SUCCESSFUL (UP TO 4 TRIES)
                        READ_SCTR          BL,0,0,2,1,<OFFSET D_BUF>,AL
                                                    ;READ 1ST FAT SECTOR
                    JNC     LP2_END                 ;QUIT LOOP WHEN
                                                    ;   READ IS SUCCESSFUL
                        RESET_DISK         BL       ;RESET DISK
                        LOOP    LP2_BEG             ;CONTINUE LOOP
        LP2_END:            ;END REPEAT (SUCCESSFUL, OR 4 TRIES)
        IF_BEG:             ;IF SUCCESSFUL, REPORT FORMAT, ELSE REPORT ERROR
                    CMP     AL, 0                   ;AL (STATUS) IS 0
                    JNE     UNS                     ;   IF SUCCESSFUL
                        MOV     AL, D_BUF           ;FIRST BYTE OF FAT
                        MOV     AH, 0               ;   INTO AX
                        CNV_UNS_STR        <OFFSET IO_BUF>, AX, 16
                                                    ;CONVERT TO HEX
                        DSPLY_STR          <OFFSET FMT_MSG>
                                                    ;DISPLAY LABEL
                        DSPLY_STR          <OFFSET IO_BUF>
                                                    ;DISPLAY FORMAT
                        DSPLY_STR          <OFFSET HEX_MSG>
                                                    ;'H' CR LF LF
                        JMP     IF_END
        UNS:                ;ELSE (UNSUCCESSFUL)
                        DSPLY_STR          <OFFSET READ_ERR>
                                                    ;ERROR MESSAGE
                        MOV     AH, 0               ;MAKE AX = STATUS
                        CNV_UNS_STR        <OFFSET IO_BUF>, AX, 16
                                                    ;CONVERT TO HEX STRING
                        DSPLY_STR          <OFFSET IO_BUF>
                                                    ;DISPLAY IT
                        DSPLY_STR          <OFFSET HEX_MSG>
                                                    ;'H' CR LF LF
        IF_END:             ;END IF

                    ;END OF MAINLINE
                        RET                         ;RETURN

        MAIN            ENDP

        CODE            ENDS                        ;END OF CODE SEGMENT

                        END     MAIN                ;END OF F11-15.ASM
                                                    ;   ENTRY POINT = MAIN
```

HARD DISKS

Many (if not most) modern systems contain one or more hard disk drives in addition to floppy drives. A system that contains one or more hard disks is capable of returning a number of error codes in addition to those listed previously in Figure 11-4. Figure 11-16 lists the additional BIOS disk service error codes supported by hard disk machines.

In order to better allow for large hard disks and to decrease the necessary cluster size, DOS version four expands the number of possible logical clusters by varying the size of FAT entries. On large hard disks, each FAT entry may be sixteen-bits (two-bytes) long rather than twelve bits. FORMAT.COM specifies the disk's FAT entry size at offset 36H of the boot block (side zero, track zero, sector one). The FAT entry size specification is an eight-byte string of the form "FATxx ", where xx is the number of bits in each FAT entry, currently either 12 or 16.

In addition to the FAT entry size, version four FORMAT and DISKCOPY also place a four-byte randomly generated serial number at offset 27H within the boot block (low word at 27H, high word at 29H). The disk serial number as displayed by DOS is merely the hexadecimal representation of the binary serial number. Since it is relatively unique, the serial number can be used to provide a simple copy-protection scheme. A copy-protected program merely reads the boot block and checks the serial number against that of the original system disk. If different, the program refuses to execute.

Figure 11-16   **BIOS Disk Services Hard Disk Error Codes**

05H	= Hard disk controller reset failed.
07H	= Bad parameter table.
0AH	= Bad sector flag.
0BH	= Bad track flag.
0CH	= Media type not found.
0DH	= Invalid number of sectors on format.
0EH	= Control-data address mark detected.
0FH	= DMA arbitration level out of range.
11H	= ECC-corrected data error.
AAH	= Drive not ready.
BBH	= Undefined error.
CCH	= Write fault.
E0H	= Status-register error.
FFH	= Sense operation failed.

SUMMARY

In this chapter, we have learned that data is stored on magnetic disk by magnetizing spots on the disk surface in either of two directions. One direction represents a zero, and the other direction represents one; thus, each magnetized spot records a single bit on the disk. The bits are recorded on the disk in circles, called tracks; a 5¼-inch double-density diskette surface contains forty tracks, numbered zero through thirty-nine. Each track is divided into nine (or eight) sectors of 512 bytes each, numbered from one through nine (or eight). Tracks are organized into cylinders; a cylinder is a collection of all the tracks that can be accessed with a single setting of the read/write heads. The number of tracks in a cylinder is equal to the number of disk surfaces (two for a double-sided diskette).

BIOS disk services, accessed through interrupt type 13H, provide non-file-structured disk access. The program must provide BIOS with the exact physical location on the disk from which to read or to which to write; the location is specified as drive, side, track, and sector. You can write a number of building blocks that use the BIOS disk service operations to provide easy non-file-structured disk access. Care must be taken when accessing a disk through BIOS; it is very easy to overwrite a DOS allocation structure, resulting in the loss of access to all data on the disk.

In order to provide file-structured disk access, DOS maintains two data structures on the disk, immediately following the one-sector boot block. The File Allocation Table (FAT) consists of a series of twelve-bit entries (sixteen bits for large hard disks formatted under DOS version four), one for each logical cluster of the data area of the disk. The first two FAT entries contain information about the format of the disk. The remaining entries (number two on) are used by DOS to form a linked list (called an allocation chain) of the clusters that are allocated to each disk file; each entry contains the logical cluster number (and FAT entry number) of the next cluster allocated to the file. A value of 000H in a FAT entry indicates that the corresponding cluster is unallocated; FF8H through FFFH indicate that the entry is the last cluster of a file, the end of the linked-list allocation chain; FF0H through FF7H, if not part of an allocation chain, indicate a bad cluster that is not to be used for data storage.

The disk directory consists of a series of thirty-two-byte entries, one for each disk file. The first byte of each entry determines its status. A value of 00H indicates that the entry has never been used; since the entries are used in order, there are no more files on the disk. E5H indicates that the entry was once used, but the file has been deleted. Any other value indicates that the entry represents an active file with the name and extension stored in bytes zero through ten. Besides the filename and extension, the directory entry also contains an Attribute byte, a reserved area for use by DOS, the date and time the file was last modified, the size of the file in bytes, and the starting cluster number, which serves as the entry point into the linked-list allocation chain in the FAT.

The data area of the disk, immediately following the root directory, is used to store all file data. It is mapped by the FAT; each FAT entry represents one logical cluster of the data area. Since FAT entry number two is the first to map the data area, the first cluster of the data area is assigned logical cluster number two. The format of the disk determines where the data area begins. On a double-sided nine-sector-per-track diskette, the data area begins in logical sector number twelve (side one/track zero/sector four).

DOS uses the directory and FAT to provide a number of services necessary for file-structured disk access. The necessary services include those for file management (Directory search, Create file, Rename file, Delete file) and for access to file data (Open file, Read logical record, Write logical record, Close file).

Whether working in assembly language or a high-level language, data files are normally accessed in one of two methods: sequentially or directly. Sequential access involves accessing the file data in order from beginning to end. In order to update data sequentially, a program must copy the entire file to a new file. Direct access allows the processing of data in any order; on each disk access, the program specifies the relative record number of the desired record, which can be anywhere within the file. A program can directly modify file data by reading the desired record, modifying it in the record buffer, and rewriting it back to the same location from which it was read.

There are three common data file organizations: fixed-length record (structured), stream (unstructured), and variable-length record or terminal format. A fixed-length record (structured) file consists of a collection of records, all of the same length and made up of the same fixed-length fields. Many problems, especially business applications, lend themselves to fixed-length record processing.

In some applications, however, the data is more free-form and is not easily structured into fixed-length units; stream files or unstructured files can better satisfy such an application. A stream file has no organization; it is simply a stream of individual characters with no predetermined structure. A terminal-format file is a stream file in which the data is organized into variable-length records by storing a CR+LF sequence at the end of each record; an ASCII SUB (26) is usually appended to the file, after the last record, as an end-of-file trailer. The sequential files created by BASIC are terminal-format files.

In the following chapter, we will discuss the extended file functions by which an application program gains access to data files.

VOCABULARY

V11-1 In your own words, define each of the following terms related to magnetic disk storage:

a) Electromagnetism

b) Permanent magnetism

c) Magnetic induction

d) Read/write head

e) Track

f) Sector

g) Cylinder

h) Non-file-structured disk access

i) DMA

V11-2   In your own words, define each of the following terms related to DOS's file-allocation structures:

a) Cluster

b) Cluster size

c) File-structured disk access

d) Dynamic disk allocation

e) Boot record

f) FAT

g) File directory

h) Data area

i) Linked list

j) Allocation chain

k) Logical sector

l) Logical cluster

V11-3   In your own words, define each of the following terms related to DOS's file-structured disk services:

a) Relative sector

b) Physical record

c) File buffer

d) Physical read, physical write

e) Logical record

f) Relative record

g) Record buffer

h) Logical read, logical write

i) File fragmentation

j) Contiguous

V11-4   In your own words, define each of the following terms related to file-access methods and file organizations.

a) Sequential access

b) Direct (random) access

c) Fixed-length record file

d) Stream file

e) Relative character

f) Variable-length record file

g) Terminal-format file

REVIEW QUESTIONS

Q11-1   Why are hard disks used in IBM-compatible PCs often called "fixed" disks?

Q11-2   How does BIOS's numbering of sectors within a track differ from its numbering of drives, sides, and tracks?

Q11-3   BIOS disk operations all require the operation code to be in which register? Which register do they use for the return status?

Q11-4   If a program performs BIOS disk operation 01H twice in a row, what would you expect to be returned in AL?

Q11-5   On a BIOS disk read (operation 02H), is it possible to have the processor examine the disk data before storing it into memory? Why?

Q11-6   Why is it not possible to write only eighty bytes of data to disk?

Q11-7   If a 5¼-inch double-density diskette has been formatted with DOS version two with no special switches, how many total sectors does it contain? How many sectors of data area? How many bytes of data area?

Q11-8   How many bytes are used by DOS for each directory entry? How does DOS know when to terminate a directory search?

Q11-9   Why is a volume label limited to eleven characters?

Q11-10   What is the purpose of the Starting-Cluster field in a directory entry?

Q11-11   When using DOS version one, what is the maximum number of files that may be stored on a double-sided diskette? Why? What about DOS version two (and above)?

Q11-12   How many subdirectories can a disk (or diskette) have?

Q11-13   How large is each entry in the File Allocation Table? What value is used to indicate that a logical sector is unused?

Q11-14   If a FAT were three sectors long, what is the maximum number of logical clusters that it could be used to map?

Q11-15   How many logical clusters are immediately allocated to a file when DOS first creates it?

Q11-16   On a double-sided, nine-sector-per-track diskette, how many bytes of data are mapped by each FAT entry?

Q11-17   Explain the difference between a logical record and a physical record.

Q11-18   Explain the difference between a logical read or write and a physical read or write.

Q11-19   Explain the difference between a record buffer and a file buffer.

Q11-20   How many bytes long is a physical record? How many bytes are contained in a logical record?

Q11-21   Where is the file buffer located, within DOS or within the application program? What about the record buffer?

Q11-22   Does a logical read always result in a physical read? Can it ever result in a physical read? Does a logical read ever result in a physical write? Explain your answers.

Q11-23   Does a logical write always result in a physical write? Can it ever result in a physical write? Does a logical write ever result in a physical read? Explain your answers.

Q11-24   Explain the statement, "Disk fragmentation is the price we pay for dynamic disk allocation."

PROGRAMMING ASSIGNMENTS

PA11-1   Create a new library (DISK.MLB and DISK.LIB) for disk storage and add two building blocks: RESET_DISK and READ_SCTR. Then write a mainline program, PA11-1.ASM, which reads and displays (in hexadecimal) the hard-disk or floppy-diskette sector specified by the user.

Ask the user for the drive, side, track, and sector to display. Read the sector and check if successful. Reset the disk and try the read three more times, if necessary. If unsuccessful after four tries, display an error message with the bad status. Otherwise, display the value in hexadecimal of each of the 512 bytes in the sector. To test your program, display a sector with <Ctrl>+<PrtSc> on for a hard copy. Then use DEBUG TO Load and then Dump the same sector; compare the results.

Remember that DEBUG's Load command requires the logical sector number; you will have to calculate it by hand:

```
Multiply the track number by the number of sides on the diskette.
Add the side.
Multiply the result by the number of sectors per track.
Add the sector number.
Subtract one.
```

PA11-2   If you have not already done so, create a disk-storage library (DISK.MLB and DISK.LIB) and add three building blocks: RESET_DISK, READ_SCTR, and GET_PRMS. Then write a program, PA11-2.ASM, which reports the parameters of a hard disk or floppy diskette. Ask the user for the drive number. If it is a hard disk (greater than 7FH), use GET_PRMS (leave TYPE blank) to get the drive parameters.

If it is a floppy drive (less than 80H), read the first sector of the FAT; reset the disk and try three more times if necessary. If still unsuccessful after four tries, display an error message with the bad status. Otherwise, examine the first byte to determine the format of the diskette in the drive; if necessary, use GET_PRMS (TYPE only) to determine if it is a 5¼-inch or 3½-inch diskette. Report the following disk or diskette information to the user:

```
Hard drive or floppy diskette.
The number of sides.
The number of tracks per side.
The number of sectors per track.
Total disk or diskette capacity in kilobytes (sides * tracks *
                                            sectors / 2).
```

PA11-3   Do PA11-1, and add another building block to your disk library: GET_PRMS. Then modify PA11-1.ASM to create PA11-3.ASM, which asks the user for the logical sector number instead of side, track, and sector. The program should then determine the disk or diskette parameters (sides, tracks per side, and sectors per track), as in PA11-2 above, and use the parameters to calculate the physical location of the sector (see Figure 11-10). Other than calculating the side, track, and sector from the logical sector number, PA11-2 should be identical to PA11-1.

PA11-4   If you have not already done so, create a disk-storage library (DISK.MLB and DISK.LIB) and add four building blocks: RESET_DISK, READ_SCTR, WRITE_SCTR, and GET_PRMS. Then write a program, PA11-4.ASM, which makes a sector-by-sector copy of a floppy diskette (similar to DISKCOPY). Ask the user for the source and destination drives; do not allow drive numbers greater than 7FH. Read the FAT from the source and destination diskettes and examine the first byte of each to determine the formats of the diskettes; if necessary, use GET_PRMS to distinguish between 5¼-inch and 3½-inch diskettes. If the source and destination diskette formats are different, report an error and terminate the program.

Otherwise, copy all sectors from the source diskette to the target diskette. Whenever reading or writing, reset the disk and try three more times before reporting any error. Your program will be faster if you read and write an entire track at a time, but you may copy one sector at a time if you wish. In either case, don't expect it to be as fast as DISKCOPY; DISKCOPY uses all available memory to read and write as many tracks as possible at one time. To check your program, use DISKCOMP to compare the two diskettes.

Note: This program requires a system with two 5¼-inch or two 3½-inch floppy diskette drives.

PA11-5   If you have not already done so, create a disk-storage library (DISK.MLB and DISK.LIB) and add three building blocks: RESET_DISK, READ_SCTR, and GET_PRMS. Then write a program, PA11-5.ASM, which reports how many sectors are either bad or are currently used for file data on a diskette.

Ask the user for the diskette drive number; ensure that it is less than 80H. Read the first sector of the FAT, look at the first byte to determine the diskette's format, and read the rest of the FAT, if necessary. Then go through the FAT, entry by entry (skip the first two entries), counting the number of entries that are not 000H. Multiply the number of allocated clusters by the cluster size, and report to the user the number of sectors that are bad or allocated.

Whenever reading any sector, reset the disk and try three more times, if necessary, before reporting any error. To check your program, run CHKDSK on the same diskette and note the number of bytes in bad sectors and system and user files. Divide by 512 to convert bytes to sectors. The result should agree with what your program reported.

PA11-6   If you have not already done so, create a disk-storage library (DISK.MLB and DISK.LIB) and add three building blocks: RESET_DISK, READ_SCTR, and GET_PRMS. Then write your own diskette directory program; call it PA11-6.ASM. Ask the user for the drive number, ensuring that it is less than 80H. Examine the first byte of the FAT to determine the location and size of the directory; use GET_PRMS if necessary to determine the diskette size (5¼-inch or 3½-inch).

Read the entire directory into memory; make sure the buffer is big enough to hold it. Then go through the directory examining each thirty-two-byte entry. If the first byte is 00H, then stop; if it is E5H, then ignore it; otherwise, display the filename. Following the filename, indicate any Attribute-byte bits that are set as: R (read only), H (hidden), S (system), V (volume label), D (subdirectory), and/or A (archive).

Whenever reading any sector, reset the disk, and try three more times, if necessary, before reporting any error.

PA11-7   If you have not already done so, create a disk-storage library (DISK.MLB and DISK.LIB) and add three building blocks: RESET_DISK, READ_SCTR, and GET_PRMS. Then write a program, PA11-7.ASM, which reports which clusters are used by a specified file on a diskette. Get the drive number (less than 80H), primary filename, and file extension from the user. Examine the first byte of the FAT (use GET_PRMS to determine the diskette size if necessary), and determine the location and size of the directory.

Read the directory into memory, and search for the specified file. Report an error if it is not found. Otherwise, obtain the starting cluster number from the directory entry and proceed through the allocation chain reporting the logical cluster number of each cluster used. Remember to report the starting cluster number. Whenever reading any sector, reset the disk, and try three more times, if necessary, before reporting any error.

PA11-8   If you have not already done so, create a disk-storage library (DISK.MLB and DISK.LIB) and add three building blocks: RESET_DISK, READ_SCTR, VERIFY_SCTR, and GET_PRMS. Then write a program, PA11-9.ASM, which verifies the integrity of a hard disk or floppy diskette. Ask the user for the drive to verify. If it is a hard disk (greater than 7FH), use GET_PRMS to determine the number of sides, tracks, and sectors.

If it is a floppy drive (less than 80H), read the FAT from the diskette and examine the first byte to determine the format of the diskette; if necessary, use GET_PRMS to distinguish between 5¼-inch and 3½-inch diskettes.

Once the format has been determined, proceed through the disk verifying all sectors. Reset the disk and repeat each verify three more times if necessary. If the verify fails after four tries, report the bad sector (side, track, and sector). Count and display the total number of bad sectors.

12

File-Structured Disk Access through DOS

INTRODUCTION

In the last chapter, we discussed the allocation structures (disk directory and File Allocation Table) that DOS maintains, as well as the manner in which DOS uses those structures to provide file-structured disk access. In this chapter, we will discuss the manner in which a program accesses data files through DOS.

First we will discuss the STRUC directive, which is very useful for defining, allocating, and addressing fixed-length data structures such as the directory-search buffer (to be discussed later). We will then discuss several more topics directly related to file access: subdirectories and paths, ASCIIZ strings (used to specify filenames and/or paths), file handles (for referencing open files), the file pointer (used by DOS to determine the current position in an open file), and the error codes returned by file-related function calls.

Finally, we will discuss the file-related DOS function calls and the building blocks we should develop to provide easy access to data files. We will learn that all file access is through the DOS function call (interrupt type 21H) and that DOS provides two distinct groups of file-related functions: the traditional functions (provided by all versions) and the extended functions (introduced with DOS version two). Our discussion will concentrate on the extended functions.

We will also see that the file-structured disk-access functions may be divided into four major groups: general file-related functions, directory-management functions, file-management functions, and file-access functions.

Recall from the last chapter that DOS uses the disk directory and File Allocation Table to keep track of the physical location of file data, and that application programs access the data by logical record rather than by physical record. DOS maintains a file buffer and performs a physical read or write, only when necessary, to transfer data between the disk and the file buffer. The program must define and maintain a record buffer for the receipt and preparation of logical records. Each logical read or write results in the transfer of data between the record buffer and the file buffer; a logical disk access does not necessarily result in a physical disk access.

THE STRUC DIRECTIVE

DOS directory-search functions, to be discussed later, require the allocation and addressing of a **fixed-length data structure** (directory-search buffer). A fixed-length data structure is an area of memory of a predetermined length and organized into fields, each of a fixed length. Actually, we have been working with simple fixed-length data structures throughout this text. Byte and word are very simple data structures, which are defined by the hardware and consist of eight and sixteen bits, respectively. Double-word (DWORD), quad-word (QWORD), and ten-byte (TBYTE) are all simple data structures that are predefined by the assembler.

The assembler also provides two directives, **STRUC** and **ENDS**, which allow for complex programmer-defined data structures. STRUC is used to inform the assembler of the beginning of a data-structure definition. The syntax is as follows:

```
Symbol     STRUC
```

Symbol becomes the name of the data structure to be defined. The STRUC directive is in many ways similar to the MACRO directive. Recall that instructions following a macro directive do not result in the allocation of memory or assembly of the instructions; rather, they result only in the definition of the macro. Memory is allocated and instructions are assembled only when the macro is invoked later in the program. Similarly, any names and data definition directives (DB, DW, etc.) following the STRUC directive do not result in the immediate allocation of memory or the definition of variables. Instead, they result in a data-structure definition with the name *symbol*.

The sum of all the define-data directives determines the length of the data structure. Any symbol in the name field of a define-data directive becomes the name of a **structure field** rather than a variable name. Thus, through the use of define-data directives and symbols within the name fields, the programmer is able to define the data structure and its fields. The ENDS directive is used to end the structure definition, much as ENDM marks the end of a macro definition. The syntax for ENDS is as follows:

```
Symbol     ENDS
```

Symbol is the name of the data structure, the symbol that was defined in the name field of the STRUC directive. Note that the directive, ENDS, may signify either the end of a data-structure definition or the end of a segment, depending on its usage. If *symbol* has been defined by a SEGMENT directive, then ENDS is interpreted by the assembler as the end of that segment; if *symbol* was defined by a STRUC directive, then ENDS is interpreted as the end of that data-structure definition. Following is a very simple data-structure definition:

```
TEST_STRUCT     STRUC

FLD_1           DB      0
FLD_2           DW      ?
FLD_3           DW      5, ?
FLD_4           DB      3 DUP (?)
FLD_5           DB      'AAAA'


TEST_STRUCT     ENDS
```

Remember that the above data-structure definition does not allocate any memory or define any variables. It does define TEST_STRUCT as a fourteen-byte data structure. It also defines the type and displacement, from the beginning of the data structure, of each of the five fields: FLD_1 (type = BYTE, displacement = zero), FLD_2 (type = WORD, displacement = one), FLD_3 (type = WORD, displacement = three), FLD_4 (type = BYTE, displacement = seven), and FLD_5 (type = BYTE, displacement = ten). The following two lines of code might be placed in the data segment, after the above structure definition, to allocate two such data structures:

```
VBL_1           TEST_STRUCT     <>
VBL_2           TEST_STRUCT     <>
```

Notice that, to allocate a previously defined data structure, the structure name is placed in the action field, with a variable name in the name field; the double angle brackets in the expression field are used to indicate to the assembler that there are no field override values, to be discussed shortly. Given our previous definition of TEST_STRUCT, the above two lines of code have an effect similar to the following:

```
VBL_1
VBL_1.FLD_1     DB      0
VBL_1.FLD_2     DW      ?
VBL_1.FLD_3     DW      5, ?
VBL_1.FLD_4     DB      3 DUP (?)
VBL_1.FLD_5     DB      'AAAA'

VBL_2
VBL_2.FLD_1     DB      0
```

```
VBL_2.FLD_2     DW     ?
VBL_2.FLD_3     DW     5, ?
VBL_2.FLD_4     DB     3 DUP (?)
VBL_2.FLD_5     DB     'AAAA'
```

A total of twenty-eight bytes are allocated with initial values as specified in the data-structure definition, and the variables, VBL_1 and VBL_2, are defined as **structure variables**. Not only are VBL_1 and VBL_2 addressable, but each field within each structure variable is also individually addressable as the structure-variable name and field name, separated by a period (.). For example, all of the following instructions are now possible:

```
MOV     VBL_1.FLD_2, 65535
ADD     AL, VBL_2.FLD_1
SUB     VBL_1.FLD_3, AX
INC     VBL_1.FLD_3+2
MOV     BX, OFFSET VBL_2
MOV     [BX].FLD_4, 'A'
```

Assuming that VBL_1 has been defined at offset ten, then VBL_2 is defined at offset twenty-four (VBL_1 occupies fourteen bytes). During assembly, each memory-mode operand in the above instructions is converted to the offset of the structure variable plus the displacement of the structure field, with the type determined by the type of the field. Thus the above instructions would be assembled as follows:

```
MOV  VBL_1.FLD_2, 65535    =>    MOV   WORD PTR [11], 65535
ADD  AL, VBL_2.FLD_1       =>    ADD   AL, BYTE PTR [24]
SUB  VBL_1.FLD_3, AX       =>    SUB   WORD PTR [13], AX
INC  VBL_1.FLD_3+2         =>    INC   WORD PTR [15]
MOV  BX, OFFSET VBL_2      =>    MOV   BX, 24
MOV  [BX].FLD_4, 'A'       =>    MOV   BYTE PTR [BX+7], 'A'
```

When allocating a data structure and defining the structure variable, the program may specify **field-override values** to override the initial field values specified in the data-structure definition. For example, VBL_3 might be allocated as a structure variable as follows:

```
VBL_3           TEST_STRUCT     <20, 30, , ,'XXXX'>
```

The above line allocates the fourteen-byte data structure, defines VBL_3 as the structure variable, and overrides the initial values of FLD1, FLD_2, and FLD_5. The resulting structure allocation is similar to the following:

```
VBL_3
VBL_3.FLD_1     DB     20
VBL_3.FLD_2     DW     30
```

```
VBL_3.FLD_3    DW    5, ?
VBL_3.FLD_4    DB    3 DUP (?)
VBL_3.FLD_5    DB    'XXXX'
```

Not only were FLD_3 and FLD_4 not overridden in the above data-structure allocation, but they cannot be overriden. FLD_3 is a multiword field consisting of two words, and FLD_4 is a multibyte field, consisting of three bytes. With one exception, a field consisting of multiple values cannot be overridden. The single exception is a multibyte field defined as a string, as in FLD_5; such a string field may be overridden by a string value. If the override string is shorter than the field string, it is padded with spaces on the right to fill the field; if the override string is longer than the field, it is truncated on the right to fit the field.

KEY TERMS TO REMEMBER

Fixed-length data structure	Structure variable
STRUC and ENDS directives	Field-override value
Structure field	

SUBDIRECTORIES AND PATHS

Version one DOS utilized a simple directory structure in which a diskette contains a single **root directory** with room for either 64 (single-sided diskette) or 112 (double-sided diskette) 32-byte directory entries, one for each file on the disk. Such a simple structure is sufficient for diskettes, but is unsatisfactory for hard disks, which often may need to contain thousands of files. Besides the need for more than 112 directory entries, hard disks present a need for the ability to logically organize data into groups of related files.

Version two and later versions of DOS satisfy the need for an unlimited number of files as well as the need to logically organize the files by providing the capability of dividing the disk (either hard disk or floppy diskette) into subdirectories. Recall from the last chapter that byte number eleven of each root-directory entry is the Attribute byte for the file. Bit four of the Attribute byte, if set, indicates that the entry is for a **subdirectory file**; the file is used to store additional directory entries, rather than data. Thus, in addition to entries for data files, the root directory may also contain entries for special directory files. Directory files are created with the DOS MKDIR (or MD) command or through function call 39H, discussed later, and may be deleted with the RMDIR (or RD) command or through function 3AH.

A subdirectory file consists of a series of 32-byte directory entries, one for each file within that directory. Each directory entry in the subdirectory file is identical to the entries in the root directory, as discussed in the last chapter. Since the subdirectory is a file, it can be any size and, consequently, can contain as many entries as desired. Thus, the root directory does not have to contain entries for all files on the disk; the disk may contain files whose directory entries are stored in directory files, rather than in the root directory.

To access such a file, within a subdirectory rather than the root directory, DOS looks first in the root directory for the entry for the subdirectory file. Using the Starting-Cluster field as an entry point into the FAT, DOS locates the directory-file data and searches through it for the directory entry of the desired data file. The Starting-Cluster field of that entry, within the directory file, then provides DOS with an entry point into the FAT for the allocation chain of the data file. That allocation chain is then used for all subsequent access to the file. Of course DOS must first know the name of the directory file as well as the data-file name in order to perform such a search.

Since each entry in a directory file is identical to the entries in the root directory, one or more of those entries may be for other directories, rather than for data files; a subdirectory may contain one or more subdirectories, which may, in turn, contain additional subdirectories. Other than total disk capacity (each directory file occupies at least one cluster of disk space), there is no limit to the number of directories a disk may contain or to the depth to which directories may be nested. Figure 12-1 illustrates the manner in which a student might use subdirectories to organize his or her disk.

Figure 12-1   Sample Directory Structure

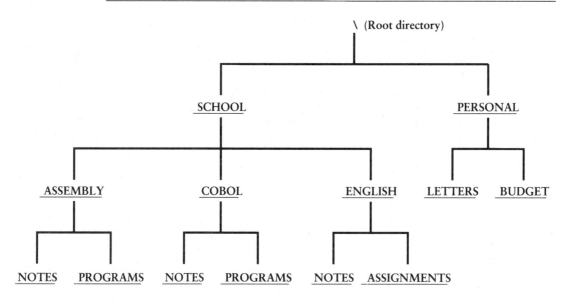

Figure 12-1 illustrates only the directory structure, sometimes called a **directory tree**; each directory file might contain one or more data-file entries in addition to the indicated directory-file entries. In the example, the root directory contains two directory-file entries, SCHOOL and PERSONAL. Each directory file contains an entry for each directory file that is immediately subordinate to it. The directory to which a subdirectory file belongs (the directory that contains the directory entry for that directory file) is often referred to as its **parent directory**. For example, ASSEMBLY's parent directory is SCHOOL, and SCHOOL's parent is the root directory.

DOS maintains a **default directory** for each disk in the system. The default directory is the directory file within which DOS will search for files, when no directory has been specified. The idea is similar to the default drive, maintained by DOS, except that a separate default directory is maintained independently for each drive. Upon booting, the default directory of each drive is its root directory, but a disk's default directory may subsequently be changed to any desired directory file, with the CHDIR (or CD) command or through function 3BH.

Any file specification, for a file that is not in the default directory, must always include a **directory path** to the file. The path lists all directory files, in order and separated by back slashes (\), through which DOS must search in order to find the entry for the desired data file. If the data file is in a directory subordinate to the current default directory, then the path may begin within the default directory. Otherwise, the path must begin within the root directory. In either case, the path must end with the directory file that contains the entry for the data file.

For example, suppose that the NOTES directory whose parent is ASSEMBLY, in Figure 12-1, contains a file called WEEK1.TXT. Suppose also that the current default directory is the root directory. Then the following command with path and filename might be used to view the file on the screen:

```
TYPE SCHOOL\ASSEMBLY\NOTES\WEEK1.TXT
```

The above path tells DOS to look in the default directory for an entry for a directory file called SCHOOL; then to look in SCHOOL for an entry for the directory file ASSEMBLY; then to look in ASSEMBLY for another directory file called NOTES; and, finally, to look within NOTES for the entry of the data file WEEK1.TXT. Another way to access the data file, WEEK1.TXT, is to first change the default directory to the directory within which it is stored. After changing the default directory, we may access the file, WEEK1.TXT, without specifying any path. Thus, the following two commands might be used to display the file:

```
CD    SCHOOL\ASSEMBLY\NOTES
TYPE  WEEK1.TXT
```

Notice that the CD command specifies only the path, without a filename. Note also that NOTES is now the new default directory. Suppose that we now wish to see a file, called PA12-1.ASM, in the PROGRAMS subdirectory whose parent is ASSEMBLY. Since PROGRAMS is not in the current default directory, we must specify a path to the file. However, PROGRAMS is not subordinate to the current default directory (NOTES); consequently, the path may not begin within the default directory and so must begin within the root directory. Such a path must begin with a back slash, to tell DOS to begin searching in the root directory rather than in the default directory, and must specify the entire path from the root directory to the file. The following path and filename would then be used to specify the file to the TYPE command:

```
TYPE \SCHOOL\ASSEMBLY\PROGRAMS\PA12-1.ASM
```

Note that the first character of the path is a back slash, specifying that it begins within the root directory rather than within the current default directory. A path consisting of only a back slash specifies the root directory itself. For example, the following command changes the default directory back to the root directory:

```
CD \
```

Remember that all paths must begin either within the root directory or within the current default directory and must specify each subordinate directory in the path to the desired directory.

ASCIIZ STRINGS

Many file-related function calls require the use of an **ASCIIZ string** for the specification of a drive and/or a directory path and/or a filename and extension. An ASCIIZ string is simply a string of ASCII characters, stored in memory, with the ASCII NUL character (00H) as a trailer. In most instances, the ASCIIZ string consists of an optional drive specifier, followed by a directory path and, in some cases, a filename and extension. The format for the string characters is the same as that required by DOS commands. For example, an ASCIIZ string might be defined within the data segment as follows:

```
FNAME          DB     'A:\SCHOOL\ASSEMBLY\PROGRAMS\TEST.DAT', 0
```

Subsequent extended function calls would specify <OFFSET FNAME> as the offset of the ASCIIZ string. Alternatively, the path and filename might be obtained from the user with our INPUT_STR building block, either accepting the default (NUL) trailer or explicitly specifying the NUL character (0) as the trailer:

```
         INPUT_STR      <OFFSET FNAME_BFR>, 64
```

If you have developed your keyboard-input building blocks to store the string with a length byte (INPUT_STRL) rather than a trailer, you will need to develop a building block to convert the input string to an ASCIIZ string with a NUL-character trailer. We will discuss such a building block later in this chapter.

FILE HANDLES

Many file-related function calls use a two-byte identifier, called a **file handle** or **token** for referring to open files or devices. When a file is opened or created, DOS returns a word value, which is then used as the file handle to identify the desired file for all subsequent file operations. Note that the file handle is determined by DOS and returned to the program; it is not determined by the program as with many high-level languages. After opening or creating a file, the program must store the file handle returned by DOS (either in a word register or in a memory variable); any subsequent file access must then provide DOS with the file handle in order to identify the desired file.

Five device handles are predefined by DOS and may be used by the program to access devices as if they were files; they are automatically opened by DOS and so do not have to be opened by the application program prior to their use. Figure 12-2 lists the handles that are predefined by DOS and the devices to which they refer.

Figure 12-2   Predefined Device Handles

0000H	Standard input device (CON). The keyboard, unless standard input has been redirected with "<" in the command line that executed the program.
0001H	Standard output device (CON). The screen, unless standard output has been redirected with ">" in the command line that executed the program.
0002H	Standard error output device (CON). Always the screen. Cannot be redirected.
0003H	Standard auxiliary device (AUX or COM1). The first asynchronous serial communications adapter.
0004H	Standard printer device (PRN or LPT1). The first parallel printer adapter.

FILE POINTER

For every open file, DOS maintains a **file pointer** to keep track of the current location, by byte, within the file. The file pointer determines the displacement from the beginning of the file for any subsequent data transfer; it specifies the relative character number of any access to the file. Upon opening or creating a file, DOS automatically initializes the file pointer to zero (first byte of the file). Each subsequent read or write transfers data to or from the file, at the location determined by the file pointer. After transferring the data, DOS automatically adds the number of bytes transferred to the file pointer, thus advancing it to the next byte after the last byte transferred.

The effect of the file pointer is to automatically provide sequential access to the file. With each file access, the file pointer automatically advances through the file stream, character by character, from beginning to end. In order to gain direct access to a file, a program must use function 42H (to be discussed shortly) to explicitly position the file pointer to the desired relative character, before the read or write.

In order to access a file directly by logical record, the program must first multiply the desired relative record number by the logical record length. The product is the relative character number of the first character of the desired record. The program must then use function 42H to position the file pointer to the relative character number thus calculated. Finally, the program performs a logical read or write, providing DOS with the address of the record buffer, and specifying the logical record length as the number of bytes to read or write.

KEY TERMS TO REMEMBER

Root directory	Directory path
Subdirectory file	ASCIIZ string
Directory tree	File handle, token
Parent directory	File pointer
Default directory	

EXTENDED-FUNCTION ERROR CODES

In general, extended file function calls return a standardized completion status in the Carry flag and the AX register. The Carry flag is cleared (NC) to indicate successful completion. If the file operation is unsuccessful, then the Carry flag is set (CY), and a standard error code is returned in AX, indicating the reason for the failure. Note that the value returned in AX should be interpreted as an error code only when the Carry flag is set. A number of function calls use AX to return some other value (file handle for example) when the function has been successful (Carry flag clear). Figure 12-3 lists the possible error codes returned in AX by DOS extended file functions.

DOS FUNCTIONS FOR FILE-STRUCTURED DISK ACCESS

As mentioned in the last chapter, modern MS-DOS provides two distinct groups of functions for file-structured disk access. The **traditional disk functions** were provided by version one DOS and are supported by all subsequent DOS versions.

The **extended disk functions** were first provided by version two DOS in order to provide better hard disk support. The traditional disk functions do not recognize subdirectories or paths and so allow access only to files within the current default directory. Due to this limitation, they are seldom used by modern programmers. Consequently, we shall restrict our discussion primarily to the extended functions, with the exception of three traditional functions for which equivalent extended functions are not provided.

Unlike the traditional functions, which treat all files as fixed-record length (structured), all extended disk functions treat data files as stream files (unstructured). Extended functions do not recognize logical records; the file is treated as a continuous stream of characters with no structure. In order to process the data as records, an application program must impose the structure by specifying the logical record length as the number of characters to read from or write to the data stream with every disk access. This characteristic of the extended functions can sometimes lead to clumsiness when accessing data by logical records. However, it does lend itself quite nicely to the processing of files that are not organized into fixed-length logical records, such as the terminal-format files maintained by BASIC interpreters and compilers.

All disk-related functions are invoked in the same manner as other DOS function calls: move the function code into AH, set up any other registers as required by the function, and execute an interrupt type 21H (DOS function call). For convenience, we have grouped the file functions into four categories: general file-related functions, directory-management functions, file-management functions, and file-access functions.

Figure 12-3   Extended-Function Error Codes

01H	Invalid function number.	10H	Attempted removal of current directory.
02H	File not found.	11H	Not same device.
03H	Path not found.	12H	No more files.
04H	Too many open files.	13H	Disk write protected.
05H	Access denied.	14H	Unknown unit.
06H	Invalid handle.	15H	Drive not ready.
07H	Memory control block destroyed.	16H	Unknown command.
		17H	Data error (bad CRC).
08H	Insufficient memory.	18H	Bad request structure length.
09H	Invalid memory block address.	19H	Seek error.
0AH	Invalid environment.	1AH	Unknown media type.
0BH	Invalid format.	1BH	Sector not found.
0CH	Invalid access code.	1CH	Printer out of paper.
0DH	Invalid data.	1DH	Write fault.
0EH	Unknown unit.	1EH	Read fault.
0FH	Invalid drive.	1FH	General failure.

Note: Many of the above error codes are not related to files and so will not occur on file-related function calls. Error codes 20H through 58H apply only to network access and are not listed here.

General File-Related Functions

The **general file-related functions** are those which do not directly modify subdirectory files or directory entries or access file data. They do, however, provide services that are useful or even necessary for the management of files and/or the accessing of file data. Following is a list with explanations of the most commonly used general file functions:

0EH - Select Default Drive (Traditional Function)

Function 0EH changes the DOS default drive. The specified drive becomes the default for all subsequent file specifications that do not include a drive specifier. The drive numbering (zero = drive A, one = drive B, etc.) follows the drive letters, whether floppy or hard disk. To select the default drive:

```
Move 0EH into AH.
Move the desired drive into DL (0 = A, 1 = B, etc.).
INT 21H.
```

Upon return, the DOS default drive has been changed to that specified by DL. In addition, the total number of logical disk drives is returned in AL. No status is returned; the Carry flag should not be interpreted as an indication of success or failure.

The specified drive will remain the default even after the program terminates and returns to DOS, unless it is subsequently changed again. In most cases, any program that changes the default drive should restore it to its original value before termination; function 19H, following, may be used to get the current default drive upon entry to the program.

Note that the value returned in AL is the number of logical disk drives, rather than physical drives, in the system. If the system contains only one floppy drive, then a value of two is returned, since the single physical drive is treated by DOS as two logical drives (A and B). Additionally, a single hard disk may often be partitioned into two or more logical drives, or a system may have installed one or more simulated disk drives (RAM disks). The value returned in AL represents the sum of all such logical disk drives.

19H - Get Default Drive (Traditional Function)

Function 19H is used to obtain the drive number of the current default drive. To get the default drive:

```
Move 19H into AH.
INT 21H.
```

The current default drive is returned in AL (zero = drive A, one = drive B, etc.). No status is returned; the Carry flag should not be interpreted as an indication of success or failure.

Any program that changes the default drive (function 0EH above) should normally obtain the current default drive before the change. Prior to termination and return to DOS, the program should set the default drive back to its original value.

1AH – Set DTA (Disk Transfer Address) (Traditional Function)

Both traditional and extended functions make use of a disk transfer address, though in a very different manner. To traditional functions, the DTA is the address of the record buffer used for the transfer of logical records to or from the file buffer. The extended functions do not use the DTA as the record buffer address; however, two extended functions (4EH and 4FH) use it as the address of a buffer to receive directory information.

Function 1AH must be used to inform DOS of the disk transfer address prior to the use of any function (traditional or extended) that makes use of the DTA. To set the DTA:

```
Move 1AH to AH.
DS must address the segment of the DTA.
Move the offset of the DTA into DX.
INT 21H.
```

No status is returned; the Carry flag should not be interpreted as an indication of success or failure.

2FH – Get DTA (Disk Transfer Address)

Function 2FH returns the current disk transfer address. The DTA is the address into which information about matching files will be placed by any subsequent extended directory search (function 4EH or 4FH) as well as the current address of the record buffer to be used by any subsequent traditional function call. To obtain the address (segment:offset) of the current DTA:

```
Move 2FH into AH.
INT 21H.
```

Upon return, the disk transfer address is in ES:BX. ES contains the segment, and BX contains the offset. No error is returned; the Carry flag is always cleared.

36H – Get Disk Allocation Information

Function 36H provides allocation information about a disk drive. To obtain the total disk capacity and the amount of free disk space:

```
Move 36H into AH.
Move drive number into DL (0 = default, 1 = A, etc.).
INT 21H.
```

Note that the drive numbering is different from that used for functions 0EH and 19H, where zero = A, one = B, and so on. Upon return, AX contains FFFFH if the drive was invalid; otherwise, no error is returned. Note that, although 36H is an extended function, the Carry flag is not used to indicate success or failure.

Any value other than FFFFH in AX indicates that the drive was valid and the total disk space and unallocated disk space are returned as follows:

```
BX = Number of available (unallocated) clusters on the disk.
DX = Total number of clusters on the disk.
AX = Cluster size—number of sectors per cluster.
CX = Number of bytes per sector.
```

Directory-Management Functions

The **directory-management functions** are those which provide services for the management of subdirectories. They do not modify directory entries or file data, but manage the subdirectory files themselves. Following is a list and explanation of the most common directory-management functions:

39H – Create a Subdirectory (MKDIR)

Function 39H creates a subdirectory file and is used by DOS to implement the MKDIR (or MD) command. It requires an ASCIIZ string containing a drive and path, ending with the desired new directory. To create a new subdirectory:

```
Move 39H into AH.
DS must address the segment of the ASCIIZ string.
Move the offset of the ASCIIZ string into DX.
INT 21H.
```

If any directory within the path does not exist, then DOS is unable to create the subdirectory; the Carry flag is set, and an error code of 03H or 05H is returned in AX (refer to Figure 12-3). Otherwise, the new subdirectory file (the last directory name in the path) is created.

3AH – Remove a Subdirectory (RMDIR)

Function 3AH removes an existing subdirectory, and is used by the DOS RMDIR (or RD) command. It requires an ASCIIZ string containing a drive and path, ending with the directory to be removed. To remove a subdirectory:

```
Move 3AH into AH.
DS must address the segment of the ASCIIZ string.
Move the offset of the ASCIIZ string into DX.
INT 21H.
```

If the path contains any directory that does not exist, or if the directory to be deleted is the current default directory or is not empty, then DOS is unable to remove the directory; the Carry flag is set, and an error code of 03H, 05H, or 10H is returned in AX (refer to Figure 12-3). Error code 05H (access denied) indicates that the directory contains one or more files and so could not be removed. Otherwise, the Carry flag is cleared and the last subdirectory in the path is removed.

3BH – Change the Default Directory (CHDIR)

Function 3BH changes the current default directory for any drive. DOS uses function 3BH to implement the CHDIR (or CD) command. It requires an ASCIIZ string containing a drive and path to become the new default directory for the drive. If no drive is specified in the ASCIIZ string, then the default directory is changed for the default drive. To change the current default directory:

```
Move 3BH into AH.
DS must address the segment of the ASCIIZ string.
Move the offset of the ASCIIZ string into DX.
INT 21H.
```

If any directory in the path does not exist, the Carry flag is set, and an error code of 03H is returned in AX (refer to Figure 12-3). Otherwise, the current directory is changed to the last directory in the path.

47H – Get the Current Default Directory

Function 47H returns the path of the current directory on the specified drive. To get the current directory:

```
Move 47H into AH.
Move drive number into DL (0 = default, 1 = A, etc.).
DS must address the segment of a 64-byte buffer.
Move the offset of the 64-byte buffer into SI.
INT 21H.
```

If an invalid drive was specified, the Carry flag is set, and an error code of 0FH is returned in AX (refer to Figure 12-3). Otherwise, the full path of the current default directory (from the root directory to the default directory) is placed into the buffer specified by DS and SI, as an ASCIIZ string. The ASCIIZ string path does not include a drive specifier and does not begin with a back slash.

MOST COMMONLY USED General and Directory-Management Functions (INT 21H)

47H – Get the current default directory
DL = drive (0 = default, 1 = A, etc), DS:SI = address of 64-byte buffer.

3BH – Change the default directory
DS:DX = address of ASCIIZ string.

1AH – Set DTA (traditional function)
DS:DX = disk transfer address.

File-Management Functions

The **file-management functions** are those which provide services for the management of files, but do not provide access to the data within those files. They all modify and/or return information about file-directory entries. Following is a list and explanation of the most common file-management functions.

41H - Delete File

Function 41H deletes a file from a directory; the directory entry is flagged as deleted and the FAT is updated to release all disk space that was allocated to the file. The file to be deleted is specified with an ASCIIZ string containing a drive, path, and the filename and extension of the file to be deleted. Only one file may be deleted at a time; the ASCIIZ string may not contain wild card characters (* or ?). To delete a file from a specified directory:

```
Move 41H into AH.
DS must address the segment of the ASCIIZ string.
Move the offset of the ASCIIZ string into DX.
INT 21H.
```

If the file cannot be deleted, the Carry flag is set, and an error code is returned in AX (refer to Figure 12-3). An error code of 05H indicates that the specified file is read-only; function call 43H must be used to change the file's attribute to zero before attempting to delete it. Otherwise the file is removed from the directory specified by the path in the ASCIIZ string, and its disk space is freed up within the FAT.

43H - Get or Change File Attribute

Function call 43H may be used to obtain a file's Attribute byte or to change the Attribute byte. This function call may be used to change the read-only, hidden-file, system-file or archive bits; it may *not* be used to change the volume-label or subdirectory bits. The function requires an ASCIIZ string containing the drive, path, and filename and extension of the file whose Attribute byte is to be read or written; if no path is specified, then DOS looks in the current default directory for the file.

To obtain a file's attribute byte:

```
Move 43H into AH.
DS must address the segment of the ASCIIZ string.
Move the offset of the ASCIIZ string into DX.
Move 0 into AL.
INT 21H.
```

Possible error codes are 02H and 03H (refer to Figure 12-3). Otherwise, DOS returns the Attribute byte in CX (CH = 0, CL = attribute). Figure 12-4 lists the meaning of each of the file Attribute-byte bits.

Figure 12-4   **File Attribute Byte**

Bit	Meaning if set
0	Read-only file
1	Hidden file
2	System file
3	Volume label
4	Subdirectory file
5	File modified since last backup (Archive bit)
6 - 7	Unused

To change a file's Attribute byte:

```
Move 43H into AH.
DS must address the segment of the ASCIIZ string.
Move the offset of the ASCIIZ string into DX.
Move 1 into AL.
Move the desired attribute into CX (attribute to CL, 0 to CH).
INT 21H.
```

DOS sets the file's Attribute byte to that specified in CL. Possible error codes are 02H, 03H, and 05H (refer to Figure 12-3). An error code of 05H indicates that an attempt was made to change the volume-label bit or the subdirectory bit. The Attribute-byte bits are as explained in Figure 12-4.

4EH – DIR First (Find first)

Function 4EH is used (with function 4FH) by the DOS DIR command. Use function 4EH to begin a directory search for a filename. An ASCIIZ string is required, containing the drive, path, and filename and extension for which to search; if no path is specified, then DOS looks in the current default directory for the file. The filename and extension may contain wild cards. In addition, a one byte attribute, to be used in the search, must be specified.

During the search, the specified Attribute byte is matched with the Attribute byte of each directory entry. If the Attribute byte is 00H, only ordinary files will be found; if the volume-label bit is set, only volume labels will be found. If any other bit (or combination of bits) is set, the appropriate types of directory entries will be found in addition to all ordinary files. The Attribute byte is explained in Figure 12-4.

Before issuing the 4EH function call, function 1AH must have previously been used to set the disk transfer address to the address of a forty-three-byte buffer to be used by DOS during the directory search. To find the first occurrence of a file:

> Move 4EH into AH.
> DS must address the segment of the ASCIIZ string.
> Move the offset of the ASCIIZ string into DX.
> Move the attribute to be used in the search into CX (attribute
> to CL, 0 to CH).
> INT 21H.

Possible error codes are 02H and 12H (refer to Figure 12-3). If the file is found, the forty-three-byte directory-search buffer (DTA) is set up by DOS as follows:

Byte(s)	Length	Description
0–20	21	Reserved
21	1	Attribute byte of matching file
22–23	2	File time
24–25	2	File date
26– 29	4	File size
30–42	13	ASCIIZ filename and extension

The first twenty-one bytes of the buffer are reserved for use by DOS in continuing the directory search; see function 4FH below. The program *must not* modify this data area if the directory search is to be continued!

Allocation and addressing of the forty-three-byte buffer, to be used during the directory search, can be greatly simplified by defining a data structure, using the STRUC directive discussed earlier. We shall call the structure DIR_BUFFER and define within it all the fields of the directory-search buffer as used by DOS. Figure 12-5 illustrates the definition of the DIR_BUFFER structure.

Figure 12-5   Directory-Search Buffer Structure

```
DIR_BUFFER      STRUC

                          DB      21 DUP (?)      ;RESERVED FOR DOS
                ATT       DB      ?               ;ATTRIBUTE BYTE
                D_TIME    DW      ?               ;FILE TIME
                D_DATE    DW      ?               ;FILE DATE
                D_SIZ_L   DW      ?               ;FILE SIZE (LEAST
                                                  ;  SIGNIFICANT WORD)
                D_SIZ_M   DW      ?               ;FILE SIZE (MOST
                                                  ;  SIGNIFICANT WORD)
                ASCIIZ    DB      13 DUP(?)       ;ASCIIZ FILENAME
                                                  ;  AND EXTENSION

DIR_BUFFER      ENDS
```

Once the directory-search buffer structure has been defined as in Figure 12-5, the allocation of a buffer for a directory search is quite simple. Put the desired name for the buffer in the name field of a source line, with the structure name (DIR_BUFFER) in the action field and angle brackets (field override values are not useful) in the expression field. The following line of code allocates a forty-three-byte directory buffer:

```
D_BFR       DIR_BUFFER   <>
```

Once the data structure has been allocated, as above, then the assembler knows the offset of the structure variable, D_BFR, as well as the displacements of the structure fields; consequently, the fields within the directory-search buffer can be easily addressed, as in the following instructions:

```
    CMP  D_BFR.ATT, 0
    MOV  CX, D_BFR.D_SIZ_M
    MOV  DX, D_BFR.D_SIZ_L
    MOV  SI, OFFSET D_BFR.ASCIIZ
```

or

```
    MOV  SI, OFFSET D_BFR
    MOV  AX, [SI].D_DATE
    MOV  BX, [SI].D_TIME
```

4FH – DIR Next (Find next)

Function 4FH is used (with function 4EH) by the DOS DIR command. It continues a directory search that was begun with function 4EH; before issuing the 4FH function call, function 1AH must have been used to set the DTA to a forty-three byte directory-search buffer, and function 4EH must have previously been used to fill in the buffer as described above. To find the next occurrence of the file:

```
Move 4FH into AH.
INT 21H.
```

The possible error code is 12H (refer to Figure 12-3). DOS finds the next directory entry matching the name and attribute specified in the ASCIIZ string of the function 4EH call. An error code of 12H is returned if no more matching files are found; otherwise, DOS sets up the directory-search buffer as described above for function 4EH.

56H – Rename File

Function 56H is used by the DOS RENAME or REN command. The rename function call requires two ASCIIZ strings. The first one specifies the drive, path, and filename and extension of the file to be renamed; the second one contains the drive, path, and new filename and extension for the file. Only one file at a time may be renamed; neither ASCIIZ string may contain wild-card characters (* or ?).

Both ASCIIZ strings must refer to the same drive (default is OK). However, the two strings may contain different paths; the rename function call may be used to "move" a file between subdirectories. Actually, the file data is not moved on the disk; its directory entry is simply removed from the first subdirectory file and added to the second subdirectory file. To rename a file:

```
Move 56H into AH.
DS must address the segment of the ASCIIZ string of the file to
                                                    be renamed.
Move the offset of the ASCIIZ string, of the file to be
                                          renamed, into DX.
Move the segment of the ASCIIZ string, with the new name, into
                                                          ES.
Move the offset of the ASCIIZ string, with the new name, into
                                                          DI.
INT 21H.
```

Possible error codes are 03H, 05H, and 11H (refer to Figure 12-3). DOS changes the name of the file, "moving" it between subdirectories if necessary.

MOST COMMONLY USED File Management Functions (INT 21H)

```
4EH - DIR First
```
    DS:DX = address of ASCIIZ string, CX = attribute,
    DTA set to 43-byte buffer.

```
4FH - DIR Next
```
    Must be preceded by function 4EH (DIR first).

```
41H - Delete File
```
    DS:DX = address of ASCIIZ string.

```
56H - Rename File
```
    DS:DX = address of ASCIIZ string (to be renamed).
    ES:DI = address of ASCIIZ string (new name).

File-Access Functions

The **file-access functions** are those which provide access to the data contained in disk files. While they may affect directory entries, their primary purpose is to allow the reading or modification of the file data. As discussed earlier, the extended functions treat all files as stream files. Each file read or write (function

3FH or 40H) must specify the number of characters to read or write as well as the location of the record buffer. DOS maintains the file pointer to automatically provide sequential access. If a program requires direct access, then it must use function 42H to position the file pointer prior to the direct-access read or write.

Before a file can be accessed, it must first be opened or created using function 3CH or 3DH. Following the file access, the file must always be closed (function 3EH) before terminating the program. Following is a list and explanation of the most common extended file-access functions.

3CH - Create File

Function 3CH creates a new file or truncates an existing file to zero bytes. After creating or truncating the file, DOS opens it for read/write access and returns its file handle. The file is ready for writing and reading data using the returned file handle. An ASCIIZ string is required, containing the drive, path, and filename and extension of the file to be created. To create or truncate a file:

```
Move 3CH into AH.
DS must address the segment of the ASCIIZ string for the file.
Move the offset of the ASCIIZ string for the file into DX.
Move the desired attribute for the file into CX (attribute to
                                        CL, 0 to CH).
INT 21H.
```

Possible error codes are 03H, 04H, and 05H (refer to Figure 12-3). An error code of 05H indicates that the directory is full (root directory) or that the file already exists and is read-only. Otherwise, DOS creates or truncates the file, opens it for read/write access, sets the file pointer to zero (first byte of the file), and returns the file handle in AX. The sixteen-bit file handle returned in AX must be used for all subsequent access to the file.

3DH - Open File

Use function 3DH to open an existing file to allow access to the data. An ASCIIZ string is required, containing the drive, path, and filename and extension of the file to be opened. The file may be opened with any of the following access modes:

0 = read (input) access only.
1 = write (output) access only.
2 = both read and write (R/W or I/O) access.

To open an existing file:

```
Move 3DH into AH.
DS must address the segment of the ASCIIZ string for the file.
Move the offset of the ASCIIZ string for the file into DX.
Move the desired access mode (0, 1, or 2) into AL.
INT 21H.
```

Possible error codes are 02H, 03H, 04H, 05H, and 0CH (refer to Figure 12-3). An error of 05H occurs if the file is read-only and the access mode in AL indicates write or read/write access (mode one or two). Otherwise, DOS opens the file for the access mode specified in AL and returns the file handle in AX. The sixteen-bit file handle returned in AX must be used for all subsequent access to the file. Any subsequent access that violates the specified access mode (attempt to read when opened for write-only or to write when opened for read-only) results in an error code of 05H.

3EH - Close File

Function 3EH closes a file that has previously been opened or created, with extended function 3CH or 3DH. Any file that has been written to must be closed before terminating the program. To close a file:

```
Move 3EH into AH.
Move the file handle, returned by open or create, into BX.
INT 21H.
```

The possible error code is 06H (refer to Figure 12-3), indicating that the handle in BX is not a valid handle for a currently open file. Otherwise, DOS flushes the file buffer to disk, updates the File-Size, File-Date, and File-Time fields of the directory entry, and releases the file handle.

3FH - Read File

Function 3FH is used to read data from a file that has been previously opened or created with extended function 3CH or 3DH. The program specifies the number of bytes to read from the data stream and the address of the record buffer to which to transfer the data. To read from a file:

```
Move 3FH into AH.
Move the file handle, returned by open or create, into BX.
Move the number of bytes to read (logical record length) into
                                                        CX.
DS must address the segment of the record buffer.
Move the offset of the record buffer into DX.
INT 21H.
```

Possible error codes are 05H and 06H (refer to Figure 12-3). An error code of 05H occurs if the file was opened for write-only access.

DOS attempts to transfer CX bytes from the file to the record buffer at DS:[DX]. Upon return, AX contains the actual number of bytes read. AX less than CX indicates that end-of-file has been reached; AX then contains the number of bytes transferred before end-of-file (zero if already at end-of-file before read).

The location within the file from which the data is taken is determined by the file pointer, which is used as a displacement from the beginning of the file (zero = first byte, one = second byte, etc.). After the read is completed, the file pointer is advanced by the number of bytes actually read, to point to the next byte after the last byte read. Since function 3FH performs a logical read, the transfer of data is from the file buffer to the record buffer, with a physical write and/or read performed by DOS only if necessary.

40H - Write File

Function 40H writes data to a file (or sets the size of a file) that has been previously opened or created, with extended function 3CH or 3DH. The program specifies the number of bytes to write to the data stream and the address of the record buffer from which to transfer the data. If zero is specified as the number of bytes to write, the file size is set to the current value of the file pointer. To write to a file or set the file size:

```
Move 40H into AH.
Move the file handle, returned by open or create, into BX.
Move the number of bytes to write into CX (zero to set the file
                                                            size).
DS must address the segment of the record buffer.
Move the offset of the record buffer into DX.
INT 21H.
```

Possible error codes are 05H and 06H (refer to Figure 12-3). An error code of 05H occurs if the file was opened for read-only access.

If CX is not zero, DOS attempts to transfer CX bytes to the file from the record buffer at DS:[DX]. Upon return, AX contains the actual number of bytes written. AX should always equal the number of bytes requested in CX. AX less than CX indicates an error condition even if the Carry flag is not set; the usual cause is a full disk.

The location within the file to which the data is written is determined by the file pointer, which is used as a displacement from the beginning of the file (zero = first byte, one = second byte, etc.). After the write is completed, the file pointer is advanced by the number of bytes actually written to point to the next byte after the last byte written. Since function 40H performs a logical write, the transfer of data is from the record buffer to the file buffer, with a physical write and/or read performed by DOS only if necessary.

If CX is initialized to zero, then no data is written to the file; the file size is set to the current value of the file pointer. If the file pointer is beyond end-of-file, the file is extended and additional clusters are allocated as necessary. If the file pointer is not at or beyond end-of-file, the file is truncated and clusters are deallocated as necessary; all file data beyond the file pointer is lost!

42H - Move File Pointer (Seek)

Function 42H is provided by DOS in order to allow direct access to file data, by altering the position of the file pointer, within a file that has been previously opened or created with extended function 3CH or 3DH. Function 42H requires a double-word displacement as well as the method for moving the pointer. The displacement must be in CX:DX, where CX is the most-significant word and DX is the least-significant word. The method for moving the pointer is indicated by a mode in AL; the three valid modes for AL, and the method of movement resulting from each, are as follows:

00H = Position pointer to absolute file location. The displacement is treated as an unsigned value, and the file pointer is positioned to the specified displacement from the beginning of the file; the unsigned displacement is moved into the file pointer.

01H = Move pointer relative to current location. The displacement is treated as a signed value, and the file pointer is moved forward or backward from its current location; the displacement is added as a signed value to the file pointer. A positive displacement moves the file pointer forward; a negative displacement moves it backward; a zero displacement has no effect.

02H = Position pointer relative to end-of-file. The displacement is treated as a signed value, and the file pointer is positioned relative to end-of-file; the current file size plus the signed displacement is moved into the file pointer. A positive displacement positions the file pointer beyond end-of-file; a negative displacement positions it before end-of file; a zero displacement positions it to end-of-file.

To position the file pointer:

```
Move 42H into AH.
Move the positioning mode (00H, 01H, or 02H) into AL.
Move the file handle, returned by open or create, into BX.
Move the MSW of the displacement into CX.
Move the LSW of the displacement into DX.
INT 21H
```

Possible error codes are 01H and 06H (refer to Figure 12-3). An error code of 01H occurs if AL contains any value other than 00H, 01H, or 02H. Otherwise, DOS positions the file pointer according to the values in AL, CX, and DX. The new position determines where subsequent reads or writes will take place, within the file.

In addition, DOS returns the new file-pointer position in DX:AX, where DX is the most-significant word and AX is the least-significant word. To obtain the current position of the pointer, use method one with a displacement of zero (AL = one, CX = zero, and DX = zero); the pointer is not moved and the current position is returned in DX:AX. Method two, with a displacement of zero, returns the current file size, but also moves the file pointer to end-of-file.

45H - Duplicate File Handle

Function 45H creates a duplicate file handle for a currently open file. To create a duplicate handle:

```
Move 45H into AH.
Move the file handle, returned by open or create, into BX.
INT 21H.
```

Possible error codes are 04H and 06H (refer to Figure 12-3). Otherwise, DOS returns the new file handle in AX. The new handle refers to the same file as the first handle, using the same file pointer and file buffer; the two handles are now synonymous. Repositioning the pointer for either handle also repositions the pointer for the other handle.

Function 45H provides an easy way to flush a file buffer and update the directory entry, without closing and reopening the file. Simply create a duplicate handle and then close it. Closing the duplicate handle causes DOS to flush the file buffer and update the directory entry for the file; the file is still open on the original handle, with the file pointer unchanged.

46H - Redirect File Handle

Function 46H redirects a file handle to refer to another open file. It is used most often to redirect one of the predefined device handles (Figure 12-2). To redirect a file handle:

```
Move 46H into AH.
Move the file handle to be redirected into CX.
Move the file handle to redirect to into BX.
INT 21H.
```

The possible error code is 06H (refer to Figure 12-3). DOS redirects the file handle in CX to refer to the same file at the same position as the handle in BX. If the handle in CX referred to an open file, then the file is closed first. Both handles now refer to the same file, originally referred to by BX, using the same file pointer and file buffer. Repositioning the pointer for either handle also repositions the pointer for the other handle.

57H - Get or Set File Date and Time

Function 57H may be used to obtain or to set the date and time of an open file. The file must have been previously opened or created with extended function 3CH or 3DH.

To obtain a file's date and time:

```
Move 57H into AH.
Move 00H into AL.
Move the file handle, returned by open or create, into BX.
INT 21H.
```

The time and date that the file was created or last modified are returned in CX and DX, respectively. The format of the date and time are the same as in the File-Date and File-Time fields of the directory entry:

Time/Date	Bit #	Meaning and Values
Time (CX):	0–4	Two-second increments (0–29)
	5–10	Minute (0–59)
	11–15	Hour (0–23)

Date (DX):	0–4	Day (0–31)
	5–8	Month (1–12)
	9–15	Year (0–119 => 1980–2099)

To set a file's date and time:

```
Move 57H into AH.
Move 01H into AL.
Move the file handle, returned by open or create, into BX.
Move the file time (formatted as above) into CX.
Move the file date (formatted as above) into DX.
INT 21H.
```

The file date and time are set to the values in CX and DX. The date and time, as set, will prevail even if the file is subsequently altered before the handle is closed. If the date (DX) is set to zero, the file date and time are not displayed on subsequent directory listings (DIR command).

The possible error codes for function 57H are 01H, 05H, and 06H. 01H is returned if AL contains any value other than 00H or 01H; 05H is returned if AL is 01H (set date and time) and the file was opened for read-only access.

MOST COMMONLY USED File-Access Functions (INT 21H)

```
3CH - Create File
```
   DS:DX = address of ASCIIZ string, CX = attribute.
   Handle or error code returned in AX.

```
3DH - Open File
```
   DS:DX = address of ASCIIZ string, AL = access mode. Handle or error code returned in AX.

```
3FH - Read File
```
   BX = handle, CX = number of bytes, DS:DX = address of record buffer.

```
40H - Write File
```
   BX = handle, CX = number of bytes, DS:DX = address of record buffer.

```
42H - Move File Pointer (Seek)
```
   BX = handle, AL = position code (0 = absolute location, 1 = relative to current position, 2 = relative to EOF), CX:DX = displacement.

```
3EH - Close File
```
   BX = handle.

BUILDING BLOCKS FOR FILE-STRUCTURED DISK ACCESS

Each of the previously discussed functions suggests a building block, to be added to your disk library (DISK.MLB and DISK.LIB) in order to provide easy access to the function call. Since many of the extended functions use the Carry flag with a standard error code, any building block that uses such a function should indicate success or failure in the same manner. Upon exit from the building block, the Carry flag should be clear to indicate success, set to indicate failure. Consequently, all such macros and procedures *must not modify* the Carry flag after the function call.

In addition, many building blocks should have an optional byte output parameter, ERROR, to receive the error code as returned by DOS. The macro header of each building block should explain the use of the Carry flag and should list and explain the possible values to be returned in ERROR. Following is a discussion of some possible building blocks to be added to your disk library (DISK.MLB and DISK.LIB).

Select the default drive:

```
SEL_DEF          MACRO     DEF_DRV, NO_DRVS
```

DEF_DRV is a byte input parameter specifying the new default drive; it should default to 0 (drive A) if omitted. The macro header should explain the drive numbering as required by DOS (0 = A, 1 = B, etc.). NO_DRVS is an optional byte output parameter to receive the number of logical disk drives as returned by DOS. The procedure should use traditional function 0EH to select the default drive.

Get the current default drive:

```
GET_DEF          MACRO     DEF_DRV
```

DEF_DRV is a byte output parameter to receive the drive number returned by DOS. The macro header should explain the drive numbering (0 = A, 1 = B, etc.). The procedure should use function 19H to obtain the default drive from DOS.

Set the disk transfer address:

```
SET_DTA          MACRO     DTA_OFF
```

DTA_OFF is a word input parameter specifying the offset of the disk transfer address, which is assumed to be in the data segment. The macro header should caution the programmer to define the DTA buffer in the data segment and to ensure that it is long enough to hold the data (logical record or directory information) that will be placed into it by DOS. The procedure uses function 1AH to set the DTA.

Alternatively, you might wish to allow the definition of the DTA in any segment by including another input parameter, DTA_SEG, for the segment half of the disk transfer address; if so, DTA_SEG should default to DS.

Get the disk transfer address:

```
GET_DTA          MACRO    DTA_OFF, DTA_SEG
```

DTA_OFF and DTA_SEG are word output parameters to receive the offset and segment of the current disk transfer address. DTA_SEG should be optional, allowing the programmer to specify only one word register to receive the DTA offset when the segment is known (data segment, for example). The procedure should use function 2FH to obtain the disk transfer address from DOS.

Get disk allocation information:

```
GET_DSK_SPACE    MACRO    DRV, FRE_CL, TTL_CL, CL_SIZ, SCT_SIZ
```

DRV is a byte input parameter specifying the drive for which allocation information is desired. It should default to zero (DOS default drive). FRE_CL, TTL_CL, CL_SIZ, and SCT_SIZ are all optional word parameters; the programmer should be able to specify word registers for the appropriate parameters to receive only the information that he or she desires.

FRE_CL receives the number of free (unallocated) clusters remaining on the disk, TTL_CL receives the total number of clusters on the disk, CL_SIZ receives the number of sectors per cluster, and SCT_SIZ receives the number of bytes per sector. The macro header should explain the drive numbering (0 = default, 1 = A, etc.) and that FFFFH is returned in CL_SIZ, if DRV specifies an invalid drive. The procedure uses function 36H to obtain the disk allocation information.

Convert a string with length byte to an ASCIIZ string:

```
CNV_STRL_ASCZ    MACRO    STR_OFF
```

CNV_STRL_ASCZ is necessary only if you have developed your string input/output building blocks to store strings with a length byte, rather than with a trailer. CNV_STRL_ASCZ converts a string, obtained from the keyboard and stored with a length byte, to an ASCIIZ string with the NUL character as a trailer.

STR_OFF is a word input parameter specifying the offset, in the data segment, of the string to be converted. Alternatively, a second input parameter, STR_SEG, might be used to allow the string in any segment; if so, it should default to DS. The procedure should move the length byte into CX (length byte to CL, zero to CH) and use MOVSB to move the string one byte to the left in the buffer. It should then use STOSB to store the NUL character (0) onto the end of the string.

Create a subdirectory:

```
MKDIR            MACRO    ASCZ_OFF, ERROR
```

ASCZ_OFF is a word input parameter specifying the offset of an ASCIIZ string in the data segment, containing the drive and path of the directory to be created. ERROR and the Carry flag are as described earlier. Alternatively, a second input parameter, ASCZ_SEG, might be used to allow the ASCIIZ string in any segment; if so, it should default to DS. The procedure uses function 39H to create the directory.

Remove a subdirectory:

```
RMDIR          MACRO     ASCZ_OFF, ERROR
```

ASCZ_OFF is a word input parameter specifying the offset of an ASCIIZ string, in the data segment, containing the drive and path of the directory to be removed. ERROR and the Carry flag are as described earlier. Alternatively, a second input parameter, ASCZ_SEG, might be used to allow the ASCIIZ string in any segment; if so, it should default to DS. The procedure uses function 3AH to remove the directory.

Change the default directory:

```
CHDIR          MACRO     ASCZ_OFF, ERROR
```

ASCZ_OFF is a word input parameter specifying the offset of an ASCIIZ string in the data segment, containing the drive and path of the directory to which the default directory is to be changed. ERROR and the Carry flag are as described earlier. Alternatively, a second input parameter, ASCZ_SEG, might be used to allow the ASCIIZ string in any segment; if so, it should default to DS. The procedure uses function 3BH to change the default directory.

Get the current default directory:

```
GET_DIR          MACRO     DRV, BUFF_OFF, ERROR
```

DRV is a byte input parameter specifying the drive for which the default directory is desired. It should default to zero (DOS default drive). BUFF_OFF is a word input parameter specifying the offset within the data segment of a sixty-four-byte buffer to receive an ASCIIZ string specifying the path of the current default directory. The macro header should explain the drive numbering (0 = default, 1 = A, etc.) and must warn the programmer to ensure that the buffer is at least sixty-four bytes in length.

ERROR and the Carry flag are as described earlier. A third input parameter, BUFF_SEG, might be used to allow the buffer in any segment; if so, it should default to DS. The procedure uses function 47H to obtain the default directory path.

Change the Attribute byte of a file:

```
CHG_ATT          MACRO     ASCZ_OFF, ATT, ERROR
```

ASCZ_OFF is a word input parameter specifying the offset of an ASCIIZ string in the data segment, containing the drive, path, and filename and extension of the file whose attribute is to be changed. ATT is a byte input parameter specifying the new Attribute byte for the file; it should default to zero (normal file attribute). The macro header should explain the significance of each bit of ATT.

ERROR and the Carry flag are as described earlier. If desired, another input parameter, ASCZ_SEG, might be used to allow the ASCIIZ string in any segment; if so, it should default to DS. The procedure should move ATT into CL and move zero into CH before using function 43H to set the file attribute.

Get the Attribute byte of a file:

```
GET_ATT          MACRO     ASCZ_OFF, ATT, ERROR
```

ASCZ_OFF is a word input parameter specifying the offset of an ASCIIZ string in the data segment, containing the drive, path, and filename and extension of the file whose Attribute byte is to be returned. ATT is a byte output parameter to receive the Attribute byte of the file. The macro header should explain the significance of each bit of ATT.

ERROR and the Carry flag are as described earlier. Another input parameter, ASCZ_SEG, might be used to allow the ASCIIZ string in any segment; if so, it should default to DS. The procedure should use function 43H to get the file attribute, returning only the low byte on the stack.

Delete a file:

```
DEL_FILE         MACRO     ASCZ_OFF, ERROR
```

ASCZ_OFF is a word input parameter specifying the offset of an ASCIIZ string in the data segment, containing the drive, path, and filename and extension of the file to be deleted. ERROR and the Carry flag are as described earlier. A second input parameter, ASCZ_SEG, might be used to allow the ASCIIZ string in any segment; if so, it should default to DS. The procedure uses function 41H to delete the file.

Rename a file:

```
REN_FILE         MACRO     OLDASCZ_OFF, NEWASCZ_OFF, ERROR
```

OLDASCZ_OFF is a word input parameter specifying the offset of an ASCIIZ string in the data segment, containing the drive, path, and filename and extension of the file to be renamed; NEWASCZ_OFF is a word input parameter specifying the offset of an ASCIIZ string in the data segment, containing the path and file-name and extension to which to rename the file. ERROR and the Carry flag are as described earlier. If desired, two additional input parameters, OLDASCZ_SEG and NEWASCZ_SEG, might be used to allow the ASCIIZ strings in any segment; if so, both should default to DS. The procedure should use function 56H to rename the file.

Define the directory-search buffer data structure:

```
DEFINE_DIR_BFR_STRUCT    MACRO
```

The building block should consist of a macro only; it does not call a procedure. The macro needs no parameters and should contain only the DIR_BUFFER data-structure definition, as shown in Figure 12-5. The macro header should explain that any source module that needs to allocate and address a directory-search buffer must include DISK.MLB on pass one and invoke the DEFINE_DIR_BFR_STRUCT macro before attempting to allocate or address the fields of a directory-search buffer.

If you work only with TASM (Turbo Assembler), you need not even define a macro. Simply include the directory-search buffer data-structure definition within DISK.MLB; the data structure is then automatically defined, without any macro invocation, for any module that includes the disk macro library.

The need for the macro, when working with MASM, is created by the fact that MASM is a two-pass assembler. We have conditioned our INCLUDE directives with IF1 to save assembly time by including the macro library only on the first pass of MASM. We are able to include macro definitions only on pass one because MASM remembers all macro definitions from pass one to pass two; however, structure definitions are effective only for the current pass. By including the structure definition within a macro, which is invoked in any module that needs it, the expansion of the macro on both passes defines the data structure for pass two as well as for pass one.

Search for the first matching directory entry:

```
DIR_FRST        MACRO    ASCZ_OFF, ATT, ERROR
```

ASCZ_OFF is a word input parameter specifying the offset of an ASCIIZ string in the data segment, containing the drive, path, and filename and extension for which to search. ATT is a byte input parameter specifying the attribute to use on the search; it should default to zero (normal attribute). The macro header should explain the use of wild cards, in the filename and extension of the ASCIIZ string, as well as the effect on the search of each bit of ATT.

ERROR and the Carry flag are as described earlier. If desired, another input parameter, ASCZ_SEG, might be used to allow the ASCIIZ string in any segment; if so, it should default to DS.

The macro header should caution the user to set the DTA before invoking the building block to a forty-three-byte buffer, to receive information about the matching file and to allow DOS to keep track of the directory search. Explain the use of DEFINE_DIR_BFR_STRUCT for facilitating the allocation and addressing of the required directory-search buffer. Also caution that the DTA must not be changed if the directory search is to be continued.

Search for the next matching directory entry:

```
DIR_NXT          MACRO    ERROR
```

ERROR and the Carry flag are as described earlier. The macro header should explain the meaning of the Carry flag and ERROR, in terms of the continuation of the search. The header also must caution the programmer to set the DTA to a forty-three-byte directory-search buffer and invoke DIR_FRST before invoking DIR_NXT; also caution the programmer not to change the DTA before completion of the search. The procedure should use function 4FH to search for the next matching directory entry.

Open a file:

```
OPEN_FILE        MACRO    ASCZ_OFF, MODE, HANDLE, ERROR
```

ASCZ_OFF is a word input parameter specifying the offset of an ASCIIZ string in the data segment, containing the drive, path, and filename and extension of the file to be opened. MODE is a byte input parameter specifying the access mode for the file. MODE should default to two (read/write access) and should allow character codes for the three file modes (R, W, and R/W or I, O, and I/O); the macro should translate the allowed codes to the proper numeric value of the access mode. The macro header should explain the allowed codes, the default value, and allowed numeric values for MODE.

HANDLE is a word output parameter to receive the sixteen-bit file handle returned by DOS. The macro header should explain the importance of HANDLE for all subsequent file access. ERROR and the Carry flag are as described earlier. If desired, another input parameter, ASCZ_SEG, might be used to allow the ASCIIZ string in any segment; if so, it should default to DS. The procedure should use function 3DH to open the file.

Create a file:

```
CREATE_FILE      MACRO    ASCZ_OFF, ATT, HANDLE, ERROR
```

ASCZ_OFF is a word input parameter specifying the offset of an ASCIIZ string in the data segment, containing the drive, path, and filename and extension of the file to be created. ATT is a byte input parameter specifying the Attribute byte for the new file; ATT should default to 20H (normal file, archive bit set).

The macro header should explain the default as well as the significance of each bit of ATT.

HANDLE is a word output parameter to receive the sixteen-bit file handle returned by DOS. The macro header should explain the importance of HANDLE for all subsequent file access. ERROR and the Carry flag are as described earlier. If desired, another input parameter, ASCZ_SEG, might be used to allow the ASCIIZ string in any segment; if so, it should default to DS. The procedure should use function 3CH to create the file.

A PAUSE IN THE ACTION

Reminder of File Organizations and Access Methods

Recall from the last chapter that there are three fundamental file organizations: stream or unstructured, fixed-length record or structured, and terminal-format or variable-length record. Also recall that data is accessed either sequentially or directly.

Sequential access involves either reading or writing data in order from beginning to end; it requires that a file be copied in order to alter the data. Direct access involves reading and/or writing data in any order, anywhere within the file; it allows the modification of data without copying the file (read a record; modify the data; rewrite the record back to the same file location).

A stream file is accessed character by character with no organization imposed on the data; it allows both sequential and direct access by character. A structured file is organized into records, all of the same length; each record is usually further organized into fixed-length fields, one field for each item of data. Fixed-length organization allows both sequential and direct access by record. A terminal-format file consists of variable-length records (lines) each terminated with a CR_LF sequence; it allows only sequential access by record (line).

Our building blocks should provide for easy access to all three file organizations and should provide direct access (as well as sequential access) for both stream and structured files. Of the following building blocks, READ_STREAM and WRITE_STREAM are intended to provide easy access to either stream or structured files (for structured files, specify the record length for BYTES). SEEK provides direct access to stream files, and RSEEK provides direct access to structured files. READ_CHR, WRITE_CHR, READ_STR, WRITE_STR, WRITE_IMMED_STR, READ_STRL, and WRITE_STRL permit the accessing of terminal-format files in much the same manner as the keyboard and screen.

Read from a file stream:

```
READ_STREAM      MACRO    HANDLE, BYTES, BUFF_OFF, ERROR
```

HANDLE is a word input parameter specifying the handle that was returned by OPEN_FILE or CREATE_FILE. BYTES is a word input/output parameter.

On input, it specifies the number of bytes to read; on output, it receives the number of bytes actually read. The macro header should explain the use of BYTES to determine end-of-file: when its value on output is less than its value on input, end-of-file has occurred. BUFF_OFF is a word input parameter specifying the offset of the record buffer to receive the file data; the macro header should caution the programmer to ensure that the buffer is at least as long as the number of bytes specified with BYTES.

ERROR and the Carry flag are as described earlier. Note that no error is returned for end-of-file; BYTES must be used to determine end-of-file. If desired, another input parameter, BUFF_SEG, might be used to allow the record buffer in any segment; if so, it should default to DS. The procedure should use function 3FH to read from the file.

Write to a file stream:

```
WRITE_STREAM     MACRO     HANDLE, BYTES, BUFF_OFF, ERROR
```

HANDLE is a word input parameter specifying the handle that was returned by OPEN_FILE or CREATE_FILE. BYTES is a word input/output parameter. On input, it specifies the number of bytes to write; on output, it receives the number of bytes actually written. The macro header should explain the result of specifying zero for BYTES (truncate or extend file) and should caution the programmer about the possible loss of data. It should also explain the use of BYTES to detect a disk-full error; when its value on output is less than its value on input, a disk-full error has occurred.

BUFF_OFF is a word input parameter specifying the offset of the record buffer containing the data to be written; the macro header should caution the programmer to prepare at least as many bytes in the record buffer as specified with the BYTES parameter. ERROR and the Carry flag are as described earlier. Note that no error is returned for disk-full; BYTES must be used to detect a disk-full error. If desired, another input parameter, BUFF_SEG, might be used to allow the record buffer in any segment; if so, it should default to DS. The procedure should use function 40H to write to the file.

Move a file pointer (seek) by character:

```
SEEK             MACRO     HANDLE, MODE, DISP_M, DISP_L, ERROR
```

HANDLE is a word input parameter specifying the handle that was returned by OPEN_FILE or CREATE_FILE. MODE is a byte input parameter specifying the method of file-pointer movement; it should default to zero and should allow the specification of the mode as BEG, CUR, or END, as well as by numeric value (0, 1, or 2 respectively). The macro header should explain the default as well as the allowed values and the method of movement resulting from each value.

DISP_M and DISP_L are both word input/output parameters. On input, they specify the most-significant word and least-significant word, respectively, of the displacement for the file-pointer movement. On output, they should receive the new position (displacement from the beginning of the file) of the file pointer. The macro header should explain the usage for output as well as the significance of the displacement. ERROR and the Carry flag are as described earlier. The procedure should use function 42H to position the file pointer.

Move a file pointer (seek) by record:

```
RSEEK           MACRO    HANDLE, MODE, R_LEN, R_DISP,ERROR
```

RSEEK is identical to SEEK, above, except that it positions the file pointer by fixed-length record rather than by character. It is used to facilitate direct access to fixed-length record files. HANDLE, MODE, ERROR, and the Carry flag are as described earlier.

R_LEN is a word input parameter specifying the record length of the file. R_DISP is a word input/output parameter. On input, it specifies the number of records for the file-pointer movement. On output, it should receive the record number (first record is number 0) of the new file-pointer position. The macro header should explain the use of R_DISP for output as well as the significance of the record length and displacement on input.

The procedure should first multiply the record displacement by the record length to calculate the displacement by character (use IMUL since R_DISP on input is a signed value and may be negative). It should then move the resulting double-word (DX:AX) displacement into the correct registers and use function 42H to position the file pointer. Finally, it should move the new position, returned by DOS, into DX:AX and divide by the record length in order to calculate the new record number that should be placed onto the stack for return to the macro.

Read a character from a terminal-format file:

```
READ_CHR        MACRO    HANDLE, CHR_ERR
```

READ_CHR is analogous to INPUT_CHR (chapter 9) except that it reads the character from a file instead of from the keyboard and uses the Carry flag to indicate an error rather than an extended-keyboard character. HANDLE is a word input parameter specifying the handle returned by OPEN_FILE or CRE-ATE_FILE. CHR_ERR is a byte output parameter to receive either the character read from the file or an error code. The Carry flag indicates whether CHR_ERR contains a character or an error. Carry clear indicates that CHR_ERR is a character; Carry set indicates that it is an error (the error returned by DOS or zero to indicate end-of-file).

The procedure must contain a data segment in which a one-byte record buffer has been defined. It should read one character into the record buffer either with READ_STREAM or by directly accessing DOS function 3FH. If a read error occurs, the procedure should leave the Carry flag set and return the DOS error on the stack.

If the read is successful, then the procedure should check the number of bytes actually read; if it is zero then the procedure should set the Carry flag and return zero on the stack in order to indicate end-of-file. Otherwise (no error or end-of-file), it should move the character from the one-byte buffer to the stack and return, being careful to leave the Carry flag clear.

Read a terminal-format file record into a string:

```
READ_STR        MACRO     HANDLE, BUFF_OFF, MAX_LEN, TRAILER, ERROR
```

READ_STR is analogous to INPUT_STR (chapter 9) except that it uses READ_CHR to read each character of the string from a file instead of from the keyboard. HANDLE is a word input parameter specifying the handle returned by OPEN_FILE or CREATE_FILE. BUFF_OFF, MAX_LEN, and TRAILER are the same as in INPUT_STR.

ERROR and the Carry flag are as described earlier, with two exceptions. The building block should return with the Carry flag set and zero in ERROR if end-of-file has been reached; if the line from the file exceeds MAX_LEN, the procedure should set Carry and return eight in ERROR. If desired, another input parameter, BUFF_SEG, might be used to allow the string buffer in any segment; if so, it should default to DS. The macro header should warn the programmer that the buffer must be at least one byte longer than MAX_LEN.

The procedure should be similar to $INPUT_STR, but with several major differences. It obtains each character using READ_CHR instead of INPUT_CHR; it does not have to worry about extended-keyboard characters and need not watch for or specially handle the BS (8) character; it does not echo characters or beep; it should terminate the input when it encounters either CR (13, end-of-record) or SUB (26, end-of-file); if the line (record) length exceeds MAX_LEN, the procedure should simply truncate it (discard the rest of the characters up to CR or SUB), set the Carry flag, and return an error code of eight. The macro header should explain that an error code of eight indicates a truncated string.

After moving BUFF_OFF into a base or index register, to be used as a buffer pointer, and initializing a character counter to zero, the procedure should begin a loop using READ_CHR to obtain a character from the file. If the Carry flag is set, the procedure should immediately exit the loop, returning the error from READ_CHR and leaving Carry set.

Otherwise, it should check the character; if the character is CR (13), it should exit the loop with the Carry flag clear. If the character is SUB (26), then the procedure should exit with the Carry flag set, returning an error code of zero to indicate end-of-file.

If the character is neither CR (13) or SUB (26), the procedure should increment the character count and then compare it with MAX_LEN; if it is greater than MAX_LEN, then the character should not be stored nor should the buffer pointer be incremented. If the character count is less than or equal to MAX_LEN, the character should be stored in the buffer, the buffer pointer should be incremented, and the loop should be repeated.

After exiting the loop, unless exited with an error, the procedure should do one more READ_CHR to throw away the LF (10) following the CR and then compare the character count with MAX_LEN. Character count greater than MAX_LEN indicates that the string has been truncated; the procedure should set the Carry flag and return an error code of eight (insufficient memory). Otherwise, the Carry flag and error code should be as returned by READ_CHR.

Finally, the procedure should store the trailer onto the end of the string in the buffer.

```
READ_STRL        MACRO    HANDLE, BUFF_OFF, MAX_LEN, ERROR
```

READ_STRL is almost identical to READ_STR, except that it stores the string with a length byte rather than with a trailer. It is analogous to INPUT_STRL (chapter 9) except that it uses READ_CHR to read the string from a file instead of from the keyboard. The macro should be very similar to READ_STR except for the lack of TRAILER as a parameter. The procedure is very similar to $READ_STR, except that it stores the string beginning with the second byte of the buffer, storing the string length into the first byte when finished. When storing the length byte, it should store MAX_LEN instead of the character count if the string has been truncated (character count greater than MAX_LEN).

Write a character to a terminal-format file:

```
WRITE_CHR        MACRO    HANDLE, CHAR, ERROR
```

WRITE_CHR is analogous to DSPLY_CHR (chapter 7) except that it writes the character to a file instead of to the screen. HANDLE is a word input parameter specifying the handle returned by OPEN_FILE or CREATE_FILE. ERROR and the Carry flag are as described earlier, except that Carry flag set with an error code of zero is used to indicate that the disk is full. CHAR is a byte input parameter specifying the character to be written, as in DSPLY_CHR.

The procedure must contain a data segment in which a one-byte record buffer has been defined. In order to write the character, the procedure should first move it into the record buffer and then write one byte from the buffer, either with WRITE_STREAM or by directly accessing DOS function 40H. It should then check the number of bytes actually written; if it is zero, the Carry flag should be set and an error code of zero should be returned to indicate a disk-full error. Otherwise, the procedure should return the DOS error code from the write, being careful not to modify the Carry flag.

Write a string to a terminal-format file:

```
WRITE_STR          MACRO     HANDLE, STR_OFF, TRAILER, ERROR
```

WRITE_STR is analogous to DSPLY_STR (chapter 8) except that it uses WRITE_CHR to write the string characters to a file instead of to the screen. HANDLE is a word input parameter specifying the handle returned by OPEN_FILE or CREATE_FILE. STR_OFF and TRAILER are the same as in DSPLY_STR. ERROR and the Carry flag are as described earlier, except that the building block should return with the Carry flag set and an error code of zero if the disk is full. If desired, another input parameter, STR_SEG, might be used to allow the string in any segment; if so, it should default to DS.

The macro header should instruct the programmer to be sure to write a CR+LF sequence to the end of each line and to write a SUB (26) character to the end of the file after all output and before closing the file. The procedure should be almost identical to $DSPLY_STR, except for the manner in which it writes each character. It should use WRITE_CHR to write each character to the file, immediately checking the Carry flag; if Carry is set by WRITE_CHR, the procedure should immediately exit, leaving Carry set and returning the error code from WRITE_CHR.

```
WRITE_STRL         MACRO     HANDLE, STR_OFF, ERROR
```

WRITE_STRL is very similar to WRITE_STR, except that it writes a string that has been stored with a length byte rather than with a trailer. It is analogous to DSPLY_STRL (chapter 8) except that it uses WRITE_CHR to write the string to a file instead of to the screen. The macro should be very similar to WRITE_STR except for the lack of TRAILER as a parameter. The procedure is very similar to $WRITE_STR, except that it uses the length byte and a repeat-n-times construct, as in DSPLY_STRL, to write the string characters to the file.

Write an immediate string to a terminal-format file:

```
WRITE_IMMED_STR  MACRO     HANDLE, STRING, TRAILER, ERROR
```

WRITE_IMMED_STR is analogous to DSPLY_IMMED_STR discussed in chapter 9. It does not require a procedure. It simply defines STRING within a data segment and invokes WRITE_STR to write it to the file.

Close a file:

```
CLOSE_FILE         MACRO     HANDLE, ERROR
```

HANDLE is a word input parameter specifying the handle returned by OPEN_FILE or CREATE_FILE. ERROR and the Carry flag are as described earlier. The macro header should explain the result and necessity of closing files. The procedure should use function 3EH to close the file.

Figure 12-6 provides an example program that uses OPEN_FILE, READ_STREAM, and CLOSE_FILE to display the contents of a data file to the screen.

Figure 12-6 Example Program Using OPEN_FILE, READ_STREAM, and CLOSE_FILE Building Blocks

```
                    TITLE F12-6.ASM
                    PAGE  55, 80

    COMMENT |       PROGRAM:       F12-6.ASM
                    PROGRAMMER:    Your name here
                    DATE:          Date here
                    CLASS:         Class name and number here
                    INSTRUCTOR:    Instructor's name here

            DISPLAYS THE CONTENTS OF A DATA FILE TO THE SCREEN

            USES INPUT_STR, DSPLY_STR, DSPLY_CHR, OPEN_FILE,
            READ_STREAM, AND CLOSE_FILE BUILDING BLOCKS

            INPUT PARAM'S:  NONE
            OUTPUT PARAM'S: NONE
                            RETURNS TO DOS, UPON COMPLETION
            |

                    IF1
                        INCLUDE CONSOLE.MLB
                        INCLUDE DISK.MLB
                    ENDIF

;STACK SEGMENT ==========================================================

STACK               SEGMENT PARA STACK 'STACK'       ;BEGIN STACK
                                                     ;  SEGMENT

                    DB      64 DUP ('*STACK* ')      ;DEFINE 512
                                                     ;  BYTE STACK

STACK               ENDS                             ;END OF STACK SEGMENT

;DATA SEGMENT ===========================================================

DATA                SEGMENT PARA PUBLIC 'DATA'       ;BEGIN DATA
                                                     ;  SEGMENT
                ;DEFINE BUFFERS AND MESSAGES
IO_BUF          DB      81 DUP('*')                  ;BUFFER FOR I/O
R_BUF           DB      '#'                          ;1-BYTE RECORD BUFFER
FN_PRMPT        DB      'File to display (may include path) ', 0
OPEN_ERR        DB      13, 10, 7, 'Unable to open file', 0
READ_ERR        DB      13, 10, 7, 'Unable to read from file', 0
CLOSE_ERR       DB      13, 10, 7, 'Unable to close file', 0
CODE_MSG        DB      ' - Error code: ', 0
HEX_END         DB      'H', 13, 10, 10, 0

DATA                ENDS                             ;END OF DATA SEGMENT
```

Figure 12-6:   (continued)

```
;CODE SEGMENT ==========================================================

CODE             SEGMENT PARA PUBLIC 'CODE'        ;BEGIN CODE
                                                   ;  SEGMENT

                 ASSUME   CS:CODE, SS:STACK
                                       ;ASSOCIATE CS AND SS
                                       ;  WITH PROPER SEGMENTS

MAIN             PROC FAR                 ;BEGIN MAINLINE
                                          ;  FAR PROCEDURE

        ;INITIALIZATION (SAME FOR ALL PROGRAMS)
        ;FIRST, SET UP FOR RETURN TO DOS VIA PSP
                 PUSH    DS               ;PUT RETURN SEG (PSP)
                                          ;  TO STACK
                 MOV     AX, 0            ;PUT ZERO RETURN
                 PUSH    AX               ;  OFFSET TO STACK
        ;NOW, ADDRESS THE DATA SEGMENT WITH DS
                 MOV     AX, DATA         ;POINT DS TO
                 MOV     DS, AX           ;  DATA SEGMENT
                 ASSUME  DS:DATA          ;ASSOCIATE DS WITH
                                          ;  DATA SEGMENT

        ;BEGIN MAINLINE CODE
        ;GET FILE NAME AND OPEN FILE
                 DSPLY_STR       <OFFSET FN_PRMPT>
                                          ;PROMPT FOR FILE SPEC
                 INPUT_STR       <OFFSET IO_BUF>, 80
                                          ;GET FILE SPEC
                 OPEN_FILE       <OFFSET IO_BUF>, R, DX, AL
                                          ;OPEN IT, READ ONLY,
                                          ;  HANDLE TO DX, ERROR
                                          ;  CODE TO AL
                 ;IF UNSUCCESSFUL, REPORT ERROR AND ABORT
                 JNC     OPEN_OK          ;GO ON IF SUCCESSFUL
                     DSPLY_STR       <OFFSET OPEN_ERR>
                                          ;REPORT OPEN ERROR
                     CALL    RPT_CODE
                                          ;REPORT ERROR CODE
                     JMP     DONE         ;ABORT
OPEN_OK:         ;END IF
        ;LOOP READING AN DISPLAYING 1 CHARACTER AT A TIME
                 MOV     CX, 1            ;NUMBER BYTES TO READ
LP_BEG:          ;BEGIN GENERAL LOOP, QUIT WHEN NO CHARACTER READ
                     READ_STREAM DX, CX, <OFFSET R_BUF>, AL
                                          ;READ 1 CHAR INTO R_BUF,
                                          ;  ERROR CODE TO AL
                     ;IF UNSUCCESSFUL, REPORT ERROR AND ABORT
                     JNC     READ_OK      ;GO ON IF SUCCESSFUL
                         DSPLY_STR       <OFFSET READ_ERR>
```

Figure 12-6:   (continued)

```
                                        ;REPORT READ ERROR
                        CALL    RPT_CODE
                                        ;REPORT ERROR CODE
                        JMP     CLOSE_IT
                                        ;CLOSE FILE AND ABORT
READ_OK:            ;END IF
                CMP     CX, 1           ;QUIT LOOP WHEN NO CHAR
                JB      LP_END          ;  READ (EOF)
                    MOV     AL, R_BUF   ;DISPLAY CHAR
                    DSPLY_CHR       AL  ; FROM FILE
                    JMP     LP_BEG      ;CONTINUE LOOP
LP_END:            ;END GENERAL LOOP
        ;CLOSE FILE AND RETURN TO DOS
CLOSE_IT:       CLOSE_FILE      DX, AL  ;CLOSE IT, ERR CODE TO AL

                ;IF UNSUCCESSFUL, REPORT ERROR
                JNC     CLOSE_OK        ;GO ON IF SUCCESSFUL
                    DSPLY_STR       <OFFSET CLOSE_ERR>
                                        ;REPORT CLOSE ERROR
                    CALL    RPT_CODE    ;REPORT ERROR CODE
CLOSE_OK:          ;END IF

        ;END OF MAINLINE
DONE:           RET                     ;RETURN

MAIN            ENDP


;-----------------------------------------------------------------
;SUBPROCEDURE TO REPORT ERROR CODE IN AL

RPT_CODE        PROC    NEAR

                PUSH    AX              ;SAVE IT
                MOV     AH, 0           ;NOW AX = CODE
                DSPLY_STR       <OFFSET CODE_MSG>
                                        ;CODE EXPLANATION
                CNV_UNS_STR     <OFFSET IO_BUF>, AX, 16
                                        ;CONVERT CODE TO HEX
                DSPLY_STR       <OFFSET IO_BUF>
                                        ;DISPLAY CODE
                DSPLY_STR       <OFFSET HEX_END>
                                        ;'H' CR LF LF
                POP     AX              ;RESTORE IT
                RET                     ;RETURN

RPT_CODE        ENDP

CODE            ENDS                    ;END OF CODE SEGMENT

                END     MAIN            ;END OF F12-6.ASM
                                        ;  ENTRY POINT = MAIN
```

SUMMARY

In this chapter we have discussed a number of concepts necessary to the understanding of data-file access. We began with the STRUC directive, which allows for the definition of fixed-length data structures and is useful for the directory-search structures required by functions 4EH (DIR first) and 4FH (DIR next). Once such a data structure has been defined, the allocation and addressing of the structure is greatly simplified.

We then discussed subdirectories and paths. A subdirectory is a file that consists of a series of 32-byte directory entries, one for each file within the subdirectory. A path is a string of subdirectory names, separated by back slashes (\), beginning in either the current default directory or in the root directory and describing the location of a file. Paths and filenames are specified to DOS with ASCIIZ strings. An ASCIIZ string is merely a string that is terminated with the NUL character.

In order to access file data, a program must first use function 3DH to open a preexisting file or function 3CH to create a new file. In either case, the desired file and path are specified with an ASCIIZ string. When the file is opened or created, DOS returns a sixteen-bit file handle or token; all subsequent access identifies the file by its handle.

Disk access consists of logical reads and writes (functions 3FH and 40H), transferring the specified number of characters between DOS's internal file buffer and the program's record buffer, whose address is specified to DOS upon each read or write. DOS performs a physical write and/or read to or from the disk only when necessary. The extended functions treat all files as a continuous stream of characters with no structure. In order to interpret the stream as logical records, the application program must specify the same logical record length on every file access.

A program gains direct access to the data by using function 42H to move the file pointer to the desired relative character within the stream. If the program needs direct access by relative record number, then it must calculate the desired relative character number before moving the file pointer.

Upon completion of the access to file data, the program must close the file (function 3EH). DOS does not physically write the last physical record from the file buffer to the disk until the file is closed. More importantly, not until the file is closed does DOS update the disk directory entry to reflect any changes in the file size, date, or time. Failure to close a file leaves its date and time unchanged, may result in the loss of data, and may also result in the loss of storage space on the disk (lost clusters), a situation that can be corrected only with CHKDSK.

VOCABULARY

V12-1   In your own words, define each of the following terms:

a) Fixed-length data structure

b) STRUC, ENDS

c) Structure field

d) Structure variable

e) Field-override value

V12-2 In your own words, define each of the following terms:

a) Root directory

b) Subdirectory file

c) Directory tree

d) Parent directory

e) Default directory

f) Directory path

g) ASCIIZ string

h) File handle

i) File pointer

j) General file-related functions

k) Directory-management functions

l) File-management functions

m) File-access functions

REVIEW QUESTIONS

Q12-1 Which data-file organization is the most flexible, fixed-length record (structured), stream (unstructured), or terminal format?

Q12-2 Give an example of a fixed-length data structure that DOS maintains on disk.

Q12-3 What are the two possible interpretations of the ENDS directive? How does the assembler know which way to interpret it?

Q12-4 How does a program address a field within an allocated structure?

Q12-5 When is a field-override value not permitted in the allocation of a structure?

Q12-6 What are the two directories within which a path may begin?

Q12-7 What are the three access modes for which a file may be opened? What access mode is provided when a file is created?

Q12-8 When a file is opened, does the program specify the file handle or does DOS determine the handle?

Q12-9 Which file handles are automatically opened and ready for use by the program?

Q12-10 What are the three modes of movement for a file pointer?

Q12-11 Describe the manner in which extended functions return errors?

Q12-12 The extended functions include a group of directory-management functions; however, no such functions are included in the traditional functions. Why?

Q12-13 Other than function 3CH, which creates a new file with zero bytes, what is the only other extended function that can be used to decrease the size of a file? What must the program do to cause the function to decrease the file size?

PROGRAMMING ASSIGNMENTS

PA12-1 Write a program to give the user a directory listing and tell the user how many entries were found. Add the following building blocks to your disk library: DEFINE_DIR_BFR_STRUCT, SET_DTA, DIR_FRST, and DIR_NXT. In addition, if your keyboard input building block stores strings with a length byte, you will have to add an additional building block, CNV_STRL_ASCZ.

Write a mainline program, PA12-1.ASM, to provide the directory listing and the count of matching entries. The program must define a directory-search buffer, in the data segment, to receive information from DOS about the matching file specifications.

Set the DTA to the directory-search buffer, then ask the user for a file specification for the directory search. Convert the string from the user to an ASCIIZ string, if necessary. Initialize a counter to zero and use DIR_FRST to search for the first matching file.

Begin a loop, repeating while the Carry flag is clear, indicating that a file has been found. Inside the loop, display the matching filename and extension from the directory-search buffer, increment the counter, and use DIR_NXT to search for the next matching file. Then repeat the loop.

After the loop, check the counter to see if any files were found. If the counter is zero, display a message, "File not found"; otherwise, convert the counter to a string, and display it with a message explaining that it is the number of matching entries.

PA12-2   Write a program to rename a file. Add the building block, REN_FILE, to your disk library. In addition, if your keyboard input building block stores strings with a length byte, you will have to add an additional building block, CNV_STRL_ASCZ. Write a mainline program, PA12-2.ASM, to do the file renaming.

Ask the user for the path and name of the file to be renamed, telling the user that wild cards are not allowed. Convert the string from the user to an ASCIIZ string, if necessary.

Ask the user for the new filename; let the user know that a different path may be specified to "move" the file to another directory but the drives must match. Convert the string from the user to an ASCIIZ string, if necessary.

Rename the file and check the Carry flag; if set, check the error code and print an appropriate message.

PA12-3   Write a program to delete a file. Add the building block, DEL_FILE, to your disk library. In addition, if your keyboard input building block stores strings with a length byte, you will have to add an additional building block, CNV_STRL_ASCZ. Write a mainline program, PA12-3.ASM, to delete the file.

Ask the user for the path and name of the file to be deleted, telling the user that wild cards are not allowed. Convert the string from the user to an ASCIIZ string, if necessary.

Delete the file and check the Carry flag; if set, check the error code and print an appropriate message.

PA12-4   Write a program to copy a user-specified file to a new file also specified by the user; use a logical record length (up to 512 bytes), which is also specified by the user. When completed, report the number of records that were copied. Add the following building blocks to your disk library: OPEN_FILE, CREATE_FILE, READ_STREAM, WRITE_STREAM, and CLOSE_FILE.

Write a mainline program, PA12-4.ASM, to copy a file. The program must allocate a 512-byte record buffer (DB DUP) within the data segment. Get the record length from the user to use on the copy; convert it to an unsigned integer. If invalid, print an error message, and try again. If less than 1 or greater than 512 (length of record buffer), print an error and try again.

Get the name of the input file (to copy from) from the user, and open it for read access only. Check the Carry flag; if set, print an appropriate error message and let the user try again. Get the name of the output file (to copy to) from the user, and create it. Check the Carry flag; if set, print an appropriate error message, and let the user try again.

Begin a loop to copy records. Read a logical record, of the length specified by the user, from the input file to the record buffer, and check the Carry flag; if set, report an appropriate error and abort the copy. Otherwise, check the number of characters actually transferred. If zero bytes were read, then stop copying. If a partial record was transferred, then do one last write to the output file, specifying the number of bytes actually read from the input file, and then stop copying. If a full record was transferred, write a full record from the record buffer to the output file, and go back to read another record. Keep a count of the number of records written to the output file. Check the Carry flag after each write; if set, print an appropriate error message and abort the copy.

When through copying (copy completed or aborted): close both files, convert the count (number of records written) to a string, and display it with a message, explaining that it is the number of records copied.

PA12-5   Write a program that quickly copies a file (up to 32,768 bytes) as one record. If you have already done PA12-4, compare the time it takes each program to copy the same file.

Add the same building blocks to your disk library as in PA12-4. Add another building block, SEEK, to position the file pointer.

Write a mainline program, PA12-5.ASM, to copy the file. The program must allocate a 32,768-byte record buffer (DB DUP) within the data segment. Get the name of the input file (to copy from) from the user and open it for read access only. Check the Carry flag; if set, print an appropriate error message, and try again.

Use SEEK to determine the size of the input file. Use mode two to move the file pointer to end-of-file, specifying Word registers containing zero for both DISP_M and DISP_L. Upon exit from the building block, DISP_M and DISP_L contain the file size. Use SEEK again to set the file pointer back to the beginning of the file; use mode zero, specifying zero for both DISP_M and DISP_L. Check the Carry flag after each SEEK; if set, print an appropriate error message, and abort the program.

Check the file size; if it is greater than 32,768 bytes, tell the user that it is too big, and abort the program. Otherwise, get the name of the output file (to copy to) from the user, and create it. Check the Carry flag; if set, print an appropriate error message, and try again.

Copy the file with one read and one write, specifying the file size as the number of bytes to transfer on each. After copying, close both files, convert the file size to a string, and display it with a message, explaining that it is the number of bytes copied.

PA12-6   Write a program to copy character-by-character from the keyboard to a stream file called A:KEYBOARD.DAT. When finished, report the number of characters copied, and display the file for the user. Add the following building blocks to your disk library: SET_DTA, DEFINE_DIR_BFR_STRUCT, DIR_FRST, CREATE_FILE, READ_STREAM, WRITE_STREAM, SEEK, and CLOSE_FILE.

Write a mainline program, PA12-6.ASM. Allocate a directory-search buffer, define a one-byte record buffer, and define the ASCIIZ string for the file, all in the data segment. Set the DTA to the directory search buffer, and invoke DIR_FRST, checking the Carry flag and error code, to determine if A:KEYBOARD.DAT already exists. If it does not exist, create it.

Otherwise, tell the user that it already exists and ask if he or she wants to overwrite it. If the user says no, abort the program; otherwise, create the file. Check the Carry flag and, if set, the error code. Abort the program with an appropriate error message, if unsuccessful.

If successful, tell the user to type <Ctrl>+<Z> when finished. Then begin a loop that uses INPUT_CHR to get a single character from the keyboard. Ignore any extended-keyboard characters. Check the character for a<Ctrl>+<Z>(26) and exit the loop if one is found. If the character is not extended or<Ctrl>+<Z>, echo it to the screen, move it into the record buffer, write it to the file, and count one more character. If the character is CR (13), then also echo, write, and count a LF (10) character.

Do not close the file after completion of the loop. Display "^Z" followed by CR and LF to the screen, then convert the character count to a string, and display it with an appropriate message.

After displaying the number of characters, use SEEK to move the file pointer back to the beginning of the file. Then, use a repeat-n-times loop to read the file, one character at a time, displaying each character to the screen. **Close** the file when finished.

PA12-7   Write a program to provide direct access, by relative record number, to a list of customer names (twenty-four bytes per name) in a file called A:CUSTOMER.DAT. When finished, report the number of names viewed and the number of names written. Add the following building blocks to your disk library: OPEN_FILE, CREATE_FILE, RSEEK, READ_STREAM, WRITE_STREAM, and CLOSE_FILE.

Write the mainline program, PA12-7.ASM. Define the necessary ASCIIZ string and a twenty-five byte record buffer, both in the data segment. Open A:CUSTOMER.DAT for read/write access, and check the Carry flag. If successful, then go on; otherwise, check the error code. If it is any error other than "File not found," provide an appropriate error message and abort the program; otherwise tell the user that the program could not find A:CUSTOMER.DAT, and ask if he or she wants to create it. If the user says no, abort the program; otherwise, create the file.

Warn the user that if he or she views a record that has not been written to the file yet, garbage may be displayed to the screen. Then begin a loop that asks the user if he or she wants to view a customer name, write a customer name, or quit. Exit the loop immediately if the user says to quit; otherwise, ask for the customer number. Use the customer number minus 1 as the relative record number. Use RSEEK with twenty-four for R_LEN to move the file pointer to the correct record.

If the user wants to view a customer name, read the record into the record buffer, specifying twenty-four as the number of bytes to read. Display the record to the screen, and increment the count of records viewed.

If the user wants to write a customer name, then input the name from the keyboard into the file buffer, limiting the user to twenty-four characters, and write it to the file specifying twenty-four characters.

When the user says to quit, close the file, and report the number of records viewed and the number written before returning to DOS.

PA12-8   Write a program, PA12-8.ASM, which reads one line at a time from a terminal-format file, displaying each line as it is read. Add the following building blocks to your disk library: OPEN_FILE, READ_CHR, READ_STR (or READ_STRL), and CLOSE_FILE. Also add CNV_STRL_ASCZ if your keyboard input building block stores strings with a length byte.

The program should ask the user for the name of the file and open the file for read-only access; if your keyboard input building block stores strings with a length byte, you will have to convert the user's input to an ASCIIZ string before opening the file. Check the Carry flag, and report any error, and let the user try again if necessary.

Otherwise, use READ_STR (or READ_STRL) to read a line from the file, limiting the string to eighty bytes, and use DSPLY_STR (or DSPLY_STRL) to display it to the screen. Then tell the user to press any key to continue, using INPUT_CHR to pause the program. Continue reading a line from the file, displaying it, and pausing until end-of-file is reached on the terminal-format file.

PA12-9   Write a program to copy a user-specified terminal-format file to a new terminal-format file, also specified by the user; copy the file one character at a time. When completed, report the number of characters that were copied. Add the following building blocks to your disk library: OPEN_FILE, CREATE_FILE, READ_CHR, WRITE_CHR, and CLOSE_FILE. Also add CNV_STRL_ASCZ if your keyboard input building block stores strings with a length byte.

Write a mainline program, PA12-9.ASM, to copy a file. Get the name of the input file (to copy from) from the user, and open it for read access only. Check the Carry flag; if set, print an appropriate error message and let the user try again. Get the name of the output file (to copy to) from the user and create it. Check the Carry flag; if set, print an appropriate error message and let the user try again. If your keyboard input building block stores strings with a length byte, you will have to convert the user's input to an ASCIIZ string before opening each file.

Begin a repeat-until loop to copy the file. Read a character from the input file and check the Carry flag; if set, check the error. If the error is end-of-file (0), simply report "EOF mark not found"; for any other error, print an appropriate message, and abort the copy.

Write the character to the output file and check the Carry flag; if set, report an appropriate error message, and abort the copy. Otherwise, repeat the loop until the character just read and written is an ASCII SUB (26) used to mark the end of terminal-format files.

When through copying (copy completed or aborted), close both files, convert the count (number of characters written) to a string, and display it with a message, explaining that it is the number of characters copied.

PA12-10   Write a program to copy a user-specified terminal-format file to a new terminal-format file, also specified by the user; copy the file one line at a time. When completed, report the number of lines that were copied. Add the following building blocks to your disk library: OPEN_FILE, CREATE_FILE, READ_CHR, WRITE_CHR, READ_STR (or READ_STRL), WRITE_STR (or WRITE_STRL), WRITE_IMMED_STR, and CLOSE_FILE. Also add CNV_STRL_ASCZ if your keyboard input building block stores strings with a length byte.

Write a mainline program, PA12-10.ASM, to copy a file. Get the name of the input file (to copy from) from the user, and open it for read access only. Check the Carry flag; if set, print an appropriate error message, and let the user try again. Get the name of the output file (to copy to) from the user, and create it. Check the Carry flag; if set, print an appropriate error message, and let the user try again. If your keyboard input building block stores strings with a length byte, you will have to convert the user's input to an ASCIIZ string before opening each file.

Begin a loop to copy the file. Read a line from the input file, and check the Carry flag; if set, check the error. If the error is line-too-long (8), simply report "Line #n too long—truncated"; for any other error, print an appropriate message, and abort the copy.

Write the line to the output file, and check the Carry flag; if set, report an appropriate error message and abort the copy. Otherwise, write a CR+LF sequence to mark the end of the record, checking the Carry flag, reporting any error and exiting as above. If no error, count the line, and repeat the loop.

Upon exiting from the loop, write one last line to the file in case the last line of the input file is immediately terminated with a SUB (no CR+LF). Then write a SUB to mark the end of the new file. Close both files, convert the count (number of lines written) to a string, and display it with a message, explaining that it is the number of lines copied.

13

Advanced Programming Topics

INTRODUCTION

This and the following chapter include a number of advanced topics, which you may not have time to cover in a semester length course. While possibly beyond the scope of an introductory course in assembly-language programming, they have been included here in order to present you with some challenging ideas for further exploration.

Unlike the executable programs developed under many operating systems designed for use with earlier microprocessors such as the Z-80, DOS executable programs are not limited to any particular memory location. The memory location at which the program is loaded and executed is not determined at the time that the program is written, assembled, and linked; rather, the program's location is determined by DOS at the time the program is executed. Thus, all DOS executable programs are **relocatable**.

When loading any file for execution, DOS determines the first available (unused) memory location at a paragraph (sixteen-byte) boundary. Thus the same program may reside at any memory location during execution, depending upon the version of DOS in use as well as upon the various memory-resident programs and/or device drivers currently installed in the system. At the first available memory location, DOS builds a 256-byte block of memory called the Program Segment Prefix or PSP. The program file is then loaded into memory, immediately following the PSP, at a displacement of 256 (100H) bytes from the first available paragraph of memory.

DOS supports two types of executable programs, those with an extension of .COM and those with an extension of .EXE. The relocatability of .COM files is provided purely by the memory segmentation of the 8086/8088 family of processors. The file structure is similar to the nonrelocatable program files of earlier microprocessors and operating systems (most notably CP/M); DOS relocates the program simply by initializing all Segment registers to the Segment address of the memory location into which the program is loaded.

.EXE files are fully relocatable in the traditional sense of the word; an .EXE file contains a relocation header providing DOS with all the information necessary to individually initialize segment and pointer registers and to modify addresses within the program to reflect the memory location at which the program has been loaded.

A .COM file, since it has no relocation header, is limited to a single segment with a maximum size of 64K. .COM files may be created with MASM, LINK, and EXE2BIN as long as the source file follows a number of rules to be discussed in this chapter. Although it is limited to a single segment, the source file may contain multiple segment directives as long as they are all combined into a single segment with the GROUP directive.

The 256-byte Program Segment Prefix, constructed by DOS in the memory immediately preceding the program, is used to provide communication between DOS and the program as well as to retain several interrupt vectors, which DOS restores upon termination of the program. Access to the PSP data can be simplified by the definition of a separate segment with a combine type of AT.

We will also discuss a number of alternate methods of program termination that DOS provides in addition to interrupt type 20H.

Finally, this chapter will discuss the interfacing of assembly language with other programming languages. Interfacing with any high-level language requires a good deal of research into the calling and parameter-passing conventions of the particular compiler. The assembly-language subprocedure, to be linked with the high-level mainline, must carefully follow all conventions of the compiler.

.COM FILES VERSUS .EXE FILES

As discussed in the introduction, DOS determines a program's location in memory at the time that it loads it for execution. At the first available paragraph boundary (multiple of sixteen) DOS builds a 256-byte (100H) Program Segment Prefix immediately followed by the program. If the program file has an extension of .EXE, then it must begin with a **Relocation Header** of at least 512 bytes (more if necessary), which was created by LINK, and which provides DOS with information necessary for the adjustment of the program code and for the initialization of segment and pointer registers.

As a minimum, the relocation header contains **segment displacement values** for both CS and SS as well as **pointer offset** values for IP and SP. Each Segment register displacement represents the number of bytes from the beginning of the program at which the segment begins. The IP offset is the offset within the code segment of the entry point to the program; the offset for SP is the length of the stack segment defined within the program.

Upon loading the .EXE program, DOS adds the CS displacement value (from the relocation header) plus 100H (length of PSP) to the segment address at which the PSP begins; CS is then initialized to the resulting segment address. Similarly, the initial value for SS is calculated by adding the SS displacement value (from the relocation header) plus 100H to the segment address of the PSP. DOS then moves the PSP segment address, without any adjustment, into both DS and ES.

The result is that DS and ES both contain the segment address of the PSP, while CS and SS contain the segment addresses at which the program's code segment and stack segment, respectively, have been loaded. IP and SP are then initialized to the IP and SP offsets contained within the relocation header. Thus, CS:IP now point to the memory location of the first program instruction, while SS:SP point to the top of the stack.

Additionally, the relocation header at the beginning of an .EXE file must contain **fix-up addresses** for any Far jumps or calls. Recall that a Near (or Short) jump or call is assembled to a machine-language instruction that specifies the target address as a displacement from the current offset. Thus, since the target is specified relative to the current offset, a Near jump or call will execute properly regardless of the memory location into which the program has been loaded by DOS. However, a Far jump or call, in machine language, specifies its target as an absolute address consisting of a segment (CS) and offset (IP).

The linker cannot know, at link time, the address at which the program will eventually be loaded; in fact, depending on outside factors, the same program file may be loaded by DOS at a different address each time it is executed. Consequently, LINK assembles any Far jump or call as if the program is to be loaded at address 0000H:0000H. It then places the address of the instruction within the relocation header. Upon loading the program, DOS uses the fix-up address to locate the instruction and then adds the segment address, at which the program has been loaded, to the segment half of the absolute target address. In this manner, each Far jump or call instruction is adjusted (or fixed up) by DOS to reflect the actual memory location at which the program will reside during execution.

A .COM file has no such relocation header. Consequently, DOS cannot perform any fix-ups of Far jumps or calls, nor can it initialize the Segment or Pointer registers to anything other than values that can be determined by DOS without any special information about the program. Upon loading the .COM program into memory immediately following the PSP, DOS initializes all Segment registers (CS, DS, SS, and ES) to the same value, the Segment address of the PSP. Additionally, DOS always initializes SP to FFFEH, and IP to 100H. Thus execution of a .COM file always begins at offset 100H, and the top of the stack is always at offset FFFEH (65534) from the beginning of the PSP.

Previously, we have created all .COM files with DEBUG and have used the assembler only for the creation of .EXE files; however, as will be discussed shortly, you can develop .COM program files much like .EXE programs, through the use of a text editor, MASM, and LINK. However, the lack of a relocation header in the .COM file and the simplicity in the way DOS prepares the program for execution result in a number of restrictions on .COM program source files. Following is a discussion of some of those limitations.

KEY TERMS TO REMEMBER

Relocatable program	Pointer offset value
Relocation Header	Fix-up address
Segment displacement value	

.COM FILE RESTRICTIONS

The fact that the program entry point is always at offset 100H places several requirements on the source program for a .COM file. Any program that is to be converted to a .COM file must always include an ORG directive at the beginning of the source file, before any instructions or data-definition directives, in order to set the assembler's location counter to 100H. The following directive tells the assembler to set its location counter to 100H so that it will properly calculate all subsequent symbol offsets for a .COM program file:

```
ORG        100H
```

Additionally, the program must begin with an instruction rather than a data directive. However, since any forward reference to data requires a PTR operator to explicitly specify the data type, it is normally desirable to place all data definitions at the beginning of the program, before the instructions that reference them. Consequently, most .COM programs begin with a jump instruction, at offset 100H, followed by all data-definition directives, followed by the remainder of the code. The jump instruction, at offset 100H, merely jumps around the data to a label or procedure name at the first instruction of the program code.

Since DOS initializes all four Segment registers to the same value (the Segment address of the 256-byte Program Segment Prefix), a .COM program may contain only one 64K segment. Thus, the sum of the PSP and program may not exceed 64K; the code, data, and stack together may not be greater than 65,280 bytes (65,536–256). .COM programs often contain only one SEGMENT directive; a .COM program may contain multiple SEGMENT directives only if a GROUP directive is used to combine them all into one segment as illustrated later in Figure 13-3.

Finally, a source program that is to be converted to a .COM file must never contain any Far jumps or calls. The FAR PTR operator must never be used with a jump or call instruction, and the PROC directive beginning all procedures, except for the mainline and any interrupt service routines, must specify a type of NEAR.

CREATING A .COM FILE - EXE2BIN.EXE

To create a .COM file, first create the source file (.ASM) observing the above restrictions. Then assemble and link the program to create an .EXE version. Note that LINK will display a warning message:

```
Warning: No STACK segment
```

Ignore the message; .COM files do not have a separate stack segment. Do not attempt to run the .EXE file; it must be converted to a .COM file before it will execute properly. A utility program, EXE2BIN.EXE, is provided on the assembler diskette for this purpose. To convert an .EXE file to a .COM file, enter the command to execute EXE2BIN, as follows:

```
EXE2BIN exefile comfile
```

Exefile is the drive and name of the .EXE file to be converted. The extension may be omitted; EXE2BIN assumes an extension of .EXE. *Comfile* is the drive and name of the .COM file to be created. The extension, .COM, must be included in the file specification; otherwise, EXE2BIN creates the file with an extension of .BIN. If *comfile* is entirely omitted, EXE2BIN creates a file with the same primary name as *exefile* and an extension of .BIN.

For example, if we were to write a program, TEST.ASM, and assemble and link it to create TEST.EXE, then the command to convert it to a .COM file, TEST.COM, would be as follows:

```
EXE2BIN TEST TEST.COM
```

EXE2BIN first checks the relocation header of TEST.EXE to ensure that the program contains only one segment and that it does not include any Far jumps or calls. If the header indicates a displacement other than zero for either CS or SP, if it specifies an offset for SP or an offset other than 100H for IP, or if it contains fix-up addresses for any Far jumps or calls, then EXE2BIN terminates without creating TEST.COM, reporting the error:

```
File cannot be converted
```

If TEST.EXE follows the rules for conversion to a .COM file, then EXE2BIN creates TEST.COM and copies TEST.EXE, minus the relocation header, into it. Thus, the resulting TEST.COM contains only the instructions and data from TEST.EXE, without the relocation header. It is now ready to be loaded and executed as a .COM file.

The following three figures (13-1, 13-2, and 13-3) provide a comparison of the source code required for .COM files with that required for .EXE files. Figure 13-1 illustrates a source file that is to be assembled and linked to an .EXE file. The program merely reports the segment address at which it has been loaded by DOS, as well as the address (segment:offset) of its entry point.

Figure 13-1   Sample .EXE Program
Display Program Segment and Entry Point

```
COMMENT \                    EXE_TST.ASM

        .EXE PROGRAM TO REPORT PROGRAM SEGMENT ADDRESS
        AND ENTRY-POINT SEGMENT:OFFSET

        \

                PAGE    55,80              ;LINES, WIDTH FOR LISTING
                TITLE   EXE_TST.ASM

                INCLUDE        CONSOLE.MLB

;STACK SEGMENT ==================================================
STACK           SEGMENT PARA STACK 'STACK'
                DB     128 DUP ('*')
STACK           ENDS

;DATA SEGMENT ===================================================
DATA            SEGMENT PARA PUBLIC 'DATA'
IO_BUF          DB     5 DUP ('#')             ;DEFINE A 5-BYTE BUFFER
DATA            ENDS

;CODE SEGMENT ===================================================
CODE            SEGMENT PARA PUBLIC 'CODE'
                ASSUME  CS:CODE, SS:STACK

MAIN            PROC    FAR

        ;INITIALIZE
                PUSH    DS                 ;SET UP
                XOR     AX, AX             ;  FOR RETURN
                PUSH    AX                 ;  TO DOS
                MOV     AX, DATA           ;ADDRESS DATA
                MOV     DS, AX             ;  SEGMENT
                ASSUME  DS:DATA            ;  WITH DS

        ;REPORT SEGMENT ADDRESS WHERE LOADED
                DSPLY_IMMED_STR <13, 10, 'Program loaded at '>
                MOV     AX, ES             ;GET PROGRAM SEGMENT
                CNV_UNS_STR    <OFFSET IO_BUF>, AX, 16
                                           ;CONVERT TO HEX STRING
                DSPLY_STR      <OFFSET IO_BUF>
                                           ;SHOW SEG ADDRESS OF
                                           ;  PROGRAM
                DSPLY_IMMED_STR <'H (seg address).', 13, 10, 10>

        ;REPORT ENTRY POINT AS SEGMENT:OFFSET
                DSPLY_IMMED_STR 'Entry point is '
```

Figure 13-1:   (continued)

```
                    MOV     AX, CS              ;GET CODE SEGMENT
                    CNV_UNS_STR    <OFFSET IO_BUF>, AX, 16
                                                ;CONVERT TO HEX STRING
                    DSPLY_STR      <OFFSET IO_BUF>
                                                ;SHOW CS
                    DSPLY_IMMED_STR 'H:'
                    MOV     AX, OFFSET MAIN
                                                ;OFFSET OF ENTRY POINT
                                                ;   INTO AX
                    CNV_UNS_STR    <OFFSET IO_BUF>, AX, 16
                                                ;CONVERT TO HEX STRING
                    DSPLY_STR      <OFFSET IO_BUF>
                                                ;SHOW ENTRY-POINT OFFSET
                    DSPLY_IMMED_STR <'H (seg:off)', 13, 10, 10>

                    RET                         ;TERMINATE

MAIN                ENDP

CODE                ENDS

                    END     MAIN               ;PROGRAM ENTRY POINT
```

Figure 13-2 illustrates the same program as in Figure 13-1, except that it has been rewritten to be converted to a .COM file. Notice that it contains only one segment, CODE. Notice also that the entry point is preceded by an ORG directive to set the assembler's location counter to offset 100H, and that the instruction at the entry point consists of a jump around all data directives to the beginning of the mainline procedure. Since the program does not contain a DATA segment, all screen output has necessarily been accomplished with the DSPLY_STR building block rather than with DSPLY_IMMED_STR (recall that DSPLY_IMMED_STR requires that the program contain a previously defined segment with the name DATA).

GROUP DIRECTIVE

Although a .COM file may have only one segment, it is often useful to use multiple segment directives with different segment names. Our DSPLY_IMMED_STR presents just such a need since its use requires the previous definition of a segment with a name of DATA. If multiple segments are to be defined with different names, then the program must use a **GROUP** directive to cause the linker to combine the multiple segments into a single segment in order to be able to convert the .EXE file to a .COM file.

Figure 13-2   Sample .COM Program
Display Program Segment and Entry Point

```
COMMENT \                   COM_TST1.ASM

               .COM PROGRAM TO REPORT PROGRAM SEGMENT ADDRESS
               AND ENTRY-POINT SEGMENT:OFFSET

               \

                       PAGE    55,80           ;LINES, WIDTH FOR LISTING
                       TITLE   COM_TST1.ASM

                       INCLUDE        CONSOLE.MLB

CODE           SEGMENT PARA PUBLIC 'CODE'
               ASSUME  CS:CODE, DS:CODE, ES:CODE

;ENTRY POINT AT 100H ===========================================
                       ORG     100H            ;ENTRY POINT MUST BE 100H
ENTRY:         JMP     NEAR PTR MAIN   ;JUMP AROUND DATA

;PROGRAM DATA ==================================================
IO_BUF         DB      5 DUP ('#')     ;DEFINE A BUFFER
MSG_1          DB      13, 10, 'Program loaded at ', 0
MSG_2          DB      'H (seg address).', 13, 10, 10, 0
MSG_3          DB      'Entry point is ', 0
MSG_4          DB      'H:', 0
MSG_5          DB      'H (seg:off)', 13, 10, 10, 0

;PROGRAM CODE ==================================================
MAIN           PROC    FAR

        ;REPORT SEGMENT ADDRESS WHERE LOADED
               DSPLY_STR       <OFFSET MSG_1>
               MOV     AX, ES          ; GET PROGRAM SEGMENT
               CNV_UNS_STR     <OFFSET  IO_BUF>, AX, 16
                                       ;CONVERT TO HEX STRING
               DSPLY_STR       <OFFSET IO_BUF>
                                       ;SHOW SEG ADDRESS OF
                                       ;PROGRAM
               DSPLY_STR       <OFFSET MSG_2>

        ;REPORT ENTRY POINT AS SEGMENT:OFFSET
               DSPLY_STR       <OFFSET MSG_3>
               MOV     AX, CS          ;GET CODE SEGMENT
               CNV_UNS_STR     <OFFSET IO_BUF>, AX, 16
                                       ;CONVERT TO HEX STRING
```

Figure 13-2: (continued)

```
                 DSPLY_STR        <OFFSET IO_BUF>
                                          ;SHOW CS
                 DSPLY_STR        <OFFSET MSG_4>
                 MOV     AX, OFFSET ENTRY
                                          ;GET OFFSET OF ENTRY
                                          ;  POINT
                 CNV_UNS_STR      <OFFSET IO_BUF>, AX, 16
                                          ;CONVERT TO HEX STRING
                 DSPLY_STR        <OFFSET IO_BUF>
                                          ;SHOW ENTRY-POINT OFFSET
                 DSPLY_STR        <OFFSET MSG_5>

                 INT     20H              ;TERMINATE

MAIN             ENDP

CODE             ENDS

                 END     ENTRY            ;ENTRY AT OFFSET 100H
```

The GROUP directive is used to combine segments with different names into one segment. The syntax is as follows:

groupname   GROUP *segname1*[, *segname2*[, *segname3*, ...]]

All segments with the specified segment names are combined into one segment as if they all had the same segment name with PUBLIC combine type. All offsets within all the segments are calculated relative to the beginning of the group. *Groupname* then becomes the name by which to refer to the resulting segment; alternatively, any one of the *segname*s grouped together may be used to reference the entire resulting segment.

The segments within a group need not be contiguous; they need not be all of the same class or contiguous within the source file. However, the entire group must be addressable as one segment; the distance between the beginning of the first segment and the end of the last segment within the group may not exceed 64K.

In Figure 13-3, the .COM program in Figure 13-2 has been rewritten with a DATA segment in order to allow the use of our DSPLY_IMMED_STR building block. Note that the program contains two segments, DATA and CODE. The presence of the DATA segment permits the use of DSPLY_IMMED_STR for screen output. Since it is to be converted to a .COM file, it begins with a jump instruction at offset 100H in order to jump around all data to the mainline procedure. It also contains a GROUP directive to combine the two segments (DATA and CODE) into one segment (P_GROUP).

Figure 13-3 **Sample .COM Program**
Display Program Segment and Entry Point
Using DSPLY–IMMED__STR Building Block

```
COMMENT  \                    COM_TST2.ASM

                ALTERNATE .COM PROGRAM TO REPORT PROGRAM SEGMENT ADDRESS
                AND ENTRY-POINT SEGMENT:OFFSET

                USES DATA SEGMENT AND GROUP DIRECTIVE TO ALLOW USE OF
                DSPLY_IMMED_STR BUILDING BLOCK

                \

                    PAGE    55, 80              ;LINES, WIDTH FOR LISTING
                    TITLE   COM_TST2.ASM

                    INCLUDE         CONSOLE.MLB

P_GROUP         GROUP   DATA, CODE
                    ASSUME  CS:P_GROUP, DS:P_GROUP, ES:P_GROUP


;DATA SEGMENT ===================================================
DATA            SEGMENT PARA PUBLIC 'DATA'

        ;PROGRAM ENTRY POINT
                    ORG     100H              ;ENTRY POINT MUST BE 100H
ENTRY:          JMP     NEAR PTR MAIN     ;JUMP AROUND DATA

        ;PROGRAM DATA
        ;DSPLY_IMMED_STR ALSO PUTS STRING DATA HERE
IO_BUF          DB      5 DUP ('#')       ;DEFINE A BUFFER

DATA            ENDS

;CODE SEGMENT ===================================================
CODE            SEGMENT WORD PUBLIC 'CODE'

        ;PROGRAM CODE
MAIN            PROC    FAR

        ;REPORT SEGMENT ADDRESS WHERE LOADED
                    DSPLY_IMMED_STR <13, 10, 'Program loaded at '>
                    MOV     AX, ES            ;GET PROGRAM SEGMENT
                    CNV_UNS_STR     <OFFSET IO_BUF>, AX, 16
                                              ;CONVERT TO HEX STRING
                    DSPLY_STR       <OFFSET IO_BUF>
                                              ;SHOW SEG ADDRESS OF
                                              ;  PROGRAM
```

Figure 13-3: (continued)

```
                          DSPLY_IMMED_STR <'H (seg address).', 13, 10, 10>

              ;REPORT ENTRY POINT AS SEGMENT:OFFSET
                          DSPLY_IMMED_STR 'Entry point is '
                          MOV     AX, CS              ;GET CODE SEGMENT
                          CNV_UNS_STR     <OFFSET IO_BUF>, AX, 16
                                                      ;CONVERT TO HEX STRING
                          DSPLY_STR       <OFFSET IO_BUF>
                                                      ;SHOW CS
                          DSPLY_IMMED_STR 'H:'
                          MOV     AX, OFFSET ENTRY
                                                      ;GET OFFSET OF ENTRY
                                                      ;  POINT WITHIN GROUP
                          CNV_UNS_STR     <OFFSET IO_BUF>, AX, 16
                                                      ;CONVERT TO HEX STRING
                          DSPLY_STR       <OFFSET IO_BUF>
                                                      ;SHOW ENTRY-POINT OFFSET
                          DSPLY_IMMED_STR <'H (seg:off)', 13, 10, 10>

                          INT     20H                 ;TERMINATE

MAIN                      ENDP

CODE                      ENDS
                          END     ENTRY               ;ENTRY AT OFFSET 100H
```

The manner in which MASM calculates offsets within a group requires some explanation, since it may not be obvious from the code in Figure 13-3. Anytime it encounters a symbol within a segment that has been combined with other segments by the GROUP directive, MASM calculates the symbol's offset from the beginning of its segment, rather than from the beginning of the group. This is no problem in COM_TST2 (Figure 13-3) since the only offsets that need to be calculated are within the segment, DATA, which is the first segment within the group. Consequently, the offsets of all strings placed within the DATA segment by DSPLY_IMMED_STR are calculated correctly. Similarly, since ENTRY is defined within DATA, the correct offset is calculated in the instruction to display the entry-point offset:

```
        MOV        AX, OFFSET ENTRY
```

However, the programmer must be very careful in referring to the offsets of any labels in the segment, CODE. Suppose, for example, that we needed to move the offset of the label, MAIN, into the AX register. We might code the following instruction:

```
        MOV        AX, OFFSET MAIN
```

Since MAIN is defined within CODE, the assembler would calculate its offset as the number of bytes from the CODE SEGMENT directive, rather than from the beginning of the entire segment formed by the GROUP directive. Fortunately, we can force the assembler to correctly calculate the offset by preceding the label name by the group name followed by a colon. In order to cause MASM to calculate the correct offset from the beginning of the group, the above instruction should be rewritten as follows:

```
MOV      AX, OFFSET P_GROUP:MAIN
```

The specification of the group causes the assembler to calculate the offset of MAIN as the number of bytes from the beginning of the group. Thus, the offset is calculated as the number of bytes from the DATA SEGMENT directive, since it is the first segment within the group.

PROGRAM SEGMENT PREFIX (PSP)

As mentioned earlier, the **Program-Segment Prefix** or **PSP** is a 256-byte block of memory that is set up by DOS when loading any file for execution. Do not confuse the PSP with the relocation header. The relocation header is constructed by LINK and is placed at the beginning of an .EXE file on disk. It is used by LINK to tell DOS how to prepare the .EXE program for execution.

The Program Segment Prefix is constructed by DOS in memory when any executable file (either a .COM file or an .EXE file) is loaded for execution. It is used by DOS to provide the program with information about its environment and the manner in which it has been executed. Figure 13-4 lists and explains the PSP fields.

Figure 13-4   Program-Segment Prefix

Byte(s)	Length	Usage
00H–01H	02H	INT 20H instruction. .EXE files normally terminate and return to DOS by executing a Far return to this instruction.
02H–03H	02H	Memory size, in paragraphs; the Segment address of the next paragraph after the last byte of available user memory in the machine.
04H	01H	Reserved.
05H–09H	05H	Far call instruction to DOS function dispatcher. This is a throwback to CP/M and is not very useful.
0AH–0DH	04H	INT 22H vector. Interrupt type 22H is the DOS termination-handler routine, which is executed by DOS upon termination of any program. Upon loading a program, and before execution begins, DOS copies the interrupt vector into the PSP; the vector is restored from the PSP upon program termination (in case it has been modified by the program).

0EH–11H	04H	INT 23H vector. Interrupt type 23H is the DOS <Ctrl>+<C> handler, which is executed by DOS whenever a <Ctrl>+<C> or <Ctrl>+<Break> is entered at the keyboard. Upon loading a program, and before execution begins, DOS copies the interrupt vector into the PSP; the vector is restored from the PSP upon program termination (in case it has been modified by the program).
12H–15H	04H	INT 24H vector. Interrupt type 24H is the DOS critical-error handler, which is executed by DOS whenever a critical hardware error (disk error for example) occurs; the critical-error-handler routine is responsible for the "Abort, Retry, Ignore" message on disk errors. Upon loading a program, and before execution begins, DOS copies the interrupt vector into the PSP; the vector is restored from the PSP upon program termination (in case it has been modified by the program).
16H–2BH	16H	Reserved.
2CH–2DH	02H	Reserved in version one DOS; in versions two and above, the segment address of the environment block.
2EH–4FH	22H	Reserved.
50H–5BH	0CH	Reserved in version one DOS; in version two, the Function Request Dispatcher, currently consisting of an INT 21H instruction, followed by a FAR RET instruction, followed by nine NUL characters.
5CH–6BH	10H	Parameter #1. Bytes 5CH through 67H contain the first parameter from the command line tail, interpreted as a file specification and stored in the manner required by traditional (version 1) functions.

Byte(s)	Contents
5CH	Drive: 0 = No drive found in parameter, 1 = A:, 2 = B:, 3 = C:, etc.
5DH–64H	Primary filename, uppercase, padded on the right with spaces.
65H–67H	File extension, uppercase, padded on the right with spaces. All spaces if no extension found.

6CH–7FH	14H	Parameter #2. Bytes 6CH through 77H contain the second parameter from the command line tail, interpreted as a file specification and stored in the manner required by traditional (version 1) functions (see above).
80H–FFH	80H	Default DTA and command line tail. Upon execution of the program, the Disk Transfer Address has been set to offset 80H of the PSP. The same PSP area also contains the unformatted command line tail. Byte number 80H contains the length of the command line tail, which begins in byte number 81H and consists of all characters, following the program name, in the command line that invoked the program. It includes the initial space(s) or tab(s) separating the program name from the first parameter and is not converted to uppercase or otherwise modified in any way.

Note that in addition to passing information in to the program DOS also uses the PSP to restore three interrupt vectors (22H, 23H, and 24H) upon termination of the program by execution of an INT 20H instruction. In order for DOS to find the PSP to properly restore the vectors, CS must contain the Segment address of the PSP at the moment of execution of the INT 20H instruction. CS always points to the PSP during execution of any .COM file; it is initialized to the PSP by DOS prior to execution of the program and is never modified by a .COM program (no Far jumps or calls). Consequently, .COM files may be terminated simply by executing an INT 20H instruction.

During execution of an .EXE file, however, CS normally does not address the PSP; it is initialized by DOS to the beginning of the code segment (the Segment address of the entry point) and may be further modified by the program through Far jumps or calls. As a result, an .EXE program must address the PSP with CS prior to terminating with an INT 20H instruction. This is the reason that .EXE programs normally begin with instructions to push DS and zero:

```
PUSH     DS          ;SET UP
XOR      AX, AX      ;  FOR RETURN
PUSH     AX          ;  TO DOS
```

Upon entry to an .EXE program, DS contains the Segment address of the PSP; thus the above three instructions set up the stack such that the Far return instruction at the end of the program causes a transfer of control to offset zero within the PSP. Thus, CS now contains the Segment address of the PSP, and the next instruction to be executed is the INT 20H at offset zero of the PSP. The program properly exits to DOS with CS addressing the PSP so that DOS may properly restore the three interrupt vectors.

ACCESSING PSP DATA

Aside from the use of the first two bytes for a proper return to DOS, the other most common usage of the PSP by a program is to access input parameters through the **command line tail**. The command line tail consists of all characters, following the name of the program, in the command line that invoked the program. For example, in order to use EXE2BIN to convert a file called TEST.EXE to a .COM file called TEST.COM, we would enter the following command:

```
EXE2BIN   TEST  TEST.COM
```

The command line tail, from the above command consists of all characters, including spaces, following the name of the program:

```
"   TEST  TEST.COM"
```

The quotes are not part of the command line tail; we have enclosed it in quotes only to emphasize that it includes all characters, including spaces and tabs, following the program name. The PSP provides two methods of accessing input parameters from the command line. While building the PSP, DOS stores the entire command line tail, exactly as entered, into bytes 80H through FFH. Offset 80H contains the length of the tail while the command line tail itself is stored into offsets 81H through FFH.

Additionally, DOS parses the command line tail, treating each of the first two parameters as a file specification. The first parameter is parsed into bytes 5CH through 68H of the PSP, with the drive specifier in byte 5CH, the primary name (uppercase, padded on the right with spaces) in bytes 5DH through 65H, and the extension (uppercase, padded on the right with spaces, or all spaces if no extension) in bytes 66H through 68H. The second parameter is similarly parsed into bytes 6CH through 78H of the PSP (byte 6CH = drive, bytes 6DH − 75H = name, bytes 76H − 78H = extension).

Sometimes, though less often, a program may need to use the PSP to determine the total user memory in the PC or to obtain information from the environment block. The total PC memory, in paragraphs, is stored by DOS into bytes 02H through 03H; the word at that location is an unsigned integer representing the number of paragraphs (one-sixteenth the number of bytes) of total user memory in the PC.

If the DOS in use is version two or higher, environment information may be obtained by using the environment-block segment address in bytes 2CH through 2DH. The **environment block** is a series of ASCIIZ strings providing information about the operating system configuration and terminated by an extra NUL character, after the last ASCIIZ string. The default environment block consists of the following data:

```
DB          'COMSPEC=d:\COMMAND.COM', 0
DB          'PATH=', 0
DB          'PROMPT=', 0
DB          0
```

The drive specifier, d in the first ASCIIZ string, is the drive from which the PC was booted unless subsequently changed with the SET COMSPEC = command. The second and third ASCIIZ strings are each modified by any PATH or PROMPT commands. Note that the word at byte number 2CH represents the Segment address of the environment block. To access the environment block, you should move the Segment address into a Segment register; the environment block then begins at offset zero within that segment.

KEY TERMS TO REMEMBER

GROUP directive	Command line tail
PSP	Environment block

Figure 13-5 provides the source code for an .EXE program that examines the PSP and displays the number of paragraphs of total user memory, the environment block, the unformatted command line tail, and each of the first two parameters as parsed into the PSP by DOS. Notice that the program defines the PSP as a segment with AT segaddress combine type. Recall that a segment with a combine type of AT segadress does not add to the program, but merely provides addressing of memory outside the program.

Since the address of the PSP is determined by DOS as the program is loaded, PSP_SEG has been given a dummy segment address of zero. Upon loading the program, DOS initializes ES and DS (as well as CS and SS, for .COM programs) to contain the actual PSP Segment address. Thus, the program uses ES as the Segment address whenever addressing the PSP.

Figure 13-5   .EXE Program that Addresses the PSP

```
COMMENT \                    EXE_PSP.ASM

         .EXE PROGRAM TO REPORT PSP INFORMATION

             \

                    PAGE    55,80           ;LINES,WIDTH FOR LISTING
                    TITLE   EXE_PSP.ASM

                    INCLUDE        CONSOLE.MLB

;PSP SEGMENT OUTSIDE PROGRAM (AT COMBINE TYPE) ===================
PSP_SEG         SEGMENT AT 0            ;0 IS DUMMY ADDRESS - ES
                                        ;  IS SET TO PSP BY DOS
INT_20_INST     DB      ?, ?            ;INT 20H INSTRUCTION
MEM_SIZE        DW      ?               ;MEMORY SIZE IN
                                        ;  PARAGRAPHS
RSV_1           DB      ?               ;RESERVED
DOS_CALL_INST   DB      5 DUP (?)       ;CP/M DOS FUNCTION CALL
TERM_ADD        DD      ?               ;INT 22H VECTOR
BREAK_ADD       DD      ?               ;INT 23H VECTOR
ERROR_ADD       DD      ?               ;INT 24H VECTOR
RSV_2           DB      22 DUP (?)      ;RESERVED
ENV_SEG_ADD     DW      ?               ;SEG ADDRESS OF
                                        ;  ENVIRONMENT BLOCK
RSV_3           DB      34 DUP (?)      ;RESERVED
FUNCT_DISP      DW      6 DUP (?)       ;DOS FUNCTION DISPATCHER
PARAM_1         DB      16 DUP (?)      ;1ST CMND-LINE PARAMETER
PARAM_2         DB      20 DUP (?)      ;2ND CMND-LINE PARAMETER
CMD_LEN         DB      ?               ;LENGTH OF COMMAND LINE
                                        ;  TAIL
CMD_LINE        DB      127 DUP (?)     ;COMMAND LINE TAIL
                ORG     80H             ;REDEFINE 80H - FFH
```

Figure 13-5: (continued)

```
DEF_DTA         DB      128 DUP (?)        ;DEFAULT DISK TRANSFER
                                           ;  ADDRESS

PSP_SEG         ENDS

;STACK SEGMENT =================================================
STACK           SEGMENT PARA STACK 'STACK'

                DB      128 DUP ('*')

STACK           ENDS

;DATA SEGMENT ==================================================
DATA            SEGMENT PARA PUBLIC 'DATA'

IO_BUF          DB      6 DUP ('#')        ;DEFINE A BUFFER

DATA            ENDS

;CODE SEGMENT ==================================================
CODE            SEGMENT PARA PUBLIC 'CODE'
                ASSUME  CS:CODE, SS:STACK, ES:PSP_SEG

MAIN            PROC    FAR

        ;INITIALIZE
                PUSH    DS                 ;SET UP
                XOR     AX, AX             ;  FOR RETURN
                PUSH    AX                 ;  TO DOS
                MOV     AX, DATA           ;ADDRESS DATA
                MOV     DS, AX             ;  SEGMENT
                ASSUME  DS:DATA            ;  WITH DS

        ;REPORT TOTAL USER MEMORY IN PARAGRAPHS
                DSPLY_IMMED_STR <13, 10, 'Paragraphs of mem: '>
                MOV             AX, MEM_SIZE
                CNV_UNS_STR     <OFFSET IO_BUF>, AX
                DSPLY_STR       <OFFSET IO_BUF>
                DSPLY_IMMED_STR <13, 10 ,10>

        ;REPORT THE ENVIRONMENT BLOCK
                DSPLY_IMMED_STR <'Environment block:', 13, 10>
                PUSH    ES                 ;SAVE IT AND
                MOV     AX, ENV_SEG_ADD ;  POINT ES:[BX]
                MOV     ES, AX             ;  TO THE
                ASSUME  ES:NOTHING      ;  ENVIRONMENT
                MOV     BX, 0              ;  BLOCK
        ;DISPLAY THE ENVIRONMENT BLOCK (ALL ASCIIZ STRINGS)
        ;BLOCK IS TERMINATED WITH EXTRA NUL CHAR
```

Figure 13-5:   (continued)

```
LP1_BEG:            ;GENERAL LOOP (QUIT WHEN AL EQ 0)
                    MOV     AL, ES:[BX] ;GET NEXT ENVIRONMENT
                    INC     BX          ;   CHARACTER
            CMP     AL, 0               ;TEST FOR TERMINATION
            JE      LP1_END             ;   OF THE LOOP
                CALL    DSP_ASCZ        ;DISPLAY ONE ASCIIZ STR
                JMP     LP1_BEG         ;CONTINUE LOOP
LP1_END:            ;END GENERAL LOOP
            POP     ES                  ;RESTORE IT
            ASSUME  ES:PSP_SEG          ;  TO PSP

        ;DISPLAY THE COMMAND LINE TAIL
                DSPLY_IMMED_STR <10, 'Command line tail: "'>
            MOV     CL, CMD_LEN         ;CMD-LINE LENGTH INTO
            MOV     CH, 0               ;  CX FOR LOOP
            MOV     BX, OFFSET CMD_LINE
                                        ;POINT ES:[BX] TO
                                        ;  COMMAND LINE
            JCXZ    LP2_END             ;SKIP LOOP IF CMD-LINE
                                        ;  LENGTH IS ZERO
LP2_BEG:            ;REPEAT CX (COMMAND LINE LENGTH) TIMES
                    MOV     AL, ES:[BX] ;GET NEXT CMD-LINE
                    INC     BX          ;   CHARACTER
                DSPLY_CHR       AL      ;DISPLAY IT
                LOOP    LP2_BEG         ;CONTINUE LOOP
LP2_END:            ;END REPEAT
            DSPLY_IMMED_STR <'"', 13, 10, 10>

        ;DISPLAY FIRST AND SECOND PARAMETERS AS FILE SPECS
            DSPLY_IMMED_STR '1st PSP parameter: '
            MOV     BX, OFFSET PARAM_1
                                        ;POINT TO 1ST PARAMETER
            CALL    DSP_PRM             ;DISPLAY IT
            DSPLY_IMMED_STR '2nd PSP parameter: '
            MOV     BX, OFFSET PARAM_2
                                        ;POINT TO 2ND PARAMETER
            CALL    DSP_PRM             ;DISPLAY IT

            RET                         ;TERMINATE TO DOS

MAIN        ENDP

;-------------------------------------------------------------
;SUBPROCEDURE TO DISPLAY AN ASCIIZ STRING
DSP_ASCZ        PROC    NEAR
```

Figure 13-5: (continued)

```
DALP_BEG:              ;REPEAT UNTIL AL EQ 0
                       DSPLY_CHR        AL ;DISPLAY ASCIIZ CHAR
                       MOV     AL, ES:[BX];GET NEXT ASCIIZ
                       INC     BX         ;  CHARACTER
                CMP     AL, 0              ;TEST FOR CONTINUATION
                JNE     DALP_BEG           ;  OF LOOP
                ;END REPEAT

                DSPLY_IMMED_STR <13, 10>
                RET                        ;RETURN

DSP_ASCZ        ENDP


;----------------------------------------------------------------
;SUBPROCEDURE TO DISPLAY A PSP PARAMETER
DSP_PRM         PROC    NEAR

                MOV     AL, ES:[BX]        ;GET DRIVE NUMBER
                ADD     AL, '0'            ;TO ASCII '0', '1', ETC.
                DSPLY_CHR        AL        ;DISPLAY IT
                DSPLY_CHR        '"'       ;QUOTE FOR NAME & EXT
                MOV     CX, 11             ;MAXIMUM CHARS IN NAME
DPLP_BEG:              ;REPEAT CX (11) TIMES
                       INC     BX          ;GET NEXT CHARACTER
                       MOV     AL, ES:[BX] ;  OF FILE SPEC
                       DSPLY_CHR        AL ;DISPLAY NAME CHAR
                       LOOP    DPLP_BEG    ;CONTINUE LOOP
                ;END LOOP
                DSPLY_IMMED_STR <'"', 13, 10, 10>
                RET                        ;RETURN

DSP_PRM         ENDP

CODE            ENDS

                END     MAIN
```

Figure 13-6 is the source code for the same program, to access and display PSP information, rewritten to be converted to a .COM program file. Notice that it contains three segments: PSP_SEG (with AT combine type), DATA, and CODE; a GROUP directive has been used to combine the three segments into one segment, P_GROUP, as required for a .COM program.

Figure 13-6   .COM Program that Addresses the PSP

```
COMMENT \      COM_PSP.ASM

               COM PROGRAM TO REPORT PSP INFORMATION
               PROGRAM MUST BE CONVERTED TO A .COM FILE WITH EXE2BIN


               \

                      PAGE    55, 80            ;LINES,WIDTH FOR LISTING
                      TITLE   COM_PSP.ASM

                      INCLUDE CONSOLE.MLB

P_GROUP               GROUP   PSP_SEG, DATA, CODE
                      ASSUME  CS:P_GROUP, DS:P_GROUP, ES:P_GROUP

;PSP SEGMENT ===================================================
PSP_SEG               SEGMENT AT 0             ;0 IS DUMMY ADDRESS - ES
                                               ;  IS SET TO PSP BY DOS
INT_20_INST           DB      ?, ?             ;INT 20H INSTRUCTION
MEM_SIZE              DW      ?                ;MEMORY SIZE IN
                                               ;  PARAGRAPHS
RSV_1                 DB      ?                ;RESERVED
DOS_CALL_INST         DB      5 DUP (?)        ;CP/M DOS FUNCTION CALL
TERM_ADD              DD      ?                ;INT 22H VECTOR
BREAK_ADD             DD      ?                ;INT 23H VECTOR
ERROR_ADD             DD      ?                ;INT 24H VECTOR
RSV_2                 DB      22 DUP (?)       ;RESERVED
ENV_SEG_ADD           DW      ?                ;SEG ADDRESS OF
                                               ;  ENVIRONMENT BLOCK
RSV_3                 DB      34 DUP (?)       ;RESERVED
FUNCT_DISP            DW      6 DUP (?)        ;DOS FUNCTION DISPATCHER
PARAM_1               DB      16 DUP (?)       ;1ST CMND-LINE PARAMETER
PARAM_2               DB      20 DUP (?)       ;2ND CMND-LINE PARAMETER
CMD_LEN               DB      ?                ;LENGTH OF COMMAND LINE
                                               ;  TAIL
CMD_LINE              DB      127 DUP (?)      ;COMMAND LINE TAIL
                      ORG     80H              ;REDEFINE 80H - FFH
DEF_DTA               DB      128 DUP (?)      ;DEFAULT DISK TRANSFER
                                               ;  ADDRESS

PSP_SEG               ENDS

;DATA SEGMENT ===================================================
DATA                  SEGMENT PARA PUBLIC 'DATA'

               ;PROGRAM ENTRY AT 100H - JUMP AROUND DATA
                      ORG     100H
ENTRY:                JMP     NEAR PTR MAIN

               ;PROGRAM DATA
               ;DSPLY_IMMED_STR ALSO PUTS STRING DATA HERE
```

Figure 13-6:   (continued)

```
IO_BUF              DB      6 DUP ('#')        ;DEFINE A BUFFER

DATA                ENDS

;CODE SEGMENT =======================================================
CODE                SEGMENT WORD PUBLIC 'CODE'

MAIN                PROC    FAR

            ;REPORT TOTAL USER MEMORY IN PARAGRAPHS
                    DSPLY_IMMED_STR <13, 10, 'Paragraphs of mem: '>
                    MOV             AX, MEM_SIZE
                    CNV_UNS_STR     <OFFSET IO_BUF>, AX
                    DSPLY_STR       <OFFSET IO_BUF>
                    DSPLY_IMMED_STR <13, 10 ,10>

            ;REPORT THE ENVIRONMENT BLOCK
                    DSPLY_IMMED_STR <'Environment block:', 13, 10>
                    PUSH    ES              ;SAVE IT AND
                    MOV     AX, ENV_SEG_ADD ;  POINT ES:[BX]
                    MOV     ES, AX          ;  TO THE
                    ASSUME  ES:NOTHING      ;  ENVIRONMENT
                    MOV     BX, 0           ;  BLOCK
            ;DISPLAY THE ENVIRONMENT BLOCK (ALL ASCIIZ STRINGS)
            ;BLOCK IS TERMINATED WITH EXTRA NUL CHAR
LP1_BEG:            ;GENERAL LOOP (QUIT WHEN AL EQ 0)
                    MOV     AL, ES:[BX] ;GET NEXT ENVIRONMENT
                    INC     BX          ;  CHARACTER
                    CMP     AL, 0           ;TEST FOR TERMINATION
                    JE      LP1_END         ;  OF THE LOOP
                      CALL    DSP_ASCZ      ;DISPLAY ONE ASCIIZ STR
                      JMP     LP1_BEG       ;CONTINUE LOOP
LP1_END:            ;END GENERAL LOOP
                    POP     ES              ;RESTORE IT
                    ASSUME  ES:PSP_SEG      ;  TO PSP

            ;DISPLAY THE COMMAND LINE TAIL
                    DSPLY_IMMED_STR <10, 'Command line tail: "'>
                    MOV     CL, CMD_LEN     ;CMD-LINE LENGTH INTO
                    MOV     CH, 0           ;  CX FOR LOOP
                    MOV     BX, OFFSET CMD_LINE
                                            ;POINT ES:[BX] TO
                                            ;  COMMAND LINE
                    JCXZ    LP2_END         ;SKIP LOOP IF CMD-LINE
                                            ;  LENGTH IS ZERO
LP2_BEG:            ;REPEAT CX (COMMAND LINE LENGTH) TIMES
                    MOV     AL, ES:[BX] ;GET NEXT CMD-LINE
                    INC     BX          ;  CHARACTER
                    DSPLY_CHR       AL  ;DISPLAY IT
                    LOOP    LP2_BEG     ;CONTINUE LOOP
LP2_END:            ;END REPEAT
                    DSPLY_IMMED_STR <'"', 13, 10, 10>
```

Figure 13-6:   (continued)

```
                ;DISPLAY FIRST AND SECOND PARAMETERS AS FILE SPECS
                DSPLY_IMMED_STR '1st PSP parameter: '
                MOV     BX, OFFSET PARAM_1
                                        ;POINT TO 1ST PARAMETER
                CALL    DSP_PRM         ;DISPLAY IT
                DSPLY_IMMED_STR '2nd PSP parameter: '
                MOV     BX, OFFSET PARAM_2
                                        ;POINT TO 2ND PARAMETER
                CALL    DSP_PRM         ;DISPLAY IT

                INT     20H             ;TERMINATE TO DOS

MAIN            ENDP


;----------------------------------------------------------------
;SUBPROCEDURE TO DISPLAY AN ASCIIZ STRING
DSP_ASCZ        PROC    NEAR

DALP_BEG:       ;REPEAT UNTIL AL EQ 0
                    DSPLY_CHR      AL  ;DISPLAY ASCIIZ CHAR
                    MOV     AL, ES:[BX] ;GET NEXT ASCIIZ
                    INC     BX          ;   CHARACTER
                CMP     AL, 0           ;TEST FOR CONTINUATION
                JNE     DALP_BEG        ;   OF LOOP
                ;END REPEAT

                DSPLY_IMMED_STR <13, 10>
                RET                     ;RETURN

DSP_ASCZ        ENDP


;----------------------------------------------------------------
;SUBPROCEDURE TO DISPLAY A PSP PARAMETER
DSP_PRM         PROC    NEAR

                MOV     AL, ES:[BX]     ;GET DRIVE NUMBER
                ADD     AL, '0'         ;TO ASCII '0', '1', ETC.
                DSPLY_CHR      AL       ;DISPLAY IT
                DSPLY_CHR      '"'      ;QUOTE FOR NAME & EXT
                MOV     CX, 11          ;MAXIMUM CHARS IN NAME
DPLP_BEG:       ;REPEAT CX (11) TIMES
                    INC        BX              ;GET NEXT CHARACTER
                    MOV        AL, ES: [BX] ; OF FILE SPEC
                    DSPLY_CHR       AL  ;DISPLAY NAME CHAR
                    LOOP    DPLP_BEG        ;CONTINUE LOOP
                ;END LOOP
                DSPLY_IMMED_STR <'"', 13, 10, 10>
                RET                     ;RETURN
```

Figure 13-6:   (continued)

```
DSP_PRM        ENDP

CODE           ENDS

               END     ENTRY
```

ALTERNATE METHODS OF PROGRAM TERMINATION

Thus far we have terminated all programs by executing an interrupt type 20H, either directly (.COM files) or by executing a Far return to the INT 20H instruction at offset zero of the PSP. DOS provides five alternate methods of terminating a program and returning to DOS. Three methods, INT 20H, INT 27H, and function call 00H, are supported by all versions of DOS; all require that CS contain the Segment address of the PSP upon termination.

Two additional methods, function calls 4CH and 31H, are supported by DOS versions two and higher; neither requires that CS point to the PSP. Additionally, functions 4CH and 31H each allow the return of a completion code to DOS. Interrupt type 27H and function call 31H each allow the program to terminate to DOS without releasing all allocated memory; they are used by terminate-and-stay-resident (TSR) programs to be discussed in the next chapter.

Following is a discussion of each of the five methods of terminating a program back to DOS:

INT 20H - Terminate to DOS (all versions of DOS):

In order for a program to terminate to DOS using INT 20H, CS must point to the PSP. If CS already points to the PSP, as in .COM files, the program merely executes INT 20H. Most .EXE programs must point CS to the PSP and so terminate by performing a Far return to the INT 20H instruction at offset zero of the PSP.

DOS flushes all file buffers, restores the interrupt vectors 22H, 23H, and 24H from the PSP, releases all memory allocated to the process, and returns control to COMMAND.COM.

Function 00H - Terminate to DOS (all versions of DOS):

The result of DOS function 00H is virtually identical to that of INT 20H. To terminate to DOS, the program should move 00H into AH and perform an INT 21H. Since CS does not normally point to the PSP, function 00H is not very useful for the termination of .EXE programs.

As with INT 20H, DOS flushes all file buffers, restores the interrupt vectors 22H, 23H, and 24H from the PSP, releases all memory allocated to the process, and returns control to COMMAND.COM.

INT 27H - Terminate and Stay Resident (all versions of DOS):

In order for a program to terminate and stay resident using INT 27H, CS must point to the PSP; the program should then set DX to the offset (from CS) of the next byte following the resident portion (number of bytes to remain resident) and execute INT 27H.

DOS flushes all file buffers, restores the interrupt vectors 22H, 23H, and 24H from the PSP, and returns control to COMMAND.COM as with INT 20H. However, instead of releasing all memory from CS:0000H, DOS releases only memory beginning with CS:DX. Any subsequent program will be loaded at that address, thus leaving intact the resident portion of the terminating program.

Since CS must point to the PSP, INT 27H may not be used as the last instruction in order to terminate an .EXE file. However, an .EXE file may terminate and stay resident by modifying the interrupt instruction at offset zero of the PSP; to change the instruction to INT 27H, the .EXE program merely moves 27H to offset one of the PSP. To terminate and stay resident, once the PSP has been modified, the program sets DX to the number of bytes to remain resident, as indicated above, prior to performing the Far return to offset zero (INT 27H) of the PSP.

Function 4CH - Terminate with Return Code (DOS version two and higher):

DOS function call 4CH requires that DOS version two or higher be in use; version one DOS does not recognize the function call. In order to terminate with a return code, the program should move 4CH into AH, move the return code into AL, and execute a DOS function call (INT 21H). Unlike INT 20H, INT 27H, and function 00H, CS need not point to the PSP.

DOS flushes all file buffers, restores the interrupt vectors 22H, 23H, and 24H from the PSP, releases all memory allocated to the process, and returns control to COMMAND.COM. Since it does not require that CS point to the PSP, DOS function 4CH may be used, instead of a Far return to the PSP, as the last instruction of an .EXE file in order to return to DOS.

The return code may subsequently be tested by a batch file with an IF ERROR-LEVEL statement. By convention, a return code of zero indicates success, while any other return code indicates an error condition.

Function 31H - Terminate and Stay Resident (DOS version two and higher):

DOS function call 31H also requires that DOS version two or higher be in use; version one DOS does not recognize the function call. In order to terminate and stay resident with a return code, the program should move 31H into AH, move the return code into AL, set DX to the size of the resident portion in paragraphs, and execute a DOS function call (INT 21H). As with function 4CH, CS need not point to the PSP.

DOS flushes all file buffers, restores the interrupt vectors 22H, 23H, and 24H from the PSP, and returns control to COMMAND.COM as with INT 20H.

However, instead of releasing all memory occupied by the program, DOS releases memory beginning with the Segment address of the PSP plus the number of paragraphs specified by DX. Any subsequent programs are loaded at that segment address, leaving the resident portion of the program intact. Since it does not require that CS point to the PSP, DOS function 31H allows the easy installation of memory-resident .EXE files.

The return code may subsequently be tested by a batch file with an IF ERROR-LEVEL statement. By convention, a return code of zero indicates success, while any other return code indicates an error condition.

INTERFACING WITH HIGH-LEVEL LANGUAGES

Interfacing assembly language with high-level languages usually involves writing a subprocedure in assembly language and a mainline program in the high-level language. The high-level mainline calls the assembly-language subprocedure to accomplish some low-level task that is difficult or impossible to perform from the high-level language. The high-level language compiler is then used to compile the mainline program to an object file, the subprocedure is assembled to another object file, and the two object files are linked to create a single executable file.

Such interfacing of an assembly-language subprocedure with a high-level language program requires an intimate knowledge of the particular high-level language's calling conventions. There is no single standard convention for all languages, or even for different implementations of the same language. Before attempting to interface with a particular compiler you must research the compiler's calling conventions. Consult the programmer's manual for the compiler. Most compiler manuals explain their calling conventions in a section entitled "Interfacing with Other Languages," "Interfacing with Assembly Language," "Mixed-Language Programming," or something similar.

Following are some hints as to the most important things to look for when researching a compiler's calling conventions:

Compiler Calling Conventions

1) Segment and group conventions. What names and classes are required for the subprocedure segments to combine properly with those created by the compiler? What GROUP directives are required?

2) Symbol naming conventions. What restrictions does the compiler place on symbol names? How long may symbols be? What characters are permitted? Is the compiler case sensitive? Your subprocedure's public symbols (to be referenced by the high-level mainline) must follow the compiler's rules.

   Additionally, some compilers alter all external symbols in some manner;

the assembly-language subprocedure must use the modified symbol. For example, C compilers add an underscore character to the beginning of every external symbol. Consequently, if the external symbol is declared as TEST within the C program, then it must be defined as _TEST within the assembly-language module.

3) Type (Near or Far) of subprocedures. Does the compiler use Near or Far calls? If Near, then the subprocedure must be Near. If the compiler uses Far calls, then the subprocedure must be Far.

4) Parameter-passing conventions (order and method). Usually the parameters will be passed in a stack hole much as we have used. Usually BP will not already point to the stack hole, however; the procedure must save BP, move SP into it, and add four (Near call) or six (Far call) to point it to the parameters. Other than the location of the stack hole, compilers differ greatly in their parameter-passing conventions.

   In what order are the parameters passed? Some compilers push the parameters from left to right; consequently, the first (left-most) parameter is at the highest memory address. Others push from right to left with the first parameter at the lowest memory address ([BP + 0] after pointing BP to the hole).

   How is each parameter passed (by Value, by Near reference, or by Far reference)? Following is an explanation of each of the three possible methods of parameter passing:

   a) By Value. A copy of the parameter value has been placed into the stack hole; the length of the parameter (and size of the stack hole) depends on the parameter's data type. The subprocedure addresses the parameter as [BP+n]. Compilers do not retrieve modified parameters from the stack; consequently, any parameter that is passed by Value cannot be altered by the subprocedure. Any parameter that has been passed by Value may be used for input only by the subprocedure.

   b) By Near reference. The stack hole contains the offset of the parameter; each offset requires two bytes of stack hole. The compiler has ensured that DS points to the segment within which the parameter is stored. The subprocedure addresses the parameter data by first moving the offset from the stack into BX, SI, or DI. It then uses BX, SI, or DI as a pointer to the parameter. Since the parameter itself is not on the stack, it may be altered by the subprocedure. For example, to add one to a word parameter passed by Near reference:

```
PUSH    SI
MOV     SI, [BP+n]
INC     WORD PTR [SI]
POP     SI
```

   c) By Far reference. The stack hole contains both the segment and the offset of the parameter; each parameter requires four bytes within the stack hole with the offset at the lower memory address and the segment at the higher address. The subprocedure cannot assume that DS is correct. It must retrieve both the segment and the offset from the stack in order to address the parameter. For example, to increment a byte parameter passed by Far reference:

```
PUSH    SI
PUSH    DS
MOV     SI, [BP+n]
MOV     DS, [BP+n+2]
INC     BYTE PTR [SI]
POP     DS
POP     SI
```

5) Closing of the stack hole. Should the subprocedure use a RET n instruction to close the stack hole? Some compilers close the stack hole within the mainline upon return from the subprocedure, in which case the subprocedure must **not** close it. Other compilers **require** that the subprocedure close up the stack.

In order to illustrate the differences between compilers, we shall examine the QuickBASIC compiler from Microsoft and the Turbo C compiler from Borland International. Our choice of these two compilers should not be construed as any indication that they are better, easier, or more common than any other compilers. Rather, we have chosen them because they are radically different from each other. Taken together, they illustrate practically every possible permutation of calling conventions: segments and groups required, symbol names, type of calls, parameter passing (order and method), and closing of the stack hole. Consult the appropriate compiler manual for interfacing with any other high-level language.

QuickBASIC requires that the data segment be named DATA and that DGROUP be declared as a group containing DATA. The code segment must be named CODE. Turbo C uses two data segments: _DATA (containing any data that is to be initialized upon entry to a block) and _BSS (uninitialized data). The GROUP directive must be used to combine both into one group called DGROUP. Turbo C requires that the code segment be named _TEXT.

QuickBASIC accesses subprocedures with Far calls. The subprocedure must be Far, and the parameters are at [SP+4] upon entry to the subprocedure. By default Turbo C uses Near calls. The subprocedure must be Near, and the parameters are at [SP+2] upon entry. However, if the subprocedure has been declared as a Far function within the C program then C uses a Far call, and the assembly-language subprocedure must be Far.

QuickBASIC pushes the parameters to the stack from left to right. Consequently, the parameter at [SP+4] is the last (right-most) parameter in the BASIC CALL parameter list. By default, C pushes parameters from right to left. The first C parameter is at [SP+2]. However, if the subprocedure has been declared as a Pascal function, then C pushes parameters from left to right.

QuickBASIC passes all parameters by Near reference. C passes all parameters by Value. If the subprocedure needs to modify a C data item, then the C program must pass a pointer to the data. To the assembly-language subprocedure, this is the same as passing the data item by Near reference (Near pointer) or by Far reference (Far pointer). C also implements all subprocedures as functions that return a value, apart from the parameter list. Upon return to C, the function takes on the value placed into AX by the subprocedure (DX:AX for data types longer than one word).

Finally, QuickBASIC requires that the subprocedure close the stack hole with RET *n*, where *n* is the size of the stack hole (twice the number of parameters). By default, C prohibits the closing of the stack hole by the procedure; it is closed by the mainline upon return. However, if the procedure has been declared as a Pascal function, then the mainline does not close the stack hole; the subprocedure must close it.

Figures 13-7 and 13-8 illustrate two versions of a simple subprocedure to be called by a high-level language program. In both cases, the subprocedure receives two signed integer values, compares them and returns the larger of the two. QBMAXINT, in Figure 13-7, is designed to be called by a QuickBASIC program.

Figure 13-7   **Subprocedure to Be Called by QuickBASIC**
                   Find the greatest of two integers.

```
COMMENT  |                          QBMAXINT.ASM


         SUBPROCEDURE TO BE CALLED BY MICROSOFT QUICKBASIC PROGRAM
         FINDS THE LARGEST OF TWO SIGNED INTEGERS

         TO USE:
                 CALL QBMAXINT(FRST.INT%, SCND.INT%, MAX.INT%)
                 QBMAXINT.OBJ MUST BE LINKED TO THE PROGRAM


         INPUT PARAMETERS:
                 FIRST INTEGER
                         SIGNED WORD
                         PASSED BY NEAR REFERENCE
                         [SP+8] = OFFSET OF INTEGER
                         (WILL BE [BP+4])
                 SECOND INTEGER
                         SIGNED WORD
                         PASSED BY NEAR REFERENCE
                         [SP+6] = OFFSET OF INTEGER
                         (WILL BE [BP+2])
         OUTPUT PARAMETERS:
                 LARGER OF THE TWO INTEGERS
                         SIGNED WORD
                         PASSED BY NEAR REFERENCE
                         [SP+4] = OFFSET OF INTEGER
                         (WILL BE [BP+0])
```

Figure 13-5: (continued)

```
                    TITLE    QBMAXINT.ASM
                    PAGE     55, 80                ;LINES, WIDTH

DGROUP              GROUP    DATA

DATA                SEGMENT WORD PUBLIC 'DATA'

        ;DEFINE ANY DATA HERE

DATA                ENDS

CODE                SEGMENT BYTE PUBLIC 'CODE'

                    ASSUME   CS:CODE, DS:DGROUP


        ;FAR PROCEDURE TO FIND AND RETURN THE BIGGEST INTEGER
QBMAXINT            PROC     FAR

                    PUBLIC   QBMAXINT           ;NEED TO REFERENCE
                                                ;  EXTERNALLY

        ;SAVE BP AND ADDRESS PARAMETERS
                    PUSH     BP                 ;SAVE IT
                    MOV      BP, SP             ;POINT BP TO STACK
                    ADD      BP, 6              ;ADJUST TO POINT TO
                                                ;  PARAMETERS
        ;SAVE ANY OTHER REGISTERS
                    PUSH     AX                 ;SAVE
                    PUSH     SI                 ;  THEM
        ;COMPARE AND RETURN THE BIGGEST INTEGER
                    MOV      SI, [BP+4]         ;POINT SI TO 1ST INT
                    MOV      AX, [SI]           ;GET 1ST INT TO AX
                    MOV      SI, [BP+2]         ;POINT SI TO 2ND INT
                    CMP      AX, [SI]           ;COMPARE THEM
                    JGE      QBM_1              ;KEEP 1ST INT IF BIGGEST
                        MOV     AX, [SI]        ;  GET 2ND INT TO AX
QBM_1:              MOV      SI, [BP+0]         ;POINT SI TO MAX INT
                    MOV      [SI], AX           ;RETURN AX (BIGGEST)
        ;RESTORE REGISTERS AND RETURN, CLOSING STACK HOLE
                    POP      SI                 ;RESTORE
                    POP      AX                 ;  THEM
                    POP      BP
                    RET      6                  ;FAR RETURN TO BASIC,
                                                ;  CLOSING STACK HOLE

QBMAXINT            ENDP

CODE                ENDS

                    END                         ;END OF QBMAXINT.ASM
```

TCMAXINT, in Figure 13-8, is the same subprocedure as in Figure 13-7 but has been rewritten to be called by a Turbo C program. Compare TCMAXINT with QBMAXINT. Although they both perform the same function, they contain major differences due to the different calling conventions of QuickBASIC and Turbo C.

Figure 13-8 **Subprocedure to Be Called by Turbo C**
Find the greatest of two integers.

```
COMMENT  |        TCMAXINT.ASM

         SUBPROCEDURE FOR A TURBO C INTEGER FUNCTION
         RETURNS THE LARGEST OF TWO SIGNED INTEGERS

         TO USE:
                 DECLARE TCMAXINT AS AN EXTERNAL INTEGER FUNCTION
                 INVOKE AS:  TCMAXINT(FRST_INT, SCND_INT)
                         BOTH PARAMETERS MUST BE INTEGER
                         TCMAXINT RETURNS LARGEST INTEGER
                 TCMAXINT.OBJ MUST BE LINKED TO THE PROGRAM

         INPUT PARAMETERS:
                 FIRST INTEGER
                         SIGNED WORD
                         PASSED BY VALUE
                         AT [SP+2]
                         (WILL BE [BP+0])
                 SECOND INTEGER
                         SIGNED WORD
                         PASSED BY VALUE
                         AT [SP+4]
                         (WILL BE [BP+2])
         OUTPUT PARAMETERS:
                 NONE
         FUNCTION VALUE of TCMAXINT:
                 LARGER OF THE TWO INTEGERS
                         SIGNED WORD IN AX
         |

                 TITLE   TCMAXINT.ASM
                 PAGE    55, 80              ;LINES, WIDTH

DGROUP           GROUP   _DATA, _BSS

_DATA            SEGMENT WORD PUBLIC 'DATA'

         ;DEFINE ANY INITIALIZED DATA HERE

_DATA            ENDS
```

Figure 13-8: (continued)

```
_BSS            SEGMENT WORD PUBLIC 'BSS'

                ;DEFINE ANY UNINITIALIZED DATA HERE

_BSS            ENDS

_TEXT           SEGMENT BYTE PUBLIC 'CODE'

                ASSUME  CS:_TEXT, DS:DGROUP

                ;NEAR PROCEDURE TO FIND AND RETURN THE BIGGEST INTEGER
_TCMAXINT       PROC    NEAR

                PUBLIC  _TCMAXINT       ;NEED TO REFERENCE
                                        ;   EXTERNALLY

                ;SAVE BP AND ADDRESS PARAMETERS
                PUSH    BP              ;SAVE IT
                MOV     BP, SP          ;POINT BP TO STACK
                ADD     BP, 4           ;ADJUST TO POINT TO
                                        ;   PARAMETERS
                ;SAVE ANY OTHER REGISTERS
                PUSH    SI              ;SAVE IT
                ;COMPARE AND RETURN THE BIGGEST INTEGER
                MOV     AX, [BP+0]      ;GET 1ST INT TO AX
                CMP     AX, [BP+2]      ;COMPARE THEM
                JGE     QBM_1           ;KEEP 1ST INT IF BIGGEST
                    MOV   AX, [BP+2]    ;   GET 2ND INT TO AX
QBM_1:
                ;RESTORE REGISTERS AND RETURN AX AS FUNCTION VALUE
                POP     SI              ;RESTORE
                POP     BP              ;   THEM
                RET                     ;NEAR RETURN TO C;
                                        ;   LEAVE STACK HOLE OPEN!
                                        ;   AX IS FUNCTION VALUE

_TCMAXINT       ENDP

_TEXT           ENDS

                END                     ;END OF TCMAXINT.ASM
```

Figure 13-9 illustrates a simple QuickBASIC program, which calls QBMAX-INT. QB2ASBLY.BAS inputs two integers from the keyboard, calls QBMAXINT to determine the larger of the two, and prints the larger integer returned by QBMAXINT. To test the subprocedure, assemble QBMAXINT to an object file, use the QuickBASIC compiler to compile QB2ASBLY to an object file, and use LINK to link the two object files into one executable file (specify QB2ASBLY+QBMAXINT for the object files).

Figure 13-9 **QuickBASIC Program that Calls QBMAXINT**

```
REM PROGRAM IDENTIFICATION SECTION ===============================
REM
REM QB2ASBLY.BAS
REM
REM QUICKBASIC PROGRAM THAT CALLS AN ASSEMBLY-LANGUAGE
REM SUBPROCEDURE TO FIND THE LARGER OF TWO INTEGERS
REM
REM 6/15/90
REM
REM VARIABLE TABLE ==============================================
REM      NAME            PURPOSE
REM      ----            -------
REM
REM      INT1%           FIRST INTEGER FROM KEYBOARD
REM      INT2%           SECOND INTEGER FROM KEYBOARD
REM      MAX.INT%        LARGER OF TWO INTEGERS
REM
REM MAINLINE PROCEDURE ==========================================
INPUT "Enter an integer: ", INT1%
INPUT "Enter another integer: ", INT2%
CALL QBMAXINT(INT1%, INT2%, MAX.INT%)      REM EXTERNAL ASSEMBLY-
                                           REM LANGUAGE SUBPROCEDURE
PRINT: PRINT
PRINT MAX.INT%; "is the biggest."
PRINT: PRINT
END
```

Figure 13-10 illustrates a simple Turbo C program that performs the same functions as QB2ASBLY in Figure 13-9. It also reads two integers from the keyboard, invokes TCMAXINT as a function to determine the larger of the two, and prints the larger integer returned by TCMAXINT. Assemble TCMAXINT, compile TC2ASBLY and link the two object files to one executable file.

SUMMARY

DOS supports two types of executable programs, .COM files and .EXE files. .COM files have a simple structure, containing only the program code and data. When such a file is loaded, DOS initializes all Segment registers to the same Segment address, the address at which the PSP and program have been loaded; IP is always initialized to 100H (the offset immediately following the PSP), and SP is always initialized to FFFEH. Due to their simplicity, all .COM files are limited to a total of 64K for the sum of the program code plus all data plus the stack plus the PSP.

Figure 13-10   Turbo C Program that Calls TCMAXINT

```
/* ===============================================================
TC2ASBLY.C

Turbo C program that uses an assembly-language function to find
the larger of two integers

6/15/90
=============================================================== */

#include <stdio.h>

extern int TCMAXINT();            /* External Assembly-language */
                                  /* function */

/* ============================================================= */
main()
{
    int nbr1,                     /* First integer from user */
        nbr2,                     /* Second integer from user */
        max;                      /* Larger of two integers */

    printf("Enter an integer: ");         /* Print to screen */
    scanf("%d", &nbr1);                   /* Input from keyboard */
    printf("Enter another integer: ");
    scanf("%d", &nbr2);
    max = TCMAXINT(nbr1, nbr2);           /* Invoke assembly funct */
    printf("\n"); printf("\n");           /* Skip 2 lines */
    printf("%d is the biggest.\n", max);
    return 0;                             /* Return 0 ERRORLEVEL */
}
```

.EXE files have a more complex structure, containing a relocation header that enables DOS to calculate the appropriate Segment addresses for CS and SS and to initialize IP and SP to the appropriate offsets within the code and stack segments. Additionally, the relocation header contains the information necessary for DOS to properly modify the segment addresses of all Far jumps and calls. .EXE files are unlimited in size and may use separate segments for code, data, and stack.

The PSP that DOS constructs within the 256 (100H) bytes immediately preceding any program (either .COM or .EXE) contains information that is retrievable by the program. Primarily, the program may access the command line tail, either unformatted or parsed as file specifications, from the PSP. The first two bytes of the PSP contain an INT 20H instruction, which is normally used by .EXE programs for termination to DOS. Additionally, DOS uses the PSP to store the initial values of three interrupt vectors (22H, 23H, and 24H); upon program termination, DOS restores the vectors from the PSP.

DOS provides five distinct methods of program termination, two of which allow the specification of the address at which to release memory and so can be used to cause the program to terminate and stay resident in memory. We will discuss TSR programs in the next chapter.

The interfacing of assembly language with high-level languages requires a good deal of research on the part of the programmer. There is no standard calling convention for all compilers. Interfacing with a particular compiler requires a knowledge of the calling conventions used by the desired compiler: segment and group conventions, symbol naming conventions, type of calls (Near or Far), parameter-passing conventions (order and method), and the closing of the stack hole (by the subprocedure or by the mainline).

VOCABULARY

V13-1   In your own words, define each of the following terms:

a) Relocatable program

b) Relocation header

c) Segment displacement value (in relocation header)

d) Pointer offset value (in relocation header)

e) Fix-up address (in relocation header)

f) Program segment prefix (PSP)

g) Command line tail

h) Environment block

i) Parameter passing by Value

j) Parameter passing by Near reference

k) Parameter passing by Far reference

REVIEW QUESTIONS

Q13-1   In your own words, describe the difference between the format of a .COM file and that of an .EXE file.

Q13-2   What is the limit, if any, on the size of a .COM file?

Q13-3   What is the limit, if any, on the size of an .EXE file?

Q13-4   Which type of executable file (.COM or .EXE) is limited to one segment?

Q13-5   For which Segment registers does an .EXE file's relocation header contain segment displacement values?

Q13-6   For which pointer registers does an .EXE file's relocation header contain pointer offset values?

Q13-7   For which instructions does an .EXE file's relocation header contain fix-up addresses?

Q13-8   What directive may be used to combine segments with different *segname*s into one segment?

Q13-9   How long is a PSP?

Q13-10   Can a program file on disk contain a PSP? If so, which type (.COM or .EXE or both)?

Q13-11   Can a program file on disk contain a relocation header? If so, which type (.COM or .EXE or both)?

Q13-12   Can a program, as loaded into memory, contain a PSP? If so, which type (.COM or .EXE or both)?

Q13-13   Can a program, as loaded into memory, contain a relocation header? If so, which type (.COM or .EXE or both)?

Q13-14   What is contained in a command line tail?

Q13-15   If a program defines a segment for its PSP, what combine type should be used?

Q13-16   Describe the location and format of the unformatted command line tail in the PSP.

Q13-17   Describe the location and format of the first two parameters of the command line tail, as parsed into the PSP by DOS.

Q13-18   Describe the manner in which total user memory is stored within the PSP.

Q13-19   Describe the format and location of the environment block.

Q13-20   List the major considerations that must be researched before attempting to interface an assembly-language subprocedure with a high-level language compiler.

Q13-21   Of the three parameter-passing methods (by Value, Near reference, Far reference), which have we previously used in our building blocks? Give an example of each.

PROGRAMMING ASSIGNMENTS

PA13-1   Rewrite PA12-2 as a .COM file. Except for being converted to a .COM file, PA13-1.COM should be identical to PA12-2.EXE.

PA13-2   Rewrite PA12-4 as a .COM file. Except for being converted to a .COM file, PA13-2.COM should be identical to PA12-4.EXE.

PA13-3   Rewrite PA12-5 as a .COM file. Except for being converted to a .COM file, PA13-3.COM should be identical to PA12-5.EXE.

PA13-4   Rewrite PA12-2 as an .EXE file that allows the user to enter the old and new file specifications in the command line, much like the REN command. The user should be able to enter a command such as:

```
PA13-4     OLDFILE.ASM     NEWFILE.ASM
```

PA13-5   Rewrite PA12-4 as an .EXE file that allows the user to enter the source and destination file specifications in the command line, much like the COPY command. The user should be able to enter a command such as:

```
PA13-5     SRCFILE.ASM     DESTFILE.ASM
```

PA13-6 Rewrite PA12-5 as an .EXE file that allows the user to enter the source and destination file specifications in the command line, much like the COPY command. The user should be able to enter a command such as:

```
PA13-6      SRCFILE.ASM      DESTFILE.ASM
```

PA13-7 Rewrite PA12-2 as a .COM file that allows the user to enter the old and new file specifications in the command line, much like the REN command. The user should be able to enter a command such as:

```
PA13-7      OLDFILE.ASM      NEWFILE.ASM
```

PA13-8 Rewrite PA12-4 as a .COM file that allows the user to enter the source and destination file specifications in the command line, much like the COPY command. The user should be able to enter a command such as:

```
PA13-8      SRCFILE.ASM      DESTFILE.ASM
```

PA13-9 Rewrite PA12-5 as a .COM file that allows the user to enter the source and destination file specifications in the command line, much like the COPY command. The user should be able to enter a command such as:

```
PA13-9      SRCFILE.ASM      DESTFILE.ASM
```

PA13-10 Write a subprocedure, similar to Figure 13-7 or 13-8, to be called by a high-level language other than QuickBASIC or C. Write a program, similar to Figure 13-9 or 13-10, in the high-level language you have chosen. Assemble the subprocedure, compile the mainline program, and link the two to create a single executable program (PA13-10.EXE).

PA13-11 Write a subprocedure (to be called by a high-level language of your choice) to perform modular arithmetic. The subprocedure should accept two positive integer values and return the remainder of the first integer divided by the second. For example:

```
15 MOD 4 should return 3
11 MOD 5 should return 1
21 MOD 7 should return 0
```

Write a mainline program in the language of your choice; then assemble the subprocedure, compile the mainline program, and link the two to create a single executable program (PA13-11.EXE).

14

Interrupt-Driven Processing

INTRODUCTION

In this chapter we will discuss interrupt-driven programs that respond to asynchronous hardware interrupts. Most of the programs we have written thus far take control of the processor upon execution and execute a fixed sequence of instructions; the program maintains full control over the sequence of events. An interrupt-driven program, on the other hand, responds to external events. The processing is controlled to a great extent by events external to the processor and outside the control of the program.

Some of the most important hardware devices in the IBM PC that are capable of controlling processing through the generation of interrupts are the 8259 Interrupt Controller, the 8255 Programmable Peripheral Interface, and the 8253 Timer. We will discuss each of these peripheral devices in some detail.

Following our discussion of interrupt-generating peripheral devices, we will discuss the design and implementation of interrupt-service routines to respond to and process hardware interrupts. Finally, we will discuss TSR (Terminate-and-Stay-Resident) programs. A TSR program is any program that remains, at least partially, in memory after its termination to DOS. The resident portion of the program normally remains passive, with no effect on the execution of subsequent programs, until it is activated by an interrupt caused by some external event. Upon activation, the TSR program takes control of the processor and responds to the interrupt, often modifying the function of the PC.

PERIPHERAL SUPPORT HARDWARE

In addition to the system (8086/8088) processor, the IBM PC contains a number of **peripheral support hardware** devices, specialized microprocessors for providing support to the system processor. Although specialized, each device can also be "programmed" to a certain degree by controlling the values in registers within each specialized processor that are connected via support hardware to predetermined I/O ports. Thus, a program communicates with and/or controls the various specialized processors through I/O ports by executing IN and OUT instructions.

Three of the most important devices, and those which we shall discuss here, are the **Intel 8259 Interrupt Controller**, the **Intel 8255 Programmable Peripheral Interface**, and the **Intel 8253 Timer.** Communication with and control of the peripheral devices are accomplished through I/O ports. Internal registers and ports within each device are mapped by support circuitry to specific I/O port addresses through which the 8086/8088 can read and/or write values from or to the peripheral devices. Figure 14-1 illustrates the I/O port assignments of each of the three devices.

In the following sections, we shall discuss each device in some detail. In general, to obtain information from any of the peripheral devices, the processor executes an IN instruction from the appropriate I/O port into the AL register; to control a device, the processor must move an appropriate value into AL and output it to the appropriate I/O port.

Figure 14-1 Peripheral Device I/O Port Addresses

Device	I/O port	Description
8259 Interrupt Controller	20H	Out—Interrupt Command register
	21H	In/Out—Interrupt Mask register
8255 Programmable Peripheral Interface	60H	In—Port PA
	61H	In/Out—Port PB
	62H	In—Port PC
8253 Timer	40H	In/Out—Channel 0 Latch register
	41H	In/Out—Channel 1 Latch register
	42H	In/Out—Channel 2 Latch register
	43H	Out—Timer Command Register

Note: "In" and "Out" are from the point of view of the 8086/8088 system processor.

8259 Interrupt Controller

The 8259 Interrupt Controller is used in the IBM PC as an interface between the 8086/8088 processor and all other hardware devices that need to be able to interrupt the processor for service. For example, every time a key is depressed or released, the keyboard needs to interrupt the processor to cause it to execute an interrupt-service routine within BIOS to capture and interpret the scan code from the keyboard and to store the appropriate character.

Recall that the 8086/8088 is capable of servicing 255 different interrupt types, each with its own four-byte vector, within the vector table beginning at absolute address 00000H. Whenever any interrupt occurs, the processor must know the interrupt type in order to retrieve the appropriate vector and so transfer control to the address of the correct interrupt-service routine. The 8086/8088 processor uses only two lines specifically for responding to external (hardware) interrupt requests, INT REQ (interrupt request) and INT ACK (interrupt acknowledge). The interrupting device is responsible for placing the appropriate interrupt type onto the eight-bit data bus. Whenever any device wishes to interrupt the 8086/8088, the following sequence must be observed:

8086/8088 Hardware-Interrupt Sequence

1) The interrupting device puts a signal onto the INT REQ line.

2) If interrupts are enabled (IF set in the Flags register), then the 8086/8088 responds with a signal on the INT ACK line.

3) The interrupting device is then responsible for placing the appropriate interrupt type (0 - 255) onto the data bus.

4) The 8086/8088 retrieves the interrupt type from the data bus and executes the interrupt just as if it were executing an INT instruction of the same type.

Rather than requiring that all peripheral devices in the PC be "intelligent" enough to observe the above sequence, IBM chose to use the 8259 Interrupt Controller as an interface between those devices and the 8086/8088. The 8259 uses eight separate input lines, called IRQ0 through IRQ7, to receive interrupt requests from up to eight peripheral devices. Each peripheral device is connected to its own dedicated IRQn line and need only place a signal on that line in order to request an interrupt of the correct type. The 8259 then observes the interrupt sequence described above in order to communicate the appropriate interrupt request to the 8086/8088.

Whenever it receives an interrupt request on any one of the eight IRQn lines, the 8259 places a signal onto the INT REQ line to the 8086/8088, waits for the

INT ACK from the 8086/8088, and then places the appropriate interrupt type, as determined by the IRQ*n* line on which the request was received, onto the data bus. A request on IRQ0 causes the 8259 to respond to the INT ACK with interrupt type 08H; IRQ1 results in an interrupt type 09H; IRQ7 causes the 8259 to generate an interrupt type 0FH. Thus, hardware-interrupt lines IRQ0 through IRQ7 result in interrupts 08H through 0FH from the 8259 to the 8086/8088. Figure 14-2 illustrates the logical configuration of the 8259 between the 8086/8088 and the peripheral devices that must be able to interrupt the processor.

Figure 14-2   8259 Interrupt Controller

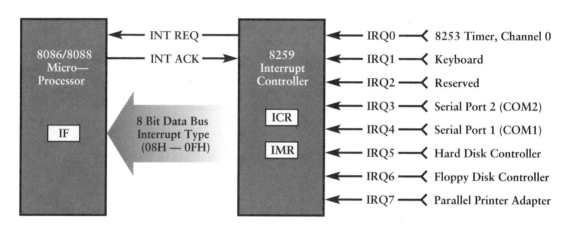

The 8259 contains two registers, the **Interrupt Command Register (ICR)** and the **Interrupt Mask Register (IMR)**, which are accessible to the 8086/8088 processor through I/O ports 20H and 21H, respectively. The two registers provide the 8086/8088 with a great deal of control over the 8259. As we will discuss shortly, the IMR allows the enabling and disabling of each of the eight peripheral devices, independently of each other. The ICR provides a great deal of flexibility in programming the 8259; however, most of its programming has already been handled by BIOS. We will discuss only one use of the Interrupt Command Register.

Because each of the devices connected to IRQ0 through IRQ7 is independent, the 8259 may receive two or more interrupt requests at the same time; the two requests may occur simultaneously or the second request may occur while the first request is still being processed. The 8259 will issue only one interrupt request at a time to the 8086/8088, holding the second request until the processor has completed servicing the first request. If two requests occur simultaneously, the lower-numbered IRQ*n* line takes precedence and is issued to the 8086/8088 immediately; the higher-numbered request is held until completion of the first request.

To implement this queuing of interrupt requests, the 8259 needs to know when the processor has completed servicing an interrupt request in order to know when it may issue any pending request. The processor notifies the 8259 of the completion of servicing of the current interrupt by outputting a value of 20H to the Interrupt Command Register (I/O port 20H). Consequently, any interrupt-service routine (for hardware interrupt types 08H through 0FH) must *always* issue an **End-of-Interrupt** signal (**EOI**) to the 8259 by outputting a value of 20H to I/O port 20H immediately before returning from the interrupt. All such interrupt-service routines must end with the following instructions:

```
                     End-of-Interrupt Sequence

        MOV      AL, 20H             ;END OF INTERRUPT SIGNAL
        OUT      20H, AL             ;   TO 8259
        POP      AX                  ;RESTORE IT
        IRET                         ;RETURN FROM INTERRUPT
```

As mentioned above, the 8259 also contains an Interrupt Mask Register (I/O port 21H) for individually enabling or disabling the eight IRQn lines. The IMR is an eight-bit register, one bit for each of the IRQn lines; bit zero controls IRQ0, bit one controls IRQ1, and so on. A value of zero in any bit enables the corresponding IRQn line; a value of one disables the line. Before responding to any interrupt request, the 8259 first checks the appropriate bit within the IMR. The interrupt request is passed on to the 8086/8088 processor only if the corresponding IMR bit is clear (zero); if the IRQn line is disabled (the corresponding IMR bit is set), then the interrupt request is ignored by the 8259.

Note that the IMR bit values are opposite to what might seem reasonable. A bit value of zero *enables* the appropriate IRQn line; a value of one *disables* the IRQn line, thus disabling interrupts from the device that is connected to that line. Note also that enabling an IRQn line (clearing its IMR bit) only ensures that its interrupt requests will be passed through the 8259 to the 8086/8088; it does not guarantee that the 8086/8088 will respond to the request. Recall that the 8086/8088 Flags register contains a bit called the Interrupt-Enable flag, which must be set (one) before the 8086/8088 will respond to any interrupts. Thus, any program that wishes to enable hardware interrupts must set the Interrupt flag (STI) as well as clear the appropriate 8259 IMR bit(s). The following three instructions enable IRQ0 and IRQ1 (timer and keyboard) while disabling all other hardware interrupts:

```
        MOV      AL, 11111100B       ;ENABLE ONLY IRQ0 AND  IRQ1
        OUT      21H, AL             ;TO 8259 IMR
        STI                          ;ENABLE INT'S IN 8086/8088
```

8255 Programmable Peripheral Interface

The 8255 is a very flexible I/O interface chip that can be configured in many ways to provide an interface between the 8086/8088 and I/O devices within the PC. It contains three ports, called **PA**, **PB**, and **PC**, which are mapped by support circuitry to I/O ports 60H, 61H, and 62H, respectively. In addition, it contains a **Command register**, which is mapped to I/O port 63H. During boot, BIOS outputs a value of 99H to the 8255 Command Register, properly configuring it such that PA and PC are input ports and PB is an input/output port. PA and PC may then be used to input device information through the 8255. Port PB is normally used as an output port to control the operation of the 8255, including selecting the source for ports PA and PC; additionally, an input from port PB obtains the last value to be output to it. Figure 14-3 illustrates the function of the 8255 ports.

Figure 14-3   8255 Ports

Port	Description	I/O Port
PB	Output - Controls 8255 (Input returns last output value)	61H

Bit #	Explanation
0	To 8253 Timer, Gate 2 (1 enables Timer channel 2)
1	To speaker (1 enables output to speaker)
2	Selects source for port PC bits 0 - 3
3	To cassette motor (0 turns motor on)
4	0 enables RAM
5	0 enables parity errors from expansion boards
6	1 enables keyboard clock signal
7	Selects source for PA Also, 1 = keyboard acknowledge

Port	Description	I/O Port
PA	Input keyboard scan code or configuration switch 1 Keyboard scan code if PB bit 7 is 0 Config switch 1 if PB bit 7 is 1 (PA bit 0 = SW1-1, Bit 1 = SW1-2, etc.)	60H
PC	Input configuration switch 2 and other	62H

Bit #	Explanation
0 - 3	Configuration switch 2 SW2-5 through SW2-8 if PB bit 2 is 0 SW2-1 through SW2-4 if PB bit 2 is 1
4	Cassette data input
5	Timer channel two output
6	1 = Parity error on expansion board
7	1 = Parity error on system board

Port PA and bits six and seven of PB are used for keyboard input. The processor obtains keyboard scan codes, as discussed in chapter 9, by inputting from port PA while the keyboard is selected as its source. PB bit six enables or disables the system clock signal to the keyboard processor. Clearing bit six (zero) disables the keyboard by cutting off its clock signal; thus bit six must always be one in order for the keyboard to operate. Bit seven of PB serves two purposes; in addition to selecting the source for PA, it also serves as a keyboard acknowledge whenever its value is set to one.

Bit seven of PB is initialized to zero by BIOS and normally remains clear except when reading configuration-switch-1 settings or acknowledging a scan code from the keyboard. To obtain a keystroke, the program inputs the scan code from port PA; the program must then send an acknowledgment to the keyboard by setting and then clearing bit seven of port PB. Following are the necessary instructions for retrieving a scan code from the keyboard:

```
IN    AL, 60H         ;GET SCAN CODE
MOV   AH, AL          ;SAVE SCAN CODE
IN    AL, 61H         ;GET PORT PB
OR    AL, 80H         ;SET BIT 7
OUT   61H, AL         ;KEYBOARD ACKNOWLEDGE
AND   AL, 7FH         ;CLEAR BIT 7
OUT   61H, AL         ;RESELECT SCAN CODE FOR PA
```

8253 Timer

The 8253 Timer chip contains three separate timer channels each of which can be "programmed" to perform one of six timing or counting functions, called mode zero through mode five. Each channel contains two registers, a **Latch register** and a **Counter register**; the three Latch registers are accessible to the processor for either input or output via I/O ports 40H through 42H. In addition, each channel receives two input signals from the system bus: a **Clock** and a **Gate**. Each channel generates one **Output** signal back to the system bus. In addition, the Timer chip contains a **Command register**, which is accessible to the processor for output only through I/O port 43H, and which is used to control the operation of all three channels of the timer.

In general, each channel operates by first loading the word value from the Latch register into the Counter register. Each subsequent cycle of the clock input decrements the Counter-register value. As the Counter register counts down to zero, a signal is generated on the Output line; the type of Output signal is determined by the mode of the channel. In addition, the mode of the channel determines the effect of the Gate signal. In modes zero, two, three, and four, a low voltage on the Gate inhibits the decrementing of the Counter register, thus temporarily stopping the clock. In modes one and five, the cycling of the Gate from low to a high causes the reloading of the Counter register with the value from the Latch register, thus restarting the count.

In modes zero, one, four, and five, the channel generates one output upon completion of the count. In modes two and four, a recurring output signal is generated; upon completion of the count, the Counter register is automatically reloaded from the Latch register and counted down again. Figure 14-4 describes the operation of the 8255 Timer channels in each of the five modes.

Figure 14-4   8253 Timer Modes

Mode   Description

0 **Countdown, Level Output, Gate Inhibit.** Output is low for n clock cycles, where n is the value in the Latch register; output is high thereafter. A low Gate signal inhibits counting of clock cycles.

   Upon output of a value to the Latch Register, it is immediately loaded into the Counter register and the Output signal is set to low (0). Each subsequent cycle of the clock signal while the Gate is high (1) decrements the Counter register; a low Gate (0) inhibits counting. When the Counter register reaches zero, the Output is raised to a high signal (1) and remains high.

1 **Countdown, Level Output, Gate Restart.** Output is low for n clock cycles, high thereafter. A low Gate signal inhibits counting; the transition of the Gate, from low to high, restarts the count.

   Upon output of a value to the Latch register, the Output signal is immediately set to low (0). When the Gate goes high, the Counter register is loaded from the Latch register and the countdown begins. If the Gate subsequently goes low, counting is inhibited; when the Gate returns to a high state, the Counter register is reloaded from the Latch register and the count begins again. When the Counter register reaches zero, the Output is raised to high and remains high.

2 **Repeated Pulse Output, Gate Inhibit.** Every n clock cycles, the Output pulses to low for the duration of one clock cycle, the Gate, if low, inhibits the counting of clock cycles.

   The Counter register is loaded from the Latch register, and the Output is set to high. Each subsequent clock cycle decrements the Counter register unless the Gate is low. When the count reaches one, the Output goes low for one clock cycle; when the count reaches zero, the output returns to high, the Counter register is reloaded from the Latch register and the countdown is repeated.

3 **Square Wave Output, Gate Ignored.** The Output is a square wave whose frequency is equal to the frequency of the clock signal divided by n, the Latch-register value.

   The Counter register is loaded from the Latch register, and the Output is set to high. Each subsequent clock cycle decrements the Counter register. When the count reaches one-half the Latch-register value, the Output goes low; when the count reaches zero, the output returns to high, the Counter register is reloaded from the Latch register, and the countdown is repeated.

4 **Countdown, Pulse Output, Gate Inhibit.** Output is high for n clock cycles, where n is the value in the Latch register, then pulses low for the duration of one clock cycle. A low Gate signal inhibits counting of clock cycles. Mode four is identical to mode zero, except that the output is a low pulse.

Upon output of a value to the Latch register, it is immediately loaded into the Counter register and the Output signal is set to high. Each subsequent cycle of the clock signal, while the Gate is high, decrements the Counter register. When the Counter register reaches zero, the Output pulses to a low signal for one clock cycle, then returns to high and remains high.

5 **Countdown, Pulse Output, Gate Restart.** Output is high for n clock cycles, then pulses low for the duration of one clock cycle. A low Gate signal inhibits counting; the transition of the Gate, from low to high, restarts the count. Mode five is identical to mode one, except that the output is a low pulse.

Upon output of a value to the Latch register, the Output signal is immediately set to high. When the Gate goes high, the Counter register is loaded from the Latch register and the countdown begins. If the Gate subsequently goes low, counting is inhibited; when the Gate returns to a high state, the Counter register is reloaded from the Latch register and the count begins again. When the Counter register reaches zero, the Output pulses to low for one clock cycle, then returns to high and remains high.

All three channels are controlled through the single Command register (I/O port 43H). The value output to the Command register determines which channel is currently being programmed, the mode for that channel, the manner in which the Latch register is to be accessed, and the manner in which the Counter register is to be counted down. Figure 14-5 illustrates the significance of the Command register bits.

Figure 14-5   8253 Command Register (I/O port 43H)

Bit(s)	Description
0	Determines whether the Counter register will be decremented as a binary or Binary-Coded-Decimal value; binary is normal. 0 equals Binary; 1 equals BCD.
1 - 3	Determines the mode of the channel. Binary values 000 through 101 result in modes 0 through 5.
4 - 5	Selects the manner in which the Latch register is to be accessed. 00 = Immediately load the Latch register with the current value of the Counter register. 01 = Input/output MSB only. 10 = Input/output LSB only. 11 = Input/output LSB followed by MSB.
6 - 7	Selects the channel to be programmed by bits 0 through 5. Binary values 00 through 10 signify channels zero through two.

Notice, from Figure 14-5, that the manner in which the processor inputs or outputs from or to the Latch register is determined by the value output to bits five and four of the Command register. Since the Latch register is a sixteen-bit register, only the high or low byte is accessible by a single input or output instruction. A binary value of 01 causes any I/O, to or from the channel's Latch-register I/O port to access only the most-significant byte of the Latch register; 10B enables access to the least-significant byte. If bits five and four are 11B, then the first input or output accesses the least-significant byte, while the next I/O accesses the MSB. Notice also that the program can cause any channel's Latch register to be immediately loaded with the current Counter-register value by clearing bits four and five (00) in the byte that is output to the Command register.

Figure 14-6 summarizes the manner in which the Clock, Gate, and Output signals of the 8253 are connected into the system bus. Note that the programmer has no control over the Clock signal received by any of the 8253 Timer channels. All three clocks are connected to a 1.19318-megahertz signal (1,193,180 cycles per second) on the system board.

Similarly, the programmer has no control over the Gate signals for channels zero or one; both are connected to a positive voltage (high) and so are always enabled. However, the channel two Gate may be controlled by setting or clearing bit zero of port PB (I/O port 61H) of the 8255 Programmable Peripheral Interface (Refer back to Figure 14-3). A value of one in PB bit zero results in a high Gate to channel two of the 8253 Timer chip; a bit value of zero results in a low Gate, inhibiting the countdown of channel two.

As indicated by Figure 14-6, the output of each Timer channel has been dedicated to a specific purpose within the IBM PC. As the PC is booted, BIOS programs channel zero for mode three with a Latch-register value of zero, which is effectively 65536 or the highest possible count value. Thus channel zero generates a square wave with a frequency of 18.2 hertz (1,193,180 / 65536 = 18.2). Channel zero Out is connected to IRQ0 of the 8259 Interrupt Controller. Consequently, channel zero generates an interrupt type eight 18.2 times per second or once every 55 milliseconds. BIOS uses this type eight interrupt to maintain the system time and date.

Note that a program should not normally intercept this type eight interrupt (we will discuss interrupt-service routines shortly). Intercepting interrupt type eight not only disables BIOS's maintenance of system time and date but also interferes with the proper functioning of the disk drives, since the system time is used in controlling the disk drive motors. Any program that must intercept the fifty-five millisecond timer tick should use interrupt type 1CH. To make this possible, BIOS's type eight interrupt-service routine contains an instruction to generate an interrupt type 1CH (INT 1CH). Thus, each type eight interrupt (IRQ0) generated by the Timer chip results in an interrupt type 1CH from BIOS.

Channel one is programmed by BIOS to function in mode two with a Latch-register value of eighteen, thus generating a pulse signal at a rate of 66.287 KHz. This pulse signal is used to cause the DMA Controller to perform a memory refresh every fifteen microseconds. A program should *never* modify the programming of channel one; modifying channel one in any way may destroy the integrity of RAM memory.

Figure 14-6   8253 Timer Chip Inputs and Outputs

Channel	Signal	From/To
0	Clock	1.19318 MHz clock.
	Gate	Positive (high) voltage.
	Output	To IRQ0 (to 8259 Interrupt Controller).
1	Clock	1.19318 MHz clock.
	Gate	Positive (high) voltage.
	Output	To Data-Request line of DMA controller (for memory refresh).
2	Clock	1.19318 MHz clock.
	Gate	8255 PPI, bit 0 of port PB (0 = low, 1 = high).
	Output	To AND gate used as input to speaker. Other AND-gate input is from 8255 PPI, port PB, bit 1.

Sound Generation

The 8253 Timer chip's channel two Out is connected to an AND gate as input to the system speaker and may be used by the programmer to generate sound effects. To generate a tone, the program should first program channel two to generate a square wave and to read/write both the LSB and MSB of the Latch register by outputting a value of B6H (10110110B) to the Timer Command register (I/O port 43H). It should then output the desired count value to the channel two Latch register (I/O port 42H), LSB first followed by MSB. The necessary count value should be calculated as 1,193,180 divided by the desired frequency.

Once channel two has been programmed for the proper Out signal, the input to the speaker must be enabled. To do so, the program should input the current value of register PB of the 8255 PPI (I/O port 61H), OR it with 03H to set bits zero and one, and output the result back to PB; bit zero set insures that channel two Gate is high, and bit one set enables the signal to the speaker. To turn the sound off, the program ANDs the current PB value with FDH (11111101B) to clear bit one and outputs the result to PB. Since bit one is zero, a low signal is generated to the speaker's AND gate, disabling any speaker output. Figure 14-7 illustrates a simple sound generation program.

Note that although SOUND.ASM in Figure 14-7 does not support frequencies above 65.535 KHz, the 8253 Timer chip is capable of generating frequencies up to 596.59 KHz (Latch-register value of two). SOUND.ASM does not support the full frequency range of the 8253, but it is capable of producing tones far beyond the capabilities of the human ear, which is limited to about 15 KHz. Note also that the speaker need not be turned off to change the frequency of the tone; once the speaker and channel two have been enabled, a program may change the pitch by merely outputting the new Latch-register value to I/O port 42H without disabling the speaker.

Figure 14-7   Sound Generation Program

```
COMMENT \                    SOUND.ASM

        GENERATES SPEAKER OUTPUT AT FREQUENCY ENTERED BY USER

        !!! MUST BE CONVERTED TO A .COM FILE !!!

        \

                PAGE    55, 80              ;LINES, WIDTH FOR LISTING
                TITLE   SOUND.ASM

                INCLUDE         CONSOLE.MLB

P_GROUP         GROUP   DATA, CODE
                ASSUME  CS:P_GROUP, DS:P_GROUP, ES:P_GROUP


;DATA SEGMENT =========================================================
DATA            SEGMENT PARA PUBLIC 'DATA'

        ;PROGRAM ENTRY POINT
                ORG     100H                ;ENTRY POINT MUST BE 100H
ENTRY:          JMP     NEAR PTR MAIN       ;JUMP AROUND DATA

        ;PROGRAM DATA
        ;DSPLY_IMMED_STR ALSO PUTS STRING DATA HERE
IO_BUF          DB      6 DUP('#')          ;INPUT BUFFER
F_MSG           DB      'Enter desired frequency '
                DB      '(19 - 65535, or 0 to quit) ', 0
INV_MSG         DB      10, 10, 'Invalid frequency - '
                DB      'Press any key to try again ', 0

DATA            ENDS

;CODE SEGMENT =========================================================
CODE            SEGMENT WORD PUBLIC 'CODE'

        ;PROGRAM CODE
MAIN            PROC    FAR

        ;GET AND CHECK FREQUENCY FROM USER
GET_F:          CLS
                LOCATE  4, 0
                DSPLY_STR       <OFFSET F_MSG>
                                            ;PROMPT TO ENTER FREQ
                INPUT_STR       <OFFSET IO_BUF>, 5
                                            ;INPUT FREQUENCY
                CNV_STR_UNS     <OFFSET IO_BUF>, BX
                                            ;CONVERT TO NUMERIC
```

Figure 14-7: (continued)

```
                    JC      INV_F              ;IF INVALID NUMERAL
                    CMP     BX, 0              ;0 TO QUIT?
                    JNE     M_1                ;NO - GO ON
                    JMP     M_RET              ;YES - QUIT
        M_1:        CMP     BX, 19             ;FREQ TOO LOW?
                    JAE     M_2                ;NO - GO ON
            ;REPORT INVALID FREQUENCY
        INV_F:      DSPLY_STR       <OFFSET INV_MSG>
                                               ;ERROR MESSAGE
                    INPUT_CHR       AL         ;PAUSE
                    JMP     GET_F              ;TRY AGAIN
            ;CALCULATE LATCH REGISTER VALUE FROM FREQUENCY
        M_2:        MOV     DX, 12H            ;SET DX:AX TO CLOCK
                    MOV     AX, 34DCH          ; FREQ (1,193,180)
                    DIV     BX                 ;DIVIDE BY FREQUENCY
                    MOV     BX, AX             ;SAVE LATCH VALUE TO BX
            ;PROGRAM TIMER CHANNEL 2 FOR SQUARE WAVE (MODE 3),
            ;BOTH BYTES OF LATCH REGISTER
                    MOV     AL, 0B6H           ;10 11 011 0B
                    OUT     43H, AL            ;TO TIMER COMMAND REG
                    MOV     AL, BL             ;LOW BYTE TO CH 2
                    OUT     42H, AL            ; LATCH REGISTER
                    MOV     AL, BH             ;HIGH BYTE TO CH 2
                    OUT     42H, AL            ; LATCH REGISTER
            ;PAUSE, THEN START TONE
                    DSPLY_IMMED_STR <10, 10, 'Any key starts tone '>
                    INPUT_CHR       AL         ;PAUSE BEFORE SOUND
                    IN      AL, 61H            ;GET PPI PORT PB
                    OR      AL, 03H            ;SET BITS 0 & 1 (HI GATE
                                               ; 2 AND SPEAKER ENABLE)
                    OUT     61H, AL            ;BACK TO PB - SOUND ON
            ;PAUSE AGAIN, THEN TURN SOUND OFF
                    DSPLY_IMMED_STR <13, 10, 'Any key stops tone '>
                    INPUT_CHR       AL         ;PAUSE WITH SOUND ON
                    IN      AL, 61H            ;GET PB
                    AND     AL, 0FDH           ;CLEAR BIT 1 (DISABLE
                                               ; SPEAKER)
                    OUT     61H, AL            ;BACK TO PB - SOUND OFF
                    JMP     GET_F              ;REPEAT

            ;TERMINATE PROGRAM
        M_RET:      DSPLY_IMMED_STR <10, 10, 'Good-bye', 13, 10, 10>
                    INT     20H                ;TERMINATE TO DOS

        MAIN        ENDP

        CODE        ENDS

                    END     ENTRY              ;ENTRY AT OFFSET 100H
```

INTERRUPT-SERVICE ROUTINES

Any program that needs to respond to interrupts must contain a specially written procedure called an **interrupt-service routine,** which executes whenever the interrupt occurs. The interrupt-service routine must follow a number of rules to be discussed shortly. In order to enable the interrupt processing, the program modifies the appropriate interrupt vector to the segment:offset of the entry point of the interrupt-service routine. Before modifying the vector, however, the program should usually save the current vector; the program should then restore the vector to its previous value prior to termination and return to DOS.

Interrupt vectors may be accessed in either of two ways, by directly addressing the vector table beginning at 0000H:0000H or by using two functions provided by the DOS function call (INT 21H). Although the latter method is preferred, an interrupt vector might be obtained as follows:

```
;READ VECTOR FOR INTERRUPT TYPE 16H INTO DX:AX
        PUSH    ES                ;SAVE IT
        MOV     AX, 0             ;SET ES:BX
        MOV     ES, AX            ; TO SEGMENT:OFFSET
        MOV     BX, 4 * 16H       ; OF THE VECTOR
        MOV     AX, ES:[BX]       ;VECTOR OFFSET TO AX
        MOV     DX, ES:[BX+2]     ;VECTOR SEGMENT TO DX
        POP     ES                ;RESTORE IT
```

An interrupt vector might be modified in a similar manner, moving the desired offset and segment **to** ES:[BX] AND ES:[BX+2]. However, the program should first disable interrupts (CLI) to prevent the execution of an interrupt while the vector is being modified. The program should then re-enable interrupts (STI) after the vector modification is finished. As mentioned above, DOS functions 25H and 35H provide a much safer method of accessing the interrupt-vector table. Following is an explanation of the two DOS function calls for accessing interrupt vectors.

Function 35H - Get interrupt vector:

To obtain an interrupt vector, move the function code 35H into AH; move the interrupt type (number) into AL; and execute an interrupt type 21H.

DOS obtains the appropriate interrupt vector from the vector table (at address 0000H:4*AL) and returns it in ES:BX, where ES is the segment and BX is the offset of the current interrupt-service routine.

Function 25H - Set interrupt vector:

To set an interrupt vector, move the function code 25H into AH; move the interrupt type (number) into AL; move the desired vector into DS:DX (segment into DS, offset into DX); and execute an interrupt type 21H.

DOS sets the desired vector by moving DS:DX into the vector table, DX (offset) to address 0000H:4*AL, and DS (segment) to 0000H:4*AL+2. Any subsequent interrupt of the type specified by AL will result in execution of the interrupt-service routine at the address specified by DS:DX.

Prior to using function 25H to set an interrupt vector, the program should first use function 35H to obtain and save the current vector. Upon completion of the program and prior to termination to DOS, the program should use function 25H again to restore the vector to its previous value.

In order to install any interrupt service, the appropriate vector must be set to the address of the service routine. Additionally, if the interrupt-service routine is to service a hardware interrupt (types 08H - 0F), the program must also ensure that the IRQn line is enabled by clearing the appropriate bit in the Interrupt Mask register of the 8259 Interrupt Controller. To do so, the program should input the current value from I/O port 21H, AND it with the appropriate value to clear the bit, and output the result back to the IMR through port 21H.

As mentioned earlier, any interrupt-service routine must follow several rules. First, the programmer must be very careful to save and restore any modified registers, especially if the routine is to service a hardware interrupt (types 08H through 0FH). All registers must be restored to their original values before returning to the code that was in execution at the moment of the interrupt.

In addition, the values of all registers, other than CS and IP, are completely unpredictable; upon entry to the service routine, the registers retain whatever value they may have contained at the moment of the interrupt. Consequently, the interrupt-service routine must make no assumptions about any registers other than CS and IP. Specifically, if the interrupt-service routine is to address data, it must either use a CS: segment override for every variable reference or must, upon entry, save DS and initialize it to the correct segment (same as CS). Typically, the service routine might begin and end as follows:

```
              Initialization of DS in Interrupt-Service Routine

              PUSH      DS                  ;SAVE IT
              PUSH      CS                  ;POINT DS TO
              POP       DS                  ; THIS SEGMENT
              ASSUME    DS:P_GROUP          ; AND ASSOCIATE IT
                .
                .
                .
              POP       DS                  ;RESTORE IT
              ASSUME    DS:NOTHING          ; AND DISASSOCIATE IT
              IRET                          ;RETURN FROM INTERRUPT
```

Since control will be transferred to the procedure by an interrupt, rather than by a call, it should terminate with an interrupt-return instruction (IRET). Additionally, if the routine is very long, you may need to re-enable interrupts before the service is complete. Since the processor clears the Interrupt-Enable flag as it executes the interrupt, the service routine may want to set it (STI) in order to allow the proper processing of other hardware interrupts (fifty-five millisecond clock tick for example).

Any service routine for a hardware interrupt (08H - 0FH) must also issue an End-of-Interrupt signal (see above) to notify the 8255 Interrupt Controller upon completion of servicing the interrupt, immediately before restoring registers and returning. Figure 14-8 illustrates a simple program that uses an interrupt-service routine to turn the PC into a stopwatch.

Figure 14-8   **Stopwatch Program**

```
COMMENT \                   WATCH.ASM

          STOPWATCH PROGRAM

          MUST BE CONVERTED TO .COM FILE USING EXE2BIN

          INCLUDES TWO INTERRUPT SERVICE ROUTINES:
                    1CH - BIOS TIMER TICK
                    09H - KEYBOARD (IRQ1)

             \

                    PAGE    55, 80              ;LINES, WIDTH FOR LISTING
                    TITLE   WATCH.ASM

                    INCLUDE          CONSOLE.MLB

P_GROUP             GROUP   DATA, CODE
                    ASSUME  CS:P_GROUP, DS:P_GROUP, ES:P_GROUP

;DATA SEGMENT ========================================================
DATA                SEGMENT PARA PUBLIC 'DATA'

          ;PROGRAM ENTRY POINT
                    ORG     100H                ;ENTRY POINT MUST BE 100H
ENTRY:              JMP     NEAR PTR MAIN       ;JUMP AROUND DATA

          ;PROGRAM DATA
INIT_MSG            DB      'S T O P W A T C H', 13, 10 ,10, 10
                    DB      'Press <Space Bar> to start clock'
                    DB      13, 10, 10
                    DB      'Press <Space Bar> again to stop clock'
                    DB      13, 10, 10
                    DB      'Press <Enter> to reset clock'
                    DB      13, 10, 10
                    DB      'Press <Esc> to quit'
                    DB      0
BLANKS              DB      '  '
```

Figure 14-8: (continued)

```
ESC_FLG           DB        0
CLCK_SWTCH        DB        0
IO_BUF            DB        7 DUP ('#')
I09H_VCTR         DD        ?
I1CH_VCTR         DD        ?
HOURS             DB        0
MINUTES           DB        0
SECONDS           DB        0
MSECS             DW        0


DATA              ENDS


;CODE SEGMENT =========================================================
CODE              SEGMENT PARA PUBLIC 'CODE'


        ;PROGRAM CODE - MAINLINE
MAIN              PROC    FAR


        ;PRINT INSTRUCTIONS AND LABELS
                  CLS                           ;CLEAR SCREEN
                  LOCATE   4, 25
                  DSPLY_STR       <OFFSET INIT_MSG>
                  LOCATE   18, 28
                  DSPLY_IMMED_STR 'Hours:'
                  LOCATE   19, 26
                  DSPLY_IMMED_STR 'Minutes:'
                  LOCATE   20, 26
                  DSPLY_IMMED_STR 'Seconds:'
                  LOCATE   21, 21
                  DSPLY_IMMED_STR 'Milliseconds:'
        ;INSTALL KEYBOARD AND TIMER INTERRUPT SERVICE ROUTINES
        ;FIRST, SAVE CURRENT VECTORS
                  PUSH     ES                ;SAVE IT
                  MOV      AH, 35H           ;GET CURRENT BIOS TIMER-
                  MOV      AL, 1CH           ;   TICK INTERRUPT VECTOR
                  INT      21H               ;   INTO ES:BX
                  MOV      WORD PTR I1CH_VCTR, BX        ;SAVE THE
                  MOV      WORD PTR I1CH_VCTR + 2, ES ;  VECTOR
                  MOV      AH, 35H           ;GET CURRENT KBRD
                  MOV      AL, 09H           ;   INTERRUPT VECTOR
                  INT      21H               ;   INTO ES:BX
                  MOV      WORD PTR I09H_VCTR, BX        ;SAVE THE
                  MOV      WORD PTR I09H_VCTR + 2, ES ;  VECTOR
                  POP      ES                ;RESTORE IT
        ;NOW, INSTALL THE NEW INTERRUPT VECTORS
                  MOV      DX, OFFSET P_GROUP:BTICK_SVC
                                             ;DS:DX = NEW VECTOR
                  MOV      AH, 25H           ;INSTALL NEW
                  MOV      AL, 1CH           ;   BIOS TIMER-TICK
                  INT      21H               ;   INT VECTOR
                  MOV      DX, OFFSET P_GROUP:KBRD_SVC
                                             ;DS:DX = NEW VECTOR
```

Figure 14-8:   (continued)

```
                        MOV     AH, 25H             ;INSTALL NEW
                        MOV     AL, 09H             ;  KEYBOARD INT
                        INT     21H                 ;  VECTOR
LP_BEG:                 ;LOOP UNTIL USER PRESSES <ESC>
            ;DISPLAY HOURS FIRST
                        LOCATE  18, 35
                        MOV     AL, HOURS
                        SUB     AH, AH
                        CNV_UNS_STR    <OFFSET IO_BUF>, AX
                        DSPLY_STR      <OFFSET IO_BUF>
                        DSPLY_STR      <OFFSET BLANKS>
            ;DISPLAY MINUTES
                        LOCATE  19, 35
                        MOV     AL, MINUTES
                        CNV_UNS_STR    <OFFSET IO_BUF>, AX
                        DSPLY_STR      <OFFSET IO_BUF>
                        DSPLY_STR      <OFFSET BLANKS>
            ;DISPLAY SECONDS
                        LOCATE  20, 35
                        MOV     AL, SECONDS
                        CNV_UNS_STR    <OFFSET IO_BUF>, AX
                        DSPLY_STR      <OFFSET IO_BUF>
                        DSPLY_STR      <OFFSET BLANKS>
            ;DISPLAY MILLISECONDS
                        LOCATE  21, 35
                        MOV     AX, MSECS
                        CNV_UNS_STR    <OFFSET IO_BUF>, AX
                        DSPLY_STR      <OFFSET IO_BUF>
                        DSPLY_STR      <OFFSET BLANKS>
                CMP     ESC_FLG, 0          ;CONTINUE LOOP
                JNE     LP_END              ;  UNTIL <ESC>
                JMP     LP_BEG              ;  IS PRESSED
LP_END:                 ;END LOOP UNTIL

            ; RESTORE INTERRUPT VECTORS AND RETURN TO DOS
                PUSH    DS                  ;SAVE IT
                MOV     DX, WORD PTR ES:I1CH_VCTR       ;DS:DX TO
                MOV     DS, WORD PTR ES:I1CH_VCTR + 2 ;  ORIG 1CH
                                                       ;  VECTOR
                MOV     AH, 25H             ;RESTORE ORIGINAL
                MOV     AL, 1CH             ;  BIOS TIMER-TICK
                INT     21H                 ;  INTERRUPT VECTOR
                MOV     DX, WORD PTR ES:I09H_VCTR       ;DS:DX TO
                MOV     DS, WORD PTR ES:I09H_VCTR + 2   ;  ORIG KBD
                                                       ;  VECTOR
                MOV     AH, 25H             ;RESTORE ORIGINAL
                MOV     AL, 09H             ;  KBD INTERRUPT
                INT     21H                 ;  VECTOR (TYPE 9, IRQ1)
                POP     DS                  ;RESTORE IT
                LOCATE  25, 0
                INT     20H                 ;TERMINATE TO DOS
```

Figure 14-8: (continued)

```
MAIN                ENDP

                    ASSUME DS:NOTHING, ES:NOTHING

;BIOS CLOCK TICK SERVICE -------------------------------------------
;INTERRUPT SERVICE FOR 55 MSEC BIOS CLOCK TICK (TYPE 1CH)

BTICK_SVC           PROC      FAR

                    PUSH      DS                ;SAVE IT
                    PUSH      CS                ;POINT DS TO
                    POP       DS                ;  THIS SEGMENT
                    ASSUME    DS:P_GROUP
                    ;IF WATCH IS ON, THEN COUNT 55 MILLISECONDS
                    ;  (IGNORE IF OFF)
                    CMP       CLCK_SWTCH, 0     ;0 = OFF
                    JE        END_IF1
                        ADD       MSECS, 55           ;COUNT 55 MSECONDS
                        ;IF MSECS GE 1000, THEN ROLL TO SECONDS
                        CMP       MSECS, 1000 ;1000 = FULL SECOND
                        JB        END_IF2
                            SUB       MSECS, 1000 ;CONVERT MSECS
                            INC       SECONDS       ;  TO SECOND
                            ;IF SECONDS GE 60, THEN ROLL TO MINUTES
                            CMP       SECONDS, 60 ;60 SECS = MINUTE
                            JB        END_IF3
                                SUB       SECONDS, 60   ;CONVERT SECS
                                INC       MINUTES         ;  TO MINUTE
                                ;IF MINUTES GE 60, THEN ROLL TO HOURS
                                CMP       MINUTES, 60   ;60 MINS = HR
                                JB        END_IF4
                                    SUB       MINUTES, 60 ;CONVERT MINS
                                    INC       HOURS         ;  TO HOUR
END_IF4:                                ;END IF
END_IF3:                            ;END IF
END_IF2:                        ;END IF
END_IF1:                    ;END IF

            ;RETURN FROM INTERRUPT
                    POP       DS                ;RESTORE IT
                    ASSUME    DS:NOTHING
                    IRET                        ;RETURN

BTICK_SVC           ENDP

;KEYBOARD SERVICE --------------------------------------------------
;INTERRUPT SERVICE FOR KEYBOARD INTERRUPT (TYPE 09H - IRQ1)

KBRD_SVC            PROC      FAR

                    PUSH      AX                ;SAVE
                    PUSH      DS                ;  THEM
```

Figure 14-8:   (continued)

```
                    PUSH    CS                  ;POINT DS TO
                    POP     DS                  ;  THIS SEGMENT
                    ASSUME  DS:P_GROUP
            ;GET THE KEY SCAN CODE AND ACKNOWLEDGE KEYBOARD
                    IN      AL, 60H             ;GET SCAN CODE (PORT PA)
                    MOV     AH, AL              ;SAVE IT
                    IN      AL, 61H             ;SEND
                    OR      AL, 80H             ;  KEYBOARD
                    OUT     61H, AL             ;  ACKNOWLEDGE
                    AND     AL, 7FH             ;  SEQUENCE TO
                    OUT     61H, AL             ;  8255 PPI
                    ;IF KEY DOWN, THEN PROCESS IT (IGNORE IF UP)
                    TEST    AH, 80H             ;BIT #7 CLEAR = DOWN
                    JNZ     END_IF5
                        ;CASE OF AH (SCAN CODE)
   C_1:                     ;CASE 1 - <SPACE BAR>
                        CMP     AH, 39H ;39H = <SPACE>
                        JNE     C_2
                            NOT     CLCK_SWTCH  ;TOGGLE CLOCK
                                                ;  ON/OFF
                            JMP C_END
   C_2:                     ;CASE 2 - <ENTER>
                        CMP     AH, 1CH  ;1CH = <ENTER>
                        JNE     C_3
                            SUB AX, AX          ;ZERO OUT
                            MOV MSECS, AX       ;  AX AND
                            MOV SECONDS, AL     ;  SET ALL
                            MOV MINUTES, AL     ;  COUNTERS
                            MOV HOURS, AL       ;  TO ZERO
                            JMP C_END
   C_3:                     ;CASE 3 - <ESC>
                        CMP     AH, 01H  ;01H = <ESC>
                        JNE     C_END
                            MOV CLCK_SWTCH, 0
                                                ;TURN CLOCK OFF
                            NOT ESC_FLG         ;  AND SET FLAG
                                                ;  TO END PROGRAM
   C_END:               ;END CASE
   END_IF5:         ;END IF
                    MOV     AL, 20H             ;SEND END-OF-INT TO 8259
                    OUT     20H, AL             ;  INTERRUPT CONTROLLER
                    POP     DS                  ;RESTORE
                    POP     AX                  ;  THEM
                    ASSUME  DS:NOTHING
                    IRET                        ;RETURN FROM INTERRUPT

   KBRD_SVC         ENDP

   CODE             ENDS

                    END     ENTRY               ;ENTRY AT OFFSET 100H
```

Sometimes it is not desirable to entirely circumvent BIOS's handling of a hardware interrupt, but rather to merely examine registers and perhaps take some action before turning the interrupt over to BIOS for proper handling. In such a case, the program need not issue an EOI or terminate with an IRET. Instead, it should use a Far Memory-mode jump to transfer control to BIOS for completion of the interrupt service. The Far jump to BIOS is accomplished by using the original interrupt vector, stored in memory by the program, to specify the target of the jump. In such a case, the service routine must always save the Flags register along with any other used registers immediately upon entry; all registers, including the Flags register, must then be restored immediately before the Far jump to BIOS.

Although WATCH.ASM in Figure 14-8 illustrates the preferred method of capturing the timer interrupt (interrupt type 1CH from BIOS Time-of-Day), we have included WATCH2.ASM, in Figure 14-9, to demonstrate an interrupt-service routine that jumps to BIOS for completion of servicing of the interrupt. BTICK_SVC, for interrupt 1CH in WATCH.ASM, is replaced by TIMER_SVC, which is installed as the service routine for the 8253 channel zero interrupt (type 08H - IRQ0). Note that TIMER_SVC saves and restores the Flags register, in addition to DS, and terminates by jumping to BIOS for completion of the interrupt service.

TERMINATE-AND-STAY-RESIDENT (TSR) PROGRAMS

A **Terminate-and-Stay-Resident (TSR)** program is any program that uses interrupt type 27H or DOS function call 31H, discussed in the previous chapter, to terminate and stay resident. Generally, the program is made up of two parts, the resident portion followed by the installation routine. The resident portion, usually consisting of one or more interrupt-service routines, is the portion of the program that remains in memory after termination. The installation routine generally modifies the necessary interrupt vectors in order to enable the interrupt-service routines within the resident portion; it then terminates with interrupt type 27H or DOS function 31H, leaving the resident portion in memory.

The entry point of the program (offset 100H if a .COM file) usually consists of a jump around the resident portion to the installation routine. In order to avoid multiple installations of the same program, the resident portion usually contains some label (sequence of byte values) by which it can be identified in memory. The installation routine then examines the destination of one of the interrupt vectors to determine if the resident portion is already in memory. If so, it terminates normally without modifying any vectors and without remaining resident.

Figure 14-10 illustrates a TSR program that can be used as a guide for any TSR program that needs to alter the behavior of the keyboard. SHFT_TGL was originally written to assist a disabled student who typed with his nose, before more sophisticated off-the-shelf typing programs for the disabled were readily available. It causes the four shift keys (<Alt>, <Ctrl>, <Left shift>, and <Right shift>) to behave as toggle keys; when one of the shift keys is pressed and released, it logically remains down until it is pressed and released again.

Figure 14-9   Stopwatch Program, Intercepting IRQ0

```
COMMENT \                    WATCH2.ASM

            STOPWATCH PROGRAM

            MUST BE CONVERTED TO .COM FILE USING EXE2BIN

            INCLUDES TWO INTERRUPT SERVICE ROUTINES:
                    08H - 8253 TIMER TICK (IRQ0)
                    09H - KEYBOARD (IRQ1)

                \

                    PAGE    55, 80              ;LINES, WIDTH FOR LISTING
                    TITLE   WATCH2.ASM

                    INCLUDE CONSOLE.MLB

P_GROUP             GROUP   DATA, CODE
                    ASSUME  CS:P_GROUP, DS:P_GROUP, ES:P_GROUP

;DATA SEGMENT ========================================================
DATA                SEGMENT PARA PUBLIC 'DATA'

        ;PROGRAM ENTRY POINT
                    ORG     100H                ;ENTRY POINT MUST BE 100H
ENTRY:              JMP     NEAR PTR MAIN       ;JUMP AROUND DATA

        ;PROGRAM DATA
INIT_MSG            DB      'S T O P W A T C H', 13, 10 ,10, 10
                    DB      'Press <Space Bar> to start clock'
                    DB      13, 10, 10
                    DB      'Press <Space Bar> again to stop clock'
                    DB      13, 10, 10
                    DB      'Press <Enter> to reset clock'
                    DB      13, 10, 10
                    DB      'Press <Esc> to quit'
                    DB      0
BLANKS              DB      ' '
ESC_FLG             DB      0
CLCK_SWTCH          DB      0
IO_BUF              DB      7 DUP ('#')
I09H_VCTR           DD      ?
I08H_VCTR           DD      ?
HOURS               DB      0
MINUTES             DB      0
SECONDS             DB      0
MSECS               DW      0

DATA                ENDS
```

Figure 14-9:   (continued)

```
;CODE SEGMENT ============================================================
CODE                    SEGMENT PARA PUBLIC 'CODE'

        ;PROGRAM CODE - MAINLINE
MAIN                    PROC    FAR

        ;PRINT INSTRUCTIONS AND LABELS
                        CLS                         ;CLEAR SCREEN
                        LOCATE  4, 25
                        DSPLY_STR       <OFFSET INIT_MSG>
                        LOCATE  18, 28
                        DSPLY_IMMED_STR 'Hours:'
                        LOCATE  19, 26
                        DSPLY_IMMED_STR 'Minutes:'
                        LOCATE  20, 26
                        DSPLY_IMMED_STR 'Seconds:'
                        LOCATE  21, 21
                        DSPLY_IMMED_STR 'Milliseconds:'
        ;INSTALL KEYBOARD AND TIMER INTERRUPT SERVICE ROUTINES
        ;FIRST, SAVE CURRENT VECTORS
                        PUSH    ES                  ;SAVE IT
                        MOV     AH, 35H             ;GET CURRENT BIOS TIMER
                        MOV     AL, 08H             ;  INTERRUPT VECTOR
                        INT     21H                 ;  INTO ES:BX
                        MOV     WORD PTR I08H_VCTR, BX      ;SAVE THE
                        MOV     WORD PTR I08H_VCTR + 2, ES ;  VECTOR
                        MOV     AH, 35H             ;GET CURRENT KBRD
                        MOV     AL, 09H             ;  INTERRUPT VECTOR
                        INT     21H                 ;  INTO ES:BX
                        MOV     WORD PTR I09H_VCTR, BX      ;SAVE THE
                        MOV     WORD PTR I09H_VCTR + 2, ES ;  VECTOR
                        POP     ES                  ;RESTORE IT
        ;NOW, INSTALL THE NEW INTERRUPT VECTORS
                        MOV     DX, OFFSET P_GROUP:TIMER_SVC
                                                    ;DS:DX = NEW VECTOR
                        MOV     AH, 25H             ;INSTALL NEW
                        MOV     AL, 08H             ;  8253 TIMER
                        INT     21H                 ;  INT VECTOR
                        MOV     DX, OFFSET P_GROUP:KBRD_SVC
                                                    ;DS:DX = NEW VECTOR
                        MOV     AH, 25H             ;INSTALL NEW
                        MOV     AL, 09H             ;  KEYBOARD INT
                        INT     21H                 ;  VECTOR
LP_BEG:                 ;LOOP UNTIL USER PRESSES <ESC>
        ;DISPLAY HOURS FIRST
                        LOCATE  18, 35
                        MOV     AL, HOURS
                        SUB     AH, AH
                        CNV_UNS_STR     <OFFSET IO_BUF>, AX
                        DSPLY_STR       <OFFSET IO_BUF>
                        DSPLY_STR       <OFFSET BLANKS>
```

Figure 14-9: (continued)

```
                ;DISPLAY MINUTES
                        LOCATE    19, 35
                        MOV       AL, MINUTES
                        CNV_UNS_STR      <OFFSET IO_BUF>, AX
                        DSPLY_STR        <OFFSET IO_BUF>
                        DSPLY_STR        <OFFSET BLANKS>
                ;DISPLAY SECONDS
                        LOCATE    20, 35
                        MOV       AL, SECONDS
                        CNV_UNS_STR      <OFFSET IO_BUF>, AX
                        DSPLY_STR        <OFFSET IO_BUF>
                        DSPLY_STR        <OFFSET BLANKS>
                ;DISPLAY MILLISECONDS
                        LOCATE    21, 35
                        MOV       AX, MSECS
                        CNV_UNS_STR      <OFFSET IO_BUF>, AX
                        DSPLY_STR        <OFFSET IO_BUF>
                        DSPLY_STR        <OFFSET BLANKS>
                CMP     ESC_FLG, 0       ;CONTINUE LOOP
                JNE     LP_END           ;  UNTIL <ESC>
                JMP     LP_BEG           ;  IS PRESSED
LP_END:                 ;END LOOP UNTIL


                ; RESTORE INTERRUPT VECTORS AND RETURN TO DOS
                        PUSH    DS               ;SAVE IT
                        MOV     DX, WORD PTR ES:I08H_VCTR       ;DS:DX TO
                        MOV     DS, WORD PTR ES:I08H_VCTR + 2 ; ORIG 1CH
                                                               ;  VECTOR
                        MOV     AH, 25H          ;RESTORE ORIGINAL
                        MOV     AL, 08H          ;  BIOS TIMER-TICK
                        INT     21H              ;  INTERRUPT VECTOR
                        MOV     DX, WORD PTR ES:I09H_VCTR       ;DS:DX TO
                        MOV     DS, WORD PTR ES:I09H_VCTR + 2 ; ORIG KBD
                                                               ;  VECTOR
                        MOV     AH, 25H          ;RESTORE ORIGINAL
                        MOV     AL, 09H          ;  KBD INTERRUPT
                        INT     21H              ;  VECTOR (TYPE 9, IRQ1)
                        POP     DS               ;RESTORE IT
                        LOCATE  25, 0
                        INT     20H              ;TERMINATE TO DOS


MAIN            ENDP

                ASSUME DS:NOTHING, ES:NOTHING

;8253 TIMER, CHANNEL 2 SERVICE -------------------------------------
;INTERRUPT SERVICE FOR 55 MSEC 8253 TICK (TYPE 08H - IRQ0)

TIMER_SVC       PROC    FAR
```

Figure 14-9: (continued)

```
                        PUSHF                   ;SAVE
                        PUSH    DS              ;  THEM
                        PUSH    CS              ;POINT DS TO
                        POP     DS              ;  THIS SEGMENT
                        ASSUME  DS:P_GROUP
                        ;IF WATCH IS ON, THEN COUNT 55 MILLISECONDS
                        ; (IGNORE IF OFF)
                        CMP     CLCK_SWTCH, 0   ;0 = OFF
                        JE      END_IF1
                            ADD     MSECS, 55        ;COUNT 55 MSECONDS
                            ;IF MSECS GE 1000, THEN ROLL TO SECONDS
                            CMP     MSECS, 1000 ;1000 = FULL SECOND
                            JB      END_IF2
                                SUB     MSECS, 1000 ;CONVERT MSECS
                                INC     SECONDS     ;  TO SECOND
                                ;IF SECONDS GE 60, THEN ROLL TO MINUTES
                                CMP     SECONDS, 60 ;60 SECS = MINUTE
                                JB      END_IF3
                                    SUB     SECONDS, 60      ;CONVERT SECS
                                    INC     MINUTES          ;  TO MINUTE
                                    ;IF MINUTES GE 60, THEN ROLL TO HOURS
                                    CMP     MINUTES, 60     ;60 MINS = HR
                                    JB      END_IF4
                                        SUB     MINUTES, 60 ;CONVERT MINS
                                        INC     HOURS       ;  TO HOUR
END_IF4:                                ;END IF
END_IF3:                                ;END IF
END_IF2:                    ;END IF
END_IF1:            ;END IF

            ;JUMP TO BIOS TO FINISH SERVICING TIMER INTERRUPT
                        POP     DS              ;RESTORE
                        POPF                    ;  THEM
                        ASSUME  DS:NOTHING
                        JMP     I08H_VCTR       ;JUMP TO BIOS

TIMER_SVC           ENDP


;KEYBOARD SERVICE -------------------------------------------------
;INTERRUPT SERVICE FOR KEYBOARD INTERRUPT (TYPE 09H - IRQ1)

KBRD_SVC            PROC    FAR

                        PUSH    AX              ;SAVE
                        PUSH    DS              ;  THEM
                        PUSH    CS              ;POINT DS TO
                        POP     DS              ;  THIS SEGMENT
                        ASSUME  DS:P_GROUP
                    ;GET THE KEY SCAN CODE AND ACKNOWLEDGE KEYBOARD
```

Figure 14-9:   (continued)

```
                    IN      AL, 60H         ;GET SCAN CODE (PORT PA)
                    MOV     AH, AL          ;SAVE IT
                    IN      AL, 61H         ;SEND
                    OR      AL, 80H         ;  KEYBOARD
                    OUT     61H, AL         ;  ACKNOWLEDGE
                    AND     AL, 7FH         ;  SEQUENCE TO
                    OUT     61H, AL         ;  8255 PPI
                ;IF KEY DOWN, THEN PROCESS IT (IGNORE IF UP)
                    TEST    AH, 80H         ;BIT #7 CLEAR = DOWN
                    JNZ     END_IF5
                        ;CASE OF AH (SCAN CODE)
        C_1:            ;CASE 1 - <SPACE BAR>
                        CMP     AH, 39H  ;39H = <SPACE>
                        JNE     C_2
                            NOT     CLCK_SWTCH   ;TOGGLE CLOCK
                                                 ;  ON/OFF
                            JMP     C_END
        C_2:            ;CASE 2 - <ENTER>
                        CMP     AH, 1CH  ;1CH = <ENTER>
                        JNE     C_3
                            SUB     AX, AX          ;ZERO OUT
                            MOV     MSECS, AX    ;   AX AND
                            MOV     SECONDS, AL  ;   SET ALL
                            MOV     MINUTES, AL  ;   COUNTERS
                            MOV     HOURS, AL    ;   TO ZERO
                            JMP     C_END
        C_3:            ;CASE 3 - <ESC>
                        CMP     AH, 01H  ;01H = <ESC>
                        JNE     C_END
                            MOV     CLCK_SWTCH, 0
                                                 ;TURN CLOCK OFF
                            NOT     ESC_FLG    ;  AND SET FLAG
                                               ;  TO END PROGRAM
        C_END:              ;END CASE
        END_IF5:        ;END IF
                    MOV     AL, 20H         ;SEND END-OF-INT TO 8259
                    OUT     20H, AL         ;  INTERRUPT CONTROLLER
                    POP     DS              ;RESTORE
                    POP     AX              ;  THEM
                    ASSUME  DS:NOTHING
                    IRET                    ;RETURN FROM INTERRUPT

        KBRD_SVC    ENDP

        CODE        ENDS

                    END     ENTRY           ;ENTRY AT OFFSET 100H
```

SHFT_TGL functions by capturing the keyboard interrupt (type 09H, IRQ1) and modifying the shift keys to behave as toggle keys. The first time the key is depressed, the interrupt-service routine jumps to BIOS for handling of the key; when the key is released, however, the program sends a keyboard acknowledge to the 8255 Programmable Peripheral Interface and an End-of-Interrupt to the 8259 Interrupt Controller and returns with an IRET. Thus, BIOS does not receive the interrupt for the release of the key and so thinks it is still down.

The second time the key is pressed, SHFT_TGL's resident interrupt-service routine acknowledges the key, sends an EOI, and returns; when it is released, SHFT_TGL jumps to BIOS, thus informing BIOS of the release of the key. Consequently, BIOS thinks that the key has remained depressed from the first time it is pressed until the second time it is released. In order to enable the user to keep track of the status of each shift key, SHFT_TGL emits a quick beep the first time a key is pressed (turned on); no beep is produced the second time it is pressed and released (turned off).

Figure 14-10   TSR Keyboard Interrupt-Service Routine

```
COMMENT \                           SHFT_TGL.ASM

            PROGRAM TO CONVERT SHIFT KEYS TO TOGGLE KEYS

            AFFECTS <LEFT SHIFT>, <RIGHT SHIFT>, <ALT>, AND <CTRL>
            AFTER INSTALLATION, SHIFT KEYS BEHAVE AS TOGGLE KEYS
            PRESSING THE KEY ONCE TURNS IT ON (LEAVES IT DOWN)
            PRESSING THE SAME KEY AGAIN TURNS IT OFF (RELEASES IT)

            PROGRAM MUST BE CONVERTED TO A .COM FILE WITH EXE2BIN

            \

                    PAGE    55, 80              ;LINES, WIDTH FOR LISTING
                    TITLE   SHFT_TGL.ASM

                    INCLUDE CONSOLE.MLB

P_GROUP             GROUP   RES_DATA, RES_CODE, DATA, CODE
                    ASSUME  CS:P_GROUP

;RESIDENT DATA SEGMENT ==========================================
RES_DATA            SEGMENT PARA    PUBLIC 'RES_DATA'

          ;PROGRAM ENTRY POINT
                    ORG     100H
ENTRY:              JMP     NEAR PTR INSTALL        ;JUMP AROUND
                                                    ;  RESIDENT PART
          ;RESIDENT DATA
```

Figure 14-10: (continued)

```
KEY_FLGS        DB      0               ;USED TO KEEP TRACK OF
                                        ;  LOGICAL STATUS OF
                                        ;  SHIFT KEYS
I09H_VCTR       DD      0               ;CURRENT KBRD VECTOR
RES_LBL         DB      'SHFT_TGL'      ;IDENTIFY RESIDENT PART

RES_DATA        ENDS

;RESIDENT CODE SEGMENT ===============================================
RES_CODE        SEGMENT PARA    PUBLIC  'RES_CODE'

        ;RESIDENT PORTION OF PROGRAM
        ;INTERCEPTS KEYBOARD INTERRUPT (TYPE 09H)
        ;JUMP TO BIOS FOR HANDLING OF ALL BUT SHIFT KEYS
        ;FIRST TIME A SHIFT KEY IS PRESSED AND RELEASED
        ;    JUMP TO BIOS WHEN PRESSED
        ;    ACKNOWLEDGE AND RETURN WHEN RELEASED
        ;    (MAKE BIOS THINK IT'S STILL DOWN)
        ;SECOND TIME A SHIFT KEY IS PRESSED AND RELEASED
        ;    ACKNOWLEDGE AND RETURN WHEN PRESSED
        ;    JUMP TO BIOS WHEN RELEASED
        ;    .(MAKE BIOS THINK IT WAS JUST RELEASED)

KBD_SVC         PROC    FAR             ;KEYBOARD INT SERVICE
                PUSHF                   ;SAVE FLAGS
                PUSH    AX              ;  AND
                PUSH    DS              ;  REGISTERS
                PUSH    CS              ;POINT DS TO
                POP     DS              ;  THIS SEGMENT
                ASSUME  DS:P_GROUP
        ;GET SCAN CODE AND CHECK FOR SHIFT KEYS
        ; (<CTRL>, <ALT>, <LEFT SHIFT> & <RIGHT SHIFT>)
                IN      AL, 60H         ;GET SCAN CODE
                MOV     AH, AL          ;SAVE IT TO AH
                AND     AL, 7FH         ;  MASK OUT BIT #7
                                        ;  (UP OR DOWN)
                ;CASE OF AL (SCAN CODE OF KEY)
C_1:            ;CASE 1 - <ALT> KEY
                CMP     AL,38H          ;38H = <ALT>
                JNE     C_2
                    MOV     AL, 1       ;00000001B FOR KEY MASK
                    JMP     SHFT_KEY            ;HANDLE IT
C_2:            ;CASE 2 - <CTRL> KEY
                CMP     AL,1DH   ;1DH = <CTRL>
                JNE     C_3
                    MOV     AL, 2       ;00000010B FOR KEY MASK
                    JMP     SHFT_KEY            ;HANDLE IT
```

Figure 14-10: (continued)

```
C_3:                    ;CASE 3 - LEFT <SHIFT> KEY
                CMP  AL,2AH           ;2AH = LEFT <SHIFT>
                JNE  C_4
                     MOV    AL, 4     ;00000100B FOR KEY MASK
                     JMP    SHFT_KEY ;HANDLE IT
C_4:                    ;CASE 4 - RIGHT <SHIFT> KEY
                CMP  AL,36H           ;36H = RIGHT <SHIFT>
                JNE  C_END
                     MOV    AL, 8     ;00001000B FOR KEY MASK
                     JMP    SHFT_KEY ;HANDLE IT
C_END:          ;END CASE


             ;JUMP TO BIOS KEYBOARD INTERRUPT SERVICE ROUTINE
             ;LET BIOS KNOW ABOUT KEYBOARD INTERRUPT
KS_BIOS:        POP      DS              ;RESTORE
                POP      AX              ;  REGISTERS
                POPF                     ;  AND FLAGS
                ASSUME   DS:NOTHING
                JMP      I09H_VCTR       ;JUMP TO BIOS


                ASSUME   DS:P_GROUP
SHFT_KEY:       ;HANDLE A SHIFT KEY
                ;IF FIRST TME FOR KEY
                TEST     KEY_FLGS, AL   ;KEY_FLAG BIT CLEAR
                JNZ      ELSE1          ;  IF FIRST TIME TIME
                   ;IF KEY WAS PRESSED (DOWN)
                   TEST  AH, 80H ;BIT #7 CLEAR
                   JNZ   ELSE2          ;  IF PRESSED
                      CALL   BEEP    ;PRESSED - BEEP, AND
                      JMP    KS_BIOS ;  TELL BIOS
ELSE2:          ;ELSE (KEY RELEASED - UP)
                   XOR     KEY_FLGS, AL    ;TOGGLE FLAG
                   JMP     KS_RET          ;DON'T TELL BIOS
END_IF2:        ;ENDI IF
ELSE1:          ;ELSE (2ND TIME)
                ;IF KEY WAS RELEASED
                TEST  AH, 80H       ;BIT #7 SET
                JZ    KS_RET         ;  IF RELEASED (UP)
                   XOR     KEY_FLGS, AL    ;TOGGLE FLAG
                   JMP     KS_BIOS ;TELL BIOS
END_IF1:        ;ENDIF


             ;ACKNOWLEDGE KEYBOARD, EOI TO 8259, RETURN FROM INT
             ;DON'T TELL BIOS ABOUT KBRD INTERRUPT
KS_RET:         IN     AL,61H         ;KEYBOARD
                OR     AL,80H         ;  ACKNOWLEDGE
                OUT    61H,AL         ;  SEQUENCE
```

Figure 14-10:   (continued)

```
                    AND     AL,7FH              ;  TO
                    OUT     61H,AL              ;  8255 PPI
                    MOV     AL,20H              ;END-OF-INT SIGNAL TO
                    OUT     20H,AL              ;  8259 INT CONTROLLER
                    POP     DS                  ;RESTORE
                    POP     AX                  ;  REGISTERS
                    POPF                        ;  AND FLAGS
                    IRET                        ;RETURN FROM INT
KBD_SVC             ENDP


;BEEP -------------------------------------------------------------
;SUBPROCEDURE TO PRODUCE QUICK BEEP WHEN KEY GOES DOWN

BEEP                PROC    NEAR                ;QUICK BEEP

                    PUSH    AX                  ;SAVE
                    PUSH    CX                  ;  THEM
                    MOV     AL, 0B6H            ;PROGRAM CH 2 TIMER
                    OUT     43H, AL             ;  COMMAND REGISTER
                    MOV     AL, 0A9H            ;LOW BYTE TO
                    OUT     42H, AL             ;  LATCH REGISTER
                    MOV     AL, 04H             ;HIGH BYTE TO
                    OUT     42H, AL             ;  LATCH REGISTER
                    IN      AL, 61H             ;ENABLE SPEAKER
                    OR      AL, 03H             ;  (SET BITS 0 AND 1
                    OUT     61H, AL             ;   OF PPI PORT PB)
                    MOV     CX, 20000           ;LOOP WITH
B_LP:               LOOP    B_LP                ;  SPEAKER ON
                    AND     AL, 0FDH            ;DISABLE SPEAKER
                    OUT     61H, AL             ;  (CLEAR PB BIT 1)
                    POP     CX                  ;RESTORE
                    POP     AX                  ;  THEM
                    RET                         ;RETURN

BEEP                ENDP

RES_CODE            ENDS

;NON-RESIDENT DATA SEGMENT ========================================

DATA                SEGMENT PARA      PUBLIC   'DATA'

        ;INSTALLATION MESSAGE TO USER (NON-RESIDENT)
INS_MSG             DB      7, '<<<<<<<<<<<<<< SHFT_TGL is now '
                    DB      'installed. >>>>>>>>>>>>>'
                    DB      13, 10, 10, 10
                    DB      'The four shift keys ( <Alt>, '
                    DB      '<Ctrl>, <Left shift>, and <Right '
                    DB      'shift> )', 13, 10
```

Figure 14-10: (continued)

```
                        DB          'will now function as toggle '
                        DB          'keys.', 13, 10, 10
                        DB          'Pressing any shift key once '
                        DB          'causes it to remain active, as if '
                        DB          'held down.', 13, 10
                        DB          'A quick beep indicates that the '
                        DB          'key is now "down".', 13, 10, 10
                        DB          'Pressing the same key, a second'
                        DB          ' time, releases it (no beep).'
                        DB          13, 10, 10
                        DB          'To type a key combination, press '
                        DB          'the keys one at a time.', 13, 10
                        DB          'For example, to type <Ctrl>+<K>:'
                        DB          13, 10
                        DB          ' Press and release <Ctrl>, then '
                        DB          '<K>; then press <Ctrl> again, to '
                        DB          'release it.', 13, 10, 10
                        DB          'To cancel SHFT_TGL, reboot the '
                        DB          'system:', 13, 10
                        DB          ' Press and release <Alt>, then '
                        DB          '<Ctrl>, then <Del>.', 13, 10, 10
                        DB          0

DATA                    ENDS



;NONRESIDENT CODE SEGMENT ==========================================
CODE                    SEGMENT PARA     PUBLIC   'CODE'

        ;NONRESIDENT PROCEDURE TO INSTALL RESIDENT PORTION
                        ASSUME   ES:P_GROUP
INSTALL                 PROC     FAR
                        CLS                         ;DISPLAY INSTALL MESSAGE
                        DSPLY_STR        <OFFSET P_GROUP:INS_MSG>

        ;GET THE CURRENT KEYBOARD (09H) VECTOR
                        MOV      AH, 35H            ;GET VECTOR CODE
                        MOV      AL, 09H            ;INT TYPE 9 (IRQ1)
                        INT      21H                ;GET VECTOR TO ES:BX
        ;SEE IF ALREADY INSTALLED
                        MOV      DI, BX             ;POINT ES:DI TO
                        SUB      DI, 8              ;  8 BYTES BEFORE
                                                   ;  INT SVC ROUTINE
                        MOV      SI, OFFSET RES_LBL
                                                   ;POINT DS:SI TO LABEL
                                                   ;  IN THIS PROGRAM
                        MOV      CX, 8              ;COMPARE
                        CLD                         ;  EIGHT
                        REP      CMPSB              ;  BYTES
```

Figure 14-10:   (continued)

```
                        ;IF ALREADY INSTALLED, TERM NORMALLY TO DOS
                        JNE       ELSE3
                              INT       20H  ;NORMAL TERM TO DOS
        ELSE3:          ;ELSE (NOT INSTALLED), INSTALL AND TSR
                              MOV       WORD PTR I09H_VCTR, BX       ;SAVE CURRENT
                              MOV       WORD PTR I09H_VCTR+2, ES     ;  VECTOR
                              MOV       DX, OFFSET P_GROUP:KBD_SVC   ;INSTALL
                              MOV       AH, 25H                     ;  NEW
                              MOV       AL, 09H                     ;  INT 09H
                              INT       21H                         ;  VECTOR
                              MOV       DX,OFFSET P_GROUP:INS_MSG    ;TERM AND
                              INT       27H                         ;  STAY RES
        END_IF3:        ;END IF

        INSTALL         ENDP

        CODE            ENDS

                        END       ENTRY             ;ENTRY AT OFFSET 100H
```

SUMMARY

Peripheral devices notify the processor of external events by generating interrupts through the 8259 Interrupt Controller. Each peripheral device is connected to a dedicated interrupt-request line (IRQ0 through IRQ7) connected to the 8259. The 8259 translates IRQn lines to the appropriate interrupt (types 08H through 0FH) to the processor. The interrupt then results in the execution of an interrupt-service routine determined by the appropriate interrupt vector.

Two other important peripheral devices are the 8255 Programmable Peripheral Interface and the 8253 Timer. The 8255 acts as an interface between the processor and several external devices, most notably the keyboard controller, the configuration switches, the speaker AND gate, and the cassette controller. The 8253 contains three channels, each of which can be programmed to produce a number of possible outputs based on two input signals, a Clock and a Gate. The frequency of a channel's output is determined by outputting an appropriate value to its Latch register; the resulting output frequency is the Clock signal (1.19318 MHz) divided by the Latch-register value.

Any program that must respond to external events does so by setting the appropriate interrupt vector to a special subprocedure within the program, called an interrupt-service routine. When a peripheral device generates an interrupt, control is passed to the interrupt-service routine, which takes the appropriate action and generates an End-of-Interrupt signal to the 8259 Interrupt Controller. A TSR program uses DOS interrupt 27H or DOS function call 31H to leave one or more interrupt-service routines within memory after termination. The resident code then processes the appropriate hardware interrupts, often altering the behavior of the PC in some manner.

VOCABULARY

V14-1   In your own words, define each of the following terms:

a) Peripheral support hardware   e) End-of-Interrupt signal

b) Intel 8253   f) Interrupt-service routine

c) Intel 8255   g) TSR program

d) Intel 8259

REVIEW QUESTIONS

Q14-1   Why is the 8259 Interrupt Controller necessary in the IBM PC?

Q14-2   What function is performed by the 8255 Programmable Peripheral Interface?

Q14-3   What three functions are served by the 8253 Timer?

Q14-4   What use do programs usually make of the 8259 Interrupt Control Register?

Q14-5   Describe the function of the 8259 Interrupt Mask Register?

Q14-6   When and why is it necessary for an interrupt-service routine to send an EOI to the 8259?

Q14-7   Name and describe the function of each of the 8255 ports.

Q14-8   Describe the function of the 8255 Command register.

Q14-9   How many channels are contained in the 8253 Timer?

Q14-10   Describe the general function and purpose of the Latch register and Counter register in each Timer channel.

Q14-11   Describe the general purpose of the Clock, Gate, and Output signals of each Timer channel.

Q14-12   List and describe the function (in terms of the Latch register, Counter register, Clock, Gate, and Output) of the 8253 channels in each of the six possible modes.

Q14-13   How many Command registers does the 8253 contain?

Q14-14   Describe the use of the 8253 Command register.

Q14-15   Describe the physical connection to the system bus of each channel of the 8253 (Clock, Gate, and Output).

Q14-16   What are the requirements for an interrupt-service routine?

Q14-17   How does a program install an interrupt-service routine?

Q14-18   What is the preferred method of capturing the fifty-five-millisecond timer tick?

Q14-19   What is meant by the term "TSR"?

Q14-20   What are the two methods for a program to terminate and stay resident? What are the restrictions on each method?

PROGRAMMING ASSIGNMENTS

PA14-1   Rewrite SOUND.ASM (Figure 14-7) to produce the desired tone for a user specified period of time. Ask the user for the sound duration (in milliseconds) as well as for the pitch.

When the program turns the sound on, it should also set a switch (byte variable) to indicate that the sound is on and move the desired number of milliseconds into a word variable to be used as a counter.

Include an interrupt-service routine for BIOS' fifty-five-millisecond timer tick (interrupt type 1CH). The interrupt-service routine should check the switch to see if the sound is currently on. If not, it should return from the interrupt without taking any action. If the switch indicates that the sound is currently on, it should subtract fifty-five from the millisecond counter; if the result is less than or equal to zero, the routine should disable the speaker and clear the sound-on switch before returning from the interrupt.

PA14-2   Rewrite WATCH2.ASM (Figure 14-9) to keep track of the time in five-millisecond increments instead of fifty-five-millisecond increments.

Install an interrupt-service routine for the 8253 channel two output (IRQ0, interrupt 08H). Then change the channel-two Latch-register value to 5966 (1,193,180 / 200) to produce a 200 hertz signal.

The IRQ0 interrupt-service routine should add five to the milliseconds counter for each interrupt. In order to avoid interfering with BIOS's time of day, the type 08H interrupt-service routine needs to jump to BIOS every eleventh five-millisecond interrupt. To do so, it should maintain a count of the number of five-millisecond interrupts, incrementing the count on each interrupt. If the count has not yet reached eleven, the routine should issue an EOI and return from the interrupt. When the count reaches eleven, the routine should set it back to zero and then jump to BIOS's time-of-day routine (original interrupt type 08H vector). Thus BIOS sees the interrupt every fifty-five milliseconds.

PA14-3   Write a program that allows the user to play music, using the bottom two rows of the keyboard as piano keys. The bottom row (<Z> through <,> should behave like one octave (from low C to middle C) of white piano keys; the appropriate keys in the second row (<S> through <J>) should behave like the corresponding black piano keys. The keyboard keys and the piano keys to which they should correspond are as follows:

```
            S   D       G   H   J
    Keys    Z   X   C   V   B   N   M   ,

                C#  D#      F#  G#  A#
    Notes   C   D   E   F   G   A   B   C
```

The program should install its own keyboard interrupt-service routine (interrupt 09H) to detect the pressing and releasing of any keys. All keys, other than <Esc> and those corresponding to notes, should be ignored. Pressing any of the assigned keys should produce the appropriate note. Following is a summary of the keys, the corresponding notes, the frequencies for the notes and the Latch-register values to produce the note:

Key	Note	Frequency	Latch value
<Z>	C (low)	131.00000	9108
<S>	C#	138.78967	8597
<X>	D	147.04253	8115
<D>	D#	155.78613	7659
<C>	E	165.04966	7229
<V>	F	174.86402	6823
<G>	F#	185.26198	6441
<B>	G	196.27823	6079
<H>	G#	207.94954	5738
<N>	A	220.31486	5416
<J>	A#	233.41546	5112
<M>	B	247.29507	4825
<,>	C (mid)	262.00000	4554

Whenever one of the above keys is depressed, the program should output the appropriate value to the channel-two Latch register and enable the speaker. Whenever the key is released, the speaker should be disabled unless another key has already been depressed, in which case the speaker should remain enabled.

The program should continue until the user presses <Esc>, at which time the program should terminate to DOS.

PA14-4 Write a TSR program that disables the <PrtSc> key. The installation routine should determine if the resident portion is already installed, terminating normally if so or installing it if necessary.

The resident portion must contain a keyboard (interrupt 09H) interrupt-service routine that obtains and examines the scan code of each key depressed. If the key is not <PrtSc>, the routine should jump to BIOS's keyboard interrupt-service routine (original 09H interrupt vector) for normal handling of the keystroke. If the key is <PrtSc> the interrupt-service routine should issue a keyboard acknowledge and an EOI and return from the interrupt, causing the <PrtSc> to be ignored.

PA14-5   Write a TSR program that prevents the accidental pressing of the <Num Lock> key by requiring that it be pressed in conjunction with either <Left shift> or <Right shift>. The installation routine should determine if the resident portion is already installed, terminating normally if so or installing it if necessary.

The resident portion must contain a keyboard interrupt-service routine (09H) that obtains and examines the scan code of each key depressed. If the key is not <Num Lock>, the routine should jump to BIOS's keyboard interrupt-service routine (original 09H interrupt vector) for normal handling of the keystroke.

If the key is <Num Lock>, the interrupt-service routine should check the status of the left and right shift keys. If neither is down, the routine should issue a keyboard acknowledge and an EOI and return from the interrupt, causing the <Num Lock> to be ignored; if either shift key is down, it should jump to BIOS's keyboard interrupt-service routine for normal handling of the <Num Lock> key.

Index

to itself. 131

SAR *dest,* **CL**—Shift *dest* right CL times, copying high bit to itself. 131

SBB *dest, source*—Subtract *source* and Carry flag from *dest.* 125

SCAS—Subtract byte or word value at ES:[DI] from value in AL or AX, setting flags, discarding difference; adjust DI. 383

SHL *dest,* **1**—Shift *dest* left once, 0 to low bit. 131

SHL *dest,* **CL**—Shift *dest* left CL times, 0's to low bit. 131

SHR *dest,* **1**—Shift *dest* right once, 0 to high bit. 130

SHR *dest,* **CL**—Shift *dest* right CL times, 0's to high bit. 130

STC—Set Carry flag. 154

STD—Set Direction flag (down). 154

STI—Set Interrupt flag (enable hardware interrupts). 154

STOS—Copy byte or word value from AL or AX to ES:[DI]; adjust DI. 382

SUB *dest, source*—Subtract *source* value from *dest.* 124

TEST *dest, source*—Logical AND *source* value with *dest* value, setting flags, discarding result of AND. 127

XCHG *dest*1, *dest*2—Swap values in *dest*1 and *dest*2. 121

XOR *dest, source*—Logical XOR *source* value with *dest.* 128